P9-CAB-194

My Native Land

THE YORKE FAMILY AT HOME, 1837

MY NATIVE LAND

Life in America, 1790–1870

COMPILED AND EDITED BY

W. S. Tryon

Phoenix Books

THE UNIVERSITY OF CHICAGO PRESS

CHICAGO AND LONDON

First published in an expanded edition as

A MIRROR FOR AMERICANS

Standard Book Number: 226-81313-4

THE UNIVERSITY OF CHICAGO PRESS, CHICAGO 60637
The University of Chicago Press, Ltd., London W.C. 1

Copyright 1952 and 1961 by The University of Chicago
All rights reserved. Published 1952. Phoenix Edition
1961. Third Impression 1969. Printed in the United
States of America

In this volume which I offer to the public, the reader is not to expect the scientific production of a philosopher, but passing observations. This species of composition has all the attractions of romance, combined with the usefulness of truth. I have always perused the book of travels with particular delight, no matter how awkward its style, or humble the adventurer.

It may be said to be a species of composition free alike to the illiterate and the learned, requiring no peculiar or appropriate style; demanding neither the dignified march of history, the brilliancy of works of the imagination, nor the precision and regularity of those which are purely scientific, yet, admitting with propriety something of them all. Men of the most common acquirements are not thought presumptuous in attempting it; for it may be the fortune of such only, to have witnessed facts of the highest interest, or to have passed through countries not likely to be visited by the learned. Hence the various modes adopted by travellers from the regular and systematic essay, down to the simple diary or journal.

HENRY M. BRACKENRIDGE,
Views of Louisiana (1814)

We will travel in steamboats, ralerodes, stage-coaches, and canal-boats, over rivers, lakes and mountains. We will visit cities, towns, and country, and see every kind of scenery, and make the acquaintance of all sorts of people; but if the trip should prove dull and uninterestin to you, you can sleep over the long stretches, and if you should git cumpletely out of patience with your auther, you can stop on the way and git aboard of the next book *that cums along.*

WILLIAM T. THOMPSON,
Major Jones's Sketches of Travel (1848)

Foreword

ACCOUNTS written by travelers are a rich depository of historical information, for they give, often in a form otherwise unavailable, an on-the-spot record of places and people by contemporary eyewitnesses. They possess value, also, by their power to project the present-day reader into that vanished past, which to sense and comprehend is the very essence of history. For the American scene the number of these travel books is both surprisingly and flatteringly large, and on their pages emerge a remarkably complete description of native life and manners.

Partly because it was a new country, partly because its institutions struck out in novel directions, the United States was visited again and again by curious and articulate Europeans who, as soon as they were safe at home, wrote down their observations, sometimes with discernment, but often with shallow prejudice. So voluminous, indeed, is this literature that there have appeared in recent years two excellent compilations which make available to modern readers pertinent and illuminating excerpts from this wealth of material. In 1923 Professor Allan Nevins edited a volume entitled *American Social History as Recorded by British Travellers,* which was reissued, with revisions, in 1948 as *America through British Eyes.* In 1949 Professor Oscar Handlin translated portions of the more outstanding Continental travelers in a work called *This Was America.* Together, these two books present an introduction to that large body of foreign observation on the United States and make it possible, thereby, to see ourselves as others see us.

It is strange that hitherto no similar effort has been made to collect and extract for present-day readers the works of those native Americans who also journeyed about their country and set down their judgments as to what their countrymen were like. Whether this is due to a failure of scholarship or to a survival of that subservience to European opinion, which makes of America "an echo of what is thought and written under the aristocracies beyond the ocean," it would be difficult to say. However it may be, the present work constitutes an effort, if not to redress the balance, at least to place side by side with the European commentaries that body of American observation which exists contemporaneously with them and so to make equally available through appropriate extracts a native view of the native scene.

Certainly Americans traveled widely in their own land. As Bayard Taylor remarked, "No people travel more than the Americans. Locomotion belongs naturally to the restless, shifting phases of the national temperament. Even our farmers are beginning to have their little after-harvest trips to the sea-shore, the Hudson, Niagara, or the West."[1] What is more, a striking number of them, on returning home, were moved to set down in writing where they had been and what they had seen. Much of this writing found its way into book form, and these printed records have made available to their posterity a valuable as well as a voluminous documentation of the American past.

The motives which occasioned their literary effort were varied. Some, with an eye to the dignity of history, set down for later generations material which they feared otherwise would be lost or distorted. "I resolved to furnish," wrote the president of Yale College, "to some of those, who will live eighty or a hundred years hence, the means of enabling them to know what was the appearance of their country during the period occupied by my journeys."[2] Others avowed a more dilettante attitude and averred they sought merely to while away the tedious hour and seek such amusement as they could find in an otherwise dull world. Many declared they wrote for the edification or entertainment of friends and, with a coyness which is not always convincing, insisted they published with reluctance and only from the importuning of others. Mrs. Anne Royall, with commendable but infrequently imitated candor, traveled and wrote to earn her bread and butter. But it was characteristic and significant that nearly all declared it was their purpose to record a true picture of their native land in order to dissipate the false and prejudiced narrations of jealous Europeans.

Seldom did Americans allow the travel accounts of Europeans to escape their wrath or irony. In addition to the general condemnation of Charles Dickens and Mrs. Trollope, other European travelers were singled out for censure as well. Thus Christian Schultz, who journeyed from New York to New Orleans, stated that it was his intention in writing down his observations to correct the *Travels in America,* by Thomas Ash, a work which Schultz "found so to abound in mistakes, misrepresentations, and fictions in almost every page" that he did not "believe that any such person ever travelled the route pretended to be described."[3] Mrs. Royall, who took the self-

---

1. Bayard Taylor, "Travel in the United States," *Atlantic Monthly,* XIX (April, 1867), 477.
2. Timothy Dwight, *Travels in New-England and New-York* (London, 1823), I, iv.
3. Christian Schultz, *Travels on an Inland Voyage* (New York, 1810), p. iv.

same trip down the Alabama River as Captain Basil Hall, poked (for her) gentle fun at the famous English tourist for his "despotic requests," his reserve, his sulkiness, and the omissions in his narrative.[4] Even the humorist William T. Thompson went out of his way to caricature another famous British traveler. "I don't believe," wrote Thompson, "I'd know any more about Virginny than Captain Marryat did about America when he went home to write his ever-lastin book of lies."[5] More general was Caroline Gilman, who, traveling in Canada and observing the misspellings of "Storeage" and "Travillers" on public signboards, wondered whether, "in the sweeping custom of foreign journalists," she might not indict the entire Canadian people for illiteracy.[6] But it was James K. Paulding, who in sarcastic anger drew up the most complete indictment of the European traveler in America in a "compendium of regulations" for the use of future foreign visitors:

Never fail to seize every opportunity to lament, with tears in your eyes, the deplorable state of religion among "these republicans."

Be very particular in noticing stage drivers, waiters, tavern keepers, and persons of importance, who, as it were, represent the character of the people. Whenever you want any deep and profound information, always apply to them.

If you dine with a hospitable gentleman, don't fail to repay him by dishing up himself, his wife, daughters, and dinner in your book. Be sure you give their names at full length; be particular in noting every dish upon the table.

Tell all the old stories which the Yankees repeat of their southern and western neighbours, and which the latter have retorted upon them. Be sure not to forget the gouging of the judge, the roasting of the negro, the wooden nutmegs. Never inquire whether they are true or not. Be sure you don't forget to say that you saw everything you describe.

If the stage breaks down with you, give the roads no quarter. If you get an indifferent breakfast at an inn, cut up the whole town where the enormity was committed, pretty handsomely.

Never read any book written by natives of the country you mean to describe. They are always partial; and besides, a knowledge of the truth always fetters the imagination.

Never suffer the hospitalities and kindness of these republicans to conciliate you. You may eat their dinners but never forget that if you praise the Yankees, John Bull will condemn your book. Charity begins at home; the first duty of a traveller is to make a book that will sell.

Never mind your geography. Your book will sell just as well if you place New York on the Mississippi, and New Orleans on the Hudson. The person most completely qualified of any we ever met with for a traveller, was a worthy Englishman, who being very near-sighted, and hard of hearing, was not led astray by the villainy of his five senses; and what was very remarkable his book contained quite as much truth as those of his more fortunate contemporaries who were embarrassed by eyes and ears.[7]

4. Anne Royall, *Mrs. Royall's Southern Tour* (Washington, 1838), p. 107.
5. William T. Thompson, *Major Jones's Sketches of Travel* (Philadelphia, 1848), p. 42.
6. Caroline Gilman, *The Poetry of Travelling in the United States* (New York, 1838), pp. 107.
7. James K. Paulding, *The New Mirror for Travellers* (New York, 1828), pp. 80–84. Perhaps the most savage attack ever made by an American on the European traveler is Frederick W. Shelton's *The Trolliopiad, or, Travelling Gentlemen in America: A Satire, by Nil Admirari* (New York, 1837). Calvin Colton's *The American* (London, 1833) is similar.

Foreword

Whatever may have been their motives, Americans, in each succeeding decade, traveled throughout their own land in ever increasing numbers. That they were able to do so was largely the result of improved means of communication, of macadamized roads, canals, and railways. And while their discomforts, not to say downright hardships, would discourage most of their descendants, they seemed to have dealt cheerfully with inconveniences and dwelt rather upon the unfolding wonders of the nineteenth century's mechanical revolution.

Their attitudes were conditioned mostly by the nationalism and the romanticism of their time. No portion of the new nation, or its expanding frontiers, was uninteresting to them. Yet, if they were annoyed by the unflattering accounts which foreigners often published about the United States, they did not themselves fall into an uncritical attitude. Their patriotism was restrained and civilized, and they often excoriated what they saw. At times one feels that, in common with all travelers, they praised and condemned on the basis of whether their accommodations and meals were good or bad or whether or not what they saw reminded them of home. Though often motivated by sectional or personal prejudice, yet, even if their accounts cannot always be regarded as "true" in every specific instance, they remained amazingly objective and on the whole have furnished trustworthy reports.

As natives in their native land they possessed certain advantages. They did not regard their compatriots as Hottentots or Esquimaux or view them primarily as curiosities. Neither were they compelled constantly to condemn or explain what they saw because it was "American" or the result of "republican institutions." They kept their feet pretty well on the ground. Only infrequently are there those tedious and vague analyses of the "American soul" with which Europeans were so concerned and the spirituality of which they ordinarily found wanting. Americans rather acutely guessed that denunciations of our cultural abyss were either the final refuge of those overwhelmed by the promise of American material greatness or the shallow observations of tourists to whom the connection between economic and spiritual values had never occurred. Amusingly, but with a certain weariness as well, James Russell Lowell wrote:

I read the other day in print the remark of a British tourist who had eaten large quantities of our salt, such as it is (I grant it has not the European savor), that the Americans were hospitable, no doubt, but that it was partly because they longed for foreign visitors to relieve the tedium of their dead-level existence, and partly from ostentation.

America was without arts, science, literature, culture, or any native hope of supplying them. We were a people wholly given to money-getting, and who, having got it, knew no other use for it than to hold it fast. We were to Europe but a huge mob of adventurers and shop-keepers. Leigh Hunt expressed it well enough when he said that he could never think of America without seeing a gigantic counter stretched all along the seaboard.

At the same time, our critics somewhat too easily forgot that material must make ready the foundation for ideal triumphs, that the arts have no chance in poor countries. The Edinburgh Review never would have thought of asking, "Who reads a Russian book?" and England was satisfied with iron from Sweden without being impertinently inquisitive after her painters and statuaries. Was it that they expected too much from the mere miracle of Freedom?[8]

In general, American travelers viewed critically but sympathetically, understood what they witnessed, and engaged in amazingly few invidious comparisons with Europe. Americans, by and large, were better and actually more urbane travelers than Europeans. They possessed better manners, accepted inhospitalities more tolerantly, and exhibited greater humor and appreciation toward differences of living.

Their chief interest was fixed upon the nation's mechanical progress, pride in its economic advance, and an often sentimental regard for the wonders of nature. On the other hand, they did not ignore the charitable and humanitarian efforts to better social conditions, nor did they neglect either the striving for intellectual advance or the everyday life and manners of the common man and woman. Whether viewing the material or the spiritual, however, optimism was the keynote of all their observations. If things at the moment were not good, they soon would be. It would be difficult to find, before 1870, any description by an American traveler of his native land marked by pessimism or despair.

Such is not surprising in a new and rapidly developing country whose greatness was in its future rather than its past, where all around lay impressive and splendid landscapes, and where its people were emotionally confident of present as well as future security. Occasionally an account dealt with personalities, as in the works of Mrs. Royall, who, though amusing, was also tediously shrewish. Not infrequently, when confronted with some important personage, like Andrew Jackson or Brigham Young, details of personal interviews result. But, for the most part, American travelers appear to have centered their attention on things, places, and people collectively rather than upon individuals.

As if conscious that "a land without ruins is a land without memories—a land without memories is a land without history," there usually obtrudes in the travel books of Americans an attempt to give the "historical background" of places visited. The result is usually a triumph for pious intent but less com-

8. James R. Lowell, "On a Certain Condescension in Foreigners," *Atlantic Monthly*, XXIII (January, 1869), 85–92.

mendable in the way of reliable fact. These excursions into history the modern reader will ignore with safety.

Though every effort was made to achieve "style," too many Americans confused purple patches, elegance of phrasing, and banal platitudes of morality for good writing. Today's reader views these excesses either with uneasiness or amusement and recognizes in them the faults of an age as much as of an individual. If Americans reported more accurately than foreign travelers, and with at least equal penetration, it must be confessed that the latter were generally the better literary craftsmen.

The arrangement of a work of this nature falls heir to all the complaints of works anthological in character. Why was this included? Why was that omitted?

Such extracts as appear were invariably selected because they seemed to possess descriptive material peculiarly significant for an understanding of the life of the American people. In general, the work had to be a genuine travel book, that is, an account by one who had actually visited the areas he described and which he published within a few years of the time in which the journey took place. Admittedly, however, the line between such a work and one merely descriptive is thin. In such cases the intent of the writer was a determining factor. Naturally much valuable material has perforce been omitted. It is hoped that the selective bibliography at the end will partially atone for this rejected material.

All material, however valuable intrinsically, which did not specifically fall into the category of a work of travel has been omitted: guidebooks, guides for emigrants, almanacs and gazetteers; "recollections" published many years later; all manuscript material in the form of diaries, journals, and letters which either still reside in the collections of great libraries or have found their way into print only at a later date; and, lastly, official reports, government surveys, and congressional documents.

Since a primary purpose of these volumes is to make available as wide a range as possible of generally inaccessible travel material, works which have enjoyed the popularity of many editions, for example, Richard Henry Dana's *Two Years before the Mast,* or works which exist in a comparatively modern reprint, such as Timothy Flint's *Recollections of Ten Years,* are not included.

The text of this collection is precisely that of the original with the following exceptions: obvious mistakes of grammar, punctuation, or spelling have been corrected, though usually only where the original obscured or impeded the meaning; passages have been frequently deleted for the sake of brevity without the usual notation of ellipses; rearrangement of material, for the sake of clearer organization, has sometimes been made; and, in a few instances, words not in the original have been added without the usual brackets to maintain continuity. It should be noted, however, that in editing the original material *no change or alteration in the thought or meaning of the author has been permitted*.

The selections are grouped into four main geographic divisions: (I) the Atlantic Northeast, including the areas north of the Potomac River and east of the Appalachian Mountains; (II) the South, including the areas south of the Potomac and Ohio rivers and extending west of the Mississippi River as far as Texas; (III) the Prairies and the Plains, including that region between the Appalachians and the Rockies; and (IV) the Pacific West, including the territory from the Rockies to the Coast and including also the Southwest. Within each geographic section the material is arranged chronologically.

Contents

Contents

II. THE COTTON KINGDOM

III. THE VALLEY OF DEMOCRACY

Contents

Part I

THE RISING CITIES OF THE ATLANTIC NORTHEAST

From the earliest days of the Republic, New England and the Middle States engendered a particular and peculiar interest for most Americans. This was not merely because of the historical role they had played in the winning of independence, for in this they shared honors with the states of the Atlantic South, but rather because of the kind of civilization they were developing with each new decade. Here were located the largest towns and cities; here were first developed new modes of transportation, improved roads, canals, and railways; here were created the new manufactures with their accumulated surpluses of capital; and here arose the first stirrings of a new national culture and the first promptings of humanitarian reform and impulse.

It was essentially an urban culture, and, accordingly, it was to the cities that most travelers to the Northeast were drawn. They did not entirely neglect the countryside, it is true; but it is clear from the records they have left that they merely journeyed through it to reach the next town on their itineraries. Of course the transportation lines, arranged primarily in reference to interurban connections, were partly responsible for the course of their travels, as also was the fact that the urban centers offered more in the way of amusements, comforts, and concentrated "sights." Yet, despite these practical considerations, the traveler, seeking the characteristic manifestations of northern life, was drawn into the cities by a sure instinct for essentials.

What they viewed depended, naturally, on the personality of the sight-seer. Some dutifully viewed the monuments and historic scenes or gathered, usually out of a local gazetteer, dull figures on the height of buildings or the width of streets. Others were prone to generalize on the culture or nature of the inhabitants, finding the ladies of Baltimore well dressed or the children of Boston well mannered. Most observed the more serious aspects of urban culture with discernment, though a few gazed upon its foibles with amusement. Even the smaller towns came in for due consideration, but it was natural that the larger cities—Baltimore, Philadelphia, Boston, and, above all, New York—should receive the greatest attention. When all the travel records are taken together, the result is an illuminating and reasonably complete description of urban manners and life.

The best accounts by American travelers into the northeastern area are in the years before the Civil War. Though the number of travel works increases after that date, the quality of the accounts falls off sharply. Sentimentalism, rose-colored romance, and the search for "quaintness" and the picturesque became the stock in trade of the narrations. Some describe the excellence of trout-fishing on an inland stream or a lazy boating trip along the coast. No one would suspect by 1890 that New England, New York, or Pennsylvania possessed huge cities and great manufacturing plants or that the population was largely of immigrant derivation. The inhabitants had become "natives," and the traveler gave way to the tourist.

I

A Southern View of Boston and Its Schools, 1793

*J*ohn *Drayton, the son of a distinguished Revolutionary soldier, was born at Drayton Hall, not far from Charleston, South Carolina. Educated, partly at Princeton, partly in London, his life was given chiefly to politics and the law. As early as 1792 he was elected a member of the House of Representatives in South Carolina, and thereafter he served his native state as a member of the state Senate, lieutenant-governor, and governor. In 1812 he was appointed a judge of the United States District Court in South Carolina, an office he occupied until his death in 1822. His chief writings are* A View of South Carolina *(1802), modeled somewhat after Jefferson's* Notes on Virginia, *and the* Memoir of the American Revolution *(1821).*

In 1793, the year before his marriage, he made a brief excursion to the North. The result, from which the following passages have been taken, was the publication in 1794 of the Letters Written during a Tour through the Northern and Eastern States of America. *The account is brief and, despite its title, covers little more than New York City, Boston, and a few of the smaller New England towns. Though not without certain conceits of the eighteenth century, it is a fairly literal narration, in parts stilted and discon-*

nected, with a spelling and punctuation free and untrammeled. Drayton was an urbane gentleman. He came to see what there was to see, and he indulges in no invidious comparisons with his own South Carolina. Indeed, he gives the impression that the South might learn much from northern institutions. His great interest in education—when governor, he was to urge and secure the establishment of a state university in South Carolina—is apparent from the full and lengthy attention he devotes to the Boston school system, a system undoubtedly superior to any other in the United States, though not so good, in 1793, as Drayton supposed.

I mentioned in my last letter, that I dined with the select men of the town, on the 8th instant. It is my intention at present to inform you upon what occasion it was, and what were the occurrences of the day. You must then know, that I had been previously invited by them, to attend the visitation of their public schools on that day. Once, every year, they are visited in this public manner, besides, being attended at other times by a committee; and happy was it for me, that their visitation took place at that auspicious moment. I enjoyed thereby a pleasure, which perhaps I may never receive again in this place.

It is to the honor of Boston, that its youth are almost entirely educated in a public manner; and at the public expence. For this purpose, a proportionate tax is laid upon the citizens sufficient to support schools: where, the poor as well as the rich, have an equal claim to the master's attention, and the benefit of the institution: without any additional expence. They are here offered by their natural, to their political parent, for the purpose of being educated; not, as may suit the whim of their relations, but, as may tend most to their country's good. To view these sources of knowledge, to encourage the exertions of the scholars, and to observe the attention of their masters, was the end of our visitation.

The procession began at 8 o'clock, A.M. and consisted of the select men of the town, the lieutenant governor, and other public officers of the commonwealth: the vice-president of the United States of America; the clergy: consuls of foreign powers; respectable gentlemen of the town; and strangers who had been invited: making I suppose near one hundred in number. Our visits were scarcely finished by 3 o'clock P.M. for we went to seven different schools. —Six, for the attainment of useful American knowledge; and the seventh, for that of the classics.

The school rooms are built at the public expence; large enough to accommodate two hundred scholars; and are oblong. The seats are disposed along the length of the room, five rows deep on each side; rising one above another, and leaving a passage way in the middle. Each bench is capable of accommodating five scholars: hence, with a glance of the eye, one may make a tolerably good guess, at the number which may be present. There are generally two of these rooms under the same roof; one below, and the other, above stairs. The one in the first floor, is for the education of girls; and the upper one, is for that of boys. Be not surprized, at my mentioning that girls are educated in this public manner. It is the pride of the citizens, that it is so done.

Children are not admissible into the public schools at Boston, until seven years old: and they are there educated, the girls until they be twelve, and the boys until they arrive at the age of fourteen. At which time, the poor boys are sufficiently acquainted with the necessary parts of education, to be put out to some trade; while the girls can follow pursuits becoming their different stations in life.

The schools for the girls, are entirely under the directions of masters; and if I be not mistaken, under those who have graduated at some college. They are here by just degrees instructed in all the solid parts of an American education, becoming their sex. I heard the dialogue between Syphax and Juba in the tragedy of Cato, read by several of them in the different schools; with a propriety and elegance commanding my greatest admiration. Poetry and prose, equally call their attention. Whether to follow Pope in his moral essays on man, or to converse with each other, in the instructive reading of dialogues they exhibited a proficiency, which in girls between seven and twelve years of age was surprising. Writing and arithmetic, claim also a portion of their time. And a knowledge of grammar, early impressed upon their minds, directs them to a proper use of their own language.

The boys were examined in grammar, arithmetic, and geography; much to their honor and my gratification. They are instructed in an accurate knowledge of their own country, as well as in the grand outlines of the United States: and I believe are made acquainted with navigation, and surveying. They excell in beautiful writing. When any boy discoveres a brightness of abilities, and desire of literary knowledge, he is removed to the Latin and Greek school; from whence, if he continue to merit the good opinion of his parents, he at a proper time is advanced to Cambridge college. There, to receive an education, still at the public expence, as far as relates to tuition. Thus we find, that the paths of knowledge are equally open here to the poor, as well as to the rich.

One part of the necessary education which the children receive, is in the particular care paid to the pronunciation of their language. That the schools in America generally teach the pronunciation, is true; but I have never known any to expose the faults of pronunciation, in so forcible a manner as those, which are the subject of the present letter. The masters have for this purpose, selected, by way of illustration, a number of words generally miscalled: with which the children are instructed to be well acquainted. They are examined upon them, from time to time, and are taught to pronounce the word first in its proper way, and then to contrast it with the mode in which it is miscalled. As for example,

Boil,	is called Boil,	and not *Bile.*
Cucumber,	Cucumber,	*Cowcumber.*
Certain,	Certain,	*Sartin.*
Merchant,	Merchant,	*Marchant.*
Molasses,	Molasses,	*Lasses.*
Onions,	Onions,	*Inions.*
Oil,	Oil,	*Ile.*
Point,	Point,	*Pint.*
Steady,	Steady,	*Study.*

From the examination of the English schools we passed to that of the Latin, and Greek; consisting of about fifty scholars. Before the examination began, a salutatory oration in Latin, was delivered by a young gentleman of the senior class. After which, an examination took place, upon the Latin and Greek grammars, Clarke's introduction, Virgil, Horace and Homer. Then, a dialogue in Latin, was delivered by the senior class. After which a valedictory oration in English was pronounced by one of that class, who bids fair to rise in literature. He is the son of a blacksmith, educated at the public expence: and deservedly rising, from meriting the favor of his countrymen.

The number of children which we saw at the different schools, inclusively amounted to eleven hundred. I am informed, that there are about fourteen hundred educated at the public expence in this place. Many of them are children of genteel families; but by far the greater part, are poor children.

The examination at every school, ended with an *exhortation,* and a prayer; delivered by two gentlemen of the clergy successively. How great an influence these had upon the hearers, is not for me to say. But for myself, I enjoyed a pleasure of devotion and patriotism, which cannot be described.

I doubt whether there be any country, where the wants of the unfortunate are more respected, than in the commonwealth of Massachusetts. Her fostering hand leads the youth into life; and is afterwards ready to be extended, when any unfortunate emergency may offer. Of their institutions for the relief of misfortune, there is none which affords me more satisfaction than one for the assistance of ship-wrecked people; called the Humane Society. It is formed by some of the most respectable men of the town, as well clergy as laity. From whose fund, small huts are built upon the islands most exposed to ship-wreck, for the relief of those, whose good fortune may bring them to land, escaped from the dangers of the sea.

These huts, are generally placed upon uninhabited islands; and are furnished with blankets, wood, tinder-box, candles, salt provisions, biscuit, and such other things, which although not the luxuries, are yet the necessaries of life. They are visited once every year, by the society, and such gentlemen as they may choose to invite: for the purpose of seeing whether the hut, and necessaries placed in them, are in good order. It was my good fortune to be of the party, which went down the harbour upon that occasion. We were in number about forty; and sailed in a packet, attended by a handsome twelve oared barge. Such is the respect paid to this society by the government, that upon these occasions it is always honored by a federal salute of cannon, from the castle; as well when going, as when returning. I am informed that these huts have already been the means of saving to the commonwealth, the lives of many of its citizens: while the society judiciously distributes rewards to those, whose exertions have served the distressed.

I did not omit paying a visit to Castle-William. It is situated in the harbour of Boston, a league below the town: upon an island containing about thirty acres of land. There is a beautiful archipelago of islands in this harbour, in number, amounting to about forty: all of which, have high grounds upon them. Upon the height of one of these islands, the castle is placed. In some parts of it, there is a stone foundation; but in others, the height of the land is only assisted with ramparts, and merlons of turf. I am informed it was formerly furnished with three tier of cannon. The first consisting of heavy ones, placed at the waters edge: and the other two upon platforms at the embrasures. But now, they are placed upon the middle battery, except thirteen small ones, which being round the flag-staff en barbette, serve for the purpose of saluting. The castle is very much out of order at present; the platforms and carriages for guns, being much injured by the weather. However, even in its present situation it is very respectable: and is well provided with mortars, cannon, bombs, ball, and double-headed shot. From its near situation to the channel, its guns can shoot with much effect, upon vessels passing to, or from the town. Here, I saw an eighteen pounder, which the British had disabled of its trunnions, re-mounted and fit for service, upon a carriage, invented for that particular purpose. It is made of white oak, and is said to answer very well.

There are now within the castle, barracks equal to the lodgement of a thousand men: besides many buildings upon the island, without its gates.

The ground within the earth, is intersected at proper distances by covered ways: and the magazine is protected from accidents. Here, are now mounted about thirty pieces of heavy cannon besides some smaller ones. It is garrisoned by a company of infantry upon pay, at the expence of the commonwealth: who also guard the convicts here sent, convicted of crimes deserving punishment less than death. They are condemned to labour for a certain term of years, or for life: of whom, seventy are now on the island, chiefly employed in the nail manufactory.

I went into the blacksmith's shop, which is a long building, with several forges in it; but, I assure you I was soon glad to leave it: for never was I attacked by such a set of importunate sturdy beggars in my life. I had no opportunity of making any observations, or asking any questions; so incessantly did their shameless demands wring in mine ears. I hastened from a place, where I saw there was nothing to be gained; and much, to be lost. For, although it be a pleasure to me in reflecting, that I have never in my life withholden assistance from the unfortunate; yet it is also my satisfaction to avoid throwing it away upon the undeserving. In the midst of such a confusion of tongues, of entreaties, and of oaths; it was impossible to make any discrimination. While some were begging, others, were as earnest, that nothing should be given them: charging them, with being unworthy of charity. Disgusted at the scene, I left them to the punishment, which their crimes had deservedly brought down, upon their heads.

A stranger at Boston, soon remarks the industry of its inhabitants; and their attention to business. While, he laments that so noted a town in the page of history, were not regulated by a better police. It is under the controul of select-men, as indeed all the other towns of the commonwealth are: but their powers, are too much abridged by reason of their town meetings, to undertake any thing of efficiency, without having recourse to the opinions of a multifarious assembly. Few lamps assist the passenger through the streets by night, and if ever they were necessary in any place, they certainly are in this. For the streets are crooked, and narrow; paved from side to side with round stones, extremely disagreeable, and inconvenient to those who walk them: and for this reason, strangers are more apt to ride about this, than any other town on the continent. In many streets there are no railings or posts, to defend one from the carriages, which are incessantly traversing them. Carts, waggons, drays, trucks, wheelbarrows, and porters, are continually obstructing the passage in these streets: While, the people concerned in this kind of business, are not apt to put themselves out of the way, for the pleasure of conferring favors. They seem so conscious that all men are equal, that they take a pride in shewing their knowledge of this principle upon every occasion. I have seen a porter with a little hand cart pursuing his destination in the street, with the utmost unconcern; at the risk of being crippled, or having his cart crushed to pieces by a carriage which was thundering in his ears. And having escaped misfortune, he reviled the coachman, and asked him if he

HARVARD SQUARE IN 1776

did not see him? The same question might have been retorted in answer, with the addition of 'did not you hear me?' Nothing, but the most sullen and unaccommodating disposition, could have hindered him from giving way to a carriage; which could turn aside less easily, than he might have done.*

* [In this respect, matters had not appreciatively improved after fifty years apparently. Thus William T. Thompson, in 1848, described his first walk through Boston streets:

"If a man could walk edgeways, he mought possibly manage to git through a square or two of Boston 'thout gittin nocked off the side-walk more'n a dozen times. Why, they aint much wider than the space between the rows of a pea-patch, and then they are so twistified that it's as much as a common sized body can do to keep both feet in the same street at the same time. And then what makes it worse, is the way the Boston peeple walks. They all go dashin along like they was gwine to die, and hadn't but a few hours left to settle ther bisness. As for givin the walk to a lady, or half of it to a gentleman, they don't think of no sich thing, and if you don't want to have your breth nocked out of you evry few steps, you mought as well take the middle of the street at once, whar, if you don't keep a monstrous sharp lookout, you is certain to be run over by ther everlastin grate, long, sheep-shear lookin carts. After bumpin along for 'bout half a square, I found myself in the street and my frend half way into a store dore, whar he was nocked by a feller what was stavin ahead with a armfull of wooden clocks" (William T. Thompson, *Major Jones's Sketches of Travel* [Philadelphia, 1848], p. 127).—Ed.]

There cannot be a greater nuisance in any town, and particularly in this, than the allowance of hucksters, to occupy part of the streets, during the day. Either the overseers of the markets and streets, are not invested with sufficient powers to remedy the evil; or some reason, of which, I am uninformed, forbids their putting them in force. One would imagine, that with such heavy taxes as the Bostonians labour under, much more, might be done for their convenience. It may truly be said, that they are taxed, not by what they are worth: but by what their appearances in life are. Hence, the reason, why some monied men among them, make no show: and are without noise continually amassing wealth, and confining it within their immediate grasp, to the disadvantage of the society at large. While others of more generous dispositions, are called upon to pay a much larger tax, than they should in justice do. The taxes are imposed by assessors upon their estate, stock in trade, and in the funds: and unless the citizens prove to their satisfaction, that they do not possess a fortune equal to their assessment, they are obliged to pay the tax. This publication they are unwilling to make, particularly mercantile men: who deem it improper that persons might thus be informed of their private circumstances. Hence, some respectable and rich citizens have left the town: an example, which may be followed by others, should this system of taxation not be altered.

No place in America is perhaps equal to Boston, for excellent hackney coaches. From nine o'clock in the morning, to the same hour in the evening, they are on the stand in State-street: and are ready at a moment's warning.

All kinds of trades, flourish in this industrious place. Among their manufactures, there are none more worthy of being noticed, than that of glass, wool-cards, sail-duck, and fishing-hooks. The machines for the making of the wool-cards, is extremely ingenious: and said to be invented by an inhabitant of the town. It is supposed to be superior to any thing of the kind in Europe. Every piece of the wooden work, is fashioned out by a particular machine; so that the utmost uniformity is observable among the different parts of the wooden work. The wires, are cut and bent, at the same time; which is considered as a great and expeditious improvement. The duck manufactory carries on a vast deal of business; and supplies much of the shipping with sails. It employs three hundred and sixty persons; seventy of whom are girls: and works twenty-seven looms. The importation of sail cloth has been greatly reduced, since this manufacture has been established; in so much, that a gentleman who had been in the habit of annually importing four thousand pieces of sail cloth from Russia, informed me, he now only imports two thousand, from that place.

There is a public walk in Boston, called the mall: which is very agreeable. It is upwards of half a mile long, and offers to your choice both a gravel, and a turf walk; shaded by beautiful elm trees. A street runs parallel with it on one side; and on the other a large common: where hundreds of cattle feed during the day. This common on the further side, rises up to a considerable height. At one end of the walk is a prospect of a large basin of water, Roxbury town, and Charles river: at the other, the town of Boston, and column upon Beacon hill.

This column has been lately erected, in commemoration of remarkable events which took place, during the American war: and in honor of its present efficient government. It is about sixty feet high: crowned on the top with a golden eagle standing upon a globe, and overlooking the arms of the United States. This spot, is the highest elevation about Boston. From it, may be seen over the tops of all the houses, the islands in the harbour, the light house, many leagues at sea, and a vast distance into the country. Bunker's hill, here heaves into view. From this hill, also is seen the bridge over Charles river, connecting Boston with Charlestown: and another partly finished, opening a more easy communication with Cambridge. The first is about a quarter of a mile long; the latter will be more than twice its length. They have each of them side ways, for foot passengers, are illuminated at night by lamps, and are built of wood: which, in all probability, will last long without repair; as the worm does not bite in these northern latitudes.

2

Life and Manners in New England, 1812

*T*hough born (1752) at Northampton, Massachusetts, Timothy Dwight belonged by lineage to the distinguished Connecticut Burrs, Edwardses, and Huntingtons. After graduation from Yale, he became a preacher and a pedagogue. Always ambitious, and with what today would be described as the "executive mind," he was appointed president of Yale in 1795. He brought renown to that institution through a term of office which lasted until his death in 1817.

He was a prolific writer. Much was in a theological vein, but he was also devoted to the belles-lettres, encouraged their study at Yale, and himself produced a considerable poetic effusion. Beginning in 1785 he published the tedious Conquest of Canaan, an epic once compared to the Iliad and the Aeneid, and in subsequent years the pastoral Greenfield Hill, and the satirical Triumph of Infidelity. Such writings ensconced him safely in that remarkable literary circle known today as the Connecticut Wits.

Dwight was undoubtedly a man of courage, possessed of good judgment, and held forthright convictions. However, his outlook on life was often narrow and not infrequently bigoted. His sobriquet, "Pope Dwight," testifies not only to his ultraconservative Federalism in politics and to his ultraconservative Calvinism in theology but as well to the crushing and lofty manner of his pronouncements.

His tours through the length and breadth of New England, with an occasional sally into neighboring New York, began in 1796. Year after year he journeyed to a different place, recording faithfully and accurately the inexhaustible details of his observations: every hamlet and town; the size of the *population; the number of churches; the amount of commerce; the state of the inns; the condition of the roads. Gathered together in 1821, this material was published in New Haven in four massive volumes as* Travels in New-England and New-York. *It is likely to remain his most enduring work, as it is certainly one of the best-known accounts by an American traveler. For the most part factual and precise, it contains, however, illuminating summaries of the New England character and morals. Its tone is sternly Federalist and Calvinist. At times hardly more than a gazetteer, it is a source of unlimited information. As a reference work, its value is unequaled, but, as literature, its style—lumbering along in massive, balanced sentences—is, frankly, dull.*

YALE COLLEGE DESCRIBED BY ITS PRESIDENT

A man of learning and benevolence cannot fail of finding a particular interest in authentic accounts of the state of learning in any country which becomes an object of his inquiries. You will therefore naturally expect from me a minute account of Yale college; both because it is one of the oldest and most respectable seminaries in this country, and because, from the office which I hold in it, you may fairly regard the story as claiming your confidence. At the same time you will remember, that the plan of education pursued throughout New-England is in substance the same. This recital therefore will serve, with a moderate number of exceptions, not very material, as a picture of all the New-England colleges.

In the year 1792, the legislature gave to the institution the arrearages of certain taxes, which had for some time been due to the state in its paper currency, on the condition, that the governor, lieutenant-governor, and six senior councillors, for the time being, should by a vote of the corporation, as well as the authority of the state, be received as members of their board; the clerical side of the board, however, retaining the power of filling up their own vacancies. The proposal was unanimously accepted by the corporation, and the following September these gentlemen took their seats. From that time to the present the trustees have consisted of the governor, lieutenant-governor, and six senior councillors, the president and ten fellows being clergymen.

The legislature in their first charter had given to the institution the annual sum of fifty pounds sterling, and continued this grant until the year 1755. In consequence of this legislative benefaction the trustees were enabled to purchase the whole front of the square on the north-western side of the green, and on this ground to erect three new academical buildings and a house for the president; to make a handsome addition to their library; to procure a complete philosophical* and chemical apparatus, and to establish three new professorships; a professorship of chemistry, in 1800; of law, in 1804; and of languages and ecclesiastical history, in 1805.

The academical buildings consist of three colleges, of four stories, each containing thirty-two rooms; named Connecticut Hall, Union Hall, and Berkely Hall; a chapel, containing in the third story a philosophical chamber and rooms for the philosophical apparatus, and a building resembling the chapel in form, and named the Connecticut Lyceum. This building contains seven recitation rooms, six for the three younger classes, and one for the senior class; a chemical laboratory, and its necessary appendages; two chambers, occupied by professors, and the library. The number of books in the library is about seven thousand volumes. Few libraries are, probably, more valuable in proportion to their size. The situation of the academical buildings is uncommonly pleasant, fronting the green on the north-western side, upon a handsome elevation, with a spacious yard before them. The buildings are plain; but so arranged as to strike the eye with pleasure.

At the same time you are to be informed, that Yale college has never received any very considerable benefactions, except from the legislature of Connecticut. Munificent donations have been given to Harvard college by several opulent gentlemen, both in Great Britain and America. About two thousand pounds sterling, plainly intended for Yale college by the Hon. Edward Hopkins, once governor of Connecticut, fell, through a series of accidents, partly into the hands of her sister seminary and partly to three grammar schools: one at New-Haven, one at Hartford, and one at Hadley, in Massachusetts. The wealthy men of this state have never been numerous, and but one of them has ever thought it proper seriously to aid this institution out of his own treasures. Everything of this nature, which has been done here, has been done by men of moderate fortunes. Upwards of two hundred youths are in this seminary continually receiving benefits from the efficacy of a moderate sum, for the real value of which millions would be a cheap price. There is not a legislature, a court, a congregation, a town-meeting, nor even a fire-side, which, however insensible of the fact, does not share in these benefits.

The course of education, pursued in this seminary, is the following:

Students are examined for admission in the works of Virgil; the Select Orations of Cicero; Clark's, or Mair's Introduction to the making of Latin; the Greek Testament; the several branches of Arithmetic; Sallust, and Collectanea Graeca Minora.

In the first, or freshman year, are studied Collectanea Graeca Minora;

* [I.e., scientific.—ED.]

Homer's Iliad, six books; Livy, the first five books; Cicero de Oratore; Adam's Roman Antiquities; Morse's Geography, vol. i; Webber's Mathematics, vol. i.

In the second, or sophomore year, Horace; Collectanea Graeca Majora, vol. i; Morse's Geography, vol. ii; Webber's Mathematics, vol. ii; Euclid's Elements; English Grammar; Tytler's Elements of History.

In the third, or junior year, Tacitus (history); Collectanea Graeca Majora; Enfield's Natural Philosophy; Enfield's Astronomy; Chemistry; Vince's Fluxions.

In the fourth, or senior year, Blair's Lectures—Logic; Chemistry, Natural Philosophy, and Astronomy; Locke on the Human Understanding; Paley's Moral Philosophy; Theology.

The professor of divinity reads no public lectures properly so called. Instead of this, he delivers a system of divinity in sermons; one every sabbath in term time through four years, the period of education in the college. The number of these discourses is one hundred and sixty: the term time in each year being forty weeks. He also delivers an informal lecture to the senior class every week; completing in this manner a system of theology each year.

The professor of mathematics and natural philosophy goes through a course of philosophical experiments with the junior class every year, and delivers two lectures to the senior class every week.

The professor of chemistry delivers one hundred and twenty lectures in that science every year to the two elder classes, so that each class hears a complete course of chemical lectures twice. These are delivered in the laboratory, a room convenient for this purpose. They have here the advantage of seeing every experiment commenced and completed. The apparatus is ample, and the establishment superior, it is believed, to any thing of the kind on this continent. The chemical professor also delivers private lectures on mineralogy. A very valuable cabinet of mineralogical specimens is a part of the collegiate apparatus.

The professor of languages and ecclesiastical history will deliver a complete course of lectures on the latter subject, commencing with the earliest period of the church, and extending to the present time.

The professor of law is required to read thirty-six lectures only, to be completed in two years, on the law of nature, the American constitution, and the jurisprudence of Connecticut.

A medical institution will be established in this seminary at the next meeting of the corporation. It will consist of three professorships beside that of chemistry: one of the materia medica and botany; one of anatomy and surgery; and one of the theory and practice of physic. In this institution the medical society of this state co-operate with the college. The students will be required to study two years, and will be examined by a committee of eight: four of them professors, the other four chosen by the medical convention. When they have heard one course of lectures, and have been approved at this examination, they will receive a license to practice physic and surgery. But, to receive the degree of M.D. they must have heard two courses of lectures. A course will be completed each year.

The three younger academical classes are divided, and have each two tutors. To them they recite three times a day, four days in the week; and twice the two remaining days. The senior class recites once a day to the president. All the classes are made responsible for the manner in which they hear, and remember the lectures; being examined at every lecture concerning their knowledge of the preceding; and accordingly are all furnished with note books, in which they take down at the time the principal subjects of every lecture. This responsibility, so far as I am informed, is rarely a part of an European system of education.

In addition to all these exercises the students in the several classes are required daily to exhibit, in succession, compositions of various kinds, all of which are examined by the respective instructors. The senior and junior classes also dispute forensically every week two questions, on some subject approved by the instructor. When the dispute is ended, the instructor discusses the question at length, and gives his own views of it, and of the several arguments on both sides, to the class. This is believed to be an exercise not inferior in its advantages to any other. The students also declaim, both publicly and privately, during their academical course. On the third Wednesday of July, annually, the senior class is examined by the professors, tutors, and other gentlemen commissioned for that purpose, in their whole course of studies. After the examination is ended a vote is taken on each, by which it is determined whether he shall receive the degree of bachelor of arts. The issue of this procedure is then reported to the president; and by him, on the Tuesday preceding the commencement, to the corporation. Such as are approved by the examiners, and have been guilty of no improper conduct in the interim, are then by an act of the corporation entitled to receive the following day the degree of bachelor of arts. All who have received this degree, and have not disgraced themselves by any improper conduct, are upon application entitled, at the end of three years, to receive that of master of arts.

On the Friday preceding the commencement, the senior class, who are regularly permitted to return home after the examination, re-assemble at the college. The following Sabbath a sermon is addressed to them by the professor of divinity.

The commencement is holden on the succeeding Wednesday, in the church belonging to the first congregation in this city. A very numerous and brilliant assembly is always collected upon this occasion. The exhibitions begin, however, on the preceding evening; when speeches selected by the students of the three younger classes, from ancient or modern orators and poets, and approved by the faculty of the college, are declaimed. The number of exhibitors is usually not far from twenty. Honorary premiums are given to three in each class, who, by judges appointed for the purpose, are declared to have declaimed best.

On the morning of the commencement day, at 9 o'clock, a procession is formed at the chapel door by the students, candidates for the master's degree, the faculty, the corporation, and a numerous train of the clergy and other gentlemen, under the conduct of the sheriff of the county; and proceeds circuitously to the church. The exercises commence with a prayer by the president and a piece of sacred music. Such candidates for the first degree as have been previously selected by the faculty for this purpose, then pronounce a series of orations, disputes, colloquies, &c., written by themselves. Another piece of sacred music concludes the exercises of the morning. The exercises of the afternoon differ little from those of the morning; except that orations are spoken by the candidates for the second degree, and that the degrees are conferred. The decorum observed on this occasion is entire, honourable to those who assemble, and strongly indicative of a refined state of society. I ought before to have observed, that all the students in the seminary are publicly examined twice every year in their several studies; and, if found seriously deficient, are liable to degradation. In this exercise a fortnight each year is very laboriously employed.

The expense of tuition is thirty-three dollars a year, or seven pounds eight shillings and six pence sterling. This sum, which is paid by every student, entitles each one to the instruction given by the professors, as well as to that of the ordinary course.

The government of Yale college is in the hands of the president and eighteen fellows, who have power to "make, repeal, and alter, all such wholesome and reasonable laws, rules, and ordinances, not repugnant to the laws of the state, as they shall think fit and proper for the instruction and education of the students, and to order, govern, rule, and manage the said college, and all matters, affairs, and things, thereunto belonging. Their acts, however, are to be laid before the legislature as often as required; and may be repealed and disallowed by the legislature whenever it shall think proper." The president, also, with the consent of the fellows, has power "to give and confer all such honours, degrees, and licenses, as are usually given in colleges or universities, upon such as they shall think worthy thereof."

The number of students is ordinarily about two hundred and sixty. The whole number graduated, to the year 1814, was three thousand four hundred and ten. Of these two hundred and seven have filled the high offices of magistracy, nine hundred and forty-one have been ministers of the Gospel, one thousand five hundred and thirty-eight have died, and one thousand eight hundred and seventy-two were still living.

EVERYDAY LIVING

The means of comfortable living are in New-England so abundant, and so easily obtained, as to be within the reach of every man who has health, industry, common honesty, and common sense. Labour commands such a price, that every labourer of this character may earn from one hundred and twenty-five to two hundred and fifty dollars a year. Hence every one may, within a moderate period, purchase himself a farm of considerable extent in the recent settlements, and a small one in those which are older. Even those, who are somewhat below the common level in these attributes, may and do acquire small houses and gardens, where they usually live comfortably.

The food of the inhabitants at large, even of the poor, is principally flesh and fish; one or other of which is eaten by a greater part of the inhabitants twice and three times a day. A breakfast, in the large towns, is chiefly bread and butter; the bread in the cool season generally toasted. In the country almost universally this is accompanied with smoked dried beef, cheese, or some species of fish or flesh broiled, or otherwise fitted to the taste of the family. So universal is this custom, that a breakfast without such an addition is considered as scarcely worth eating. At dinner, the vegetables continually succeed each other in their varieties. Fruits also, which are very numerous and various, as well as very rich and luscious, are brought upon the dinner-table, or are eaten in other parts of the day, throughout most of the year. Supper, in mosts parts of the country, is like breakfast, except that it is made up partially of preserved fruits, different kinds of cake, pies, tarts, &c. The meats, used at breakfast and supper, are generally intended to be dainties.

Puddings, formed of rice, flour, maize, and sometimes of buck-wheat, very frequently constitute a part of the dinner.

Pork, except the hams, shoulders, and cheeks, is never converted into bacon. I do not know that I ever saw a flitch of bacon cured in New-England in my life. The sides of the hog are here always pickled, and by the New-England people are esteemed much superior to bacon. The pork of New-England is fatted upon maize, a sweeter and richer food for cattle of all kinds than any other, is more skillfully cured, and is, therefore, better than that of any other country. It is also a favourite food with most of the inhabitants.

Tea and coffee constitute a part of the breakfast and supper of every class, and almost of every individual. The principal drink of the inhabitants is cyder. Wine, which is here very cheap, is extensively used; so in the mild season is punch. Porter, also, is drunk by fashionable people; and, in small quantities, ale. In the large towns, particularly in Boston, dinners are given without number, but much more unfrequently in the smaller ones. The favourite entertainment in them is the supper. For this there are two potent reasons. One is, every body is here employed in business through the day. The evening, being the only season of leisure, furnishes the best opportunity for that agreeable intercourse, which is the primary object of all entertainments. The other is, the want of a sufficient number of servants to take the burthen of superintending the preparation of dinners from the mistress of the family. I have been present at a very great multitude of entertainments of both kinds, and am compelled to say, that those of the evening are much the most pleasant and rational. There is less excess, and more leisure; the mind is more cheerful, and the conversation almost of course more sprightly, interesting, and useful.

The hours of breakfast vary in the country from six to eight in the summer, and from seven to nine in the winter; those of dinner from twelve to two; those of supper from five to eight. In the large towns all these hours vary still more. The most fashionable people breakfast late, and dine from three to four. The food of such people is principally taken at a single meal. In the summer many of the labouring people make their principal meal at supper.

The proportion of animal food, eaten in this country, is, I think, excessive.

At entertainments, the dining-table is loaded with a much greater variety of dishes than good sense will justify. A fashion, which it is difficult to resist, prevails, in this respect, over every rational consideration.

The quantity of ardent spirits, consumed chiefly by the middle and lower classes of people, is scandalous to its character.

The dress of the inhabitants is chiefly formed of the manufactures, and made up in the fashions of Europe, particularly of Great Britain.

The principal amusements of the inhabitants are visiting, dancing, music, conversation, walking, riding, sailing, shooting at a mark, draughts, chess, and unhappily, in some of the larger towns, cards, and dramatic exhibitions. A considerable amusement is also furnished in many places by the examination and exhibitions of the superior schools; and a more considerable one by the public exhibitions of the colleges.

Our countrymen also fish and hunt.

Journies taken for pleasure are very numerous, and are a favourite object.

Boys and young men play at foot-ball, cricket, quoits, and at many other sports of an athletic cast, and in the winter are peculiarly fond of skating. Riding in a sleigh, or sledge, is also a favourite diversion in New-England.

People of wealth, and many in moderate circumstances, have their children taught music, particularly on the piano-forte; and many of the young men play on the German flute, violin, clarionet, &c. Serenading is not unfrequent.

Visiting, on the plan of sociality and friendship, is here among all classes of people, especially among those who are intelligent and refined, a very agreeable and very rational source of enjoyment.

Reading also is a favourite employment with persons in almost all conditions of life. A considerable collection of books, throughout a great part of this country, is furnished to the inhabitants by social libraries. Private libraries are undoubtedly much more limited than in Great Britain. Many of them are, however, sufficient collections to extend much useful information, and to supply not a small fund of pleasure to their proprietors and others. By these means a great number of persons are enabled to read as extensively as their other avocations will permit. The reading of newspapers in this country is undoubtedly excessive, as is also the number of papers annually published.

Marriages were formerly festivals of considerable significance in this country. It was customary to invite even remote relations of the parties, all their particular friends, and a great number of their neighbours. A dinner was made, in form, by the parents of the bride for the bridegroom and a numerous suite. The marriage was celebrated in the evening. Cake and wine were plentifully distributed among the guests; and the festivity was concluded with dancing. At the present time the guests are usually few.

Justices of the peace are throughout New-England authorized to marry, but are rarely if ever employed to perform this service when a clergyman can be obtained.

At the funerals in New-England, the friends and neighbours attend of course. When the assembly is gathered by the ringing of the parish bell, a prayer is made at the house in which the deceased lived, by the clergyman, and is always adapted to the occasion. The corpse is then conveyed to the grave, either upon a hearse or upon men's shoulders. In the latter case, the young men of the town always voluntarily offer their services in sufficient numbers. A solemn procession accompanies it, and to a great exent it is attended by pall-bearers. After the corpse is committed to the grave, in many places a solemn address is made by the clergyman to the assembly, and the thanks of the surviving family are returned to those who are present for their attendance. Sometimes the procession is formed anew, and accompanies the mourners to their habitation; but more frequently the company disperses.

The persons of the New-Englanders, their complexion, manners, and language, so much resemble those of Englishmen, that the similarity has been the subject of not a little discussion on both sides of the Atlantic, in the knotty case of impressing seamen. Differences however exist, which are discernible without much difficulty. The English are, as a body, fairer than we; have oftener hair of a light colour, and blue eyes. They are more frequently fleshy. Our countrymen are taller, more agile, have frequently dark hair and black eyes, and the muscles are more strongly marked, both in the limbs and in the face.

BOSTON BEFORE 1845

The climate of this country, and perhaps the mode of living, have, I think, had a perceptible influence on both the complexion and figure of the New-England people. Still, a multitude of very fair complexions are found everywhere; and flaxen, auburn, golden, and still lighter-coloured hair, is seen in very numerous instances.

The natives of New-England are generally straight, and well-formed. Deformed persons are found here; but, I have good reason to believe, as rarely as in any country under Heaven. There is however one particular, in which we are said to fall behind most nations. It is supposed that our teeth more generally decay at an untimely period.

The women of New-England are generally well, and often elegantly formed. Their features have usually a good degree of regularity, are comely, and frequently handsome. A vast number of them have complexions inferior to none in the world. In great numbers they have fine eyes, both blue and black; and generally possess that bloom, which health inimitably suffuses over a beautiful countenance. They are said to be too feminine; and are certainly less masculine than most of their sex in England or in Europe. To us, this is a delightful part of their character.

Their manners are in entire symmetry with their minds and faces. An universal sweetness and gentleness, blended with sprightly energy, is their most predominant characteristic. There is nothing languid in their deportment, and rarely any thing affected. They are affable, obliging, and cheerful; while they are at the same time grave, discreet, and very rarely betrayed into any impropriety.

The employments of the women of New-England are wholly domestic. The business, which is abroad, is all performed by men, even in the humblest spheres of life. That of the house is usually left entirely to the direction of the women, and is certainly managed by them with skill and propriety. The houses in this country are, with their furniture, almost all kept in good order; and a general neatness prevails, even among those who are in humble circumstances. Indeed, a great part of the women in this country exert quite as much industry as is consistent with the preservation of health.

It is said, and I suspect with truth, that the American women lose their beauty and the brilliancy of youth at an earlier period of life than in England. A great part of them are slender. Multitudes lose their teeth at an untimely date; and many of them part with their bloom before thirty years of age.

To the character, which I have given of the women of New-England, there are unquestionably many exceptions. We have homely women, we have ignorant women, we have silly women, we have coarse women, and we have vicious women. At the same time we have no reason, in these particulars, to dread a comparison with other countries. In the most fashionable life we have frivolous women, who, having nothing to do, or choosing to do nothing of a useful nature, find time hang heavily on them. To relieve themselves from the ennui, flowing of course from the want of regular and useful engagements, women of this description crowd to the theatre, the assembly-room, the card-table, routs, and squeezes; flutter from door to door on ceremonious visits, and from shop to shop to purchase what they do not want, and to look at what they do not intend to purchase; hurry to watering places, to recover health which they have not lost; and hurry back again in pursuit of pleasure which they cannot find. Happily, the number of these is not very great, even in our cities.

3

A Scientist among the Shakers, 1819

*W*hen Benjamin Silliman made his brief excursion northward to Quebec, he was already established as the most influential scientist in America. Born in Trumbull, Connecticut, in 1779, a graduate of Yale at seventeen, he was appointed professor of chemistry and natural history at his alma mater in 1802. A great teacher, a popular lecturer on science, founder and editor of the American Journal of Science (*1818———*), *his fame as a disseminator and defender of scientific studies was unlimited. He traveled widely in the United States and Europe, on the latter, publishing the popular* Journal of Travels in England, Holland, and Scotland (*2 vols., 1810*) *and* A Visit to Europe in 1851 (*1853*) *and, on the former,* Remarks Made on a Short Tour, between Hartford and Quebec in the Autumn of 1819 (*1820*), *from which comes the account of the Shakers.*

The air was filled with projects for reform by means of communal "association," and among the earliest and most famous was the religious society of the Shaking Quakers. Established at New Lebanon, New York, forty years before Silliman visited them, the Shakers had aroused widespread interest and comment from many foreign as well as American travelers. In the course of a leisurely journey from Connecticut to Canada, largely devoted, as was to be expected, to an observation of geological phenomena, Silliman dropped in on the Shaker community in New Lebanon, New York. As a scientist, he viewed their arrangements dispassionately, buttressing his views with quotations from other sources; but, as a deeply religious man, he found their theology incomprehensible and, as a man of vigorous physique, with strong family ties, their doctrines of celibacy repugnant.

As we ascended a mountainous ridge, two miles on the road to New-Lebanon, a fine retrospect occurred. Immediately below, was a spacious and deep basin, environed by mountains, which, receding one behind another, presented in one view, brilliant forest green, in another, dark hues, almost black, and farther off, ridges and summits struggling through clouds and mist, and rain, in obscure and gloomy grandeur. Beautifully contrasted with these, was the bright cluster of buildings in Lenox, compact, blended by perspective into one rich group, in which turrets, and Gothic pinnacles and Grecian pillars were conspicuous.

The lofty Hoosack, with its double summit—the highest mountain in this region, appeared at a distance on our right;—on our left, the fertile vales of Richmond, a scattered agricultural town, and almost before we were aware of it, we wound our way down the steep declivity of the mountain, which bounds the south-east side of the vale of New-Lebanon. We had already passed upon our right, a small village belonging to the people, ludicrously called Shakers or Shaking Quakers.

We did not deviate into this first settlement, because their principal establishment, in this quarter, was immediately before us, and we were indeed not fully clear of the mountain, before we found ourselves in the midst of their singular community. Their buildings are thickly planted, along a street of a mile in length. All of them are comfortable, and a considerable proportion are large. They are, almost without an exception, painted of an ochre yellow, and, although plain, they make a handsome appearance. The utmost neatness is conspicuous in their fields, gardens, court yards, out houses, and in the very road; not a weed, not a spot of filth, or any nuisance is suffered to exist. Their wood is cut and piled, in the most exact order; their fences are perfect; even their stone walls are constructed with great regularity, and of materials so massy, and so well arranged, that unless overthrown by force, they may stand for centuries; instead of wooden posts for their gates, they have pillars of stone of one solid piece, and every thing bears the impress of labour, vigilance and skill, with such a share of taste, as is consistent with the austerities of their sect. Their orchards are beautiful, and probably no part of our country presents finer examples of agricultural excellence. They are said to possess nearly three thousand acres of land, in this vicinity. Such neatness and order I have not seen any where, on so large a scale, except in Holland, where the very necessities of existence impose order and neatness upon the whole population; but here it is voluntary.

Besides agriculture, it is well known, that the Shakers occupy themselves much, with mechanical employments. The productions of their industry and skill, sieves, brushes, boxes, pails and other domestic utensils are every where exposed for sale, and are distinguished by excellence of workmanship. Their garden seeds are celebrated for goodness, and find a ready market. They have many gardens, but there is a principal one of several acres which I am told exhibits superior cultivation.

Their females are employed in domestic manufactures and house work, and the community is fed and clothed by its own productions.

The property is all in common. The avails of the general industry are poured into the treasure of the whole; individual wants are supplied from a common magazine, or store house, which is kept for each family, and ultimately, the elders invest the gains in land and buildings, or sometimes in money, or other personal property, which is held for the good of the society.

It seems somewhat paradoxical to speak of a family, where the relation upon which it is founded is unknown. But still, the Shakers are assembled in what they *call* families, which consist of little collections, (more or less numerous according to the size of the house) of males and females, who occupy separate apartments, under the same roof, eat at separate tables, but mix occasionally for society, labour or worship. There is a male and a female head to the family, who superintend all their concerns—give out their provisions—allot their employments, and enforce industry and fidelity.

The numbers in this village, as we were informed by one of the male members, are about five hundred, but there are said to be fifteen hundred, including other villages in this vicinity. Their numbers are sustained by voluntary additions, and by proselyting. Poor and ignorant people, in the vicinity, and on the neighbouring mountains in particular, are allured, it is said, by kindness, and presents, to join the society; and destitute widows, frequently come in, with their children, and unite themselves to this community. Where a comfortable subsistence for life, a refuge for old age, and for infancy and childhood, the reputation (at least with the order) of piety, and the promise of heaven are held out to view, it is no wonder that the ignorant, the poor, the bereaved, the deserted, the unhappy, the superstitious, the cynical and even the whimsical, should occasionally swell the numbers of the Shakers.

Their house of public worship is painted white, and is a neat building, which in its external appearance, would not be disreputable to any sect.

Their worship, which I did not have an opportunity of seeing, is said to be less extravagant than formerly; their dancing is still practised, but with more moderation, and for a good many years, they have ceased to dance naked, which was formerly practised, and even with persons of different sexes. Their elders exercise a very great influence over the minds of the young people. The latter believe (as I was assured by a respectable inhabitant of New-Lebanon, but not a Shaker) that the former hold a direct and personal intercourse with Christ and the Apostles, and that the elders possess the power of inspecting their very thoughts, and their most secret actions. Perhaps this will account for the reputed purity of the Shakers, for whatever may be imagined, it does not appear that any scandalous offences do *now* occur among them, or, at least, that they are brought to light, and it must be allowed that if they were frequent, they could not be concealed.

They profess, it is said, to believe, that Christ has already appeared the second time on the earth, in the person of their great leader, mother Ann Lee, and that the saints are now judging the world.

They have no literature among them, nor do we hear that they are ever joined by people of enlightened minds. We met a party of children apparently coming from school, and I enquired of a Shaker, a middle aged man of respectable appearance, whether the children belonged to the Society; he answered in the affirmative; "But," I replied, "how is that, since you do not have children of your own? Are these children the offspring of parents who after becoming such, have joined your society, and brought their children with them?" "Yea," was the answer, with a very drawling and prolonged utterance, and at the same time, there was a slight faultering of the muscles of his face, as if he were a little disposed to smile. The children were dressed in a plain costume as the whole society are.

This singular people took their rise in England, nearly half a century ago, and the settlement at New-Lebanon, is of more than forty years standing.

They first emigrated to America in the year 1774, under their spiritual mother, Ann Lee, a niece of the celebrated General Charles Lee, who made a distinguished figure, during the American Revolutionary War.

The order, neatness, comfort and thrift, which are conspicuous among them, are readily accounted for, by their industry, economy, self-denial and devotion to their leaders, and to the common interest, all of which are religious duties among them, and, the very fact that they are, for the most part, not burdened with the care of children, leaves them greatly at liberty, to follow their occupations without interruption.*

But—where is the warrant, either in reason or in scripture, by which whole communities, (not, here and there, individuals, peculiarly situated,) withdraw themselves from the most interesting and important of the social relations—from the tender charities of husband and wife—from the delightful assiduities of parental love—from that relation, on which society stands, and on which, as on a fruitful stock, is grafted, every personal and domestic virtue, and every hope, both for this world and a better!

They rarely publish any thing respecting their own principles and habits, and we are indebted chiefly to those who have seceded from their community, for the more precise information which we possess respecting them.

Among various publications of this nature—"An account of the people called Shakers, their faith, doctrines and practices, &c. by Thomas Brown," who was, for several years, a member of their society, is probably one of the best. It has every appearance of being written with candor and truth, and although an unpolished performance, exhibits considerable ability.

If this book be considered as a fair account of the Shakers, it is manifest, that notwithstanding all the commendation to which they are entitled, for their moral virtues and their habits of order, industry and economy, they are the subjects of the wildest fanaticism, and of the most degrading superstition. If it be idolatry and blasphemy, to pronounce a woman, of at least questionable character, to be the Saviour of the world, at his second coming, and thus, in the person of this woman, to blend the attributes of the Son of God, with at least occasional drunkenness, it will be very difficult to acquit the Shakers of these crimes. I am aware of the ignorance of many of these people, and am not disposed to doubt, that there is real piety among them, any more than I am to deny that industry, sobriety, economy and occasional humanity are conspicuous traits of their characters. They have however, been known to act in a very inhuman manner, in separating and alienating children from parents, and in severing the other dearest ties of our common nature, for the purpose of building up their own sect.

The conclusion of Mr. Brown's book contains the following summary of facts respecting them. Speaking of their conversion he says: "After a number have believed, the next principal labour of the leaders is to gather them into a

* They have another collection of houses in the vicinity, where I was told they place offending members, who being under discipline, are for the time, excluded from the community, and whom they style *backsliders;* they designate them by saying, "they are *out of the gift."* I am told that they are not offended by being called Shakers, and do not regard it as an opprobrious epithet. Indeed, I have never heard of a milder or more respectable name, by which they either are called, or even wish to be.

united interest and order. They assemble every sabbath in their public meeting-house.

They walk to the meeting-house, in order, two and two, and leave it in the same order. Men enter the left hand door of the meeting-house, and women the right hand. In each dwelling-house, is a room called the meeting-room, in which they assemble for worship every evening; the young believers assemble morning and evening, and, in the afternoon of the sabbath, they all assemble in one of these rooms, in their dwelling-house, to which meeting spectators, or those who do not belong to the society, are not admitted, except friendly visitors. Their houses are well calculated and convenient.

In the great house at Lebanon there are near one hundred; the men live in their several apartments on the right, as they enter into the house, and the women on the left, commonly four in a room. They kneel in the morning by the side of the bed, as soon as they arise, and the same before they lie down; also before and after every meal. The brethren and sisters generally eat at the same time at two long tables placed in the kitchen, men at one, and women at the other; during which time, they sit on benches and are all silent. They go to their meals walking in order, one directly after the other; the head of the family, or elder, takes the lead of the men, and one called elder sister takes the lead of the women. Several women are employed in cooking and waiting on the table—they are commonly relieved weekly by others. It is contrary to order for a man or woman to sleep alone, but two of the brethren sleep together, and the sisters the same. It is contrary to order for a man to be alone with a woman, also to touch one another. If a man presents any thing to a female, or a female to a male, due care must be taken by each one not to touch the other. It is contrary to order for a woman to walk out alone, or to be alone. A man and woman are not allowed to converse together, except in the presence of some of the brethren and sisters. They sometimes have what they call union meetings, when several of the brethren and sisters meet together, sit and converse and smoke their pipes. If a man is on the road alone from home, in a carriage, it is contrary to order for him to admit a woman to ride with him on any account whatever. It is contrary to order, or the gift as they call it, to leave any bars down, or gates open, or leave any thing they use, out of its proper place, consequently they seldom have any thing lost. It is according to the gift or order, for all to endeavour to keep all things in order; indolence and carelessness they say is directly opposite to the gospel and order of God; cleanliness in every respect is strongly enforced—it is contrary to order even to spit on the floor. A dirty, careless, slovenly or indolent person they say, cannot travel in the way of God, or be religious. It is contrary to order to talk loud, to shut doors hard, to rap at a door for admittance, or to make a noise in any respect; even when walking the floor, they must be careful not to make a noise with their feet. They go to bed at nine or ten o'clock, and rise at four or five; all that are in health go to work about sun-rise, in-door mechanics, in the winter, work by candlelight; each one follows such an employment as the deacon appoints for him. Every man and woman must be employed, and work steadily and moderately. When any are sick they have the utmost care and attention paid to them. When a man is sick, if there is a woman among the sisters, who was his wife before he believed, she, if in health, nurses and waits upon him. If any of them transgress the rules and orders of the church, they are not held in union until they confess their transgression, and that often on their knees, before the brethren and sisters.

Each church in the different settlements has a house called the office, where all business is transacted either among themselves or with other people; each family deposit in the office all that is to be spared for charitable purposes, which is distributed by the deacon to those whom he judges to be proper objects of charity. He never sends the poor and needy empty away.

Mr. Brown is of opinion that they will not "soon become extinct." "Their general character" (he adds,) "of honesty in their temporal concerns, and their outward deportment and order being such, that many may be induced to join them; and as industry and frugality are two great points in their religion, it is likely they will become a rich people." In proof of his opinion he remarks: "See the once uncultivated wilderness waste of Niskeuna, and other places now turned into fruitful fields—see their neat public edifices towering amidst the surrounding elegance and neatness of their more private habitations—See their ability in their munificent donations to the poor in New-York; ——— ——— judging of their future prosperity from their present flourishing state and from their being a much more orderly people, (than formerly) it is possible they may increase in number and acquire a prevailing influence in the future destinies of this country."

4

A Resolute Woman Observes the
Atlantic Cities, 1824–29

The contributions of women to American life have been greatly neglected, and none more so than those of Mrs. Anne Royall. This remarkable woman was born in Maryland in 1769, though her life, at least until she was fifty, was associated with the frontier areas of western Virginia, Pennsylvania, and Alabama. These fifty years were entirely undistinguished. An uneducated servant, she married her wealthy and cultivated master, who, bequeathing her his property at his death, left her apparently well off at the age of forty-seven. The heirs of Royall, however, broke the will, and the widow, at fifty-four, found herself impoverished. It was then that she displayed the grit, the resolution, and the character for which she is remembered.

She determined to earn her living by traveling and selling the accounts of her observations, and in the prosecution of her objectives she was indefatigable. For seven years she pursued her way through nearly every portion of the United States, and hardly a town existed which she did not sketch with her pen. The result was embodied in five extensive works: Sketches of History, Life, and Manners in the United States (1826), *perhaps the best of her writings;* The Black Book (3 vols., 1828–29), *presumably a sequel to the* Sketches; Mrs. Royall's Pennsylvania (2 vols., 1829); Mrs. Royall's Southern

Life in the East

Tour (*3 vols., 1830–31*); *and* Letters from Alabama (*1830*). *In 1831 she settled in Washington and edited successively until her death, at the age of eighty-five, two periodicals,* Paul Pry *and* The Huntress.

Mrs. Royall's books have all the faults and virtues of the woman herself. Her innocence in matters of punctuation, grammar, and spelling was the consequence of her lack of education. The poor format of her volumes, cheap paper, printing, and binding, came from ill-considered ideas of making money. Her extremely dubious indulgence in personalities, while sometimes amusing, was more often in bad taste, frequently tedious, and on occasion hardly above a species of blackmail. She praised extravagantly those whom she liked, notably the Masons, and those who bought her books. She damned relentlessly the objects of her dislike, and none more than the Presbyterian clergy, whom she detested.

Nonetheless the value of her accounts is very great. For the social historian she is highly informative about frequently ignored aspects of American life. Not only did she go everywhere, but she observed with a keen eye, and her accounts are accurate and detailed. As the champion of all kinds of causes, she was particularly interested in prisons, orphan asylums, hospitals, and charitable institutions. Without pretense herself, she was alive to the actual life of the people and caught amazingly the color and vigor of American manners. One readily forgives her her faults when contemplating this highly alert and courageous woman, at nearly sixty years of age, undergoing the hardships of travel in the America of the 1820's, or on reading the voluminous and significant record she left. Few writers as neglected as Mrs. Royall deserve more to be recovered today.

The following excerpts come chiefly from the Sketches of History, Life, and Manners *but partly from her* Pennsylvania *and* Alabama. *The reader will have little difficulty in following her various journeys northward from Washington, D.C., through Baltimore, Philadelphia, eastern Pennsylvania and New York, to Boston.*

THE FEDERAL CAPITAL

The conveyance from Richmond to Washington, by way of Fredericksburg, is partly by land and partly by water. The steam-boat which takes you in at Potomac Creek, at 8 o'clock, P.M. lands at Washington about day-light— by which means we lost the pleasure of an approaching view of the city, which the river commands. When the steam-boat lands her passengers on the shore of the Potomac, they are a mile, at least, from the inhabited part of the city, with the exception of a few scattered dwellings. To remedy this inconvenience, the proprietors of the line have provided a large vehicle, something like a stage coach; it is called a carry-all, and would carry twenty persons. This vehicle soon brought us in view of the "mighty city," which is nothing more than distinct groups of houses, scattered over a vast surface, and has more the appearance of so many villages, than a city.

It was not long before the towering dome of the capitol met my eye: its glassy columns and walls of glittering white. The next object that strikes the eye of a stranger, is the President's house, on the left, while the capitol is on the right, as you advance in an eastern direction. Another object of admiration is the bridge over the Potomac. The capitol, however, which may aptly be called the eighth wonder of the world, eclipses the whole. This stupendous fabric, when seen at a distance, is remarkable for its magnitude, its vast dome rising out of the centre, and its exquisite whiteness.—The President's house, like the capitol, rivals the snow in whiteness. It is easily distinguished from the surrounding edifices, inasmuch as they are of brick. The War Office, Navy Office, the Treasury department, the Department of State, the General Post Office, and the City Hall are all enormous edifices. These edifices, the elevated site of the city; its undulating surface, partially covered with very handsome buildings; the majestic Potomac, with its ponderous bridge, and gliding sails; the eastern branch with its lordly ships; swelling hills which surround the city; the spacious squares and streets, and avenues adorned with rows of flourishing trees, and all this visible at once; it is not in the power of imagination to conceive a scene so replete with every species of beauty.

The Capitol

I am almost deterred from attempting to give even a sketch of the exterior of this vast edifice. It stands on an elevation of eighty feet above the tide-water of the Potomac, and covers nearly two acres of ground. It stands north and south, presenting an east and west front. The ascent to it is on the west, nearly a perpendicular, and parallel to its whole length; whilst the ground on the east front is perfectly horizontal. On the east principally lies the capitol square, enclosed with iron railing.

The east front will (for it is not yet finished,) present a colonade of one hundred and sixty feet, consisting of twenty-five Corinthian columns, twenty-five feet in height. The ceiling is vaulted, and the whole edifice is of solid masonry, of hewn free stone, of the Corinthian order. Both the inside and out is painted white, and reflects a lustre dazzling to the eyes. All the steps, stairs and floors are stone, with the exception only of the Senate chamber and Congress hall. No wood is found in any part of the building but the doors, sash, and railing, which last is mahogany. The covering is of copper; the domes are also of copper. The great centre dome in shape resembles an inverted wash-bowl; only magnify a wash-bowl to the size of ninety-six feet in diameter, and you will have correct idea of its figure. What would be the rim of the top, is of solid stone. The rim of the bottom which is a balustrade is of wood; this encircles the sky-lights; the great body of the dome is copper, with steps leading from the bottom to the top, from which you have one of the grandest views in nature. The two wings are likewise ornamented with domes and sky-lights; they are low compared to that of the centre. The sky-lights of these last are finished in a style of inimitable taste and beauty; their snowy graces charm and attract the eye of every beholder.

The Representative Hall is in the form of a semi-circle; upon the middle of the segment stands the chair of the Speaker, considerably elevated. Over

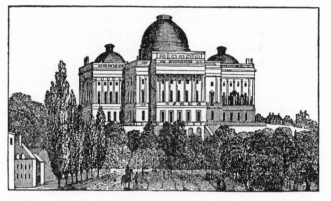

THE CAPITOL

the chair is a canopy of the richest crimson silk, trimmed with fringe equally rich; the canopy is supported by four upright posts, higher than the tallest man's head. From the top of these, the canopy drops to the bottom in copious folds of the same brilliant material. This would completely conceal the Speaker from view, were it not gracefully festooned on each side, and even then, he can only be seen in front. Precisely in front of the chair, stands the Clerk's table, also elevated above the floor of the Hall, but much lower than the chair, so as not to intercept the view between it and the members. At this table sits the Clerk and his assistants, with their backs to the chair, and so near to it, that the Speaker by looking over can read the documents.

On the right and left of the chair sit the members, (a goodly number,) in semi-circular rows, one behind another, extending from the chair to the door of entrance, leaving a straight line open from one to the other. The members are encompassed by the bar of the *house;* behind the bar is a lobby quite round the hall. The sergeant-at-arms stands outside the bar, and the door-keepers outside of the door of Congress Hall. Each member has a chair to himself, and before him is a mahogany table with drawers and places for pen, ink, and paper; these seats are arranged in regular rows. The Hall is heated by furnaces; I saw two fire places only.

The Senate Chamber is similar to the Hall, and furnished in like manner also, with the exception of the President's chair, which is quite plain, compared with that of the Speaker's. I attended a few times to hear the debates, but was unable to hear, at least, distinctly, owing to the noise made in the galleries, lobbies, and that made by the slamming of the doors. I was greatly surprised that so little order was maintained; such running to and fro, both by visitors and members.

Scandalous Conditions

If you are poor, you have no business in Washington, and unless you are well dressed, you will have good luck if you be not kicked out of doors by the servants, should you attempt to enter a house. These servants, which are nothing more than so many bullies, swarm in every boarding house, and so much do they and the proprietor resemble, differing only in slight shade of colour, that it would be difficult for one (if he were much frightened) to distinguish one from the other. In point of politeness, the advantage is often on the side of the former. In short, ignorance, impudence and pride, are decided traits in the bulk of the citizens of Washington. One is astonished upon going into the shops and stores, which are spacious buildings, to meet with the most unpolished, uncouth looking people, particularly the Irish women. They are certainly the most disgusting in their appearance and manners, of any females I have seen; they have a fierce, savage countenance, quite appalling to those unaccustomed to foreigners; though the Irish men are generous and humane, very much so.

It is certainly not to be expected, that the Metropolis of the United States should be exempt from evils common to every large city, but I will venture to say that no city of the same age has kept pace with it in vice and dissolute manners. And what is still more astonishing, is, that it should erect its empire in the very capitol itself. In the first place, there are about two hundred hands engaged at work, on that part of it which remains to be finished, and out of the whole number, there are perhaps not half a dozen sober men. They do however work during the day, but when their day's work is ended, they hie to the grog-shops and taverns, and usually spend their day's wages, sitting up to a late hour, and often committing broils in the streets, to the great annoyance of the citizens.

Besides these there are a number of strangers who flock to Washington during the sessions of Congress, with a view of begging money from the members; and so great is the infatuation of those unfortunate creatures, that they will implore even a cent in the most emphatic language. They will sell the coat off of their backs and hat off their heads to purchase drink. And for the mutual accommodation of all parties, spirituous liquors are permitted to be retailed in the capitol!

But of all sights that ever disgraced a city, a house of Legislation I mean, and one which most astonishes a stranger, is the number of abandoned females, which swarm in every room and nook in the capitol, even in day-light. One would think that, within the precincts of a legislative body, supposed to comprise all the wisdom and talent of the nation, at least some regard would be paid to decorum. I have seen these females with brazen fronts, seated in the galleries listening to the debates. They used (I have been told) to mix promiscuously with the respectable class of females, until Mr. Clay (the Speaker,) assigned them a place by themselves. Mr. Clay certainly does deserve much credit for this public homage to virtue, as does Mr. ———, for submitting a resolution for banishing those retailers of spirituous liquors from the capitol: the fate of this resolution will hardly be credited; it was lost.

Near to the very door of the Representatives Hall, immediately fronting it, is a temple dedicated to one of those females; it is a circular apartment, lighted with sky-lights. The opening fronting the Hall is always displayed; and no matter who comes or who goes, president, foreign minister, respectable citizen or stranger, this *Hortensis* proclaims the frightful progress of vice! She commands the pass to the gallery and the hall; and all who pass from the latter to the Senate chamber, or from thence to the hall, must necessarily pass through this temple; here she stands or sits in her chair of state, with a table spread with accommodation, and a maid to attend her. I have seen her surrounded by her smiling votaries in dozens. One of the members informed me, that when an effort was made to expel those retailers of spiritous liquors, &c. from the capitol, it was alleged "that it was a place of general privilege, over which Congress had no control."

PHILADELPHIA—ITS MARKETS AND CHARITIES

Journey to Philadelphia

We left Baltimore about sun-down, and arrived in Philadelphia about sun-rise next morning, the distance between ninety and an hundred miles; fare $4. This journey is performed partly by steam-boats and partly by stages. You leave Baltimore in a steam-boat, land at Frenchtown, to take the stage to

Newcastle, Delaware; then the steam-boat again, sailing up the Delaware to Philadelphia.

About midnight we came to shore at Frenchtown, and here was pulling, hauling, settling bills and fare. An hundred people were in motion, men, women, children, and parrots. Here was every one running to get their ticket; "I want my ticket, give me my ticket"; they overset me several times. Nothing could equal the uproar and confusion which now took place; such running with porters, band-boxes, trunks, and portmanteaus, flying in all directions; such pushing, elbowing, and trampling on one's toes; it was emphatically every one for himself. And what made the matter worse, we had but one lantern! After encountering a number of disasters, we were seated in the stage, and the man came round for our tickets, but it would have been the easiest thing in life to have cheated him, it being so dark, that one could not see their hand before them. The cavalcade now set forward, in a solemn walk, without one lamp amongst seven or eight, perhaps ten stages, whilst we prayed for an opposition line. It seemed an age before we reached Newcastle, and here we had to get out in the dark, and grope our way to the steam-boat, which we did not quit till we landed at Philadelphia.

Streets and Markets

The site of Philadelphia is a perfect level, excepting a slight elevation at the southern end; this, and the streets, which are wide and straight, to mathematical nicety, and the numerous squares, adorned with handsome trees, gives to Philadelphia that beauty, so much admired by travellers. Besides the streets, it has numerous courts and alleys, (a court is like an alley, but is only open at one end,) which cross about the middle of each square; the latter run from street to street. These are wide enough for a cart to pass, and have neat side walks. The streets are swept every day, and the pavements washed; nothing could be neater.

Of all these streets, Market-street is the most interesting, as in it is the greatest market in the United States. The market-house, which is nothing more than a roof supported by pillars and quite open on each side, runs one mile, that is, eight squares in length! It must be understood, however, that the market house stops at the edge of every square, (so as not to interfere with the cross streets,) and begins on the next square. On market days, of which there are two in the week, a strong chain is drawn quite across the street, at the end of the market-house, and no horse or carriage is permitted to pass. No one, who has not seen it, can form an idea of the variety, abundance, or neatness of the Philadelphia market. Nothing can exceed the whiteness of the benches and stalls; the meat is exquisitely neat, cut with the greatest care, and disposed upon tables, on cloths as white as the whitest cambric. The butchers wear a white linen frock. The vegetables excel in neatness and perfection, and consist of the whole vegetable kingdom; fruit of all sorts, and fish of every kind, besides a variety of game, butter, cheese and milk. Here I saw milk brought to market in churns. These churns differ in size, but are as white as a curd, bound with copper hoops, as bright as sand and hands can make them. Every one who comes to sell, has one particular place assigned him in the market, from which they never move. The butcher stands at his table, the woman sits in her stall; no moving except that of the citizens, who are coming and going continually, from early in the morning till nine o'clock at night. The whole of this mighty scene is conducted with perfect order; no contention, no strife or noise—presenting one of the most interesting sights perhaps in the world. Although there are but two days in the week which are styled market-days, yet there is market every day except Sunday; but this is trifling, compared with the set days—indeed there is a market on Sunday morning, for milk only. Market-street is so wide as to afford a passage for carriages on each side, independent of the footway.

The most amusing part is what is called the Jersey Market as that part of the market-house next to the Delaware is chiefly occupied by people from that state. On the great market days (which is twice in the week) toward the afternoon, the New Jersey women exhibit a rare show. They are mostly great overgrown, shapeless women, who love a drop of the comfortable, and by that time, are all pretty well *corned,* as they call it, and sit fast asleep in their stalls. This being harvest time for the plunderers, wags, thieves, and saucy children, will walk through the market and rob the old women of their fruit, cakes, nuts, or whatever they may have. Sometimes Mrs. Red Face will wake up and catch them, and the plunderer takes to his heels, while old Mrs. Lovedram makes a direful sputtering, and sets the neighborhood in a roar. These females are a great curiosity, being rather thicker than long, and their faces like lady moon at the full.

Having disposed of Market-street, I shall drop a few remarks upon the city generally. Philadelphia exhibits a very different appearance from all our other great towns, presenting a much greater variety of the human species. It would seem that the *lame,* the *blind* and *diseased* of all nations flock to Philadelphia. In walking the streets you meet some with one arm, others with one eye, some with no eyes, some limping, some with wooden legs, some with long legs and short bodies, others with long bodies and short legs, some reel footed, some club footed, others with long noses and some without any, some with black patches on the nose, while others have the patch upon mouth, lip or cheek. Here a Bolivar with a forest or flower garden on the top, there a little scooped out thing called a bonnet, then the high-crowned dandy hat, and next the broad brim, and every variety of cloth, cut and color.

But there is another show in Philadelphia, which combines a little of the terrible; this is the practice of young gentlemen and boys, rolling hoops on the pavements. Armies of these almost grown men take possession of the sidewalks and drive the people into the open streets. It is the only city where young gentlemen roll hoops.

The most business, as well as most fashion and opulence, is found in Chestnut-street, next to Market-street, south, and parallel with it. The warehouses are principally upon the Delaware river. Very large vessels can come up to Philadelphia; these ascend the Delaware—very few are able to ascend the Schuylkill, it being much smaller than the former. That part of the city adjacent to the Schuylkill is very thinly settled, and the streets near it are mostly unpaved: all the others are paved with stone, and the side-walks are neatly paved with brick, are wide and well lighted. The profusion of merchandize which lines the streets and windows is incredible. Dry goods are strewed along the side-walks, near the store doors; flannels, cloths, muslins, silks and calicoes, are hung up over the doors in whole pieces, hanging down on each side to the pavement; others are placed in rolls, side by side, on boxes standing each side of the door; barrels of sugar, coffee, raisins and fruit, stand out of doors. These are intermingled with shoe-shops, book-stores, merchant tailors, where clothes are ready made; add to these jeweller's shops, china-shops, saddlery, tin, iron and copper ware, to say nothing of millineries, upholsteries and groceries. The windows are low, large, and project into the streets some distance. Some are filled with the most splendid plate, glass and china ware; some with caps, ruffs, bonnets and ribbons; others with liquid medicine, contained in vast glass bottles of every colour, and look exceedingly beautiful at night. The windows have different rows of shelves on the inside, from the bottom to the top, and upon these shelves the articles are disposed. But it is at night that the wealth and splendor of Philadelphia appears to the best advantage; the windows being lighted with numerous lamps and gas-lights, which, with the lamps in the streets, and the lustre of the glittering wares in the windows, present a scene of astonishing beauty.—The houses are principally of brick; large, well built, and many of them elegant. But the glory of the city is the water-works.

Fair Mount Water Works

What is called the water works, are two reservoirs on the top of a hill, which supply the city with water. This scheme unites both beauty and utility, and is one that none but Philadelphians would have thought of. In 1819, the sum of $350,000 was voted, to carry the plan into effect, and was undertaken by A. Coley, Esq., who died when he had nearly completed the work. In the first place, a dam is thrown across the Schuylkill, in a diagonal line. By the power of this water, several wheels are put in motion, which, by the aid of double force pumps, is conveyed upon the top of a vast hill, into two reservoirs, which communicate with each other. From these reservoirs, the water is conveyed to leaden pipes under ground, to every part of the city, by means of hydrants. The city uses one million gallons per day.

I saw the old water-works; they were at the centre square of the city; nothing remains of them but a romantic edifice, resembling a temple; it occupies a whole square itself. It is the only building on the square, which is enclosed, planted with trees, and forms one of the many ornaments of the city. It is seen from every point.

The Mint

I called for the first time, at the United States' Mint. This is called the United States' Mint merely for the sake of parade, as the U.S. it appears, has little or nothing done in it. The specie coined here is principally owned by individuals. The building is quite small and very indifferent. No one would take it for any thing but an old wash house, nor is it half so gay as some I have seen. Its appearance, however, is worse in front, the principal part of the building, such as workshops and forge-houses extending some distance back. The keeper or head man was by no means extraordinary, though he did happen to know a bar of gold from one of silver. But he was unqualified to give an accurate and satisfactory account of the process.

I saw large wedges of bullion, that is gold and silver, roughly cast into bars. The silver was from one to two feet in length, and very rough. I was greatly surprised upon trying to raise one of them from the ground. It proved much heavier than I would have supposed a piece of double the size: the gold particularly: a small piece no larger than one's hand, was almost as much as I could lift. I am not aware of the quantity of copper mixed with the bullion, but the quantity is proportioned with the utmost exactness.

The furnace where the bullion is melted is not larger than a common stove, though it was not in blast. It was quite a simple looking thing.

When the metal is mixed it is beat out into long bars, very much like bars of iron or steel, and is formed in width and thickness precisely to that of a dollar, half dollar, or whatever may be intended. The process is very simple, required few hands and very little ingenuity.

The only difficulty or care required is to have the exact weight in the finished pieces; this appears to be subjected to the most scrutinizing inspection.

I saw not more than half a dozen hands. Some were cutting the bars into square pieces; others were rounding them off, and some were engraving the face of the coins. It appears that in order to ascertain whether the proper weight is in the coins, a number of pieces are deposited together—one or perhaps more, is taken from the sum and weighed, and if it lacks the smallest particle the manager forfeits a heavy fine, and perhaps a prosecution.

I was more astonished at this than anything about the mint, which is by no means so interesting as one would have imagined. The chief of the money coined belongs to the merchants of Philadelphia, who purchase the bullion for the purpose. It has no guard in day time, nor am I clear that it has one at all, and is only enclosed in rear with a slight wall, being quite open to the street in front. It is an old yellow building of brick.

Museum

It may readily be supposed, that the idea of seeing a place so celebrated as the museum of Philadelphia, inspired me with no common curiosity: that, and the market, to me, were objects of the first interest, which I had long and ardently wished to see. The museum is in Chestnut-street, near the corner of South fourth-street. I soon discovered it by a sign, and after crossing a gallery, came to a stair-case, wide enough to admit a waggon and team. I made but a few steps, before one of them springing under my feet, rung a bell, to my great surprise, and upon gaining the stairs, I was met by a man whose business it is to receive the money paid, which is twenty-five cents. The first object of my inquiry, was the mammoth skeleton, but I was greatly disappointed in its appearance. The skeleton is indeed as large as is represented, but it had not that formidable, dread-inspiring aspect which my romantic turn led me to expect, and with which I expected to be overwhelmed: I beheld it without surprise or emotion. It is standing upon its feet in a small room, which is lighted by a large window, enclosed with a rail as high as one's breast, and presenting its side foremost. The whole has a very dark appearance, and in many parts it is quite black. In some instances the bone is as hard as iron, while other parts seem to be in a mouldering condition.

This skeleton was found by accident, in Ulster county, N.Y. on a farm belonging to Mr. John Mastin, as he was digging for marl. It was in a morass, and the water flowed in so fast upon him that he was forced to desist from digging. In 1801, Mr. C. W. Peale, of Philadelphia, purchased the right of digging for the skeleton, and after six weeks of intense labour, his efforts were crowned with success. He obtained the skeleton perfect, except two ribs.

Although I was not thrown into hysterics at the sight of the mammoth skeleton, I found enough of the marvellous in the museum to remunerate for the disappointment. Amongst these were the sea-lion, the skeleton of a horse, which when living, measured 20 hands in height, with a human figure on its back! a sheep weighing 214 lbs., the devil-fish—in short, ten thousand things wonderful and pleasing, including 200 portraits of our most distinguished men. Of all the portraits, I was particularly struck with those of Commodore Perry, Doctor Rush, Latrobe, and Albert Gallatin.

The museum was founded by Mr. Peale, in 1784; this indefatigable man has done more since that time, than one would suppose could be done by a whole nation—the collection is endless. I had not the pleasure of seeing Mr. Peale, but was much gratified in the acquaintance of his son, and by seeing a full length portrait of the old gentleman, painted by himself—it stands in the museum. The young Mr. Peale is a small man, upon whom, however, nature and art have lavished their favours; I met with him in the museum, and received from him those marks of politeness and attention, which none but the learned and the refined know how to bestow. After paying once, you have free liberty of the museum as often as you choose to call.

Prison

The prison of Philadelphia is celebrated throughout the world. I had often heard of it, and was now within the reach of that gratification which interesting objects inspire. It consists of two vast buildings, with a large space between, which is enclosed with a high stone wall, and open at the top. At one end of this yard is that part of the prison designed for women, at the other, stands that for men. The sexes are on no account permitted to mix or visit each other. In that part appropriated to women, I found 84 females, from which to 480, is the usual number, and from four to five hundred men. The women were in a very long room, in two lines, one on each side of the room, leaving a space between; they sat on long benches close to the wall, and every one with a little wheel, (viz. a flax wheel) before her, spinning as fast as though they were spinning for a wager. One side of the room was lighted by windows, the other side was divided into lodging rooms, where they slept at night. These rooms were furnished with neat and comfortable beds; they have another large room where they eat, besides a kitchen to cook and wash in. Several of them were employed in cooking, washing, and cleaning the prison. Several black women were amongst them, and all well clothed, and cheerful: one of the blacks asked me for money; I inquired of her what was done with her when she did not perform her task? (they are all tasked so much per day;) she replied, "that they put her in a dark room, where she could see no body, and fed her on bread and water; 'But,' said she, laughing,

'I be bound da never gets me dare again.' The whole establishment was remarkably clean. These females spin, weave, and make their own clothing: they also make coarse carpeting, which is sent to the stores for sale. The men work at their respective trades. I did not visit their prison, being refused admittance by the keeper. I saw a number of them, however, at work in the yard, from the door of the female department; they were engaged in cutting and splitting stone. The whole of the prisoners eat three times a day, as follows:—"Rye coffee and bread, for breakfast; meat and soup for dinner; mush, molasses, and water, for supper." None but criminals are confined in this prison. The prisoners are overlooked with great care, by men appointed for that purpose. All was peace and stillness, no strife or loud talking was heard throughout the prison.

Hospital

Of all the benevolent institutions of Philadelphia, the hospital is the most interesting; both it and the prison are nearly in the heart of the town. There were few in it when I called; and after what has been said of the humanity and benevolence of the place, it would be needless to give a minute description of it. It is a very large building, disposed into apartments similar to that of Baltimore, but has a handsome botanical garden attached to it, and like it enclosed with a wall. I was admitted without paying any thing, to a door which was opened by a most heavenly-looking female. This lady then led me into a spacious parlour, where, and the adjoining one, I beheld a sight unequalled, perhaps, in the world!—It was the lying in hospital. I found eight females sitting at dinner; some were convalescent, and some were soon to be confined. But the neatness of the parlour, the furniture, the dinner, servants attending, the attention paid to the females by the aforesaid lady, was something altogether unexpected: but guess my astonishment, upon being told by the lady, that "those were poor women, who were unable to support themselves during their confinement, and that they were nursed, fed and furnished with medical aid throughout the whole time, gratis!" She then conducted me into another large apartment, which might vie with a king's palace, for comfort and beauty. Here was a number of females indeed, closely confined. But in the cradles I saw a most interesting sight; this was the dear little infants, 4 in each cradle. How clean, how exquisitely neat those sweet little creatures looked; how comfortably they lay and slept, whilst both they and their mothers were watched with the tenderest care. Immediately beneath those apartments were two others; the same size, appropriated to the same purpose, and attended to in like manner, by a matron and servants; it also contained a number of females and infants. This astonished me the more, as I was wholly unprepared for such a display of disinterested charity. I observed the finest bread, veal, chicken, and wine on the tables, and every other article of food and drink, suited to their situation. Here, as in Baltimore, strangers are prohibited from seeing the insane.

As we walked back, my friend pointed out the grave of Mrs. Girard of Philadelphia: she died in the hospital, being deranged some time previous. Although Girard is said to be worth $10,000,000, yet this grave is undistinguished by the least mark of respect.

A full statue of William Penn, the founder of Philadelphia, is on the Hospital-square. He is standing on a pedestal, with his Quaker hat on, in full Quaker dress. In his hand he holds a roll, on which is written, "Toleration to all sects, equal rights and justice to all." The statue was presented to Philadelphia, by the nephew of Penn. It was made in England. The hospital has a library of 5,000 volumes, and an anatomical museum.

Deaf and Dumb Institution

I shall notice but one more of the institutions of Philadelphia, as, to describe them all, would be impossible in a work like this. Besides, it would only be a repetition of the same thing; so nearly do they resemble, that a description of one may serve for the whole, I mean so far as benevolence and the most exalted charity is concerned. The number of charitable institutions is twenty-seven, the institution for the deaf and dumb, is amongst the number. It is a place where deaf and dumb children are taught, fed, and clothed gratis, a few only being able to pay for tuition. Besides literary pursuits, the females are taught all sorts of domestic work, such as sewing, knitting, but mostly the manufacturing of straw bonnets. When I knocked at the door, it was opened by a little girl of about twelve years old, who I perceived was one of the pupils; she bowed her head gracefully, and beckoned to me to come in, and with a second motion of her hand, invited me to follow her, turning round often as she advanced through the gallery, to see if I kept the right way. When she opened the door of the sitting room, she pointed to a lady and then to me alternately, which was in effect an introduction to the matron of the mansion. Having done this, she betook herself to her task, which was that of plaiting straw for bonnets. This lady-matron possessed all the sweetness and meek-eyed charity of her sisters of the hospital, and answered my inquiries with the most obliging condescension. Her vocation she said only extended to the care of the female pupils when out of school. During school hours, they were under the care of their respective teachers, but the moment school was out, they came into her part of the building. Whilst with her, they were employed in making and mending their clothes, and plaiting straw for bonnets, or to whatever their fancy led them. None, however, were allowed to be idle. There were two long tables in the room; at one of these were seated those engaged in bonnet-plaiting, and at the other, those who were engaged in sewing. I drew near to those who were plaiting straw, with a view of inspecting their work. It was truly interesting to perceive not only the skill and ingenuity, displayed in the accomplishment of their pursuit, but the pleasure they took in my approbation of it.

One of the pupils, a full grown young lady, (a number of them are women grown,) was writing a letter. I took the pen out of her hand, with an intention of conversing with her in writing. When she discovered my design, she jumped up and brought me a slate and pencil, upon which I wrote the following sentence and handed it to her. "Did you find it hard to learn to read and write." She looked at it some time, and then handed it across the table to a girl apparently thirteen years old, pointing to the word *hard,* which it appeared she either did not know the meaning, or could not make out the hand. The little girl to whom she gave the slate, instantly understood it, and explained it to her friend, by throwing her face into that contortion occasioned by lifting a heavy weight, which contracts the muscles of the face. The former then took the slate and wrote under it the following: "Yes, it was very hard." She answered several questions in the same manner.

Being desirous of seeing the boys of the institution, the lady-matron sent for the principal teacher to her room. He appeared well pleased with my visit, and an exhibition being to take place the next day, he very politely presented me with a ticket, referring to the exhibition, as a place better suited to my purpose and feelings. At my request, however, he repeated in a few words, the system of education, viz. 1st, they taught the pupil the thing, 2d, the name, 3d, the quality, and 4th, its use, until they have learned them the names of all things.

Next day I attended at Mr. Wilson's church, which, from its amazing size, afforded a fine opportunity for the exhibition. The exhibition was to commence at a certain hour, previous to which, every thing was suitably arranged for the accommodation of the spectators, who, to the amount of two thousand, at least, took their seats in the pews and galleries fronting the pupils, who were all arranged at one end of the church, the boys on one side, and the girls on the other, of their teachers, who were some in the pulpit, and some on a temporary rostrum fronting it, where the pupils were to exhibit. On the opposite side of the rostrum from the audience, in full view, were placed large, long slates, upon which the pupils were to exhibit. In the first place, an eloquent and feeling oration was delivered. Then the pupils, from four to six at a time, stood up to exhibit. The teacher gave out a sentence, first to the audience, and then by signs to the pupils, and in an instant, they wrote it on the slates, conjugating the verbs, and declining the nouns. After the grammar class had got through, examples in arithmetic were exhibited, then ancient and modern history, several gentlemen present putting questions in each, through the teachers. The exhibition took up about three hours, but they were the pleasantest I ever spent. Of all the institutions of Philadelphia, this sheds the brightest lustre on its citizens.

Next day being Sunday, I went to hear the Quakers or Friends, as they are called. Here was a direct contrast to the preceding; nought but silence reigned; not a word was said; all was solemn as midnight. Amongst them were a number of the most fashionable people of Philadelphia. I had been at Quaker meetings before, but never saw such a display of beauty and dress. Nothing could exceed the richness and neatness of that of the young Quaker ladies. The richest silks and satins, so uniform, and made so exquisitely neat, mostly white; their plain small round crowned bonnets; their neat square handkerchiefs, of the finest muslin, gave them a celestial appearance. The church was amazingly large, and yet it was filled to overflowing; the men, that is the Quakers, all wear their hats. The elderly men and women sat at one end of the building upon elevated seats, and during the meeting seemed deeply engaged in thought. Their countenances bespoke minds wholly withdrawn from outward objects. After sitting in this manner nearly two hours, two of the old men shook hands, the signal for breaking up.

Education

When accosted, the Philadelphians are polite and condescending, whether abroad or at home. I found them very easy of access, much more so than in Washington. But from the limited opportunity I had of judging, I am inclined to think education does not receive that attention we might expect, in a city so devoted to the public good. The dialect of the citizens, particularly of the children, gave rise to this opinion; it is very defective, and the young misses are detestably affected in their manners, dress and dialect. I questioned a few on the subject of grammar, geography, and history, who were said to be engaged in these studies, and found them wretchedly defective. They have, withal, a whining tone in their speech, extremely disgusting; though the higher classes pronounce the English language with purity and even elegance.

EASTERN PENNSYLVANIA: A RAILROAD AND THE GERMANS
The Mauch Chunk Rail Road

Easton has every appearance of becoming one of the first commercial towns in the state, and bids fair to outstrip all her rivals. All the Lehigh coal must pass through Easton. The Lehigh canal, by which this coal is to be transported to Philadelphia and from thence to other places, begins at Easton and extends to the mines at Mauch Chunk, 36 miles from hence. This is called the Lehigh Canal, which, including the cost expended on the Lehigh river is rising $800,000! It has fifty locks! This was done by the enterprising Messrs. White & Hazard of "The Lehigh Coal and Navigation Company," at their private expense. At Mauch Chunk the rail-road connects the canal with the mines.

And now for the ride upon this rail-road at Mauch Chunk, the mines, and the ride back. We were placed in pleasure carriages, which have seats like sleighs, and precisely like the sleigh, but longer, and without the back and front, and have small iron wheels. These carriages are fastened together, as many as you please—one horse to every twenty persons, which he pulls with ease, at a brisk trot—no horse is used in returning.

The distance from the town to the mines is nine miles, the mountain being an oblong; the rail road runs parallel with its length, which resembles what we call a spur. The road runs on the side of this ridge, and partly on the top, as it happens to sink or rise—the highest summit is about one thousand feet, and the road rises one foot in seventy.

It was a delightful afternoon, when, seated in the *front* of the *front* carriage, supported by two strangers at my back, a little beau next to them, an old-maid, &c&c.&c., the owner of the carriages, and driver in front of all, and off we go upon the rail road. But of all modes of travelling or sailing, it is the most pleasing; so steady, so swift; not a jolt, jar, or movement, to the right or left. To say it was delightful, would scarcely convey the idea; nor can it be conveyed by language, to other than those who have travelled on one. I shall ever, after this, be the warm advocate of rail-roads! Rail-roads! rail-roads! give me a rail-road!

As we drove on, I happened to ask the owner of the wagon "What would be the result were we to meet a wagon?" "We would call out to the driver to hold up," there being a sort of machine which locks the wheel, one end of which the driver, who always sits in front, holds in his hand; by this means the wagons can be made to go fast or slow, or stopped. This part of the story I can scarcely believe, when applied to the coal wagons—from their great weight and velocity when running down, I doubt whether any power on earth could stop them.

As we draw near the mines we descend a little, and have a beautiful prospect of the plains and hills around us, from our high situation.

The coal mines is matter enough to satisfy the most capacious mind, and gratify the most unbounded curiosity—one whole mountain of solid coal, which continues, it is said, across the country to the Schuylkill. Wherever they have made the experiment, they find the same unbroken mass of coal. The excavation already made comprises seven acres, to a great depth, in some places 70 or an 100 feet, and yet there is no alteration in the coal—it lies unbroken and unmixed by the least particle of stone, earth, or any thing whatever.

A vast many hands are employed in loosening the coal, loading the wagons, and gathering them together, to send to the river. These hands do not work under ground—they begin on the surface, and dig and haul off as they go. There is, at first, on the surface of the mountain, a few feet of earth, which is carefully removed, but when they once get to the coal, the earth ceases—it is so easy to dig, that one good hand can dig 100 bushels per day— the instruments used are a pick-axe and a crow-bar; these are light and sharp, which the men handle with much ease. It is surprising to see how fast they can loosen and throw it out.

They receive from 80 to 90 cents per day. Some of the workmen are Irish, some Germans, and some Yankees; they work, drink whiskey, fight, receive their money in the fall, go home, spend the winter, and return in the spring. They have no boss, (as an overlooker is called in the Atlantic country.) I asked "if they drew their wages by the day, or the bushel?" they replied, "they drew the same wages, whether they worked or played."

A number of railroads run in all directions over the excavation, to facilitate the removal of the coal to the rail-road which is to convey it to the river. The rail road is thus described by a traveller, who called nearly at the same time; and to save trouble I copy it from a paper, as I am aware it is correct.

A road is first cut along the side of the mountain, on which billets of wood are laid transversely (like our swamp cause ways;) and on them, parallel with the road, the rails of pine, 6 by 4 inches thick, are placed. On the upper surface and inner edge of these rails, narrow bars or plates are screwed for the wheels to run on. The cost $4,500 per mile. The cars for carrying the coal are made of sheet iron, with strong wheels about two feet in diameter.

The bodies of the wagons are very deep, and wider at the top than the bottom. A driver or steersman always sits in front to guide the wagon upon the road where it makes short or crooked turns. The wheels, I find, have often to be greased.

The ride up is, in comparison, nothing to our ride down. The company and myself being again seated in the carriages the horse was again put to for a little way, when he was again taken out, and away we flew; at first slow, but soon like the wind. There are a few scattering houses near the mines, in imitation of a town, and a solitary one here and there for a little further on, also a meadow, where we saw several mules feeding.

The wheels, going up, make very little noise, but going down they make a considerable hollow rumbling sound, which I presume must be heard some distance. It was no little amusement to me to see birds, cats, dogs, and cows flying for their lives before us. We were 30 minutes running down.

But of all the wonders of Mauch Chunk I was most astonished at the rapidity of the wheels upon a road apparently level, as any person in the world, with no more knowledge of rail-roads than myself, would be at a loss to distinguish which way the road descended. It has all the appearance of a perfect level. We pay 50 cents each for our ride.

The Pennsylvania Germans

Easton is settled by Germans, though the most of them use the English language, and are well educated. The professional men, particularly, are greatly superior to those of New-York, and not inferior (if they do not excel) those of any other state or town. There is a plain, unmoved, though intelligent independence about them, similar to the people of the western states.

It would seem that good sense, good size, good manners and hospitality had fled for shelter to this part of the state; and nothing proves the truth of the remark more clearly than their freedom from priest-craft. I find no pious education societies here. These Germans I find are too wise for priests. In religion they are Lutherans, who do not suffer those religious pirates to come amongst them. They remind me of the French people, particularly the young men and women, being very sprightly and fond of music and dancing. You hear the violin or Piano Fort, of an evening, almost in every house.

The landlord, White, was what is called an Englishman in Pa. It must be remembered all are called English in Pa. though American born, who are not Germans or of German descent. This distinction is used from the custom of those Germans, speaking the German language. And though most of the Germans understand and converse in the German language, they also pronounce the English language with elegance and ease—There are a few Germans, however, who neither understand nor can converse in the English language.

The Germans in Pennsylvania have a custom amongst them, which they observe with religious care—this is called a *Fair,* which they hold twice a year. These are distinct from the fairs for selling wares and cattle, and are something like the Thanksgiving in New England, that is, a kind of merry-making. It differs, however, from the Thanksgiving in this—the people make pies, cake, &c. and remain at home, or go to church. The Germans all (that is the young people) repair from the country to the nearest town, and, instead of going to church, go to balls and dance, sometimes two or three days and nights.

One of these took place at Reading while I was there. The first thing I heard in the morning was music in the bar-room; being informed of the occasion, I stepped to the bar-room door, and there sat two young men playing on violins, and two or three young men and women sitting on a long bench, and three or four others dancing to the music. Being partial to the violin, and fond of seeing young people happy, I stood some time in the door to indulge my feelings.

GERMANTOWN, PA., 1793

While I remained there, the young men and women *poured* into the bar-room—the men threw off their cloaks, the ladies threw off their shawls and bonnets, and to dancing they went. This was continued till night set in—the bar-room! see what custom does! In some parts of the United States a lady would think herself disgraced forever, were she to sit down for a minute in a bar-room. This is all affectation, as virtue sanctifies every place it honors with its presence, and very possibly these same finnicken ladies might do a worse thing in a better place. Nothing, however, could exceed the ease and grace of the females. The men did not dance so well, yet they danced well for people who worked, as doubtless they were all farmers' sons; but the females hopped as light as a feather; they were mostly fair, round faced, and rather low, and far from being squeezed to death in the waist. The day being unfavorable, they were mostly dressed in calico—the young men were better dressed and better shaped; and both were small to what I would have expected; nor did they possess that glow of health which I witnessed in many parts of the State; but the downcast modest blush and innocence of the young women was ravishing—such a picture of innocence never fell in my way. They danced two, three, and four couple; the women, as in olden times, would cut out and fairly dance the men down. The girls conversed little or none, and very few, I was told, could speak English—the young men were more gay and lively; but the room, at length, became so full, that they had scarcely room for more than one or two to dance at a time.

Meantime there is a market at the market-house, and everything that can be mentioned, either to eat or to drink, can be found there; and there the parties hie, and the sweetheart treats his fair one to the best. Every young lady has the privilege (as in the Christmas and New Year presents) to ask the young man to give her a "Fairing," meaning a present.—The whole is a scene of throng, mirth, and gaiety, and the most appropriate for youth and innocence—shoals of these were coming and going all the day.

At night, after supper, the party adjourned to the dining room, which being very large, they were better accommodated. They danced nearly all night, and renewed it again next day and night. This was the case at all the taverns, and many parties were at private houses: meantime everything in the streets and shops wears a face of gaiety—the children dressed up, and groups of boys, with cherry faces, all seemed to bring happiness to the fair, instead of the fair bringing happiness to them.

Many, in fact, most of these, when they marry, receive from 10 to $30,000 (and in many instances more) from their parents—not in cash—the German, dull and ignorant as he is, takes care of that; he never trusts wife nor child with money; but he purchases a good tract of land, generally limestone, as it is known to be good. He then builds a barn, which in worth, is a handsome fortune of itself. If there be no house, a small one is erected next, and the son goes into it, and he and his wife go to work furnished with stock and every thing to his hand for farming or housekeeping; he lays up his money, too; as his father did, so does *he,* taking care of every cent, and lays it out for *his* children in like manner.

The chief strength of Pennsylvania lies in the astonishing fertility of her lands, the industry, sobriety, and union of her citizens. This is altogether owing to the nature of its inhabitants, and chiefly to the Germans. The Quakers are also wealthy, but they mostly reside in the towns. You may soon discover the difference between the farm of a German and that of any other nation, or his cattle and horses. Look at an Irishman's horse, and look at the German's, and you may readily tell one from the other. In short, the Germans are the main stay of Pennsylvania. The German differs from all other nations that have settled in America; he is not fond of change; he sticks to his old way. All others, Scotch, French, Irish, and English, are always changing from one thing to another, and from one place to another. The German sticks to the same place, and pursues the same business—*they* speculate, and are rich to-day, and poor to-morrow. The German never ventures his cash—*they* are given to drink and gambling. The German is sober, and never gambles—*they* are sometimes of one sect, and sometimes of another. The German is always the same honest and independent Lutheran—*they* will run in debt and cheat, and are ambitious. The German avoids all these: he is in politics as he is in religion, firm and steady: he chooses his man, and sticks to him, and these are the ignorant *Dutch*. Show me a more industrious, sensible, or judicious man, than the German—they are the cream of our country.

But the most distinguished trait in the character of a German is, that he is master in his own house: there lies the secret of his wealth. If these Germans (I thought, when I discovered their great farms, three story stone barns, with their great glass windows and corresponding wealth,) are so ignorant, how comes it they are the wealthiest people in the country? and setting myself to search into the cause, I traced it to his authority over his wife and children. This independence is found amongst no other set of men—nor are they so ignorant: I find them as well informed as other people, and generally more so; and no females are more exemplary in industry, innocence, and modesty. As to charity and hospitality, you may travel through the whole State and not pay one cent, particularly if you are poor; and one farm is worth a whole county in the southern states. If a person were taken up from the old fields of Virginia and Maryland, and set down on some farms I have seen in Pennsylvania, he would think he was in Paradise!

NEW YORK: JAILS AND FIRES

Competition en Route to New York

After spending two weeks to a day in Philadelphia, I entered my name on the waybill, paid my passage over night, and set off for New-York in the steam-boat next morning, sailing up the Delaware. Shortly I went down to enjoy the comforts of the stove-room for it was freezing! I found about fifty strange faces below, independent of those on deck—ladies and gentlemen all in one large room. I took a seat in silence amongst them, admiring the republican simplicity of their manners. The ladies, unembarrased, modest, and discreet, conversing familiarly with the gentlemen, all mingled together, leaving it difficult to tell who were, or who were not their husbands. In this respect they differ greatly from their more southern neighbours, who would have taken it as an insult, were they reduced to sit in the same room with gentlemen, particularly where men of all classes are passengers. Here was no silly affectation amongst the females, no impertinent frowardness amongst the men; they cracked their nuts and eat their apples very much at their ease; these I thought must be New-Yorkers, which proved to be the case. My meditations, however, were soon interrupted by a call upon the passengers to come and receive their tickets, as it appeared we had to leave the Delaware, take stages and proceed by land across the country to the Raritan river, (New-Jersey,) where we take the steam-boat again. Every one, even the passengers seemed to testify the most eager desire to beat the other line, whose passengers had just left the shore in their stages as we arrived.

When we began to draw near the Raritan, we had a view of the other line, and it is probable they had a view of us, from the rate they were driving. Each line was running on elevated ground, in view of each other, during some miles; but all in vain, we got to the river first, and I was almost carried to the boat by the porters, in their eagerness to conquer the other line. The foremost stage of the opposition made two desperate attempts to pass us within a few yards of the Raritan; they came so near effecting their purpose that the forewheel struck the hind wheel of ours, the one I was in, and nothing but the narrowness of the pass prevented their success. These opposition lines are certainly an advantage to travellers, and a great one too, but it is one of great hazard.

No sooner were we in the boats, (which was almost at the same instant,) than the steam was liberally plied to the wheels, and a race between the "Legislator" and the "Olive Branch," commenced for New-York. The former was our heroine, and a stately boat she was; but although she seized upon the middle of the channel, her rival drew up alongside somewhat boldly, and sometimes had the presumption to run ahead, which her ability to sail in shoal water enabled her to do; often, however, she lagged behind. It was quite an interesting sight to see such vast machines, in all their majesty, flying as it were, their decks covered with well-dressed people, face to face, so near to each other as to be able to converse. It is well calculated to amuse the traveller, were it not for a lurking fear that we might burst the boilers. I confess for one, I would rather lose the race than win it, (which we did,) under such circumstances.

Without noticing or being noticed, I took a seat by the stove, with true republican independence; ladies and gentlemen all mingled promiscuously together—some sitting, some walking about, some lying down on the settees, as their leisure served. Two gentlemen sat upon the same seat which I had taken, engaged in conversation upon the approaching presidential election. One (as I took it) was of New-Jersey, the other of New-York. He of New-York expressed some surprise at the result of the New-Jersey election. "I was led to believe," said he, "that your state would have supported Mr. Adams."—the vote, it appeared, was in favour of Gen. Jackson. "Do you think," replied he of N.J. warmly, "that we would vote for a man who doesn't believe in the Christian religion? No sir, we are not come to that yet, and I hope never will." "Not believe in the Christian religion!" answered N.Y. "why how is that? I don't understand you." "I mean," said N.J. "that John Q. Adams is a Unitarian."

New York City

We landed in the city of New-York about 3 o'clock, and I took up my lodgings in Front-street, at the house of Mr. Jacques. On entering a large room, I found an assembly of ladies and gentlemen sitting before a blazing fire, (no unwelcome sight.) The old men were smoking their pipes, and the younger ones were amusing the ladies with anecdotes, perfectly regardless of the copious draughts of tobacco smoke. To diversify the picture, one of the young ladies sat down to her piano forte! Never did I witness such independence of manners, even in the land of Jackson; our western heroes, when it comes to smoking, withdraw from the company of the ladies.

Next day, after breakfast, I bent my course toward the far famed Broadway; it is four miles long, and the side walks paved with flag, (the middle of the street in all the towns and cities in this country are paved with common round stone.) Next to Broadway, in point of beauty, is Hudson, Washington, Greenwich, and the Bowery; this last runs in a diagonal line, and joins Broadway. Pearl street, with many others first laid out, are narrow and crooked; there are, however, many handsome streets which cross at right angles, viz: Market, Grand, and Canal streets. Of all these streets, Pearl street does the most business, being the principal mart of the merchants. Wall street is also a place of much business; in it are the banking houses, exchange, brokers, insurance, auctioneers, and custom house offices; in short, all commercial business is transacted there. Nothing can exceed the throng of gentlemen in Wall street; particularly when their merchant ships arrive; on such occasions it is dangerous to walk in Wall street; here the commercial papers are read, and ship news detailed. This street alone, may give a stranger an idea of the business and trade of New-York. Broadway, on the other hand, is distinguished for the fashionable, the gay, and the idle, as Pearl street and Wall street are for men of business. It is likewise the seat of much business; the lower stories of most of the houses being occupied by retail shops, and book stores, for upwards of two miles; the principal booksellers are in this street. The broad windows are filled with china and glass ware, plate, millinery, fruit, confectionary; in short, every thing, and much more abundant than in Philadelphia. But shops, furniture, superb buildings with their marble fronts, are completely eclipsed by the teeming fair ones, from morning till ten o'clock at night. It is impossible to give even an idea of the beauty and fashion displayed in Broadway on a fine day; the number of females, the richness and variety of dress, comprising all that can be conceived of wealth or skill, mocks description. Here the earnest merchant steps, there the gay cook and merry chamber-maid, with some scores of honest tars, hucksters, rude boys, and chimney sweeps, with the rolling coaches, and the rattling carts, may give some idea of this life-inspiring city.

But all this is only a drop in the bucket compared to that on the wharves or slips, (as they are called here,) the warehouses, docks, ship-yards, and auction stores, which occupy South, Front, and Water streets, pouring a flood of human beings. Here the sound of axes, saws, and hammers, from a thousand hands; there the ringing of the blacksmith's anvil; hard by the jolly tar with his heavo; the whole city surrounded with masts; the Hudson, East river, and the bay covered with vessels, some going out and some coming in, to say nothing of the steam-boats; in short, imagine upwards of an hundred thousand people, all engaged in business; add to these some thousand strangers which swarm in the streets and public houses; such is New-York.

State Prison

The state prison of New-York, stands on the Hudson river, in Greenwich-street. It is built of free stone, in the Doric style; two stories in height, the buildings and yard cover four acres of ground; the whole is enclosed with a stone wall.

The prisoners do not work out of doors as at Philadelphia; the most of them are kept at weaving; the first stocking-loom I ever saw was in this prison, but such was the intricacy of the thing that I am unable to describe it. Besides weavers, there are turners, brushmakers, coopers, blacksmiths, tailors, painters, shoemakers, carpenters, and many card and spin; they eat three times a day, mush and molasses for supper, cocoa sweetened with molasses, with bread, for breakfast, beef shins, made into soup, thickened with beans or rice, for dinner, and once a week they have a pork dinner, and always plenty of potatoes; some instances of industry are rewarded by a pint of beer. Good behaviour generally shortens the term of confinement; the young and the old, who are illiterate, are carefully instructed. The prison is warmed by stoves; they have pumps and fire engines in the yard.

No convict, sentenced for a less term than three years, can be put in this prison: when a convict arrives, he is stripped, washed clean, and dressed in new clothes, and after taking a description of his person, which is entered in the prison book, he is put to work. In the summer, they work from 6 o'clock A.M. till 6 P.M.: on beat of drum, at 9 o'clock, in the summer, and 8 in the winter, they retire to their beds, which are neat and comfortable. There were 500 in when I called; amongst these were very few women; many of them were fine looking men, one of them in particular, in reply to an observation I dropped, that people of their inoffensive looks should be guilty of crimes, "ah," said he, "many of the people you see here are put in for very little."

A sentinel parades on the wall during the day with fixed bayonet, but at night fifty men stand guard. Many instances occur of the same person being put in the second, third, fourth, and even fifth time! a number are put in for life; the crimes which subject a convict for life, are rape, robbery, burglary, sodomy, maiming, house-breaking, forging proof of deeds, or public securities, and counterfeiting gold or silver. Until very lately they received no compensation for their labor!

The supreme judges and the attorney general of the state, regulate the laws of the institution, which, with all deference to them, are very rigid. A physician and surgeon reside in the prison, and others visit there daily from the city, none of which receive compensation.

Bridewell and the Jail

Bridewell and the jail are in the park, near the city hall; and two black, dismal looking edifices they are; one stands at one end of the hall, and the other at the other end: they are both built of stone, and painted black. Bridewell is a small building; in it are confined all those who are committed for trial, also those under sentence of death; likewise the higher class of convicts: besides these, are a number of poor, constantly in bridewell, who are picked up daily by the watch and constables in the streets, and put in here until they can be sent to the alms-house; I saw about 15 of these, whom the keeper told me were brought in that morning! It appears to be the pride of New-York, to have no poor seen in the streets.

Although the sessions are held monthly, they cannot empty bridewell: 170 prisoners are arraigned on an average, and often 200 tried. I found about 200 in this abode of wretchedness, white and black, male and female, about one half of whom were females. The males presented nothing in their appearance different from their equals in the streets; indeed, I was struck with the innocence and modesty of their looks and behaviour: pointing to one of them, I asked the keeper "if it were possible that one of his interesting appearance, could be guilty of a crime?" his reply was, that he was charged with forgery. There were about forty females in bridewell. They were the most abandoned, vicious, impudent; they were audacity itself, without one particle of aught besides. They laughed, they romped, they giggled, and saluted me with the familiarity of an old acquaintance! asked "if I came to keep them company?" And this is the effect of great cities! Some of these females are quite young, not more than fourteen or fifteen years of age.

The Fire Department

The Fire Company is at once, the most respectable and useful society in the city. It consists of Fire Companies in every Ward, under the control of one *Chief* Engineer. The common council carry a wand, with a gilded flame at the top. The engineers wear a leathern cap, painted white, with a gilded front, and a fire engine blazoned thereon, and carry a speaking trumpet, painted black, with the words "engine, No. 1," (or as the case may be,) in white, painted on their caps. The fire wardens wear a hat, the brim black, and the crown white, with the city arms blazoned on the front, and carry speaking trumpets, painted white, with the word "warden," in black: the firemen also have badges. When a building takes fire in the night, the watchmen cry "Fire," the bells are set to ringing; the companies attend as above described, with all possible dispatch, with their engines, which are pulled by the firemen running at full speed. Every man, even the mayor of the city are under the control of the fire corporation, during a fire. They use no buckets, or at least rarely, the rivers being so near, and their hose[*] extending from one engine to another, and finally to the river, it is conveyed through them to the fire. The engineers, chief engineers, and fire wardens only direct; they are constantly running to and fro, directing the firemen. The firemen when they are fixed each in his station, stand still and play the engine; their superiors speaking to them through the trumpets, for the noise and crackling of the fire, and that of the multitude which gather, would effectually drown their voice. None but the fire companies join in extinguishing fires; the citizens which gather in crowds, are kept as a distance by the city officers. The engines are the most superb piece of mechanism in the city, most of them being richly gilded, and the fire companies consist wholly of reputable men. The membership is deemed one of honour, but it is one dearly bought; the smoke from the fires, as near as they are obliged to approach, would strangle any one else. Very little damage has accrued from fire, since the department has been organized upon its present plan.

[*] A leathern pipe, from four to five inches in circumference, of great length.

THE ATHENS OF AMERICA

Boston, rising up as it were, out of the water, makes a fine display from whatever point it is approached. The state-house, a grand edifice with a lofty dome, stands upon the highest ground in the city, nearly in the centre; this, and the cupolas of Fanueil Hall, the old state-house, and a dozen others, with about 70 white steeples which pierce the clouds in every part of the town, gives Boston a decided advantage over any city, in point of beauty, at this distance. We took the middle bridge, which soon landed us in Boston, where beauty diminished as we drew near; and still more so when we found ourselves lost in narrow streets, with houses mountain high on each side of us. I was no little afraid of being dashed to pieces by the stages and carriages which come meeting us, for want of room to pass.

It was some time in the afternoon of the following day, before I ventured to walk over the city, which, independent of the scenery that surrounds it, is by no means handsome. The streets are very short, narrow, and crooked, and the houses are so high, (many of them five stories), that one seems buried alive. The side-walks are narrow, and badly paved, and the town is badly lighted; in this respect, it is greatly behind New-York or Philadelphia. They have a custom amongst them as old as the city, singular enough; that is, shutting up their shops at dark, winter and summer, which gives the city a gloomy appearance, and must be doubly so during the long winter nights. I should be at a loss to conjecture how their clerks and young men dispose of themselves, during their long winters. New-York and Philadelphia do as much business after dark as they do in the day, and perhaps more; for the young people then take time to amuse themselves, and the lights which illuminate the shops and stores, give life and activity to the whole city.

The site of the city is nearly circular, its greatest width being not more than a mile and a half, or perhaps three quarters; but the houses are closely built, and so high, that they contain a great number of people. There are, however, some handsome streets, such as Washington-street, State-street, Green and Congress-streets: but the glory of the streets is the colonade on the side of the mall. Beacon-street is also, for its length, unrivalled, bordering on the mall likewise, and being on elevated ground, it commands one of the finest views in the city: it runs in front of the state-house.

The citizens of Boston are at present engaged in making great improvements in the city. They are reclaiming the land from the water, and have succeeded to an astonishing degree, having realiized about 70 acres of made land where the mill-pond formerly flowed. They are likewise pulling down houses, widening the streets, and erecting large and durable buildings. The town is chiefly built of brick, though there are many elegant free-stone buildings, which, for beauty and size, excel any private buildings in the United States. These stand mostly on Mount Vernon, Beacon-street and the Colonade. The exterior of the houses is nothing compared with the costly furniture within them: plate, China ware, mahogany, the finest cut glass, and rich carpeting, are paltry things with them; their houses are adorned with nymphs, Naiads, shepherds, cupids and goddesses, of the finest alabaster; portraits, the finest paintings, and the choicest books, settees and chairs; damask curtains, of the richest fashion; every room is filled with the "softly speaking marble"; these beautiful images meet you wherever you turn: they are standing in niches on the stair-cases and up-stairs as well as below. The marble assuming every shape and every grace: here you see a nymph stretched on a couch, there a Naiad standing with a gilded cup in her hand, and a third in the act of dancing.

Boston, however, has been losing ground in commerce, for a few years back; and its merchants are vesting their capital in manufacturing establishments, upon the most extensive and comprehensive scale. They have several grand manufactures of glass, cotton, dyeing and calico printing, in which vast sums are invested. The Chelmsford factory, near Boston, belongs to a number of wealthy merchants, amounting to a capital of $100,000. The Waltham factory is in complete operation; it also belongs to a company of merchants, and is confined to the manufacturing of cotton shirting and sheeting. This factory was established in 1814: the capital stock is $600,000. It employs 400 persons, chiefly females; has in operation 7800 spindles, 240 looms, and makes about 1,700,000 yards annually. The whole of the machinery is performed by water! The looms are entirely of iron, and make such a noise when they are in full operation, that it is with great difficulty you can make yourself heard. This is a most astonishing invention. Besides the factory just mentioned, there is an extensive bleaching establishment at Waltham, where the cloth is whitened and prepared for market.

Buildings and Public Institutions

The wharves of Boston are among the first public buildings in the city, and a subject of admiration to all who visit them: they extend to a great distance in the water, to wit, central and long wharf, 1,240 feet. The India wharf is also of considerable length. These wharves are lofty brick houses, with a street on each side, for the lading of vessels, the water being too shallow for vessels to come near the shore, as they do at New-York. The wharves are all four stories high, and of brick, but the central wharf being more recently built, is more showy. Nothing can look more grand than these wharves stretching out into the bay to such an amazing length.

The state-house is called the *new* state-house, to distinguish it from the old one. It stands upon a lofty eminence, called Mount Vernon, at the head of the mall. It is built of brick. Very high in proportion to its relative size, it has a splendid dome and cupola of astonishing height. It fronts the mall, with a colonnade of singular beauty. The mall (which is often called the common,) is an extensive plot of ground, enclosed and designed for the amusement of the citizens: it is very large, comprising between 11 and 12 acres, nearly square; it has a gentle descent from the state-house to the water, which spreads out into a wide sheet at its lowest extremity. It is planted with beautiful flourishing trees, and has a large pond fed by a spring in the centre. Here the citizens repair in sultry weather, to breathe the refreshing breeze from the ocean. Here may be seen the young and the old of both sexes, particularly of an evening; the gay dresses of the ladies are now fluttering in the wind before me. The spruce beau, the pert apprentice, the statesman, and the beggar, all tread the mall in the pride of independence.

The old state-house is a large brick building, at the head of State-street, which runs east and west; it stands about the middle of the city, has a cupola, and looks venerable from age. It is now used as a masonic hall, and sundry public offices are kept in it. Formerly the general court, (as the legislature is called in Massachusetts,) held their sittings in it.

At the foot of State-street, a little to the left, stands Fanueil hall, a large building of brick; the basement story is now, and always has been, used as a market-house. It is open on all sides, and filled with butcher's meat; the second story comprises the hall, with one or two small offices at one end. The upper one, or third story, contains the city arms. The market of Boston yields to none, and in many things it excels, particularly in its fish. The meat and vegetables also are fine and plentiful, with early fruit of delicious flavor. While the butchers assemble under Faneuil Hall, and another place adjoining, the vendors of vegetables line themselves in rows at random, or sell out of carts the best way they can; the fishmongers have a kind of a shed, with a long bench near to which they have large tubs of water with the finest salmon fresh from the ocean, and every kind of fish that can be mentioned. The fish market is exemplary for neatness.

The Massachusetts general hospital is a vast building of stone, at the north west extremity of the city. It is handsomely ornamented with a glass cupola, and is the most spacious building in the city. It differs little from the Philadelphia hospital in the neatness and convenience of the apartments.

The institution has not as yet been able to extend relief to paupers; each boarder pays at least three dollars per week, every thing included. The attending physicians and surgeons, with the superintendent, must reside in the hospital. No operation is performed, but in the presence of many individuals. Not a medicine is prepared but by prescription, which is placed on record; not a patient remains in the hospital who is not visited once a week by the visiting committee, and personally examined by them; no change in food or in disease, and no medical application, but what are noted in a book, and exhibited to the board of visiters and to the public. No one can be elected acting physician, surgeon, or superintendent, who is not above twenty-six years of age, shall have studied physic and surgery seven years or more, and have been recommended by the consulting physicians as a proper person. A record of all their doings is carefully kept in a book. There were but 70 patients in the hospital when I called; I did not visit the insane.

Boston has struck out a new path with respect to the poor. They have attached a large farm to the establishment, which is worked by the paupers, and by means of this, and articles furnished for spinning and making clothes, they are little or no charge to the city. Many indigent persons who are unable to purchase wood or other necessaries of life, go to the poor-house, and ultimately prove an advantage to the establishment; these come and go when they choose: The homeless and all are taken in there. The paupers are mostly men and women advanced in years, who work a little every day; they work at their ease, no one offering to extort more from them than they are able and willing to perform. It is surprising to witness how neat their farm and gardens appear. They plant a great quantity of potatoes, beans and peas, and every species of vegetables. This is the work of the men; the women stay within doors, they wash, iron, mend, and cook. The poor-house is a large stone building in South Boston, several stories, with a chapel in the upper story, where divine service is performed every Sunday. From 200 to 300 paupers are supported in this manner, annually, being little expense to the community. I never saw more happiness, ease and comfort, than exists in the poor-house in Boston.

There are in Boston two permanent orphan asylums, established by the legislature, though wholly supported by subscription. One of these is for the support and education of female orphans, supported by the ladies of Boston; the other is for male orphans, and supported by the gentlemen. Being told no material difference distinguished these benevolent establishments, I only visited the female asylum. The building is by no means adequate to the number of children in this asylum. There are too many in the school-room. Neither do I approve of keeping children so very young as those are, (some of them not more than four years of age,) so closely confined: what I mean is, that children of their age are too young to be kept at close study so great a portion of the day, as these children are. Something is wrong in the management of the establishment, I would suppose, from the appearance of the children, they do not look healthy and vigorous.

The state prison of Massachusetts is organized upon the same plan as those of New-York and Philadelphia, with this difference, however, the convicts of the former are more lively and active, perform their work with more cheerfulness, and receive the full amount of their labor. The prison is in Charlestown, and like those mentioned, has a large yard for the prisoners to perform their labor. The out-door laborers are chiefly stone-cutters, and never did men exceed them in application to business. The prison-yard is in one continual roar of hammers and chisels. Not a man lifted his head to look at me, as I walked through the sheds, while the dust or sand, raised by the instruments, almost blinded me. The mechanics work in shops, which make a part of the prison wall, some hundred feet in length. In these shops mechanics of every description are at work, even at jewelry, printing, and engraving: many of these convicts clear their expenses, and have money to take with them when they are discharged.

The penitentiary is built of stone. It consists of a principal building and two wings. The centre of principal building, is divided into apartments for the accommodation of the officers and overseers. The two wings form the prison. These cells in the ground story, are appropriated for the convicts during their sentence to solitary, and when confined as a punishment for disorderly behaviour. Half of the upper story of the east wing is appropriated for a hospital, where the sick are comfortably situated, tenderly nursed, and skilfully attended. The other half of this story is the apartments for the females, who are always locked in, and not suffered to go into the work yard where the male convicts are. Competent judges pronounce this to be one of the strongest and best built prisons in the world. It is guarded at night by 24 men.

The whole of the prison is neatly plastered and whitewashed, even to the floors: from two to four sleep in one cell, upon straw beds, with pillows and blankets, and stools to sit on. They eat three times a day, mush with molasses and milk, for breakfast; supper the same; a pork or fish, with beans or peas, and bread, for dinner; all who labor hard, drink beer. None are put in for life. The number of prisoners in when I called, was about 300–280 is about the average. This is the best prison, and the best kept, of any in the U.States, at least, that I have seen. The wardens and keepers are gentlemen of education, and discharge their trust with great humanity.

But the pride of Boston is the Athaeneum. Here the citizens "drink deep of the Pierian Spring." It contains a library of 19,000 volumes, of the best authors, both ancient and modern. The books are classed in different rooms, and you have only to name those you wish to read, when you are shewn into that part of the building which contains them. No one is permitted, not even the proprietors, to take a book so much as from one room to another; those, and those only, who are proprietors, can go into the Athenaeum without special leave from one of their number. The privilege is certainly one of the greatest treats; the building being one of the largest in the city, pleasantly shaded with trees, the rooms spacious, and as silent as night; no one is allowed to speak above their breath lest they might interrupt the readers. Besides the library, the Athenaeum contains a choice collection of statuary and painting.

Manners and Characteristics

In no city, perhaps, in America, are to be found a greater body of what may be called gentlemen than in Boston: whatever can be conceived of wealth, whatever can be conceived of talent, or intellect embellished by education or improved by business, is eminently displayed in the gentlemen of Boston. They are affable, mild, and liberal, in every sense of the word. They are mostly Unitarians and Universalists in religion, the most humane and benevolent sects I have met with; the former, however, predominate. The ladies, like the gentlemen, are not exceeded by any on the continent; in accomplished manners, they possess all the yielding softness of the southern ladies with warmer hearts, and minds improved by travelling, most of them having made the tour of Europe. As to beauty, the ladies of Boston are celebrated throughout the world. But that which deserves our greatest applause, is their unbounded benevolence and charity towards the distressed.

What may be called the lower class, for their opportunity, are ignorant, proud, and abrupt in their manners, particularly the men; nor do they mix at all with the higher class, or have any intercourse with them, more than with the inhabitants of a distant country. They do not know them in the streets, they are as absolutely separated as though an impassable gulph lay between them. Though they can read and write, and many, in fact, all, I am told, go to the grammar schools; a chambermaid will read as correct as the most finished scholar, and yet their dialect is wretchedly defective. Here are a few of their phrases: *Hadn't ought,* ought not, *I be,* I am, *do what you'r mine'to,* use your pleasure, *on to it,* on it, with a number of such. But *guess,* and *what'say,* are their favorites, and make a part of every sentence. It is amusing enough to hear about a dozen of their *what'says* and *guesses* assembled together. What'-say is a substitute for sir or madam, (which amongst them you seldom hear,) and answers to the *how* of New-York; it is a habit they have contracted from asking a question to be repeated again, although they have heard it distinctly.

A Harvard College "Exhibition"

Cambridge is chiefly remarkable for being the seat of Harvard University. It is the most richly endowed of any literary institution in the Union; and consists of six large edifices, besides buildings for the president, professors, and students. It has a president, twenty professors, six tutors, a proctor, and a regent. It has a library of 28,000 volumes, the largest in America! It has a philosophical and chemical apparatus also, the most complete one in our country; the philosophical apparatus alone cost nearly 1500 £. It has besides an anatomical museum, an observatory, a cabinet of minerals, and a botanical garden of 8 acres. It has usually between three and four hundred students.

An exhibition of students took place while I was in Boston, of which I availed myself with no small degree of pleasure. The hall was filled when I arrived, although it wanted several minutes of the time, and it was with difficulty I obtained a seat. The musicians sat in the gallery, music being a part of the exhibition. The president had not made his appearance and I indulged the interval in viewing the audience, which could not have been short of a thousand; beside a vast number who were unable to get in for want of room. The students, dressed in the richest black silk gowns, sat by themselves under the gallery, except the pierian sodality that were to perform on instruments, who sat above. These were easily distinguished by the uniformity of their dress, and their modest deportment. I never saw such an assembly of fine looking people, not only as respects size and figure, but in mien and countenance: genius and intelligence shone in every face.

Meantime my ear was saluted with the most ravishing sounds; the music in the gallery began to play, and continued till the president of the university entered the hall, and took his seat in the desk. He entered the hall in a flowing robe of shining black silk, like those worn by the students. President Kirkland is of middling age and stature, portly figure, and fair complexion, his face round and comely, with a blue eye, his mouth small, his teeth regular and beautiful, his countenance noble, frank, and intelligent. On his head he wore something I shall never be able to describe: it was a cap (or something like one) made of black silk or velvet. Supposing this cap to fit the head precisely, upon the top of this, that is, upon the crown of his head, sat something quadrangular in shape, thin as pasteboard, and black as the other. This part of the head dress was about ten inches each way, and adhered horizontally to the sound part. He wore it one corner foremost, from whence dropped one of the richest tassels, which I thought interrupted his Rev.

LLDship very much, by getting into his eyes. The whole, however, was very becoming and gave him quite a dignified appearance. When he had advanced about half way up the hall, he took off the thing, whatever it be, and saluted the audience by a gentle inclination of his head, with great dignity and grace; he then proceeded up the hall with a slow, majestic step, mounted the rostrum, and stepped from thence into his desk, with the utmost composure and self-possession, while a pleasant smile sat upon his countenance, and every eye seemed to hail his arrival.

After being seated, he put on his head-piece, the music stopped, and the students began the exhibition, the president calling them separately by name in Latin. As they mounted the rostrum, they bowed first to the president, and then turning round, with a cheerful countenance, bowed respectfully to the audience, and immediately commenced speaking, perfectly unembarrassed, whilst a thousand eyes were upon them. Sometimes one, but often two, three, or four, would mount the rostrum together, though but one at a time exhibited. Some spoke in Greek, some in Latin, and others in English.

The subjects were orations upon history, philosophy, and the fine arts; also dissertations, disquisitions, and conferences were likewise held by three or four in debate. Essays, dialogues, astronomical, and mathematical excercises; among others, a dialogue in Greek, translated from Moliere's Marriage Force, and spoken by three young gentlemen, and though all Greek to me, it gave universal satisfaction, particularly to the president, who could not forbear laughing as they seemed to quarrel, and were sometimes upon the point of fighting. An interval in the exhibition of the speakers, gave place for the music, performed by the sodality.

I should be at a loss to say which I admired most, the beauty and modesty of the youths, the richness of their dress, the display of eloquence, or the sweet rolling music: from never having witnessed a display of this nature, I was doubtless more affected with the exhibition than any one present. Amongst the students, I was particularly affected with Charles F. Adams, son of the president.

5

The Pleasures of New York, 1828

Cultivated, urbane—"sophisticated" might be the adjective today—James Kirke Paulding was a leading member of the New York literati, the Knicker-bocker group. He wrote much and well enough to have written better. Born in Putnam County, New York, in 1778, most of his active literary life was associated with New York City. In 1807 and 1808 he collaborated with Washington Irving in the Salmagundi Papers. *Thereafter he turned out in profusion poems, satires, works on travel, and a great many novels. Though marred by haste, they are, nevertheless, of a considerably greater merit than most of the contemporary American output. In middle age he enjoyed politi-cal appointments, even being briefly Secretary of the Navy under Van Buren. The declining years of his life were spent in mellow retirement on his estate near Hyde Park. He died in 1860.*

In 1828 he published anonymously The New Mirror for Travellers; and Guide to the Springs. By an Amateur. *This satirical jeu d'esprit, surveying first New York City and then, by easy stages, the Hudson River and the fashionable watering resorts at Saratoga, is not quite a travel book in the usual sense. But the often clever lampoons do, nonetheless, reveal an intimate side of the life of the day less frequently treated in more serious works.*

DINING AND DANCING

The people of New York are very hospitable. They give you a great dinner or evening party, and then "let you run." These dinners seem to be in the nature of a spasmodic effort, which exhausts the purse or the hospitality of the entertainer, and is followed by a collapse of retrenchment. Mr. ——— has a fine house, the inside of which looks like an upholsterer's shop, and lives in style. He gave me an invitation to dinner, at a fortnight's notice, where I ate out of a set of China, my lady assured me cost seven hundred dollars, and drank out of glasses that cost a guinea a piece. In short, there was nothing on the table of which I did not learn the value, most especially the wine, some of which mine entertainer gave the company his word of honour, stood him in eight dollars a bottle, besides the interest, and was half a century old.

There can be no doubt these dinners are genteel and splendid, because every body here says so. But between ourselves, I was ennui. The dinner lasted six hours, at the end of which, the company was more silent than at the beginning, a sure sign of something being wanting. For my part, I may truly affirm, I never was at a more splendid dinner, or one more mortally dull.

From the dinner party, which broke up at nine, I accompanied the young people to a tea party, being desirous of shaking off the heaviness of that modern merry making. We arrived about a quarter before ten, and found the servant just lighting the lamps. There was not a soul in the room but him. He assured me the lady would be down to receive us in half an hour, being then under the hands of Monsieur Manuel, the hair dresser, who was engaged till nine o'clock with other ladies. You must know this Manuel is the fashionable hair dresser of the city, and it is not uncommon for ladies to get their heads dressed the day before they are wanted, and sit up all night to preserve them in their proper buckram rigidity. Monsieur Manuel, as I hear, has two dollars per head, besides a dollar for coach hire, it being utterly impossible for monsieur to walk. His time is too precious.

We had plenty of leisure to admire the rooms and decorations, for Monsieur Manuel was in no hurry. I took a nap on the sopha, under a superb lustre which shed a quantity of its honours upon my best merino coat, sprinkling it handsomely with spermaceti. About half past ten the lady entered in all the colours of the rainbow, and all the extravagance of vulgar finery. I took particular notice of her head, which beyond doubt, was the master piece of Monsieur Manuel. It was divested of all its natural features, which I suppose is the perfection of art. There was nothing about it which looked like hair, except it was petrified hair. All the graceful waving lightness of this most beautiful gift of woman, was lost in curls stiff and ungraceful as deformity could make them, and hair plastered to the head till it glistened like an overheated "gentleman of colour." She made something like an apology for not being ready to receive us, which turned however pretty much on not expecting any company at such an early hour. Between ten and eleven the company began to drop in; but the real fashionables did not arrive till about half past eleven, by which time the room was pretty well filled. It was what they call a conversation party, one at which there was neither cards nor dancing. The thing is intrinsically ill bred, and should this practice continue to gain ground, there is not the least doubt that the number of old bachelors and maidens will continue to increase and multiply in a manner quite contrary to Scripture. To conclude this heart rending subject, I venture to affirm, that assemblages of this kind, ought to be called eating, instead of tea drinking, or conversation parties. Their relative excellence and attraction is always estimated among the really fashionable, refined people, by the quality and quantity of the eatables and drinkables. One great requisite, is plenty of oysters; but the *sine qua non,* is oceans of champagne, for there was little conversation, a great deal of eating, and the champagne so plenty, that nine first rate dandies got so merry, that they fell fast asleep on the benches of the supper table up stairs.

I have since been at several of these first rate fashionable conversationes, where there was almost the same company, the same eatables and drinkables, and the same lack of pleasing and vivacious chit-chat. I sidled up to several little groups, whose loud laugh and promising gestures, induced me to believe, there was something pleasant going on. But I assure you nothing could equal the vapid insignificance of their talk. There was nothing in it, but "La, were you at the ball last night?"—and then an obstreperous roar of ill bred, noisy laughter. There is no harm in people talking in this way, but it is a cruel deceit upon the unwary, to allure a man into listening. In making my observations, it struck me, that many of the young ladies looked sleepy, and the elderly ones did certainly yawn most unmercifully.

It is not to be wondered at, that the indefatigable votaries of fashion should look sleepy at these parties. Some of them have sat up all the night before perhaps, in order not to discompose the awful curls of Monsieur Manuel. Others, and I am told the major part of them, have been at parties five nights in the week, for two or three months past. You will recollect, that owing to the absurd and ridiculous aping of foreign whims and fashions, these evening parties do not commence till the evening is past, nor end till the morning is come. Hence it is impossible to go to one of them, without losing a whole night's rest, which is to be made up, by lying in bed the greater part of the next day. It is no wonder their persons are jaded, their eyes sunk, their chests flattened, their sprightliness repressed by midnight revels, night after night, and that they supply the absence of all these, by artificial allurements of dress, and artificial pulmonic vivacity.

The crying absurdity of this arrangement, in a society where almost every person at these parties, has business or duties of some kind to attend to by nine o'clock the next day, must be apparent. The whole thing is at war with the state of society here, and incompatible with the system of domestic arrangements, and out door business. It is a pitiful aping of people abroad, whose sole pursuit is pleasure, and who can turn day into night, and night into day, without paying any other penalty but the loss of health, and the abandonment of all pretensions to usefulness. If our travelled gentry cannot bring home something more valuable than these mischievous absurdities, they had better stay at home.

Among the most disgusting of these importations is, the fashion of waltzing, which is becoming common here of late. It was introduced as I understand, by a party of would be fashionables, that saw it practised at the operas, with such enchanting langour, grace and lasciviousness, that they fell in love with it, and determined to bless their country by transplanting the precious exotic. I would not be understood to censure those nations among whom the waltz is, as it were, indigenous—a national dance. Habit, example and practice from their earliest youth, accustom the women of these countries to the exhibition, and excuse it. But for an American woman, with all her habits and opinions already formed, accustomed to certain restraints, and brought up with certain notions of propriety, to rush at once into a waltz, to brave the just sentiment of the delicate of her own and the other sex, with whom she has been brought up, and continues to associate, is little creditable to her good sense, her delicacy or her morals. Every woman does, or ought to know, that she cannot exhibit herself in the whirling and lascivious windings of a waltz, without calling up in the minds of men, feelings and associations unworthy the dignity and purity of a delicate female. The lascivious motions—the up turned eyes—the die away langours—the dizzy circlings—the twining arms—and projecting front—all combine to waken in the bosom of the spectators analogies, associations, and passions, which no woman, who values the respect of the world, ought ever wilfully challenge or excite.

I must not forget one thing that amused me, amid all this aping and ostentation. I was at first struck with the profusion of servants, lamps, and China, and silver forks at these parties, and could not help admiring the magnificence of the entertainer, as well as his wealth. But by degrees, it began to strike me, that I had seen these things before; and at last I fairly detected a splendid tureen, together with divers elegant chandeliers and lamps, which I had actually admired the night before at a party in another part of the town. As to my old friend Simon, and his squires of the body, he and I are hand and glove. I see him and his people, and the tureen, and the China, and the lamps, every where. They are all hired, in imitation of the fashionable people abroad. They undertake for every thing here, from furnishing a party, to burying a Christian. I can't help thinking it is a paltry attempt at style.

A SOUTHERN LADY DELIGHTS IN THE CITY

I could live in New York forever. We have a charming suit of rooms fronting on Broadway, that would be a perfect Paradise, were it not for the noise which prevents one's hearing oneself speak, and the dust which prevents one's seeing. But still it *is* delightful to sit at the window with a Waverley,* and see the moving world forever passing to and fro, with unceasing footsteps. Every body appears to be in motion, and every thing else. The carriages rattle through the streets; the carts dance as if they were running races with them; the ladies trip along in all the colours of the rainbow; and the gentlemen look as though they actually had something to do. They all walk as if they were in a hurry, and on my remarking this to my uncle, he replied in his usual sarcastic manner, "Yes, they all seem as if they were running away from an indictment." I did not comprehend what he meant.

My bonnet and curls seem to have almost conquered Stephen, who declares he has seen nothing equal to my "costume," as he calls it, since he left Paris. He has actually offered to walk with me in Broadway, and did us the honour to go with us to the theatre, one stormy night. The sublime actions of the Flying Dutchman, and Peter Wilkins, and the sublime displays in "I've been roaming," cannot fail to enlighten the understanding, refine the taste, and improve the morals of all the rising generation, in an equal if not greater degree, than bridewell or the penitentiary. The bashful ladies generally shut both their eyes, at "I've been roaming." Those who retain a fragment of the faculty of blushing, only open one eye; but such as are afraid of nothing, use a quizzing glass that nothing may escape them. To be sure, Madame —— danced. You never saw such droll capers, I declare I hardly knew which way to look. But the ladies all applauded; so I suppose I dont know what is proper, not having seen much of the world. Stephen was in ecstacies, and bravoed and encored, till my uncle bade him be quiet, and not make a jackanapes of himself. I was delighted with the theatre; it is lighted with gas; and the play was one of the finest shows I ever beheld; —processions—thunder and lightning, and dancing—fighting—rich dresses— a great deal of fiddling, and very little poetry, wit, or sense. I was a little disappointed at this—but Stephen says, nothing is considered so vulgar as a sensible, well written play.

* [I.e., with one of Sir Walter Scott's Waverley novels.—Ed.]

My head is now full of finery, and all my senses in a whirl. I wish you could see me. My hat is so large that there is no bandbox on the face of the earth, big enough to accommodate it; and yet you will be surprised to hear that it is neither fit for summer or winter, rain or sunshine. It will neither keep off one or the other, and so plagues me when I go into the street, that I hardly know which way to turn myself. Every puff of wind nearly oversets me. There are forty-two yards of trimmings, and sixty feathers to it. My dress is a full match for my hat. It took twenty three yards of silk, and five yards of satin. I am so beflounced, that my uncle laughs at me whenever I come where he is, and declares, that a fine lady, costs more to fit her out now a days, than a ship of the line. What between hat and flounces, &c. a lady has a time of it when the wind blows, and the dust is flying in clouds, as it does in Broadway all day long. I encountered a puff, at the corner of one of the streets, and there I stood, holding my hat with one hand, and my cardinal cloak, which has fifty-six yards of various commodities in it, with the other. I thought I should have gone up like a balloon; and stood stark still until I came near being run over by a great hog, which was scampering away from some mischievous boys. At last a sailor took compassion on me, and set me down at the door of a store. As he went away, I heard him say to his companion: "D——n my eyes, Bill, what a press of canvass the girls carry now a days."

O its delightful to travel. We had such a delightful sail in the steam boat, though we were all sick; and such a delightful party, if they only had been well. Only think of sailing without sails, and not caring which way the wind blows; and going eight miles an hour let what would happen. It was quite charming; but for all this I was glad when it was over, and we came into still water. Coming into the Narrows, as they are called, was like entering a Paradise. On one side is Long Island, with its low shores, studded with pretty houses, and foliage of various kinds, mixed up with the dark cedars. On the other, Staten Island, with its high bluff, crowned by the telegraph and signal poles; and beyond, the great fort that put me in mind of the old castles which Stephen talks about. We kept close to the Long Island shore, along which we glided, before wind and tide with the swiftness of wings. Every moment some new beauty opened to our view. Signior Maccaroni, as my uncle calls him, looked at it with perfect nonchalance. The bay was nothing to the bay of Naples; and the castle, less than nothing, compared with Castel Nuovo. Thank Heaven, I had not been abroad to spoil my relish.

The moment we touched the wharf, there was an irruption of the Goths and Vandals, as my uncle called the hackney coachmen, and the porters,

who risked their necks in jumping aboard. "Carriage, sir,"—"Baggage, sir,"
—"City Hotel sir,"—"Mansion House,"—"Mrs. Mann's,"—were reiterated a
thousand times; and I thought half a dozen of them would have fought for
our trunks, they disputed and swore so terribly. My uncle called them hard
names, and flourished his stick, but it would not do. When we got to the
hotel I thought we had mistaken some palace for a public house. Such mirrors
—such curtains—such carpets—such sophas—such chairs! I was almost afraid
to sit down upon them. My uncle says, all this finery comes out the cotton
plantations and rice swamps; and that the negroes of the south, work like
horses, that their masters may spend their money like asses in the north.

6

The Great Water Highway through
New York State, 1829

*The following account is not technically a travel "book," for it was pub-
lished in a Philadelphia periodical,* The Ariel, *in 1829–30 under the title
"Notes on a Tour through the Western Part of the State of New York." The
author is unknown, though the narration makes it clear he was a Pennsyl-
vanian, probably from Bristol. It is an unvarnished, unadorned record, without pretension to literary style. Yet, despite the plain manner in which it is*

presented, it contains an extremely vivid picture of the modes of travel between New York City and the West.

For purposes of comparison, two brief notes, one on Hudson River steamboats and the other on the canal and stage route from Albany to Buffalo, are appended. These excerpts come from a manuscript diary written by Thomas S. Woodcock in 1836 but not printed until 1938 by the New York Public Library under the editorship of Deoch Fulton.

Steamboats had been running since 1807 on the Hudson, and by the time the "Notes" were written in 1829 such transportation had been well developed. Both day and night steamers made the voyage, but it is apparent from our two accounts that travelers wishing to see the sights preferred the former.

The Erie Canal had only been opened along its complete length for four years when the traveler of the "Notes" used it. Though we have today the impression that tourists went on board in Albany and remained until Buffalo was reached, it is clear from the two accounts that a combination of stagecoaches was frequently made with the canal boats because of the slowness of the latter. Two types of canal boat existed. The slow-moving, less-expensive, freight-and-passenger combination, known as "Line Boats," was used by our traveler of 1829; the faster, more luxurious, passenger service, known as "Canal Packets," was employed by Woodcock.

May 5th.—In New York I took my lodging at Mrs. *Man's* boarding house, No. 61, Broadway. After making some improvements in my appearance, such as brushing up my hat and coat, and brushing off my beard, I issued forth into the splendid avenue, where all the beauty and fashion of this gay city daily promenade, to enjoy the pleasure of a walk. After walking and walking, and walking further, until my feet exhibited an alarming regiment of *blisters,* I wended my tedious way back to my lodgings—took a peep at the medley of boarders that thronged the house—looked at (but did no more than *taste*) the shaved dried beef and prepared bread-and-butter on the supper-table—for the former was cut in true Vauxhall style, one pound to cover half an acre, and the latter was only alarmed by butter—sipped a dish of tea, and made my escape to bed, ruminating on the horrors of an empty stomach tantalized by a New York supper.

May 6th.—Got up early, fresh and active—had a good night's rest, in spite of a slim supper—paid for that and my bed—*one dollar*—just four times as much as the whole was worth. Pushed off to the North America steamboat, and took passage to *Albany*—fare, two dollars. The night boats, as they are called, that is, the boats which go in the night, are some of them as low as one dollar, board included; but you lose the pleasure which even common

Life in the East

minds must feel when gazing on the glorious scenery that fringes the borders of the mighty Hudson, and which, to a stranger, fully makes up the difference. The North America is a splendid and superior boat, far surpassing all others that ply upon the Hudson, and ploughs her majestic course through the waves at the rate of fifteen miles an hour. I should estimate the number of passengers on board to-day at *three hundred,* all of whom had the appearance of belonging to the higher order of society, as the low-priced boats are favored with the rabble, who move about here so often, and in such numbers, as to give those boats a good support. We left the wharf about seven and passed by the grand Pallisadoes and the Highlands. After leaving Newburg, many very beautiful and highly cultivated *seats* are passed, on the east side of the river. As we approached the Catskill mountains, which are the highest I have ever seen, the celebrated mountain house, called *Pine Orchard,* was pointed out to me. It is located on one of the most elevated points, and is distant twelve miles from the river. But I came to the conclusion that the fatigue of climbing to the summit would be infinitely greater than the pleasure which its airy situation could afford.

After leaving the city of *Hudson,* the country gradually sinks, on each side, and appears in some places tolerably fertile—but I much prefer looking at, to living on, such a soil.

We arrived at *Albany* about eight in the evening: but, it being dark and rainy, I left the boat immediately, and took up my abode at Welch's Connecticut Coffee-House. As the rain kept me in doors, I went to roost early, and got a comfortable night's rest.*

* [Exactly seven years later, in 1836, Thomas S. Woodcock described the same route up the Hudson, which offers an interesting comparison (*New York to Niagara, 1836: The Journal of Thomas S. Woodcock, Edited, with Notes, by Deoch Fulton* [New York: New York Public Library, 1938], p. 5):

"Left New York in the Steam Boat Albany at 7 O Clock A.M. for the City of Albany the Distance is 145 Miles and the fare is $3 Meals extra. there are two lines of Boats up the River, one being a day and the other a Night line. the night line leaves at 5 O Clock and is fitted up with elegant Berths for sleeping and is certainly the most convenient way of travelling, unless as in my case the Traveller has not previously been up the river, and is desirous of seeing, its highly picturesque scenery. Our Boat though not the swiftest and most elegant of the line, is still a very handsome affair. she is upwards of 200 feet long, and has an engine of 200 horse power. she has boilers on both sides of her, the quantity of *Wood* consumed in a trip is enormous, and being pine, seems to burn as fast as it can be put in. unlike the steamboats in the Irish channel, her machinery is all on deck, and ascending a flight of steps, there is another deck called the promenade Deck. it is supported by pillars, and has an awning spread over it to keep of(f) the rays of the Sun. as she has her Machinery on Deck, it allows her to have a cabin the whole of her length, for though some of her Machinery must unavoidably come through it is so boxed up as to be no detriment to her appearance. in the forward part, is a bar room where Gentlemen can obtain refreshments, and lounge on the settees, as it is against the rules of the Boat to lounge in the Dining Cabin. the Cabin immediately aft is the Ladies Saloon or retiring room. next is the Ladies Cabin, in which Gentlemen in Company with Ladies, may enjoy their society. the Dining Cabin which is very large fills the rest of the space. this is well fitted up. Between the windows in the Cabin are some large and very respectable oil pictures, by

7th.—Got up with the sun, to allow time to survey the place, as my stay was limited. The first, and in fact the only object worthy of particular notice, (at least that I saw,) is the spacious Basin of the great *Clinton* Canal—improperly called *Erie* Canal. This is formed by a section of the river, taken therefrom by means of an extensive wharf running parallel with the shore, about one hundred yards from the same, and in length about three quarters of a mile, having a lock at the lower end, to receive and let out vessels of considerable burden. This wharf, if I may so call it, is about thirty yards wide, having extensive store-houses built upon it, from one end to the other. Several bridges are thrown across the Basin, opposite to some of the principal streets, in order to facilitate the communication with the wharf. It is truly astonishing to behold with what ease vessels may be loaded and unloaded.

Albany is certainly in a very thriving condition. But I did not see one building that could be called a splendid edifice. Even the State Capitol is nothing more than a plain, and not *very large,* but substantial stone building. The other public buildings that may be thought conspicuous, are, the Academy, Lancastrian School, and several churches with handsome steeples. The beauty of the place is greatly lessened by the many old Dutch buildings, with their gable ends fronting the streets. But it is much larger than I had supposed, and upon a general view, is a rather handsome city than otherwise.

I had contemplated taking my passage at Albany, on board a canal boat; but was disuaded therefrom in consequence of the tediousness of the passage, to *Schenectady,* having to surmount an elevation of *forty* locks, in a distance of twenty-eight miles, and occupying twenty-four hours. I therefore took my seat in the stage for Schenectady, distance fifteen miles by turnpike, fare sixty-two cents. There are now running between the two last-named places, upwards of *thirty* four-horse stages, (quite a match, if not superior to the Philadelphia and New York Union line stages,) which go and return daily, generally well crowded. This may serve to give an idea of the trade of Albany with the west. I left the city about ten A.M., making one of nine tolerably large men, of which, by the way, I must confess, I was rather more than the average size. After leaving the suburbs of Albany, we entered what are called the *Pine Plains,* but which in justice should be called the *Albany Desert* —for, of all miserable, sterile, sandy, barren wastes that ever I beheld, it caps the climax. Nor is there a single object to relieve the eye, to interest the traveller, or to merit attention, until you arrive at Schenectady, save the uniform

Native Artists. contrary to the custom prevailing in Europe the helmsman is forward instead of aft, which enables him to have a better lookout. he has a small room elevated above the Deck and entirely separate from the passengers. the helmsman or Pilot has *three* assistants the wheel being double and requiring two men to each wheel."—ED.]

straightness of the turnpike, (which is very good,) and a row of large, towering Lombardy poplars, about forty feet apart, on the north side of the road, in a direct line for the whole distance of fifteen miles. I inquired of a passenger the object of planting them. He replied that he supposed their roots would be some security to the road, and prevent its being blown away!

We arrived at Schenectady about one o'clock. As *all* the passengers in our stage were bound to Utica, one of the number proposed that he be appointed to bargain for our passage in one boat, as the opposition runs very *high,* or to speak more correctly, very *low* on the canal, and it required some policy, as we were soon convinced, to avoid imposition. As soon as the stage stopped at the Hotel, even before the driver with all his activity to undo the door, up stepped a large muscular fellow, and bawled out at the highest pitch of polite etiquette, "Gentlemen, do you go to the West?" "We do." "The packet starts at 2 o'clock, gentlemen; you had better take your passages and secure your births; only 3½ cents a mile, gentlemen, and two shillings a meal, with best accommodations, and a very superior boat, gentlemen." "Hang his boat, gentlemen, don't take passage in her," said a second fellow. "I'll take you for less than half the money in a devlish fine boat, and charge you but a shilling a meal." By this time there were at least a half a dozen more, all anxious for us to engage our passage with them at almost any price we pleased. But our *Contractor* very properly remarked, that he must see the boats himself before he would take passage in any. We therefore all sallied forth to the canal, which passes at right angles through the town. We selected a very superior boat of the Clinton Line, calculated to accommodate thirty persons. This boat is calculated for carrying freight, and the cabins are furnished in good style. The Captain actually engaged to take us to Utica, a distance of 89 miles, for one cent and a quarter per mile! a York shilling for each meal extra, and to make no charge for births, which are a very necessary accommodation, as the boats run day and night. "Thinks I to myself" this will make up for the shaved dried beef, and prepared bread and butter. I had only time to take a casual peep at Schenectady, but it appears to be a thriving, pleasant town, and is located principally between the Mohawk and the Canal. Very few persons take the boats between this place and Albany, on account of the delay occasioned by the numerous locks. We "set sail by horse power," as the Irish man has it, about 2 o'clock P.M., the horses being attached to a rope about 30 yards long, made fast to the boat amidships, with our ideas pleasingly elevated at the thought of traveling on the *Grand Clinton Canal* for the first time. The afternoon was cool and pleasant and never was I more delightfully situated as a traveller than on this occasion. A majority of my companions were Western merchants, well informed respecting the localities and prospects of the country we were passing through, and ready and willing to give the required information. The Canal, this afternoon's passage, has been for the most part immediately on the south bank of the Mohawk, which flows through a narrow valley of good land, but the hills on either side have a poverty-stricken appearance.

At the close of twilight we arrived at Schoharie creek. This is the first place of danger I have yet observed. The creek is about 30 yards wide at this place, and is crossed by means of ropes stretched across the stream, which ropes are your only security; should they give way, you must inevitable go

STEAMBOAT, 1835

down the current and pass over a dam immediately below, of several feet perpendicular descent. In times of a freshet it is very dangerous. Two or three boats have already been forced involuntarily over it, and so far in safety. The horses are ferried over in scows, pulled by the same ropes. As darkness soon covered the face of nature, I retired to the cabin, and after sketching my observations, and enjoying a pleasant confab with my fellow travellers, retired to my birth, while our boat skimmed its peaceful way along this artificial and wonderful water communication.

8th.—I arose early, having but a disturbed rest during the night, owing to the continued blowing of trumpets and horns at the approach of every lock, and now and then a tremendous jar received in passing a boat; but there is the strictest caution and observation of rules respecting the mode of passage, &c., a precaution highly important, or, owing to the immense number of boats, great confusion and no little danger would be the consequence. The boats on the canal have a beautiful appearance at night, being each illuminated by two large reflecting lamps on either side of the bow, which has much the appearance of a street brilliantly illuminated. I endeavored to count the boats which we passed yesterday, but I soon gave it up for a troublesome job. On going on deck this morning, I found a cold air and a heavy frost; we were just passing the village of Conojoharie, being the most considerable place since leaving Schenectady. I shall not attempt a description of all the numerous villages growing along our route. We are still in the valley of the Mohawk, which is narrow and fertile, but the surrounding country has nothing to boast of as to soil. The river at this place is not, I should suppose, over 50 or 70 yards wide, and is, wherever I have seen it, chequered with little islands, which give it a pleasing appearance. The locks and bridges are very numerous, and it requires great attention and care in passing them, or you may be knocked down, and rise up without your head on your shoulders, which, before you can say "look out," may be in possession of the canal fishes. The bridges being low—the highest of them not more than 10 feet above the water, and some not even over 8 feet, while the boat is full seven, we have occasionally only one foot between the two objects, which hardly admit a boy to pass under them. The bridges are cheap structures, being nothing more than two stone abutments, having sleepers thrown across the canal covered with planks, and a handrail on each side. The main width of the canal at the water line is about 40 feet, and the locks 25. The captain informs me that six persons have lost their lives by being crushed between the bridges, which is a greater number than have been killed during the same time by the bursting of steam engines in the waters of the middle or eastern States.

The locks I shall not attempt to describe. They are very simple, very strong, well built, and permanent, being uniformly about one hundred feet long. Our boat, which is of a superior class for freight boats, is about 80 feet long by 20; the bow and stern are 4 feet lower than the middle section, which is divided into three apartments—the two end ones for the accommodation of passengers, the stern to eat in, and the bow to sleep and sit in, each about 23 feet long, and sufficiently high for a six-footer to stand erect with his hat on. The roof is in the form of the back of a tortoise, and affords a handsome promenade, excepting when the everlasting bridges and locks open their mouths for your head. The centre apartment is appropriated to merchandise. The only difference between this and a passage or packet boat, is, that their centre cabins are also for the accommodation of passengers, and in some instances a little more expensively finished, and travel at the rate of 4 miles an hour, while we rarely exceed 3¼, they with three horses, and we with only two. It is evident the freight boats very much injure the packets by the cheapness with which they run, but as they go with freight, their passage money is clear gain, and competition is the result. The packets pay heavier tolls, and of course levy it on their cargo of live stock. We really live *well* in our little house, and have an obliging captain and steward, with every convenience, but short necks, that we could ask or desire.

It takes 5 hands to manage a boat of this size: they are the steward, the helmsman, and two drivers, who relieve each other as occasion may require: we have relays of horses every 20 miles, and thus we are gliding to the West. At 12 a.m. we arrived at the little falls of the Mohawk, distant 88 miles from our place of embarkation, and this being the wildest place on the canal, I shall notice it particularly. The river falls in less than half a mile 50 feet, by one continued rapid, which is surrounded by five locks, one directly above the other. There being about 20 boats waiting to pass the locks, which would occupy some time, the captain very politely offered to accompany me to the village situated on the opposite side of the river, which is crossed by a very handsome aqueduct of hewn stone, to supply the canal as a feeder. The village is of considerable size, with several very pretty buildings. There is a splendid water power at this place, but the most interesting sight was to see the fountains which are before almost every house, supplied from a rivulet led from the mountains, and which are spouting in all directions.

The rapids at the Little falls are divided just below the village by an elevated island of everlasting rocks, which arrests its progress and causes an incessant roar and foam. The canal for a mile below this spot is a perfect encroachment upon the bed of the river—the wall which divides it from the river is powerful and strong, that the labor and expense attending its erection must have been immense. The country still continues poor on both sides, while the narrow valley of the Mohawk presents very fine land. The passenger can supply himself with provisions and grog at all the lockhouses along the line at a very low rate. We arrived at 5 o'clock at the long level commencing at the village of Frankford; the canal is now one entire uninterrupted sheet of water for 70 miles, without a solitary lock; we have passed enough however to suffice for a while, having ascended upwards of 40 since leaving Schenectady, a distance of 80 miles. Very soon after entering the long reach, which is the summit level of the canal, the country begins to assume a different appearance, and the view is not so confined as heretofore. As the afternoon is a very pleasant one, the prospect is truly delightful.

We arrived at Utica just at sunset, and found our water course literally choked up with boats, and as there was considerable freight on board ours to be discharged here, we were notified that she would be detained about two hours, of which space we determined to avail ourselves by taking a peep at the town, all agreeing to continue our voyage with the obliging Captain and steward. Accordingly we stepped on shore, and took a bird's eye view of the attractions of the place. As I never had heard much said respecting this same town of Utica, I was truly astonished, and not a little pleased with it. I never saw so many fine buildings in any other town. It is really a beautiful place, and to my apprehension is not much smaller than Albany. The streets are many of them very wide, being at right angles, nearly in a direction North, South, East and West, with the exception of State street, which runs in an oblique direction, and appears to be the Broadway of Utica, and truly for two or three squares it is in no respect inferior to that celebrated avenue of New York. The Mohawk runs immediately on the north side of the place, and the canal directly through the centre. Nothing can exceed the facility with which boats are loaded and discharged. There is a walk on each side of the canal about 10 feet wide; a boat stops opposite a store, a tackle descends from an upper story, which by means of a rope and windlass within the building, managed by one man, can raise and lower heavy weights with wonderful dispatch.

We left Utica at 10 P.M. and the ear was saluted from a great distance up and down the canal by the music of bugles, horns and trumpets, some of the boatmen sounding their instruments most sweetly. After enjoying these sounds for some time, I tumbled into my birth to partake of the necessary blessing of a nap.

9th.—I awoke about sunrise and ascended our deck; there had been another heavy frost. We were just passing Bull fort, and had entered the *Black Snake,* so called from the serpentine course of the canal. We have passed, during the night, Rome, and now had before us one uninterrupted white pine and hemlock swamp for something like 20 miles, and it really looks to me as if you might cut and hawl wood and logs to eternity without exhausting the supply. In the course of the last 10 miles, we have passed several squads of Onondaga and Oneida Indians. Among these numbers were frequently seen little children, and we diverted ourselves for miles together in making them run after the packet, by occasionally throwing out a cent, which made great scratching and scrabbling to see who would get it. We could not prevail on them to converse by the offer of any bribe whatever.

At six o'clock we arrived at what may be called one of the wonders of this part of the world—the extensive salt establishment, belonging to the state, situated immediately at the head of Onondaga Lake. Here are located the villages of Syracuse, Salina, and Geddesburg, all within a mile of each other. Syracuse is in a very prosperous condition. It was a very agreeable and novel sight to me to behold at this place upwards of 200 acres actually covered with vats filled with salt water in the act of evaporation. The quantity of salt sent to market from this shop is immense. The salt water is obtained from two springs or wells, and is pumped by water power obtained from the canal, carried through horizontal logs in every direction for a half a mile to a mile and a-half, to supply the vats. Soon'after leaving this place it became dusk, and I took to my couch.*

10th.—The Captain called me at peep of day, to say I was near my place of landing. I had scarcely time to equip myself before it was necessary to

* [The journey on the Erie Canal, made by a "packet boat," was described by Wood-cock (*ibid.*, pp. 7–9) as he continued his trip from Albany in 1836:

"Left Albany at 9 O Clock by the Railway for Schenectady, a distance of 17 Miles, for which 62½ cents is charged. we were drawn by horses about 2 Miles, being a steep ascent. we then found a Steam Engine waiting for us (built by Stephenson and called the John Bull) the road is then quite level for 14 Miles through the poorest Country I ever saw. the sand banks are so loose that trees have been cut down and laid upon them, to promote vegetation and prevent the sand from drifting. we at length stop to have our carriages attached to a stationary Engine which lets us down an inclined plane, from the top of which we have a fine view of Schenectady and part of the Valley of the Mohawk. it is chiefly built of Bricks and is in a low flat situation, and I think a place of no great importance. we arrived at this place at ½ past 10. from the cars we proceeded to enter our names for the Packet Boat. these boats are about 70 feet long, and with the exception of the Kitchen and bar, is occupied as a Cabin. the forward part being the ladies Cabin, is separated by a curtain, but at meal times this obstruction is removed, and the table is set the whole length of the boat. the table is supplied with everything that is necessary and of the best quality with many of the luxuries of life. on finding we had so many passengers, I was at a loss to know how we should be accommodated with berths, as I saw no convenience for anything of the kind, but the Yankees ever awake to contrivances have managed to stow more in so small a space than I thought them capable of doing. the way they proceed is as follows—The Settees that go the whole length of the Boat on each side unfold and form a cot bed. the space between this bed and the ceiling is so divided as to make room for two more. the upper berths are merely frames with sacking bottoms, one side of which has two projecting pins, which fit into sockets in the side of the boat. the other side has two cords attached one to each corner. these are suspended from hooks in the ceiling. the bedding is then placed upon them—the space between the berths being barely sufficient for a man to crawl in, and presenting the appearance of so many shelves. much apprehension is always entertained by the passengers when first seeing them, lest the cords should break. such fears are however groundless. the berths are allotted to the way bill the first on the list having his first choice and in changing boats the old passengers have the preference. the first Night I tried an Upper berth, but the air was so foul that I found myself sick when I awoke. afterwards I choose an under berth and found no ill effects from the air. these Boats have *three* Horses, go at a quicker rate and have the preference in going through the locks, carry no freight, are built extremely light, and have quite Genteel men for their Captains, and use *silver* plate. the distance between Schenectady and Utica is 80 Miles the passage is $3.50 which includes board. there are other Boats called Line Boats that carry at a cheaper rate, being found for ⅔ of the price mentioned. they are larger Boats carry freight have only two horses, and consequently do not go as quickly, and moreover do not have so select a company. some Boats go as low as 1 cent per Mile the passengers finding themselves. The Bridges on the Canal are very low, particularly the old ones, indeed they are so low as to scarcely allow the baggage to clear, and in some cases actually rubbing against it. every Bridge makes us bend double if seated on anything, and in many cases you have to lie on your back. the Man at the helm gives the Word to the Passengers. 'Bridge' '*very* low Bridge' 'the lowest in the Canal' as the case may be. some serious accidents have happened for want of caution. a young English Woman met with her death a short time since, she having fallen asleep with her head upon a box had her head crushed to pieces. such things however do not often occur, and in general it affords amusement to the passengers who soon imitate the cry, and vary it with a command, such as 'All Jackson men bow down.' after such commands we find very few Aristocrats. The Canal was within sight of the Mohawk River, in some cases only the towing path being between, the wall rising from the Channel of the river and being elevated 20 or 30 feet. This is the valley of the Mohawk. so narrow is it in some places that there seems scarcely room for the River the Road and the Canal which pass through it.—Ed.]

jump ashore, and I soon found myself on the road to Auburn, distant 9 miles
—stage fare 25 cents only.

11th.—I was awakened about midnight by the landlord, and informed that
the great Western Mail, which was to carry me to Buffalo, was ready, on
which I rose, paid my fare, and was crowded as usual, with eight others, into
a comfortable stage. The country is low meadow land, in the possession of
the Pioneers of the land, and looks more like what is generally supposed in
my county, to be the appearance of the clime generally, than any I have seen;
but there is no mistake about the soil's being good—tho' I should rather suppose it to be unhealthy, as the Natives are very dirty and beastly. Further we
ascended a considerable eminence, and from the summit *Erie* was distinctly
seen on the left, and *Niagara* on the right, and the town of Buffalo full in
view before us. I cannot say that I admire the country nor do I think it is
sufficiently watered, and, by the by, that which I tasted, I never wish to
taste more, as it set my bowels in an uproar prodigiously, to my great inconvenience and pain. At Buffalo, which supports six extensive Hotels, a Theatre
and three Churches, the grand Canal terminates by another spacious Basin,
filled with boats.

7

In America All Women Are Ladies, 1835

*F*rancis Lieber was born in Berlin, Germany, in 1800. Caught in the tur-
moil of liberal sentiments, he fought in the Waterloo campaign and in the
Greek War for Independence. Constantly suspected by a reactionary Prussian
government for his liberal ideas, he underwent persecution and police surveil-
lance until even earning his living had become difficult. He removed, after a

Life in the East

short stay in England, to the United States in 1827. Engaged first in Boston and then in Philadelphia in teaching and literary activities, he was finally appointed to a professorship in history and government at South Carolina College in 1835. There he remained, not always outwardly happy, until he was called to Columbia in 1857.

Lieber was a prolific author. Though most of his books deal with history, politics, and political theory, there were many others, of which the present The Stranger in America *is an example. He had wit and humor—of a somewhat heavy Teutonic quality, it is true—but even in his lighter works he tends to overelaboration and discursiveness. Yet he was discerning and keenly intelligent and, even when straying furthest from his subject, invariably interesting. When Lieber wrote* The Stranger in America, *a work dealing with a voyage to New York, up the Hudson, and across New York State to Buffalo, he had been in the United States but eight years. Much of what he saw is undeniably through the eyes of a German exile. Yet it is apparent that he considered himself a bona fide American, and most of his reactions are those of a permanently adopted citizen.*

It is a good and very beneficial trait of the Americans, that they hold women in great esteem. An American is never rude to a woman; let a single woman travel from Philadelphia to Cincinnati, and if she be of respectable appearance, she will not only meet with no molestation on her way, but very soon some gentleman or other will take her under his protection, and she may proceed with perfect safety. The consequence is that many very respectable females, of course not ladies of the higher circles, travel alone in the United States. Nay, if those who have no claim to a respectful treatment move from place to place, they assume invariably a respectable appearance, without inconveniencing that part of the company, unacquainted with their history.

The Americans are not a race of French agility, and, therefore, cannot be expected to show that pliant politeness toward women which depends, in a great degree, upon this peculiar quality; they are not easily excitable, and, consequently, not versatile in conversation; they, therefore, cannot show that quick politeness which depends upon this inventive brightness of the moment; but they are essentially and substantially polite, ready to serve a woman, of whatever class, and to show the greatest regard to the female sex in general.

I have seen a hundred times a woman enter a stage-coach, wait, without saying a word of apology, until a gentleman had removed from a back seat, and then, with equal silence, place herself in the vacated situation. Here I must observe that, in my opinion, an American lady accepts with greater *nonchalance* any act of politeness, than the women of other countries; by which they imprudently deprive their social life of much of its charm. A smile, a friendly glance, a gentle word—who cares for holding the stirrup if he cannot expect thus much. Yet, as you may imagine, there are many sweet and lovely exceptions. Women belonging to the industrial classes in America, I have observed to be, in comparison with those of a similar rank in other countries, particularly imperturbable by politeness, perhaps owing to a certain shyness, and, perhaps, it is more observed because you are brought more into contact with people of all classes in this country than in others; for here all the world travels, the richest and the poorest, the blackest and the whitest. (By a report made to the New Jersey legislature, on the 7th of February, 1834, we find that nearly *one hundred and ten thousand passengers* were conveyed between the cities of New York and Philadelphia, by the Camden and Amboy rail-road line, during the year 1833.) How often have I handed a lady into the stage-coach, or picked up a handkerchief, or handed her some dish at dinner, when travelling, without receiving as much as a word in return.

I met lately with a pleasing instance of the regard paid to the female sex in the United States. A separate place has been appropriated to the delivery of letters to females, in New York, and an editor noticing this arrangement and approving of it, suggests the propriety of having an awning or covering of some description to protect the applicants from the sun. Of course, only women who have no servants to send, or no home so fixed that the carrier may take the letters to them, go in *propria persona* to the post-office, and for them was this considerate arrangement made. Had the arrangement in question been made, not for the convenience of females, but in order to separate certain women, always busy about the post-office, from the place of general delivery, the considerate regard for the community would have been equally praiseworthy.

I once saw a young, gay gentleman taking, in a stage-coach, a baby from a lady and holding it in his lap, I should think at least half an hour. I thought it, of course, very amiable, but really I was also barbarian enough to think it quite sufficient, in all conscience, to bear good-humoredly the act of travelling in company of a non-domestic baby.

I have always considered Mahomed very impolite for denying women a soul, but I really wish ladies would keep out of the way where they are not in their sphere. A poor fellow of a traveller wants, for instance, to hear the great men of the nation "talk." He goes to Washington; by eleven o'clock, the morning after his arrival, he proceeds to the senate, though its business only begins by twelve o'clock. He thinks he has secured a seat. But by that time ladies begin to drop in; presently they seize upon all the seats. Very well, allow the poor fellow but a fair *stand;* but no, he is obliged to squeeze himself in a corner, pressed in from all sides; mercy, ye gentle souls, allow him but a free passage from his ear to the debaters, and treat the rest of his body as though it were a bale of cotton under the hydraulic press! The prayer is said; he stretches his neck like a turtle, and turns his eyes away, in order to bring his ear the better into a position that it may catch a sound, which Echo, more merciful than the ladies, may throw into it. His twisted neck begins to ache; his eyes are closed, he thinks "now for the treat," when, un-happily, some officer of the senate taps him on the shoulder: "Sir, there are ladies coming," at the same time, shuffling and pushing chairs over the heads of innocent listeners and constituents, crammed in like the camomile flowers of the shaking-quakers. At last, the officer succeeds in working a passage, and, lo! as if a canal of bonnets, feathers, and veils, had broken through, in they rush; there is no use in resistance. Without a single "I beg your pardon," or betraying the least sorrow at disturbing you, the ladies drive the poor man out of his last retreat. He must needs give way, the contrary would be rude. The poor man who has come, say five hundred miles, to hear the senate, is standing, by this time near the door, with a longing look toward the presi-dent, if he has found an opportunity to turn his head back again; and now the debates begin, but, alas! the ladies, also, begin, and our unlucky traveller retires, all he has heard of the senate having been a lisping from sweet lips, directed, perchance, to a polite senator himself. I truly and sincerely think, that legislative halls are, generally speaking, not places calculated for ladies, for many and, I think, very weighty reasons.

Suppose, the same disappointed man, whom we have seen swimming, without success, against the current in the senate-house, is desirous of hearing an oration on some political subject, to be delivered in a public hall or church. He starts early, to be certain of a place, but oh Jove, protector of the strangers! when he arrives, all seats, below and in the first rank above, are already taken by the ladies, whose pretty heads are in as quick motion as their fans, which gives to the whole scene the appearance of an agitated sea be-tween the breakers. But the stranger espies a yet empty space; to this he directs his course; it is difficult, and may cost him a flap of his coat, but, never mind, he is anxious to hear the orator of the day. He penetrates, at length, to the spot where he expects to rest in peace. "Sir," says, very politely, a man with a short stick in his hand, "these seats are reserved for the gentlemen who form the procession." Confound it, internally exclaims the disappointed man, and makes his exit. I remember, I was once unable, on occasion of the de-

livery of a Latin oration at a public commencement of some college, to penetrate a crowd of ladies, composed, almost without exception, not of mothers,
but of young fashionables. I am resolved to do my best to get up a *Polite
anti-ladies thronging-poor-men-out-of-every-chance-of-seeing-any-thing-Soci-
ety.*

Every female person in the United States is a lady. But a few days ago, my
boy went out with a colored servant, and as they had not returned when it
began to grow dark, I felt uneasy, and went to the ferry, on which they had
intended to cross the Delaware. I asked the ferryman: "Has a colored woman
with a child gone across this afternoon?" describing both. "No colored lady
has gone to the other shore," was the answer, not with the intention to correct me, but because the words were more natural to his lips. He repeated,
afterwards, "No, sir, no colored lady has gone across, within the last two
hours."

I'll tell you more. They had, notwithstanding what had been said, gone
across, but in another boat. My boy found a little girl on board the ferry, with
whom he soon made acquaintance, and speaking to the gentleman who was
in charge of her, said, "I wish I had a sweet little sister like this little girl."
"Have you no sister?" asked the gentleman. "No," said my boy, "but I have
begged God to give me one." The colored girl, mentioned above, told at home
this innocent story, and added, "I did not know where I should look, when
the little boy said, he had begged God to give him a sister." *Voilà de la
delicatesse!*

These are anecdotes, and must be taken as evidence is taken in court, for
what they are worth. I dislike very much picking up anecdotes and gen-
eralizing them—the common method of travellers who think themselves very
sagacious. It is a poor way of reasoning and observing, and has done infinite
mischief in judging of individuals and events, both in history and in our own
times, but these are anecdotes of a generic character. I know the state of
things, independently of their evidence, and give them because they elucidate
the fact; I do not reason from them, but add them by way of illustration.

There are strange inconsistencies in the character of every nation, and one
of the strangest in the Americans is the immense freedom young ladies enjoy
upon some points and their primness in others. Nothing is more common
here than for the young lady of the house, perhaps seventeen years old, to
give invitations to a ball in her own name, to single gentlemen as well as
others, though there may not be the slightest reason for the mother or father
not issuing them in their name. I fancied I had made a great impression
upon some unknown beauty when I received my first invitation from Miss
So and So. "I invited by Miss X.Y.Z.? She writing my name?" such were

my thoughts. It was not long, however, before I discovered my mistake. The mother is put quite in the background. This is village-like, and is rapidly growing out of fashion in the best educated families. As soon as the lady is married, she drops like a Cactus grandiflorus after twenty-four hours blowing; she recedes to give the ground to other young ladies yet unmarried. This is *mauvais ton,* no one denies, and you see less of it in New York than in Philadelphia, in Philadelphia less than in Boston.

An American girl is never embarrassed; a child of ten years,—and I would hardly except a single class of the inhabitants,—receives you with a frankness and good breeding which is astonishing, and I can assure you, not unpleasing. So perfectly self-possessed are they, that blushing is decidedly of little occurrence. My attention was lately drawn to a young friend of mine, a most amiable girl who blushed; and I then thought how rarely I had seen it. I could remember but a very few girls of a large acquaintance that will now and then be seen blushing, I mean when nothing but false *embarras* is the cause. This pleasing ease and sensible frankness sometimes degenerate, as you may suppose, into unbecoming and ungraceful forwardness.

American ladies are possessed of much natural brightness, and converse very freely, infinitely more so than gentlemen. Altogether, boys and girls are earlier *developed* here than in Europe, partly perhaps owing to the climate, partly because they are allowed more freedom,—left more to themselves. A young man of twenty has a much more advanced position in life here than in England.

Good education among ladies is general. Not a few are truly superior in this respect. I think there must be numbers who are bright and fluent letter-writers, to judge from my own correspondence. I know several ladies whose attainments and natural powers would be a great ornament to society any where, whom I count among the most superior minds with whom it has ever been my good fortune to become acquainted.

You wish the ladies described too? I know that we wish as much to become acquainted with the appearance of the female sex of a country as with their character. But this is no easier task than to give, in a few lines, a description of the scenery of a country; it is, in fact, much more difficult. Yet I will try it; only remember that descriptions of this kind are to be taken as general assertions, admitting of innumerable exceptions. To begin then.—It must be allowed, in the first place, that American women have generally a fine, and—more frequently than the women of other countries—a genteel, rarely an imposing appearance. Their shoulders are generally not wide enough, and too sloping; their busts not sufficiently developed, but the waist is small and round, and the lower parts of the body finely formed; their feet

FASHIONS FOR JUNE, 1856

are not particularly good—they are better than German feet indeed, and better than the English. Yet so capricious are exceptions! The smallest pair of correctly shaped feet, so small as would be justly criticized if an artist were to give them to a work of his imagination, and the neatest pair of ankles, with corresponding hands and wrists, that I ever beheld, I saw on this side of the Atlantic.

Their walk is much better than the ungraceful dipping and pitching of the English ladies. Their arms—where are fine arms any longer to be found? Sleeves have spoiled them. Their color—I do not now speak of the arms—is generally delicate, which contributes to give, even to the lowest classes, an air of gentility. Their eyes are not as large as the Spanish, yet they are fine, well-cut, and well set, and of much mental expression. They look bright, and are generally of a fine dark brown color. The general expression of the face is again that of handsomeness and delicacy rather than of great and striking beauty. From all this you will see that American ladies look better in the street than in the ball-room, yet I can assure you you find there also many charming faces. It is a peculiarity of the United States which has often struck me, that there are more pretty girls than in any other large country, but fewer imposing beauties than in Europe.

Before I close my chapter on American beauty—a chapter which, I dare say, has proved very unsatisfactory to you, although I gave you fair warning that it is very difficult for a conscientious writer to generalize such things—I must mention the fact, that American women make most exemplary wives and mothers, and strange, be a girl ever so coquettish—yea, even a positive flirt, who in Europe, would unavoidably make her future husband unhappy as soon as she were married, here she becomes the domestic and retired wife. That unhappy marriages seem to be comparatively rare in America may be partly owing to the great patience of an American husband, which is again referrible to the greater want of excitability, but it is undoubtedly owing also, and probably in a greater degree, to the temper of the women.

The American women are kind and very charitable; I think they are peculiarly so. Married ladies do not only give, if a case of misfortune happens to present itself, but they undergo considerable personal trouble in compliance with their charitable disposition. And again, I have known here several ladies of the most worldly appearance, living, apparently, but to gain admiration, who, nevertheless, would visit the poor and sick in their humblest dwellings.

Mourning dress among the ladies is carried here to excess. A traveller is surprised at seeing so many people dressed in black. I met, one day, a lady of my acquaintance, in Rockaway, a village on the sea-shore, not far from New York. She was in mourning; she told me the reason of her sombre dress; some distant relation had died. "But," said I, "I saw you in mourning half a year ago: for whom was that?" "We were then in mourning for—Mary, my dear," turning to her sister, "for whom were we in mourning, then?"

A proper regard for our departed friends, shown by external signs, is, undoubtedly, becoming for a civilized man, and agrees with our feelings. But if mourning is carried to such an extent as in the United States, it has no more meaning than the going into mourning of a court, ordered by the high-chamberlain, for some prince. Besides, it causes a state of things which may seriously interfere with the whole life of an individual. A female is born to be married, marriage requires previous acquaintance, and, as things now stand, acquaintance cannot, generally, take place without social intercourse; mourning, however, throws a young lady out of society. I have known families in which young ladies continued to wear mourning for some very distant cousins, from their seventeenth year to their twenty-first: a very serious affair in a country where ladies cease much earlier to be considered as floating on the full tide of marriageableness than in other parts of the world. Some avoid this inconvenience by going to balls in semimourning, which never fails to make on me a very unpleasant impression. There is a mockery in such a contrast, which shows too plainly—I mourn, but I do not grieve.

8

The Metropolis, 1837

*A*sa Greene is a writer virtually forgotten today, though he does not entirely deserve such neglect. He was born in Ashby, Massachusetts, about 1789, graduated from Williams College in 1813, and, nearly ten years later, received an M.D. degree from Brown University. For a time he practiced medicine

*and published newspapers in the Berkshire region, but he apparently had a
distaste for the former and no great success in the latter. When he was about
forty years old, he removed to New York, and there, practicing as a physician,
a bookseller, and a newspaperman, became a literary figure as well. In quick
succession appeared* The Life and Adventures of Dr. Dodimus Duckworth,
a satire on the medical profession; Travels in America by George Fibbleton,
Ex-Barber to the King of Great Britain, *an attack upon the English travelers
in America;* A Yankee among the Nullifiers; *and two accounts of New York,*
The Perils of Pearl Street *and* A Glance at New York. *The last, from which
comes the following extract, was published anonymously in the year of his
death, 1837. This volume is marked by much of the satirical wit which was
characteristic of Greene's fiction, together with his sense for the unusual
which he treats in a highly realistic way.*

THE SIDEWALKS OF NEW YORK

Not more than a sixth part of the island of Manhattan is compactly covered with houses, stores, and paved streets. The rest is occupied with farms
and gardens; though the limits of the city comprise the whole island; and
the farmers and gardeners of the upper five-sixths are included in one of
the wards of the city, are subject to the government of the mayor and corporation, and enjoy the same municipal privileges as their more crowded neighbors, who walk on paved streets, and are surrounded with all the bustle of
city life.

The streets of the ancient parts of New York are narrow, crooked, and irregular—running into and crossing each other at all sorts of angles except a
right angle. As a specimen of the narrow, the irregular and the crooked,
Pearl Street may be taken—Pearl Street, that great mart of business and principal scene of wholesale operations. The new parts of the city are more regularly laid out. The streets and avenues are broad and straight; and the squares
have generally right angles.

Broadway is a noble street, 80 feet wide and straight as an arrow, extending
from the Battery northward nearly two miles, and uniting with the fifth
avenue.

But broad as Broadway is, it is now quite too narrow for the immense
travel, business, and locomotion of various kinds, of which it is the constant
scene. This is particularly the case with that part below Canal-street; and
more particularly so south of the Park. Here the attempt at crossing is almost
as much as your life is worth. To perform the feat with any degree of safety,
you must button your coat tight about you, see that your shoes are secure at

the heels, settle your hat firmly on your head, look up street and down street, at the self-same moment, to see what carts and carriages are upon you, and then run for your life. We daily see persons waiting at the crossing places, for some minutes, before they can find an opening, and a chance to get over, between the omnibuses, coaches, and other vehicles, that are constantly dashing up and down the street; and, after waiting thus long, deem themselves exceedingly fortunate if they can get over with sound bones and a whole skin.

Another great thoroughfare is the Bowery. But this street is wider than Broadway; and as fewer people pass therein, either in the way of business or pleasure, it is not so much crowded, and there is not the same difficulty and danger in crossing it.

"New York, I perceive"—said a gentleman the other day, scraping the mud from his boots—"still holds her own. She had, as far back as I can remember, the reputation of being the dirtiest city in the Union; and she maintains it still. I have been recently in Boston, Philadelphia, Baltimore, and several other cities; but I have seen nothing in the way of foul streets, to compare with New York."

But this should hardly be taken for gospel. Some allowance should be made for the disposition of editors to exaggerate. But after all, it must be owned, that, until within a few years, New York was shamefully dirty. Even as late as the year '32, she had not greatly improved. The first thorough cleansing she ever had, was in the summer of that year; and for this cleansing the cholera is to be thanked.

While the cholera was on the way from Canada, the fathers of the city began to bethink themselves of abating the fury and shortening the stay of that dread enemy, as much as possible, by divesting the city of that foul aliment on which the pestilence delights to feed.

They resolved to clean the streets; and the streets were cleaned. For the first time, within the memory of living man, the stones of the pavement every where showed their heads. The rain had occasionally washed them bare, but, in the more level streets, the stones, after having once been fixed in the pavior, rarely had shown themselves again to mortal eyes. In 1832, after the arrival of the cholera, they were first scraped and swept clean; and the filth carted away.

Formerly there were no street scavengers. There was a law requiring each householder as often, we believe, as once a week to sweep before his own door; not only the side-walk, but also half way across the street, where his opposite neighbor was to meet him. The dirt, swept in heaps, was to be carried away by the carts. We well remember that the householders swept as often as they pleased; and for the matter of being carried away, the dirt often remained in heaps for several days; or rather the heaps were trodden and scattered about again; and required to be swept and collected anew.

How surprised, then, were the citizens of New York, in the summer of '32, to behold the tidiness of their streets. "Where in the world did all these stones come from?" said an old lady who had lived all her life in the city; "I never knew that the streets were covered with stones before. How very droll!"

But the cleanliness of New York, during that cholera summer, it must be confessed, was in part ascribable to the want of business and the scarcity of inhabitants: the first having almost entirely disappeared, and the latter in great numbers, by reason of the pestilence. Seventy-five thousand human beings, and several thousand horses, carts, and other vehicles, make a very considerable difference in the generation of street-dirt. Having been once, therefore, thoroughly swept and cleansed, it was comparatively easy to keep streets clean, until the return of the inhabitants and the revival of business.

New York has never entirely relapsed into those abominably dirty habits, for which she was so long notorious. Her system of street management is improved. Regular scavengers are now employed; and they may be seen, sometimes, busily engaged with their hoes and their brooms. New York is at least fifty per cent more tidy than she was previous to 1832.

HOTELS

In New York, as in all other cities, hospitality, or anything resembling it, is unknown. And this is the result, not of any native churlishness or want of fellow feeling; but simply of the particular circumstances, the peculiar social condition, of the inhabitants of cities. "What is every body's business is nobody's." The citizens live too close together, too crowded, to allow room for hospitality. The scattered condition of people living on farms and plantations renders them hospitable. Bring the southerner to New York—make him a citizen of this great metropolis—and he would no more entertain strangers than Mr. John Smith, or any of the other thousands of our citizens who keep house, and whose names figure in the Directory.

The number of hotels in New York is exceedingly limited when we consider the size and business of the place, and the great number of strangers to be accommodated. There are not in all, we believe—or at least all that deserve the name of hotels—much above thirty. There are, indeed, hundreds of places where spirituous liquors are sold, and which perhaps are designated, in flaming characters over the door, as "hotels." There are other places again, of great respectability, where good eating is to be had, and which are generally denominated "refectories." But of public houses, where meat and lodging are furnished, in genteel, respectable, or decent style, there are not, as we have just said, much above thirty.

This, for a population of 300,000 and 20,000 strangers who are frequently in the city at a time, we repeat, is a very small number. If we allow them, on an average, to accommodate 200 persons apiece,—which we believe is a sufficiently liberal allowance—there are only 6000 of the 20,000 strangers provided for; to say nothing of the citizens, who, in great numbers, both married and single, both clerks and business men, and men of no business, occupy a room and a seat at the board of some one of the hotels.

The boarding houses, of which there are many of great respectability in different parts of the city, accommodate a pretty large number of strangers. But, after all, we do not see where all of them find the conveniences of bed and board. Meat they may find at the eating houses, and that at all hours, and whenever they are hungry. For lodgings they must do as heaven pleases. If they find accommodations, as doubtless they must somewhere, we confess our utter ignorance of the whereabouts.

That persons from abroad are often straightened for a lodging, we see exemplified every spring and fall, when the city is most amply filled with strangers. They arrive in great numbers by the steamboats. They order their luggage to be carried, each one, to such or such a hotel; "We are full," says the landlord. "The mischief you are!" says the stranger; "but hav'nt you some snug little corner you can stow me into? You know I always put up with you."—"I know you do," says the landlord, "and I am sorry that I can't accommodate you now. But I'm full from cellar to garret. There is not room enough to get in a shad edgeways."

The consequence of this is, that the keepers of hotels, are enabled to charge for their accommodations whatever sums they please. About two years ago—though they had previously been doing an excellent business—they, by a simultaneous movement, raised their prices thirty-three and a third per cent.

But as the gentility of the house is always estimated by the extravagance of its charges, and as the strife of gentility is somewhat prevalent in our growing country, so those hotels which lay on the largest price, are pretty certain to be thoroughly filled. All, or nearly all these hotels are situated in the southerly part of the city, and most of them are in the three lower wards. There they are convenient to the steamboat landings, and also to the business operations of the city. Nearly half of the whole number are situated in Broadway; and these, with three exceptions, no further north than the Park.

Three hotels are kept on the "European plan," or in the English mode, of separating the two important concerns of bed and board. In taking the first, you are under no obligations to take the last. You may eat at your landlord's if you please, and you may order what you please; but this has no connection with your bill for lodging, and you pay down on the nail for what you have eaten. This plan has been only introduced here within five or six years.

The other hotels are kept on the old plan. A long table—or what is called in France a *table d'hote*—is furnished daily, at a certain hour, which, in most of the houses, is 3 o'clock. A few, out of Broadway, dine at 2; and some of those in Broadway—such as the Astor House, the American, and perhaps some others, set an extra table at 5, for the accommodation of foreigners, or such aspiring Americans as are anxious to prove their aristocracy by going hungry to that late hour.

The table d'hote is more sociable than the refectory. At the latter you discuss your beefsteak, your chicken, or whatever you have ordered, alone, and with plenty of elbow room. At the former you eat in company with one or two hundred, to the music of as many knives and forks, and usually so crowded together that your elbows are pinned down to your sides like the wings of a trussed fowl. But, besides the greater sociability of eating in a crowd, there is another advantage, particularly to an irresolute or absent minded man, in dining at the table d'hote—it saves him the necessity of studying the particular dish he would prefer, since every thing is spread out to his eye, and the laborious effort, either of thinking or of memory, is not required in making the choice.

The price of lodging per week, at the Custom House Hotel, is $2,50. At Tammany Hall and at Lovejoy's it varies from $2,50 to 3,50, according as your room is situated, up one or more pair of stairs—the price being lower, the nearer you approach heaven; and higher, the closer you cling to earth. In the eating department of these houses, the price of a meal consisting of one dish, varies from 12½ to 31½ cents.

In the hotels on the old plan the price of bed and board, per day, varies from $1,50 to $2,50. The latter is the price at the Astor House. The other houses in Broadway, for the most part, if not all, charge $2,00. The Clinton Hotel does the same. In the other streets, from $1,50 to $1,75 is the price.

DANDIES

Like other great cities, New York has her share of this class of the biped without feathers. They abound more or less in every part of the city, from Corlaer's Hook to the Battery, and from Blooming Dale to White Hall. But they are mostly to be seen in public places—at the corners of streets, on the door-steps of hotels, and in the various public walks.

Dandies may be divided into three classes, namely: *chained* dandies, *switched* dandies, and *quizzing-glass* dandies. These are so distinguished, as the reader will readily conceive, from those harmless pieces of ornament which they severally wear about their persons or carry in their hands.

The chained dandy is so called from a golden—or a gilded—or a brazen—chain, of light workmanship, which he wears about his neck, and which is attached to a watch if he is able to wear one; and to nothing at all, if his pecuniary condition happens to be better suited to that convenience.

The switched, or caned, dandy is so denominated from a slender cane, or switch, about the size of a pipe-stem, made of whale-bone, or of steel, of a shiny black, neatly polished, with an ivory head, a brass foot, a golden eye, and a tassel of silk; which cane or switch, he constantly carries and switches about him.

The quizzing-glass dandy is so styled from a small glass, either of a circular or elliptic shape, set in gold or in brass, which he carries suspended to his neck by a chain or riband; and which he whips from his bosom, and applies to his eye, as often as he is introduced to a stranger of either sex, and as often as he sees a female who has any pretension either to youth or beauty.

In respect to numbers, the three classes are nearly equally divided. In many cases, they are united in the same person. The tasseled switch, the gilded chain, the everlasting quizzing-glass, combine to ornament the self-same character. He is a dandy of the first water. He is the triple, or compound, dandy; and his head is found, on dissection, to possess three times the vacancy of the single, simple, or uncompounded dandy.

Dandies are supposed, by many, to be on the increase in New York. But of that we are not certain. The truth is, the race is not particularly admired, and especially by the ladies. The consequence is, that they have little chance of getting married and thus propagating the species. It is believed, therefore, that in time they will run out.

WATER AND OTHER LIQUIDS

The cry of the citizens of New-York for water—"pure and wholesome water"—has been unceasing. There is not perhaps in the Union a city more destitute of the blessing of good water than New-York.

The present supply, such as it is, comes from three sources, to wit: the town pumps, the Manhattan Company, and Knapp's spring. To this we should add a fourth source, namely, the clouds; from which the chief supply for washing is obtained.

The town pumps are conveniently situated at the corners of the streets, every where throughout the city; so that no person who is athirst, need perish for want of water, if he will take the trouble of walking the length of a square. If he stand in need of physic at the same time, the pump will furnish that also—without money. Besides the virtue derived from the neighboring sinks, the pump-water is also impregnated with certain saline properties, which render it peculiarly efficacious in certain complaints.

Little less so is that—if we may judge from its peculiar hue and taste— which is called Manhattan water. This is ready pumped by the Manhattan Banking Company, which was chartered many years ago, for the purpose of

CENTRAL PARK, NEW YORK

supplying the city with "pure and wholesome water." Not that the people get it gratis, as they do the town pump beverage. But they can have it brought to their houses in pipes, on application to the Manhattan Company, and paying the regular price. The pumping up of this water from the depths of the Collect, is an expensive affair. It requires the constant employment of a powerful steam engine, and the constant operation of a still more powerful banking company; which company is provided with a perpetual charter to issue bank bills and discount notes. By perpetual, meaning of course, as long as they shall keep the great steam pump in operation. With such an induce-ment to keep their stream of "pure and wholesome water" constantly run-ning, it is not likely that this source will soon fail. But "pure and wholesome" as it is, by the express terms of the charter, the people generally prefer that from the town pumps, except for the purposes of washing; and for that, most people use rain water.

The third source, namely Knapp's Spring, furnishes the only tolerable water in the city. This is conveyed about the streets in hogsheads, and sold, we believe, at a penny a gallon. Small as this price seems, their supply of spring water, we are informed, costs some of the larger hotels more than $300 each, per annum. The hotels, boarding houses, and respectable private families make use of this water for tea, coffee, and ordinary drink. The poor all resort to the street pumps.

Such is, such has been, and such is likely to be for some years to come, the condition of New York, in regard to the indispensable article of water. The great difficulty in supplying the city properly is the very great distance from which it must be brought. Very recently, it was resolved, after a scientific survey of the river and the ground, and duly calculating the expense, to bring hither the waters of the Croton. For this purpose an act has been obtained from the legislature; and if money can be raised, the water will probably be forthcoming, sometime within the life-lease of the present generation.

That part of the Croton river from whence the water is to be taken, is about forty-four miles, in a northerly direction, from the City Hall. The water is to be conveyed by a covered aqueduct of strong mason work, to a rise of land on the island, called Murray Hill; from whence, by the force of its own gravity, it will distribute itself through all the streets and avenues of the city. The length of pipe, required for the distribution, is estimated at 167 miles. The amount of water, which the Croton will furnish, is set down at 30,000,000 gallons daily, in the driest times; and 50,000,000 daily, in times of ordinary plenty.

The Croton water is found, by chemical analysis, to be exceedingly pure, and such as will prove highly agreeable to the tastes of all hydro-epicures. Free from impurities, the Croton water will be a great inducement to personal cleanliness. Having it running pure into their very bedrooms, the citizens will find it an agreeable pastime, instead of a disgusting labor, to wash themselves of a morning. The Philadelphians shall not then have occasion to make the invidious comparison between their delightful Schuylkill water and the vile slops wherewith our bedrooms are furnished. Yet the expense will be enormous—no less than $5,500,000—the labor will be immense, and some years must elapse before we shall quench our thirst and lave our limbs in the Croton.

This delay is to be regretted on many accounts; and very particularly, as it will afford an excuse to many persons for continuing the excessive use of strong drink. The water is now so bad, they plead, that it is absolutely necessary to qualify it with a drop of ardent spirits, to render it potable. But a single drop will not suffice; and many drops, even to a full stream, are added to the cup.

To give the greater foundation for the excuse, and at the same time to render it more available, the principal topers get their qualifying drops at those cheap resorts where rum, brandy, gin, and whiskey may be had for three cents per glass; and where the water is usually derived from the town-pumps.

What is the entire number of dram-shops in New York, we know not. But they may be found at almost every corner throughout the city, and at almost every door of the buildings bordering on the North and East rivers. Besides those places devoted to the mere sale and swilling of liquors; almost every grocery is likewise a dram-shop. Not only tea, coffee, sugar, molasses, butter and cheese are sold at these establishments; but likewise ardent spirits of all sorts, by the gallon and the glass. And the trade in these latter articles is thought to be the most lucrative of the two.

But if the bad water is an excuse for drinking ardent spirits, the bad quality of the spirits should be a still stronger excuse for letting them alone. The world, perhaps, does not afford, nor has the brain of man conceived, more villanous mixtures than are constantly sold at the groceries and dram-shops of this city. Nay, for the matter of that, the hotels themselves are not much better. They purchase the liquors of the grocers, but it is a part of the modern grocer's business to adulterate his liquors: and what he sells under the name of Cogniac, Jamaica, or Port, has a small mixture of either of those liquors as can well be imagined.

In speaking of other liquids besides water—whereof the number used as beverage is pretty large—we must not forget tea, coffee, wine, and beer. There are few, or no families in New York, where the former are not drunk, such as they are; the coffee in the morning and the tea at night. It is not so easy spoiling the latter by any process of making; and therefore it is, in general, quite possible to drink it. We cannot say as much for the liquid called coffee. It is, in most cases, triply ruined: first, in the burning, secondly, in the boiling; and finally in the mixture therewith, of that very doubtful liquid denominated milk.

Wine in New York is better; and, if we except that compound called Port, is the best liquor in the city. The Madeira is very fine; as even those most grumbling and fastidious of guests—the British journalists—acknowledge. The Claret in New York is good also. So are the Sherry and the Champagne. Of the latter and of Madeira large quantities are drunk. The sound-headed old wine-drinkers prefer the Madeira; the dashing young blades choose Champagne. How often they are cheated by a substitution of bottled cider, it matters not to say.

The last beverage we shall touch upon is beer; a liquid we very seldom touch at all, and should not do so now, except for the purpose of the present work. This liquid—under the names of porter and ale—is much drunk in this city; especially in the cold season. Small beer is not unfrequently substituted in the summer.

9

A Georgia Planter among the Yankees, 1845

*W*illiam T. Thompson, *except for his birth in Ravenna, Ohio, in 1812, and a few years of his youth in Philadelphia, was associated throughout his long life with the South. In 1835 he moved to Georgia, where he became owner of a variety of periodicals, of which the* Savannah Morning News, *founded in 1850, was the most important. Though he pursued agriculture enough to consider himself a planter, it is evident that his main labors were in the field of literature. As an editor he defended slavery vigorously and, after 1860, secession and the Confederacy as well. As an author his three humorous works on the exploits of "Major Jones," published between 1843 and 1848, gave him a considerable, though now forgotten, popularity. After the war he endeavored to ameliorate the worst horrors of Reconstruction. He died in 1882.*

Of all forms of literature, humor is, perhaps, the most ephemeral. It is a testimony to Thompson's skill that his "Major Jones" still lives as a recognizable character and that his books not only are highly readable but offer a valuable commentary on the passing scene. Though some of his mannerisms are distasteful to a modern generation (the unalleviated use of the word "nigger," for example), Thompson was actually neither a southern firebrand nor a sectional bigot. He had, obviously, independence of judgment and a ready discernment as well as wit. Far from being the untutored bucolic he pretends to be, Thompson was a cultivated and dignified gentleman and behind that staple of American humor—the misspelled word—Major Jones leaves a candid and unforgettable record of the American scene.

DEMOCRACY AND THE ARTS IN THE CAPITAL CITY

In a few minits more we was in sight of Washington city, with the great umbrella top of the Capitol loomin up into the heavens, grand, gloomy, and peculiar. We wasn't long gettin to the wharf, and after a terrible encounter with 'bout five hundred cab-men and porters, I made out to git my baggage into a hack and druv to Gadsby's hotel, whar I got a good supper and soon went to bed.

It was pretty late before I got up this mornin, and then it was 'bout a ower before I found my way down stairs after I did git up. You hain't no idee what a everlastin heap of rooms and passages and stairways ther is to these big hotels, and to a person what aint use to 'em it's 'bout as difficult to navigate through 'em as it is to find one's way out of a Florida hammock.

As soon as I got my breckfust I sot out for the Capitol, what stands on the hill, at the upper eend of the Avenue, as they call it, which is a grate wide street runnin rite through the middle of the city. When I looked up to it—from the street—it seemed like it wasn't more'n twenty yards off, but before I got to it I was pretty tired walkin. The gates was open, and I walked into the yard, and follered round the butiful paved walks til I cum to the steps. The yard, round the bildin, is all laid off in squares and dimonds, and is all sot out with trees. Rite in frunt of the bildin, on the side towards the city, is a curious kind of a monument, standin in a basin of water, with little babys and angels, all cut out of solid marble, standin all round on the corners of it, pintin up to a old eagle what looks like he'd gone to roost on the top of it. It's a very pretty thing, and the water what it stands in is full of little red fishes, playin all about as lively as tadpoles in a mill pond. I looked at the monument sum time, and red sum of the names on it, but sum I couldn't make out and the rest I've forgot.

After gwine up two or three more pair of stone stairs, I cum to the door of the Capitol. I couldn't see nobody about, so I nocked two or three times, but nobody didn't answer. I waited awhile and then nocked agin with my stick, but nobody never sed a word. Thinks I, they can't be home. But the door was open—so thinks I, I'll go in and see the bildin any how. Well, in I went, and the fust thing I met was two pair of stairs agin, both gwine the same way. I tuck one of 'em, and after gwine a little ways I cum to another green door. Thinks I, it won't do to be too bold. So I nocked agin, louder and louder, but nobody answered. Well, thinks I, the government can't be to home sure enuff, and I was jest thinkin what a bominable shame it was for them to neglect their bisness so, when here cum a feller, what had whiskers all over his face, with three or four galls, laughin and gigglin at a terrible rate, and in they went, without ever nockin a lick. Well, thinks I, I've got as good a right here as any body else what don't belong to the administration, so I follered into the rotunda.

I tell you what, this rotunda is a monstrous tall bildin jest of itself. Why you could put the Pineville court-house inside of it, and it wouldn't be in the way a bit. A full grown man don't look no bigger in it than a five year old boy, and I cum very near nockin a pinter dog in the hed for a rat, he looked so little. The sides is all hung round with picters, and over the doors ther is some sculptures representin William Penn swindlin the Ingins out of ther land, and Columbus cumin ashore in his boat, and old Danel Boon killin off the aborigenes with a butcher knife, and other subjects more or less flatterin to the national character. The figers is all cramped up like they'd been whittled down to fit ther places, and don't look well to my likin at all. The picters is very good, and it's worth a trip from Georgia to Washington to see them great national paintins, the Signers of the Declaration of Independence, the Surrender of Cornwallis, Washington givin up his Commission, the Baptism of Pocahontas, and the Pilgrim Fathers on board ther ship.

I went out on the portico, and what do you think! the very first thing I seed was a woman without so much as a pettycoat on! Not a real live woman, but one cut out of marble, jest as nateral as life itself. Thar she was, sort of half standin and half squattin by the side of a man dressed off in armour and holdin a round ball in his hand. At first I never was so tuck aback in my life, and I looked all round to see if anybody was lookin at me. I couldn't help but look at it, though it did make me feel sort o' shamed all alone by myself. Every now and then somebody would cum by, and then I would walk off and look tother way. But sumhow I couldn't go away. The more I looked at it the handsumer it got, til bimeby I seemed to forgit every other thought in the contemplation of its beauty. Ther was sumthing so chaste, and cold, and pure about that beautiful figure, that I begun to be in love with it, and I couldn't help but think if I was Columbus and wasn't marble myself, I'd be tempted to give her a hug now and then, if she *was* a squaw.

Ther is two other statues standin on the east frunt of the Capitol, one representin the godess of Peace, and the other General Mars, the god of War. They are both very handsome. Mars carrys his hed like a genwine South Carolina militia captain, and Peace looks like she wouldn't hurt anybody for the world; but ther is something tame about 'em—they look somehow like they was cast in a mould.

After lookin at them a while, I went out to the bildin what stands in the yard, and tuck a look at Mr. Greenough's Washington, and to tell you the truth, I never was so disappinted in my life. This statue has some terrible bad faults, and on first view, before one has time to study and understand the design of the artist, creates any thing but a favorable impression. In the fust place the position is out of keepin with the character of Washington; in the second place, the costume is worse than the position, and in the next place, the mouth is not good, and destroys the character and expression of the face. Ther ain't nothing Washington about it, to my notion. The idea of puttin a Roman togy on Gen. Washington, is ridiculous; as if he wasn't jest as much entitled to be a type of his age and generation, as Julius Caesar or any other Roman hero is of the age when ther was no tailors to make coats. It made me feel bad when I looked up and saw Washington's bare busum. The veneration which Americans feel for the character of Washington is shocked at the exposure of that noble breast, whose every throb was for his country. It seems like a desecration to represent him in any other way than as he was, when he was alive; and though ther is something imposin and grand in the artist's design, the effect is destroyed by the want of fidelity to the character of the man. I tried my best to overcum my prejudices agin the Washington, because it was an American work, but it was no go, and I went back and tuck another look at Columbus and his Ingin gall, before I went down to my hotel.

FOOD AND DRINK IN BALTIMORE

I waked up this mornin bright and early in the Exchange Hotel in Baltimore, but I felt so monstrous tired that I didn't git rite out of bed. Well, while I was layin thar, lookin round the room at the fine furniture—at the splendid mahogany burow and wardrobe, the marble-top'd washstand and the cast-iron fire-place, and a heap of other curious fixins—I seed a green cord with a tossel on the eend of it, hangin down by the hed of my bed. Thinks I, that must be to pull the winder blinds, to let the light in, and as it was rayther dark, I tuck hold of it and pulled it easy two or three times; but the thing seemed to be hitched sumwhar, and the blinds didn't move a bit. I wasn't more'n done pullin it, before sumbody nocked at my dore, and as I didn't know who it mought be, I covered up good, and ses I, "Cum in."

A nigger feller opened the dore and stood thar for 'bout a minit, lookin at me like he wanted sumthing, 'thout saying a word.

"Well, buck," ses I, "what's the matter," beginnin to think he had a monstrous sight of imperence.

"I cum to see what the gemmen wants," ses he.

"Well," ses I, "I don't want nothin."

He looked sort o' sideways at me and put out.

After studyin a bit to try to make out what upon yeath could brung him to my room, I put my hand out and tried the curtains agin; and the fust thing I know'd here cum the same chap back agin.

This time I looked at him pretty sharp, and ses I—"What upon yeath do you mean?"

With that he begun bowin and scrapin and scratchin his hed, and ses he— "Didn't you ring, sir?"

"Ring what?" ses I.

"Your bell," ses he.

By this time I begun to spicion thar was sumthing rong; and shore enuff, cum to find out, I'd been pullin a bell-rope all the time, what kep up a terrible ringin down stairs, though I couldn't hear the least sign of it myself. I'd seen them things hangin round in the rooms at the Charleston Hotel, and at Gadsby's, but I never know'd what they was before. Well, thinks I, live and larn—I'll know a bell-rope when I see it agin.

After brushin and combin a little, I went out into the readin-room and looked over the papers til breckfast. I was settin on the sofa readin in the National Intelligencer, when the fust thing I know'd I thought the whole roof of the bildin was cumin down on top of my hed—whow! row! whow-wow! went sumthing like the very heavens and yeath was cumin together. I couldn't hear myself think, and I was makin for one of the winders as fast as I could, when the everlastin rumpus stopped. I ax'd sumbody what in the name of thunder it was. "O, you needn't be larmed," ses he, "it's nothin but the breckfust gong." I was jest about as wise then as I was before, but I know'd it had sumthing to do with breckfust, and my appetite soon cum back to me agin.

You know I always used to drink coffee, and I'm monstrous fond of it yet; but being as I didn't feel very well this mornin, when the waiter ax'd me which I'd have, I sed "tea."

"Black or green?" ses he.

I looked at the feller, and ses I—"What?"

"Will you have black or green tea?" ses he.

I didn't know whether he was projectin with me or not, so ses I, "I want a cup of tea, jest plain tea, without no fancy colerin about it."

That settled the bisness, and in a minit he brung me a grate big cup of tea that looked almost as strong as coffee; but it was monstrous good, and I made out a fust rate breckfust.

After breckfust I tuck a walk out to see the city, and shore enuff it is a city! I turned up Baltimore street, whar the fine stores is kep, and whar the galls all go a shoppin and perminadin in the afternoons to show ther new dresses. Well, I can tell you what's a positiv fact, it would take a French dancin master to git along in Baltimore street without runnin agin sumbody, and even he couldn't shassay his way round through the troops of galls without runnin a fowl of one now and then, or rakin his shins all to pieces on the pine boxes what is piled all along the sidewalk, after you git above Charles street. I done the very best dodgin I could, but every now and then I ran spang agin sumbody, and then while I was bowin and scrapin a apology to 'em, ten to one if I didn't knock sum baby over in the gutter what was cumin along with its ma, behind me, or git my cote-tail fast in among the crates and boxes so tite that I run a monstrous risk of losin it bowdaciously. But I wasn't the only one what got hung—two or three galls got ther dresses hitched up, on the nails and hoops, so they blushed as red as fire, and a old gentleman with a broad-brimmed hat, and his stockings over his trowses, tumbled over a wheel-barrow rite into a pile of boxes and tore his clothes dredful. It tuck the old man sum time to gether himself up, and git out of the jam he was in. When he got out he never cussed a word, but he fetched a groan that sounded like it cum from way down below his waistbands, and went on.

I thought, at fust, that the store-keepers must be doin a terrible sight of bisness, to be shure, to be sendin off and receivin so much goods, but I knocked on sum of the boxes with my cane, and they sounded as holler as a old empty bee-gum. I spose the city gits a fust rate rent for the pavement, but if the merchants was to keep ther empty boxes in ther sellers, it would be a great deal more convenient for the people to pass along, and I should think it wouldn't hurt ther contents a bit. The fact is a body can't git into the stores to buy nothing, for the piles of boxes round the doors. I wanted a piece of tobacker myself, but I couldn't see no store what I could git into without runnin the risk of breakin my neck or tearin my trowses.

After gwine up as far as Youtaw street, I crossed over and cum down on tother side of the street, lookin along at one thing and another til I got most down to Charles street. By this time I begun to be monstrous dry, and as I'd heard tell a good deal about the sody water they have in the big cities, I

thought I'd try a little at the fust place whar they sold it. Well, the fust
doctor's shop I cum to had a Sody water sign up, and in I went to git sum.

Ses I, "I want a drink of your sody water."

"What kind of syrup will you have?" ses he, puttin his hand on a bottle
of molasses.

"I don't want no syrup," ses I, "I want sody water."

"Ah," ses he, "you want extra sody."

And with that he tuck a glass and put sum white stuff in it, and then held
it under the spout til it was full, and handed it to me.

I put it to my hed and pulled away at it, but I never got sich a everlastin
dose before in all my life. I got three or four swallers down before I begun to
taste the dratted stuff, and you may depend it liked to killed me right ded in
my tracks. It tuck the breth clean out of me, and when I cum to myself, my
tongue felt like it was full of needles, and my stummick like I'd swallered
a pint of frozen soapsuds, and the tears was runnin out of my eyes in a
stream.

I drapped the glass and spurted the rest out of my mouth quicker'n
lightnin, but before I could git breth to speak to the chap what was standin
behind the counter starein at me with all his might, he ax'd me if I wasn't
well.

"Well! thunder and lightnin," ses I, "do you want to pisen me to deth and
then ax me if I'm well?"

"Pisen!" ses he.

"Yes," ses I, "pisen! I ax'd you for sum sody water, and you gin me a dose
bad enough to kill a hoss."

"I gin you nothin but plain sody," ses he.

"Well," ses I, "if that's what you call sody water I'd be dadfetch'd if I'll
try any more of it. Why, it's worse nor Ingin turnip juice stew'd down
six gallons into a pint, cooled off in a snow-bank and mixed with a harry-
cane."

Jest then some bilin hot steam come up into my throte, that liked to
blow'd my nose rite out by the roots.

Ses he, "Maybe you ain't used to drinkin it without syrup."

"No," ses I, "and what's more, I never will be."

"It's much better with sassypariller, or gooseberry syrup," ses he. "Will
you try some with syrup?"

"No, I thank you," ses I, and I paid him a thrip* for the dose I had, and
put out.

I wanted some tobacker monstrous bad: so I stepped into a store and ax'd

* [Slang for a three-cent piece.—Ed.]

for sum. The man said he didn't sell nothin but staples, but he reckoned I'd find some a little further down, at Smith's. Well, I went along lookin at the signs till I cum to Shaw, Smith & Co. Thinks I this must be the place. So in I went and ax'd a very good lookin man with whiskers, what was standin near the door, if he had any good chewin tobacker.

"No sir," ses he, "we haint got any more of that article on hand than we keep for our own use; but we would like to sell you some carpets to-day."

"Carpets?" ses I; and shore enuff, come to look, ther wasn't another thing but carpets and oil cloths, and mattins and rugs and sich things in the store; and I do blieve ther was enuff of 'em of all sorts and figers to furnish all the houses in Georgia.

After a little explanation he told me the Smith I wanted was J. C. Smith, down opposite to the Museum. He said I'd find lots of tobacker and segars thar, and I'd know the place by a big Ingin standin out before the door. Shore enuff, when I went thar I got some fust rate segars and tobacker, and a box to put it in.

That's the way they do bisness here. They don't keep dry goods and groceries, calicoes, homespun, rum, salt, trace chains and tobacker all together like they do in Pineville, but every kind of goods has a store to itself. If you ever come to Baltimore and want some tobacker or segars, you must go to the stores what's got little painted Ingins or Niggers standin out by the doors; for you mought jest as well go to a meetin house to borrow a hand-saw, as go to any of the stores here for any thing out of ther line. I spose, like the sody water, it's well enuff to them that's used to it, but monstrous aggra-vokin to them what aint.

As I hadn't been down in the lower part of the city, I thought I'd git into one of the omminybuses and ride over to Fells' Pint, and see how it looked. Well, it's a good long stretch from one eend of Baltimore to the other I can tell you. I noticed when anybody wanted to git out they jest pulled a leather strap and the omminybus cum to a halt. So when we got down to Fell street, I tuck hold of the strap and gin it a jerk, but the hosses went on fast as ever, so I jest laid my wait on the strap to stop 'em. "Hellow!" ses the driver out-side, "do you want to pull me in two?" Cum to find out the strap was hitch'd to the man instead of the hosses, and I liked to draw'd him through the hole whar he took his money. He was mad as a hornit, but when he looked in and seed who it was, he had nothin more to say.

I expect some parts of Fells' Pint would suit Mr. Dickens fust rate. It's old as the hills, and crooked as a ram's horn, and a body can hear jest as much bad English that as he could among the cockneys of London, and can find sum fancy caracters, male and female, that would do honor to St. Gileses or any other romantic quarter of the British metropolis.

By the time I got back it was two o'clock, and I begun to have a pretty good appetite agin. I made out to get back to the Exchange and pretty soon after I got thar that everlastin gong rung agin, and we all went in to dinner. I never seed sich a handsum table in all my life before. It was long enuff for a fourth of July barbecue, and all dressed out like a weddin-supper. Evry thing looked in order, like a army formed in line of battle. The plattoons of ivory-handled knives, and silver forks, and cut-glass goblets, and wine-glasses,

BALTIMORE IN 1834

was all ranged in two long columns on each side, with a napkin standin at each place like a file-closer, crimped up as handsum and lookin as white and fresh as a water-lily. In the middle was the baggage-train, which was made up of a long row of bright covers, with elegant silver casters and tureens, large glass vases full of sallary, and lots of other dishes. I felt jest like I was gwine into battle; and whether Mr. Dorsey, like Lord Nelson, expected every man to do his duty or not, I was termined to do mine. Well, the table was soon surrounded, and then the attack commenced. It was a terrible carnage. The knives and forks rattled like small arms, the corks popped like artillery, and the shampane flew like blood at evry discharge. General Jennings manoovered his troops fust rate—carrying off the killed and wounded as fast as possible, and supplyin ther places with reinforcements of fresh dishes. He had a regular Wellington army, made up of English, French, American, German, Itallian, and all kinds of dishes; but, like Napoleon at Waterloo, he was doomed to come out second best, and in a short time his splendid army was cut to pieces, routed, dispersed, and demolished, horse, foot, and dragoons, or rather, roast, boiled, and stewed.

You know I've fit the Ingins in Florida, and can stand my hand as well as the next man in a bush-fight, but I never was in jest sich a engagement before, and I made rather a bad job of it in the beginning. I hadn't more'n swallered my soup when he cums a nigger pokein a piece of paper at me, which he sed was a bill. Thinks I, they're in a monstrous hurry 'bout the money, so I told him I hadn't time to look it over then. The feller looked and grinned like he didn't mean no offense, and ax'd me what I'd be helped to. Well, I know'd they didn't have no bacon and collards, so I told him to bring a piece of roast beef. By the time I got fairly gwine on my beef, Mr. Dorsey cum in and tuck a seat at the eend of the table, not far from me, and ax'd me how I was pleased with Baltimore. I told him very well, and was passin a word or two with him, when the fust thing I know'd my plate was gone, and when I turned round to look for it, the nigger poked the bill at me agin. I begun to think that was carryin a joke a leetle too fur, and I ses—

"Look here, buck; I told you once I hadn't no time to tend to that now, and I'd like to know what in the devil's name you tuck my plate away for?"

"What'll you be helped to?" ses he, like he didn't understand me.

"I ax'd for sum beef," ses I, "but—" and before I could git it out he was off, and in a minit he brung me another plate of roast beef.

Well, by the time I got it salted to my likin, and while I was takin a drink of water, away it went agin. I jest made up my mind I wouldn't stand no such nonsense any longer, so I waited til he brung me a clean plate agin, and ax'd me what I wanted.

"Sum more beef," ses I.

I kep my eyes about me this time, and shore enuff, the moment I turned to nod to sum gentlemen what Mr. Dorsey introduced me to, one of the niggers made a grab at my plate. But I was too quick for him that time.

"Stop!" ses I.

"Beg pardon, sir," ses he; "I thought you wanted another plate."

"I've had enuff plates for three or four men already," ses I; "and now I want sum dinner."

"Very well, sir," ses he; "what'll you have?"

"Well," ses I, "I want you to jest keep a eye on my plate, and not let anybody grab it off til I'm done with it, and then I'll tell you what I want next."

Jest then Mr. Dorsey called him to him and sed sumthing in his ear, and here he cum with Mr. Dorsey's compliments and a bottle of shampane, and filled one of my glasses, and then tuck his stand so he could watch my plate, grinnin all the time like he'd found a mare's nest or sumthing.

The plan worked fust rate, and after that I got a fair showin at the beef. Then I ax'd the waiter what else ther was, and he brung me the bill agin, and told me I'd find it on thar. Shore enuff, it was a bill of things to eat, insted of a bill of expenses. Well, I looked it over, but I couldn't tell the *rari de poulets à la Indienne,* or the *Pigeons en compote,* or the *Anguelles a la Tartare* from any thing else, til I tasted 'em, and then I didn't hardly know the chickens from the eels, they was cooked so curious. Ther was plenty that I did know though, to make out a fust rate dinner, and long before they brung in the custards, and jellies, and pies, my appetite was gone. I was jest goin to leave the table, when Mr. Dorsey ax'd me if I liked Charlotte Roose. I told him I hadn't the pleasure of her acquaintance. "Well, Majer," ses he, "you better try a little"; and with that he sent me a plate with sumthing on it made out of pound-cake and ice-cream 'thout bein froze, which was a little the best thing I ever eat in my life.

A SOUTHERN VIEW OF THE NORTHERN FREE NEGRO

I've always had a great curiosity to see how the free niggers git along in the Northern States. So after breckfust this mornin, I ax'd whar was the best place to see 'em; for I'd heard gentlemen what had been in Filladelfy say that ther was whole squares in this city whar nobody but niggers lived. I was told if I wanted to see free niggers in all ther glory, I must go down Sixth street til I come to 'em.

Well, I started, and sure enuff, I hadn't gone many squares before I begun to smell 'em, and never will I forget the sight I saw down in Small street, and sum other streets in that neighborhood. Gracious knows, if anybody wants to git ther simpathies excited for the pore nigger, all they have got to do is to go to this part of Filladelfy. I've been on the big rice plantashuns in Georgia, and I've seed large gangs of niggers that had the meanest kind of masters, but I never seed any pore creaters in sich a state of retchedness in all my life. I couldn't help but feel sorry for 'em, and if I was able, I'd been willin to paid the passage of the whole generation of 'em to Georgia, whar they could get good masters that would make the young ones work, and would take care of the old ones.

Thar they was, covered with rags and dirt, livin in houses and cellars, without hardly any furniture; and sum of 'em without dores or winders. Pore, miserable, sickly-lookin creaters! it was enuff to make a abolitionist's hart ake to see 'em crawlin out of the damp cellar-dores til they got able to start out to beg or steal sumthing to eat, while them that was able was cussin and fightin about what little they had. You couldn't hardly tell the men from the wimmin for ther rags; and many of 'em was diseased and bloated up like frogs, and lay sprawlin about like so many cooters in a mud-hole, with ther red eyes peepin out of ther dark rooms and cellars like lizards in a pile of rotten logs.

This, thinks I, is nigger freedom; this is the condition to which the filanthropists of the North wants to bring the happy black peeple of the South! Well, one of two things is certain:—either the abolitionists is a grand set of hippocritical scoundrels, or they are totally ignorant of the condition of the slaves what they want to git away from ther masters. Materially considered, the niggers of Georgia is as much better off than the niggers of Pensylvany, as the pore peeple of America is better off than the pore peeple of Ireland; and, morally considered, the advantage is equally as great in favor of the slaves of the South over the pore free niggers of the North. For whar social equallity cannot possibly exist, the black peeple are miserable jest in the degree that they approach to equality in wealth and edication with the whites, and are enabled to understand their degraded position. What's the use to talk about equallity when no such thing exists. Ther is as much prejudice agin coler here as anywhar else. A body sees that in ther churches, and theatres, and courts, and evrywhar else. Nobody here that has any respect for themselves, treats a nigger as ther equal, except a few fannyticks. At the South, the relation between the two races is understood by both parties, and a white man ain't at all jealous of the pretensions of his servants; but here, ther is a constant jealous enmity existin between the whites whose occupations brings 'em in contact with 'em, and the niggers, who is all the time aspirin to a social equality.

For my part, I've got as much feelin for the niggers as anybody can have. But one thing is monstrous certain, if my niggers wasn't better off and happyer on my plantation than these Northern free niggers is, I wouldn't own 'em a single day longer. My niggers has got plenty of hog and hommony to eat, and plenty of good comfortable clothes to wear, and no debts to pay, with no more work than what is good for ther helth; and if that ain't better than freedom, with rags, dirt, starvation, doctor's bills, lawsuits, and the five thousand other glorious privileges and responsibilities of free nigger citizenship, without the hope of ever turnin white and becomin equal with ther superiors, then I ain't no filossofer.

After lookin into sum streets that I wouldn't risk my life in gwine through, and seein scenes of destitution and misery enuff to make one's very hart sick, I went back to my hotel.

THE MILLS AND THE GIRLS OF LOWELL

Lowell is the handsumest small town I was ever in. We tuck rooms at the Merrymack House, one of the best hotels, and, before tea, tuck a walk over the place. It was a pleasant afternoon, and as we walked along on the bank of the canal what carries the water from the river to the factories, we couldn't help but notice the clean and healthy appearance of the town. The clear cool water went sweepin along, deep and strong, in its rock-banks, over which the green grass and flowers hung to dip themselves in the stream, while a roarin sound, that cum from the direction of the great blocks of five-story factories, reminded us that it was no idle stream, runnin to waste its usefulness on the desert shore, but that it gave its power to aid the industry of man, and to contribute to the wealth of the nation.

We tuck a stroll on the banks of the Merrymack, below the town. From different pints we got a fine view of the place. We was passin up Merrymack street to our hotel when the bells rung, and the fust thing we know'd the whole town was full of galls. They cum swarmin out of the factories like bees out of a hive, and spreadin in evry direction, filled the streets so that nothin else was to be seen but platoons of sun-bonnets, with long capes hangin down over the shoulders of the factory galls. Thousands upon thousands of 'em was passin along the streets, all lookin as happy, and cheerful, and neat, and clean, and butiful, as if they was boardin-school misses jest from ther books. It was indeed a interestin sight, and a gratifyin one to a person who has always thought that the opparatives as they call 'em in the Northern factories, was the most miserable kind of peeple in the world.

It was a butiful moonlight night, and after tea we walked out into the street agin. The stores was all lit up and the galls was walkin about in pairs, and half dozens, and dozens, shoppin from store to store, and laughin and talkin about ther purchases, as if it didn't hurt 'em to spend ther earnins no more'n other peeple. Under ther curious lookin cracker-bonnets thar was sum lovely faces and eyes, that looked better by moonlight than any I have seed sense I left Georgia. By ten o'clock not a cracker-bonnet was to be seen in the streets, though the moonlight was as bright as day and I couldn't help but feel sorry for the six thousand little nimphs of the spindles, who had no lovers thar to court 'em on sich a night.

The next mornin the sun was jest up when we went down on to the corporashuns, as they call 'em here, whar the mills are. It was a most lovely mornin. The factorys was all still. The yards in frunt of the bildins was clean, and the little flower-gardens by the dores was glitterin with due, as the fust bees of the mornin cum to suck the honey from the blossums. Ther wasn't many peeple to be seed in the streets. Now and then we could see sum men gwine to the countin-rooms and offices, or to the factorys, but the cracker-bonnets was in eclipse. The galls was at breckfust at their boardin-houses, which are neat two, and sumtimes three-story brick houses, what stand in blocks near the factorys, and is owned by the proprietors of the mills.

Bimeby the bells rung. In a minit more the streets leadin to the mills was swarmin with galls. Here they cum in evry direction, laughin and talkin to one another in groops and pairs, or singly, all lookin as merry and happy as if they was gwine to a frollic, insted of to ther work.

They poured into the mills by thousands, like bees into a hive, and in a few minits more the noise of the machinery begun to git louder and louder, until each factory sent out a buzzin sound, with which all other sounds soon becum mixed up, until it seemed we was into a city whar men, wimmin and children, water, fire, and light, was all at work, and whar the very air breathed the song of industry.

After breckfust we went to one of the mills, whar we got a little boy to show us the way. The little feller tuck us from one room to another all over the mill, and sich other contraptions I never seed before. The machinery made sich a noise that we couldn't hear ourselves think, let alone sayin any thing to one another, and then we was so cumpletely dumbfounded by what we seed, that we couldn't a found a word to say even if we could heard one another talk. Thar was the galls tendin the looms and the spindles, mixed all up among the cranks and wheels, and drum-heds and crossbands, and iron fixins, that was all agwine like lightnin, and ther little white hands flying about like they was part of the machinery. Bissy as they was, though, they found time now and then to steal a sly glance at us, and then I could see a mischievous smile playin round sum of ther pretty mouths, as much as to say, what green fellers we was that never seed a cotton-mill before. I tried to git the hang of sum of the machinery, but it wasn't no use. Evrything I seed, from the ceilin to the floor, was whirlin, and whizzin, and rattlin, and dashin, as if it would tear evry thing to pieces; but what they was doin or what set 'em agwine, was more'n I could make out.

After gwine through three or four of the mills, which was all pretty much alike, we went into one whar they print calicos. This part of the bisness ain't the nicest work in the world, though it is very interestin. We went into the dryin-room as they call it, but we didn't stay thar but a very short time. If the *other* country is much hotter than this dryin-room, it is not much misrepresented in the accounts we have of it. When I stepped in I felt the hot air, as I breathed it into my lungs, like boilin water, and my hair crisped up like I was in a bake-oven. My friend, who takes a good deal of pains with his whiskers, dassent risk 'em in the dryin-room more'n a minit; and when we got out I felt jest like I'd cum out of a steam-bath.

The next place we went to was the whip manufactory, whar we seed a cover braided onto a whip-stalk, by machinery, in about two minits. From thar we went to another place, whar they made cotton and woolen cards. That machine banged any thing I ever seed in all my life. I've always thought that a machine that could make any thing as well as it could be made with hands was pretty considerable of a machine. But to see a little iron contraption take a piece lether and a coil of wire, and cut off the wire and bend it double, punch the holes in the lether, put the wire in the holes, push 'em in and bend 'em, and fasten 'em thar quicker and better than five men could do it, went a little ahead of any thing I ever heard or dreamed of. The man that invented that machine could invent one to eat shad without swallerin the bones.

The next place we went into was a machine carpenter's shop, whar the rough boards cum into one dore in a cart and went out at the other in panel-dores, winder-sashes, pine boxes, &c. Saws and plainers and chissels and awgers was sawing, plainin, chisselin and borin in evry direction by machinery, with men to tend 'em; and for one that wasn't acquainted with the bearins of the place, it was necessary to keep a pretty sharp look-out to prevent having a shavin tuck off of him sumwhar, or to keep from bein dove-tailed, or havin a awger-hole put rite through him fore he know'd what hurt him.

In the evenin we tuck a walk to look at the town. Passin by a book-store, we went in to git sumthing to read. The old gentleman what keeps the store show'd us sum numbers of the "Lowell Offering," what he sed was made up of the writins of the factory galls. My friend sed he'd bet that gall he seed readin in the mills was one of the writers, and he told the man to let him have all the numbers. Hearin us say we would like to see sum of the writers, Mr. Davis, who is a monstrous clever, obligin man, sed he would be very happy to interduce us to sum of 'em. We tuck him at his word, and in a few minits more he show'd us into a neat little parlor, whar we was soon made acquainted with Miss Harriet F——* the editor of the Offering, and her mother. Miss F—— promised Mr. Davis to take good care of us, and to see that none of the Lowell galls stole our harts, and he went back to his store. We spent a ower in very agreeable chat with Miss F——, who is a true specimen of a New England gall. She has worked in the mills for several years, but now devotes herself to the magazine what she edits, supportin her mother by her industry. After awhile she proposed to interduce us to sum more of the literary factory galls, and takin my arm, she carried us through several of the mills, and interduced us to the galls who was at ther work.

As we was passin the great machine carpet factory, she ax'd us if we had seed 'em weavin carpets on the power-looms. We told her no—that we went thar in the day, but they wouldn't let us in.

---

* [Harriet Farley, editor of the *Lowell Offering* until December, 1845.—ED.]

"Oh!" sed she, "they didn't know you was Southerners, or they wouldn't been 'fraid of your stealin ther patent."

I didn't know zactly whether she meant that as a compliment or not.

We went to the office, and ses Miss F——:

"Mr. Peters, here's a couple of Southern frends of mine, what wants to see the carpet-looms."

"Well, but, Miss F——," ses he, "you know its entirely agin the rules for anybody to be admitted to see the machinery."

"Yes; but," ses she, "I don't care for the rules—these gentlemen are all the way from Georgia, and they *must* see the looms."

"But—" ses the old man.

"I don't care," ses she; "I'll be answerable for all the damage."

"Well," ses Mr. Peters, "you can go into that room, (pinting to a dore,) and when you're in the packin-room, I guess you can find the way into the looms without my *lettin you in.*"

That was sufficient, and in we went. I ax'd Miss F—— if that man wasn't a Yankee inventor.

"O, no," ses she; "he's only a ordinary genius in these parts."

The carpet-looms is a grate specimen of American ingenuity, bein the only power-looms for weavin carpetin in the world; but my hed was so full of wonders that I had seen durin the day, that I hadn't no room for the carpet-looms. Besides, they is such thunderin grate big, smashin iron things, and go at such a terrible rate, that I expected evry minit to git my branes nocked out by 'em.

After takin a look at 'em for a few minits, we went out, and visited sum more of the literati. Miss F—— interduced me to Miss Lucy L——,* the author of *"The Wasted Flowers,"* one of the prettyest little allegorys in the English language. Miss L—— was in the packin-room of one of the mills, as clerk, checkin off the goods as they were bein put up into bales. She had worked in the mills several years. I never met with a more interestin young lady, though I spose she wouldn't thank me for callin her a *lady,* as she gin me her autograf in a very different spirit. It reads——

Major Jones:
    Sir—I have the honor to be, yours, very respectfully, a *bona-fide* factory girl,
                                           Lucy L——.

We found the place still more attractive as our acquaintance extended, yet soon after we bid 'em all good-by, when we parted with 'em for our hotel.

* [Lucy Larcom, later to be famous as author of *A New England Girlhood.*—Ed.]

10

A Charlestonian in Babylon, 1852

*A*ccording to its title-page, Glimpses of New-York City *was written "By a South Carolinian." The text makes it clear that the South Carolinian was a native of Charleston, and the copyright notice suggests that the name of the author was William M. Bobo. Of Bobo, or whoever was the author, nothing is known.*

Though many writers used the artifice of "Letters to a Friend," as the vehicle for their travelogues, Bobo employed "Conversations." Much of his volume is in this narrative, conversational form; but, for all its outward appearance, it is a travel book. The author endeavors to be "literary," without marked success, and indulges in a considerable amount of Victorian moralizing; yet, with all his obvious faults, he gives an extensive account of oft-hidden material and appears to have viewed far more than the conventional sights. His efforts to re-create the actual scene and to catch colloquial expressions give to his work a far greater value than many a more orthodox narrative. For a southerner, writing after 1850, the work is refreshingly free from sectional prejudice.

The Five Points

Now we will take a look at *"The Five Points,"* both by day and night. The contrast with that which we have been seeing and talking about will be striking. We have seen the glory of the North, now we shall see the shame. We shall not need our hack, as it is only a short distance from the City Hall. Have you got a good supply of cigars?—if not, get some, as we shall need them while prowling among the filthy cellars and the malaria which envelopes that region of the city.

Up and down Orange-street, you will observe make two of the points, then Cross-street coming diametrically across Orange, makes two more, and Anthony intersecting precisely the cross, makes the five. As we approached this place you remarked that every house became worse in appearance after we left Broadway, till we crossed Centre-street. There it sinks into sameness—like the degrees of crime, till you reach infamy, positive and hopeless. You begin to see the squalid, roisterous-looking, drunken females, sitting upon the door-steps, or standing round the counter of a drinking hole. The groups are from three to four, in number, not more. The children, poor little fellows, half naked, winter and summer, it is all the same, are seen moving from place to place, with a make-shift of a toy, or a piece of bread or a bone in their clutches, gnawing it like young dogs around a kitchen yard.

See the squalid females, sottish males and half-starved urchins, perching about the windows, stoops and cellar doors, like buzzards on dead trees, viewing the dead carcass beneath. The population of the Points is about evenly divided between whites and blacks. The blacks however are, for the most part, the rulers; they own and keep a majority of the drinking and dance-houses.

We now pass through this alley into the area and up a flight of rickety stairs. There lies a drunken female, screaming and yelling—only a fit of delirium tremens. The next flight brings us upon a drunken beast in the shape of a man, rolling and pitching about upon the floor like a catfish in mud. Near by you see a poor little boy *pulling* at a piece of meat, the only meal he has had probably for twenty-four hours. Another flight. We enter an eight-by-ten room; what a scene presents itself—five or six bloated and haggard-looking brutes in human form are sitting or lying around the room talking, all cursing and swearing in the most blasphemous manner. At the stove sits a female, cooking a meal consisting of greens and pork. See that pallet of straw, with nothing but a blanket for *clothes,* and it looks as if it had never seen water. What destitution! Not two shillings worth of furniture in the room, including the clothes upon *the bodies* of the inmates. These poor wretches pay a few shillings per week, and take the chances whether they get a meal or not; they get a place upon the floor when they sleep at all events.

But now it is time for Pete William's ball to open. Let us go down. We enter a cellar, where we see a few males and females, black, yellow, and white, seated or swaggering about the room; as many males smoking segars and swearing off some story of the day. Upon a sort of platform sit two or three negoes representing the orchestra, and opposite is the bar, behind which stands a negro, or Pete (who is a negro) himself, dealing out whiskey, tobacco, beer, and segars, at three cents a glass, or a penny apiece. The music commences, and out sally two or three cotillions of this piebald party, and away they whirl in a most disgusting and revolting manner.

The records of the courts will show that there are more cases of crime presented at its bar, in the city of New-York alone, than in all the South put together. In fact, there is more poverty, prostitution, wretchedness, drunkenness, and all the attending vices, in this city, than the whole South. This is a comment upon Northern institutions. When the Abolitionists have cleared their own skirts, let them hold up their hands in holy horror at the slave-holder, and the enormity of his sins.

To give a correct and critical description of the Five Points would only disgust. I have told enough, in God's name, to convince you that the Points are the most disgusting in America. Here is the last *quarterly* report of the Chief of Police, and it appears that during the quarter ending June 30th, 9,087 arrests were made, as follows:—55 for assault and battery with intent to kill; 1,291 for assault and battery; 72 for assaulting policemen; 26 for aiding and assisting to escape; 9 for attempting to commit rape; 46 for attempting to steal; 17 for attempting burglary; 61 for abandonment; 55 for burglary; 1 for bigamy; 53 for bastardy; 4 for constructive larceny; 1,337 for disorderly conduct; 5 for deserting from the army and navy; 24 for driving without a license; 7 for embezzlement; 14 escaped convicts; 14 for forgery; 5 for felonies; 13 for fraud; 218 for fighting in the streets; 175 for grand larceny; 34 for gambling; 91 for insanity; 2,165 for intoxication; 1,708 for do. and disorderly conduct; 15 for indecent exposure of person; 14 for insulting females; 53 for keeping disorderly houses; 220 for miscellaneous misdemeanors; 13 for murder; 35 for obtaining goods by false pretences; 818 for petit larceny; 20 for picking pockets; 18 for passing counterfeit money; 2 for perjury; 5 for rape; 16 for robbery in the first degree; 16 for receiving stolen goods; 13 apprentices for running away; 1 for selling liquor without a license; 6 for selling lottery policies; 9 for threatening life; 260 for violation or corporation ordinances; 775 for vagrancy; 12,402 persons were lodged at the different station houses; 1,300 lost children were restored.

There are 6,004 places in the city where spirituous liquors are sold; 1,566 of them being unlicensed—and 4,185 are open on Sundays.

The effective police force on the 1st of July was as follows: Captains, 19; Assistant Captains, 38; Sergeants, 76; Policemen, 803. Total, 936.

Sewing Girls

Now we will look at the difficulties which beset the poor working girls, such as tailoresses' and milliners' apprentices, hat and cap and shoe liners, &c., &c.

See here—read this advertisement—"WANTED, 500 girls wanted to work on pantaloons. Apply at No. —— —— street." Now let me explain, and you can be able to judge what kind of an establishment this is. An hour after the time for calling passes, you can see hundreds of girls flocking up stairs to get the work. I will give you the history of one, and it will serve as a portrait of tens of thousands during the year.

"You advertised for hands on pantaloons this morning?" she trembling asks of the man with the quill behind his ear.

"Yes, we want some hands this week; do you want a job?" he replies.

"Yes, sir; I would like to have something to do this week," answers the girl.

"How many pair can you make?"

"I will try to get six pair done."

The work being already cut out and rolled up into bundles, is handed by "the cutter" to the man at the desk, who remarks—

"You are a stranger to us, and before we can let you have the work, you must give some security for the return of it."

"How much is necessary?" she inquires.

"Why, eight shillings will do."

If the poor victim has the amount, forthwith she hands it over and departs with the goods, if not, she hurries back home, and takes her bonnet or dress and carries it to the pawnbroker's, where she gets the required sum, and again returns for the work which she receives, and goes home with a light and buoyant heart.

This is the case precisely with at least three hundred and fifty girls on the day the advertisement appears, together with the day after, save in a few dozen instances where the poor girl cannot raise the dollar, having pawned her last frock, may be, a week previously.

You ask how there are so many who want work, or are out of employment. Why, I will explain, while my girl is finishing her job, as we are not done with her yet, by a long ways; her history is only one quarter told.

She had bound herself for six months to a first-class milliner in the city, but after the six months expired, was turned off to give place to other apprentices.

"How was that?" you ask. Well, she had to work the six months to learn the trade, and *find* herself. The employer now has to give her wages, if she remains, but sooner than pay her for what he can get done for nothing, turns her off, and takes another apprentice for six months, on the same terms, *"to learn the trade."*

She now sees the advertisement, applies, as I have told you, and has probably let the pawnbroker have the last article she had upon the earth, which would bring one dollar, to get this job. She, you must know, has had to support herself for the last six months *at least,* if not longer, out of the wages she got, where she nursed for some "pious family up town."

We now see her returning with her bundle; I will follow and hear what passes between her and the "inspector," who, by the way, is a sour, crabbed, ill-grained foreigner, or blue-skinned Yankee, (just as bad.)

He takes the bundle, unrolls it, turns up his nose, as if he had smelt a dead rat, and remarks, in the crossest manner possible, *"You have ruined the job,"* makes the whole lot up together, and contemptuously throws it under the counter.

The girl entreats, with tears standing in her eyes, as large as mountains (to her), by saying that she has worked for "Mrs. or Mr. So-and-so, and they never found any fault with my work."

"You never worked for *us* before, Miss, and it does not suit. We would rather you had not touched the cloth—you have ruined the job, and there's an end of it—please stand aside, as there are others waiting for *their* pay."

She then asks for her money back, but only receives a threat in return, with a low, muttering grumble, that you have damaged us already eight or ten dollars, and we will retain your dollar, as it is all we shall ever get for our goods, which you have spoilt.

This thing is enacted over and over and over, throughout the two *"pay days,"* the firm having, may be, some twenty or thirty persons whom they pay on those days—but let me follow the goods and my poor girl.

The goods are thrown, as I said before, under the counter, and probably fall through a trap-door into the pressing room, where they are ironed out, assorted, and packed up for the southern trade, in nine cases out of ten, before the girl gets to the street. You see the merchant not only gets his work done for nothing, but three hundred and fifty dollars in cash to ship it off with, into the bargain. I understand that an indictment has been issued against a large firm in Broadway, but twenty-five or fifty dollars at farthest will *stop it*—that is the last you will hear of the case.

It is no hard matter to depict the situation of our poor girl, when we add that her board has not been paid for two weeks. What is a lone girl to do in this case? She reasons somewhat in this manner:—I have lived honestly, worked hard for my first employers, done all I could to satisfy their demands, and I am now left without a place to lay my head, a cent in my pocket, or a friend to ask for assistance. I see I cannot live by honest means, and will, (*must live,*) by dishonest ones, rather than go to the poor-house. She deliberately walks out and sells herself for gold.

This is the history of thousands upon thousands in New-York, and yet there is no effort made to put a stop to it. If the employer does pay her for her work, it is not enough to support her decently, and she falls, because the labor of a working girl will not give her more than bread. Why is this thing so? Simply because she is a *woman,* and *man* can impose upon her.

No girl can make a living at the wages paid by shirt venders and manufacturers of ready-made clothing, hats, caps, shoes, bonnets, &c., it is out of the question. Nor will it be any better till the strong arm of the law is resorted to. There is another species of fraud practised upon the poor girls, known as the "shop-tenders." These are generally fascinating girls, who are told to talk and act in such a manner as to entice young men to frequent the shop, to make their purchases of cigars and tobacco, or their brandy and water as the case may be. The employer tells them, that if they fail to get up a custom or trade, they will lose their places. Don't you frequently see "a bartender" advertised for, who is "tidy" and "can influence trade,"—it is *not unfrequent.* The poor girl is literally compelled to use, not only her physical labor, but her personal charms and wits, and ingenuity for her employers, thereby blunting the finer feelings of her nature.

There is no part of the human race or class of our people so much imposed on and maltreated as the young females in large cities. They have no parents, nor any male friends to take their part; they are ignorant of their rights, and are first reduced to dependence, then led on step by step, to an untimely and disgraceful end.

Chatham-Street and the Bowery

Chatham-street commences at Centre street, and extends to the junction of East Broadway and Bowery-streets, which is about a quarter of a mile; and I would venture to assert that there is more to be seen within that quarter of a mile, than in twice the distance on any other street of New-York. This part of the city is sometimes called Jerusalem, from the fact that the Jews do most, if not all the business on this street.

Here is a string of mock auction establishments and is it not strange that hundreds will suffer themselves to be decoyed into these barefaced swindling shops, when they have heard so much of their operations, and too, when the Mayor has men carrying a great placard up and down the streets in front of these places, with "Strangers beware of mock auctions" on it, from morning till night.

On the right-hand it seems that every house is a ready-made clothing establishment, and I do not see any other kind till we get to the National Theatre, when the furniture houses commence, which continue to Oliver-street.

On the left are silver-smith and jewelry stores—shirt, boot, shoe, and hat, do.—and all other kinds of commodities, from pea-nuts to double-barrel shot guns. The variety nor amount does not so much astonish you, as the little space it is all crowded into; a room six by twelve is plenty large to expose a general assortment. Here you can see at a glance every thing in the old furniture line, from a Brussels carpet to cracked penny whistle—yea, even one of the veritable powder-horns used by the hunters of Kentucky at the Battle of New Orleans. We not only see more wares and merchandise huddled here together, but we see more people on the sidewalks hurrying to and fro. Here you see Jew and Gentile, Priest and Levite, as well as all other classes—the old and young of the nations upon earth, and all the conditions and hues of the *genus homo*. How all can possibly make a living honestly is beyond my conception. You rarely ever see them selling any thing; at least I never have, and I have passed here repeatedly; however, I am always in a hurry when I go through this street; I am afraid of being run over, or having my pockets picked. Chatham-street is a sort of museum or old curiosity shop, and I think Barnum would do well to buy the whole concern, men, women, and goods, and have it in his world of curiosities on the corner of Ann and Broad-way.

Look at that fellow—he is an Italian, I would judge, with his store upon his back. What a lot of suspenders, fiddle-strings, razorstrops, buttons, thread, dumb watches, pinch-beck jewelry, and pocketbooks he has hanging about him or in his tray upon top of his head, all of which he will *"shell sheap,"* no doubt.

Then that Book-store Man on the corner. His store is made by putting two planks upright against the wall and making shelves for the books, with a falling door, and a lock. This is the storehouse, and by it sets or stands the proprietor from morning till night. The books are all old, and most of them out of print, yet among them you may find some valuable works. Following the example of his more fashionable and wealthy brother chips of Broadway, he keeps indelible ink, the morning papers, a few envelopes, cornplasters and toothache drops.

Over there is a shell-store and there is now in that lot a sample of all the shell animals in the known world. Here is the sign of the three golden balls

—it is a pawnbroker's sign. It contains thousands and thousands of all sorts of articles of clothing, jewelry, pistols, guns, and in fact every thing that will bring one red cent in the market. Just above is the Franklin Museum, as it is called, but nothing more than a place where a set of men and women play, and sing a few negro songs in a sickly manner, and a few disgusting women pretend to expose themselves as model artists.

We have now got to Church-street. I do not believe that there is one respectable house on this street. Such a mixture of negroes and whites. On that side the drinking houses, dancing houses, and houses of bad character. Look in that negro hotel if you want to see the effects of a night's debauchery. A woman half dressed, and lying upon the floor in a state of beastly intoxication, not able to move hand or foot. That fellow sitting on the "stoop" (the little portico is called a stoop, why I am not able to say) looks as if he has suffered from his night's frolic; no doubt he has, badly too. I think he is a stranger.

"Halloo, my friend, what seems to be the matter? Are you sick, or is it the old drunk?"

"Gentlemen, I am from ——— county, Ohio, and came to this city day before yesterday with a lot of flour and bacon hams, which I sold to Mr. ———, No. —— ——— street, and he paid me half the purchase money, the other half he is to pay in thirty days; here's his note.

"Yesterday, after dinner, as I was walking up Broadway, I met a fellow, and asked him if he could show me the way to the Mansion Hotel. 'Oh yes,' said he, 'I am well acquainted with this village of ours; come along. Ah,' says he, 'here is my sister, she is just going home, and passes right by your hotel. I believe I will go down town myself;' and away he went full tilt. We (his sister and I) came here to this house, where she said she lived, and that there was agoing to be a party at night, and invited me to stay to it—that it should not cost me a red cent, but that the others who came would have to pay a dollar. So I concluded to stop, and I did.

"After tea was over, the brother came in and cut a few shines about the rooms, hugging this sister and kissing that sister; got mighty loving all at once. He asked if I was going to stay to the ball. 'Oh yes,' said the sister. 'Well,' said he, 'let's have a bottle of wine.' Directly a bottle was brought and drank, I joining in. After awhile I thought it would look sorter sneaky not to go my part like a man, so I asked if they had any more of that wine. 'Oh yes'; and in a little less than no time another cork hit the ceiling, and we began to feel tolerable rich and clever.

"The ladies now began to assemble for the ball, and after the music was ordered to commence, we fell to dancing. I was kinder scared at first; but I found the fellows were so free with their partners, that I just let myself out, and took a wide row. I began to feel my wine; and after drinking some '*first-rate old whiskey,*' all at once I got sleepy, and was carried up stairs, thrown into a room, and this is all I remember.

"I find that I am minus one hundred and forty dollars in cash, a first-rate silver lever watch of a neighbor's of mine, which I brought along to get a mainspring put in, and a first-rate umbrella, and my ring, which a girl gave me the Sunday before I left home."

This Church-street is a hard place, and I advise all strangers, and everybody else, to avoid it as they would a bed of snakes.

Here we are at *the Bowery* No. 1, so look out for what passes. The houses are not so high, so costly, or so substantially built in this street as in Broadway, there being no fine stone fronts over here. The great majority are two and three-story houses, with open fronts, as you will observe the whole block, *under* the awning, looks like one store. Broadway is unquestionably a fine street, but in point of spaciousness, view, and variety, it is not to be compared with the Bowery. Yet there are thousands of inhabitants of this good city who would not for any reasonable consideration confess having ever been here, or in fact *knowing* precisely where it is. The rush and clatter of omnibuses, the chattering and bartering crowds within the well-filled shops, the hurrying throng upon the sidewalks, are at any hour of the day or night as great as in Broadway; and to a stranger visiting New-York for the first time, and being put down in the Bowery, would take it for granted that he was in the principal thoroughfare of the great metropolis.

The Bowery presents probably a greater number and variety of shops than any other street in the world. Fancy bread, cheap jewelry, splendid looking-glasses, furniture, hardware, and china, straw bonnets, ready-made clothing, cooking-stoves, and "doll-babies," fiddles and cocktails, new music and Shrewsbury oysters are to be had here for the turning of your hand (provided there is any thing in it), and without stepping out of your way. Indeed, on a fine spring day, this noted thoroughfare, filled with its stalwart men, and buxom, bright-eyed lasses, tripping along with a step as free and elastic as a country milkmaid, looks like a vast holiday fair two miles long.

Another important feature of the Bowery, is that every thing can be bought 15 or 20 per cent. cheaper than in Broadway, and equally fine in appearance, and as good in the quality.

The Bowery has, too, its fashionable side; although the absurd solitude to which custom (or rather the want of it) dooms one side of Broadway, does not make a desert of the east side of the Bowery, yet the belles and b'hoys of this region take pretty good care to see that they are on the right side of *the street* as well as *each other*. And I would venture the assertion that the searcher for the beautiful would find more to please the eye, gratify the taste, and amuse the mind, in a half hour's stroll in the Bowery on a bright afternoon, than can be met in Broadway in a lunar month.

Here comes the "fashionable" promenader of this street; that's him, in the very last agony of the "ton"—black silk hat, smoothly brushed, sitting precisely upon top of the head, hair well oiled, and lying closely to the skin, long in front, short behind, cravat a-la-sailor, with the shirt collar turned over it, vest of fancy silk, large flowers, black frock coat, no jewelry, except in a few instances, where the insignia of the engine company to which the wearer belongs, as a breastpin, black pants, one or two years behind the fashion, heavy boots, and a cigar about half smoked, in the left corner of the mouth, as nearly perpendicular as it is possible to be got. He has a peculiar swing, not exactly a swagger, to his walk, but a swing, which nobody but a Bowery boy can imitate, and is always upon the *qui vive*—never caught napping.

The Broadway dandy is rigged, as well as I can recollect, somewhat after this manner:—Fine patent-leather boots, rather short, very large striped pants, tight, except round the boot, a flashy vest, very short, watch-chain and seal, with a large bunch of "charms," and a heavy finger-ring suspended on the guard chain, fancy cravat, of the "broad-tie" style, standing shirt collar, coat of some fancy pattern, on the sack order, just covering the hips, sleeves large and loose over the hand, all the beard that can be raised left, to prove that he is not a woman, quizzing-glass over the left eye, hair befrizzled to the utmost, a short walking-stick under the arm, all topped off with one of Leary's white hats, placed on the left side of the head, and you have the real Simon siwassee Broadway fop. He ambles or rather reels when he walks, as if his feet were blistered, and is never seen to speak with any one upon the street.

The Bowery man speaks to every acquaintance he meets, and is hail-fellow-well-met with every body, from the mayor to the beggar.

Another grand difference in these two specimens of humanity. The Bowery boy is a fair politician, a good judge of horse flesh, tragedy, comic acting, music as well as dancing, and renders himself essentially useful as well as ornamental, at all the fires in his ward, and if necessary, in his neighbor's; does a kind, generous act when in his power, pays his board, and splits the Third Avenue wide open occasionally with "Old Pumpkins." The Broadway representative is not only a fop but a ninny, knows about as much of what is going on, out of the very limited circle of his lady friends, as a child ten years old. He ambles up and down Broadway twice or thrice in twenty-four hours, smokes a cigar after dinner, and drives, if he can raise the means for so doing, waits upon a lady friend, if he should be lucky enough to have one, when she will let him, and this is the extent of all his actions and ambition.

The female fops of each, partake of the ingredients of the above representatives in all particulars except in case of rendering assistance at fires in the first instance, but the latter makes it up, by assisting in keeping the sidewalks clean, with the skirts of her dress. You see this street has all the requisites to make it a great business mart; here are several banks, insurance offices, &c. &c. and if the Bowery had a judicial tribunal of her own, it would be a separate kingdom, and as a matter of course, an independent one. Whenever a person who lives upon this street sees an acquaintance getting "large for his size," he is most sure to say, *"You are aping Broadway now";* and vice versa, the Broadway man says, by way of derision, "That's the Bowery touch," no matter whether it be a bank officer or a street loafer, the same sentiment exists in all.

Take this street, up one side and down the other, and you will find more true, genuine independence, generous hospitality, wit, humor, nobleness of disposition, and liberality than any other portion of the city of New-York. These people feel a sort of "State pride," and where that exists you always find a free, open-hearted, noble, and independent spirit.

COTTON PLANTATION

Part II

THE COTTON KINGDOM

The spreading territory below the Mason and Dixon Line and south of the Ohio River—in large part the areas which made up the Confederacy—was considered in the popular mind as a great Cotton Kingdom. That it was not all given over to the production of cotton, the tobacco plantations of Virginia and the rice and sugar plantations of South Carolina and Louisiana testify. But since nearly all the vast section was agrarian in economy, dominated by a planting aristocracy, and involved in the "peculiar institution" of slavery, it was natural enough that it should be conceived as a unit.

It was an area which, decade after decade, diverged continuously from the general patterns of American development. It set up a localistic states' rights *politique* in opposition to the rising nationalism of the North and West; it created a class system from planter aristocrat to Negro slave in contrast to the democratic spirit elsewhere in the nation; and it turned its back on the rising industrialism and urbanization of the North and East to maintain a persistent agricultural and rural way of life. Its unique position, and the contrast it afforded to the rest of the United States, excited a wide curiosity, and, accordingly, the South was much visited and described, especially by northerners.

In general, the observations and interests of travelers were absorbed in the spectacle of the planter and his slaves, sometimes to the neglect of other legitimate aspects of southern life. Because the subject was highly controversial, and became increasingly more so as the century advanced, it was natural that the observer's already preconceived notions colored his views. For that reason, if no other, a single account of the South is unsatisfactory; many accounts need to be compared before a balanced picture can be secured. Most travelers from the outside condemned slavery, and, certainly, very few unstintedly praised it. On the other hand, it should not be overlooked that there was a considerable number of northerners who, upon contact with the slave society, found it was not so bad as it had been painted and who mellowed their views about it. Perhaps because of the unusual amount of prejudice, for or against the system, there were many efforts to obtain "a record of the South as it really was." Of this type, Olmstead's narration is a classic.

Not all travelers were overwhelmed by the South's slave system. Occasionally there are observations about the poor whites and the mountain whites, though usually in their connection to the planter class, and such cities as the South possessed came under surveillance. Charleston and Savannah received due attention, and New Orleans, because of its exotic and almost foreign flavor, entranced the tourist. It is interesting to note, too, the distinction the travelers found between the older and settled Old South of the Atlantic Coast and the frontier, western character which survived in the newer plantations of the Gulf and Mississippi region.

Like New England, the South suffered in the quality of its observers once Reconstruction was over. The tendency was to emphasize the "quaint" or to embower in a nostalgic scent of magnolia blossoms, the virtues of the ante bellum South. By the close of the century few appeared to recognize either the economic and social changes or the needs of the Cotton Kingdom.

II

A Boston Brahmin Dines with
the Virginia Democracy, 1815

George Ticknor (1791–1871), in the great age of New England's "flower-
ing," was one of the most brilliant members of Boston's literary circle. Born
into a family of wealth, a graduate of Dartmouth College, he was endowed
by nature with both physical and mental charm. Nor did anything in his life
ever destroy the rich promise of his inheritance. He traveled widely and was
as much at home in Europe as in his fine mansion on Park Street, Boston.
Cultivated, urbane, and dignified, this Boston Brahmin was the very essence
of enlightened aristocracy. Following an extended tour abroad, Ticknor in
1819 was inducted into the professorship of the French and Spanish languages
at Harvard. He did much to promote a knowledge of European, and espe-
cially Romance, culture among his less enlightened fellow-Americans. He was
a prime mover in the founding of the Boston Public Library and he was the
author of the History of Spanish Literature *(1849), a work regarded highly*
by his contemporaries, and not without value today.

When he was a youth of twenty-three, long before his later fame was
achieved, he resolved to visit "at the South, to see the men the cities contain,
and get some notion of the state of my own country." His observations were
set down in letters to his father and contain a graphic as well as elegant grace

characteristic of his later writing. The journey, well prepared for by introductory letters from ex-President John Adams, occurred at the conclusion of the War of 1812 as references to the burned capitol at Washington and the Battle of New Orleans make clear. Though bred in a deep-dyed Boston Federalism, he noted with little prejudice the two arch-leaders of Jeffersonian Democracy. It may well have been the unconscious reaction of one gentleman to another.

As we drew near to the metropolis of Washington I got out and rode forward with the driver, that I might see all that was strange and new. We were travelling on the very road by which the British had approached before us. We crossed the bridge at Bladensburg by which they had crossed, and saw on its right the little breastwork by which it was so faintly and fruitlessly defended. The degree and continuance of the resistance were plainly marked by the small mounds on the wayside, which served as scanty graves to the few British soldiers who fell; and the final struggle, which took place about a mile from the spot where the opposition commenced, was shown by the tomb of Barney's captain and sailors. These few mounds, which the winters' frosts and rains will quickly obliterate, are all the monuments that remain to us in proof of the defence of the capital of the country.

We drove forward three miles farther, and in the midst of a desolate-looking plain, over which teams were passing in whatever direction they chose, I inquired of the driver where we were. "In the Maryland Avenue, sir." He had hardly spoken when the hill of the Capitol rose before us. I had been told that it was an imperfect, unfinished work, and that it was somewhat unwieldy in its best estate. I knew that it was now a ruin, but I had formed no conception of what I was to see,—the desolate and forsaken greatness in which it stood, without a building near it, except a pile of bricks on its left more gloomy than itself,—no, not even a hill to soften the distant horizon behind it, or a fence or a smoke to give it the cheerful appearance of a human habitation.

Soon after my arrival in Washington I dined with President Madison. About half the company was assembled when I arrived. The President himself received me, as the Secretary was not on hand, and introduced me to Mrs. Madison, and Mrs. Madison introduced me to Miss Coles, her niece. This is the only introduction, I am told, that is given on these occasions. The company amounted to about twenty. There were two or three officers of the army with double epaulets and somewhat awkward manners, but the rest were members of Congress, who seemed little acquainted with each other.

The President, too, appeared not to know all his guests, even by name. For

some time there was silence, or very few words. The President and Mrs.
Madison made one or two commonplace remarks to me and others. After
a few moments a servant came in and whispered to Mr. Madison, who went
out, followed by his Secretary. It was mentioned about the room that the
Southern mail had arrived, and a rather unseemly anxiety was expressed
about the fate of New Orleans, of whose imminent danger we heard last
night. The President soon returned, with added gravity, and said that there
was no news! Silence ensued. No man seemed to know what to say at such
a crisis, and, I suppose, from fear of saying what might not be acceptable,
said nothing at all.

Just at dark, dinner was announced. Mr. Madison took in Miss Coles,
General Winder folowed with Mrs. Madison. The Secretary invited me to go
next; but I avoided it, and entered with him, the last. Mrs. Madison was of
course at the head of the table; but, to my surprise, the President sat at her
right hand, with a seat between them vacant. Secretary Coles was at the foot.
As I was about to take my place by him, the President desired me to come
round to him, and seeing me hesitate as to the place, spoke again, and fairly
seated me between himself and Mrs. M. This was unquestionably the result
of President Adams's introduction. I looked very much like a fool, I have no
doubt, for I felt very awkwardly.

As in the drawing-room before dinner, no one was bold enough to venture
conversation. The President did not apparently know the guest on his right,
nor the one opposite to him. Mrs. Madison is a large, dignified lady, with
excellent manners, obviously well practised in the ways of the world. Her
conversation was somewhat formal, but on the whole appropriate to her
position, and now and then amusing. I found the President more free and
open than I expected, starting subjects of conversation and making remarks
that sometimes savored of humor and levity. He sometimes laughed, and I
was glad to hear it; but his face was always grave. He talked of religious sects
and parties, and was curious to know how the cause of liberal Christianity
stood with us, and if the Athanasian creed was well received by our Episcopalians. He pretty distinctly intimated to me his own regard for the Unitarian
doctrines. The conversation, however, was not confined to religion; he talked
of education and its prospects, of the progress of improvement among us, and
once or twice he gave it a political aspect, though with great caution. He spoke
to me of my visit to Monticello, and, when the party was separating, told me
if I would go with him to the drawing-room and take coffee, his Secretary
would give me the directions I desired. So I had another *tête-à-tête* with
Mr. and Mrs. Madison, in the course of which Mr. M. gave amusing stories
of early religious persecutions in Virginia, and Mrs. M. entered into a defence

and panegyric of the Quakers, to whose sect she once belonged. At eight o'clock I took my leave.

I passed the whole of this morning in the Supreme Court. The room in which the Judges are compelled temporarily to sit is, like everything else that is official, uncomfortable, and unfit for the purposes for which it is used. They sat—I thought inconveniently—at the upper end; but, as they were all dressed in flowing black robes, and were fully powdered, they looked dignified. Judge Marshall is the Chief Justice of the United States, the first lawyer—if not, indeed, the first *man*—in the country. You must then imagine before you a man who is tall to awkwardness, with a large head of hair, which looked as if it had not been lately tied or combed, and with dirty boots. You must imagine him, too, with a strangeness in his manners, which arises neither from awkwardness nor from formality, but seems to be a curious compound of both; and then, perhaps, you will have before you a figure something like that of the Chief Justice. His style and tones in conversation are uncommonly mild, gentle, and conciliating; and soon I had forgotten the carelessness of his dress and person, and observed only the quick intelligence of his eye, and the open interest he discovered in the subjects on which he spoke, by the perpetual variations of his countenance.

We left Charlottesville on Saturday morning for Mr. Jefferson's. He lives on a mountain, which he has named Monticello, and which is a synonyme for Carter's mountain. The ascent of this steep, savage hill, was as pensive and slow as Satan's ascent to Paradise. We were obliged to wind two thirds round its sides before we reached the artificial lawn on which the house stands; and, when we had arrived there, we were about six hundred feet, I understand, above the stream which flows at its foot. It is an abrupt mountain. The fine growth of ancient forest-trees conceals its sides and shades part of its summit. The prospect is admirable. The lawn on the top, as I hinted, was artificially formed by cutting down the peak of the height. In its centre, and facing the southeast, Mr. Jefferson has placed his house, which is of brick, two stories high in the wings, with a piazza in front of a receding centre. It is built, I suppose, in the French style. You enter, by a glass folding-door, into a hall which reminds you of Fielding's "Man of the Mountain," by the strange furniture of its walls. On one side hang the head and horns of an elk, a deer, and a buffalo; another is covered with curiosities which Lewis and Clark found in their wild and perilous expedition. On the third, among many other striking matters, was the head of a mammoth, or, as Cuvier calls it, a mastodon, containing the only *os frontis,* Mr. Jefferson tells me, that has as yet been found. On the fourth side, in odd union with a fine painting of the Repentance of Saint Peter, is an Indian map on leather, of the southern waters of the Missouri, and an Indian representation of a bloody battle, handed down in their traditions.

Through this hall—or rather museum—we passed to the dining room, and sent our letters to Mr. Jefferson, who was of course in his study. Here again we found ourselves surrounded with paintings that seemed good.

We had hardly time to glance at the pictures before Mr. Jefferson entered; and if I was astonished to find Mr. Madison short and somewhat awkward, I was doubly astonished to find Mr. Jefferson, whom I had always supposed to be a small man, more than six feet high, with dignity in his appearance, and ease and graciousness in his manner. He rang, and sent to Charlottesville for our baggage, and, as dinner approached, took us to the drawing-room,— a large and rather elegant room, twenty or thirty feet high,—which, with the hall I have described, composed the whole centre of the house, from top to bottom. The floor of this room is tessellated. It is formed of alternate diamonds of cherry and beech, and kept polished as highly as if it were of fine mahogany.

Here are the best pictures of the collection. Over the fireplace is the Laughing and Weeping Philosophers, dividing the world between them; on its right, the earliest navigators to America,—Columbus, Americus Vespucius, Magellan, etc.,—copied, Mr. Jefferson said, from originals in the Florence Gallery. Farther round, Mr. Madison in the plain, Quaker-like dress of his youth, Lafayette in his Revolutionary uniform, and Franklin, in the dress in which we always see him. There were other pictures, and a copy of Raphael's Transfiguration.

We conversed on various subjects until dinner-time, and at dinner were introduced to the grown members of his family. These are his only remaining child, Mrs. Randolph, her husband, Colonel Randolph, and the two oldest of their unmarried children, Thomas Jefferson and Ellen; and I asssure you I have seldom met a pleasanter party.

The evening passed away pleasantly in general conversation, of which Mr. Jefferson was necessarily the leader. I shall probably surprise you by saying that, in conversation, he reminded me of Dr. Freeman. He has the same discursive manner and love of paradox, with the same appearance of sobriety and cool reason. He seems equally fond of American antiquities, and especially the antiquities of his native State, and talks of them with freedom and, I suppose, accuracy. He has, too, the appearance of that fairness and simplicity which Dr. Freeman has; and, if the parallel holds no further here, they will again meet on the ground of their love of old books and young society.

On Sunday morning, after breakfast, Mr. Jefferson asked me into his library, and there I spent the forenoon of that day as I had that of yesterday. This collection of books, now so much talked about, consists of about seven thousand volumes, contained in a suite of fine rooms, and is arranged in the catalogue, and on the shelves, according to the divisions and subdivisions of human learning by Lord Bacon. In so short a time I could not, of course, estimate its value, even if I had been competent to do so.

Perhaps the most curious single specimen—or, at least, the most characteristic of the man and expressive of his hatred of royalty—was a collection which he had bound up in six volumes, and lettered "The Book of Kings," consisting of the "Memoires de la Princesse de Bareith," two volumes; "Les Memoires de la Comtesse de la Motte," two volumes; the "Trial of the Duke of York," one volume; and *"The Book,"* one volume. These documents of regal scandal seemed to be favorites with the philosopher, who pointed them out to me with a satisfaction somewhat inconsistent with the measured gravity he claims in relation to such subjects generally.

On Monday morning I spent a couple of hours with him in his study. He gave me there an account of the manner in which he passed the portion of his time in Europe which he could rescue from public business; told me that while he was in France he had formed a plan of going to Italy, Sicily, and Greece, and that he should have executed it, if he had not left Europe in the full conviction that he should immediately return there, and find a better opportunity. He spoke of my intention to go, and, without my even hinting any purpose to ask him for letters, told me he was now seventy-two years old, and that most of his friends and correspondents in Europe had died, but that he would gladly furnish me with the means of becoming acquainted with some of the remainder, and regretted that their number was so reduced.

The afternoon and evening passed as on the two days previous; for everything is done with such regularity, that when you know how one day is filled, I suppose you know how it is with the others. At eight o'clock the first bell is rung in the great hall, and at nine the second summons you to the breakfast-room, where you find everything ready. After breakfast every one goes, as inclination leads him, to his chamber, the drawing-room, or the library. The children retire to their school-room with their mother, Mr. Jefferson rides to his mills on the Rivanna, and returns about twelve. At half past three the great bell rings, and those who are disposed resort to the drawing-room at the second call of the bell, which is at four o'clock. The dinner was always choice, and served in the French style; but no wine was set on the table till the cloth was removed. The ladies sat until about six, then retired, but returned with the tea-tray a little before seven, and spent the evening with the

The Cotton Kingdom

gentlemen; which was always pleasant, for they are obviously accustomed to join in the conversation, however high the topic may be. At about half past ten, which seemed to be their usual hour of retiring, I went to my chamber, found there a fire, candle, and a servant in waiting to receive my orders for the morning, and in the morning was waked by his return to build the fire.

To-day, Tuesday, we told Mr. Jefferson that we should leave Monticello in the afternoon. He seemed much surprised, and said as much as politeness would permit on the badness of the roads and the prospect of bad weather, to induce us to remain longer. It was evident, I thought, that they had calculated on our staying a week. At dinner, Mr. Jefferson again urged us to stay, not in an oppressive way, but with kind politeness; and when the horses were at the door, asked if he should not send them away; but as he found us resolved on going, he bade us farewell in the heartiest style of Southern hospitality. I came away thinking, with General Hamilton, that he was a perfect gentleman in his own house.

A little incident which occurred while we were at Monticello should not be passed by. The night before we left, young Randolph came up late from Charlottesville, and brought the astounding news that the English had been defeated before New Orleans by General Jackson. Mr. Jefferson had made up his mind that the city would fall. He had gone to bed, like the rest of us; but of course his grandson went to his chamber with the paper containing the news. But the old philosopher refused to open his door, saying he could wait till the morning; and when we met at breakfast I found he had not yet seen it.

There is a breathing of notional philosophy in Mr. Jefferson,—in his dress, his house, his conversation. His setness, for instance, in wearing very sharp toed shoes, corduroy small-clothes, and a red plush waistcoat, which have been laughed at till he might perhaps wisely have dismissed them.

So, though he told me he thought Charron, "De la Sagesse," the best treatise on moral philosophy ever written, and an obscure Review of Montesquieu, by Dupont de Nemours, the best political work that had been printed for fifty years,—though he talked very freely of the natural impossibility that one generation should bind another to pay a public debt, and of the expediency of vesting all the legislative authority of a State in one branch, and the executive authority in another, and leaving them to govern it by joint discretion,—I considered such opinions simply as curious *indicia* of an extraordinary character.

12

A New England Poet in Virginia
and Kentucky, 1818

*H*enry C. Knight's life was both brief and outwardly uneventful. He was
born in Newburyport, Massachusetts, in 1789. Though his education was
extensive, it was apparently unrewarding, but he did manage to get a degree
from Brown University eventually. He wrote a great deal of poetry, good
enough to be published but not good enough to be remembered. When he
was twenty-five, he began a long and leisurely trip through the South—a
trip which lasted five years. On his return he was ordained in the Episcopal
church and served out the few remaining years of his life as a priest in that
church. He died in 1835.

The Letters from the South and West *was the result of his observations in
the South. It is a brief account of Philadelphia, Washington, Virginia and
Kentucky (which states he reached in 1818), New Orleans, and the sea
voyage home to Boston. Packed into the pages of this short work is a tremendous amount of information, much of it unusual. Perhaps because he was a
poet, Knight possessed the special power of making the scene he described
come to life. He wrote well, despite eccentricities of style and punctuation,
often with wit, always with discernment. In consequence the* Letters *is his
most valuable and enduring work, as it is one of the most interesting travel
books by an American.*

The Cotton Kingdom

LIFE AND MANNERS IN THE OLD DOMINION

Almost every gentleman's seat, even if not presidential, has some romantic appellation, as—Farmer's Hall, Hunter's Hill, Mount-Pleasant; but you need not suppose all these *swells* to be mountains. In walking around a plantation, you deviate into a hundred narrow Indian-like foot, or bridle-paths; and, in going from one plantation to another, you ride through an infinite of swing-gates. Now, for me, rather less land, and better cultivated.

The plantation houses, in general, are of frame, and unexpensive; having the chimney-stacks outside, and therefore no closets inside; and the roof-shingles *shelled* on the edges. The kitchen is usually detached a few rods from the house. Mine Honourable Landlord's mansion, however, is of brick, and one hundred feet in front. In his garden, and orchard, he has more fruits, than most gentlemen in Virginia:—the fig bush, the hard and soft shelled almond; varieties of cherries; peaches, white-blossomed and double-rose-blossomed, rich and luscious that they melt two inches before they reach your lips. He has an apricot, and a nectarine from Pope's garden at Twickenham. Peach orchards, of from fifteen hundred to some thousands, are common here; for distillation into brandy. Pears, but not apples, are scarce. Most planters have a small patch of tobacco, and of cotton, for domestic use; the former plant being extensively cultivated in the southern borders of this state. The white vegetable wool of the cotton-plant is prefered to the nankin-coloured boll.

The young Virginian ladies take pleasure in nurturing their hortulan shrubbery, and fostering their parlour pot-plants. Here are breathing beds of mignionette, and there the geranium "boasts her crimson honours"; and here vie, in their ranges, the orange-tree, the union or red and white York and Lancaster rose, the moss rose, the yellow rose, the undying globe amaranth, the Otaheite plant with its long-hanging filmy veiny tendrils, the coiling snake plant, the sparkling ice or dewplant, the prickly pear, whose beauty consists in its ugliness, and the evervarying and superb hydrangea. Indeed, the smiling damsels run about among their flowers, until they look as fresh and glowing, as their own rosebushes.

As to the *Manners* of the Virginians, they are a sallow, mercurial, liberal race; abroad, extravagant in dress; at home, slouching in homespun; the children of rich planters not disdaining to wear check not quite tartan. They ride fine horses; a wealthy landlord keeping his saddle, his racing, his car-riage, and his plough horses, distinct. They teach the riding horses to pace over their smooth sands, and dislike trotters; ride without cruppers, and, about home, with *one* spur; thinking that if they get one side along, the other will not hang ashank. Instead of a chaise, they use a chair, which is very light, but unsocial, as they are usually single; and which, moreover, being without a top, exposes them to the weather.

Wherever the Virginians go, a slave or two moves behind as their shadow, to hold the horses, pull off their boots and pantaloons at bed time, and, if cold, to blow up the fire in their bed-rooms with their mouths; bellows being unknown in a slave state. All are fox-hunters, and duck shooters; some keeping parks of deer, and others a ducker for the season. As game is plenteous near their enclosures, on a cloudy drizzly day, or a clear frosty night, when the hounds can scent the trail along the dew, out start young lads and bring home the partridge, the groundhog, the rabbit, and the opossum with her offspring not bigger than a bean clinging to her teats in her false pouch.

Accustomed from boyhood to athletic sports, the Virginians are muscular and elastic in limb; and leaving draughts, whist, backgammon, and chess, for the evening; they are out at sling-fist, and sling-foot; or outjumping, or outrunning each other. I saw a young man betted upon, for five hundred dollars, at a foot race. Indeed, every thing is by wager. Dr. and Maj. wagered, whether a serpent ejected his poison from the sac through a groove in the inner side of the tooth, or through a hollow up the middle of the tooth? Maj. lost a year's medical practice upon his family, and Dr. won his gray poney. What would a northern man think, to see a father, and a sensible, and a re-spected one too, go out with a company, and play at marbles? At some cross-roads, or smooth-shaven greens, you may see a wooden-wall, high and broad as the side of a church, erected for men to play ball against.

Most young Virginians are too convivial; and not a few, however splendid in talents and fortune, are open "votaries of Bacchus," and devotees "of the Paphian Dame." But among the lower classes, worse than this is sometimes met, the pandemonium of a whiskey-shop; where houseless, pennyless, famished idlers endeavour to "keep their spirits up, by pouring spirits down."

The Virginians are fierce marksmen, and duelling is not discountenanced. They sometimes meet, and shoot at a target for a fish-fry. Fish-fries are held about once in a fortnight, during the fish season; when twenty or thirty men collect, to regale on whiskey, and fresh fish, and soft crabs, cooked under a spreading tree, near a running stream, by the slaves. At these fries, the talk is of slaves, crops, shooting-matches, and quaffing revels; their ideas ever in a muddy channel.

A more genteel festival is the barbecue, expensive and elegant; where a numerous party of ladies and gentlemen assemble by invitation, or ticket, and feast, and dance, in beautiful decorum, under an artificial arbour. This, as the Virginians, living so isolated, are fond of company, produces a course of visiting for weeks afterwards. A Virginian visit is not an afternoon merely; but they go to week it, and to month it, and to summer it. Nothing is contracted about the Virginians. Although all classes are proverbially hospitable, yet there is a wide disparity between the different *castes* in this state. The haughty and purse-proud landlords form an aristocracy over the dependent democracy of the poorer planters. Their gymnastic education insures all to be bold riders, and brave fighters; but leaves a more than moiety surprisingly wanting in literature. Latin is not uncommon but rare is any Greek. At William and Mary College, where the course is but *three,* instead of *four* years as with us, there is now no funded professorship of languages. They care but little for belles-lettres.

As to religion, the Virginians are less zealous than were our Plymouth sires. Being brought up without many churches, too few regard the sabbath, except as a holiday; or wherein to begin or end a journey. In some places, toward Norfolk, shops are kept open, only the buyer may walk round to the side door, to evade the law. Yet the Virginians are sticklers for orthodoxy. For example, Richmond is faith without works; Boston works without faith. But do not conclude, that there are no christians in Virginia. There are many; many, who will cheerfully ride twenty miles to hear one sermon.

As they reside so far apart, each plantation has its God's acre, or *corner of graves;* and the funeral service is not infrequently performed a month after the deceased is buried; as they must send, perhaps, a score or two of miles for a clergyman.

It is very common for rich planters to remain bachelors. In families, the mistress usually carries about a ponderous bunch of keys; as articles are kept under lock from the slaves, and doled out each day for use. Where there are children, each single babe, if there be a dozen, has its particular nurse, or black *mamma;* to spy it, and *tote* it up and down all day upon her shoulder, until it is three or four years old. The matrons, in the upper classes, are industrious, affable, and accomplished, in a high degree. The young ladies, with their pensive, but imaginative countenances, frequently dip into the heart. What is amiable, I have seen a little miss sit down at the side-table, on an evening, to instruct an aged house-slave to spell in the Bible. When out on the green terraces, or in the orchards, the young girls run wild as the boys; wearing, to preserve their delicacy, broad sun-bonnets, deep enough for small cradles; so that they appear all head and feet. They will run up a tree like a squirrel.

The chief sickness, in this *ancientest dominion,* is in the autumn; when you may chance to shake, on one day, so that you cannot hold yourself in your chair; and, on the next, to burn so as to scorch your clothes. In this vicinity, they do not often suffer from hydrophobia; although surrounded by families of hounds, pointers, and spaniels.

As to the *Diet* of the Virginians, I may tell you what I observe. Once for all, they are plentiful livers. The first thing in the morning, with many, is the silver goblet of mint-julap. At breakfast, besides their wheaten rolls, they usually have, in their seasons, apple-bread, or hominy, with a relish of honey or herring. They have none of the rye-and-indian loaves, the rural bread of New England.—At dinner, which is about three o'clock, whatever other varieties they may have, a tureen of soup, and a chine, jole, or ham of bacon, imbedded with greens about it, are standing dishes. A meat-house is one of the first houses built; hung on all sides with chines, middlings, joles, and hams; perhaps finer flavoured for having run wild, and fed chiefly upon mash. One of the common petty larcencies of the slaves, is breaking into the smoke-house. It is remarked that, north of the Potomac, one may find good beef, and bad bacon; and south of the Potomac, good bacon and bad beef. They do not here eat the terrapin, which is esteemed a luxury at the north; but they highly relish the sturgeon, which is seldom eaten at the east. They never fail of having hominy, which is broken corn and beans mixed; coarse or fine ground; fried, baked, or boiled. It is a good substitute for potatoes, which do not here keep sound throughout the winter, although fine in the summer, which will sometimes, it is said, grow so large, that you may sit on one end, and roast and eat the other. They seldom have any puddings, or pastries; but have, for variety, six or seven kinds of meats, flesh, fowl, and fish; frequently, in its season, the exquisite canvass-back duck, with rich catsups, and anchovies. They have no cider or common beverage for table-drink; but, instead, for the ladies, water unqualified, weak toddy, and for the gentlemen, either whiskey, or apple or peach brandy, of their own distilling. Instead of a glass before the plate of each person, as with us, the decanters rest upon the sideboard until you call upon the waiter. Most planters have an ice-house, and contrive to keep the ice cool all summer.

As the kitchens are some rods removed from the dining-hall, at dinner-hours you may count long trains of slaves pacing to and fro, with the different viands, for a long time; for, although they have so much help, they are ever in getting a thing done; and thus the dinner is comfortably cool before you sit down to it. And one need not to be over-fastidious, since, however neat the mistress, good luck is it if the kitchen is not lined with little half-naked smutchy implings, rolling and clawing about, and listening with impatient delight to the slow revolutions of the spits, and the soft warblings of the caldrons. It is difficult to get over first prejudices against black servants.

As the Virginians expend all their strength upon dinner, their supper is a mere ceremony. They have not, as we have, a table, and toast, and pies, and cake; but, at about dusk, is sent around to each one, as he sits in the hall, or under the piazza, a cup of coffee, or tea, or both. Then follows round a plate of biscuits on a tray, hot, and about as large as a small letter-waifer; and perhaps a Virginian may sip a whole cup, and nibble a half or even a whole biscuit; but as frequently neither. Some epicures, after this apology, have a flesh or crawfish supper, at ten o'clock, to sleep on, and to accommodate them with the fashionable dyspepsy.

You will expect me to say something of the *Slaves*. The plantations are blotched over, every twenty or forty rods, with slave-cabins. These cabins, as they are called, are built of small straight timbers, crossed four-square, and interlocked at the corners, very like children's cob-houses; and daubed at the interstices with clay, having a chimney of rough stones at one end outside, and a hard dry ground floor. They are cheap and mean, but healthy and comfortable. The industrious slaves have little garden-plats, and keep poultry. The field slaves are allowed a cap, shirt, and drawers, and a blanket in winter. The field-slaves are the plebians; the house-slaves the patricians. It is amusing that the blacks monopolize the most classical and romantic names; Caesar, Plato, Pompey, Cato; Flora, Florilla, Rose and Lily; our cook is Minerva, and our waiting-boy McIvor, out of Waverly.

On a plantation, is usually one of each trade; a coachman, a gardener, and a vulcan; and if one breaks off a leg, they make a tailor, or a shoemaker, out of him. The house-servants and nurses, although they do not work so hard as a labouring-slave, and live better, yet are they more stinted in leisure. The house-slaves frequently sleep down before the embers, in a row, on rough rugs. With the field-slaves, Sunday is usually a holiday; wherein they deck themselves out for a frolic, or for their unintelligible methodist meetings; where those, who are tender in spirit, are said to be "seeking." Where they have kind masters, the slaves look cheerful, and happy; and do not labor harder than a free white labourer. The little ones, which in summer wear nothing more than a remnant of a shirt, and not infrequently go literally nude, and look like little imps, will yet be seen singing, and kicking, and wallowing about in the yellow sand right merrily.

In slave states, there is little economy of labour; and, though overrun with help, it seems as if nothing could ever be done in season. Although extravagant, and even princely, in many expenditures, the planters seldom have a well, or pump, near the house; but the slaves must go twenty or thirty rods, twenty or thirty times every day, to a spring-house, and *tote* up a tub, or a huge stone-jar, upon their heads, on which they sustain all weights. Instead of having a cheap apple-mill for cider, they scoop out a long trough, and into this empty the apples; and then may you see long rows of slaves, of both sexes, arranged up and down the sides, with ponderous pounders, and their shining black arms lifted up and down in order, as they quash the pomace; and, as they drink what juice they please, they get merry, and sing lustily to the strokes of their tall weighty wooden pestles.

Sometimes you will see three or four slaves on each side of a long horizontal tree-body, cutting in a row; one axe playing up, as the other axe is playing down, in alteration; so that, when the logs are of equal diameter, they all get done at one time.

When a slave dies, the master gives the rest a day, of their own choosing, to celebrate the funeral. This, perhaps a month after the corpse is interred, is a jovial day with them; they sing and dance and drink the dead to his new home, which some believe to be in old Guinea. Indeed, a wedding, and a funeral, are equally agreeable to those not personally interested in them, as then comes a holiday. It appears to be an instinct of these creatures to dance, to equivocate, and to pilfer; but, for the two latter propensities, ignorance and necessity plead loudly. The slaves have black tempers when affronted, and no white man is near by; they will jabber, and rave, and fight, like madmen.

The treatment of the slaves is quite different under different masters, and overseers. It is certified, that a black overseer is always more domineering, and more of an eye-servant, in the bad sense of the word, than a white one. This is true also in the treatment of their own children, and dogs; which they frequently delight to abuse. What slaves I have seen, have fared coarsely, upon their hoe-cakes and ash-pone; but have been treated humanely, and not hard tasked.

There are many planters, who wish there never had been a slave brought into the country; and who would make great sacrifices to emancipate them, if it could be safely done. But this must be done gradually, and provision be made for them when free; or they would soon wish to be re-inthralled. The planters stand in dread of the free blacks in the state, who act as a kind of medium of intrigue between the slaves and the whites; and on this account they approve of a Colonization Society, in order to induce the free negroes to quit the country.*

I know not whether the slaves, in general, are not as happy as their masters. They have no thought of to-morrow for a whole life, and have provision for sickness, and for old age; whereas a poor white, or black free labourer, if sick for a week, or when become infirm from age, perhaps breaks the hopes and dependence of a whole family, or casts them upon the county. In fine,

---

* [A reference to the American Colonization Society, founded in 1817, which, with influential support, proposed to solve the Negro problem by transporting all the blacks to Africa.—Ed.]

although I certainly hold a high estimation of the Virginian character, in many respects; and of their thousand-and-one acre plantations; yet, I never should covet to live so secluded in the woods; and to have my eye offended, and my heart pained, by the degradation of so many of the human species.

NATURAL BRIDGE, VA.

The Virginian *phraseology* sounds a little peculiar to a northern ear at times. There is the executive *belittle* for demean, which, however, being an expressive word, the ex-president hath rather *belarged* his fame by adding it to our vocabulary. As the New Englanders guess, so do the Virginians reckon. What in New England is called the husk of corn, in Virginia is called the *shuck;* and what we call cob, they call husk. The Virginians use clever for intelligent; whereas we use it for a kind of negative character of weak intellect, but good disposition; the correct meaning is rather with them, than with us, as shrewd, cunning, dextrous. What they call chamber, is the room where the madam sleeps, and is usually *below* stairs; and what we call afternoon, they call evening, making no quarter divisions of the day. *Tote,* a slave word, is much used; implying both sustension and locomotion. They say—to grow a crop, for, to raise a crop; he was raised, for, he was educated; mad for angry, as do the Irish; and madam and mistress, instead of our abbreviations. Children learn from the slaves some odd phrases; as, every which way; will you *all* do this? and the epithet *mighty* is quite popular with old and young, as, for instance, mighty weak. Nor is their pronunciation without some slight peculiarities, as, stars for stairs, arr for air, bar for bear; and Talliaferro, a surname, of which they had a governor, is pronounced Tollifer.

The Cotton Kingdom

OLD KENTUCKY HOME

On the map, this country appears like a new world, divided from the Atlantic states by the everlasting Alleghanies, which seem to uplift an impassable separation wall between the east, and the west. Of this state, and some of the other western states, the growth is almost a miracle. About thirty years ago, there were only one hundred and seventy returned militia, on the east side of Kentucky river. I was informed, by a lawyer of Lexington, that, thirty years ago also, three thousand acres of prime land, but ten miles from the town, were sold by a young woman, for as little money as would buy her a *new silk gown* to attend a ball in. Patrick Henry, of Virginia, moreover, sold, to his brother-in-law, about fifty years since, more than three thousand acres, and another parcel of two thousand acres of land, in this Scott county, for *two brood mares.*

The larger towns in this state, as Lexington and Frankfort, and especially Cincinnati, in a neighbouring state, across the Ohio river, are very city-like, and thriving; and in them, as also among many of the planters, is much wealth, and gentility. One indication of a new country is, that the shops are variety-shops; each one keeping piece-goods, groceries, cutlery, porcelain, and stationery, in different corners; there not yet being that partition of trade, which we meet in older states.

The plantation-mansions are in general mean; so that many a rich planter, were it not for his far-spreading fields, would by a northern man, be accounted poor. The houses are usually of hewn timber, with stone chimnies outjutting from the end walls, and the out-doors opening directly into the parlours, so that in winter they are quite comfortless. Some few of the plantation-seats, however, are of brick, and are accommodated with ample out-buildings. There is commonly in the front yard a horse-rack, with bridle pins over head for a dozen steeds; and upon one of which, from my casement, I now see a peacock perched on his long black legs, and screeching for joy.

This is not yet a country of books. Most professional gentlemen here, for want of early opportunity, have little taste for literature; but the lawyers are well grounded in land-claims, the most general and lucrative part of their practice. In lieu of three or five years, as they have or have not received degrees, county pettifoggers here sometimes come forth to plead, and to counsel, after perhaps six months of desultory reading. As to Latin, ten years ago, very few were the youths, who advanced farther than the *licet recedere;* and, as to Greek, rare was the native minister, attorney, or physician, that ever dreamed in any language but English. Such are now entitled buck-eyes; yet often well succeed, by an undiverted application of their mental faculties, and an un-abashed assurance.

In the lower counties, you may meet with young men, urbane, fashionable, and enterprising, who cannot indite a familiar epistle passably; and others, who cannot read nor write; as one of wealthy exterior said to me, when I offered him a state-trial, that I was perusing:—"He was not *scribe* enough to *read*." This is not mentioned from marvel, but from regret; since the deficiency originated in the paucity of means in the early modes of a new country, and is a constant disquietude to them. In the towns, and among rich planters, no people are more liberal in support of public, and private tutors.

If the young men cannot easily translate the Iliad of War, they can readily construe the Oeilaid of Love. The Kentuckians frequently marry very young; men at eighteen or twenty; girls at fourteen or sixteen; and, on the day after the wedding, at the bridegroom's father's hall, is usually a sumptuous festival, called an *inn-fare*.

The men of this state have iron-bound constitutions; they are a people of enterprise, and of bravery; none were braver in the last war. Military titles are here inflicted upon one; few escaping the honour of either captain, major, colonel, or general. A gun is a child's play-thing. Let a little Western lad espy but the velvet ear of a gray-squirrel, which he has *tree'd,* on the top bough of a hackberry, and he *downs him,* as he calls it. These early habits of the youths lead to a venturousness of disposition, which is not found in more refined, and effeminate states, where sedentary philosophy and literature have prevailed.

Among the lower classes of society, the Canaan richness of the land is productive, among better fruits, of much indolence. Too many, instead of resting one day in seven, work only on one day in six; and therefore ever remain poor. In some of the inferior hovels, are seen little once-white boys sitting at table in their long shirts; and running half the summer with nothing else on; which freedom renders them hardy. Some mothers here *hip* their infants. Men of this rank, if they cannot thrive in one occupation, often commute it for another; never distrusting their capabilities. Among this class, the riotous roisters, or, as they are here called, *rowdies,* will fight, not only from patriotism, but from mere love of fighting; it being one of their habitual amusements. These merry Shamgars are said to have fifteen ribs upon each side. A pistol, and a dirk, are as familiar, as a watch, and a penknife. When maddened, an affront is followed by a battery upon the bones; for, as they cannot comprehend reason, their arguments are generally palpable. I have heard of more pugnacious affrays during the past year, than in all my life before. The impious and senseless duel-murder is frequent in this state.

Whiskey slays many a strong man here; and too many of the groceries are grogeries. I lately saw an advertisement for a pedagogue; and, in a *nota bene:* —"One that is not addicted to ardent spirits would be prefered." At elections, where they vote *viva voce,* not by ballot, you may see a barrel afloat, offered by the successful candidates, and the vulgar portion of the voters crowding, and dipping up the spirit, if not in their hats and shoes, in their palms. At such times, they feel their freedom, and vociferate their propensities. At the polls, not an age since, as the candidates sat in the clerk's office, to thank each voter for his suffrage, according to custom, one voter cried out, as he obliquely eyed them:—"I vote for that little black man, over that huge yellow man."

Most wealthy planters in this state keep their coach and pair; their chaises are here called gigs. But, on account of the roughness of the roads in a lately settled country, the men, in general, travel on horseback, with their valise behind them, and no cruppers. To prevent the mire from dishonouring their legs, the horsemen wear short galligaskins, or long cherevalls; though they mar these words into uncouth sounds. The youths, from early practice, ride gracefully; not like clodhoppers, the rider in a gallop, the horse in a long trot. Like their progenitors, the Virginians, they are partial to pacers. The little maidens here, of eight or ten years old, will pace, or canter off, on their side-saddles, like young huntress Dianas.

You meet in this country with more renowned names, than a late wilderness might promise. Scarce a lad, or damsel, but is called after some redoubtable scholar, philosopher, statesman, or warrior; some nymph of mythology, or maid of romance: Cyrus, Junius, Newton, Manlius Valerius, Euclid, Darwin, Napoleon; characters, which frequently were all "unknown to mam', or daddy O."

The Kentuckians in general have numerous families, the fruitfulness of the climate extending even to the wives; and, it is noticed, that brides, who were as Rachels in the Atlantic states, having migrated to the west, become as Leahs; and that they esteem it no unusual compliment to receive even the double blessing of Rebeccahs. From the poorer states, when there is a famine in the land, they are fain to send to this Egypt to buy corn. In this state, all are plentiful, and bountiful livers. Sugar is eaten by spoonfuls, the maple-sugar not cloying like the cane-sugar. Melons here ofttimes expand their cheeks to unedible compass. At table, is a huge pitcher of mantling milk, towering in the middle of a circle of glasses. Here is sometimes used frumenty, a pottage of wheat and milk seethed. Bonny-clabber, in its season, is with *some* a favourite cooling-dish. If their coarse ash-pones irritate the palate as they descend, their soft waffles, with their hollow cheeks floating in honey, soothe all again. In fine, the rich Kentuckians live like lords.

Camp-meetings are common in Kentucky, and are doleful curiosities. The ministers are a species of without-method Methodists; happy compounds of illiterateness and fanaticism. If the weather be rainy, and it be convenient, they enter a meeting-house; many of which are built with a door back of the pulpit, so that the preacher may turn, and exhort those, who chose to lie grouped out on the grass; and which houses have long parallel seats, instead of pews, which are deemed too aristocratical. But, in fine weather, the preachers, and their followers, encamp in the woods, or fields, for some days, or even weeks; migrating from one county to another. They preach in part-coloured suits, gray or drab, with yellow or white buttons. With most of these apostles, the text is but a pitching of the tones to the nasal key; for, although they name a text when they commence, that is commonly the last you hear of it. Their long harangues are ludicrously solemn, and sometimes accidently sensible. When the whole vast circumvened crowd lift up their voices, they outsing all music. At a baptism, they appear to imagine an immersion into a creek an ablution of sin. The shores are lined with the picturesque multitudes, and you would smile in sadness, at the blushing unhallowed mode of submerging the women. For, as they do not close gather the borders of their white flannel robes, nor sink them by leaden knobs, when a female wades into the stream, her robe opens, and spreads, like an umbrella. The gospel is indeed, in a too literal sense, revealed unto babes and sucklings, if such have it.

In slave states, the white conversation is apt to be darkened in its complexion; indeed, three quarters of sociable discourse is often engrossed by the topic of slaves. If a young widow be inquired of, it is asked, is she a good manager? and instead of the phrase, how rich? how many slaves has she? Although, south and west, men boast of being most democratic, yet what is more contradictory to their principles, than their tyranny over three fifths of their population?

I saw one slave corded up to a tree, with his hands above his head, for wagging an evil tongue at a white man, and stripped, and knouted with a raw-hide thong, until his back was carbonadoed into ridges, and crimson. If two slaves are found quarrelling, it is customary to tie their left wrists together, and order them to lash each other, until one asks of the other pardon. A mistress is often obliged to wield the cowskin over her refractory young female house servants; and the practice is, when they scream aloud, to chastise them until they smother their sobs. Yet, in truth, as might be expected, almost every slave is an eye-servant, more easily governed by fear, than by affection; and, as the mansion, and yard, and plantation, are overrun with them, there could be, perhaps, no safety without severity.

The Phraseology in this state is sometimes novel. When you arrive at a house, the first inquiry is, where is your plunder? as if you were a bandit; and out is sent a slave to bring in your plunder; i.e. your trunk, or valise. Instead of saying of a promised mother, with Shakespearean delicacy, that she is "nigh fainting under the pleasing punishment, that women bear"; the hint is quite Shaker-like, that she is "about to tumble to pieces." I have often heard the word *human* used here as a noun. The word *great* is sometimes used to signify *little;* as, that a lady has a great foot, meaning, without irony, a little foot. Many from habit, like the Virginians, tuck a *t* at the end of such words as onct, twict, skifft. They here call a river, a run; a lot, a section of land; they say to stall, i.e. overload, a horse; and cupping for milking. Some words are used, even by genteel people, from their imperfect educations, in a new sense; and others, by the lower classes in society, pronounced very uncouthly, as:—to eat a liquid, to quile for to quiet, to suspicion one, to legerize an account, to prize for to raise by a lever, to fayz for to fix, offer for the candidacy, best book I have ever read after, well liked of, heap of times, did done do it, done done did it, painter for panther, varmont for vermin, contràry, hȳmn, breethren, an oxen, I seen, I brung, exhibitation, schrowd, yearth, yearn for earn, bresh, hommer, sketes, drap, fotch, mought, and so forth.

13

Sundry Observations on Southern Life, 1818–29

Mrs. Royall was an indefatigable traveler. Between 1818 and 1822 she visited Alabama, mostly in the area along the Tennessee River. Later she journeyed northward (see p. 48) and, again in 1828 and 1829, made an extensive trip through the Atlantic and Gulf South, from Virginia southward through the Carolinas and Georgia, then westward along the Gulf to Mobile.

Mrs. Royall was certainly not without her prejudices. On the other hand, when stripped of their invective and personalities, her observations cannot be ignored, for she described features of southern life too frequently omitted by other travelers. Almost alone in the travel literature of the South, she refused to be absorbed by the institution of slavery, recognizing that other phenomena existed in the southern community. She caught in her lively way the frontier aspects of Alabama; she searched into the educational and humanitarian conditions of Charleston; she saw people, too, in their everyday life. Considering how bitterly she could attack what she did not like, it is remarkable how detached and universal were her interests, with what adroitness she escaped being engulfed by the single theme of the plantation, and with what lively insight she could re-create the life of the people.

AN ALABAMA REVIVAL

I have met with several excellent orators since I have been in this country; the best I ever heard, men of handsome delivery. These are methodists. I was truly astonished, as I never saw one of that sect, before, hardly worth hearing.

The Cotton Kingdom

The baptists, and the Cumberland presbyterians, are continually preaching and *covaulting* also. When that busybody, Mr. *They say,* reported Mr. Porter was to preach here to day, that is, out at the stand in the woods, I observed, "I will go and hear Mr. Porter."

"Oh," said a bystander, "it is another preacher than Mr. Porter that preaches to-day—there is not such another preacher in the known world—he's a monstrous fine preacher."

As I had heard some fine preaching, for the oratory I went to hear this none-such. But never was I so disappointed. I placed myself in front of the preacher, (a great rough looking man,) and the congregation sat some on fallen timber, some on benches carried there for the purpose—some sat flat on the ground, and many stood up—about 500 in all. His text was, "He that hath ears to hear, let him hear." The people must have been deaf indeed that could not have heard him. He neither made division nor subdivision. He is one of the Cumberland presbyterians. They are Calvinists, it is said, but do not deem education a necessary qualification to preach the Gospel. But to the sermon: he began low but soon bawled to deafening. He spit in his hands, rubbed them against each other, and then would smite them together, till he made the woods ring. The people now began to covault, and dance, and shout, till they fairly drowned the speaker. Many of the people, however, burst out into a laugh. Seeing this, the preacher cried out, pointing to them with his finger, "Now look at them sinners there—You'll see how they will come tumbling down presently—I'll bring them down." He now redoubled his strength; spit in his hands and smote them together, till he made the forest resound, and took a fresh start; and sure enough the sinners came tumbling down. The scene that succeeded baffles description. Principally confined to women and children, the young women had carefully taken out their combs, from their hair, and laid them and their bonnets in a place of safety, as though they were going to set in for a fight; and it was much like a battle. After tumbling on the ground, and kicking sometime, the old women were employed in keeping their clothes civil, and the young men (never saw an old man go near them) would help them up, and taking them by each hand, by *their* assistance, and their own agility, they would spring nearly a yard from the ground at every jump, one jump after another, crying out, glory, glory, as loud as their strength would admit; others would be singing a lively tune to which they kept time—hundreds might be seen and heard going on in this manner at once. Others, again, exhausted by this jumping, would fall down, and here they lay cross and pile, heads and points, yelling and screaming like wild beasts of the forest, rolling on the ground, like hogs in a mire,—very much like they do at camp meetings in our country, but more shameless; their clothes were the color of the dirt; and like those who attend the camp meetings, they were all of the lower class of the people. I saw no genteel person among them. Are not people of education answerable for this degradation of society? It appears to me, since I have had opportunities of mixing with the world, that there are a certain class of citizens, whose interest it is to keep their fellow men in ignorance. I am very sure, half a dozen words of common sense, well applied, would convince those infatuated young women that they were acting like fools. In fact a fool is more rational. Not one of those but would think it a crying sin to dance.

The noise of the preacher was effectually drowned at length, and a universal uproar succeeded louder than ever.—Whilst this was going on, I observed an old woman near me, snivelling and turning up the whites of her eyes, (she was a widow—all the widows, old and young, covaulted,) and often applying her handkerchief to her eyes, and throwing herself into contortions, but it would not do, she could not raise the steam.

I pointed to one young woman, with a red scarf, who had tired down several young men, and was still covaulting, and seeing she jumped higher than the rest, I asked "who she might be?" One of the gentlemen, a Mr. Gallagher, who was standing near, gave such an account of her (men know these things) as would shock a modest ear. "D——n her, she gets converted every meeting she goes to." How much better had she been at a ball, (if they must dance,) where they would be obliged to behave decent, and where vile characters dare not appear.

Shortly after they began to rear and covault, a daughter of my host began too. He walked up to her, and left her off some distance, and sat her down at the root of a tree. When he returned, I inquired "if she was sick?"

"No," he answered, "but she was beginning to go on as the rest, and I told her if she wished to worship God, to do it there, and not to expose herself before faces."

The preacher having spent all his ammunition, made a pause, and then called upon all the sinners to approach and be prayed for. Numbers went forward, all women and children, (children of ten years old get religion!) and the priest began to pray; when a decent looking man approached the stand, and took a female by the arm, and led her away. As he walked along, the preacher pointed to him, and said, "God, strike that sinner down!" The man turned around, and in an angry tone said, "God has more sense than to mind such a damned fool as you are!" and resumed his course.

Being tired of such an abominable scene, I proposed returning home, and, taking a near cut through a slip of woodland, we surprised the red scarf lady in a manner that gave us no favorable opinion of her piety.

There is a great deal of preaching here; and a great many ill natured remarks pass between the presbyterians and methodists; but whether it be to determine which shall save the most souls, or receive most money, I am too ignorant to discover. From what I have heard, it appears the methodists have braved every danger, and preached to the people gratis, in the settling of the country; and now that there is no danger, and the people have become wealthy, those sly fellows, the presbyterians, are creeping in to reap the harvest. But the methodists have a great advantage, in point of talent, many of them being the best orators in the country. But they all draw too many women after them, in my humble opinion.

THE LADIES OF RALEIGH TAKE SNUFF

My pen is now to give pain, not only to the parties concerned, but to all that part of mankind not lost to feeling: I allude to a strange infatuation of the females in Raleigh, from the oldest to the youngest, in an unbounded use of snuff!!!—real tobacco snuff! They do not snuff it up the nose, but take it into the mouth—they call it dipping. It was first resorted to, to clean the teeth, and has grown into a confirmed habit! It is simply dipping a small wooden brush, a little stick (bruised or chewed at one end) into a common box of snuff and rubbing the teeth, and they are so besotted, that they sit for hours rubbing their teeth, merely as it is said, for the pleasure of intoxication—like a toper over his bottle, which is affirmed to be the effect. But why snuff would occasion intoxication when grown into a habit, more than *chewing* tobacco, I cannot discover: some say it is more apt to reach the system by the saliva. Let this be as it may, it has a powerful effect on the system, and must finally destroy the health. The ladies of Raleigh are deadly, pale, and emaciated, old and young; even little girls look like ghosts. A knott of young ladies will assemble in a room as though it were a tea party and lock themselves in, and dip for hours, chatting and amusing themselves all the while with anecdotes and stories—cooks, chamber-maids and washer-women, all dip. I have seen little girls walking in the streets, with their lips besmeared with snuff and saliva, which rendered them objects of disgust, and it evidently distends the mouth.

Besides the expense and loss of health, and color, it evidently must engross all their time. These little and big girls never go without their box, and the stick in it, either in their reticule or their bosom; and the cook hardly waits to get her dinner dished, till she is eagerly engaged in *dipping*. It is strange they do not take some measures to stop the evil amongst the children, that the mania might end with the mother. This lamentable practice is said to be spreading into the neighborhood of Raleigh; and, some do say, it is in use in some of the adjoining towns. They generally strive to keep it a secret but it is, alas, but too well known. Several respectable gentlemen, married and single, with deep felt regret, mentioned the ruinous habit to me; and requested me to expose a habit so offensive, and one which threatened to destroy the intercourse of the sexes. The young men of Raleigh, seemed to deplore the unfortunate habit.

This is one of the many proofs we have, that women and not men rule the nation. I hope my fair Sisters will never require another public lecture, and that the prospect of dying old maids may induce them to quit *dipping*.

SAVANNAH

Savannah being built upon a bluff, makes a handsome appearance as we approach it; the steeples first,—the houses soon after become visible. The river spreads out to a great width, and the harbor exhibited a number of steam-boats, and some shipping, and almost rivals the beauty of Charleston harbor.

The streets of Savannah are one sea of sand; the novelty of this, and the pride of China (*alias* China-tree) in full bloom, filling the air with the sweetest fragrance, the profusion of its foliage, and the soft tinge of its exuberant flowers, the hum of insects, the fruit shops, the genial shade, and the pleasant sunshine,—I have no name for the scene!

Savannah is the garden spot of the south, whether as to opulence, trade, refinement, hospitality, or site. The buildings of Savannah are rather indifferent, like those of Charleston, and much inferior to those of Augusta. They seem to take most pride in decorating their streets with those beautiful trees, and their despatch of business. Of all people, they take the most pleasure in an unwearied attention to business. The business season commences late in the fall, and ends in June, and such is their industry, that they scarcely leave time for refreshment or repose. After the business season is over, they then enjoy themselves with their friends—travel to the north, or amuse themselves as they please, till the business season comes round again. This is the routine of all the southern towns. Though Savannah is an even sandy plain, this plain is considerably elevated above the river, and rises still higher in the rear.

From the top of the Exchange, we have one of the handsomest prospects in the southern country, and by a long way the most extensive. For the distance of eight miles, you see one continued plain of rice and cotton fields. Splendid mansions, groves of live oak, magnolia gardens, the river with its islands, steamboats, and shipping, the whole city with its squares, and regular streets, lined with the pride of Savannah, (I would say instead) of China, with the endless cotton warehouses, the marble monument, erected to the memory of Green and Pulaski, present to the eye, a most ravishing picture of beauty, or rather novelty to a traveller. The harbor excepted, it greatly exceeds any view of Charleston. Its chief beauty consists in the symmetry, extent, and uniform evenness of the great rice and cotton plantations, and the alternate rows of those exquisitely variegated trees and houses.

The wharves and streets near the river, were alive with people and drays.

Having often mentioned the china-tree, I never saw it in bloom till now, and one of them, growing opposite my window, so near that I could put out my hand and pluck the flowers. The China-tree is in symmetry and attitude, something like the apple tree, if we allow it about twice its height, and it would grow much taller, but they are topped from time to time, and neatly pruned. The color and form of the flower, is much like the liloc. It is, how-ever, more deeply tinged with red—on the outside of its tiny petals, which are exactly like those of the liloc, and like it, grows in large bunches, the stem not so long, nor is the body of the flower so pointed—very narrow hair stripes of a blood red, appear on the outward part of the petal, and it is some-what deeper shaded than the liloc. These hang in bunches on the boughs of the tree, as thick as the leaves, which are in heavy clusters of a beautiful bright green, in shape like the elder,—thus mingled and shaded, the tree is extremely beautiful and very ornamentive.

Market is held on Sunday morning in Savannah, all the negroes (who reap the benefit) for many miles round come in, and the market is numerously attended. It is hardly necessary to say this is a special privilege of leniency, and accommodation to the slaves, who cannot attend with their own per-quisites and manufactures in the week; and it is also a day of visits and finery. This privilege is not the only one they are allowed: the poorer sort traverse the streets during Sunday, with brooms, and various other manufactures of their own.

Among the novelties of Savannah, I was amused with the gait of the peo-ple, as they walked the streets. They are so much accustomed to wade through the sand, that they have contracted a habit, something like a wading step, as one would walk through a bed of tough brick-mortar. Their gait is slow and regular, their step long, their head thrown back—the better to breathe, I suspect—and they rise and fall every step. This is more strongly marked in the men. My visit to Savannah happened to be at one of the busiest seasons in the year: in those times, the people scarcely take time to eat, or sleep. All the produce of the State and a large portion of South Carolina, comes here to be shipped, and the time being limited, they work themselves nearly to death.

All the streets cross at right angles, laying the city off into squares. The streets are wide, and paved on the sides; but such is the depth of the sand in the middle of the street, that carriages sink into it, and people can scarcely drag themselves through it; and yet this difficulty is entirely eclipsed by the beauty of the trees, which line the streets, and the profusion of delicious fruit.

To sum up the whole in a few words, so far as I have travelled, Savannah is the first city of the south, by a long way. The citizens are wealthy, sober, intelligent, hospitable, industrious, and high-minded, to a degree which few towns in the United States, can ever reach. I cannot say the society is better than in Camden, S.C. and Wilmington, N.C. but it greatly excels in wealth and numbers. I met with more of what we call gentlemen in Savannah, than in any town in the United States.

14

A Yankee Falls in Love with the South, 1835

*J*oseph H. Ingraham is remembered today, when he is remembered at all, *as the prolific writer of superdramatic and sensational novels, of which La-fitte: The Pirate of the Gulf and the later, religious Prince of the House of David are representative. Contemporary opinion recognized that his writings were enormously popular and totally without literary merit. Longfellow notes in his diary for April 6, 1846: "Ingraham the novelist called. A young, dark man, with soft voice. He says he has written eighty novels, and of these* twenty during the last year; till it has grown to be merely mechanical with him. These novels are published in the newspapers. They pay him something more than three thousand dollars a year."

Ingraham was born in Portland, Maine, in 1809 and attended Bowdoin College. His career was somewhat varied. In his youth he was a sailor. Later he became a schoolteacher—which accounts for the title "Professor" found on the title-pages of his works—married the daughter of a wealthy Mississippi planter, and ended his career as an Episcopalian clergyman. He died at Holly Springs, Mississippi, in 1866.

When still a young man in his twenties, he visited New Orleans and the Natchez area of Mississippi. The result was his first and, without much doubt, his best book, the anonymous The South-West. By a Yankee. Stylistically, the book is wordy, "over literary," and displays many of the romantic notions which appear so prominently in his later fiction. At the same time, with a novelist's insight, he catches vividly the color and vitality of the half-foreign, half-strange life of New Orleans and the Mississippi plantations. He was certainly not the type of New Englander who went to disapprove of what he saw in the South. He tended to palliate slavery and to dwell on the picturesque features of plantation life. Yet, if he undoubtedly surveyed the South with rose-colored glasses, he was most assuredly not blind to the evils of southern life; and many of his comments show both shrewdness and insight.

SHIPS ON THE LEVEE AT NEW ORLEANS

Double lines of market and fish-boats, secured to the Levée, form a small connecting link with the long chain of shipping and steamboats that extend for a league in front of New Orleans. At the lower part of the town lie generally those ships, which having their cargoes on board, have dropped down the river to await their turn to be towed to sea. Fronting this station there are no stores, but several elegant private dwellings, constructed after the combined French and Spanish style of achitecture, almost embowered in dark, green foliage, and surrounded by parterres. The next station above, and immediately adjoining this, is usually occupied by vessels, which, just arrived, have not yet obtained a berth where they can discharge their cargoes; though not unfrequently ships here discharge and receive their freight, stretching some distance up the Levée to the link of market-boats just mentioned.

From the market to the vicinity of Bienville-street, lies an extensive tier of shipping, often "six deep," discharging and receiving cargo, or waiting for freight. The next link of the huge chain is usually occupied by Spanish and

French coasting vessels,—traders to Mexico, Texas, Florida, &c. These are usually polaccas, schooners, and other small craft—and particularly black, rakish craft, some of them are in appearance.

Next to this station (as you will perceive, the whole Levée is divided into *stations* appropriated to peculiar classes of shipping,) commences the range of steamboats, or steamers, as they are usually termed here, rivaling in magnitude the extensive line of ships below. The appearance of so large a collection of steamboats is truly novel, and must always strike a stranger with peculiar interest.

The next station, though it presents a more humble appearance than the others, is not the least interesting. Here are congregated the primitive navies of Indiana, Ohio, and the adjoining states, manned (I have not understood whether they are *officered* or not) by "real Kentucks"—"Buckeyes"—"Hooshers"—and "Snorters." There were about two hundred of these craft without masts, consisting of "flat-boats," and "keel-boats," which are one remove from the flat-boat, having some pretensions to a keel; they somewhat resemble freighting canal-boats. Besides these are "arks," most appropriately named, their *contents* having probably some influence with their god-fathers in selecting an appellation, and other non-descript-craft. These are filled with produce of all kinds, brought from the "Upper country," (as the north western states are here termed) by the farmers themselves who have raised it;—also, horses, cattle, hogs, poultry, mules, and every other thing raiseable and saleable are piled into these huge flats, which an old farmer and a half a dozen Goliaths of sons can begin and complete in less than a week, from felling of the first tree to the driving of the last pin.

These boats, on arriving here, are taken to pieces and sold as lumber, while their former owners with well-lined purses return home as deck passengers on board steamboats. An immense quantity of whiskey from Pittsburgh and Cincinnati, besides, is brought down in these boats, and not unfrequently, they are crowded with slaves for the southern market. The late excellent laws relative to the introduction of slaves, however, have checked, in a great measure, this traffic here, and the Mississippi market at Natchez has consequently become inundated, by having poured into it, in addition to its usual stock, the Louisianian supply.

The line of flats may be considered the last link of the great chain of shipping in front of New-Orleans, unless we consider as attached to it a kind of dock adjoining, where ships and steamers often lie, either worn out or undergoing repairs. From this place to the first station I have mentioned, runs along the Levée, fronting the shipping, an uninteresting block of stores, (except where they are intersected by streets,) some of which are lofty and elegant, while others are clumsy piles of French and Spanish construction, browned and blackened by age.

THE STREETS OF NEW ORLEANS BY NIGHT

We commenced our long, delightful walk just as the loud report of the evening gun broke over the city, rattling and reverberating through the long massively built streets, like the echoing of distant thunder along mountain ravines. On a firm, smooth, gravelled walk elevated four feet, by a gradual ascent from the street—one side open to the river, and the other lined with the "Pride of China," or India tree, we pursued our way to Chartres-street, the "Broadway" of New-Orleans. The moon shone with uncommon brilliancy, and thousands, even in this lower faubourg, were abroad, enjoying the beauty and richness of the scene. Now, a trio of lively young Frenchmen would pass us, laughing and conversing gayly upon some merry subject, followed by a slow moving and stately figure, whose haughty tread, and dark *roque-laure* gathered with classic elegance around his form in graceful folds, yet so arranged as to conceal every feature beneath his slouched *sombrero,* except a burning, black, penetrating eye,—denoted the exiled Spaniard.

We passed on—and soon the lively sounds of the French language, uttered by soft voices, were heard nearer and nearer, and the next moment, two or three duenna-like old ladies, remarkable for their "embonpoint" dimensions, preceded a bevy of fair girls, without that most hideous of all excrescences, with which women see fit to disfigure their heads, denominated a "bonnet"— their brown, raven or auburn hair floating in ringlets behind them.

As we passed on, the number of promenaders increased, but scarcely a lady was now to be seen. Every other gentleman we met was enveloped in a cloud, not of bacchanalian, but tobacconalian incense, which gave a peculiar atmosphere to the Levée.

Every, or nearly every gentleman carried a sword cane, apparently, and occasionally the bright hilt of a Spanish knife, or dirk, would gleam for an instant in the moon-beams from the open bosom of its possessor, as, with the lowering brow, and active tread or wary suspicion, he moved rapidly by us, his roundabout thrown over the left shoulder and secured by the sleeves in a knot under the arm, which was thrust into his breast, while the other arm was at liberty to attend to his segar, or engage in any mischief to which its owner might be inclined. This class of men are very numerous here. They are easily distinguished by their shabby appearance, language, and foreign way of wearing their apparel. In groups—promenading, lounging, and sleeping upon the seats along the Levée—we passed several hundred of this *canaille* of

Orleans, before we arrived at the "Parade," the public square in front of the cathedral. They are mostly Spaniards and Portuguese, though there are among them representatives from all the unlucky families which, at the building of Babel, were dispersed over the earth. As to their mode and means of existence, I have not as yet informed myself; but I venture to presume that they resort to no means beneath the dignity of "caballeros"!

After passing the market on our right, a massive colonnade, about two hundred and fifty feet in length, we left the Levée, and its endless tier of shipping which had bordered one side of our walk all the way, and passing under the China-trees, that still preserved their unbroken line along the river, we crossed Levée-street, a broad, spacious esplanade, running along the front of the main block of the city, separating it from the Levée, and forming a magnificent thoroughfare along the whole extensive river-line.

We entered Rue St. Pierre, which issues from it south of the grand square. This square is an open green, surrounded by a lofty iron railing, within which troops of boys were playing. The front of this extensive square was open to the river, bordered with its dark line of ships; on each side were blocks of rusty looking brick buildings of Spanish and French construction, with projecting balconies, heavy cornices, and lofty jalousies or barricaded windows. The lower stories of these buildings were occupied by retailers of fancy wares, vintners, segar manufacturers, dried fruit sellers, and all the other members of the innumerable occupations, to which the volatile, ever ready Frenchman can always turn himself and a *sous* into the bargain. As we passed along, these shops were all lighted up, and the happy faces, merry songs, and gay dances therein, occasionally contrasted with the shrill tone of feminine anger in a foreign tongue, and the loud, fierce, rapid voices of men mingling in dispute, added to the novelty and amusement of our walk. I enumerated ten, out of seventeen successive shops or *cabarets,* upon the shelves of which I could discover nothing but myriads of claret and Madeira bottles, tier upon tier to the ceiling; and from this fact I came to the conclusion, that some of the worthy citizens of New-Orleans must be most unconscionable "wine-bibbers," if not "publicans and sinners," as subsequent observation has led me to surmise.

On the remaining side of this square stood the cathedral, its dark moorish-looking towers flinging their vast shadows far over the water. The whole front of the large edifice was thrown into deep shade, so that when we approached, it presented one black mingled mass, frowning in stern and majestic silence upon the surrounding scene.

Leaving this venerable building at the right, we turned into Chartres-street, the second parallel with the Levée, and the most fashionable, as well as greatest business street in the city. As we proceeded, *cafés,* confectioners, fancy stores, millineries, parfumeurs, &c. &c., were passed in rapid succession; each one of them presenting something new, and always something to strike the attention of strangers, like ourselves, for the first time in the only "foreign" city in the United States.

At the corner of one of the streets intersecting Chartres-street—Rue St. Louis I believe—we passed a large building, the lofty basement story of which was lighted with a glare brighter than that of noon. In the back ground, over the heads of two or three hundred loud-talking, noisy gentlemen, who were promenading and vehemently gesticulating, in all directions, through the spacious room—I discovered a bar, with its peculiar dazzling array of glasses and decanters containing "spirits"—not of "the vasty deep" certainly, but of whose potent spells many were apparently trying the power, by frequent libations. This building—of which and its uses more anon—I was informed, was the "French" or "New Exchange." After passing Rue Toulouse, the streets began to assume a new character; the buildings were loftier and more modern—the signs over the doors bore English names, and the characteristic arrangements of a northern dry goods store were perceived, as we peered in at the now closing doors of many stores by which we passed. We had now attained the upper part of Chartres-street, which is occupied almost exclusively by retail and wholesale dry goods dealers, jewellers, book-sellers, &c., from the northern states, and I could almost realize that I was taking an evening promenade in Cornhill, so great was the resemblance.

As we successively crossed Rues Conti, Bienville and Douane, and looked down these long straight avenues, the endless row of lamps, suspended in the middle of these streets, as well as in all others in New-Orleans, by chains or ropes, extended from house to house across, had a fine and brilliant effect, which we delayed for a moment on the flagstone to admire, endeavouring to reach with our eyes the almost invisible extremity of this line of flame. Just before we reached the head of Chartres-street, near Bienville, our way was impeded by a party of gentlemen in violent altercation in English and French, who completely blocked up the "trottoir." "Sir," said one of the party—a handsome, resolute-looking young man—in a calm deliberate voice, which was heard above every other, and listened to as well—"Sir, you have grossly insulted me, and I shall expect from you, immediately—before we separate— an acknowledgment, adequate to the injury." "Monsieur," replied a young Frenchman whom he had addressed, in French, "Monsieur, I never did insult you—a gentleman never insults! you have misunderstood me, and refuse to listen to a candid explanation." "The explanation you have given, sir," reiterated the first speaker, "is not sufficient—it is a subterfuge"; here many voices mingled in loud confusion, and a renewed and more violent altercation ensued which prevented our hearing distinctly; and as we had already crossed to the opposite side of the street, having ladies under escort, we rapidly passed on our way, but had not gained half a square before the clamour increased to an uproar—steel struck steel—one, then another pistol was discharged in rapid succession—"guards," "gens d'armes, gens d'armes," "guards! guards!" resounded along the streets, and we arrived at our hotel, just in time to escape being run down, or run through at their option probably, by half a dozen *gens d'armes* in plain blue uniforms, who were rushing with drawn swords in their hands to the scene of contest, perfectly well assured in our own minds, that we had most certainly arrived at NEW-ORLEANS!

Though affairs of the kind just described are no uncommon thing here, and are seldom noticed in the papers of the day—yet the following allusion to the event of last evening may not be uninteresting to you, and I will therefore copy it, and terminate my letter with the extract.

"An affray occurred last night in the vicinity of Bienville-street, in which one young gentleman was severely wounded by the discharge of a pistol, and another slightly injured by a dirk. An *'affaire d'honneur'* originated from this, and the parties met this morning. Dr. —— of New-York, one of the principals, was mortally wounded by his antagonist M. Le —— of this city."

NEW ORLEANS COFFEE HOUSES AND GAMBLING HELLS

A French coffee-house is a place well worth visiting by a stranger, more especially a Yankee stranger. I will therefore detain you a little longer and introduce you for a moment into this café and to its inmates. As the coffee houses here do not differ materially from each other except in size and richness of decoration, though some of them certainly are more fashionable resorts than others, the description of one of them will enable you perhaps to form some idea of other similar establishments in this city. Though their usual denomination is "coffee-house," they have no earthly, whatever may be their spiritual, right to such a distinction; it is merely a *"nomme de profession,"* assumed, I know not for what object. We entered from the street, after passing round a large Venetian screen within the door, into a spacious room, lighted by numerous lamps, at the extremity of which stood an extensive bar, arranged, in addition to the usual array of glass ware, with innumerable French decorations. There were several attendants, some of whom spoke English, as one of the requirements of their station. This is the case of all *employés* throughout New-Orleans; nearly every store and place of public resort being provided with individuals in attendance who speak both languages. Around the room were suspended splendid engravings and fine paintings, most of them of the most licentious description, and though many of their subjects were classical, of a voluptuous and luxurious character. This is French taste however. There are suspended in the Exchange in Chartres-street—one of the most magnificent public rooms in the city—paintings which, did they occupy an equally conspicuous situation in Merchant's Hall, in Boston, would be instantly defaced by the populace.

Around the room, beneath the paintings, were arranged many small tables, at most of which three or four individuals were seated, some alternately sipping negus and puffing their segars, which are as indispensable necessaries to a Creole at all times, as his right hand, eyebrows, and left shoulder in conversation. Others were reading newspapers, and occasionally assisting their comprehension of abstruse paragraphs, by hot "coffee," alias warm punch and slings, with which, on little japanned salvers, the active attendants were flying in all directions through the spacious room, at the beck and call of customers. The large circular bar was surrounded by a score of noisy applicants for the liquid treasures which held out to them such strong temptations. Trios, couples and units of gentlemen were promenading the well sanded floor, talking in loud tones, and gesticulating with the peculiar vehemence and rapidity of Frenchmen. Others, and by far the majority, were gathered by twos and by fours around the little tables, deeply engaged in playing that most intricate, scientific, and mathematical of games termed "Domino." This is the most common game resorted to by the Creoles. In every café and cabaret, from early in the morning, when the luxurious mint-julep has thawed out their intellects and expanded their organ of combativeness, till late at night, devotees to this childish amusement will be found clustered around the tables, with a tonic, often renewed and properly sangareed, at their elbows. Enveloped in dense clouds of tobacco-smoke issuing from their eternal segars—those inspirers of pleasant thoughts,—to whose density, with commendable perseverance and apparent good will, all in the café contribute,—they manoeuvre their little, dotted, black and white parallelograms with wonderful pertinacity and skill.

There are certainly one hundred coffee-houses in this city—how many more, I know not,—and they have, throughout the day, a constant ingress and egress of thirsty, time-killing, news-seeking visitors. As custom authorized this frequenting of these popular places of resort, the citizens of New-Orleans do not, like those of Boston, attach any disapprobation to the houses or their visitors. And as there is, in New-Orleans, from the renewal of one half of its inhabitants every few years, and the constant influx of strangers, strictly speaking no exclusive *clique* or aristocracy, to give a tone to society and establish a standard of propriety and respectability, as among the worthy Bostonians, one cannot say to another, "It is not genteel to resort here—it will injure your reputation to be seen entering this or that café." The inhabitants have no fixed criterion of what is and what is not "respectable," in the northern acceptation of the term. They are neither guided nor restrained from following their own inclinations, by any laws of long established society, regulating their movements, and saying "thus far shalt thou go, and no farther." Consequently, every man minds his own affairs, pursues his own business or amusement, and lets his neighbours and fellow-citizens do the same; without the fear of the moral lash (not law) before his eyes, or expulsion from "caste" for doing that "in which the soul delighteth."

Thus you see that society here is a perfect democracy, presenting variety and novelty enough to a stranger, who chooses to mingle in it freely, and feels a disposition impartially to study character.

Proceeding along the corridor, we left the billiard-room on our left, in which no sound was heard (though every richly-carved, green-covered table was surrounded by players, while numerous spectators reclined on sofas or settees around the room) save the sharp *teck! teck!* of the balls as they came in contact with each other, and the rattling occasioned by the "markers" as they noted the progress of the game on the large parti-coloured "rosaries" extended over the centre of the tables. Lingering here but a moment, we turned an angle of the gallery, and at the farther extremity came to a glass door curtained on the inner side, so as effectually to prevent all observation of the interior. Entering this,—for New Orleans,—so carefully guarded room, we beheld a scene, which, to an uninitiated, ultra city-bred northerner, would be both novel and interesting.

The first noise which struck our ears on entering, was the clear ringing and clinking of silver, mingled with the technical cries of the gamblers, of "all set"—"seven red"—"few cards"—"ten black," &c.—the eager exclamations of joy or disappointment by the players, and the incessant clattering of the little ivory ball racing its endless round in the roulette-table. On one side of the room was a faro-table, and on the opposite side a roulette. We approached the former, which was thronged on three sides with players, while on the other, toward the wall, was seated the dealer of the game—the "gentleman professeur." He was a portly, respectable looking, jolly-faced Frenchman, with so little of the "black-leg" character stamped upon his physiognomy, that one would be far from suspecting him to be a gambler by profession. This is a profession difficult to be conceived as the permanent and only pursuit of an individual. Your conception of it has probably been taken, as in my own case, from the fashionable novels of the day; and perhaps you have regarded the character as merely the creation of an author's brain, and "the profession" *as* a profession, existing nowhere in the various scenes and circumstances of life.

There are in this city a very great number of these *infernos,* (*anglicè* "hells") all of which—with the exception of a few private ones, resorted to by those gentlemen who may have some regard for appearances—are open from twelve at noon till two in the morning, and thronged by all classes, from the lowest blackguard upward. They are situated in the most public streets, and in the most conspicuous locations. Each house has a bank, as the amount of funds owned by it is termed. Some of the houses have on hand twenty thousand dollars in specie; and when likely to be hard run by heavy losses, can draw for three or four times that amount upon the directors of the "bank company." The establishing of one of these banks is effected much as that of any other. Shares are sold, and many respectable moneyed men, I am informed, become stockholders; though not ambitious, I believe, to have their names made public. It is some of the best stock in the city, often returning an enormous dividend. They are regularly licensed, and pay into the state or city treasury, I forget which, annually more than sixty thousand dollars. From six to twelve well-dressed, genteel looking individuals, are always to be found in attendance, to whom salaries are regularly paid by the directors; and to this salary, and this occupation, they look for as permanent a support through life as do members of any other profession. It is this class of men who are emphatically denominated "gamblers and black legs." The majority of them are Frenchmen, though they usually speak both French and English. Individuals, allured by the hope of winning, are constantly passing in and out of these houses, in "broad noon," with the same indifference to what is termed "public opinion," as they would feel were they going into or out of a store.

Those places which are situated in the vicinity of Canal-street and along the Levée, are generally of a lower order, and thronged with the *canaille* of the city, sailors, Kentucky boatmen, crews of steam-boats, and poor Gallic gentlemen, in threadbare long-skirted coats and huge whiskers. The room we were now visiting was of a somewhat higher order, though not exclusively devoted to the more genteel adventurers, as, in the very nature of the thing, such an exclusion would be impossible. But if unruly persons intrude, and are disposed to be obstreperous, the conductors of the rooms, of course, have the power of expelling them at pleasure.

Being merely spectators of the game, we managed to obtain an advantageous position for viewing it, from a vacant settee placed by the side of the

THE LEVEE AT NEW ORLEANS

portly dealer, who occupied, as his exclusive right, one side of the large table. Before him were placed in two rows thirteen cards; the odd thirteenth capping the double file, like a militia captain at the head of his company, when marching "two by two"; the files of cards, however, unlike these martial files of men, are *straight*. You will readily see by the number, that these cards represent every variety in a pack. The dealer, in addition, has a complete pack, fitting closely in a silver box, from which, by the action of a sliding lid, he adroitly and accurately turns off the cards in dealing. The players, or "betters," as they are termed, place their money in various positions as it respects the thirteen cards upon the table, putting it either on a single card or between two, as their skill, judgment, or fancy may dictate.

As I took my station near the faro-board, the dealer was just shuffling the cards for a new game. There were eleven persons clustered around the table, and as the game was about to commence, arm after arm was reached forth to the prostrate cards, depositing one, five, ten, twenty, or fifty dollars, according to the faith or depth of purse of their owners. On, around, and between the cards, dollars were strewed singly or in piles, while the eyes of every better were fixed immoveably, and, as the game went on, with a painful intensity, upon his own deposit, perhaps his last stake. When the stakes were all laid, the dealer announced it by drawling out in bad English, "all saat." Then, damping his forefinger and thumb, by a summary process—not quite so elegant as common—he began drawing off the cards in succession. The card taken off does not count in the game; the betters all looking to the one turned up in the box to read the fate of their stakes. As the cards are turned, the winners are paid, the money won by the bank swept off with a long wand into the reservoir by the side of the banker, and down go new stakes, doubled or lessened according to the success of the winners—again is drawled out the mechanical "all set," and the same routine is repeated until long past midnight, while the dealers are relieved every two or three hours by their fellow-partners in the house.

At the right hand of the dealer, upon the table, is placed what is denominated "the bank," though it is merely its representative. This is a shallow, yet heavy metal box, about twenty inches long, half as many wide, and two deep, with a strong network of wire, so constructed as to cover the box like a lid, and be secured by a lock. Casting my eye into this receptacle through its latticed top, I noticed several layers of U.S. bank notes, from five to five hundred dollars, which were kept down by pieces of gold laid upon each pile. About one-fifth of the case was parted off from the rest, in which were a very large number of gold ounces and rouleaus of guineas. The whole amount contained in it, so far as I could judge, was about six thousand dollars, while there was more than three thousand dollars in silver, piled openly and most temptingly upon the table around the case, in dollars, halves, and quarters, ready for immediate use. From policy, five franc pieces are substituted for dollars in playing; but the winner of any number of them can, when he ceases playing, immediately exchange them at the bank for an equal number of dollars. It often happens that players, either from ignorance or carelessness, leave the rooms with the five franc pieces; but should they, five minutes afterward, discover their neglect and return to exchange them, the dealer exclaims with an air of surprise—"Saar! it will be one mistake, saar. I nevair look you in de fas before, saar!" Thousands of dollars are got off annually in this manner, and a very pretty interest the banks derive from their ingenious method of *franking*.

Having seen some thousands of dollars change hands in the course of an hour, and, with feelings somewhat allied to pity, marked the expression of despair, darkening the features of the unfortunate loser, as he rushed from the room with clenched hands and bent brow, muttering indistinctly within his teeth fierce curses upon his luck; and observed, with no sympathizing sensations of pleasure, the satisfaction with which the winners hugged within their arms their piles of silver, we turned from the faro, and crossed the room to the roulette table. These two tables are as inseparable as the shark and the pilot fish, being always found together in every gambling room, ready to make prey of all who come within their influence. At faro there is no betting less than a dollar; here, stakes as low as a quarter are permitted. The players were more numerous at this table than at the former, and generally less genteel in their appearance. The roulette table is a large, long, green-covered board or platform, in the centre of which, placed horizontally upon a pivot, is a richly plated round mahogany table, or wheel, often inlaid with ivory and pearl, and elaborately carved, about two feet in diameter, with the bottom closed like an inverted box cover. Around this wheel, on the inner border, on alternate little black and red squares, are marked numbers as high as thirty-six, with two squares additional, in one a single cipher, in the other two ciphers; while on the green cloth-covered board, the same numbers are marked in squares. The dealer, who occupies one side of the table, with his metal, latticed case of bank notes and gold at his right hand, and piles of silver before him, sets the wheel revolving rapidly, and adroitly spins into it from the end of his thumb, as a boy would snap a marble, an ivory ball, one quarter the size of a billiard ball. The betters, at the same instant, place their money upon such one of the figures drawn upon the cloth as they fancy the most likely to favour them, and intently watch the ball as it races round within the revolving wheel. When the wheel stops, the ball necessarily rests upon some one of the figures in the wheel, and the fortunate player, whose stake is upon the corresponding number on the cloth, is immediately paid his winning, while the stakes of the losers are coolly transferred by the dealer to the constantly accumulating heap before him; again the wheel is set revolving, the little ball rattles around it, and purses are again made lighter and the bank increased.

As we were about to depart, I noticed in an interior room a table spread for nearly a dozen persons, and loaded with all the substantials for a hearty supper. The dealers, or conductors of the bank, are almost all bachelors, I believe, or ought to be, and keep "hall" accordingly, in the same building where lies their theatre of action, in the most independent and uproarious style. After the rooms are closed, which is at about two in the morning, they retire to their supper table, inviting all the betters, both winners and losers, who are present when the playing breaks up, to partake with them. The invitations are generally accepted; and those poor devils who in the course of the evening have been so unfortunate as to have "pockets to let," have at least the satisfaction of enjoying a good repast, *gratis,* before they go home and hang themselves.

SUNDAY IN NEW ORLEANS

The spacious bar-room of our magnificent hotel, as I descended to it on Sabbath morning, resounded to the footsteps of a hundred gentlemen, some promenading and in earnest conversation—some hastening to, or lounging about the bar, on which was displayed a row of rapidly disappearing glasses, containing the tempting, green-leaved, mint-julep—while others, some *tête à tête,* some smoking, were sipping in quiet their morning potation. A few, with legs *à la Trollope,* upon the tables, were reading stray papers, at the farther extremity of the hall.

My northern friend met me at the door of the hotel, around which, upon the side-walk, was gathered a knot of fashionably dressed, cane-wearing young men, talking, all together, of a duel. The morning was cloudless, the air mild. The sun shone down warm and as we passed from Camp-street across Canal, into Chartres-street, all the gay inhabitants, one would verily believe, had turned out as to a gala. The long, narrow streets were thronged with moving multitudes, and flashing with scarfs, ribbons, and feathers. Children, with large expressive eyes, their heads surmounted with tasselled caps and fancy hats, arrayed in their "brightest and best," bounded along behind their more soberly arrayed, but not less gay parents, followed by gaudily dressed slaves, who chattered incessantly with half-suppressed laughter to their acquaintances on the opposite trottoir. Clerks, just such looking young men as you will meet on Sabbath mornings in Broadway, or Cornhill—released from their six day's confinement—lounged by us arm in arm, as fine as the tailor and hair-dresser could make them. Crowds, or gangs of American and English sailors, mingling most companionably, on a cruise through the city, rolled jollily along—the same careless independent fellows that they are all the world over. I have observed that in foreign ports, the seamen of these once hostile nations link together like brothers. This is as it should be. The good feeling existing generally among all classes of Americans toward the mother country, must be gratifying both to reflecting Americans and to Englishmen.

These sons of Neptune were all dressed nearly alike in blue jackets, and full white trowsers, with black silk handkerchiefs knotted carelessly around their necks, and confined by some nautical breast-pin, in the shape of a foul anchor, a ship under her three top-sails, or plain gold hearts, pierced by arrows. Sailors are very sentimental fellows on shore! In direct contrast to these frank-looking, open-browed tars, who yawed along the side-walk, as a landsman would walk on a ship's deck at sea, we passed, near the head of Bienville-street, a straggling crew of some Spanish trader, clothed in tarry pantaloons and woollen shirts, and girt about with red and blue sashes, bucanier fashion, with filthy black whiskers, and stealthy glowing eyes, who glided warily along with lowering brows. The unsailor-like French sailor—the half horse and half alligator Kentucky boatman—the gentlemanly, carelessly-dressed cotton planter—the pale valetudinarian, from the north, whose deep sunken eye told of suicidal vigils over the midnight lamp—a noble looking foreigner, and a wretched beggar—a troop of Swiss emigrants, from the grandsire to the infant, and a gang of Erin's toil-worn exiles—all mingled *en masse*—swept along in this living current; while, gazing down upon the moving multitude from lofty balconies, were clusters of bright eyes, and sunny faces flashed from every window.

As we approached the cathedral, a dark-hued and finely moulded quadroon, with only a flowing veil upon her head, glided majestically past us. The elegant olive-browned Louisianese—the rosy-cheeked maiden from *La belle riviere*—the Parisian gentil-homme—a dignified, light-mustachoed palsgrave, and a portly sea-captain—the haughty Englishman and prouder southerner—a blanketed Choctaw, and a negro in uniform—slaves and freed-men of every shade, elbowed each other very familiarly as they traversed in various directions the crowded side-walks.

Crossing rue St. Louis, we came in collision with a party of gens d'armes with drawn swords in their hands, which they used as walking canes, leading an unlucky culprit to the callaboose—that "black-hole" of the city. Soldiers in splendid uniforms, with clashing and jingling accoutrements, were continually hurrying past us to parade.

At the corner of Toulouse-street we met a straggling procession of bareheaded, sturdy-looking priests, in soiled black surplices and fashionable boots, preceded by half a dozen white-robed boys, bare-legged and dirty. By this dignified procession, among which the crowd promiscuously mingled as they passed along, and whose august approach is usually notified by the jingling of the "sacring bell," was borne the sacred "host." They hastily passed us, shoved and jostled by the crowd, who scarcely gave way to them as they hastened on their ghostly message. These things are done differently in Buenos Ayres or Rio Janeiro, where such a procession is escorted by an armed guard, and a bayonet thrust, or a night in a Spanish prison, is the penalty for neglecting to genuflect, or uncover the heretical head.

As we issued from Chartres-street—where all "nations and kingdoms and tongues" seemed to have united to form its pageant of life—upon the esplanade in front of the cathedral, we were surprised by the sound of martial music pealing clearly above the confusion of tongues, the tramp of feet, and the rattling of carriages. On and around the noble green, soldiers in various uniforms, some of them of a gorgeous and splendid description, were assembling for parade. Members of the creole regiment—the finest body of military men I ever beheld, with the exception of a Brazilian regiment of blacks—were rapidly marshalling in the square. And mounted huzzars, with lofty caps and in glittering mail, were thundering in from the various streets, their spurs, chains and sabres, ringing and jingling warlike music, as they dashed up to the rendezvous.

At the head of this noble square, so variegated and tumultuous with its dazzling mimicry of war, rose in solemn and imposing grandeur the venerable cathedral, lifting its heavy towers high above the emmet-crowd beneath. Its doors, in front of which was extended a line of carriages, were thronged with a motley crowd, whose attention was equally divided between the religious ceremonies within the temple and the military display without. We forced our way through the mass, which was composed of strangers like ourselves—casual spectators—servants—hack-drivers—fruit sellers, and some few, who, like the publican, worshipped "afar off."

"Do you attend the *Theatre d'Orleans* to-night?" inquired a young Bostonian, forgetful of his orthodox habits—twirling while he spoke a ticket in his fingers—"you know the maxim—when in Rome"—

"I have not been here quite long enough yet to apply the rule," said I; "is not the theatre open on other evenings of the week?"

"Very seldom," he replied, "unless in the gayest part of the season—though I believe there is to be a performance some night this week; I will ascertain when and accompany you."

You are aware that the rituals, or established forms of the Roman church, do not prohibit amusements on this sacred day. The Sabbath, consequently, in a city, the majority of whose inhabitants are Catholics, is not observed as in the estimation of New-Englanders, or Protestants it should be. The lively Orleanese defend the custom of crowding their theatres, attending military parades, assembling in ballrooms, and mingling in the dangerous masquerade on this day, by wielding the scriptural weapon—"the Sabbath was made for man—not man for the Sabbath"; and then making their own inductions, they argue that the Sabbath is, literally, as the term imports, a day of rest, and not a day of religious labour.

That evening as I entered my room, I discovered, lying upon my table, a ticket for the American or Camp-street theatre, folded in a narrow slip of a play-bill, which informed me that the laughable entertainment of the "Three Hunchbacks," with the interesting play of "Cinderella," was to constitute the performance of the night: In a few moments afterward my Boston friend, who had left the ticket in my room, came in with another for the French theatre. I decided upon attending both, dividing the evening between them.

After tea we sallied out, in company with half of those who were at the supper-table, on our way to the theatre. The street and adjacent buildings shone brilliantly, with the glare of many lamps suspended from the theatre and coffee houses in the vicinity. A noisy crowd was gathered around the ticket-office—the side-walks were filled with boys and negroes—and the curbstone was lined with coloured females, each surrounded by bonbons, fruit, nuts, cakes, pies, gingerbread, and all the other et cetera of a "cake-woman's commodity." Entering the theatre, which is a plain handsome edifice, with a stuccoed front, and ascending a broad flight of steps, we passed across the first lobby, down a narrow aisle, opened through the centre of the boxes into the pit or *parquette,* as it is here termed, which is considered the eligible and fashionable part of the house. This is rather reversing the order of things as found with us at the north. The pews, or slips—for the internal arrangement, were precisely like those of a church—were cushioned with crimson materials, and filled with bonnetless ladies, with their heads dressed *à la Madonna.* We seated ourselves near the orchestra. The large green curtain still concealed the mimic world behind it; and I embraced the few moments of delay previous to its rising, to gaze upon this Thespian temple of the south, and a New Orleans audience.

The "parquette" was brilliant with bright eyes and pretty faces; and upon the bending galaxy of ladies which glittered in the front of the boxes around it, I seemed to gaze through the medium of a rainbow. There were, it must be confessed, some plain enough faces among them; but, at the first glance of the eye, one might verily have believed himself encircled by a gallery of houris. The general character of their faces was decidedly American; exactly such as one gazes upon at the Tremont or Park theatre; and I will henceforward eschew physiognomy, if "I guess" would not have dropped more naturally from the lips of one half who were before me, while conversing, than "I reckon."

There were but few French faces among the females; but, with two or three exceptions, these were extremely pretty. Most of the delicately-reared Creoles, or Louisiana ladies, are eminently beautiful. Their style of beauty is *unique,* and not easily classed. It is neither French nor English, but a combination of both, mellowed and enriched under a southern sky.

The interior of the house was richly decorated; and the paneling in the interior of the boxes was composed of massive mirror-plates, multiplying the audience with a fine effect. The stage was lofty, extensive, and so constructed, either intentionally or accidentally, as to reflect the voice with unusual precision and distinctness. The scenery was in general well executed: one of the forest scenes struck me as remarkably true to nature. While surveying the gaudy interior, variegated with gilding, colouring, and mirrors, the usual cry of "Down, down?—Hats off," warned us to be seated.

The performance was good for the pieces represented. The company, with the indefatigable Caldwell at its head, is strong and of a respectable character. When the second act was concluded we left the house; and passing through a parti-coloured mob, gathered around the entrance, and elbowing a gens d'armes or two, stationed in the lobby—we gained the street, amidst a shouting of "Your check, sir! your check!—Give me your check—Please give me your check!—check!—check!—check!" from a host of boys, who knocked one another about unmercifully in their exertions to secure prizes, which, to escape a mobbing, we threw into the midst of them; and jumping into a carriage in waiting, drove off to the French theatre, leaving them embroiled in a *pêle mêle,* in which the sciences of phlebotomy and phrenology were being "tested" by very practical applications.

After a drive of half a league or more through long and narrow streets, dimly lighted by swinging lamps, we were set down at the door of the Theatre d'Orleans, around which a crowd was assembled of as different a character, from that we had just escaped, as would have met our eyes had we been deposited before the *Theatre Royale* in Paris. The street was illuminated from the brilliantly lighted cafés and cabarets, clustered around this "nucleus" of gayety and amusement. As we crossed the broad *pavé* into the vestibule of the theatre, the rapidly enunciated, nasal sounds of the French language assailed our ears from every side. Ascending the stairs and entering the boxes, I was struck with the liveliness and brilliancy of the scene, which the interior exhibited to the eye. "Magnificent!" was upon my lips— but a moment's observation convinced me that its brilliancy was an illusion, created by numerous lights, and an artful arrangement and lavish display of gilding and colouring. The whole of the interior, including the stage decorations and scenic effect, was much inferior to that of the house we had just quitted.

The boxes—if caverns resembling the interior of a ship's longboat, with one end elevated three feet, and equally convenient, can be so called—were cheerless and uncomfortable. There were but few females in the house, and none of these were in the pit, as at the other theatre. Among them I saw but two or three pretty faces; and evidently none were of the first class of French society in this city. The house was thinly attended, presenting, wherever I turned my eyes, a "beggarly account of empty boxes."

After remaining half an hour, wearied with its tiresome *ritornello* of a popular French air—listening with the devotion of a "Polytechnique" to the blood-stirring Marseillaise hymn—amused at the closing scene of a laughable comédie, and edified by the first of a pantomime, and observing, that with but one lovely exception, the Mesdames *du scene* were very plain, and the Messieurs very handsome, we left the theatre and returned to the hotel, whose deserted bar-room, containing here and there a straggler, presented a striking contrast to the noise and bustle of the multitude by which it was thronged at noonday. In general, strangers consider the *tout ensemble* of this theatre on Sabbath evenings, and on others when the élite of the New-Orleans society is collected there, decidedly superior to that of any other in the United States.

A LOUISIANA SUGAR PLANTATION

A gentleman to whom I brought a letter of introduction called yesterday and invited me to ride with him to his plantation, a few miles from New Orleans. He drove his own phaeton, which was drawn by two beautiful long-tailed bays. After a drive of a mile and a half, we cleared the limits of the straggling, and apparently interminable faubourgs, and, emerging through a long narrow street upon the river road, bounded swiftly over its level surface, which was as smooth as a bowling-green—saving a mud-hole now and then, where a crevasse had let in upon it a portion of the Mississippi. An hour's drive, after clearing the suburbs, past a succession of isolated villas, encircled by slender columns and airy galleries, and surrounded by richly foliaged gardens, whose fences were bursting with the luxuriance which they could scarcely confine, brought us in front of a charming residence situated at the head of a broad, gravelled avenue, bordered by lemon and orange trees, forming in the heat of summer, by arching naturally overhead, a cool and shady promenade. We drew up at the massive gate-way and alighted. As we entered the avenue, three or four children were playing at its farther extremity, with noise enough for Christmas holidays; two of them were trundling hoops in a race, and a third sat astride of a non-locomotive wooden horse, waving a tiny sword, and charging at half a dozen young slaves, who were testifying their bellicose feelings by dancing and shouting around him with the noisiest merriment.

After playful and affectionate congratulations between the noble little fellows and their parent, we walked toward the house, preceded by our trundlers, with the young soldier hand-in-hand between us, followed close behind by the little Africans, whose round shining eyes glistened wistfully —speaking as plainly as eyes could speak the strong desire, with which their half-naked limbs evidently sympathized by their restless motions, to bound ahead, contrary to decorum, "wid de young massas!"

Around the semi-circular flight of steps, ascending to the piazza of the dwelling,—the columns of which were festooned with the golden jasmine and luxuriant multiflora,—stood, in large green vases, a variety of flowers, among which I observed the tiny flowerets of the diamond myrtle, sparkling like crystals of snow, scattered upon rich green leaves—the dark foliaged Arabian jasmine silvered with its opulently-leaved flowers redolent of the sweetest perfume,—and the rose-geranium, breathing gales of fragrance upon the air. From this point the main avenue branches to the right and left, into narrower, yet not less beautiful walks, which, lined with ever-green and flowering shrubs, completely encircled the cottage.

The proprietor of the delightful spot which lay spread out around me—a lake of foliage—fringed by majestic forest trees, and diversified with labyrinthyne walks,—had, the preceding summer, consigned to the tomb the mother of his "beautiful ones." They were under the care of a dignified lady, his sister, and the widow of a gentleman formerly distinguished as a lawyer in New-England. But like many other northern ladies, whose names confer honour upon our literature, and whose talents elevate and enrich our female seminaries of education, she had independence enough to rise superior to her widowed indigence; and had prepared to open a boarding school at the north, when the death of his wife led her wealthier brother to invite her to supply a mother's place to his children, to whom she was now both mother and governess.

The history of this lady is that of hundreds of her country-women. There are, I am informed, many instances in the south-west, of New-England's daughters having sought, with the genuine spirit of independence, thus to repair their broken fortunes. In this country the occupation of instructing, whether invested in the president of a college or in the teacher of a country school, is degraded to a secondary rank. In New-England, on the contrary, the lady of a living collegiate president is of the élite, decidedly, if not at the head, of what is there termed "good society." Here, the same lady, whether a visitor for the winter, or a settled resident, must yield in rank—as the laws of southern society have laid it down—to the lady of the planter. The south-erners, however, when they can secure one of our well-educated northern ladies in their families, know well how to appreciate their good fortune. In-mates of the family, they are treated with politeness and kindness; but in the soirée, dinner party, or levée, the governess is thrown more into the back-ground than she would be in a gentleman's family, even in aristocratic England; and her title to an equality with the gay, and fashionable, and wealthy circle by whom she is surrounded, and her challenge to the right of *caste,* is less readily admitted. This illiberal jealousy is the natural consequence of the crude state of American society, where the line of demarcation be-tween its rapidly forming classes is yet uncertainly defined, and each in-dividual who is anxious to be of the better file has to walk circumspectly lest he should be found mingling with the canaille.

After a kind of bachelor's dinner, in a hall open on two sides for ventila-tion, sumptuous enough for Epicurus, and served by two or three young slaves, who were drilled to a glance of the eye, crowned by a luxurious dessert of fruits and sweet-meats, and graced with wine, not of the vintage common in New England, but of the pure *outre-mer,* we proceeded to the sugar-house or *sucrérie,* through a lawn which nearly surrounded the ornamental grounds about the house, studded here and there with lofty trees, which the good taste of the original proprietor of the domain had left standing in their forest majesty. From this rich green sward, on which two or three fine saddle-horses were grazing, we passed through a turn-stile into a less lovely, but more domestic enclosure, alive with young negroes, sheep, turkies, hogs, and every variety of domestic animal that could be attached to a plantation. From this diversified collection, which afforded a tolerable idea of the interior of Noah's ark, we entered the long street of a village of white cottages, arranged on either side of it with great regularity. They were all exactly alike, and separated by equal spaces; and to every one was attached an enclosed piece of ground, apparently for a vegetable garden; around the doors decrepit and superannuated negroes were basking in the evening sun—mothers were nursing their naked babies, and one or two old and blind negresses were spinning in their doors. In the centre of the street, which was a hundred yards in width, rose to the height of fifty feet a framed belfry, from whose summit was suspended a bell, to regulate the hours of labour. At the foot of this tower, scattered over the grass, lay a half score of black children, *in puris naturalibus,* frolicking or sleeping in the warm sun, under the surveillance of an old African matron, who sat knitting upon a camp-stool in the midst of them.

We soon arrived at the boiling-house, which was an extensive brick building with tower-like chimneys, numerous flues, and a high, steep roof, reminding me of a New England distillery. As we entered after scaling a barrier of sugar-casks with which the building was surrounded, the slaves, who were dressed in coarse trowsers, some with and others without shirts, were engaged in the several departments of their sweet employment; whose fatigues some African Orpheus was lightening with a loud chorus, which was instantly hushed, or rather modified, on our entrance, to a half-assured whistling. A white man, with a very unpleasing physiognomy, carelessly leaned against one of the brick pillars, who raised his hat very respectfully as we passed, but did not change his position. This was the overseer. He held in his hand a short-handled whip, loaded in the butt, which had a lash four or five times the length of the staff. Without noticing us, except when addressed by his employer, he remained watching the motions of the toiling slaves, quickening the steps of a loiterer by a word, or threatening with his whip, those who, tempted by curiosity, turned to gaze after us, as we walked through the building.

The season of sugar-making is termed by the planters of the south, the "rolling season"; and a merry and pleasant time it is too. It commences about the middle or last of October, and continues from three weeks to as many months, according to the season and other circumstances; but more especially the force upon the plantation, and the amount of sugar to be made. As the season approaches, every thing assumes a new and more cheerful aspect. The negroes are more animated, as their winter clothing is distributed, their little crops are harvested, and their wood and other comforts secured for that season; which, to them, if not the freest, is certainly the gayest and happiest portion of the year. As soon as the corn crop and fodder are harvested, every thing is put in motion for the grinding. The horses and oxen are increased in number and better groomed; the carts and other necessary utensils are overhauled and repaired, and some hundred or thousand cords of wood are cut and ready piled for the manufacture of the sugar. The *sucrérie,* or boiling house, is swept and garnished—the mill and engine are polished—the kettles scoured—the coolers caulked, and the *purgerie,* or draining-house, cleaned and put in order, where the casks are arranged to receive the sugar.

The first labour in anticipation of grinding, is that of providing plants for the coming year; and this is done by cutting the cane, and putting it in *matelas,* or matressing it, as it is commonly called. The cane is cut and thrown into parcels in different parts of the field, in quantities sufficient to plant several acres, and so arranged that the tops of one layer may completely cover and protect the stalks of another. After the quantity required is thus secured, the whole plantation force, nearly, is employed in cutting cane, and conveying it to the mill. The cane is divested of its tops, which are thrown aside, unless they are needed for plants, which is often the case, when they are thrown together in rows, and carefully protected from the inclemencies of the weather. The stalks are then cut as near as may be to the ground, and thrown into separate parcels or rows, to be taken to the mill in carts, and expressed as soon as possible. The cane is sometimes bound together in bundles, in the field, which facilitates its transportation, and saves both time and trouble. As soon as it is harvested, it is placed upon a cane-carrier, so called, which conveys it to the mill, where it is twice expressed between iron rollers, and made perfectly dry. The juice passes into vats, or receivers, and the *baggasse* or cane-trash, (called in the West Indies *migass,*) is received into carts and conveyed to a distance from the sugar-house to be burnt as soon as may be. Immediately after the juice is expressed, it is distributed to the boilers, generally four in succession, ranged in solid masonry along the sides of the boiling-room, where it is properly tempered, and its purification and evaporation are progressively advanced. The French have commonly five boilers, distinguished by the fanciful names of *grande—propre—flambeau—sirop,* and *battérie.*

In the first an alkali is generally put to temper the juice; lime is commonly used, and the quantity is determined by the good judgment and experience of the sugar-maker. In the last kettle—the *teach* as it is termed—the sugar is concentrated to the granulating point, and then conveyed into coolers, which hold from two to three hogsheads. After remaining here for twenty-four hours or more, it is removed to the *purgerie,* or draining-house, and placed in hogsheads, which is technically called *potting.* Here it undergoes the process of draining for a few days or weeks, and is then ready for the market. The molasses is received beneath in cisterns, and when they become filled, it is taken out and conveyed into barrels or hogsheads and shipped. When all the molasses is removed from the cistern, an inferior kind of sugar is re-manufactured, which is called *cistern-sugar,* and sold at a lower price. When the grinding has once commenced, there is no cessation of labour till it is completed. From beginning to end, a busy and cheerful scene continues. The negroes work from eighteen to twenty hours though to lighten the burden as much as possible, the gang is divided into two watches, one taking the first, and the other the last part of the night; and notwithstanding this continued labour, the negroes improve in condition, and appear fat and flourishing. They drink freely of cane-juice, and the sickly among them revive and become robust and healthy.

After the grinding is finished, the negroes have several holidays, when they are quite at liberty to dance and frolic as much as they please; and the cane-song—which is improvised by one of the gang, the rest all joining in a prolonged and unintelligible chorus—now breaks night and day upon the ear, in notes "most musical, most melancholy." This over, planting recommences, and the same routine of labour is continued, with an intermission—except during the boiling season, as above stated—upon most, if not all plantations, of twelve hours in twenty-four, and of one day in seven throughout the year.

Leaving the sugar-house, I returned with my polite entertainer to the house. Lingering for a moment on the gallery in the rear of the dwelling-house, I dwelt with pleasure upon the scene which the domain presented.

The lawn, terminated by a snow-white paling, and ornamented here and there by a venerable survivor of the aboriginal forest, was rolled out before me like a carpet, and dotted with sleek cows, and fine horses, peacefully grazing, or indolently reclining upon the thick grass, chewing the cud of contentment. Beyond the lawn, and extending farther into the plantation, lay a pasture containing a great number of horses and cattle, playing together, reposing, feeding, or standing in social clusters around a shaded pool. Beyond, the interminable cane-field, or plantation proper, spread away without fence or swell, till lost in the distant forests which bounded the horizon. On my left, a few hundred yards from the house, and adjoining the pasture, stood the stables and other plantation appurtenances, constituting a village in themselves—for planters always have a separate building for everything. To the right stood the humble yet picturesque village or "Quarter" of the slaves, embowered in trees, beyond which, farther toward the interior of the plantation, arose the lofty walls and turreted chimneys of the sugar-house, which, combined with the bell-tower, presented the appearance of a country village with its church-tower and the walls of some public edifice, lifting themselves above the trees. Some of the sugar-houses are very lofty and extensive, with noble wings and handsome fronts, resembling—aside from their lack of windows—college edifices. It requires almost a fortune to construct one.

The whole scene before me was extremely animated. Human figures were moving in all directions over the place. Some labouring in the distant field, others driving the slow-moving oxen, with a long, drawling cry—half naked negro boys shouting and yelling, were galloping horses as wild as themselves —negresses of all sizes, from one able to carry a tub to the minikin who could "tote" but a pint-dipper, laughing and chattering as they went, were conveying water from a spring to the wash-house, in vessels adroitly balanced upon their heads. Slaves sinking under pieces of machinery, and other burdens, were passing and repassing from the boiling-house and negro quarter. Some were calling to others afar off, and the merry shouts of the black children at their sports in their village, reminding me of a school just let out, mingled with the lowing of cows, the cackling of geese, the bleating of lambs, the loud and unmusical clamour of the guinea-hen, agreeably varied by the barking of dogs, and the roaring of some young African rebel under maternal castigation.

Passing from this plantation scene through the airy hall of the dwelling, which opened from piazza to piazza through the house, to the front gallery, whose light columns were wreathed with the delicately leaved Cape-jasmine, rambling woodbine and honeysuckle, a lovlier and more agreeable scene met my eye. I stood almost embowered in the foliage of exotics and native plants, which stood upon the gallery in handsome vases of marble and China-ware. The main avenue opened a vista to the river through a paradise of althea, orange, lemon, and olive trees, and groves and lawns extended on both sides of this lovely spot, terminating at the villas of the adjoining plantations.

The Mississippi—always majestic and lake-like in its breadth—rolled past her turbid flood, dotted here and there by a market-lugger, with its black crew and clumsy sails. By the Levée, on the opposite shore, lay a brig, taking in a cargo of sugar from the plantation, whose noble colonnaded mansion rose like a palace above its low, grove-lined margin, and an English argosy of great size, with black spars and hull, was moving under full sail down the middle of the river.

As I was under the necessity of returning to the city the same evening, I took leave of the youthful family of my polite host, and rolling like the wind over the level road along the banks of the river, arrived in the city a few minutes after seven.

The Cotton Kingdom

A MISSISSIPPI STEAMBOAT: NEW ORLEANS TO NATCHEZ

Once more I am floating upon the "Father of rivers." New-Orleans, with its crowd of "mingled nations," is seen indistinctly in the distance. We are now doubling a noble bend in the river, which will soon hide the city from our sight; but scenes of rural enchantment are opening before us as we advance, which will amply and delightfully repay us for its absence.

Below us a few miles, indistinctly seen through the haze, a dense forest of masts, and here and there a tower, designate the emporium of commerce— the key of the mighty west. The banks are lined and ornamented with elegant mansions, displaying, in their richly adorned grounds, the wealth and taste of their possessors; while the river, now moving onward like a golden flood, reflecting the mellow rays of the setting sun, is full of life. Vessels of every size are gliding in all directions over its waveless bosom, while graceful skiffs dart merrily about like white-winged birds. Huge steamers are dashing and thundering by, leaving long trains of wreathing smoke in their rear. Carriages filled with ladies and attended by gallant horsemen, enliven the smooth road along the Levée; while the green banks of the Levée itself are

RIVERBOAT AT A "WOODING STATION"

covered with gay promenaders. A glimpse through the trees now and then, as we move rapidly past the numerous villas, detects the piazzas, filled with the young, beautiful, and aged of the family, enjoying the rich beauty of the evening, and of the objects upon which my own eyes rest with admiration.

The passengers have descended to the cabin; some to turn in, a few to read, but more to play at the ever-ready card table. The pilot (as the helmsman is here termed) stands in his lonely wheelhouse, comfortably enveloped in his blanket-coat—the hurricane deck is deserted, and the hands are gathered in the bows, listening to the narration of some ludicrous adventure of recent transaction in the city of hair-breadth escapes. Now and then a laugh from the merry auditors, or a loud roar from some ebony-cheeked fireman, as he pitches his wood into the gaping furnace, breaks upon the stillness of night, startling the echoes along the shores. How readily do we accustom ourselves to circumstances! The deep trombone of the steam-pipe—the regular splash of the paddles—and the incessant rippling of the water eddying away astern, as our noble vessel flings it from her sides, no longer affect the senses, unless it may be to lull them into a repose well meet for contemplation.

The plantations along the river extend from the Levée to the swamps in the rear; the distance across the belt of land being, from the irregular encroachment of the marshes, from one to two or three miles. These plantations have been, for a very long period, under cultivation for the production of sugar crops. As the early possessor of large tracts of land had sons to settle, they portioned off parallelograms to each; which, to combine the advantages of exportation and wood, extended from the river to the flooded forest in the rear. These, in time, portioned off to their children, while every occupant of a tract erected his dwelling at the head of his domain, one or two hundred yards from the river. Other plantations retain their original dimensions, crowned, on the borders of the river, with noble mansions, embowered in the ever-green foliage of the dark-leaved orange and lemon trees. The shores, consequently, present, from the lofty deck of a steamer,—from which can be had an extensive prospect of the level country—a very singular appearance.

As we approach Baton Rouge, the character of the scene changes. Hills once more relieve the eye, so long wearied with gazing upon a flat yet beautiful country.

We are now nearly opposite the town, which is pleasantly situated upon the declivity of the hill, retreating over its brow and spreading out on a plain in the rear, where the private dwellings are placed, shaded and half embowered in the rich foliage of that loveliest of all shade-trees, "the pride of China." The stores and other places of business are upon the front street, which runs parallel to the river. The site of the town is about forty feet above the highest flood, and rises by an easy and gentle swell from the water. The barracks, a short distance from the village, are handsome and commodious, constructed around a pentagonal area—four noble buildings forming four sides, while the fifth is open, fronting the river. The buildings are brick, with lofty colonnades and double galleries running along the whole front. The columns are yellow-stuccoed, striking the eye with a more pleasing effect, than the glare of red brick. The view of these noble structures from the river, as we passed, was very fine.

The rich and luxuriant character of the scenery, which charms and attracts the eye of the traveller as he ascends the Mississippi from New-Orleans to Baton Rouge, is now changed. A broad, turbid flood, rolling through a land of vast forests, alone meets the eye, giving sublime yet wild and gloomy features to the scene. On looking from the cabin window, I see only a long, unbroken line of cotton trees, with their pale green foliage, as dull and void of interest as a fog-bank. The opposite shore presents the same appearance; and so it is, with the occasional relief of a plantation and a "landing place," comprising a few buildings, the whole distance to Natchez. A wretched cabin, now and then, varies the wild appearance of the banks—the home of some solitary wood-cutter.

Having secured a berth in one corner of the spacious cabin, where I could draw the rich crimsoned curtains around me, and with book or pen pass the time somewhat removed from the bustle, and undisturbed by the constant passing of the restless passengers, I began this morning to look about me upon my fellow-travellers, seeking familiar faces, or scanning strange ones.

Our passengers are a strange medley, not only representing every state and territory washed by this great river, but nearly every Atlantic and trans-Atlantic state and nation. In the cabin are the merchants and planters of the "up country"; and on deck, emigrants and return-boatmen. There are about forty passengers of both sexes. Two of the most genteel-looking among them, so far as dress goes, I am told, are professed "black-legs"; or, as they more courteously style themselves, "sporting gentlemen."—There is an organized body of these *ci-devant* gentry upon the river, who have local agents in every town, and travelling agents on board the principal steamboats. In the guise of gentlemen, they "take in" the unwary passenger and unskilful player, from whom they often obtain large sums of money. As the same sportsmen do not go twice in the same boat, the captains do not become so familiar with their persons as to refuse them passage, were they so inclined. It is very seldom, however, when they are known, that they are denied a passage, as gambling is not only permitted but encouraged on most of the boats, by carrying a supply of cards in the bar. Even the sanctity of the Sabbath is no check to this amusement: all day yesterday the tables were surrounded with players, at two of which they were dealing "faro"; at the third playing "brag." Indeed the day was utterly disregarded by nearly every individual on board. Travelling is a sad demoralizer.

There are several French gentlemen on board; one important looking personage, who bears the title of general, and seems to feel the dignity it confers; three or four Mississippi cotton planters, in large, low-crowned, broad-brimmed, white fur hats, wearing their clothes in a careless, half sailor-like, half gentleman-like air, dashed with a small touch of the farmer, which style of dressing is peculiar to the Mississippi country gentleman. They are talking about negroes, railroads, and towing shipping. There is also a travelling Yankee lawyer, in a plain, stiff, black coat, closely buttoned up to his chin, strait trowsers, narrow hat, and gloves—the very antipodes, in appearance, to the *non chalant,* easy, care-for-nothing air of his southern neighbours.

A Methodist minister, in a bottle-green frock coat, fancy vest, black stock, white pantaloons and white hat, is sitting apart by the stove, deeply engaged upon the pages of a little volume, like a hymn-book. Any other dress than uniform black for a minister, would, at the north, be deemed highly improper, custom having thus so decided; but here they wear just what Providence sends them or their own taste dictates.

There are two or three fat men, in gray and blue—a brace of bluff, manly-looking Germans—a lynx-eyed, sharp-nosed New-York speculator—four old French Jews, with those noble foreheads, arched brows, and strange-expressioned eyes, that look as though always weeping—the well-known and never to be mistaken characteristic of this remarkable people. The remainder of our passengers present no peculiarities worth remarking. So I throw them all in, tall and short, little and big, and all sorts and sizes, to complete the motley *"ensemble"* of my fellow-travellers.

Among the ladies are a beautiful, dark-eyed, dark-haired Virginian, and an intelligent, young married lady from Vermont, accompanied by her only child, a handsome, spirited boy, between four and five years of age. His mother possessed a highly cultivated mind, and her full share of Yankee inquisitiveness. She was always resolved that nothing worthy of observation should escape her. She was a pure New-England interrogative. With a southerner I might have journied from Montreal to Mexico, without being questioned as often as I have been in this short passage. When a northerner is not inquisitive, the fact may generally be ascribed to intellectual dullness; in a southerner to constitutional indolence.

THE PLANTERS OF MISSISSIPPI

The towns and villages of Mississippi, as in European states, are located perfectly independent of each other, isolated among its forests, and often many leagues apart, leaving in the intervals large tracts of country covered with plantations, and claiming no minuter subdivision than that of "county." Natchez, for instance, is a corporation one mile square, but from the boundaries of the city to Woodville, the next incorporated town south, there is an interval of thirty-eight miles. It is necessary for the planters who reside between towns so far asunder, to have some more particular address, than the indefinite one arising from their vicinity to one or other of these towns. Hence has originated the pleasing custom of naming estates, as in England; and the names so given are always regarded by the planters themselves, and by the community, as an inseparable part of their address. These names are generally selected with taste, such as "Monmouth," "Laurel-hill," "Grange," "Magnolia grove," "The Forest," "Cottage," "Briars," "Father land," and "Anchorage"—the last given by a retired navy officer to his plantation. The name is sometimes adopted with reference to some characteristic of the domain, as "The Oaks," "China grove," "New Forest," &c., but more frequently it is a mere matter of fancy.

Towns in this state have usually originated from the location of a county seat, after the formation of a new county. Here the court-house is placed, and forms the centre of an area which is soon filled with edifices and inhabitants. If the county lies on a river, another town may arise, for a shipping port, but here the accumulation of towns usually ceases. A county seat, and a cotton mart, are all that an agricultural country requires. The towns in this state are thus dispersed two or three to each county, nor so long as this is a planting country, will there be any great increase in their number.

Each town is the centre of a circle which extends many miles around it into the country, and daily attracts all within its influence. The ladies come in their carriages "to shop," the gentlemen, on horseback, to do business with their commission merchants, visit the banks, hear the news, dine together at the hotels, and ride back in the evening. The southern town is properly the "Exchange" for the neighbouring planters, and the "Broadway" for their wives and daughters. And as no plantation is without a private carriage, the number of these gay vehicles, filling the streets of the larger towns on pleasant mornings in the winter, is surprising. I have counted between thirty and forty private carriages in the streets of Natchez in one morning. Showy carriages and saddle horses are the peculiar characteristics of the "moving spectacle" in the streets of south-western towns.

Every village is a nucleus of southern society, to which the least portion is generally contributed by itself. When a public ball is given by the bachelors, in one of these towns—for private parties are scarcely known—the tickets of invitation fly into the retirement of the plantations, within the prescribed circle, often to the distance of thirty miles. Thus families, who reside several leagues apart, meet together, like the inhabitants of one city. This state of things unites, in a social bond, the intelligent inhabitants of a large extent of country, who are nearly equally wealthy, and creates a state of society in the highest degree favourable to hospitality and social feeling. During the season of gayety, in the winter months, the public assemblies and private coteries of Natchez are unsurpassed by those of any other city, in the elegance, refinement, or loveliness of the individuals who compose them.

But fashion and refinement are not confined to Natchez. In nearly every county reside opulent planters, whose children enjoy precisely the same advantages as are afforded in the city. Drawn from the seclusion of their plantations, their daughters are sent to the north; whence they return, in the course of time, with cultivated minds and elegant manners. Hence every village can draw around it a polished circle of its own; for refinement and wealth do not always diminish here, as in New-England, in the inverse ration of distance from a metropolis—and elegant women may often be found blooming in the depths of forest far in the interior.

It is worthy of remark that those communities composed principally of young Mississippians, are distinguished by much less dissipation and adherence to the code of honour than such as are formed of young men principally from the northern and Atlantic southern states. The young Mississippian is not the irascible, hot-headed, and quarrelsome being he has generally been represented, although naturally warm-hearted and full of generous feelings, and governed by a high sense of honour. He is seldom a beau or a buck in the city acceptance of those terms, but dresses plainly—as often in pantaloons of Kentucky jean, a broad brimmed white hat, brogans and a blanket coat, as in any other style of vesture. Nevertheless he knows how to be well-dressed; and the public assemblies of the south-west boast more richly attired young gentlemen than are often found in the assembly-rooms of the Atlantic cities. He is educated to become a farmer—an occupation which requires and originates plainness of manners—and not to shine in the circles of a city.

I made several excursions to plantations two hour's ride from the city of Natchez. In the first mile a huge colonnaded structure, crowning an abrupt eminence near the road, struck my eyes with an imposing effect. It was the abode of one of the wealthiest planters of this state; who, like the majority of those families who now roll in their splendid equipages, has been the maker of his fortune. The grounds about this edifice were neglected; horses were grazing around the piazzas, over which were strewed saddles, whips, horse blankets, and the motley paraphernalia with which planters love to lumber their galleries. On nearly every piazza in Mississippi may be found a washstand, bowl, pitcher, towel, and water-bucket, for general accommodation. But the southern gallery is not constructed, like those at the north, for ornament or ostentation, but for use. Here they wash, lounge, often sleep, and take their meals.—Here will the stranger or visitor be invited to take a chair, or recline upon a sofa, settee, or form, as the taste and ability of the host may have furnished this important portion of a planter's house.

I once called on a planter within an hour's ride of Natchez, whose income would constitute a fortune for five or six modest Yankees. I entered the front yard—a green level, shaded with the relics of a forest—the live oak, sycamore, and gum trees—through a narrow wicket in a white-washed paling, the most common fence around southern dwellings. In the front yard were several sheep, colts, calves, two or three saddle and a fine pair of carriage-horses, negro children, and every variety of domestic fowl. The planter was sitting upon the gallery, divested of coat, vest, and shoes, with his feet on the railing, playing, in high glee, with a little dark-eyed boy and two young negroes, who were chasing each other under the bridge formed by his extended limbs. Three or four noble dogs, which his voice and the presence of his servant, who accompanied me to the house, kept submissive, were couching like leopards around his chair. A litter of young bull-headed pups lay upon a blanket under a window opening into a bed-room, white with curtains and valances; while a domestic tabby sat upon the window-sill, gazing musingly down upon the rising generation of her hereditary foes, perhaps with reflections not of the most pleasing cast. A hammock, suspended between an iron hook driven into the side of the house and one of the slender columns which supported the sloping roof of the gallery, contained a youth of fourteen, a nephew of the planter, fast locked in the embraces of Morpheus; whose *aid-de-camp,* in the shape of a strapping negress, stood by the hammock, waving over the sleeper a long plume of gorgeous feathers of the pea-fowl—that magnificent bird of the south, which struts about the ground of the planter, gratifying the eye with the glorious emblazonry upon his plumage by day, and torturing the ear with his loud clamours by night. A pair of noble antlers was secured to one of the pillars, from whose branches hung broad-brimmed hats, bridles, a sheep-skin covering to a saddle, which reposed in one corner of the piazza, a riding whip, a blanket coat or capote, spurs, surcingle, and part of a coach harness. A rifle and a shot-gun with an incredibly large bore, were suspended in beckets near the hall entrance; while a couple of shot-pouches, a game-bag, and other sporting apparatus, hung beside them. Slippers, brogans, a pillow, indented as though recently deserted, a gourd, and a broken "cotton slate," filled up the picture, whose original, in some one or other of its features, may be found in nearly every planter's dwelling in this state.

There are many private residences, in the vicinity of Natchez, of an equally expensive character with the one which furnished the above description, whose elegant interiors, contrasting with the neglected grounds about them, suggest the idea of a handsome city residence, accidentally dropped upon a bleak hill, or into the midst of a partially cleared forest, and there remaining, with its noble roof grasped by the arms of an oak, and its windows and columns festooned by the drooping moss, heavily waving in the wind. Thus are situated many of the planters' dwellings, separated from the adjacent forests by a rude, white-washed picket, enclosing around the house an un-ornamented green, or grazing lot, for the saddle and carriage-horses, which can regale their eyes at pleasure, by walking up to the parlour windows and gazing in upon handsome carpets, elegant furniture, costly mantel ornaments, and side-boards loaded with massive plate; and, no doubt, ruminate philosophically upon the reflection of their figures at full-length in long, richly-framed mirrors. Very few of the planters' villas, even within a few miles of Natchez, are adorned with surrounding ornamental shrubbery walks, or any other artificial auxiliaries of the natural scenery, except a few shade trees and a narrow, gravelled avenue from the gate to the house. A long avenue of trees, ornamenting and sheltering the approach to a dwelling, is a rare sight in this state, though very frequently seen in Louisiana. Every plantation residence is approached by an avenue, often nearly a mile in length; yet so little attention is paid to this species of ornament and comfort, in a climate where shade is a synonym for luxury, that scarcely one of them is shaded, except where, in their course through a forest, nature has flung the broad arms of majestic trees across the path.

You will judge from this state of things, that the Mississippi planters are not a showy and stylish class, but a plain, practical body of men, who, in general, regard comfort, and conformity to old habits, rather than display and fashionable innovations; and who would gaze with more complacency upon an acre of their domain, whitened, like a newly-washed flock, with cotton, than were it spread out before them magnificent with horticulture, or beautifully velveted with green. They never relax their exertions to add to their incomes; and this ever will be the case with the planter, so long as he can, by his efforts, annually increase his revenue ten or twenty thousand dollars. To the immense profit which every acre and the labour of every slave yield the planter, and to no other cause, is to be referred the anomalous result manifested in neglecting to improve their estates: for an acre, that will yield them sixty dollars per annum, and a slave, whose annual labour will yield from two to five hundred dollars, are, by the laws which regulate the empire of money, to be appropriated to the service of interest, to the entire exclusion of the claims of taste.

A plantation well stocked with hands, is the *ne plus ultra* of every man's ambition who resides at the south. Young men who come to this country, "to make money," soon catch the mania, and nothing less than a broad plantation, waving with the snow white cotton bolls, can fill their mental vision, as they anticipate by a few years in their dreams of the future, the result of their plans and labours. Hence, the great number of planters and the few professional men of long or eminent standing in their several professions. In such a state of things no men grow old or gray in their profession if at all successful. As soon as the young lawyer acquires sufficient to purchase a few hundred acres of the rich alluvial lands, and a few slaves, he quits his profession at once, though perhaps just rising into eminence, and turns cotton planter. The bar at Natchez is composed, with but few exceptions, entirely of young men. Ten years hence, probably not four out of five of these, if living, will remain in their profession. To the prevalence of this custom of retiring so early from the bar, and not to want of talent, is to be attributed its deficiency of distinguished names. There is much talent now concentrated at this bar, and throughout the state. But its possessors are young men; and this mania for planting will soon deprive the state of any benefit from it in a professional point of view. As the lawyers are young, the judges cannot of course be much stricken in years. The northerner, naturally associates with the title of "Judge," a venerable, dignified personage, with locks of snow, a suit of sober black, and powdered queue, shoe-buckles, and black silk stockings. Judge my surprise at hearing at the public table a few days since, a young gentleman, apparently not more than four or five and twenty, addressed as "judge"! I at first thought it applied as a mere *"soubriquet,"* till subsequently assured that he was really on the bench.

Physicians make money much more rapidly than lawyers, and sooner retire from practice and assume the planter. They, however, retain their titles, so that medico-planters are now numerous, far out-numbering the regular practitioners, who have not yet climbed high enough up the wall to leap down into a cotton field on the other side. Ministers, who constitute the third item of the diploma'd triad, are not free from the universal mania, and as writing sermons is not coining money, the plantations are like the vocative in Latin pronouns. The merchant moves onward floundering through invoices, ledgers, packages, and boxes. The gin-wright and overseer, also have an eye upon this Ultima Thule, while the more wealthy mechanics begin to form visions of cotton fields, and talk knowingly upon the "staple." Even editors have an eye that way!

Cotton and negroes are the constant theme—the ever harped upon, never worn out subject of conversation among all classes. But a small portion of the broad rich lands of this thriving state is yet appropriated. Not till every acre is purchased and cultivated—not till Mississippi becomes one vast cotton field, will this mania, which has entered into the very marrow, bone and sinew of a Mississippian's system, pass away. And not then, till the lands become exhausted and wholly unfit for farther cultivation. The rich loam which forms the upland soil of this state is of a very slight depth—and after a few years is worn away by constant culture and the action of the winds and rain. The fields are then "thrown out" as useless. Every plough-furrow becomes the bed of a rivulet after heavy rains—these uniting are increased into torrents, before which the impalpable soil dissolves like ice under a summer's sun. By degrees, acre after acre, of what was a few years previous beautifully undulating ground, waving with the dark green, snow-crested cotton, presents a wild scene of frightful precipices, and yawning chasms, which are increased in depth and destructively enlarged after every rain. There are many thousand acres within twenty miles of the city of Natchez, being the earliest cultivated portions of the country, which are now lying in this condition, presenting appearance of wild desolation, and not unfrequently, of sublimity. This peculiar feature of the country intrudes itself into every rural prospect, painfully marring the loveliest country that ever came from the hand of nature. Natchez itself is nearly isolated by a deep ravine, which forms a natural moat around the town. It has been formed by "washing," and though serpentine and irregular in its depth, it is cut with the accuracy of a canal. It is spanned by bridges along the several roads that issue from the town.

From the loose and friable nature of this soil, which renders it so liable to "wash," as is the expressive technical term here, the southwest portion of this state must within a century become waste, barren, and wild, unless peradventure, some inventing Yankee, or other patentee may devise a way of remedying the evil and making the wilderness to "blossom like the rose." A thick bluish green grass, termed Bermuda grass, is used with great success to check the progress of a *wash* when it has first commenced. It is very tenacious of the soil, takes firm and wide root, grows and spreads rapidly, and soon forms a compact matted surface, which effectually checks any farther increase of the ravines, or "bayous," as these deep chasms are usually termed; though bayou in its original signification is applied to creeks, and deep glens, with or without running water.

When this state was first settled, tobacco was exclusively cultivated as the grand staple. But this plant was found to be a great exhauster of the soil; cotton rapidly superseded its culture, and it was shortly banished from the state, and found a home in Tennessee, where it is at present extensively cultivated. It has not for many years been cultivated here. Planters have no room for any thing but their cotton, and corn, on their plantations, and scarcely are they willing to make room even for the latter, as they buy a great part of their corn, annually, from the Kentucky and Indiana flat boats at the "Landing."*

Among northerners, southern planters are reputed wealthy. This idea is not far from correct—as a class they are so; perhaps more so than any other body of men in America. Like our Yankee farmers they are tillers of the soil. "But why" you may ask, "do they who are engaged in the same pursuits as the New-England farmer, so infinitely surpass him in the reward of his labours?" The northern farmer cannot at the most make more than three per cent on his farm. He labours himself, or pays for labour. He *must* do the first or he cannot live. If he does the latter, he can make nothing. If by hard labour and frugal economy, the common independent Yankee farmer, such as the traveller meets with any where in New-England, lays up annually from four to seven hundred dollars, he is a thriving man and "getting rich." His daughters are attractive, and his sons will have something "handsome" to begin the world with.

But the southern farmer can make from fifteen to thirty per cent by his farm. He works on his plantation a certain number of slaves, say thirty, which are to him what the sinewy arms of the Yankee farmer are to himself. Each slave ought to average from seven to eight bales of cotton during the season, especially on the new lands. An acre will generally average from one to two bales. Each bale averages four hundred pounds, at from twelve to fifteen cents a pound. This may not be an exact estimate, but it is not far from the true one. Deducting two thousand and five hundred dollars for the expenses of the plantation, there will remain the net income of eleven thousand dollars. Now suppose this plantation and slaves to have been purchased on a credit, paying at the rate of six hundred dollars apiece for his negroes, the planter would be able to pay for nearly two-thirds of them the first year. The second year, he would pay for the remainder, and purchase ten or twelve more; and the third year, if he had obtained his plantation on a credit of that length of time, he would pay for that also, and commence his fourth year with a valuable plantation, and thirty-five or forty slaves, all his own property,

* Near this spot is a silver mine lately re-discovered, after the lapse of a third of a century. The owner found it difficult, however, to engage the neighbouring planters in his scheme of working it, for what planter would exchange his cotton fields for a silver mine?

with an increased income for the ensuing year of some thousands of dollars. Henceforward, if prudent, he will rank as an opulent planter.

Success is not however always in proportion to the outlay or expectations of the aspirant for wealth. It is modified and varied by the wear and tear, sickness and death, fluctuations of the market, and many other ills to which all who adventure in the great lottery of life are heirs. In the way above alluded to, numerous plantations in this state have been commenced, and thus the wealth of a great number of the opulent planters of this region has originated. Incomes of twenty thousand dollars are common here. Several individuals possess incomes of from forty to fifty thousand dollars, and live in a style commensurate with their wealth. The amount is generally expressed by the number of their negroes, and the number of "bales" they make at a crop. To know the number of either is to know accurately their incomes. And as this is easily ascertained, it is not difficult to form a prompt estimate of individual wealth. So you perceive that a Yankee farmer and a southern planter are birds of a very different feather.

Men here seem to feel the truth of the maxim of Bacon, that "territory newly acquired and not settled, is a matter of burthen rather than of strength": for they are spreading over it like a cloud, and occupying the vast tracts called "the Purchase," recently obtained from the Indians, previous to their removal to the west. The tide of emigration is rapidly setting to the north and east portions of the state. Planters, who have exhausted their old lands in this vicinity, are settling and removing to these new lands, which will soon become the richest cotton growing part of Mississippi. Parents do not now think of settling their children on plantations near Natchez, but purchase for them in the upper part of the state. Small towns, with "mighty names," plucked from the ruins of some long since mouldered city of classic fame and memory, are springing up here and there, like mushrooms, amidst the affrighted forests. Sixteen new counties have lately been created in this portion of the state, where so recently the Indian tracked his game and shrieked his warwhoop; and as an agricultural state, the strength and sinew of Mississippi must be hereafter concentrated in this fresher and younger portion of her territory.

THE MISSISSIPPI SLAVE TRADE

"Will you ride with me into the country?" said a young planter. "I am about purchasing a few negroes, and a peep into a slave-mart may not be uninteresting to you." I readily embraced the opportunity and in a few minutes our horses were at the door.

Crossing Cotton Square we entered upon the great northern road leading to Jackson. Here a sudden clanking of chains, startled our horses, and the next instant a gang of negroes, in straggling procession, followed by an ordinary looking white man armed with a whip, emerged from one of the streets. Each negro carried slung over his shoulder a polished iron ball, suspended by a heavy ox chain five or six feet in length and secured to the right ancle by a massive ring. They moved along under their burthen—some with idealess faces, looking the mere animal, others with sullen and dogged looks, and others again talking and laughing. This galley-looking procession was what is very appropriately termed the "Chain gang," a fraternity well known in New-Orleans and Natchez, and valued for its services in cleaning and repairing the streets. In the former city however there is one for whites as well as blacks. These gangs are merely moving penitentiaries, appropriating that amount of labour, which at the north is expended within four walls, to the broader limits of the city. In Natchez, negro criminals only are thus honoured—a "coat of tar and feathers" being applied to those white men who may require discipline not provided by the courts.

"The Chain gang," consists of insubordinate negroes and slaves, who, having run away from their masters, have been taken up and confined in jail, to await the reclamation of their owners; during the interval elapsing between their arrest and the time of their liberation by their masters, they are daily led forth from the prison to work on the streets, under the charge of an overseer. The punishment is considered very degrading, and merely the threat of the Calaboose, or the "ball and chain," will often intimidate and render submissive the most incorrigible.

When a runaway is apprehended he is committed to jail, and an advertisement describing his person and wearing apparel, is inserted in the newspaper for six months, if he is not claimed in the interim; at the expiration of which period he may be sold at auction, and the proceeds, after deducting all expenses, go to the use of the county. Should the owner subsequently claim and prove his property, the amount paid into the treasury, on account of the sale, is refunded to him. An owner, making his claim before the six months have expired, and proving his property before a justice of the peace, is allowed to take him away on producing a certificate to that effect from the justice, and paying the expenses incurred in the apprehension and securing of his slave. All runaways, or suspected runaways, may lawfully be apprehended, and carried before a justice of the peace, who at his discretion may either commit them to jail, or send them to the owner, and the person by whom the arrest was made, is entitled to six dollars for each, on delivering him to his master.

A mile from Natchez we came to a cluster of rough wooden buildings, in the angle of two roads, in front of which several saddle-horses, either tied or held by servants, indicated a place of popular resort.

"This is the slave market," said my companion, pointing to a building in the rear; and alighting, we left our horses in charge of a neatly dressed yellow boy belonging to the establishment. Entering through a wide gate into a narrow court-yard, partially enclosed by low buildings, a scene of a novel character was at once presented. A line of negroes, commencing at the entrance with the tallest, who was not more than five feet eight or nine inches in height—for negroes are a low rather than a tall race of men—down to a little fellow about ten years of age, extended in a semicircle around the right side of the yard. There were in all about forty. Each was dressed in the usual uniform of slaves, when in market, consisting of a fashionably shaped, black fur hat, roundabout and trowsers of coarse corduroy velvet, precisely such as are worn by Irish labourers, when they first "come over the water"; good vests, strong shoes, and white cotton shirts, completed their equipment. This dress they lay aside after they are sold, or wear out as soon as may be; for the negro dislikes to retain the indication of his having recently been in the market. With their hats in their hands, which hung down by their sides, they stood perfectly still, and in close order, while some gentlemen were passing from one to another examining for the purpose of buying. With the exception of displaying their teeth when addressed, and rolling their great white eyes about the court—they were so many statues of the most glossy ebony.

As we entered the mart, one of the slave merchants—for a "lot" of slaves is usually accompanied, if not owned, by two or three individuals—approached us, saying "Good morning, gentlemen! Would you like to examine my lot of boys? I have as fine a lot as ever came into market."—We approached them, one of us as a curious spectator, the other as a purchaser; and as my friend passed along the line, with a scrutinizing eye—giving that singular look, peculiar to the buyer of slaves as he glances from head to foot over each individual—the passive subjects of his observations betrayed no other signs of curiosity than that evinced by an occasional glance. The entrance of a stranger into a mart is by no means an unimportant event to the slave, for every stranger may soon become his master and command his future destinies. But negroes are seldom strongly affected by any circumstances, and their reflections never give them much uneasiness. To the generality of them, life is mere animal existence, passed in physical exertion or enjoyment. This is the case with the field hands in particular, and more so with the females than the males, who through a long life seldom see any other white person than their master or overseer, or any other gentleman's dwelling than the "great hus," the "white house" of these little domestic empires in which they are the subjects. To this class a change of masters is a matter of indifference;—they are handed from one to another with the passiveness of a purchased horse. These constitute the lowest rank of slaves, and lowest grade in the scale of the human species. Domestic and city slaves form classes of a superior order, though each constitutes a distinct class by itself. I shall speak of these more fully hereafter.

"For what service in particular did you want to buy?" inquired the trader of my friend, "A coachman." "There is one I think may suit you, sir," said he; "George, step out here." Forthwith a light-coloured negro, with a fine figure and good face, bating an enormous pair of lips, advanced a step from the line, and looked with some degree of intelligence, though with an air of indifference, upon his intended purchaser.

"How old are you, George?" he inquired. "I don't recollect, sir, 'zactly—b'lieve I'm somewhere 'bout twenty-dree.'" "Where were you raised?" "On master R——'s farm in Wirginny." "Then you are a Virginia negro." "Yes, master, me full blood Wirginny." "Did you drive your master's carriage?" "Yes, master, I drove ole missus' carage, more dan four year." "Have you a wife?" "Yes, master, I lef' young wife in Richmond, but I got new wife here in de lot. I wishy you buy her, master, if you gwine to buy me."

Then came a series of the usual questions from the intended purchaser. "Let me see your teeth—your tongue—open your hands—roll up your sleeves —have you a good appetite? are you good tempered? "Me get mad some-time," replied George to the last query, "but neber wid my horses." "What do you ask for this boy, sir?" inquired the planter, after putting a few more questions to the unusually loquacious slave. "I have held him at one thousand dollars, but I will take nine hundred and seventy-five cash. The bargain was in a few minutes concluded, and my companion took the negro at nine hundred and fifty, giving negotiable paper—the customary way of paying for slaves—at four months. It is, however, generally understood, that if servants prove unqualified for the particular service for which they are bought, the sale is dissolved. So there is in general perfect safety in purchasing servants untried, and merely on the warrant of the seller.

George, in the meanwhile, stood by, with his hat in his hand, apparently unconcerned in the negotiations going on, and when the trader said to him, "George, the gentleman has bought you; get ready to go with him," he appeared gratified at the tidings, and smiled upon his companions apparently quite pleased, and then bounded off to the buildings for his little bundle. In a few minutes he returned and took leave of several of his companions, who, having been drawn up into line only to be shown to purchasers, were now once more at liberty, and moving about the court, all the visiters having left except my friend and myself. "You mighty lucky, George," said one, congratulating him, "to get sol so quick," "Oh, you neber min', Charly," replied the delighted George; "your turn come soon too."

"You know who you' master be—whar he live?" said another. "No, not zactly; he lib on plantation some whar here 'bout." After taking leave of his companions, George came, hat in hand, very respectfully, to his purchaser, and said, "Young master, you never be sorry for buy George; I make you a good servant. But—beg pardon, master—but—if master would be so good as buy Jane—" "Who is Jane?"—"My wife, since I come from Wirginny. She good wife and a good girl—she good seamstress an' good nurse—mek de nice shirts and ebery ting."

"Where is she, George?" "Here she be, master," said he, pointing to a bright mulatto girl, about eighteen, with a genteel figure and a lively countenance, who was waiting with anxiety the reply of the planter. Opposite to the line of males was also a line of females, extended along the left side of the court. They were about twenty in number, dressed in neat calico frocks, white aprons and capes, and fancy kerchiefs, tied in a mode peculiar to the negress, upon their heads. Their whole appearance was extremely neat and "tidy." They could not be disciplined to the grave silence observed by the males, but were constantly laughing and chattering with each other in suppressed voices, and appeared to take, generally, a livelier interest in the transactions in which all were equally concerned. The planter approached this line of female slaves, and inquired of the girl her capabilities as seamstress, nurse, and ironer. Her price was seven hundred and fifty dollars. He said he would take her to his family; and if the ladies were pleased with her, he would purchase her. The poor girl was as much delighted as though already purchased; and, at the command of the trader, went to prepare herself to leave the mart. Some other negroes were purchased, several of whom appeared merely powerful combinations of bone and muscle, and the only idea suggested to the mind, in gazing upon them, was of remarkable physical energy. In the dull eye and fleshy mouth there was no expression indicative of intellect.

The increased demand for slaves led many farmers in Virginia, whose lands were unavailable, to turn their attention to raising slaves, if I may so term it, for the south-western market. Hence a nursery for slaves has been imperceptibly forming in that state, till now, by a sort of necessity, a vast amount of its capital is involved in this trade, the discontinuance of which would be as injurious in a pecuniary point of view, to those who raise them, as the want of the facilities which the trade affords, would be to the planter. Thus Virginia has become the field for the purchaser, and the phrase—"he is gone to Virginia to buy negroes," or "niggers," as is the elegant and equally common phraseology, is as often applied to a temporarily absent planter, as "he is gone to Boston to buy goods," to a New-England country merchant.

Negroes are transported here both by sea and land. Alexandria and Norfolk are the principal depots of slaves, previous to their being shipped. To these cities they are brought from the surrounding country, and sold to the slave-trader, who purchases them for about one-half or one-third less than he expects to obtain for them in the southern market. After the resident slave-dealer has collected a sufficient number, he places them under the care of an agent. They are then shipped for New-Orleans, with as comfortable accommodations as can be expected, where one or two hundred are congregated in a single merchant vessel. I have seen more than one hundred landing from a brig, on the Levée, in New-Orleans, in fine condition, looking as lively and hearty as though a sea voyage agreed well with them. They are transferred, if destined for the Mississippi market, to a steamboat, and landed at Natchez. The debarkation of a hundred slaves, of both sexes and all ages, is a novel spectacle to a northerner. Landing on the Levée, they proceed, each with his bundle, under the charge of their temporary master or conductor, toward the city, in a long straggling line, or sometimes in double files, in well-ordered procession, gazing about them with curiosity and wonder upon the new scenes opening before them, as they advance into the city, and speculating upon the advantages afforded as their home, by the beautiful country to which they find themselves transplanted. Nothing seems to escape their attention, and every few steps offer subjects for remark or laughter; for the risible muscles of the negro are uncommonly excitable.

On arriving on the "Hill," in view of the city, and obtaining a glimpse of a fine country spread out around them, their delight is very great. Full of the impression, which they early imbibe, that the south is emphatically the grave of their race, and daily having it held up before their imaginations at home, *in terrorem,* to keep them in the line of duty, if insubordinate, they leave home, as they proudly and affectionately term Virginia, with something of the feelings of the soldier, allotted to a "forlorn hope." It cannot be denied that many have died shortly after being brought into this country; but this was owing to indiscretion, in transporting them at the wrong season of the year—in the spring, after a winter spent at the north; or in autumn, during the prevalence, in former years, of the epidemics, which once were almost annual visitants of this country. Experience has taught those who introduce slaves, in late years, to bring them quite late in autumn. Hence, the two great causes of mortality being removed, the effects have, in a great measure, ceased; and slaves, when they arrive here, and gaze with surprise upon the athletic figures and gray heads of their fellows, who meet them at every step, as they advance into the city—find that they can live even in the south, and grow old on other plantations than those in "Ol' Wirginny." "I see no dead nigger yet, Jef."—"No—nor no coffin pile up neider in de street,"—said another of a gang of negroes passing through the streets, peering on all sides for these ominous signs of this "fatal" climate, as they trudged along to their quarters in the slave-market.

Passing through the city in procession, sometimes dressed in a new uniform, purchased for them in New-Orleans, but often in the brown rags in which they left Virginia, preceded by a large wagon, carrying the surplus baggage; they are marched beyond the city limits, within which, till recently, they were publicly sold, the marts being on nearly every street. Arriving at their quarters, which are usually old unoccupied buildings, and often tents or booths, pitched upon the common, beside some stream of water, and under the shade of trees, they resort, in the first place, to a general ablution, preparatory to being exposed for sale. The toilet arrangements of one hundred negroes, just from a long voyage, are a formidable affair. Both the rivers, Alpheus and Peneus, would hardly suffice for the process. Two or three days are consumed in it; after which, all appear in new, comfortable, uniform dresses, with shining faces, and refreshed after the fatigue of travel. They are now ready for inspection and sale. To this important period, the day of sale, they cheerfully look forward, manifesting not a little emulation to be "sol' fust." The interim between their arrival and sale—for they are not sold at auction, or all at once, but singly, or in parties, as purchasers may be inclined to buy—is passed in an *otium cum dignitate* of a peculiarly African character, involving eating, drinking, playing, and sleeping. The interval of ease enjoyed in the slave-market is an oasis of luxury in their existence, which they seldom know how to appreciate, if we may judge from the wishful manner in which they gaze upon gentlemen who enter the mart, as though anxious to put a period to this kind of enjoyment, so congenial to their feelings and temperament.

Probably two-thirds of the first slaves came into this state from Virginia; and nearly all now introduced, of whom there are several thousands annually, are brought from that state. Kentucky contributes a small number, which is yearly increasing; and since the late passage of the slave law in Missouri, a new market is there opened for this trade. It is computed that more than two hundred thousand dollars' worth of slaves will be purchased in Missouri this season, for the Natchez market. A single individual has recently left Natchez with one hundred thousand dollars, for the purpose of buying up negroes in that state to sell in Mississippi.

The usual way of transporting slaves is by land, although they are frequently brought round by sea; but the last is the most expensive method, and therefore, to "bring them through," is accounted preferable. This is done by forming them into a caravan at the place where they are purchased, and conducting them by land through the Indian nations to this state. The route is for the most part through a continuous forest, and is usually performed by the negroes, on foot, in seven or eight weeks. Their personal appearance, when they arrive at Natchez, is by no means improved, although they are usually stouter and in better condition than when they leave home, for they are generally well fed, and their health is otherwise carefully attended to, while on the route. Arrived within two or three miles of Natchez, they encamp in some romantic spot near a rivulet, and like their brethren transported by sea, commence polishing their skins, and arraying themselves in the coarse but neat uniform, which their master has purchased for them in Natchez.

A few Sabbaths ago, while standing before a village church in the country, my attention was drawn to a long procession at the extremity of the street, slowly approaching like a troop of wearied pilgrims. There were several gentlemen in company, some of them planters, who gazed upon the singular spectacle with unusual interest. One sooty brown hue was cast over the whole horde, by the sombre colour of their tattered garments, which, combined with the slow pace and fatigued air of most of those who composed it, gave to the whole train a sad and funereal appearance.

First came half a dozen boys and girls, with fragments of blankets and ragged pantaloons and frocks, hanging upon, but not covering their glossy limbs. They passed along in high spirits, glad to be once more in a village, after their weary way through the wilderness; capering and practising jokes upon each other, while their even rows of teeth, and the whites of their eyes—the most expressive features in the African physiognomy—were displayed in striking contrast to their ebony skins.

These were followed by a tall mulatto, with high cheek-bones, and lean and hungry looks, making rapid inroads into a huge loaf of bread, whose twin brother was secured under his left arm. A woman, very black, very short, and very pursy, who breathed like a porpoise, and whose capacity for rapid movement was equal to that of a puncheon, trudged along behind, evidently endeavouring to come up with the mulatto, as her eye was fixed very resolutely on the spare loaf; but its owner strode forward deliberately and with perfect impunity. She was followed by another female, bearing an infant in her arms, probably born in the wilderness. Close behind her came a covered wagon, from which she had just descended to walk, drawn by two fine horses, and loaded with young negroes, who were permitted to ride and walk alternately on the journey. Behind the wagon, at a long distance, came an old patriarch, at least eighty years of age, bent nearly double with the weight of years and infirmity. By his side moved an old negress, nearly coeval with him, who supported her decrepit form by a staff. They were the venerable progenitors of the children and grandchildren who preceded them. This aged couple, who were at liberty to ride when they chose, in a covered wagon behind them, were followed by a mixed crowd of negroes of all ages, and of both sexes, with and without staff, hatless and barefooted. The office of the negro's hat is a mere sinecure—they love the warm sun upon their heads—but they like to be well shod, and that with boots, for the lower region of their limbs about the ancles is very sensitive.

Behind these came a wretched cart, covered with torn, red-painted canvass, and drawn by a mule and a horse;—Sancho Panza's mule and Rosinante—I mean no insult to the worthy knight or his squire—if coupled together, would have made precisely such a pair. This vehicle contained several invalids, two of whom were reclining on a matrass laid along the bottom. Around it were many young slaves of both sexes, talking and marching along in gleeful mood. Two or three old people followed, one of whom, who walked with both hands grasping a long staff, stopped as he passed us, and with an air of affecting humility, and with his venerable forehead bowed to the earth, addressed us, "hab massas got piece 'bacca' for ol' nigger?" An old gentleman standing by, whose locks were whitened with the snows of sixty winters, having first obtained leave to do so from the owner of the drove, mounted on a fine blooded horse, rode carelessly along behind them, gave the old slave all he had about him, which, fortunately for the petitioner, happened to be a large quantity, and for which he appeared extremely grateful. Several other negroes, walking along with vigorous steps, and another white conductor, with a couple of delicately limbed race-horses, enveloped in broidered mantles, and ridden by bright-eyed little mulatto boys, and two or three leashes of hounds, led by a slave, completed the train. They had been seven weeks on the road, travelling by easy stages, and encamping at night. Old people are seldom seen in these "droves." The young and athletic usually compose them. But as in this instance, the old people are sometimes allowed to come with the younger portion of their families, as a favour; and if sold at all, they are sold with their children, who can take care of them in their old age, which they well do—for negroes have a peculiarly strong affection for the old people of their own colour.

Probably of the two ways of bringing slaves here, that by land is preferable; not only because attended with less expense, but by gradually advancing them into the climate, it in a measure precludes the effect which a sudden transition from one state to the other might produce. All slaves, however, are not brought here by negro traders. Many of the planters prefer going on and purchasing for themselves, for which purpose it is not unusual for them to take on from twenty to forty and fifty thousand dollars, lay out the whole in slaves, and either accompany through the wilderness themselves on horseback, or engage a conductor. By adopting this method they purchase them at a much greater advantage, than at second-hand from the professional trader, as slaves can be bought for fifty per cent less there, than after they are once brought into this market. The number of slaves introduced into the southwestern market is annually increasing. Last year more than four thousand were brought into the state. The prices of slaves vary with the prices of cotton and sugar. At this time, when cotton brings a good price, a good "field hand" cannot be bought for less than eight hundred dollars, if a male; if a female, for six hundred. "Body servants" sell much higher, one thousand dollars being a common price for them. Children are valued in proportion to their ages. An infant adds one hundred dollars to the price of the mother; and from infancy the children of the slaves increase in value about one hundred dollars for every three years. All domestic servants, or "house servants," which class includes coachmen, nurses, hostlers, gardeners, footmen, cooks, waiting-maids, &c.,—all indispensable to the *menage* of a wealthy planter—are always in great demand, and often sell for eighteen hundred and two thousand dollars apiece, of either sex. But these are exceptions, where the slave possesses some peculiarly valuable trait as a domestic.

Negro traders soon accumulate great wealth, from the immense profit they make on their merchandise. Certainly if any earn their gold, it is the slave-dealer. One of their number, who, for the last fifteen years, has supplied this country with two-thirds of the slaves brought into it, has amassed a fortune of more than a million dollars by this traffic alone. He is a bachelor, and a man of gentlemanly address, as are many of these merchants, and not the ferocious fellows, we Yankees have been apt to imagine them. Their admission into society, however, is not recognized. Planters associate with them freely enough, in the way of business, but notice them no further.

A CLASS SYSTEM AMONG THE NEGROES

There are properly three distinct classes of slaves in the south. The first, and most intelligent class, is composed of the domestic slaves, or "servants," as they are properly termed, of the planters. Some of these both read and write, and possess a great degree of intelligence: and as the negro, of all varieties of the human species, is the most imitative, they soon learn the language, and readily adopt the manners, of the family to which they are attached.

In the more fashionable families, negroes feel it their duty—to show their aristocratic breeding—to ape manners, and to use language, to which the common herd cannot aspire. An aristocratic negro, full of his master's wealth and importance, which he feels to be reflected upon himself, is the most aristocratic personage in existence. He supports his own dignity, and that of his master, or *"family,"* as he phrases it, which he deems inseparable, by a course of conduct befitting coloured gentlemen. Always about the persons of their masters or mistresses, the domestic slaves obtain a better knowledge of the modes of civilized life than they could do in the field, where negroes can rise but little above their original African state. It is from this class that the friends of wisely-regulated emancipation are to seek material for carrying their plans into effect.

The second class is composed of town slaves; which not only includes domestic slaves, but also all negro mechanics, draymen, hostlers, labourers, hucksters, and washwomen, and the heterogeneous multitude of every other occupation—for slaves are trained to every kind of labour. The blacksmith, cabinet-maker, carpenter, wheelwright—all have one or more slaves labouring at their trades. The negro is a third arm to every working man, who can possibly save enough money to purchase one. Even free negroes cannot do without them: some of them own several, to whom they are the severest masters.

"To whom do you belong?" I once inquired of a negro whom I had employed. "There's my master," he replied; pointing to a steady old negro, who had purchased himself, then his wife, and subsequently his three children, by his own manual exertions and persevering industry. He was now the owner of a comfortable house, a piece of land, and two or three slaves, to whom he could add one every three years. It is worthy of remark, and serves to illustrate one of the many singularities characteristic of the race, that the free negro, who "buys his wife's freedom," as they term it, from her master, by paying him her full value, ever afterward considers her in the light of property.

"Thomas, you are a free man," I remarked to one who had purchased himself and wife from his master, by the profits of a poultry yard and vegetable garden, industriously attended to for many years, in his leisure hours and on Sunday. "You are a free man; I suppose you will soon have negroes of your own."

"Hi! Hab one now, master." "Who, Tom?"—"Ol' Sarah, master." "Old Sarah! she is your wife." "She my nigger too; I pay master five hun'red dollar for her."

Many of the negroes who swarm in the cities are what are called "hired servants." They belong to planters, or others, who, finding them qualified for some occupation in which they cannot afford to employ them, hire them to citizens, as mechanics, cooks, waiters, nurses, &c., and receive the monthly wages for their services. Some steady slaves are permitted to "hire their own time;" that is, to go into town and earn what they can, as porters, labourers, gardeners, or in other ways, and pay a stipulated sum weekly to their owners, which will be regulated according to the supposed value of the slave's labour. Masters, however, who are sufficiently indulgent to allow them to "hire their time," are seldom rigorous in rating their labour very high. But whether the slave earn less or more than the specified sum, he must always pay that, and neither more nor less than that to his master at the close of each week, as the condition of this privilege. Few fail in making up the sum; and generally they earn more, if industrious, which is expended in little luxuries, or laid by in an old rag among the rafters of their houses, till a sufficient sum is thus accumulated to purchase their freedom. This they are seldom refused, and if a small amount is wanting to reach their value, the master makes it up out of his own purse, or rather, takes no notice of the deficiency. I have never known a planter to refuse to aid, by peculiar indulgences, any of his steady and well-disposed slaves, who desired to purchase their freedom. On the contrary, they often endeavor to excite emulation in them to the attainment of this end. This custom of allowing slaves to "hire their time," ensuring the master a certain sum weekly, and the slave a small surplus, is mutually advantageous to both.

The majority of town servants are those who are hired to families by planters, or by those living in town who own more than they have employment for, or who can make more by hiring them out than by keeping them at home. Some families, who possess not an acre of land, but own many slaves, hire them out to different individuals; the wages constituting their only income, which is often very large. There are indeed few families, however wealthy, whose incomes are not increased by the wages of hired slaves, and there are many poor people, who own one or two slaves, whose hire enables them to live comfortably. From three to five dollars a week is the hire of a female, and seventy-five cents or a dollar a day for a male. Thus, contrary to the opinion at the north, families may have good servants, and yet not own one, if they are unable to buy, or are conscientious upon that ground, though there is not a shade of difference between hiring a slave, where prejudices are concerned, and owning one. Those who think otherwise, and thus compound with conscience, are only making a distinction without a difference. Northern people, when they come to this country, who dislike either to hire or purchase, often bring free coloured, or white servants (helps) with them. The first soon marry with the free blacks, or become too lofty in their conceptions of things, in contrasting the situation of their fellows around them, with their own, to be retained. The latter, if they are young and pretty, or even old and ugly, assume the fine lady at once, disdaining to be servants among slaves, and Hymen, in the person of some spruce overseer, soon fulfils their expectations. I have seen but one white servant, or domestic, of either sex, in this country, and this was the body servant of an Englishman who remained a few days in Natchez, during which time, John sturdily refused to perform a single duty of his station.

The expense of a domestic establishment at the south, would appear very great in the estimation of a New-Englander. A gardener, coachman, nurse, cook, seamstress, and a house-maid, are indispensable. Some of the more fashionable families add footmen, chamber-maids, hostler, an additional nurse, if there be many children, and another seamstress. To each of these officials is generally attached a young neophyte, while one constantly stumbles over useless little negroes scattered all about the house and court-yard. Necessary as custom has made so great a number of servants, there seems to be much less domestic labour performed in a family of five, such perfect "eye-servants" are they, than in a northern family, with only one "maid of all work." There are some Yankee "kitchen girls"—I beg their ladyships' pardon for so styling them—who can do more house-work, and do it better, than three or four negro servants, unless the eye of their mistress is upon them. As nearly all manual labour is performed by slaves, there must be one to each department, and hence originates a state of domestic manners and individual character, which affords an interesting field of contemplation to the severer northerner. The city slaves are distinguished as a class, by superior intelligence, acuteness, and deeper moral degradation. A great proportion of them are hired, and, free from restraint in a great degree, compared with their situations under their own masters, or in the country, they soon become corrupted by the vices of the city, and in associating indiscriminately with each other, and the refuse of the white population. Soon the vices of the city, divested of their refinement, become their own unmasked. Although they may once have ranked under the first class, and possessed the characteristics which designate the decent, well-behaved domestic of the planter, they soon lose their identity. There are of course exceptions to these characteristics, as also in the other classes. Some of these exceptions have come within my knowledge, of a highly meritorious character.

The third and lowest class consists of those slaves, who are termed "field hands." Many of them rank but little higher than the brutes that perish, in the scale of intellect, and they are in general, as a class, the last and lowest link in the chain of the human species. Secluded in the solitude of an extensive plantation, which is their world, beyond whose horizon they know nothing—their walks limited by the "quarters" and the field—their knowledge and information derived from the rude gossip of their fellows, straggling runaways, or house servants, and without seeing a white person except their master or overseer, as they ride over the estate, with whom they seldom hold any conversation—they present the singular feature of African savages, disciplined to subordination, and placed in the heart of a civilized community. Mere change of place will not change the savage. Moral and intellectual culture alone, will elevate him to an equality with his civilized brethren. The African transplanted from the arid soil of Ebo, Sene-Gambia, or Guinea, to the green fields of American, without mental culture, will remain still the wild African, though he may wield his ox-whip, whistle after his plough, and lift his hat, when addressed, like his more civilized fellows. His children, born on the plantation to which he is attached, and suffered to grow up as ignorant as himself, will not be one degree higher in the scale of civilization. The next generation, though they may have thrown away the idols of their country, and been taught some vague notions of God, are in almost every sense of the word Africans. This has been, till within a few years, the general condition of "field hands" in this country, though there have been exceptions on some plantations highly honourable to their proprietors.

THE MISSISSIPPI POOR WHITE

Cotton is often conveyed to Vicksburg from a distance of one hundred miles in the interior. The teamsters camp every night, in an enclosure formed by their waggons and cattle, with a bright fire burning. Many are small farmers who form a peculiar class, and include the majority of the inhabitants in the east part of this state. With the awkwardness of the Yankee countryman, they are destitute of his morals, education, and reverence for religion. With the rude and bold qualities of the chivalrous Kentuckian, they are destitute of his intelligence, and the humour which tempers and renders amusing his very vices. They are in general uneducated, and their apparel consists of a coarse linsey-woolsey, of a dingy yellow or blue, with broad-brimmed hats; though they usually follow their teams barefooted and bare-headed, with their long locks hanging over their eyes and shoulders, giving them a wild appearance. Accost them as they pass you, one after another, in long lines, cracking their whips, which they use instead of the goad—perhaps the turn-out of a whole district, from the old, gray-headed hunter, to the youngest boy that can wield the whip, often fifteen and twenty feet in length, including the staff—and their replies will generally be sullen or insulting. There is in them a total absence of that courtesy which the country people of New-England manifest for strangers. They will seldom allow carriages to pass them, unless attended by gentlemen, who often have to do battle for the high-way. Ladies, in carriages or on horseback, if unattended by gentlemen, are most usually insulted by them. They have a decided aversion to a broad-cloth coat, and this antipathy is transferred to the wearer. There is a species of warfare kept up between them and the citizens of the shipping ports, mutually evinced by the jokes and tricks played upon them by the latter when they come into market; and their retaliation, when their hour of advantage comes, by an encounter in the back woods, which they claim as their domain.

At home they live in log-houses on partially cleared lands, labor hard in their fields, sometimes owning a few slaves, but more generally but with one or none.—They are good hunters, and expert with the rifle, which is an important article of furniture in their houses. Whiskey is their favourite beverage, which they present to the stranger with one hand, while they give him a chair with the other.

They are uneducated, and destitute of the regular administration of the gospel. As there is no common school system of education adopted in this state, their children grow up as rude and ignorant as themselves; some of whom, I have caught in the cotton market at Natchez, and questioned upon the simple principles of religion and education which every child is supposed to know, and have found them wholly uninformed. This class of men is valuable to the state, and legislative policy, at least, should recommend such measures as would secure religious instruction to the adults, and the advantages of a common education to the children, who, in thirty years, will form a large proportion of the native inhabitants of Mississippi.

15

Sensible Reflections on Southern
Society, 1852–58

*F*rederick Law Olmsted possesses fame today for two diverse reasons: as
the most dispassionate commentator on the South before the Civil War and
as the great landscape architect of the park systems of the United States. He
was born in Hartford, Connecticut, in 1822. For nearly thirty years his life
seems to have been without fixed purpose while he "found himself." He was
a desultory student at Yale, a sailor, a businessman, and a farmer. In 1850 he
commenced his travels which, within a decade, were to make him famous.
Beginning with England, he wrote Walks and Talks of an American Farmer
in England *(1852) and was thereupon commissioned by the* New York Times
*to travel throughout the South to report for northern readers what the Cotton
Kingdom was really like. Three books were the result:* A Journey in the Seaboard States *(1856),* A Journey through Texas *(1857), and* A Journey in the
Back Country *(1860).*

*These three works—from which come the following extracts—comprise a
thorough, unbiased description of southern life, especially in its social and
economic phases, with chief attention centered upon the plantation, the
Negro, and the institution of slavery. From every point of view it is a remarkable survey. The 1850's were a period of passionate controversy between
North and South. Vilification was rampant on both sides of the Mason and
Dixon Line. The air was filled with recriminations, denunciation, partisan
politics, and economic self-interest. It was, indeed, a decade in which it would*

appear that no participant could be found who would judge of the issues raging between North and South with either calmness or objectivity. Yet such an observer was Olmsted. He seldom entered into the troubled waters of the moral issue of slavery, but he did, with serenity and reason, observe what life was actually like, to white and black, in a slave society and what were the effects of that institution upon economic and social progress. His conclusions are plain. He found slavery wasteful and expensive. But he clearly saw facts, indulged in no romantic nonsense about the Negro, and opposed immediate emancipation as impractical and as likely to create more harm than good. It is a great pity that North and South alike did not derive more knowledge from the pages of Olmsted and less from the sentimental Uncle Tom's Cabin *or the vitriolic* Impending Crisis of the South. *But if by 1860 rampant emotionalism had destroyed all rationality, it is pleasing to recognize that some few minds still kept their heads, as the classic pages of Olmsted's travels reveal.*

After the Civil War, Olmsted turned to the other of his interests. It was he who designed Central Park for New York, Prospect Park for Brooklyn, the great park systems of Boston, Buffalo, and Chicago, and launched the state and national public reservations with the Yosemite in California. He died at an advanced age in 1903.

A JAMES RIVER FARM

This morning I visited a farm, some account of which will give a good idea of the more advanced mode of agriculture in Eastern Virginia. It is situated on the bank of James River, and has ready access, by water or land-carriage, to the town of Richmond.

The labor of this farm was entirely performed by slaves. I did not inquire their number, but I judged there were from twenty to forty. Their "quarters" lined the approach-road to the mansion, and were well-made and comfortable log cabins, about thirty feet long by twenty wide, and eight feet wall, with a high loft and shingle roof. Each, divided in the middle, and having a brick chimney outside the wall at each end, was intended to be occupied by two families. There were square windows, closed by wooden ports, having a single pane of glass in the center. The house-servants were neatly dressed, but the field-hands wore very coarse and ragged garments.

During three hours, or more, in which I was in company with the proprietor, I do not think there were ten consecutive minutes uninterrupted by some of the slaves requiring his personal direction or assistance. He was even obliged, three times, to leave the dinner-table.

"You see," said he, smiling, as he came in the last time, "a farmer's life, in this country, is no sinecure." This turning the conversation to Slavery, he observed, in answer to a remark of mine, "I only wish your philanthropists would contrive some satisfactory plan to relieve us of it; the trouble and the responsibility of properly taking care of our negroes, you may judge, from what you see yourself here, is anything but enviable. But what can we do that is better? Our free negroes—and, I believe it is the same at the North as it is here—are a miserable set of vagabonds, drunken, vicious, worse off, it is my honest opinion, than those who are retained in slavery. I am satisfied, too, that our slaves are better off, as they are, than the majority of your free laboring classes at the North."

I expressed my doubts.

"Well, they certainly are better off than the English agricultural laborers or, I believe, those of any other Christian country. Free labor might be more profitable to us: I am inclined to think it would be. The slaves are excessively careless and wasteful, and, in various ways—which, without you lived among them, you could hardly be made to understand—subject us to very annoying losses.

"To make anything by farming, here, a man has got to live a hard life. You see how constantly I am called upon—and, often, it is about as bad at night as by day. Last night I did not sleep a wink till near morning; I am quite worn out with it, and my wife's health is failing. But I cannot rid my-self of it."

I asked why he did not employ an overseer.

"Because I do not think it right to trust to such men as we have to use, if we use any, for overseers."

"Is the general character of overseers bad?"

"They are the curse of this country, sir; the worst men in the community. But lately, I had another sort of fellow offer—a fellow like a dancing-master, with kid gloves, and wrist-bands turned up over his coat-sleeves, and all so nice, that I was almost ashamed to talk to him in my old coat and slouched hat. Half a bushel of recommendations he had with him, too. Well, he was not the man for me—not half the gentleman, with all his airs, that Ned here is"—(a black servant, who was bursting with suppressed laughter, behind his chair).

"Oh, they are interesting creatures, sir," he continued, "and, with all their faults, have many beautiful traits. I can't help being attached to them, and I am sure they love us." In his own case, at least, I did not doubt it; his manner towards them was paternal—familiar and kind; and they came to him like children who have been given some task, and constantly are wanting to be encouraged and guided, simply and confidently. At dinner, he frequently addressed the servant familiarly, and drew him into our conversation as if he were a family friend, better informed, on some local and domestic points, than himself.

He informed me that able-bodied field-hands were hired out, in this vicinity, at the rate of one hundred dollars a year, and their board and clothing. Four able-bodied men, that I have employed the last year, on my farm in New York, I pay, on an average, one hundred and five dollars each, and board them; they clothe themselves at an expense, I think, of twenty dollars a year;—probably, slaves' clothing costs twice that. They constitute all the force of my farm, hired by the year (except a boy, who goes to school in Winter), and, in my absence, have no overseer except one of themselves, whom I appoint. I pay the fair wages of the market, more than any of my neighbors, I believe, and these are no lower than the average of what I have paid for the last five years. It is difficult to measure the labor performed in a day by one, with that of the other, on account of undefined differences in the soil, and in the bulk and weight of articles operated upon. But, here, I am shown tools that no man in his senses, with us, would allow a laborer, to whom he was paying wages, to be encumbered with; and the excessive weight and clumsiness of which, I would judge, would make work at least ten per cent. greater than those ordinarily used with us. And I am assured that, in the careless and clumsy way they must be used by the slaves, anything lighter or less rude could not be furnished them with good economy, and that such tools as we constantly give our laborers, and find our profit in giving them, would not last out a day in a Virginia corn-field—much lighter and more free from stones though it be than ours.

So, too, when I ask why mules are so universally substituted for horses on the farm, the first reason given, and confessedly the most conclusive one, is, that horses cannot bear the treatment that they always *must* get from negroes; horses are always soon foundered or crippled by them, while mules will bear cudgeling, and lose a meal or two now and then, and not be materially injured, and they do not take cold or get sick if neglected or overworked. But I do not need to go further than to the window of the room in which I am writing, to see, at almost any time, treatment of cattle that would insure the immediate discharge of the driver, by almost any farmer owning them at the North.

A SOUTH CAROLINA RICE PLANTATION

I left Charleston yesterday morning, on horseback, with a letter in my pocket to Mr. X., a rice planter, under whose roof I am now writing. Nowhere in the world could a man live more pleasantly than where I am. I was awakened this morning by a servant making a fire for me to dress by. Opening the window, I found a clear, brisk air, but without frost. There was not a sign of winter, except that a few cypress trees were leafless. A grove which surrounded the house was all in dark verdure; and there were green oranges on trees near the window; the buds were swelling on a jessamine-vine, and a number of camilia-japonicas were in full bloom. Sparrows were chirping, doves cooing, and a mocking bird whistling loudly.

Mr. X. has two plantations on the river, besides a large tract of poor pine forest land, extending some miles back upon the upland, and reaching above the malarious region. In the upper part of this pine land is a house, occupied by his overseer during the malarious season, when it is dangerous for any but negroes to remain during the night in the vicinity of the swamps or rice-fields. Even those few who have been born in the region, and have grown up subject to the malaria, are generally weakly and short-lived. The negroes do not enjoy as good health on rice plantations as elsewhere; and the greater difficulty with which their lives are preserved, through infancy especially, shows that the subtle poison of the miasma is not innocuous to them; but Mr. X. boasts a steady increase of his negro stock of five per cent. per annum, which is better than is averaged on the plantations of the interior.

As to the degree of danger to others, "I would as soon stand fifty feet from the best Kentucky rifleman and be shot at by the hour, as to spend a night on my plantation in summer," a Charleston gentleman said to me.

The plantation which contains Mr. X.'s winter residence, has but a small extent of rice land, the greater part of it being reclaimed upland swamp soil, suitable for the culture of Sea Island cotton, which, at the present market, might be grown upon it with profit. But, as his force of slaves has ordinarily been more profitably engaged in the rice-fields, all this has been for many years "turned out," and is now overgrown with pines. The other plantation contains over five hundred acres of rice-land, fitted for irrigation; the remainder is unusually fertile, reclaimed upland swamp, and some hundred acres of it are cultivated for maize and Sea Island cotton.

There is a "negro settlement" on each; but both plantations, although a mile or two apart, are worked together as one, under one overseer—the hands being drafted from one to another as their labor is required. Somewhat over seven hundred acres are at the present time under the plow in the two plantations: the whole number of negroes is two hundred, and they are reckoned to be equal to about one hundred prime hands—an unusual strength for that number of all classes. The overseer lives, in winter, near the settlement of the larger plantation, Mr. X. near that of the smaller.

It is an old family estate, inherited by Mr. X.'s wife, who, with her children, were born and brought up upon it in close intimacy with the negroes, a large proportion of whom were also included in her inheritance, or have been since born upon the estate. Mr. X. himself is a New England farmer's son, and has been a successful merchant and manufacturer. He is also a religious man, without the dementifying bigotry or self-important humility, so frequently implied by that appellation to a New Englander, but generous, composed and cheerful in disposition, as well as conscientious.

The patriarchal institution should be seen here under its most favorable aspects; not only from the ties of long family association, common traditions, common memories, and, if ever, common interest, between the slaves and their rulers, but, also, from the practical talent for organization and administration, gained among the rugged fields, the complicated looms, and the exact and comprehensive counting-houses of New England, which directs the labor.

The house-servants are more intelligent, understand and perform their duties better, and are more appropriately dressed, than any I have seen before. The labor required of them is light, and they are treated with much more consideration for their health and comfort than is usually given to that of free domestics. They live in brick cabins, adjoining the house and stables, and one of these, into which I have looked, is neatly and comfortably furnished. Several of the house-servants, as is usual, are mulattoes, and good-looking. The mulattoes are generally preferred for in-door occupations. Slaves brought up to house-work dread to be employed at field-labor; and those accustomed to the comparatively unconstrained life of the negro-settlement, detest the close control and careful movements required of the house-servants. It is a punishment for a lazy field-hand, to employ him in menial duties at the house, as it is to set a sneaking sailor to do the work of a cabin-servant; and it is equally a punishment to a neglectful house-servant, to banish him to the field-gangs. All the household economy is, of course, carried on in a style appropriate to a wealthy gentleman's residence—not more so, nor less so, that I observe, than in an establishment of similar grade at the North.

It is a custom with Mr. X., when on the estate, to look each day at all the work going on, inspect the buildings, boats, embankments and sluice-ways, and examine the sick. Yesterday I accompanied him in one of these daily rounds.

After a ride of several miles through the woods, in the rear of the plantations, we came to his largest negro-settlement. There was a street, or common, two hundred feet wide, on which the cabins of the negroes fronted. Each cabin was a framed building, the walls boarded and whitewashed on the outside, lathed and plastered within, the roof shingled; forty-two feet long, twenty-one feet wide, divided into two family tenements, each twenty-one by twenty-one; each tenement divided into three rooms—one, the common household apartment, twenty-one by ten; each of the others (bedrooms), ten by ten. There was a brick fire-place in the middle of the long side of each living room, the chimneys rising in one, in the middle of the roof. Besides these rooms, each tenement had a cock-loft, entered by steps from the household room. Each tenement is occupied, on an average, by five persons. There were in them closets, with locks and keys, and a varying quantity of rude furniture. Each cabin stood two hundred feet from the next, and the street in front of them being two hundred feet wide, they were just that distance apart each way. The people were nearly all absent at work, and had locked their outer doors, taking the keys with them. Each cabin has a front and back door, and each room a window, closed by a wooden shutter, swinging outward, on hinges. Between each tenement and the next house, is a small piece of ground, inclosed with palings, in which are coops of fowl with chickens, hovels for nests, and for sows with pig. There were a great many fowls in the street. The negroes' swine are allowed to run in the woods, each owner having his own distinguished by a peculiar mark. In the rear of the yards were gardens—a half-acre to each family. Internally the cabins appeared dirty and disordered, which was rather a pleasant indication that their home-life was not much interfered with, though I found certain police regulations were enforced.

The cabin nearest the overseer's house was used as a nursery. Having driven up to this, Mr. X. inquired first of an old nurse how the children were; whether there had been any births since his last visit; spoke of two convalescent young mothers, that were lounging on the floor of the portico, with the children, and then asked if there were any sick people.

"Nobody, oney dat boy, Sam, sar."

"What Sam is that?"

"Dat little Sam, sar; Tom's Sue's Sam, sar."

"What's the matter with him?"

"Don' 'spec dere's noting much de matter wid him now, sar. He came in Sa'dy, complainin' he had de stomach-ache, an' I gin him some ile, sar; 'spec he mus' be well, dis time, but he din go out dis mornin'."

"Well, I'll see to him."

Mr. X. went to Tom's Sue's cabin, looked at the boy, and, concluding that he was well, though he lay abed, and pretended to cry with pain, ordered him to go out to work. Then, meeting the overseer, who was just riding away, on some business off the plantation, he remained some time in conversation with him, while I occupied myself in making a sketch of the nursery and the street of the settlement in my note-book. On the verandah and the steps of the nursery, there were twenty-seven children, most of them infants, that had been left there by their mothers, while they were working their tasks in the fields. They probably make a visit to them once or twice during the day, to nurse them, and receive them to take to their cabins, or where they like, when they have finished their tasks—generally in the middle of the afternoon. The older children were fed with porridge, by the general nurse. A number of girls, eight or ten years old, were occupied in holding and tending the youngest infants. Those a little older—the crawlers—were in the pen, and those big enough to toddle were playing on the steps, or before the house. Some of these, with two or three bigger ones, were singing and dancing about a fire that they had made on the ground. They were not at all disturbed or interrupted in their amusement by the presence of their owner and myself. At twelve years of age, the children are first put to regular field-work; until then no labor is required of them, except, perhaps, occasionally, they are charged with some light kind of duty, such as frightening birds from corn. When first sent to the field, one-quarter of an able-bodied hand's day's work is ordinarily allotted to them, as their task.

But very few of the babies were in arms; such as were not, generally lay on the floor, rolling about, or sat still, sucking their thumbs. The nurse was a kind-looking old negro woman, with, no doubt, philo-progenitiveness well developed; but she paid very little attention to them, only sometimes chiding the older ones for laughing or singing too loud. I watched for half an hour, and in all that time not a baby of them began to cry; nor have I ever heard one, at two or three other plantation-nurseries which I have visited.

From the settlement, we drove to the "mill"—not a flouring mill, though I believe there is a run of stones in it—but a monster barn, with more extensive and better machinery for threshing and storing rice, driven by a steam-engine, than I have ever seen used for grain on any farm in Europe or America before. Adjoining the mill-house were shops and sheds, in which blacksmiths, carpenters, and other mechanics—all slaves, belonging to Mr. X. —were at work. He called my attention to the excellence of their workmanship, and said that they exercised as much ingenuity and skill as the ordinary mechanics that he was used to employ in New England. He pointed out to me some carpenter's work, a part of which had been executed by a New England mechanic, and a part by one of his own hands, which indicated that the latter was much the better workman.

I was gratified by this, for I had been so often told, in Virginia, by gentlemen, anxious to convince me that the negro was incapable of being educated or improved to a condition in which it would be safe to trust him with himself—that no negro mechanic could ever be taught, or induced to work carefully or nicely—that I had begun to believe it might be so.

We were attended through the mill-house by a respectable-looking, orderly, and gentlemanly-mannered mulatto, who was called, by his master, "the watchman." His duties, however, as they were described to me, were those of a steward, or intendant. He carried, by a strap at his waist, a very large number of keys, and had charge of all the stores of provisions, tools, and materials of the plantations, as well as of all their produce, before it was shipped to market. He weighed and measured out all the rations of the slaves and the cattle; superintended the mechanics, and himself made and repaired, as was necessary, all the machinery, including the steam-engine.

In all these departments, his authority was superior to that of the overseer. The overseer received his private allowance of family provisions from him, as did also the head-servant at the mansion, who was his brother. His responsibility was much greater than that of the overseer; and Mr. X. said, he would trust him with much more than he would any overseer he had ever known.

When we were leaving the house, to go to church, on Sunday, after all the white family had entered their carriages, or mounted their horses, the head house-servant also mounted a horse—as he did so, slipping a coin into the hands of the boy who had been holding him. Afterwards, we passed a family of negroes, in a light wagon—the oldest among them driving the horse. On my inquiring if the slaves were allowed to take horses to drive to church, I was informed that, in each of these three cases, the horse belonged to the negroes who were driving them. The old man was infirm, and Mr. X. had given him a horse, to enable him to move about.

But the watchman and the house-servant had bought their horses with money. The watchman was believed to own three horses; and, to account for his wealth, Mr. X.'s son told me that his father considered him a very valuable servant, and frequently encouraged him in his good behavior, with handsome gratuities. He receives, probably, considerably higher wages, in fact (in the form of presents), than the white overseer. He knew his father gave him two hundred dollars at once, a short time ago. The watchman has a private house, and, no doubt, lives in considerable luxury.

After passing through tool-rooms, corn-rooms, mule-stables, store-rooms, and a large garden, in which vegetables to be distributed among the negroes, as well as for the family, are grown, we walked to the rice-land. It is divided by embankments into fields of about twenty acres each, but varying somewhat in size, according to the course of the river. The arrangements are such that each field may be flooded independently of the rest, and they are subdivided by open ditches into rectangular plats of a quarter acre each. We first proceeded to where twenty or thirty women and girls were engaged in raking together, in heaps and winrows, the stubble and rubbish left on the field after the last crop, and burning it. The main object of this operation is to kill all the seeds of weed, or of rice, on the ground. Ordinarily it is done by tasks—a certain number of the small divisions of the field being given to each hand to burn in a day; but owing to a more than usual amount of rain having fallen lately, and some other causes, making the work harder in some places than others, the women were now working by the day, under the direction of a "driver," a negro man, who walked about among them, taking care that they left nothing unburned. Mr. X. inspected the ground they had gone over, to see whether the driver had done his duty. It had been sufficiently well burned, but, not more than quarter as much ground had been gone over, he said, as was usually burned in task-work,—and he thought they had been very lazy, and reprimanded them for it. The driver made some little apology, but the women offered no reply, keeping steadily, and it seemed sullenly, on at their work.

In the next field, twenty men, or boys, for none of them looked as if they were full-grown, were plowing, each with a single mule, and a light, New-York-made plow. The soil was very friable, the plowing easy, and the mules proceeded at a smart pace; the furrows were straight, regular, and well turned. Their task was nominally an acre and a quarter a day; somewhat less actually, as the measure includes the space occupied by the ditches, which are two to three feet wide, running around each quarter of an acre. The plowing gang was superintended by a driver who was provided with a watch; and while we were looking at them he called out that it was twelve o'clock. The mules were immediately taken from the plows, and the plow-boys mounting them, leapt the ditches, and cantered off to the stables, to feed them. One or two were ordered to take their plows to the blacksmith, for repairs.

The plowmen got their dinner at this time: those not using horses do not usually dine till they have finished their tasks; but this, I believe, is optional with them. They commence work at sunrise, and at about eight o'clock have breakfast brought to them in the field, each hand having left a bucket with the cook for that purpose. All who are working in connection leave their work together, and gather in a social company about a fire, where they generally spend about half an hour, at breakfast time. The provisions furnished them consist mainly of meal, rice and vegetables, with salt and molasses, and occasionally bacon, fish, and coffee. The allowance is a peck of meal, or an equivalent quantity of rice per week, to each working hand, old or young, besides small stores. Mr. X. says that he has lately given a less amount of meat than is now usual on plantations, having observed that the general health of the negroes is not as good as formerly, when no meat at all was customarily given them. The general impression among planters is, that the negroes work much better for being supplied with three or four pounds of bacon a week.

Leaving the rice-land, we went next to some of the upland fields, where we found several other gangs of negroes at work; one entirely of men engaged in ditching; another of women, and another of boys and girls, "listing" an old corn-field with hoes. All of them were working by tasks, and were overlooked by negro drivers. They all labored with greater rapidity and cheerfulness than any slaves I have before seen; and the women struck their hoes as if they were strong, and well able to engage in muscular labor. The expression of their faces was generally repulsive, and their *tout ensemble* anything but agreeable to the eye. The dress of most of them was uncouth and cumbrous, dirty and ragged; reefed up, at the hips, so as to show their heavy legs, wrapped round with a piece of old blanket, in lieu of leggings or stockings. Most of them worked with bare arms, but wore strong shoes on their feet, and handkerchiefs on their heads; some of them were smoking, and each gang had a fire burning on the ground, near where they were at work, to light their pipes and warm their breakfast by. Mr. X. said this was always their custom, even in summer. To each gang a boy or girl was also attached, whose business it was to bring water for them to drink, and to go for anything required by the driver. The drivers would frequently call back a hand to go over again some piece of his or her task that had not been worked to his satisfaction, and were constantly calling to one or another, with a harsh and peremptory voice, to strike harder or hoe deeper, and otherwise taking care that the work was well done. Mr. X. asked if Little Sam ("Tom's Sue's Sam") worked yet with the "three-quarter" hands, and learning that he did, ordered him to be put with the field-hands, observing that though rather short, he was strong and stout, and, being twenty years old, well able to do a man's work.

The field-hands are all divided into four classes, according to their physical capacities. The children beginning as "quarter-hands," advancing to "half-hands," and then to "three-quarter hands"; and, finally, when mature, and able-bodied, healthy and strong, to "full hands." As they decline in strength, from age, sickness, or other cause, they retrograde in the scale, and proportionately less labor is required of them. Many, of naturally weak frame, never are put among the full hands. Finally, the aged are left out at the annual classification, and no more regular field-work is required of them, although they are generally provided with some light, sedentary occupation. I saw one old woman picking "tailings" of rice out of a heap of chaff, an occupation at which she was literally not earning her salt. Mr. X. told me she was a native African, having been brought when a girl from the Guinea coast. She spoke almost unintelligibly; but after some other conversation, in which I had not been able to understand a word she said, he jokingly proposed to send her back to Africa. She expressed her preference to remain where she was, very emphatically. "Why?" She did not answer readily, but being pressed, threw up her palsied hands, and said furiously, "I lubs 'ou mas'r, oh, I lubs 'ou. I don't want go 'way from 'ou."

The field hands are nearly always worked in gangs, the strength of a gang varying according to the work that engages it; usually it numbers twenty or more, and is directed by a driver. As on most large plantations, whether of rice or cotton, in Eastern Georgia and South Carolina, nearly all ordinary and regular work is performed *by tasks:* that is to say, each hand has his labor for the day marked out before him, and can take his own time to do it in. For instance, in making drains in light, clean meadow land, each man or woman of the full hands is required to dig one thousand cubic feet; in swamp-land that is being prepared for rice culture, where there are not many stumps, the task for a ditcher is five hundred feet; while in a very strong cypress swamp, only two hundred feet is required; in hoeing rice, a certain number of rows, equal to one-half or two-thirds of an acre, according to the condition of the land; in sowing rice (strewing in drills), two acres; in reaping rice (if it stands well), three-quarters of an acre; or, sometimes a gang will be required to reap, tie in sheaves, and carry to the stack-yard the produce of a certain area, commonly equal to one fourth the number of acres that there are hands working together.

These tasks certainly would not be considered excessively hard, by a Northern laborer; and, in point of fact, the more industrious and active hands finish them often by two o'clock. I saw one or two leaving the field soon after one o'clock, several about two; and between three and four, I met a dozen women and several men coming home to their cabins, having finished their day's work.

Under this "Organization of Labor," most of the slaves work rapidly and well. In nearly all ordinary work, custom has settled the extent of the task, and it is difficult to increase it. The driver who marks it out, has to remain on the ground until it is finished, and has no interest in over-measuring it; and if it should be systematically increased very much, there is danger of a general stampede to the "swamp"—a danger the slave can always hold before his master's cupidity. In fact, it is looked upon in this region as a

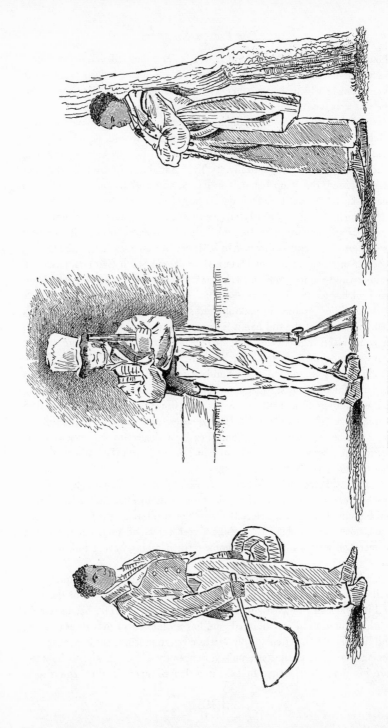

TWO SLAVE DRIVERS AND A BACKWOODSMAN

proscriptive right of the negroes to have this incitement to diligence offered them; and the man who denied it, or who attempted to lessen it, would, it is said, suffer in his reputation, as well as experience much annoyance from the obstinate "rascality" of his negroes. Notwithstanding this, I have heard a man assert, boastingly, that he made his negroes habitually perform double the customary tasks. Thus we get a glimpse again of the black side. If he is allowed the power to do this, what may not a man do?

It is the driver's duty to make the tasked hands do their work well. If, in their haste to finish it, they neglect to do it properly, he "sets them back," so that carelessness will hinder more than it will hasten the completion of their tasks.

In the selection of drivers, regard seems to be had to size and strength—at least, nearly all the drivers I have seen are tall and strong men—but a great deal of judgment, requiring greater capacity of mind than the ordinary slave is often supposed to be possessed of, is certainly needed in them. A good driver is very valuable and usually holds office for life. His authority is not limited to the direction of labor in the field, but extends to the general deportment of the negroes. He is made to do the duties of policeman, and even of police magistrate. It is his duty, for instance, on Mr. X.'s estate, to keep order in the settlement; and, if two persons, men or women, are fighting, it is his duty to immediately separate them, and then to "whip them both."

Before any field of work is entered upon by a gang, the driver who is to superintend them has to measure and stake off the tasks. To do this at all accurately, in irregular-shaped fields, must require considerable powers of calculation. A driver, with a boy to set the stakes, I was told, would accurately lay out forty acres a day, in half-acre tasks. The only instrument used is a five-foot measuring rod. When the gang comes to the field, he points out to each person his or her duty for the day, and then walks about among them, looking out that each proceeds properly. If, after a hard day's labor, he sees that the gang has been overtasked, owing to a miscalculation of the difficulty of the work, he may excuse the completion of the tasks; but he is not allowed to extend them. In the case of uncompleted tasks, the body of the gang begin new tasks the next day, and only a sufficient number are detailed from it to complete, during the day, the unfinished tasks of the day before. The relation of the driver to the working hands seems to be similar to that of the boatswain to the seamen in the navy, or of the sergeant to the privates in the army.

Having generally had long experience on the plantation, the advice of the drivers is commonly taken in nearly all the administration, and frequently they are, *de facto,* the managers. Orders on important points of the plantation economy, I have heard given by the proprietor directly to them, without the overseer's being consulted or informed of them; and it is often left with them to decide when and how long to flow the rice-grounds—the proprietor and overseer deferring to their more experienced judgment. Where the drivers are discreet, experienced and trusty, the overseer is frequently employed merely as a matter of form, to comply with the laws requiring the superintendence or presence of a white man among every body of slaves; and his duty is rather to inspect and report, than to govern. Mr. X. considers his overseer an uncommonly efficient and faithful one, but he would not employ him, even during the summer, when he is absent for several months, if the law did not require it. He has sometimes left his plantation in care of one of the drivers for a considerable length of time, after having discharged an overseer; and he thinks it has then been quite as well conducted as ever. His overseer consults the drivers on all important points, and is governed by their advice.

Mr. X. said, that though overseers sometimes punished the negroes severely, and otherwise ill-treated them, it is their more common fault to indulge them foolishly in their disposition to idleness, or in other ways to curry favor with them, so they may not inform the proprietor of their own misconduct or neglect. He has his overseer bound to certain rules, by written contract; and it is stipulated that he can discharge him at any moment, without remuneration for his loss of time and inconvenience, if he should at any time be dissatisfied with him. One of the rules is, that he shall never punish a negro with his own hands, and that corporeal punishment, when necessary, shall be inflicted by the drivers. The advantage of this is, that it secures time for deliberation, and prevents punishment being made in sudden passion. His drivers are not allowed to carry their whips with them in the field; so that if the overseer wishes a hand punished, it is necessary to call a driver; and the driver has then to go to his cabin, which is, perhaps, a mile or two distant, to get his whip, before it can be applied.

I asked how often the necessity of punishment occurred?

"Sometimes, perhaps, not once for two or three weeks; then it will seem as if the devil had got into them all, and there is a good deal of it."

As the negroes finish the labor, required of them by Mr. X., at three or four o'clock in the afternoon, they can employ the remainder of the day in laboring for themselves, if they choose. Each family has a half-acre of land allotted to it, for a garden; besides which, there is a large vegetable garden, from which they are supplied. They are at liberty to sell whatever they choose from the products of their own garden, and to make what they can by keeping swine and fowls. Mr. X.'s family have no other supply of poultry and eggs than what is obtained by purchase from his own negroes; they frequently, also, purchase game from them. The only restriction upon their traffic is a "liquor law." They are not allowed to buy or sell ardent spirits. This prohibition, like liquor laws elsewhere, unfortunately, cannot be enforced; and, of late years, grog shops, at which stolen goods are bought from the slaves, and poisonous liquors—chiefly the worse whiskey, much watered and made stupefying by an infusion of tobacco—are clandestinely sold to them, have become an established evil, and the planters find themselves almost powerless to cope with it.

So far as I have observed, slaves show themselves worthy of trust most, where their masters are most considerate and liberal towards them. Mr. X.'s slaves are permitted to purchase fire-arms and ammunition, and to keep them in their cabins; and his wife and daughters reside with him, among them, the doors of the house never locked, or windows closed, perfectly defenseless, and miles distant from any other white family.

I do not think, after all I have heard to favor it, that there is any good reason to consider the negro the moral inferior of the white; or, that if he is so, it is in those elements of character which should prevent us from trusting him with equal social munities with ourselves.

MOUNTAIN WHITES

Extreme poverty is rare in the mountains, but a smaller proportion of the people live in a style corresponding to that customary among what are called in New England "fore-handed folks," than in any other part of the civilized world which I have visited. The number who can be classed as moderately well-informed, using the New England rural standard, is extremely small. I did not meet in a whole month more than two or three natives who seemed to have enjoyed equal advantages of education with the lowest class of New England (native) working people. Each of those above the average in this respect I shall speak of distinctly.

The great majority live in small and comfortless log huts, two detached cabins usually forming the habitation of a family. These are rarely provided with glass windows, many are even without a port; yet the winter is more severe than that of England. The interior of one frame house, in which I spent a night, forty by thirty feet in dimensions, and two stories in height, occupied by a family of much more than the usual wealth, received light in the lower story only by the door and the occasional interstices of the boarding, and in the upper, by two loopholes, unfurnished with shutters.

The table is usually abundantly provided, its only marked difference from that of the lower country being the occasional presence of unleavened rye bread, made with saleratus and fat, unlike any rye bread I have eaten elsewhere, but more palatable to me than the usual corn bread. Butter is always offered in the mountains, and is usually good.

The women, as well as the men, generally smoke, and tobacco is grown for home use. They are more industrious than the men, often being seen at work in the fields, and at spinning wheels and hand-looms in almost every house. I was less troubled by vermin than in the low country, yet so much so that I adopted the habit of passing the night on the floor of the cabins, rather than in their beds. The furniture of the cabins is rather less meager than that of a similar class of habitations in the lower region. In the northern parts, it is common to see a square frame in which are piled a dozen bed quilts. Notwithstanding the ignorance of the people, books are more common than even in the houses of the slave owners of the planting districts. They seemed fond of reading aloud, those who were able—in a rather doleful and jolting manner. Their books are generally the cheapest and tawdriest of religious holiday books, as Mr. Sears' publications, Fox's "Martyrs," the "Biography of Distinguished Divines," with such others as "The Alarm to the Unconverted" and "The Cause and Cure of Infidelity"; not such as *Pilgrim's Progress,* or *Robinson Crusoe,* neither of which did I ever meet with.

I rode late last night, there being no cabins for several miles in which I was willing to spend the night, until I came to one of larger size than usual, with a gallery on the side toward the road and a good stable opposite it. A man on the gallery was about to answer (as I judged from his countenance), "I reckon you can," to my inquiry if I could stay, when the cracked voice of a worryful woman screeched out from within, "We don't foller takin' in people."

"No, sir," said the man, "we don't foller it."

"How far shall I have to go?"

"There's another house a little better than three quarters of a mile further on."

To this house I proceeded—a cabin of one room and a loft, with a kitchen in a separate cabin. The owner said he never turned anybody away, and I was welcome. He did not say that he had no corn, until after supper, when I asked for it to feed my horse. The family were good-natured, intelligent people, but very ignorant. The man and his wife and the daughters slept below, the boys and I in the cock-loft. Supper and breakfast were eaten in the detached kitchen. Yet they were by no means poor people. The man told me that he had over a thousand acres of rich tillable land, besides a large extent of mountain range, the most of which latter he had bought from time to time as he was able, to prevent the settlement of squatters near his valley-land. "There were people who would be bad neighbors I knew," he said, "that would settle on most any kind of place, and every body wants to keep such as far away from them as they can." (When I took my bridle off, I hung it up by the stable door; he took it down and said he'd hang it in a safer place. "He'd never had any thing stolen from here, and he didn't mean to have—it was just as well not to put temptation before people," and he took it into the house and put it under his bed.)

Besides this large tract of land here, he owned another tract of two hundred acres with a house upon it, rented for one third the produce, and another smaller farm, similarly rented; he also owned a grist mill, which he rented to a miller for half the tolls. He had also a considerable stock of cattle and large crops of grain, so that he must be considered a very respectable capitalist for a mountaineer. He told me that he had thought a good deal formerly of moving to new countries, but he had been doing pretty well and had staid here now so long, he didn't much think he should ever budge. He reckoned he'd got enough to make him a living for the rest of his life, and he didn't know any use a man had for more'n that.

I did not see a single book in the house, nor do I think that any of the family could read. He said that many people here were talking about Iowa and Indiana; "was Iowa (Hiaway) beyond the Texies?" I opened my map to show him where it was, but he said he "wasn't scollar'd enough" to understand it, and I could not induce him to look at it. I asked him if the people here preferred Iowa and Indiana to Missouri at all because they were free States. "I reckon," he replied, "they don't have no allusion to that. Slavery is a great cuss, though, I think, the greatest there is in these United States. There ain't no account of slaves up here in the west, but down in the east part of this State about Fayetteville, there's as many as there is in South Carolina. That's the reason the West and the East don't agree in this State; people out here hates the eastern people."

"Why is that?"

"Why you see they vote on the slave basis, and there's some of them nigger counties where there ain't more'n four or five hundred white folks, that has just as much power in the Legislature as any of our mountain counties where there'll be some thousand voters."

He made further remarks against slavery and against slave-holders. When I told him that I entirely agreed with him, and said further that poor white people were usually far better off in the free States than in the slave, he seemed a little surprised and said, "New York ain't a free State, is it?"

A MISSISSIPPI COTTON PLANTATION

As a general rule, the larger the body of negroes on a plantation or estate, the more completely are they treated as mere property, and in accordance with a policy calculated to insure the largest pecuniary returns. Hence, in part, the greater proportionate profit of such plantations, and the tendency which everywhere prevails in the planting districts to the absorption of small, and the augmentation of large estates. It may be true, that among the wealthier slaveowners, there is oftener a humane disposition, a better judgment, and a greater ability to deal with their dependents indulgently and bountifully, but the effects of this disposition are chiefly felt, even on those plantations where the proprietor resides permanently, among the slaves employed about the house and stables, and perhaps a few old favorites in the quarters. It is more than balanced by the difficulty of acquiring a personal interest in the units of a large body of slaves, and an acquaintance with the individual characteristics of each, The treatment of the mass must be reduced to a system, the ruling idea of which will be, to enable one man to force into the same channel of labor the muscles of a large number of men, of various, and often conflicting wills.

The estate I am now about to describe, was situated upon a tributary of the Mississippi, and accessible only by occasional steamboats, even this mode of communication being frequently interrupted at low stages of the rivers. The slaves upon it formed about one twentieth of the whole population of the county, in which the blacks considerably out-number the whites. At the time of my visit, the owner was sojourning upon it, with his family and several invited guests, but his usual residence was upon a small plantation, of little productive value, situated in a neighborhood somewhat noted for the luxury and hospitality of its citizens, and having a daily mail, and direct railroad and telegraphic communication with New York. This was, if I am not mistaken, his second visit in five years.

The property consisted of four adjoining plantations, each with its own negro cabins, stables and overseer, and each worked to a great extent independently of the others, but all contributing their crop to one gin-house and warehouse, and all under the general superintendence of a bailiff or manager, who constantly resided upon the estate, and in the absence of the owner, had vice-regal power over the overseers, controlling so far as he thought fit, the economy of all the plantations.

The manager was himself a gentleman of good education, generous and poetic in temperament, and possessing a capacity for the enjoyment of nature and happiness in the bucolic life. I found him a delightful companion. The gang of toiling negroes to him, however, was as essential an element of the poetry of nature as flocks of peaceful sheep and lowing kine.

The overseers were superior to most men of their class, and, with one exception, frank, honest, temperate and industrious, but their feelings toward negroes were such as naturally result from their occupation. They were all married, and lived with their families, each in a cabin or cottage, in the hamlet of the slaves of which he had especial charge. Their wages varied from $500 to $1,000 a year each.

These five men, each living more than a mile distant from either of the others, were the only white men on the estate. Of course to secure their own personal safety and to efficiently direct the labor of such a large number of ignorant, indolent, and vicious negroes, rules, or rather habits and customs, of discipline, were necessary, which would in particular cases be liable to operate unjustly and cruelly. It is apparent, also, that, as the testimony of negroes against them would not be received as evidence in court, that there was very little probability that any excessive severity would be restrained by fear of the law.

In the main, the negroes appeared to be well taken care of and abundantly supplied with the necessaries of vigorous physical existence. A large part of them lived in commodious and well-built cottages, with broad galleries in front, so that each family of five had two rooms on the lower floor, and a loft. The remainder lived in log-huts, small and mean in appearance, but those of their overseers were little better, and preparations were being made to replace all of these by neat boarded cottages. Each family had a fowl-house and hog-sty (constructed by the negroes themselves), and kept fowls and swine, feeding the latter during the summer on weeds and fattening them in the autumn on corn *stolen* (this was mentioned to me by the overseers as if it were a matter of course) from their master's corn-fields.

I several times saw gangs of them eating the dinner which they had brought, each for himself, to the field, and observed that they generally had plenty, often more than they could eat, of bacon, cornbread, and molasses. The allowance of food is weighed and measured under the eye of the manager by the drivers, and distributed to the head of each family weekly: consisting of—for each person, 3 pounds of pork, 1 peck of meal; and from January to July, 1 quart of molasses. Monthly, in addition, 1 pound of tobacco, and 4 pints of salt. No drink is ever served but water, except after unusual exposure, or to ditchers working in water, who get a glass of whiskey at night.

All hands cook for themselves after work at night, or whenever they please between night-fall and daybreak, each family in its own cabin. Each family has a garden, the products of which, together with eggs, fowls and bacon, they frequently sold, or used in addition to their regular allowance of food. Most of the families bought a barrel of flour every year. The manager endeavored to encourage this practice, and that they might spend their money for flour instead of liquor, he furnished it to them at rather less than what it cost him at wholesale. There were many poor whites within a few miles who would always sell liquor to the negroes, and encourage them to steal, to obtain the means to buy it of them. These poor whites were al-

KING COTTON

ways spoken of with anger by the overseers, and they each had a standing offer of much more than the intrinsic value of their land, from the manager, to induce them to move away.

The first morning I was on the estate, the manager invited me to ride with him on his usual daily round of inspection through the plantations. On reaching the nearest "quarters," we stopped at a house, a little larger than the ordinary cabins, which was called the loom-house, in which a dozen negroes were at work making shoes, and manufacturing coarse cotton stuff for negro clothing. One of the hands so employed was insane, and most of the others were cripples, invalids with chronic complaints, or unfitted by age, or some infirmity, for field work.

We went to another cabin and entered a room where a woman lay on a bed, groaning. It was a very dingy, comfortless room, but a musquito bar, much patched and very dirty, covered the bed. The manager asked the woman several times what was the matter, but could get no distinct reply. She appeared to be suffering great pain. The manager felt her pulse and looked at her tongue, and after making a few more inquiries, to which no intelligible reply was given, told her he did not believe she was ill at all. At this the woman's groans redoubled. "I have heard of your tricks," continued the manager; "you had a chill when I came to see you yesterday morning; you had a chill when the mistress came here, and you had a chill when the master came. I never knew a chill to last the whole day. So you'll just get up now and go to the field, and if you don't work smart, you'll get a dressing; do you hear?"

We then left. The manager said that he rarely—almost never—had occasion to employ a physician for the people. Never for accouchements; the women, from their labor in the field, were not subject to the difficulty, danger, and pain which attended women of the better classes in giving birth to their offspring.

Each overseer regulated the hours of work on his own plantation. I saw the negroes at work before sunrise and after sunset. At about eight o'clock they were allowed to stop for breakfast, and again about noon, to dine. The length of these rests was at the discretion of the overseer or drivers, usually, I should say, from half an hour to an hour. There was no rule.

The number of hands directed by each overseer was considerably over one hundred. The manager thought it would be better economy to have a white man over every fifty hands, but the difficulty of obtaining trustworthy overseers prevented it. Three of those he then had were the best he had ever known. He described the great majority as being passionate, careless, inefficient men, generally intemperate, and totally unfitted for the duties of the position. The best overseers, ordinarily, are young men, the sons of small planters, who take up the business temporarily, as a means of acquiring a little capital with which to purchase negroes for themselves.

The plowing, both with single and double mule teams, was generally performed by women, and very well performed, too. I watched with some interest for any indication that their sex unfitted them for the occupation. Twenty of them were plowing together, with double teams and heavy plows. They were superintended by a male negro driver, who carried a whip, which he frequently cracked at them, permitting no dawdling or delay at the turning; and they twitched their plows around on the head-land, jerking their reins, and yelling to their mules, with apparent ease, energy, and rapidity. Throughout the Southwest the negroes, as a rule, appear to be worked much harder than in the eastern and northern slave States. I do not think they accomplish as much daily, as agricultural laborers at the North usually do, but they certainly labor much harder, and more unremittingly. They are constantly and steadily driven up to their work, and the stupid, plodding, machine-like manner in which they labor, is painful to witness. This was especially the case with the hoe-gangs. One of them numbered nearly two hundred hands (for the force of two plantations was working together), moving across the field in parallel lines, with a considerable degree of precision. I repeatedly rode through the lines at a canter, with other horsemen, often coming upon them suddenly, without producing the smallest change or interruption in the dogged action of the laborers, or causing one of them to lift an eye from the ground. A very tall and powerful negro walked to and fro in the rear of the line, frequently cracking his whip, and calling out, in the surliest manner, to one and another, "Shove your hoe, there! shove your hoe!" But I never saw him strike any one with the whip.

The whip was evidently in constant use, however. There were no rules on the subject, that I learned; the overseers and drivers punished the negroes whenever they deemed it necessary, and in such manner, and with such severity, as they thought fit. "If you don't work faster," or "If you don't work harder," or "If you don't recollect what I tell you, I will have you flogged," are threats which I have often heard.

I said to one of the overseers, "It must be very disagreeable to have to punish them as much as you do?"

"Yes, it would be to those who are not used to it—but it's my business, and I think nothing of it. Why, sir, I wouldn't mind killing a nigger more than I would a dog."

I asked if he had ever killed a negro?

"Not quite," he said, but overseers were often obliged to. Some negroes are determined never to let a white man whip them, and will resist you, when you attempt it; of course you must kill them in that case.

Once a negro whom he was punishing, insulted and threatened him. He went to the house for his gun, and as he was returning, the negro, thinking he would be afraid to spoil so valuable a piece of property by firing, broke for the woods. He fired at once, and put six buck-shot into his hips. He always carried a bowie knife, but not a pistol, unless he anticipated some unusual act of insubordination. He always kept a pair of pistols ready loaded over the mantel-piece, however, in case they should be needed.

The severest corporeal punishment of a negro that I witnessed at the South, occurred while I was visiting this estate. I suppose however, that punishment equally severe is common—in fact, it must be necessary to the maintenance of adequate discipline on every large plantation. It is necessary because the opportunities of hiding away and shirking labor, and of wasting and injuring the owner's property without danger to themselves are great, but above all, because there is no real moral obligation on the part of the negro to do what is demanded of him.

The manner of the overseer who inflicted the punishment, and his subsequent conversation with me about it, indicated that it was by no means an unusual occurrence with him. I had accidentally encountered him, as he was showing me his plantation. In going from one side of it to the other, we had twice crossed a deep gully, at the bottom of which was a thick covert of brushwood. We were crossing it a third time, and had nearly passed through the brush, when the overseer suddenly stopped his horse exclaiming, "What's that? Hallo! who are you there?"

It was a girl lying at full length on the ground at the bottom of the gully, evidently intending to hide herself from us in the bushes.

"Who are you there?"

"Sam's Sall, sir."

"What are you skulking there for?"

The girl half rose, but gave no answer.

"Have you been here all day?"

"No sir."

"How did you get here?"

The girl made no reply.

"Where have you been all day?"

The answer was unintelligible.

After some further questioning, she said her father accidently locked her in, when he went out in the morning.

"How did you manage to get out?"

"Pushed a plank off, sir, and crawled out."

The overseer was silent for a moment, looking at the girl, and then said, "That won't do—come out here." The girl arose at once, and walked toward him; she was about eighteen years of age. A bunch of keys hung to her waist, which the overseer espied, and he said, "Ah, your father locked you in; but you have got the keys."

After a little hesitation, the girl replied that these were the keys of some other locks; her father had the door-key.

Whether her story was true or false, could have been ascertained in two minutes by riding on to the gang with which her father was at work, but the overseer had made up his mind as to the facts of the case.

"That won't do," said he, "get down on your knees."

The girl knelt on the ground; he got off his horse, and holding him with his left hand, struck her thirty or forty blows across the shoulders with his tough, flexible, "raw-hide" whip. They were well laid on, as a boatswain would thrash a skulking sailor, or as some people flog a baulking horse, but with no appearance of angry excitement on the part of the overseer.

At every stroke the girl winced, and exclaimed, "Yes, sir!" or "Ah, sir!" or "Please, sir!" not groaning or screaming.

At length he stopped and said, "Now tell me the truth."

The girl repeated the same story.

"You have not got enough yet," said he, "pull up your clothes—lie down."

The girl without any hesitation, without a word or look of remonstance or entreaty, drew closely all her garments under her shoulders, and lay down upon the ground with her face toward the overseer, who continued to flog her with the rawhide, across her naked loins and thighs, with as much strength as before. She now shrunk away from him, not rising, but writhing, groveling, and screaming, "Oh, don't, sir! oh, please stop, master! please, sir! please, sir! oh, that's enough, master! oh, Lord! oh, master, master! oh, God, master, do stop! oh, God, master! oh, God, master!"

A young gentleman of fifteen was with us; he had ridden in front, and now, turning on his horse looked back with an expression only of impatience at the delay. It was the first time I had ever seen a woman flogged. I had seen a man cudgeled and beaten, in the heat of passion, before, but never flogged with a hundredth part of the severity used in this case. I glanced again at the perfectly passionless but rather grim business-like face of the overseer, and again at the young gentleman, who had turned away; if not indifferent he had evidently not the faintest sympathy with my emotion. Only my horse chafed with excitement. I gave him rein and spur and we plunged into the bushes and scrambled fiercely up the steep acclivity. The screaming yells and the whip strokes had ceased when I reached the top of the bank. Choking, sobbing, spasmodic groans only were heard. I rode on to where the road coming diagonally up the ravine ran out upon the cotton-field. My young companion met me there, and immediately afterward the overseer. He laughed as he joined us, and said,

"She meant to cheat me out of a day's work—and she has done it, too."

"Did you succeed in getting another story from her?"

"No; she stuck to it."

"Was it not perhaps true?"

"Oh no, sir, she slipped out of the gang when they were going to work, and she's been dodging about all day, going from one place to another as she saw me coming. She saw us crossing there a little while ago, and thought we had gone to the quarters, but we turned back so quick, we came into the gully before she knew it, and she could do nothing but lie down in the bushes."

"Was it necessary to punish her so severely?"

"Oh yes, sir," (laughing again.) "If I hadn't punished her so hard she would have done the same thing again to-morrow, and half the people on the plantation would have followed her example. Oh, you've no idea how lazy these niggers are; you northern people don't know any thing about it. They'd never do any work at all if they were not afraid of being whipped."

I inquired about the increase of the negroes on the estate, and the manager having told me of deaths and births the previous year, which gave a net increase of four per cent—on Virginia estates it is often twenty per cent.—I asked if the negroes began to have children at an early age.

"Sometimes at sixteen," said the manager.

"Yes, and at fourteen," said the overseer; "that girl's had a child"—pointing to a girl that did not appear older than fourteen.

"Is she married?"

"No."

"You see," said the manager, "negro girls are not remarkable for chastity; their habits indeed rather hinder them from having children. They'd have them sooner than they do if they would marry or live with but one man, sooner than they do. They often do not have children till they are twenty-five years old."

"Are those who are married true to each other?" I asked.

The overseer laughed heartily at the idea, and described a disgustingly "Free Love" state of things.

"Do you not try to discourage this?"

"No, not unless they quarrel."

"They get jealous and quarrel among themselves sometimes about it," the manager explained, "or come to the overseer and complain, and he has them punished."

"Give all hands a damned good hiding," said the overseer.

"You punish adultery, then, but not fornication?"

"Yes," answered the manager, but "No," replied the overseer, "we punish them for quarreling; if they don't quarrel I don't mind anything about it, but if it makes a muss, I give all four of 'em a warming."

16

The Pleasures of Southern Society, 1856

The span of John Milton Mackie's life extends from 1813 to 1894. He was born in Wareham, Massachusetts, graduated from Brown University, and, after study in Berlin, taught at Brown for some years. He wrote at least four biographies, the best of which is a Life of von Leibnitz (1845); a travel book, Cosas de España, or Going to Madrid (1848); *and* From Cape Cod to Dixie. *This last of his works is a record of certain aspects of southern life—and the West Indies—from impressions gained in a tour just before the Civil War, though the book was not published until 1864. The account pretends to no profundities and admittedly surveys only the lighter and more superficial aspects which would normally come under the observations of a hasty traveler. Yet it possesses a certain humor and lightness of touch and recaptures the ante bellum South in its more genial aspects.*

A FASHIONABLE VIRGINIA PLEASURE RESORT

In the height of the season, there are a hundred arrivals a day at the White Sulphur Springs. Then, when nobody can get accommodations, everybody will insist on being there; for, in the month of August, the most beautiful ladies of Virginia and the South hold their court of love at this fountain; and, their fame going abroad through the mountains, the guests of the other Springs hasten to this centre of attraction. All the generals and judges of the Southern country, too, then come to drink at these waters. Nobody is of a lower grade than a colonel; and, to be called esquire, would argue a man of doubtful consideration.

But not even the being addressed by the very highest titles, will, at this part of the season, save a single man the necessity of sleeping—two in a chamber. There are no adequate accommodations for all these fine ladies and gentlemen. At night, the floors of drawing rooms and parlors are strewn with mattresses; and lucky is the guest who can secure one. Trunks are piled up, ceiling high, in the halls and passages; so that, excepting the fortunate inmates of the pretty private cottages, the thousand and one visitors are, of all men, by no means the most miserable, but probably, the most uncomfortable.

One August morning, as I was standing in the doorway of the office, a well-dressed gentleman drove up in a buggy, and, getting out, asked for a room.

"We cannot accommodate you, sir," said the clerk, looking at the stranger with an air of disinterested unconcern.

"But you can give me a mattress, or a sofa?" was the confident rejoinder.

"Impossible! not one left; and the last three chairs in the house taken half an hour ago!"

"Boy," said the rejected, but not disconcerted new comer, turning his quid from one cheek to the other, at the same time that he turned on his heel toward a servant, "unstrap my trunk."

"It really is of no use, sir," continued the clerk, calmly; "we cannot accommodate you."

"Carry my trunk under that oak tree, yonder," no less quietly added the stranger, and still addressing the black boy.

"Now," said he, sitting down on the trunk, which had been deposited under the protection of the branches, "fetch my buffalo robe; and I'll be d——d if I can't sleep here!"

This proof of pluck was an indirect appeal to the generous and hospitable sentiments which no true Virginian could withstand. There was a general clapping of hands on the utterance of this Diogenic resolution to take things as they came, and the luck of the pot with them; and one of the bystanders immediately stepping forward, politely offered to share his quarters with the tenant of the buffalo robe, who, accordingly, instead of living under an oak, like a Druid, now found himself the fortunate possessor of an apartment in one of the prettiest cottages on the grounds.

In the very height of the season there is no such thing as dining satisfactorily at some of the Springs, however well a person may fare there at all other times. Then, you fee the waiters, and still they bring you nothing. Poor fellows, they have nothing to bring! for the flour has given out; the cows have been milked dry; the mutton has run off into the mountains; and the chief cook has gone distracted! If you can manage to seize upon a bit of beef, and a slice of bread, 'tis your main chance, and hold on to it. Do not run any risks in looking about for vegetables, much less for side dishes, or pepper, or salt. For, while you are vainly endeavoring to accomplish impossibilities, some light-fingered waiter, under the pretence of changing your plate, will run off with your only chance of a dinner.

The scene presents a most ludicrous struggle for bones, and cold potatoes. Or, rather, it is fearful to witness such a desperate handling of the knife; to see so many faces red with rage at getting nothing; and ladies' cheeks pale with waiting; and starving gourmands looking stupefied into the vacuum of the platters before them; and disappointed dyspeptics leaving the table with an expression on their faces of "I'll go hang myself." Add, besides, to what one sees, that which he hears—the maledictions heaped liberally upon the heads of cook, and provider; the clatter of what knives and forks succeed in getting brought into action; the whistling and roaring of Sambo, and the rattling of his heels; with, now and then, an awful crash of chinaware, a slide of plates, or an avalanche of whips and custards; for, where there are several dozens of waiters running up and down the hall, like race horses, there must be occasional collisions; and these, again, lead to fights, at least once, or more, in the season, when a couple of strapping black boys knock each other's noses flatter, and make their mutual wool fly. Truly, the Frenchman who dines on the hair of his mustache, and the end of his toothpick, in front of the *Café de Paris,* is a lucky fellow, and has something under his jacket, compared with these boarders at two dollars per diem.

But it is still worse dining, when it rains. The ancient roofs of some of these halls and piazzas are not made of caoutchouc; and you cannot then sit at meat without two black boys at your back—one to keep off the flies, and the other to hold over your head an umbrella. There is a good excuse for the soup being thin on such days. 'Tis, in fact, mere rain water, with, possibly, a fly, or two, in it.

All the doctors lay down the rule, that the patient must drink mineral waters on an empty stomach; and, by my troth, it is easy following it, during the height of the season, at some of these Springs. That organ is rarely so much occupied in its legitimate business as to be in an unfit state to receive a glass from the fountain. It is said that Chinamen, when hard pushed for other articles of food, can subsist tolerably well on water diet; and, in spending the month of August here, one comes gradually to comprehend how the thing can be done.

Still, one likes to be at the fashionable Springs when the crowd is greatest. The more colonels, the better. The more pretty ladies, the gayer. He wants to talk upon politics with all the judges; attack or defend Sebastopol with all the generals; dance attendance on all the well-bred dames, and waltz with all their daughters. Half the pleasure is in the excitement which proceeds from the great number of persons collected together. Let the fashionable crowd dwindle down to a few dozens, and you leave also. Then you can have an entire suite of rooms, and excellent dinners, with a waiter at each elbow. But, no. When you see the trunks brought down, and hear the farewells said, you are as homesick as anybody, and crowd into the ninth place in the coach, rather than run the risk of being the last man to leave the mountains. So unreasonable are we all.

As for amusements here, do they not consist in drinking the waters, bathing, and, three times a day, supplying the wants of nature by vigorous efforts with the trencher? A few persons bring their books with them as an additional source of entertainment; but most are satisfied with occasionally looking through a newspaper, a magazine, or some learned treatise that may be lying about, on the use of mineral waters. The gentlemen sit half the morning through in easy, wicker-bottom chairs, under the trees, conversing on the subject of politics, estimating the amount of the cotton and rice crops, smoking cigars, drinking juleps, commenting on a passing lady, a horse, or a stage coach. Rarely does a Virginian propose a walk. He prefers to sit, two hours together, beneath the shade. An active, inquisitive Yankee will go out, and explore a mountain, or look at a neighboring farm, and, returning, find the Southerner in the seat where he left him. An alligator in the State from which he comes, would not lie on a log longer. The Northern-born man, rising, perhaps, not much later than the sun, racing up hill and down to get what he calls a little exercise, climbing the pathless mountains for views of the scenery, and scouring the valley without any purpose whatever, unless it be the getting rid of half a day he knows not what to do with, is thought by him of the *terra caliente* a sort of madcap, flibbertigibbet, a personification of unreason. The latter will make as much effort as may be necessary to back a horse; if there is game, he will occasionally go out with dog and gun; and, in a few instances, I have seen him wet a line for trout, or it might have been catfish. At tenpins, and at billiards, also, he will play. But, on the whole, it is an axiom with him, that too much exercise, as well as too much learning, will make a man mad. He, therefore, disparages both.

For any man living on the sunny side of the Union, to do nothing seems to be no labor; and he kills his time, apparently, without the pains of giving it a thought. After a while, indeed, all the visitors at these Springs learn more or less of the art of getting through the summer day easily. One begins with taking no note of the hour of the day, then lets his watch run down, and finally forgets the day of the week, and the month—all being alike, save Sunday. The morning papers he has ordered from town, come to hand several days old, and with such irregularity that, generally, the contradiction of the news arrives before the news itself; so that, at last, he comes to the conclusion that at the end of the watering season nothing of importance will have happened, and he sets his mind at rest.

As for the ladies, without knowing all the little ways they have of amusing themselves, one sees in their sweet faces that they are happy. They are, also, the cause of by far the greater part of the happiness there is in these watering places. If, by any strange fatality, the air of the Alleghanies should become fatal to ringlets, and the mineral waters wash the red out of the peach in the cheek, how soon would all these fair scenes revert to the original savages! But, fortunately, while woman lends a portion of her grace to the mountains, the grateful rocks repay the gift by endowing her with powers of enchantment superior even to those of old conferred on the Medea of the Caucasus. In the eyes of some man or other, every lady here is an enchantress. Scarcely was there a young man in the mountains, during the two seasons I spent there, who did not seem, at times, to be under the influence of illusions, more or less soft and roseate. Even my boy, Custopol, was obliged to confess to me, one day, that when, on the preceding Saturday night, Mary Jane came out in her yellow skirt and green bodice with a basque to it, a purple kerchief twisted round her braided hair, on her feet red morocco slippers, and gold drops pendent from her ears; and when he put his arm around her waist, and they went down the boards together, while Pompey, in the corner, "picked" his banjo, and all the "darkeys" in the place stood up and down the kitchen; and when Mary Jane, turning softly up her eyes, let him look by the half minute together into the whites of them; or, dancing round, poked her elbow in his ribs, and, grinning, pulled his whisker—even Custy was obliged to confess that he felt the tender passion.

Love-making, therefore, may fairly be set down as one of the amusements of the Virginia Springs; whether it turn out to be really diverting to the parties concerned—*cela dépend*.

Another source of pleasure upon which none of the guests can refrain from relying, more or less, is the arrival of the stage coach. Let it happen however often in the day, it is still an important event. One expects his friends; or, if not, somebody may come he has met before; at any rate he must see who is there.

Down gets the first gentleman from the coach. He is tall, with a large proportion of bone in him, and only a moderate supply of muscle. His rather long brown hair is brushed, like a Methodist minister's, off his forehead, which is a high one, but not broad. The well-tanned face indicates vigorous health, though a little sulphur water will be no disadvantage to the owner's liver. The air of calm self-possession marks the man accustomed to command; while the slow gait and quiet motions suggest the habit of overseeing work instead of performing it. The blue dress coat with brass buttons, which is neither old nor new, together with light-colored pantaloons, black satin vest, dark silk cravat, and broad-brimmed felt hat, belong evidently to a gentleman somewhat careless of personal appearance, but of independent circumstances; in short, it requires no epaulettes to convince you at a glance that the stranger is a colonel from one of the eastern counties of Virginia.

When his luggage is taken down, you will find that it consists of a leather trunk covered with small brass knobs and marked with the owner's name, in full, together with those of his county and State; on the top of it is strapped a heavy overcoat, while at one end dangle an extra pair of boots. The colonel travels without a hatbox; but has, instead, a well-worn pair of saddle bags, which are filled with the smaller articles of his wardrobe and such "traps" as he may very likely want on the journey.

On acquaintance, he proves to be a man of good plain sense, who belongs to what he denominates the Jeffersonian party in politics, tills the paternal acres very much after the fashion of his father before him, has, generally, a suit or two pending in the courts of law, but is as goodnatured as he is highminded, and really hates nobody. Once introduced, he will ask you to take a julep with him.

The general moves in more state; he arrives in his own coach and two, or even four—for this old-fashioned turnout has not yet entirely disappeared in the progress of civilization and the rail. He may, also, have two or three outriders, in the shape of sons, on ponies, and black boys riding mares. Sons, servants, mares and horses, they are all of his own raising; but the carriage, possibly, may have belonged to his father or some of his ancestors; for it is after the ancient English model, round topped, heavily timbered, and possessing the property, like Homer's heroes, of never growing old. The trunks being piled up behind, and to them attached a water pail, the footman is obliged to squeeze himself into what of the narrow seat in front is left by the driver.

When this whole affair sweeps up to the door of the hotel, the excited landlord, especially if it be a four-in-hand, rings his bell with a fury which indicates that something extraordinary has happened; and the servants come running, as if they expected to witness the arrival of a dozen stage coaches at once. But 'tis even more than that; 'tis a Virginian general, with horses and mares, black boys and maids, wife and children. The hair of every waiter in the house would stand straight on end, but for the curl in it!

The landlord opens the carriage door himself, hat in hand; and the general gets out. He is a shorter man than the colonel by a half inch, or more. He has a broader and still more open face, a wider back, and carries a respectable corporation before him. His clothes are thin, the colors light, and his face is red; while down out of his fob hangs a heavy gold chain, with two ponderous, ancestral seals, and a key between. The general takes off his white beaver courteously to the colonel, who instantly steps forward to shake him by the hand.

While these congratulations are being exchanged, down the carriage steps carefully comes Dinah. She is dressed mostly in white, and has a cotton kerchief of this color, striped with blue, tied so completely over her hair, that only enough of it remains in sight to show that it is becoming silvered o'er with the pale cast of age; while, over the kerchief and directly on the back of her head, is set a bonnet of open straw and muslin, originally made for the general's pretty daughter when she entered her teens, and so small, withal, that it serves merely to cover the good dame's cerebellum.

The baby is then handed out to Dinah; the rest follow; and when the trunks have been taken down, and the carriage pockets emptied, Cuffy, the coachman, effects his exit with a crack of the whip, such as makes not only his own horses, but all those within an eighth of a mile, jump—each one as though it were about his own ears the lash was playing.

And when, any time within the next half hour, the respectable Virginia farmer, or esquire, well-to-do at home, rides up to the hotel door on his nag, a greatcoat rolled up and tied, together with an umbrella, behind the saddle, and a pair of leathern bags, containing a scanty change of apparel, projecting beneath his thighs, the careless landlord scarcely deigns to touch the bell once. A sleepy-looking negro holds the new comer's bridle while he dismounts; another, lazily taking the saddle bags on his shoulders, and the roll under his arm, conducts him to his chamber; and there is no more noise made over the arrival, compared with the previous excitement, than might be likened to the blowing of a horn reversed.

The springs are of all waters, having for their principal ingredients sulphur, alum, iron, magnesia, or salt. They are also tri-colored, with deposits, white, red, and blue. Some are used for drinking, and some for bathing. The invalid may have his choice; and whatever his complaint, say the doctors, it makes no difference—he is sure to be cured. The cripple is set up at the Hot Springs, and the *malade imaginaire* is made whole at the Warm. The dyspeptic is put on alum water, and the Southwesterner, with bile in his blood and jaundice in his eyes, is ordered to drink of the White Sulphur or the Salt. The Healing Spring is good for the gout; ladies, weary after the winter's dancing, are strengthened by bathing in the two Sweet Waters; the Blue Sulphur, taken before eating venison steaks, is said to be excellent against all devils of the same color; and ever since the publication of the learned Dr. Burke's book, it is every man's own fault if he don't know that the Red Sulphur is a certain cure for consumption.

CHARLESTON BEFORE THE WAR

First of all I went to the races. For I had begun to hear the February races in Charleston talked of as far north as Washington, and had been told much of the fine horses, much of the beautiful women, who, in *grande toilette,* grace these festive occasions. Unfortunately, the twelve of February brought with it gentle showers of rain; but, heavy as was the course, I had rarely seen in the States better running. The horses were ridden by slips of black boys, whom, at first sight, I thought scarcely equal to the task, but who, in the end, proved themselves to be born Jehus. Like the steeds, they must have been bred specially for the race course.

As to the ladies, they were not to be cheated out of their holiday by rain. They were there in full feather; in ermine and point lace; in the light brocades and cashmeres of India. They were there in the latest *nouveautés;* gay with flowers and graceful with fringes, as well as in perfect little loves of parasols, and fans fluttering with coquetry. One or two dowagers sported their diamonds and jewels more appropriate to the ballroom. Nearly all, as it seemed to me, were rather over-dressed for the occasion; though, as it is the fashion of the Charlestonians to put on new bonnets for the February races, as the Philadelphians do at Easter, perhaps the temptation to make too much of the toilet at this time might well be irresistible. Still, bright colors do not harmonize with dark skies. But at the Charleston race course, nothing was gorgeous save the silks and ribbons; for, while heavens of lead over-hung an earth scarcely yet green, even the cheeks of the fair were pale, and their eyes lacked lustre. They were, however, sufficiently pretty and high-bred.

The lords of this part of creation, likewise, were tall and fine-looking; though it struck me that their easy morning costumes, if adapted to the occasion, were not quite in harmony with the elaborate toilets of the other sex. Certain it is, that the tip-top beaux were generally dressed in overcoats, sacks, raglans, sticks, and umbrellas. I could but think, also, that many of them carried a trifle too much weight in the watch chain, and, in some instances, selected their waistcoats of a crimson slightly too emphatic for the black of their pantaloons. But, on the whole, the crowd of clubmen were well attired; and I did not see among them a single specimen of the black-satin vest gentry.

For the rest, considering that ladies came to the race in full dress, I was a little surprised at seeing that the floor of the saloon wherein they were assembled was, in places, wet with tobacco juice,* and sprinkled with nutshells. Lads, whose bringing up in the best families of the town should have taught them better, threw the shells on the floor as unceremoniously as if they had been in a beer garden. Even a lady arrayed in ermine, and deep frills of Chantilly lace, who was holding court, at the moment, consisting of four gentlemen, all in waxed mustaches, suffered two out of four to stand in her presence munching peanuts.

With few exceptions, the elegantly arrayed ladies present to witness the running, and receive the admiration of the handsome members of the Jockey Club, were unmarried; the presence of a somewhat larger number of matrons would have imparted a little more dignity to the festivity, without detracting too much from its grace.

To return to town. My first impression of Charleston was extremely agreeable. It was pleasant to find an American city not wearing the appearance of having all been built yesterday. The atmosphere, charged with an unusual dampness in consequence of the low position of the town on coast and river bank, helps materially to deepen the marks of years; soon discoloring the paint upon the house and facilitating the progress of the green moss, which here is ever creeping over the northern side of roofs and walls. The whole town looks picturesquely dingy, and the greater number of buildings have assumed something of the appearance of European antiquity. The

---

* [Chewing and spitting tobacco was widely commented on. Mackie, a few weeks earlier, when visiting the White House, observed:

"But what is this I see before me at the threshold? Is it a spittoon? By my troth, an enormous one! A perfect monster in capacity, suggestive of quids of the very largest size, and a great many of them. A gentle hint, this, no doubt, to the stranger just arrived from Texas, or the Upper Mississippi, that he will please unpack his cheek before coming into the presence of democratic Majesty.

"But here are more spittoons in the anteroom! It would seem, then, that it is not expected that the American people, on coming to pay their respects to their chief upper servant, should for a moment relinquish their right to chew tobacco whenever and wherever it may please them; and they are accordingly provided with conveniences for expectoration within five-and-forty feet of the foot of the throne. This is as it should be—and strongly democratic. If there be anything wrong about it, it is, perhaps, that there are not vessels of this kind enough to supply the demand for them; and I would most respectfully suggest that the principal avenue to the White House should be lined with rows of them, as the approaches to European palaces are set out with rare plants and flowers."—Ed.]

heavy brick walls and the high gateways are such as one sees in London or Paris. Many front doors and piazzas had been wrought after the graceful models brought from England in the old colonial period. The verandas, story above story, and generally looking toward the south, or the sea, form another pleasant feature in the prevailing style of building. Nor less attractive are the gardens and courtyards invariably attached to the best houses, where, in winter, the hedges are green with pitosporum and the dwarf orange; and where blow the first fragrant violets and daffodils of spring. Here, in February, I beheld with delight the open rose, and camellias so numerous as to redden the ground they fell upon; also, the wild orange bursting with white buds, and the peach tree in full blossom, as well as the humble strawberry at its foot. Stopping at one of these lofty gateways, and looking through the quaint, old-fashioned gratings, I could not help repeating the lines of Goethe

> Ein sanfter Wind vom blauen Himmel weht, 10
> Die Myrte still und hoch der Lorber steht.

These charming gardens, in connection with the piazzas resting on ornamental pillars, make the whole town graceful. One sits, in the morning, in these open chambers, inhaling the refreshing air from the sea, its perfume mingled with that of the flowers below; and, at midday, closing the Venetian shutters to exclude the sun, he rests in grateful shade. Here, too, throughout the longer portion of the year, may be spread, at evening, the tea table; while the heavens still glow with the purple and amber of the sunset. And here lingers the family until the bells from the tower of St. Michael's, sweetly ringing their silver chimes through the calm, starry air, announce, at last, the hour of repose.

Many invalids from the North, delighted with these Southern balconies and these melodious evening bells, with this soft air and genial sunshine, with the lovely promenade of the ever grass-green Battery, and with the pleasing prospect of the bay, never the same with its coming and going ships, are tempted to linger here the winter through, nor go farther southward in their search for health or pleasure. But the climate of Charleston, if soft—soft, even, as that of Rome—is damp, and exceedingly variable. The consumptive invalid, therefore, should never dally long with these sea breezes, nor stay to pluck these flowers. He should proceed onward as far as St. Augustine, or inland to the dry, sandy hill country.

In winter, many of the wealthy South Carolinian planters come to Charleston to enjoy the gay season of February; and a few spend several months here for the sake of the greater advantages in educating their children. But all come to town with less parade than did the grand seigneurs of the generation preceding. For a quarter of a century, the number of coaches and four has been gradually diminishing. Fewer outriders herald the planter's advance. The family carriage has grown a little rickety, and the worse for wear; though the horses are still well blooded, and Sambo holds the reins with cheeks as full, and shoulders as widely spreading. Comparatively few are the masters who nowadays pass through the country with a retinue of from fifteen to twenty servants; who, at a wedding, or other festive oc-

STAGE COACH AND TEAM

casion, open wide their doors to all comers, entertaining troops of friends, twoscore and more, with for every one a couch, as well as for every one a month's welcome. Fiddling, indeed, has not died out; and Pompey still draws his bow, and beats his banjo with as much ardor as in the days of yore. At the merry-makings, there is dancing every night in the parlor, as well as plenty of giggling and roaring in the kitchen. Five-and-twenty varieties of corn cake may be served at breakfast; the pot of hominy, like the widow's cruse, is inexhaustible; the bacon makes the table groan; though certainly the number of pipes of wine annually laid down is getting every year less; nor do I believe there can be many nabobs left, who, in purchasing their supplies in town at the beginning of the season, do not fail to include a hogshead of caster oil for their little negroes.

The February balls in Charleston are scarcely less known to fame than the races. The most select and fashionable are those of the Saint Cecilian, and they have been given here from times running back past the memory of all the dancers now living. Only the gentry and the more favored strangers are admitted. They go at ten o'clock, and stay until three. The attendance, however, is principally confined to the younger portion of the fashionable community, who, before setting off for the dance, see the mammas and papas comfortably to bed. I observed that even the young married ladies attracted but little attention from the beaux; and, in fact, I was repeatedly told, that whenever a bride was led to the altar, she, afterward, went in society, as a matter of course, to the wall. Even the bride, who comes from other parts of the country to find in this hospitable city a home, runs imminent risk of receiving but few marks of courtesy from any gentleman not married. She may be beautiful, accomplished, and elegantly dressed; but the beaux will look at her, if they deign to look at her at all, with blank, mute admiration. This, in a city so famed as Charleston is for gallantry of manners, struck me as a little singular. I saw many fair young ladies among the dancers, and the prevailing style of toilet was characterized by simplicity as well as elegance. Some waltzing, also, I noticed, as graceful as that which may be seen in the countries where the waltz is at home. Of flowers, however, whether as an ornament for the person, or the apartments, there were quite too few; and it seemed as though the profusion with which nature, in the more genial seasons of the year, furnishes these decorations, had led to the neglect of their cultivation by artificial means in winter.

From the presence of two races, the streets of Charleston have a pepper-and-salt aspect. The blacks are almost as numerous as the whites, but are generally of smaller stature. I saw very few slaves, either male or female, who were of large size; still fewer who were good-looking. As an exception, however, in the matter of size, I noticed one portly dame striding down the street in broad-brimmed hat, and staff, who appropriated to her own use nearly the whole of the sidewalk, and swaggered with an importance which plainly marked her as having authority in the kitchen of one of the proudest families of Charleston. On Sunday, the negroes I saw airing themselves on their way to church appeared to good advantage, being respectful in manners, and, for the most part, becomingly plain in dress. The aged dames were in turbans containing only a few modest stripes, though worn pretty high. The younger damsels showed, of course, more love for dressing like white folks. One dainty miss, with large, liquid eyes, and the deep red breaking through her colored cheek, like the vermilion streaming through dark clouds that lie athwart the sunset, made herself gay in a French cashmere; another displayed her jaunty modesty in Canton crape; while the principal colored belle of the promenade held up her rich black silk to exhibit an elaborately embroidered petticoat. The other sex were decently clad, and scarcely in a single instance that came under my observation, grotesquely. They showed, occasionally, a little red in their cravats—sometimes a little buff. But not even on the coach box did Pompey go much beyond a brass buckle in his hat, and purple plush in his waistcoat. On the whole, therefore, the colored palmetto gentry seemed to me to have learned demureness from their betters; though there was, perhaps, as much grinning and giggling as was decent on a Sunday.

It was but a sorry entertainment to visit the slave market; yet, one fine morning, attracted by the auctioneer's flag, I dropped in. There was but one small lot on the block, evidently a badly damaged lot of merchandise; and I did not hear a single bid for them. One old woman, however, by trade a cook, was put up for sale separately. She was, at the time, half seas over, and might very likely have been thus exposed by her master for the sake of frightening her into better behavior. But, if such had been the purpose, the failure of the experiment was complete; for, when she saw that not a single bid was made for such a sinner, she exclaimed, with a prodigiously broad leer of satisfaction, "Nobody want dis ole nigger? Well, I goes back to massa."

We passed along the Battery, the principal promenade of the Charlestonians, and a truly beautiful one. Two rivers, the Cooper and the Ashley, flow past it into the bay, which here spreads out to view a pleasant expanse of waters. Almost entirely landlocked, the Palmetto Islands bound it on the south; to the eastward project into the water the two salient points of Forts Sumter and Moultrie; while in the west, when I first saw it, lay diffused over all the beautiful tints of the sunset. And, night after night, as I returned to the Battery at that hour, the sky was ever aglow with the same hues of purple and salmon color, of saffron, rose, and green. On the first evening, too, the full moon, rising above the eastern horizon, scattered innumerable sparkling points of light in a line across the dancing waves, laying a necklace of diamonds on the bosom of the bay. A little later in the year, all the fashion of Charleston will be met, at the hour of twilight, promenading on this smoothly laid sea wall. Nightly the cool breeze from the water fans them, and refreshes their languid spirits, when May-day introduces the season of hot weather. And hence has grown up the proverb, that the Charlestonians live but during two months of the year—in February, for the sake of the races, and in May, for that of the promenade upon the Battery.

17

General Sherman Destroys a Civilization, 1864

*D*avid P. Conyngham was born in Ireland in 1840 and emigrated to New *York at an early age. When only twenty-four, he was commissioned by the* New York Herald *to write an on-the-spot record of the war; and, with the rank of captain, he moved with Sherman's army from Chattanooga through the Georgia and Carolina campaigns. His observations appeared in book form as* Sherman's March through the South *(1865). After the war his pursuits were almost exclusively literary. He was editor of the* New York Tablet *and author of a half-dozen volumes, both of fiction and of fact, dealing with Ireland and the Irish. The year which saw his last book published,* Ireland Past and Present, *was also the year of his death (1883).*

Portions of Sherman's March *deal with the factual material of the day-by-day advance of the army, but mostly his interest centers on pictures of camp life, incidents in the lives of soldiers, the reaction of war on civilian populations, and the Negroes. Though given on occasion to a bit of Irish romance, his account possesses power and a tragic realism. His sympathy was naturally with the Union army he accompanied, but, nevertheless, it is evident that he had an abiding hatred for war and an infinite compassion for the helpless souls caught in the struggle.*

THE RED BADGE OF COURAGE

Night had set in. The ground was strewn with the dead and wounded. Our men slept beside their arms, for the rebel lines were quite close to them. The living, the dying, and the dead slept beside one another. Rebel and Union officers and men lay piled together; some transfixed with bayonet wounds, their faces wearing that fierce, contorted look that marks those who have suffered agony. Others, who were shot dead, lay with their calm faces and glassy eyes turned to heaven. One might think they were but sleeping.

Others had their skulls crushed in by the end of a musket, while the owner of the musket lay stiff beside them, with the death grip tightened on the piece.

Clinging to one of the guns, with his hand on the spoke, and his body bent as if drawing it, lay a youth with the top of his head shot off. Another near him, with his body cut in two, still clung to the ropes.

Men writhing in pain, men stark and cold; broken caissons, rifles, and bayonets; bloody clothes and torn haversacks, with all the other debris of war's havoc, were the price we paid for two old cannon.

A battle-field, when the carnage of the day is over; when the angry passions of men have subsided; when the death silence follows the din and roar of battle; when the victors have returned triumphant to their camps to celebrate their victory, regardless of the many comrades they have left behind; when the conquered sullenly fall back to a new position, awaiting to renew the struggle,—is a sad sight. It is hard to listen to the hushed groans and cries of the dying, and to witness the lacerated bodies of your fellow-soldiers strewn around, some with broken limbs, torn and mangled bodies, writhing in agony. How often has some poor fellow besought me to shoot him, and put him out of pain! It would be a mercy to do so, yet I dared not.

Piled up together in a ditch, near a battery which they supported with their lines, I found several rebel dead and wounded. I dragged some of the wounded out under the shelter of the trees.

The ghouls of the army were there before me; they had rifled the pockets of the dead and wounded indiscriminately.

I gave many a poor fellow a reviving drink, amidst silent prayers.

In one place I found a mere boy of about fifteen. His leg was shattered with a piece of shell. I placed his knapsack under his head. Poor child! what stories he told me of his mother, away down in Carolina; and his little sisters, how glad they would be, now that he was wounded, to see him home.

They never saw him home, for he went to the home where the weary are at rest.

I came up to the corpse of a rebel soldier, over whom a huge Kentuckian federal soldier was weeping.

"My man," I exclaimed, "why do you weep over him? Look at your comrades around you."

"True, sir," he replied, wiping his eyes; and pointing to a federal soldier near, he said, "There is my brother; this man shot him: I killed him in return. He was my bosom friend. I loved him as a father loves his child."

Next morning, as we were removing our wounded to hospital, I saw a group collected. I rode up, and found that they were some raw troops jeering and insulting rebel wounded. Veteran troops will never do this, but share their last drink and bite with them. I rated them pretty roundly, and ordered the cowardly sneaks to their regiments. After another battle or two, these very boys would feel indignant at such conduct.

It is an affecting sight to witness the removal of the dead and wounded from a battle-field, and the manner in which the former are interred. In some cases, deep pits are sunk, and, perhaps, a hundred or more bodies are flung promiscuously into it, as if no one owned them, or cared for them.

In other cases, where the bodies had been recognized, they were buried with some semblance of decency. I was once riding with a column over a battle-field, in which the skeletons of the hastily buried dead were partly exposed.

SHERMAN'S MARCH: THE BURNING OF ATLANTA, NOVEMBER 15, 1864

The arm and hand of a man protruded from one of these sunken graves.

I have often met skeletons in the woods, with the bones stretched out, and the old rotten knapsacks under the heads, and the remnants of the clothes still clinging around the bones.

These were poor fellows who got wounded in the heat of battle, and retired to the shelter of the forest. Here they lay; and not being discovered, and being unable to get away, they died, inch by inch, for carrion birds to pick their bodies. What must be the suffering of these poor fellows, with their festering wounds, crawling with maggots, without a hand to tend them, without a drop of water to cool their parched lips, with the ravens and turkey-buzzards croaking around them, watching, until they would be too helpless to defend themselves, to pounce on them, and pluck out their eyes, or drag the quivering flesh from their frames.

I have seen others, particularly at the battle of Chancellorsville, who fell, wounded, out in the woods, and who were burned up when the woods took fire, and whom we could not assist, as the rebel skirmishers and sharp-shooters took down every man who dared to put out his head.

Their shrieks and groans, as they writhed in the fiery furnace, still ring in my ears.

Women and children were dreadfully frightened at the approach of our army. It was almost painful to witness the horror and fear depicted on their features. They were schooled up to this by lying statements of what atrocious murders we were committing.

The country people trembled at our approach, and hid themselves away in woods and caves. I rode out one evening alone to pay a visit to another camp which lay some six miles beyond us. In trying to make a short way through the woods, I lost the road, and rambled on through the forest, trying to recover it. This is no easy matter, as I soon discovered; for I only got deeper and deeper into the forest. I then turned my horse's head down a valley that I knew would lead me out on a camp somewhere.

In riding along this, I thought I saw a woman among the trees. I rode in the direction, and saw her darting like a frighted deer towards a thick copse of tangled briers, wild vines, and underbrush.

Fearing some snare, I followed, with pistol in hand; and heavens, what a sight met my view! In the midst of the thicket, sheltered by a bold bluff, were about a dozen women, as many children, and three old men, almost crazy with fear and excitement.

Some of them screamed when they saw me, and all huddled closer, as if resolved to die together. I tied my horse, and assured them that they had no cause for fear; that I was not going to harm them, but would protect them, if needed. Thus assured, they became somewhat communicative.

They told me that they thought the soldiers would kill them, and that they hid here on our approach. Thinking that we were only passing through, they had brought nothing to eat or to cover them. They were here now near three days, and had nothing but the berries they picked up in the woods. They looked wretched, their features wan and thin, their eyes wild and haggard, and their lips stained from the unripe wild fruit. Some of them were lying down, huddled together to keep themselves warm; their clothes were all saturated from the dew and a heavy shower of rain which fell during the day.

I do not think one could realize so much wretchedness and suffering as that group presented. Some of the women were evidently planters' wives and daughters; their appearance and worn dresses betokened it; others were their servants, or the wives of the farm-laborers.

There were two black women, and some three picaninnies. Under the shelter of a tree, I saw a woman sitting down, rocking her body to and fro, as she wept bitterly.

I went over to her. Beside her was a girl of some fourteen years, lying at full length. As I approached, she looked so pale and statuelike, I exclaimed,—

"What's the matter. Is she in a faint?"

"Yes; in one that she won't waken from," said an old crone near.

"Dead!" I exclaimed.

"Well, stranger, I reckon so; better for her go, poor darling, than have the Yankees cotch her."

It was so. She was dead. I understood she was delicate; and the hunger and cold had killed her. So much were they afraid of being discovered that they had not even a fire lighted.

I inquired my way to the camp, and soon returned with some provisions. The dead body was removed, and the sorrowing group returned to their homes; but some of them had no homes, for the soldiers, on the principle that all abandoned houses belong to rebels, had laid them in ashes.

Many of my readers have not seen a vast army encamped. What a sight it presents! Here are some showy headquarters, with their numerous surroundings of white tents. Look into these and you will find that officers do not fare so badly even in the field. Neat beds are contrived; some are cots; others lithe saplings or frames covered with a cotton tick, and plenty of covering, probably contributed by some plantation house. On one side is a table laden with books, a box of cigars, and most likely a bottle of "commissary." These, with a looking glass and the officers' equipments, compose the furniture of the tent. Four flies form a mess tent; and as the general and staff are going to dine, we will just see what kind of fare they have. It consists of stewed beef, hashed potatoes, and a couple of chickens, which the Georgian housekeepers were kind enough to rear for them, and most likely a few bottles of old rye, which the planters were kind enough to leave in their cellars for our especial benefit—all these flanked by a respectable force of negro waiters.

Officers and orderlies are always lounging or riding about headquarters, which gives it a very gay and stirring appearance. At some distance from these are the less pretentious headquarters of some brigadier general, or colonel, while a little farther on are the modest tents of the rank and file and company officers arranged in streets.

The men around these are collected in groups, listening to long yarns beside the cook fire, or are formed into little parties playing cards, pitch and toss, or a thousand other games, known only in the army; others, are dining, grumbling at their rations while dining on turkey. The cooks are busy around a huge tin caldron, placed on the fire, in which a joint of bacon and some peas are bubbling and bubbling around as if they were patriotic enough to enjoy being eaten for the good of the soldiers. A smaller vessel simmers near it, but as the lid is on it I cannot see its contents—most likely a brace of chickens under the wing of a fat turkey. This is the way our troops lived on Sherman's campaign.

The tents themselves had a very picturesque appearance, scattered over hill and valley, in streets and in clumps, looking like so many canvas villages, or huge gypsy encampments. The groups of soldiers, the lines of soldiers marching to or from picket, the sentries moving stately on their beats, generals and officers gayly dashing about, make a camp scene gorgeously imposing and impressive.

How greatly is the effect of a camp scene improved by night! For miles around you the camp fires glitter and sparkle like the lamps of a city. If standing on a hill, one circle of dancing lights and sparkling fireflies encompasses you; while from the valleys beneath you the fires also glow, and the noise of song and merriment, of the harmony of music, floats around you.

The effects of fear, amounting almost to insanity, sometimes developed in action, are very extraordinary. In General Harker's brigade, the men were under orders to advance, when a sergeant retired to his tent, and shot himself through the head. I have known several cases of the kind. It appears strange that a man from fear of going into battle should kill himself. I have often seen men strip themselves stark naked, and run crazy out of a battle-field. I might suspect their sincerity, but I have seen them rush in this manner, under fire, into the rebel lines. This is caused, no doubt, by the stunning effect of shells bursting around them, and killing their comrades. So great is the terror produced by the explosion of several shells, that I have seen a horse that was under a very heavy fire, tremble, the sweat at the same time bursting out of every pore, and then drop down dead, without being touched by ball or shell.

On one occasion General Johnston sent a flag of truce to Sherman, in order to give time to carry off the wounded and bury the dead, who were festering in front of their lines.

A truce followed, and Rebels and Federals freely participated in the work of charity. It was a strange sight to see friends, to see old acquaintances, and in some instances brothers, who had been separated for years, and now pitted in deadly hostility, meet and have a good talk over old times, and home scenes, and connections. They drank together, smoked together, appeared on the best possible terms, though the next day they were sure to meet in deadly conflict again.

Even some of the generals freely mixed with the men, and seemed to view the painful sight with melancholy interest.

An officer, speaking of this sad burial, said, "I witnessed a strange scene yesterday in front of Davis's division. During the burial of the dead, grouped together in seemingly fraternal unity, were officers and men of both contending armies, who, but five minutes before, were engaged in the work of slaughter and death."

Under the shelter of a pine, I noticed a huge gray Kentuckian rebel, with his arm affectionately placed around the neck of a Federal soldier, a mere boy. The bronzed warrior cried and laughed by turns, and then kissed the young Federal.

Attracted by such a strange proceeding, I went over to them, and said to the veteran, "Why, you seem very much taken by that boy; I suppose he is some old friend of yours."

"Old friend, sir! Why, he is my son!"

I have often seen a rebel and a Federal soldier making right for the same rifle-pit, their friends on both sides loudly cheering them on. As they would not have time to fight, they reserved their fire until they got into the pit, then woe betide the laggard, for the other was sure to pop him as soon as he got into cover. Sometimes they got in together, and then came the tug of war; for they fought for possession with their bayonets and closed fists. In some cases however, they made a truce, and took joint possession of it.

It was no unusual thing to see our pickets and skirmishers enjoying themselves very comfortably with the rebels, drinking bad whiskey, smoking and chewing worse tobacco, and trading coffee and other little articles. The rebels had no coffee, and our men plenty, while the rebels had plenty of whiskey; so they very soon came to an understanding. It was strange to see these men, who had been just pitted in deadly conflict, trading, and bantering, and chatting, as if they were the best friends in the world. They discussed a battle with the same gusto they would a cock-fight, or horse-race, and made inquiries about their friends, as to who was killed, and who not, in the respective armies. Friends that have been separated for years have met in this way. Brothers who parted to try their fortune have often met on the picket line, or on the battle-field. I once met a German soldier with the head of a dying rebel on his lap. The stern veteran was weeping, whilst the boy on his knee looked pityingly into his face. They were speaking in German, and from my poor knowledge of the language, all I could make out was, they were brothers; that the elder had come out here several years before; the younger followed him, and being informed that he was in Macon, he went in search of him, and got conscripted; while the elder brother, who was in the north all the time, joined our army. The young boy was scarcely twenty, with light hair, and a soft, fair complexion. The pallor of death on his brow, and the blood was flowing from his breast, and gurgled in his throat and mouth, which the other wiped away with his handkerchief. When he could speak, the dying youth's conversation was of the old home in Germany, of his brothers and sisters, and dear father and mother, who were never to see him again.

In those improvised truces, the best possible faith was observed by the men. These truces were brought about chiefly in the following manner. A rebel, who was heartily tired of his crippled position in his pit, would call out, "I say, Yank!"

"Well, Johnny Reb," would echo from another hole or tree.

"I'm going to put out my head; don't shoot."

"Well, I won't."

The reb would pop up his head; the Yank would do the same.

"Hain't you got any coffee, Johnny?"

"Na'r a bit, but plenty of rot-gut."

"All right; we'll have a trade."

They would meet, while several others would follow the example, until there would be a regular bartering mart established. In some cases the men would come to know each other so well, that they would often call out,—

"Look out, reb; we're going to shoot," or, "Look out, Yank, we're going to shoot," as the case may be.

On one occasion the men were holding a friendly *réunion* of this sort, when a rebel major came down in a great fury, and ordered the men back. As they were going back, he ordered them to fire on the Federals. They refused, as they had made a truce. The major swore and stormed, and in his rage he snatched the gun from one of the men, and fired at a Federal soldier, wounding him. A cry of execration at such a breach of faith rose from all the men, and they called out, "Yanks, we couldn't help it." At night these men deserted into our lines, assigning as a reason, that they could not with honor serve any longer in an army that thus violated private truces.

THE SIEGE OF ATLANTA

From several points along the lines we could plainly see the doomed city, with the smoke of burning houses and bursting shells enveloping it in one black canopy, hanging over it like a funeral pall.

The scene at night was sublimely grand and terrific! The din of artillery rang on the night air. In front of General Geary's headquarters was a prominent hill, from which we had a splendid view of the tragedy enacting before us. One night I sat there with the general and staff, and several other officers, while a group of men sat near us enjoying the scene, and speculating on the effects of the shells. It was a lovely, still night, with the stars twinkling in the sky. The lights from the campfires along the hills and valleys, and from amidst the trees, glimmered like the gas-lights of a city in the distance. We could see the dark forms reclining around them, and mark the solemn tread of the sentinel on his beat. A rattle of musketry rang from some point along the line. It was a false alarm. The men for a moment listened, and then renewed their song and revelry, which was for a while interrupted. The song, and music, and laughter floated to our ears from the city of camps, that dotted the country all round.

Sherman had lately ordered from Chattanooga a battery of four and a half inch rifles, and these were trying their metal on the city.

Several batteries, forts, and bastions joined in the fierce chorus. Shells flew from the batteries, up through the air, whizzing and shrieking, until they reached a point over the devoted city, when down they went, hurling the fragments, and leaving in their train a balloon-shaped cloud of smoke. From right, and left, and centre flew these dread missiles, all converging towards the city. From our commanding position we could see the flash from the guns, then the shells, with their burning fuses, hurtling through the air like flying meteors.

"War is a cruelty," said the general beside me; "we know not how many innocents are now suffering in this miserable city."

"I'm dog gone if I like it," said a soldier, slapping his brawny hand upon his thigh; "I can fight my weight of rattlesnakes; but this thing of smoking out women and children, darn me if it's fair."

On the night of September 1, Hood blew up all the magazines and ammunition, destroyed all the supplies he could not move, comprising eight locomotives, and near one hundred cars laden with ammunition, small arms, and stores, and then retreated. Our troops, advancing near the city, met with no resistance. Observing that it was evacuated, they entered it about 11 o'clock on the morning of September 2, 1864.

Atlanta was now in our hands, the crowning point of Sherman's great campaign. Hood had been outgeneraled, outmanoeuvred, and outflanked, and was now trying to concentrate his scattered army. On the night of the 1st, when the rebel army was vacating, the stampede was frightful to those engaged, but grandly ludicrous to casual spectators.

Even war has its laughable scenes amidst all its horrors, and the retreat from Atlanta was an illustration of that. Conveyances were bought at fabulous sums, and when all were crowded, those who could not procure any—men, women, and children, old and young—followed the procession, bearing bundles of all contents and sizes. The delicate drawing-room miss, that could never venture half a mile on foot, with her venerable parents, now marched out, joining the solemn procession. Confusion and disorder prevailed in every place, considerably increased by the eighty loads of ammunition now blowing up.

Shrieking, hissing shells rushed into the air, as if a thousand guns were firing off together. We plainly heard the noise at Jonesboro'. How terrifying must it be to the trembling, affrighted fugitives, who rushed to and fro, and believed, with every report, that the Yankees were upon them—to slay, ravage, and destroy them.

But yesterday, they had exultingly gazed upon our abandoned works; to-night, how changed!

The city had suffered much from our projectiles. Several houses had been burned, and several fallen down. In some places the streets were blocked up with the rubbish. The suburbs were in ruins, and few houses escaped without being perforated. Many of the citizens were killed, and many more had hair-breadth escapes. Some shells had passed through the Trout House Hotel, kicking up a regular muss among beds and tables.

One woman pointed out to me where a shell dashed through her house as she was sitting down to dinner. It upset the table and things, passed through the house, and killed her neighbor in the next house.

Several had been killed; some in their houses, others in the streets.

When the rebels were evacuating, in the confusion several of our sick and wounded escaped from the hospitals, and were sheltered by the citizens.

Almost every garden and yard around the city had its cave. These were sunk down with a winding entrance to them, so that pieces of shells could not go in. When dug deep enough, boards were placed on the top, and the earth piled upon them in a conical shape, and deep enough to withstand even a shell. Some of these caves, or bomb-proofs, were fifteen feet deep, and well covered. All along the railroad, around the intrenchments and the bluff near the city, were gopher holes, where soldiers and citizens concealed themselves.

In some cases it happened that our shells burst so as to close up the mouths of the caves, thus burying the inmates in a living tomb.

SHERMAN'S MARCH: THE 14TH AND 20TH CORPS MOVE OUT OF ATLANTA

Sherman's comprehensive mind was already clearing the way for the Georgian campaign. He knew that Atlanta might again be rendered formidable in the hands of the enemy, and had resolved to destroy, or, to use his own words, "to wipe it out." War is at best a horrid cruelty, and cannot be refined. Expediency and necessity justify acts savage enough to make the angels weep. Friends and foes suffer indiscriminately from its ravages, and too often the innocent suffer, while the guilty escape.

As soon as General Sherman had issued his order, several families prepared to go south at once. The cars taking them down were loaded with a miscellaneous cargo. In some were crowded together tottering old age and maidens in their youthful bloom. The former fretted very much at being thus rudely torn away, root and branch, from the soil on which they grew, and in which they hoped soon to rest their wearied hearts. In addition, the wagons were crowded with a heterogeneous medley of poodle dogs, tabby cats, asthmatic pianos, household furniture, cross old maids, squalling, wondering children, all of which, huddled together, made anything but a pleasant travelling party, which I accompanied.

On Sherman's return to Atlanta he issued an order for its immediate evacuation by all citizens who had not left in compliance with his first order.

The depot presented a scene of confusion and suffering seldom witnessed. Women and children were huddled together, while men, who had lately been millionaires, were now frantically rushing about, trying to procure transportation, and forced to give their last dollar to some exacting conductor or railway official. An order had been issued by General Easton providing all these people with free transportation; but several of his employees could not see it in that light. They saw the thing could be made to pay, and they did make it pay.

The refugees were afraid to complain. Anxious to get off, dishonest employees told them for days that the next train would be the last that would go. In some cases they gave all they had to be let go, and in many cases paid as high as one hundred dollars to conductors, though all the time provided with free passages. In some cases they managed to divide families, so that they could extort the more from the remaining.

I wanted myself to get a poor soldier, who was going home to die, inside one of the cars. Though they were full of strapping, healthy negroes, who were either servants to the extortioners, or had the almighty dollars to pay their way, I could not gain admittance for the poor fellow. A few dollars in a conductor's pocket were of more importance than his comfort or safety. I gave him my blanket and oilcloth, but I have since learned he never reached home, for when taken off the top of the cars at Chattanooga he was found dead.

I simply mention these facts as a caution to generals not to place too much confidence in employees, unless they are well tried and tested. The first fire burst out on the night of Friday, the 11th of November, in a block of wooden tenements on Decatur Street, where eight buildings were destroyed.

Soon after, fires burst out in other parts of the city. These certainly were the works of some of the soldiers, who expected to get some booty under cover of the fires.

The fire engines were about being shipped for Chattanooga, but were soon brought in, and brought to bear on the burning districts.

The patrol guards were doubled, and orders issued to shoot down any person seen firing buildings. Very little effort had been made to rescue the city from the devouring elements, for they knew that the fiat had gone forth consigning it to destruction. Over twenty houses were burned that night, and a dense cloud of smoke, like a funeral pall, hung over the ruins next morning.

General Slocum offered a reward of five hundred dollars for the apprehension of any soldier caught in the act of incendiarism. Though Slocum knew that the city was doomed, according to his just notions of things it should be done officially. No officer or soldier had a right to fire it without orders.

It was hard to restrain the soldiers from burning it down. With that licentiousness that characterizes an army they wanted a bonfire.

On Sunday night a kind of long streak of light, like an aurora, marked the line of march, and the burning stores, depots, and bridges, in the train of the army.

The Michigan engineers had been detailed to destroy the depots and public buildings in Atlanta. Everything in the way of destruction was now considered legalized. The workmen tore up the rails and piled them on the smoking fires. Winship's iron foundery and machine shops were early set on fire. This valuable property was calculated to be worth about half a million of dollars.

An oil refinery near by next got on fire, and was soon in a fierce blaze. Next followed a freight warehouse, in which were stored several bales of cotton. The depot, turning-tables, freight sheds, and stores around, were soon a fiery mass. The heart was burning out of beautiful Atlanta.

The Atlanta Hotel, Washington Hall, and all the square around the railroad depot, were soon in one sheet of flame.

Drug stores, dry goods stores, hotels, negro marts, theatres, and grog shops, were all now feeding the fiery element. Worn-out wagons and camp equipage were piled up in the depot, and added to the fury of the flames.

A stone warehouse was blown up by a mine. Quartermasters ran away, leaving large stores behind. The men plunged into the houses, broke windows and doors with their muskets, dragging out armfuls of clothes, tobacco, and whiskey, which was more welcome than all the rest. The men dressed themselves in new clothes, and then flung the rest into the fire.

The streets were now in one fierce sheet of flame; houses were falling on all sides, and fiery flakes of cinders were whirled about. Occasionally shells exploded, and excited men rushed through the choking atmosphere, and hurried away from the city of ruins.

At a distance the city seemed overshadowed by a cloud of black smoke, through which, now and then, darted a gushing flame of fire, or projectiles hurled from the burning ruin.

The sun looked, through the hazy cloud, like a blood-red ball of fire; and the air, for miles around, felt oppressive and intolerable. The Tyre of the south was laid in ashes, and the "Gate City" was a thing of the past.

ATLANTA TO THE SEA

It was pretty well known that Sherman was going to cut loose from all communications, and to destroy all the factories, founderies, railroads, mills, and all government property, thus preventing the rebels from using them in his rear. After the troops destroyed Rome, Kingston, and Marietta, tore up the track, and set fire to sleepers, railroad depots, and stores, Sherman issued a special field order:

"The army will forage liberally on the country during the march. To this end each brigade commander will organize a good and efficient foraging party, under command of one or more discreet officers. To regular foraging parties must be intrusted the gathering of provisions and forage at any distance from the roads travelled.

"As for horses, mules, wagons, &c., the cavalry and artillery may appropriate freely and without limit. Foraging parties may also take mules or horses to replace the jaded animals of their trains, or to serve as pack-mules for the regiments or brigades."

These orders were all right, if literally carried out; but they were soon converted into licenses for indiscriminate plunder. The followers of an army, in the shape of servants, hangers-on, and bummers, are generally as numerous as the effective force. Every brigade and regiment had its organized, foraging party, which were joined by every officer's servant and idler about the camps.

These, scattered over the country, without any order or discipline, pounced like harpies on the unfortunate inhabitants, stripping them of all provisions, jewelry, and valuables they could discover.

In most instances they burned down houses to cover their depredations, and in some cases took the lives of their victims, as they would not reveal concealed treasures. These gangs spread like locusts over the country. In all cases where the foraging parties were under the command of a respectable officer, they acted with propriety, simply taking what provisions and necessaries they needed. They might as well have stripped the place, though, for soon came the bummers, and commenced a scene of ruin and pillage. Boxes were burst open; clothes dragged about; the finest silks, belonging to the planters' ladies, carried off to adorn some negro wenches around camp; pictures, books, furniture, all tossed about and torn in pieces. Though these wretches were acting against military orders, there was no one to complain. The planter and his family were thankful if they escaped with their lives; and as to their comrades, they were too deep in the pie themselves to complain of a system which was enriching them.

The first day's march was rather slow, in order to give time to sluggard wagons and teams to get into position. The troops were noisy and cheerful; full of hope and excitement. Though all superfluous baggage and trains had been sent to the rear, still our train numbered about two thousand wagons, and would, if stretched out in one line, extend about twenty miles.

"Living off the country" was fast becoming the order. The men knew that Sherman had started with some sixteen days' supplies, and they wished to preserve them if possible; besides, they thought that a change of diet would be good for their health. There was nothing to be got the first two days' march, as the country all around Atlanta had been foraged by Slocum's corps while hemmed in there. Now we were opening on a country where pits of sweet potatoes, yards of poultry and hogs, and cellars of bacon and flour, were making their appearance. A new spirit began to animate the men; they were as busy as so many bees about a honey-pot, and commenced important voyages of discovery, and returned well laden with spoils. Foragers, bummers, and camp followers scattered over the country for miles, and black clouds of smoke showed where they had been. Small lots of cotton were found near most of the plantation houses. These, with the gins and presses, were burned, oftentimes firing the houses and offices. Near Madison we passed some wealthy plantations; one, the property of a Mr. Lane, who was courteous enough to wait to receive us, was full of decrepit, dilapidated negroes, presided over by a few brimstone-looking white ladies. They were viciously rabid, and only wished they could eat us with the same facility that the troops consumed all the edibles on the place, and eloped with plump grunters and indignant roosters, and their families.

The 20th corps encamped near Madison that night. The cavalry had the advance, burned the depot, and cleared out the town pretty well. Madison is situated on the Augusta line, and was a town of near two thousand inhabitants before the war.

Our troops entered the town next morning, and a brigade was detailed to destroy all the works around the depot and railroad track, also to burn a pile of nearly two hundred bales of cotton in a hut near. While this work was being executed, the stragglers, who manage to get to the front when there is plunder in view, and vagabonds of the army, crowded into the town, and the work of pillage went on with a vengeance. Stores were ripped open; goods, valuables, and plate, all suddenly and mysteriously disappeared. I say mysteriously, for if you were to question the men about it, not one of them admitted having a hand in it. Grinning negroes piloted the army, and appeared to be in their element. They called out, "Here, massa; I guess we gwine to get some brandy here." The doors would at once be forced open, the cellars and shelves emptied, and everything tossed about in the utmost confusion. If a good store chanced to be struck, the rush for it was immense. Some of those inside, being satisfied themselves, would fling bales of soft goods, hardware, harness, and other miscellaneous articles, through the windows. I have seen fellows carry off a richly gilt mirror, and when they got tired of it, dash it against the ground. A piano was a much prized article of capture. I have often witnessed the ludicrous sight of a lot of bearded, rough soldiers capering about the room in a rude waltz, while some fellow was thumping away unmercifully at the piano, with another cutting grotesque capers on the top-board. When they got tired of this saturnalia, the piano was consigned to the flames, and most likely the house with it. The wreck of Madison was pretty effective, too. All the stores were gutted, and the contents scattered and broken around. Cellars of rich wine were discovered, and prostrate men gave evidence of its strength, without any revenue test. A milliner's establishment was sacked, and gaudy ribbons and artificial flowers decorated the caps of the pretty fellows that had done it. Their horses and the negro wenches, too, came in for a share of the decorative spoils.

The left wing had destroyed the Augusta line along their march. The right wing had moved by McDonagh to Jackson without encountering an enemy. The rebels were making some little show to the cavalry on our flanks, but did not as yet attempt to give battle. The negroes were joining us in crowds. Near every cross-road and plantation, we would meet groups of old men and women, and young children, who received us with shouts of joy, exclaiming, "Glory be to de Lord; bress de Lord, de day of jubilou is come; dis nigger is off to glory," and fell in with their sable friends in the rear, without even asking where we were going, or what we would do with them. Such was their simple faith that they trudged along, "bressing de Lord, de day of jubilou is come." Many of them had reason to regret their desire for liberty. With them, liberty too often meant plenty to eat and wear, and nothing to do. They found that it meant hardship, hunger, and cold; for many of them perished along the way from fatigue and the hardship of the march.

The country lying between Madison, Covington, and Milledgeville, is a perfect garden; and though not literally teeming with milk and honey, it was teeming with something better—farmyards well stocked with hogs and poultry, stacks of corn fodder, corn-houses, and bins filled with corn and grain. Sweet potatoes and negroes seemed to grow spontaneously. Hogs grunted a welcome on every side—fine, sleek hogs, that strutted about with snobbish dignity; young, petulant hogs, that cocked up their noses in disdain at the Yankees. The Yankees, not to be outdone in politeness, soon cocked up their feet. Poor, timid sheep, and submissive cattle, swinging huge bells, as if tolling a requiem over the desolation around, looked wonderingly upon the foragers as they came down in fell swoop upon the farmyard, and patiently submitted to their fate.

The left column was now closing on Milledgeville. They had struck the Eatonton Branch Railroad, twenty-two miles from Milledgeville.

We revelled in the splendid homes and palatial residences of some of the wealthy planters here. The men, with that free and easy, devil-may-care sort of way, so characteristic of soldiers, made themselves quite as much at home in the fine house of the planter as in the shanty of the poor white trash or the negro. They helped themselves, freely and liberally, to everything they wanted, or did not want. It mattered little which.

It takes an old raider to appreciate how completely and quickly a railroad can be destroyed. At the first start of railroad raids, the rails were simply turned over,—the men ranging themselves at one side, and raising in one huge swath hundreds of yards at a time, and then tossing it over. This only caused some delay, but left the material for use again. We improved on the thing like all other sciences of war. The rails were torn from the sleepers by a kind of drag, with a lever attached for a handle. Then the sleepers were piled up, and set on fire.

The rails were placed on top, and soon became so soft that they could be twisted like a corkscrew, or wound around a tree like an anaconda. Future antiquarians will rack their brains conjecturing how these iron monsters twisted themselves around the trees. I should not wonder if some Barnum of the twenty-fifty century should exhibit an immense rail as the "fungated boa-constrictor found buried in the heart of a huge oak tree, where it must have lain for hundreds of years," with, perhaps, another that has been modelled into a duck of a corkscrew, as "a corkscrew used by the aborigines of America in the days when there were giants upon the earth."

Our campaign all through Central Georgia was one delightful picnic. We had little or no fighting, and good living. The farm-yards, cellars, and cribs of the planters kept ourselves and animals well stored with provisions and forage, besides an occasional stiff horn of something strong and good, which, according to the injunctions of holy writ, we took "for our stomachs' sake."

Indeed, the men were becoming epicures. In passing through the camp one night, I saw a lot of jolly soldiers squatted outside the huts in true gypsy style, and between them a table richly stocked with meats and fowls of different kinds, flanked by several bottles of brandy.

They were a jolly set of scamps—talked, laughed, jested, and cracked jokes and bottles in smashing style.

A planter's house was overrun in a jiffy; boxes, drawers, and escritoirs were ransacked with a laudable zeal, and emptied of their contents. If the spoils were ample, the depredators were satisfied, and went off in peace; if not, everything was torn and destroyed, and most likely the owner was tickled with sharp bayonets into a confession where he had his treasures hid. If he escaped, and was hiding in a thicket, this was *prima facie* evidence that he was a skulking rebel; and most likely some ruffian, in his zeal to get rid of such vipers, gave him a dose of lead, which cured him of his Secesh tendencies. Sorghum barrels were knocked open, bee-hives rifled, while their angry swarms rushed frantically about. Indeed, I have seen a soldier knock a planter down because a bee stung him. Hogs are bayonetted, and then hung in quarters on the bayonets to bleed; chickens, geese, and turkeys are knocked over and hung in garlands from the saddles and around the necks of swarthy negroes; mules and horses are fished out of the swamps; cows and calves, so wretchedly thin that they drop down and perish on the first day's march, are driven along, or, if too weak to travel, are shot, lest they should give aid to the enemy.

Should the house be deserted, the furniture is smashed in pieces, music is pounded out of four hundred dollar pianos with the ends of muskets. Mirrors were wonderfully multiplied, and rich cushions and carpets carried off to adorn teams and war-steeds. After all was cleared out, most likely some set of stragglers wanted to enjoy a good fire, and set the house, debris of furniture, and all the surroundings, in a blaze. This is the way Sherman's army lived on the country. They were not ordered to do so, but I am afraid they were not brought to task for it much either.

We now come to Sherman's last and crowning campaign through the Carolinas. There can be no denial of the assertion that the feeling among the troops was one of extreme bitterness towards the people of the State of South Carolina. It was freely expressed as the column hurried over the bridge at Sister's Ferry, eager to commence the punishment of "original secessionists." Threatening words were heard from soldiers who prided themselves on "conservatism in house-burning" while in Georgia, and officers openly confessed their fears that the coming campaign would be a wicked one. Just or unjust as this feeling was towards the country people of South Carolina, it was universal. I first saw its fruits at Rarysburg, where two or three piles of blackened brick and an acre or so of dying embers marked the site of an old revolutionary town; and this before the column had fairly got its "hand in."

Our columns were now fast closing in about Columbia.

Early on the morning of the 15th, Major General Hazen threw forward his skirmishers, and ascertained that the enemy had fallen back behind the Congaree, burning the fine bridge that spanned the river just on the edge of Columbia. Hazen had now occupied the front with detachments from his command. Major Generals Howard, Logan, Blair, and others rode to the front, to join Hazen and reconnoitre the position, though the rebel battery was sweeping the road with round shot and canister.

Colonel Ross, chief of artillery, 15th corps, ordered up Captain De Grass's battery. This splendid battery, under its dashing young captain, took up position, and silenced the rebel battery that commanded the road. A section was placed close to the bridge, so as to sweep the streets of the city, which were crowded with soldiers, citizens, and wagons, clearing out of the town. We were within five hundred yards of the city, which was situated on a rising bluff on the other side of the river, so that we could smash it to pieces in a short time by bringing sufficient artillery to bear on it. It appeared to be Sherman's intention to shed as little innocent blood as possible.

We expected every moment that the city would be surrendered, for it now lay hopelessly in our power.

It was a lovely sight; the morning sun rose glowing and beautiful, its sparkling rays lighting up the house-tops of the doomed city, and dancing over the bright waters like diamond gems, bathing the river with its silvery rays. The shadows of the forest trees advanced along the sparkling waters as the boats shot over its surface, and the click of the rifle and whir of the bullet echoed around.

As soon as the pontoon was laid, General Sherman, accompanied by several other generals, their staffs and orderlies, forming a brilliant cavalcade, rode into the city amidst a scene of the most enthusiastic excitement. Ladies crowded the windows and balconies, waving banners and handkerchiefs. They were the wives and sisters of the few proscribed Union people of Columbia. As for the rich, haughty secessionists, they had all fled. Negroes were grouped along the streets, cheering, singing, and dancing in the wild exuberance of their newborn freedom. Perhaps the most flattering compliment paid to us was by a negro, whom, with upturned features and clasped hands, I heard exclaim, "At last! at last! our saviours!" Ringing cheers and shouts echoed far and wide, mingled with the martial music of the bands as they played "Hail, Columbia," "Yankee Doodle," and other national airs. It was, indeed, an exciting scene, and one well worth living to witness.

Our march through the city was so orderly that even the southerners began to bless their stars that the reign of terror was over, and that a reign of peace and security, like that at Savannah, was about being inaugurated. Alas that the scenes of the night should mar so auspicious a beginning!

Towards night, crowds of our escaped prisoners, soldiers, and negroes, intoxicated with their new-born liberty, which they looked upon as a license to do as they pleased, were parading the streets in groups.

As soon as night set in there ensued a sad scene indeed. The suburbs were first set on fire, some assert by the burning cotton which the rebels had piled along the streets. Pillaging gangs soon fired the heart of the town, then entered the houses, in many instances carrying off articles of value. The flame soon burst out in all parts of the city, and the streets were quickly crowded with helpless women and children, some in their night-clothes. Agonized mothers, seeking their children, all affrighted and terrified, were rushing on all sides from the raging flames and falling houses. Invalids had to be dragged from their beds, and lay exposed to the flames and smoke that swept the streets, or to the cold of the open air in back yards.

The scene at the convent was a sad one indeed. The flames were fast encompassing the convent, and the sisters, and about sixty terrified young ladies, huddled together on the streets. Some of these had come from the north, previous to the war, for their education, and were not able to return. The superioress of the convent had educated General Sherman's daughter Minnie. He had assigned them a special guard of six men; so they felt secure, and were totally unprepared for the dreadful scene that ensued. Some Christian people formed a guard around this agonized group of ladies, and conducted them to the Park.

I trust I shall never witness such a scene again—drunken soldiers, rushing from house to house, emptying them of their valuables, and then firing them; negroes carrying off piles of booty, and grinning at the good chance, and exulting, like so many demons; officers and men revelling on the wines and liquors, until the burning houses buried them in their drunken orgies.

I was fired at for trying to save an unfortunate man from being murdered.

The frequent shots on every side told that some victim had fallen. Shrieks, groans, and cries of distress resounded from every side. Men, women, and children, some half naked, as they rushed from their beds, were running frantically about, seeking their friends, or trying to escape from the fated town. A troop of cavalry, I think the 29th Missouri, were left to patrol the streets; but I did not once see them interfering with the groups that rushed about to fire and pillage the houses.

True, Generals Sherman, Howard, and others were out giving instructions for putting out a fire in one place, while a hundred fires were lighting all round them.

How much better would it have been had they brought in a division or brigade of sober troops, and cleared out the town, even with steel and bullet!

General Wood's 1st division, 15th corps, occupied Columbia. Colonel Stone's brigade was the first to enter the city and hoist the flag over the capitol—enviable notoriety, had not the drunken, riotous scenes of the night sullied its honor.

This scene continued until near morning, and then the town was cleared out, when there was nothing more to pillage or burn.

In the hospitals were some hundreds of rebel wounded. The agony and terror of the poor, helpless fellows while the fire raged around them were fearful; but, fortunately, the buildings did not catch fire.

While the streets were crowded with murdering groups of demons from all the corps in the army, hundreds of noble-minded officers and civilians were exposing their own lives to save the lives and property of the citizens.

The 18th of February dawned upon a city of ruins. All the business portions, the main streets, the old capitol, two churches, and several public and private buildings were one pile of rubbish and bricks. Nothing remained but the tall, spectre-looking chimneys. The noble-looking trees that shaded the streets, the flower gardens that graced them, were blasted and withered by fire. The streets were full of rubbish, broken furniture, and groups of crouching, desponding, weeping, helpless women and children.

The Park and Lunatic Asylum, as affording the greatest chance of safety, were crowded with these miserable outcasts. In one place I saw a lady richly dressed, with three pretty little children clinging to her. She was sitting on a mattress, while round her were strewn some rich paintings, works of art, and virtu. It was a picture of hopeless misery surrounded by the trappings of refined taste and wealth. General Sherman ordered six hundred head of cattle and some stores to be left for the nuns and the destitute.

The scene of desolation the city presented next morning was fearful. That long street of rich stores, the fine hotels, the court-houses, the extensive convent buildings, and last the old capitol, where the order of secession was passed, with its fine library and state archives, were all in one heap of unsightly ruins and rubbish. Splendid private residences, lovely cottages, with their beautiful gardens, and the stately rows of shade trees, were all withered into ashes.

The ruins alone, without the evidences of human misery that everywhere met the view, were enough to inspire one with feelings of deep melancholy.

Here was desolation heightened by the agonized misery of human sufferings.

There lay the city wrapped in her own shroud, the tall chimneys and blackened trunks of trees looking like so many sepulchral monuments, and the woe-stricken people, that listlessly wandered about the streets, its pallid mourners.

Old and young moved about seemingly without a purpose. Some mournfully contemplated the piles of rubbish, the only remains of their late happy homesteads.

Old men, women, and children were grouped together. Some had piles of bedding and furniture which they saved from the wreck; others, who were wealthy the night previous, had not now a loaf of bread to break their fast.

Children were crying with fright and hunger; mothers were weeping; strong men, who could not help either them or themselves, sat bowed down, with their heads buried between their hands.

The scenes I witnessed in Columbia—scenes that would have driven Alaric the Goth into frenzied ecstasies, had he witnessed them—made me ponder a little on the horrors of war.

Those who are unacquainted with war cannot realize the fearful sufferings it entails on mankind. They read of it in papers and books, gilded over with all its false glare and strange fascinations, as a splendid game of glorious battles and triumphs, but close their eyes to its bloody horrors. The battlefield is to them a field of honor, a field of glory, where men resign their lives amidst the joys of conquest, which hallow the soldier's gory couch and light up his death-features with a smile. This sounds well in heroic fiction, but how different the reality! Could these fireside heroes but witness a battle-field, with its dead, its dying, and wounded, writhing in agonizing tortures, or witness the poor victims under the scalpel-knife, with the field-hospital clodded with human gore, and full of the maimed bodies and dissected limbs of their fellow-creatures, war would lose its false charms for them. Could many a tender mother see her darling boy, uncared-for, unpitied, without one kind hand to stay the welling blood or wipe the death-damp from his brow, her gentle, loving heart would break in one wail of anguish. War, after all, has horrors even greater than the battlefield presents. The death-wound is mercy compared to the slow torture of languishing in prison-houses—living charnel-houses of slow putrefaction—pale, spiritless, uncared-for, unpitied, gasping and groaning away their lives in hopeless misery. And then think of the sacked and burned city; think of helpless women and children fleeing in terror before the devouring element, without a home to shelter them, without bread to feed them; think of the widows and orphans that water their scant bread with the tears of sorrow; think of all the sufferings, misery, ruin, death, war entails on mankind, and you will curse its authors, and wish that God had otherwise chastised his people. Though war may enrich the Shylock shoddies, paymasters, contractors, and speculative politicians, who sport gorgeous equipages and rich palaces out of the blood of their countrymen, it crushes the people under its wheels, like the car of Juggernaut, and oppresses the millions with taxation.

18

Gone with the Wind: Yankees and Rebels, 1865

*T*hough *born in Sheffield, Massachusetts, in 1835, the youth and young manhood of Sidney Andrews were spent outside New England. Educated in Illinois and at the University of Michigan, he became a newspaperman, first at Alton, Illinois, and then in Washington, D.C., where he was made a correspondent for the* Chicago Tribune. *In 1865 he was commissioned by the* Tribune *and the* Boston Daily Advertiser *to write on the conditions of the war-torn South. His findings were later gathered into book form,* The South since the War, *and published in 1866. The later portion of his life was spent in Boston in various editorial and political capacities. He died in 1880.*

There was a considerable and natural curiosity in the North directly after the close of hostilities for firsthand knowledge about southern conditions. Many travelers sought to supply this information. Among the earliest, and the best, was the account by Andrews. He traveled through North and South Carolina and Georgia from September to November, 1865. His account is a splendid piece of reporting. Clear and well organized, it covers a wide range of information on political, economic, and social matters—the attitudes of white rebels, the freedmen, state conventions, and race relations. In view of the fact that the passions of war had scarcely subsided, it is amazingly objective. He sometimes expected too much in the way of food, considering the prostrate economic position of the South; and his attitude toward the Negro and race relations reflects his Radical Republicanism. But there is no attitude of "Woe to the Vanquished" or any spirit of vindictiveness.

From Charleston to Orangeburg Court House is seventy-seven miles. Route, South Carolina Railroad. Time, seven and a half hours. Fare, five dollars. There is one train per day each way. Our train consisted of five freight-cars, the baggage-car, a box freight-car with seats for negroes, and one passenger-coach. The down train, which we met at Branchville,—where Sherman's army was to find its doom,—consisted of seven freight-cars, four of which were filled with troops on the way to Charleston and home, the baggage-car, and two passenger-coaches. Our one car was uncomfortably full when we started; but only eleven of the passengers came through.

"What sort of accommodations can I get at Orangeburg?" I asked of a friend in Charleston.

"You're not going to stop up there? O you can't do it!"

"Well, I shall try it, at all events."

"Don't do it; Orangeburg is just as good as any of these towns; but I advise you to shun all of 'em. The accommodations are awful: push right on to Columbia."

I wasn't to be put down that way, for I had consulted a gazetteer, and learned that "Orangeburg is a pleasant and thriving town on the northeast bank of the north fork of the Edisto River. It is in the midst of a farming district, and is the centre of a large cotton trade. Population two thousand seven hundred." That was before the war, and I knew the place had been partly burned; but I felt confident that my friend exaggerated.

We left the city at seven and a half o'clock in the morning. Twenty miles out, the conductor came through the car, and collected our fares; for no tickets are sold at Charleston. In front of me sat a good-looking young woman, of about twenty-two, I judged. Hearing her very plainly say that she was going to Orangeburg, I determined to ask her about the town and its hotel accommodations.

"Yes, I live there," she said.

"Is there a hotel in the town, or any place at which a person can stop?"

"O yes, there's a hotel," she said; and after a pause, she added, "but it's hardly such a place as a gentleman would choose, I think."

She spoke pleasantly enough, and, having answered my question, might have dropped the conversation; instead of which, she went on to say that persons who had occasion to stop in town for some days frequently took a room at a private house, and were much better suited than at the hotel.

I did the only thing I well could do,—the thing that it was perfectly natural I should do. I asked her if she could mention one or two private houses at which I might ask for accommodations, if the hotel proved unendurable.

I fully expected that she would say her mother sometimes accommodated gentlemen; and I may as well own that I had determined what reply I should make to that announcement.

Instead, however, she turned in her seat so as to face me, and said, with considerable vim, "Are you a Yankee?"

The question surprised me; and I simply answered, "From the North."

"By what right do you presume to speak to me, sir?" she asked, in a clear and snapping tone, that caught the ears and eyes of most of the passengers.

The strangeness of the question, no less than the remarkable change in her manner, coupled with the fact that I knew myself to be under the observation of thirty or more persons of Southern birth and feeling, embarrassed me to such degree that I could only stammer, "By the right which I supposed a gentleman always had to ask a lady a civil question."

"Well, sir, I don't choose to talk with you."

And she settled herself sharply into her seat, jerked her little body into a very upright position, and squared her shoulders in a very positive manner, —while I sat flushed and confused.

What should I do about it? That was a question I asked myself twenty times per hour for the next thirty miles. I was seriously inclined to apologize (though I hardly knew for what; but didn't, for I feared the little Rebel might snub me again, if I gave her an opportunity. In front of her sat a young man who had been a captain in the Rebel army. Him she soon engaged in conversation, and they cheered the slow miles with most lively chat. Surely, thought I, this is beginning the three months' journey unfortunately. I could have borne her indignation quite easily; but each individual in the car soon made me aware that my Yankee baseness was well known and thoroughly appreciated.

The forenoon wore away, and the crazy old engine dragged itself along. Little Miss was vivacious and entertaining; the ex-officer was evidently in a cheerful frame of mind; I sat alternating between repentance and indignation. Finally the whistle sounded for Branchville.

Missy rose in her seat, shook out her skirts, drew on her small thread glove, turned to me,—mind you, not to the ex-officer, but to me,—and asked me if I would be good enough to hand out her basket for her.

Here was another surprise. Queer creatures, these little Rebels, said I to myself, as I followed her out,—carrying the not heavy basket. She didn't stop when we reached the platform of the station-house, but walked on towards its upper end; and I followed, demurely, but wonderingly. Fifteen or twenty yards away from the car, she suddenly stopped, and turned quickly upon me with "Thank you; I want to apologize to you; I was rude."

And here was the greatest surprise of all! It caught me in confusion; but I managed to say something to the effect that perhaps I was too forward in asking the question I did.

"No, you were not. It was right that you should ask it, and I was rude to answer you so uncivilly. But you caught me at a disadvantage; I hadn't spoken to a Federal since Sumter was taken."

"Well, it didn't hurt you very much, did it?" said I. Whereat she laughed and I laughed, and then the engine whistled.

"I'm going to stop here a day or two," she remarked; and then, "You'll shake hands, won't you?" as I started for the car. So we shook hands, and I left her standing on the platform.

I hadn't learned much about my chances for comfort in Orangeburg, however.

We got here at three o'clock in the afternoon. I was determined to stop, let the accommodations be what they would, and firmly said "No" when the stage agent at the depot urged me to take a seat for Columbia.

There were five passengers with baggage. Twenty-five negroes crowded around us, and troubled the hot air with harsh clamor. "Give yer baggage here, sir." "Luf dis yer nig tote yer plun'er, Mass'r." "Have yer balese toted to de hotel, sah?" "Tuk a hack up town, Mass'r?"

I found the "hack" to be a rickety old short-boxed spring wagon, with two rough board seats, on the back one of which was a worn-out cushion, over both being a canvas supported on sticks nailed to each corner of the box. This establishment was drawn by a scrawny lame mule, and we were seventeen minutes in accomplishing the half-mile, which the boy called it, up to the hotel.

I was a little distrustful about the hotel; and learning from the driver that boarders were sometimes taken at another house, I stopped there and asked the white girl of fifteen, whom I found on the piazza, if they could give me meals and lodgings for about three days. She thought they could, but would call her mother. So much of the house and grounds as I could see presented an inviting appearance, and I indulged in visions of a pleasant chamber and many dreamy hours on the broad piazza. Presently "mother" appeared. She was a plump woman of thirty-three, perhaps.

"Yes, sir, we have a couple of rooms, and we sometimes take transient boarders," said she, answering the question I put to the girl.

"I am stopping three or four days in town, and had much rather be at a pleasant private house than at the hotel," I said.

"Are you a Yankee or a Southerner?"

"O, a Yankee, of course," I answered, smiling, though I saw breakers ahead.

"No Yankee stops here! Good day, sir!" And she turned and walked into the house.

The negro boy, who stood with my valise on his head, volunteered the remark, "Haf to go to de hotel, sah"; and I followed him back to the "hack."

At the "hotel" was a negro boy washing the steps from the piazza into the basement. I told him what I wanted. He would call the Missus. She was somewhere in the lower part of the house; and after her head came into sight above the level of the floor on which I stood, she stopped and washed her hands in the dirty water with which the boy had just finished scrubbing the stairway, smoothing her hair with them and wiping them on her apron.

I made known my desires, paid my driver his charge of seventy-five cents, and was shown by Robert, him of the wash-rag and scrubbing-brush, to room No. 8, the figure being at least a foot in length and rudely done in white chalk.

The room is about fourteen feet square, has one window fronting the southeast, and is in the third story. Lath and plaster there are not, on this floor at least. The partitions are of rough unmatched pine, with strips of cloth over the larger cracks, and a cheap wall paper on the boards all round. The ceiling is also of wood, and was once painted white, but is now, like the wall paper, of a smoky yellow. The paper is much broken by the shrinkage of the boards, and large patches of it have been torn off in a dozen places. The walls and ceiling are handsomely decorated with wasp's mud nests and sooty-branched cobwebs. The bed is a dirty cotton mattress in an old-fashioned high-post bedstead. There are no sheets, and in fact nothing but a cotton-stuffed pillow and a calico spread. This establishment is the abode of a numerous and industrious colony of the Improved Order of Red Men, to whom I nightly pay a heavy blood tribute. Beside the bed there is for furnishing of the room one cane-seat chair, a seven-by-ten looking-glass, and a three-foot-square and breast-high plain pine table, on which are a cracked wash-bowl and a handleless and noseless water-pitcher, to which I prevailed on Robert to add a cracked tumbler. In the window are six sound panes of glass, four cracked ones, and the remnants of five panes more. I suppose I should add also to the furniture several very social and handsome mice, and a healthy and lively swarm of uncommonly large mosquitoes.

The house has three stories and a basement dining-room. The first and second floors have broad piazzas on each side of the house. The first floor has four rooms, and the second and third have five each. Robert says mine is the best on the upper floor,—in which fact there is much consolation. Glimpses into the second floor rooms have not bred in me any desire to move down. In the so-called drawing-room there are three old chairs, a round and rickety centre-table, a sort of writing-desk, the wreck of a piano, and several pieces of carpet. In the dining-room are two twelve-foot plain pine tables, and twenty-three chairs of five different patterns. The table-spread of this noon was the same we had on the evening of my arrival, three days ago, and it was horribly filthy then. The dining-room itself is airy and clean.

The hotel grounds consist of a large yard, the gate of which is always open, and within which all the stray stock of the town has free ramble. At the bottom of the broad steps on the upper side of the house is a large mud-puddle, in which dogs and hogs alternately wallow, there being at least five of the former and nine of the latter running about. The dogs are gaunt and wolfish,—the hogs are slab-sided, half-grown, and very long of nose. There is in the yard about everything one can name, except grass and cleanliness,—bits of wood and crockery, scraps of old iron, wisps of straw and fodder, old rags, broken bottles, sticks, stones, bones, hoofs, horns, nails, etc., etc., *ad infinitum*. The barber throws the sweepings of his shop on one side the house, and the cook is equally free with her slops on the other side.

The "Missus" is the head of the house. She is tall and angular, with a complexion sallow to the last degree of sallowness, eyes in which there is neither life nor hope, hair which I am sure has not felt either comb or brush during my stay. Her dress is a greasy calico, of the half-mourning variety, to which she sometimes adds an apron which isn't more repulsive only because it can't be. She is a type of women, thank God, without counterpart in the North. She goes about the house in a shuffling, shambling manner, with the cry "Robert—Robert—Robert," or " 'Manda—'Manda—'Manda," always on her tongue. There is no variety of accent in this cry, but only one of length, as "Robert—Ro-be-rt—R-o-b-e-r-t." During meals she stands at the head of the table, and serves out the allowance of tea or coffee, and sugar and milk, with an unending string of such talk as this: "Robert, tend the hominy"; "Gal, get the gemman's cup and sasser"; " 'Manda, mind the flies"; "Goodness gracious, nigger, why don't ye pass them biled eggs"; "Now, Robert, do see them flies"; " 'Manda, look arter them squeet pertaterses"; "Now, ye good-for-nuthin' nigger, can't ye brush away them flies?" She complains, in whining, listless fashion, to everybody, about the "niggers," telling how idle, shiftless, and ungrateful they are. She has a husband, who takes special pains to inform everybody that he hasn't anything to do with the hotel; and whose sole occupations, so far as I can see, are smoking, complaining about "the niggers," and doctoring a poor old blind, spavined horse.

The genius of the house is Robert, who stands on his head as well as on his feet; who is trim, pert, wide-awake; who picks out a Northern man with unerring instinct, and is always ready and prompt to serve him; but who is forever out of the way, or very busy when that cry of "Robert—Ro-be-rt— R-o-b-e-r-t" shuffles up through the house. What trick of stealing sugar he hasn't learned isn't worth learning. "*She* talk about the niggers,—bah!" he exclaims, as he goes about his work.

The table is wretched. The tea, eggs, and waffles are the only articles even passably good. Bread and biscuit are alike sour and leaden, and all the meats are swimming in strong fat. The cook is a large and raw-boned negro-woman, who is aided by the "Missus," the boy Robert, and the girl 'Manda. I suppose Sarah cooks quite to the satisfaction of her mistress; but I doubt if it would be possible for any Northern girl, even with twenty years of training, to make of herself a cook so utterly bad as Sarah is. She certainly exhibits most remarkable ability in spoiling everything in the line of eat-ables.

The general management of the house, I scarcely need add, is hopelessly miserable. Everything is forever at sixes-and-sevens, and the knowledge of where anything was yesterday gives not the least indication of its present whereabouts. The establishment, not less in its several parts than in its aggregate whole, is an unclean thing. Shiftlessness has here his abode, and there is neither effort nor desire to dispossess him. And the traveller's bill is three dollars and a half per day!

I have not drawn this picture except for a purpose. I hear, already, in this Southern trip, a great deal about the superior civilization of the South. This hotel is a part of its outgrowth. Orangeburg was a place of twenty-five hundred to three thousand inhabitants. It is the county seat. Here is the State Orphan Asylum. The place is midway between Charleston and the capital. Let any one consider what is the character of the only public house in any Northern town of the same size, and similarly situated, and then the quality of this boasted Southern civilization will be apparent. Nor can it be said that the war is responsible for the condition of things here, for the house was full from the beginning, and has not suffered any loss from either army. It could not receive a week's support in any community of any State from Maine to the Rocky Mountains. Yet here it lives on and on, year after year, a witness for Southern civilization. Let us call things by their right names,— then shall we say *Southern barbarism.*

Part III

THE VALLEY OF DEMOCRACY

Writing in 1888, Lord Bryce, author of the distinguished *American Commonwealth,* declared that "the West may be called the most distinctively American part of America, because the points in which it differs from the East are the points in which America as a whole differs from Europe." Although he admitted that "it is impossible to draw a line between the East and the West, because the boundary is always moving westward," it is clear that he was referring primarily to the great area watered by the Upper Mississippi and its tributaries. Certain fringes of that area are less easily allocated—Kentucky or Missouri, for example—because as border states, and before 1865, connected as they were by slavery and its concomitants with the South, they did not wholly share the cultural outlook of the great valley. Yet, compared to South Carolina or Louisiana, they seem alien to the dominant developments of the Cotton Kingdom and appear to be, as actually they were, more "western" than southern.

Without falling into the excesses of the frontier historians, the comment of Lord Bryce remains intrinsically true. Many of those institutions, such as democracy, nationalism, and reform, which one thinks of as so distinctly American found either their origin in or a sympathetic development through the inhabitants of the Middle West. To an even greater though less tangible degree, such attributes as practicality, materialism, aggressive optimism, the go-getter spirit, or kindly hospitality, which comprise so much of the "American character," found their chief development in the West.

Foreigners were quick to observe this fact that Europe extended to the Alleghenies and that beyond them lay America. Americans, even more, were aware of the distinction between the eastern and western sections; and, as the great tide of emigration crossed the mountains, native travelers promptly commenced their tours to report back to the curious at home what this new life was like. They did an amazingly thorough job of it and in the totality of their accounts left little unvisited or unrecorded.

In thinking of Ohio, of Illinois, or of Minnesota, one largely conceives this frontier as a farming community and pictures log cabins, Indian wars, fields of corn, and unending, boundless prairies. To a large degree the Middle West, especially in the earlier period, was true to this notion, and American travelers duly described precisely these elements. However, it is worthy of especial note that they did not make the mistake of assuming that this was all there was to the record. They were perfectly well aware that urban movements were developing rapidly on this frontier and that many emigrants had no intention of becoming farmers and proposed, rather, to build towns. They were aware, too, that towns implied problems of transportation and culture, to cite but two; and so travelers took equally in their stride cities as well as farms, canals and railways as well as prairies, and colleges and churches as well as Indians and fur-traders.

While the West was western, these travel books are filled with significant and pertinent observation. As the valley commenced to lose its distinctive character and to take on increasingly the economic and social patterns of the older East, the Middle West became less interesting alike to travelers and to the readers of their accounts. Its drabness of life, the uniformity of its towns, and the monotony of its flat countryside were increasingly emphasized, until by the close of the century one has the impression that the entire region between the Appalachians and the Rockies was just so much to be endured until the transcontinental trains reached really "interesting" scenery on the Pacific Coast.

19

Religious Ecstasy on the Frontier, 1804–5

Among the most famous characteristics associated with the frontier were its frenetic religious revivals, and among the most celebrated preachers connected with these revivals was Lorenzo Dow. He was born in 1777 in Coventry, Connecticut. If he was a dynamic character, he was also a strange and stormy one as well. In and out of the Methodist persuasion, he did much to spread the tenets of that sect, though in the end he attacked them as "badly tainted with popery"! He traveled widely on his preaching expeditions through New England, Canada, Ireland, and England and the mountain areas of the South and West. Indeed, so much a man of God was he that he left his first wife on the next morning after his wedding to continue his itinerant preaching. History does not record what his wife thought of this. Self-centered and self-interested, for all his seeming humility, he wrote much, though, except for his Travels (1806), little of it is readable today. His record is pedestrian, dry, and matter of fact; yet, as a participant in the events he describes, it is not without interest or importance. His description of the religious ecstasies he encountered makes somewhat different reading from that which Mrs. Royall observed with such irony and distaste. After his second marriage he settled down, mostly in Connecticut, though his death occurred in Maryland in 1834.

I had heard about a singularity called the *jerks* or *jerking exercise* which appeared first near Knoxville, Tennessee, in August last, to the great alarm of the people, which reports at first I considered as vague and false; but at length, like the Queen of Sheba, I set out, to go and see for myself.

When I arrived in sight of that town, I saw hundreds of people collected in little bodies; and observing no place appointed for meeting, before I spoke to any, I got on a log, and gave out a hymn; which caused them to assemble round, in solemn attentive silence: I observed several involuntary motions in the course of the meeting, which I considered as a specimen of the jerks.

Thus I got on to meeting; and after taking a cup of tea gratis, I began to speak to a vast audience, and I observed about thirty to have the *jerks,* though they strove to keep still as they could; these emotions were involuntary and irresistible, as any unprejudiced eye might discern.

Hence to Mary's-ville, where I spoke to about fifteen hundred, and many appeared to feel the word, but about fifty felt the jerks; at night, I lodged with one of the Nicholites, a kind of Quakers who do not feel free to wear coloured cloaths; I spoke to a number of people at his house that night. Whilst at tea, I observed his daughter, (who sat opposite to me at the table,) to have the jerks, and dropped the teacup from her hand, in the violent agitation: I said to her, "young woman, what is the matter?" she replied, "I have got the jerks." I asked her how long she had it? she observed, "a few days," and that it had been the means of the awakening and conversion of her soul, by stirring her up to serious consideration about her careless state, &c.

Soon after I spoke again in Knoxville, to hundreds more than could get into the Court house, the Governor being present; about one hundred and fifty appeared to have the jerking exercise, amongst whom was a circuit preacher, who had opposed them a little before, but he now had them powerfully; and I believe that he would have fallen over three times had not the auditory been so crowded that he could not, unless he fell perpendicularly.

After meeting, I rode eighteen miles, to hold meeting at night: The people of this settlement were mostly Quakers: and they had said, (as I was informed) the Methodists and Presbyterians have the jerks, because they *sing* and *pray* so much, but we are still peaceable people, wherefore we do not have them: However, about twenty of them came to meeting, to hear one, as was said, somewhat in a Quaker line; but their usual stillness and silence was interrupted; for about a dozen of them had the jerks as keen and powerful as any I had seen, so as to have occasioned a kind of grunt or groan when they would jerk. It appears, that many have undervalued the great revival, and attempted to account for it altogether on natural principles; therefore it seems to me, (from the best judgment I can form), that GOD hath seen proper to take this method, to convince people that he will work in a way to shew his power; and had sent the *jerks* as a sign of the times, partly in judgment for the people's unbelief, and yet as a mercy to convict people of divine realities.

I have seen Presbyterians, Methodists, Quakers, Baptists, Church of England, and Independents, exercised with the *jerks;* Gentleman and Lady, black and white, the aged and the youth, rich and poor, without exception; from which, I infer, as it cannot be accounted for on natural principles, and carries such marks of involuntary motion, that it is no trifling matter: I believe that those who are the most pious and given up to GOD, are rarely touched with it; and also those naturalists, who wish and try to get it to philosophize upon it, are excepted; but the lukewarm, lazy, half-hearted, indolent professor, is subject to it; and many of them I have seen, who when it came upon them, would be alarmed and stirred up to redouble their diligence with GOD; and after they would get happy, were thankful it ever came upon them. Again, the wicked are frequently more afraid of it than the small-pox or yellow fever; these are subject to it; but the persecutors are more subject to it than any, and they have sometimes cursed, and swore, and damned it, whilst jerking. There is no pain attending the jerks, except they resist it, which if they do, it will weary them more in an hour than a day's labour; which shews that it requires the *consent* of the *will* to avoid suffering.

I passed by a meeting house, where I observed the undergrowth had been cut up for a camp-meeting, and from fifty to an hundred saplings left breast high; which appeared to me so slovenish, that I could not but ask my guide the cause, who observed they were topped so high, and left for the people to jerk by; this so excited my attention, that I went over the ground, to view it; and found where the people had laid hold of them, and jerked so powerfully, that they had kicked up the earth as a horse stamping flies. I observed some emotion, both this day and night, among the people; a Presbyterian minister (with whom I stayed,) observed, "yesterday, whilst I was preaching, some had the jerks, and a young man from N. Carolina mimicked them out of derision, and soon was seized with them himself, (which was the case with many others) he grew ashamed, and on attempting to mount his horse to go off, his foot jerked about so, that he could not put it into the stirrup; some youngsters seeing this, assisted him on, but he jerked so that he could not sit alone, and one got up to hold him on, which was done with difficulty; I observing this, went to him, and asked him what he thought of it? said he, 'I believe GOD sent it on me for my wickedness, and making so light of it in others'; and he requested me to pray for him."

I observed his wife had it; she said, she was first attacked with it in bed. Dr. Nelson said, he had frequently strove to get it, (in order to philosophize upon it,) but could not; and observed they could not account for it on natural principles.

Next day, a gentleman gave me some money, and sent a horse with me several miles; and then I took to my feet, and went on to Greenville, and so on to Abington, in Viriginia. The last jerks that I saw, was a young woman, who was severely excercised during meeting; she followed me into the house, I observed to her the indecency and folly of such public gestures and grunts; and requested, (speaking sternly, to make impression on her mind) if she had any regard for her character, to leave it off; she replied, "I will, if I can." I took her by the hand, looking her in the face, and said, "do not tell lies." I perceived, (by the emotion of her hand) that she exerted every nerve, to restrain it, but instantly she jerked as if it would have jerked her out of her skin, if it were possible; I did this to have an answer to others on the subject.

20

An Early View of the Missouri
Country, 1810–11

*H*enry M. Brackenridge (1786–1871) *was the distinguished son of a distinguished father, Hugh Henry Brackenridge, the author of* Modern Chivalry. *The son, born in Pittsburgh, Pennsylvania, voyaged often and extensively through the western country, came to know it well, and left many valuable observations about it. By profession he was a lawyer and, sufficiently active in public and political matters, achieved the no mean distinction of incurring the hostility of both John Quincy Adams and Andrew Jackson. The former dismissed him as "a mere enthusiast," and the latter was the subject of an attack by Brackenridge in* Letters to the Public *(1832).*

During the years 1810–14 Brackenridge lived in the newly acquired Territory of Louisiana, and, in the course of gathering many facts about it, he journeyed in 1811 up the Missouri River to the Missouri Fur Company's post. The Journal *of that expedition he published both separately and as a part of the more extensive* Views of Louisiana *(1814). The* Journal *is on the whole the more interesting, though the* Views, *which is somewhat in the nature of a compendium, is valuable. In 1834 Brackenridge published his most famous work,* Recollections of Persons and Places in the West, *which is hardly a travel book, though it partakes of the nature of one. It affords valuable historical material on the West and autobiographical information about the author.*

A MISSOURI FRONTIER FAMILY

On leaving St. Genevieve, I drew near a settlers cabin, and discovered a group of persons seated by a large fire, which was burning under an enormous tree. "Here he comes," several voices cried out at once; and the settler coming forward requested me to alight, with an appearance of good will which made me feel that it was sincere. The dogs who were at first very noisy, now whined a kind of welcome as if they would second the hospitality of their master. I gladly excepted the invitation, having been a good deal chilled by the cold night dews. The family consisted of the mother and fourteen children, the eldest apparently about eighteen years of age a blooming girl; the youngest an infant. They were all glowing with health. I made up an acquaintance in a few moments with a half a dozen young rogues, and passed the time agreeably. The innocence, the cheerfulness and content, which prevailed in this charming family, almost seemed to be without alloy. The scene will never fade from my recollection. They were neatly dressed in new cotton cloth, and had nothing of that wretchedness or poverty, or stupid ignorance, which is but too common in the unfortunate peasantry of most countries. Looking around, I found myself in the midst of the woods; a few trees were felled round the house, which was built of unhewn logs, the interstices not closed up.

The good man having secured my horse in a kind of shed, and given him a bundle of reeds which he had cut, returned to the fire and resumed his seat. I conversed with him on various subjects, and was much impressed at the good sense as well as various information which he possessed. He gave me a brief account of his reasons for settling here. He was a native of Connecticut, had sold a small property, which he owned in the vicinity of Hartford, and had removed to Ohio, with the intention of purchasing a tract of land on which to support his increasing family. But on his arrival, he had found the price beyond his means, after the expenses he was obliged to incur in transporting his family. He had therefore come to the resolution of proceeding to the extreme frontier, and a few months before had reached New Madrid. Here he had followed the example of others, and selected a spot on the public lands, in the hope of being able to make as much by the cultivation of the soil, as would pay for it by the time the office for the sale of the public domain, should be opened. If it should not prove successful, the improvements on the land would render it more valuable to some one else, and in the meanwhile, he would be able to support his family. Supper being now announced, we all entered the cabin, where the table was spread, and rough benches placed around it. A tin cup filled with rich milk, was placed before each of us, and cakes of the Indian meal were smoking on the board. The good man said grace in a reverend manner, and we did ample justice to the simple and wholesome fare provided for us. Surrounded by health, innocence, and benevolence, who could complain?

After supper, we returned to the fire underneath the spreading tree, and whiled away the time in sprightly and mirthful conversation; the Yankee girls were very talkative, the whole family appeared to be delighted with our company in this lonely place, where they so seldom saw any strangers but their neighbours, the bears and wolves. The hour for retiring at length arrived. My host arose. "Gentlemen," said he, "it is the practice of our family to give a half an hour to religious devotion every evening: should you think proper to join us, we will be glad, if not, keep your seats, and excuse us for the present." Who could have declined such an invitation? I, with shame it is confessed, far from being as good as I ought to be, felt a desire to join in the good man's devotions, if not for the first time, at least never with so much sincerity. We again entered the house, where they sung one of Watts' pious hymns, after which, our host poured out a prayer that seemed to flow from the very bottom of his heart. The evening service was concluded by another hymn, after which, it being time to retire to rest, we were shewn up to the loft, to which we ascended by a ladder. A few blankets and bear skins had been provided for us; we resigned ourselves to sleep, in the consciousness that even such wretches as we could not fail of experiencing the care of the protecting angel, set once to guard this charming family from the approach of guile.

Truth compels me to relate some further particulars respecting this interesting family, which will be painful to the reader. The autumn following, I had to visit New Madrid, and anticipated much pleasure in seeing these worthy people. But alas! as I drew near the house, every thing appeared still about it, and on my making a noise, the good man, emaciated to a skeleton, crawled out, and after recognizing, informed me in the most pathetic, yet composed manner, of a train of misfortunes which had befallen him. His whole family had been assailed by violent bilious fevers, his wife and five of his children were no more, and the rest, with the exception of two boys, who were then extremely ill, had been kindly taken away by some of the old settlers, that they might be the better attended to; but, said he, "God's will be done—it is all for the best."—I could have wept like Niobe.

I must also add, that the season was more unhealthy than had been known for twenty years, and that the settler had unfortunately built his cabin on the border of a pond, which became stagnant in summer.

THE OLD FRENCH AFTER THE PURCHASE OF LOUISIANA

The French inhabitants of the Mississippi have little resemblance to the gay, and perhaps frivolous, Frenchmen of Louis the fifteenth and sixteenth, and still less to those who have felt the racking storm of the revolution.

The present inhabitants are chiefly descendents of the settlers who were induced to remove hither from Canada. In consequence of the misfortunes of France, the settlements of the Illinois experienced a sudden and rapid decay; which was again accelerated by the conquest of General Clark for the United States, in 1779. The greater number of the wealthy and respectable inhabitants descended the Mississippi, and settled in New Orleans, and the lower country. Others crossed the Mississippi, and established St. Louis and St. Genevieve. Scarcely any but natives of the country remained. The foreigners chiefly returned to the countries from whence they first emigrated.

Such is the origin of the greater part of that class of the population of this territory, which I have denominated the ancient inhabitants. They are chiefly natives of the country; but few families are immediately from France, or even from New Orleans or Canada.

In the character of these people, it must be remembered, that they are essentially Frenchmen; but, without that restlessness, impatience and fire, which distinguishes the European. There is, even in their deportment, something of the gravity of the Spaniard, though gay, and fond of amusements. From the gentle and easy life which they led, their manners, and even language, have assumed a certain degree of softness and mildness: the word *paisible* expresses this characteristic. In this remote country, there were few objects to urge to enterprise, and few occasions to call forth and exercise their energies. The necessaries of life were easily procured, and beggary was unknown. Hospitality was exercised as in the first ages. Ambition soared far hence, for here there was no prey. Judges, codes of law, and prisons, were of little use, where such simplicity of manners prevailed, and where every one knew how far to confide in his neighbour. In such a state of things, to what end is learning or science? The schools afforded but slender instruction; the better sort of people acquired in them reading, writing, and little arithmetic. The number of those who were lovers of knowledge, and make it a profession, was small. From the habits of these people, it would naturally be expected, that they would have been unaccustomed to reason on political subjects; they were in fact, as ignorant of them, as children are of life and manners. These inhabitants were as remarkable for their tame and peaceable disposition, as the natives of France are for the reverse.

Amongst their virtues, we may enumerate honesty and punctuality in their dealings, hospitality to strangers, friendship and affection amongst relatives and neighbours. Instances of abandonment on the female side, or of seduction, are extremely rare. The women make faithful and affectionate wives, but will not be considered secondary in the matrimonial association. The advice of the wife is taken on all important, as well as on less weighty concerns, and she generally decides. In opposition to these virtues, it must be said, that they are devoid of public spirit, of enterprise, display but little ingenuity or taste, and are indolent and uninformed.

They are catholics, but, very far from being bigoted or superstitious. They were perhaps more strict observers, formerly, of the rules and discipline of their church, and of the different holy days in the calendar. Their *fetes,* or celebration of these days, were considered, as the most interesting occasions; the old and young engaged in them with the greatest delight, and certainly contributed to their happiness. Of late, this attention to the ceremonies of their religion is considerably relaxed, since other objects of pursuit and interest have been opened to their view. The catholic worship is the only one yet known in the territory, except in private families, and in a few instances of itinerant preachers.

There was scarcely any distinction of classes in the society. The wealthy and more intelligent, would of course be considered as more important personages, but there was no difference clearly marked. They all associated, dressed alike, and frequented the small ball room. They were in fact nearly all connected by the ties of affinity or consanguinity: so extensive is this that I have seen the carnival, from the death of a common relation, pass by cheerless and unheeded. The number of persons excluded was exceedingly small. What an inducement to comport ones self with propriety and circumspection! The same interest at stake, the same sentiments that in other countries influence the first classes of society, were here felt by all its members. Perhaps as many from unmerited praise have been formed into valuable characters, as others from having been unjustly despised have become truly despicable.

Their wealth consisted principally in personal property, lands were only valuable when improved. Slaves were regarded in the light of *bien foncier,* or real property, and in fact, as the highest species. Lead and peltry were frequently used as the circulating medium.

There was but little variety in their employments. The most enterprising and wealthy were traders, and had at the same time trifling assortments of merchandise for the accommodation of the inhabitants, but there were no open shops or stores, as in the United States. There were no tailors or shoemakers; such as pursue these occupations at present, are from the United States. The few mechanics, exercising their trades, principally carpenters and smiths, scarcely deserved the name. The lead mines, I have already observed, engaged a considerable number. The government gave employment to but few, and those principally at St. Louis. By far the greater proportion of the population was engaged in agriculture; in fact, it was the business of all, since the surplus of produce of the country was too inconsiderable to be depended upon. A number of the young men for some time, embraced the employment of boatmen, which was by no means considered degrading; on the contrary, it was desirable for a young man to have it to say, that he had made a voyage in this capacity: and they appeared proud of the occupation, in which they certainly are not surpassed by any people in dexterity. It is highly pleasing to see them exerting themselves, and giving encouragement to each other, by their cheering songs.

But this occupation, amongst many other changes, has been reduced to the same footing as with the Americans. Arising probably from the simple cause, of there having arisen objects of more generous emulation.

What is somewhat strange, there were no domestic manufactures among them; the spinning wheel and the loom were alike unknown. So deficient were they in this respect, that although possessed of numerous herds, they were not even acquainted with the use of the churn, but made their butter by beating the cream in a bowl, or shaking it in a bottle.

Their amusements, were cards, billiards, and dances: this last of course the favourite. The dances were cotillions, reels, and sometimes the minuet. During the carnival, the balls follow in rapid succession. They have a variety of pleasing customs, connected with this amusement. Children have also their balls, and are taught a decorum and propriety of behaviour, which is preserved through life. They have a certain ease and freedom of address, and are taught the secret of real politeness, *self denial;* but which by the apes of French manners, is mistaken for an affected grimace of complaisant regard, and a profusion of bows, scrapes and professions.

Their language, every thing considered, is more pure than might be expected; their manner of lengthening the sound of words, although languid, and without the animation which the French generally possess, is by no means disagreeable. They have some new words, and others are in use, which in France have become obsolete.

In their persons, they are well formed, of an agreeable pleasant countenance; indicating cheerfulness and serenity. Their dress was formerly extremely simple; the men wore a blanket coat, of coarse cloth or coating, with a cape behind, which could be drawn over the head; from which circumstance it was called a *capote*. Both sexes wore blue handkerchiefs on their heads: but no hats, or shoes, or stockings; mockasins, or the Indian sandals, were also used. The dress of the females was generally simple and the variations of fashion, few: though they were dressed in a much better taste than the other sex. These manners will soon cease to exist, but in remembrance and description: every thing has changed. The American costume is generally introduced into the best families, and among the young girls and young men universally. I never saw any where greater elegance of dress than at the balls of St. Louis. We still see a few of both sexes in their ancient habiliments; capots, mockasins, blue handkerchiefs on their heads, a pipe in the mouth, and the hair tied up in a long queue. These people exhibit a striking difference when compared with the unconquerable pertinacity of the Pennsylvania Germans, who adhere so rigidly to the customs, manners and language of their fathers. A few years have effected a greater change with the inhabitants of this territory than has been brought about amongst the Germans in fifty years.

The Americans have communicated to them, their industry and spirit of enterprize, and they in turn, have given some of their more gentle and amiable customs. Upon the whole, the American manners, and even language, begin to predominate. The young men have already been formed by our government, and those growing up will have known no other. A singular change has taken place, which, one would think, ought not to be the result of a transition from a despotism to a republican government: luxury has increased in a wonderful degree, and there exists something like a distinction in the classes of society. On the other hand, more pains are taken with the education of youth; some have sent their sons to the seminaries of the United States, and all seem anxious to attain this desirable end. Several of the young men have entered the army of the United States, and have discovered talents. The females are also instructed with more care, and the sound of the piano is now heard in their dwellings for the first time.

It may be questioned, whether the poorest class has been benefitted by the change. Fearless of absolute want, they always lived in a careless and thoughtless manner: at present the greater part of them obtain a precarious subsistence. They generally possess a cart, a horse or two, a small stock of cattle, and cultivate some spots of ground. At St. Louis they have more employment than in the other villages; they make hay in the prairies, haul wood for sale, and are employed to do trifling jobs in town; some are boatmen or patrons. At St. Genevieve, they depend more upon their agriculture, and have portions in the great field, but this will probably soon be taken from them by the great industry of the American cultivators, who are continually purchasing, and who can give double the sum for rent; they are sometimes employed in hauling lead from the mines, but it will not be sufficient for their support. A number have removed to the country, and, in imitation of the Americans, have settled down on public lands, but here they cannot expect to remain long. Those who live in the more remote villages, are less affected by the change, but there is little prospect of their being better situated.

If I am asked, whether the ancient inhabitants are more contented, or happy, under the new order of things, or have reason to be so, I should consider the question a difficult one, and answer it with hesitation. It is not easy to know the secret sentiments of men, and happiness is a relative term. It is true, I have heard murmurings against the present government, and something like sorrowing after that of Spain, which I rather attributed to momentary chagrin, than to real and sincere sentiment: besides, this generally proceeds from those who were wont to bask in the sunshine of favour. Yet I have not observed those signs which unequivocally mark a suffering and unhappy people. The principal source of uneasiness arises from the difficulties of settling the land claims by the commissioners on the part of the United States. The principal inhabitants have lost much of that influence which they formerly possessed, and are superseded in trade and in lucrative occupations by strangers; their land claims, therefore, constitute their chief dependence. The subject on which the claimants are feelingly alive. This anxiety is a tacit compliment to our government, for under the former, their claims would be scarcely worth attention. The general complaint is, the want of sufficient liberality in determining on them. Six years have passed away without the final adjustment of the claims, and even those that have been decided upon, will give rise to lawsuits; it is probable there will be as copious a harvest of these as ever was furnished by any of the states.

The lower class have never been in the habit of thinking beyond what immediately concern themselves; they cannot, therefore, be expected to foresee political consequences. They were formerly under a kind of dependence, or rather vassalage, to the great men of villages, to whom they looked up for their support and protection. Had they been more accustomed to think it possible, that by industry it was in their power to become rich, and independent also, the change would have been instantly felt in their prosperity. But they possess a certain indifference and apathy, which cannot be changed till the present generation shall pass away. They are of late observed to become fond of intoxicating liquors. There is a middle class, whose claims or possessions were not extensive, but sure, and from the increased value of their property, have obtained since the change of government, a handsome competence. They, upon the whole, are well satisfied; I have heard many of them express their approbation of the American government, in the warmest terms. They feel and speak like freemen, and are not slow in declaring that formerly the field of enterprize was occupied by the monopolies of a few, and it is now open to every industrious citizen.

There are some things in the administration of justice, which they do not yet perfectly comprehend; the trial by jury, and the multifarious forms of our jurisprudence. They had not been accustomed to distinguish between the slow and cautious advances of *even handed justice,* and the despatch of arbitrary power. In their simple state of society, when the subjects of litigation were not of great value, the administration of justice might be speedy and simple; but they ought to be aware, that when a society becomes extensive, and its occupations, relations and interests, more numerous, people less acquainted with each other, the laws must be more complex. The trial by jury is foreign to the customs and manners of their ancestors; it is therefore not to be expected that they should at once comprehend its utility and importance.

The chief advantages which accrued from the change of government, may be summed up in a few words. The inhabitants derived a security from the Indians; a more extensive field, and a greater reward was offered to industry and enterprize; specie became more abundant, and merchandise cheaper. Landed property was greatly enhanced in value. In opposition, it may be said, that formerly they were more content and had less anxiety; there was more cordiality and friendship, living in the utmost harmony, with scarcely any clashing interests. This, perhaps, is not unlike the notions of old people, who believe that in their early days every thing was more happily ordered.

The idea of their becoming extinct, by dissolving before a people of a different race, and of losing their *moeurs cheries,* might excite unhappy sensations. Already the principal villages look like the towns of the Americans. Are not the customs and manners of our fathers, and of our own youth, dear to us all? Would it not fill our hearts with bitterness, to see them vanish as a dream? Sentiments like these, doubtless sometimes steal into their hearts.

THE INDIANS OF THE UPPER MISSOURI

The men are large and well proportioned, complexion somewhat fairer than that of Indians generally—usually go naked:—the dress they put on seems intended more for ornament than as essential; this consists of a sort of cassoc or shirt, made of the dressed skin of the antelope, and ornamented with porcupine quills, died a variety of colors; a pair of leggings, which are ornamented in the same way. A buffaloe hide dressed with the hair on, is then thrown over the right shoulder, the quiver being hung on the other, if armed with a bow.* They generally permit their hair to grow long; I have, in one or two instances, seen it reach to their heels, when increased by artificial locks of horse hair; and is then usually divided into several braids, matted at intervals, with a white tenacious clay; sometimes it is rolled up in a ball, and fixed on the top of the head. They always have a quantity of feathers about them; those of the black eagle are most esteemed. They have a kind of crown made of feathers, such as we see represented in the usual paintings of Indians, which is very beautiful. The swan is in most estimation for this purpose. Some ornament the neck with necklaces made of the claws of the white bear. To their heels they sometimes fasten foxes' tails, and on their leggings suspend deers' hoofs, so as to make a rattling noise as they move along. On seeing a warrior dressed in all this finery, walking with his wife, who was comparatively plain in her dress or ornaments, I could not but think this was following the order of nature, as in the peacock, the stag, and almost all animals, the male is lavishly decorated, while the female is plain and unadorned. I intend this as a hint to some of our petit maitres.

The dress of the female consists of a long robe made of the dressed skins of the elk, the antelope, or the agalia, and ornamented with blue beads, and stripes of ermine, or in its place, of some white skin. The robe is girded round the waist with a broad zone, highly ornamented with porcupine quills, and beads. They are no better off than were the Greeks and Romans, in what we deem at present so essential, but like them they bathe themselves regularly, twice a day. The women are much fairer than the men; some might be considered handsome any where; and exceed the other sex in point of numbers; the dreadful consequence of the wars in which the nation is constantly engaged.

Polygamy is general, they have often four or five wives. Their courtship and marriage resemble that of most of the Indian nations; if the parties are mutually agreeable to each other, there is a consultation of the family; if this be also favourable, the father of the girl, or whoever gives her in marriage, makes a return for the present he had received from the lover—the match is then concluded.

Their government is oligarchical, but great respect is paid to popular opinion. It is utterly impossible to be a great man amongst them without being a distinguished warrior; and though respect is paid to birth, it must be accompanied by other merit, to procure much influence. They are di-

* A warrior is seldom seen without his arms, even in the village.—His bow, spear, or gun, is considered part of his dress, and to appear in public without them, is in some measure disgraceful.

INDIAN CHILDREN AT SCHOOL

vided into different banks or classes; that of the pheasant, which is composed of the oldest men; that of the bear, the buffaloe, the elk, the dog, &c. Each of these has its leader, who generally takes the name of the class, exclusively. Initiation into these classes, on arriving at the proper age, and after having given proofs of being worthy of it; is attended with great ceremony. The band of dogs is considered the most brave and effective in war, being composed of young men under thirty.

War parties are usually proposed by some individual warrior, and according to the confidence placed in him, his followers are numerous or otherwise. In these excursions they wander to a great distance, seldom venturing to return home without a scalp, or stolen horses. Frequently when unsuccessful they "cast their robes," as they express it, and vow to kill the first person they meet, provided he be not of their own nation. In crossing the river, they use canoes made of the buffaloe hide, or a few pieces of wood fastened together. They usually leave some token, as a stake, which is marked so as to convey some idea of their numbers, the direction which they have taken, &c. To avoid surprise, they always encamp at the edge of a wood; and when the party is small, they construct a kind of fortress, with wonderful expedition, of billets of wood, apparently piled up in a careless manner, but so arranged as to be very strong, and by this means to withstand an assault from a much superior force.

Their weapons consist of guns, war clubs, spears, bows, and lances. They have two kinds of arrows, one for the purpose of the chase, and the other for war; the latter differs in this particular, that the barb or point is fastened so slightly, that when it enters the body, it remains in, and cannot be drawn out with the wood; therefore, when it is not in a vital part, the arrow is pushed entirely through. They do not poison them. Their bows are generally very small; an elk's horn, or two ribs of a buffaloe, often constitute the materials of which they are made. Those of wood are of willow, the back covered with sinews.

With respect to their religion, it is extremely difficult, particularly from the slight acquaintance I had with them, to form any just idea. They have some notion of a supreme being, whom they call the "Master of Life," but they offer him no rational worship, and have but indistinct ideas of a future state. Their devotion manifests itself in a thousand curious tricks of slight of hand, which they call magic, and which the vulgar amongst them believe to be something supernatural. They are very superstitious. Beside their magic, or medicine lodge, in which they have a great collection of magic, or sacred things, every one has his private magic in his lodge, or about his person. Any thing curious is immediately made an amulet, or a talisman; and is considered as devoted or consecrated, so as to deprive the owner of the power of giving it away.

To give an account of the vices of these people, would only be to enumerate many of the most gross which prevail amongst us, with this difference, that they are practised in public without shame. The savage state, like the rude uncultivated waste, is contemplated to most advantage at a distance. Mr. Bradbury had been an enthusiast, as most philanthropic Europeans are, on the subject of Indian manners, and I was myself not a little inclined to the same way of thinking, but now both agreed that the world would lose but little, if these people should disappear before civilized communities. In these vast plains, throughout which are scattered so many lovely spots, capable of supporting thousands such nations as the Arikara, or wandering Sioux, a few wretches are constantly roaming abroad, seeking to destroy each other. To return to the subject of their moral characters—they have amongst them their poor, their envious, their slanderers, their mean and crouching, their haughty and overbearing, their unfeeling and cruel, their weak and vulgar, their dissipated and wicked; and they have also, their brave and wise, their generous and magnamimous, their rich and hospitable, their pious and virtuous, their kind, frank, and affectionate, and in fact, all the diversity of characters that exists amongst the most refined people; but as their vices are covered by no veil of delicacy, their virtues may be regarded rather as the effect of involuntary impulse, than as the result of sentiment. In some respects they are extremely dissolute and corrupt; whether this arises from refinement in vice, or from the simplicity of nature, I cannot say; but much are they mistaken who look for primitive innocence and simplicity in what they call the state of nature. It is true that an intercourse with the whites, never fails to render these people much worse than before; this is not by imparting any new vices, but by presenting temptations which easily overcome those good qualities, which "sit so loosely about them." Want of constancy, and uniformity of character, is the defect universally remarked with regard to the Indians, and this naturally arises from the want of fixed principles of virtue.

One thing I remarked as constituting the great difference between the savage and the civilized state, *their youth undergo no discipline,* there are no schools, and the few instructions which are given by parents, are directed only to the mere physical man, and have little to do with the mind, unless it be to inculcate fortitude and courage, or rather ferocity and thirst for blood: no genuine virtues are *cultivated* and the evil propensities of the individual are suffered to mature without correction, while he wanders about a vagabond, responsible to no one for the waste of time; like a young colt, he is considered as unfit for employment until he attains his growth. The lessons of morality are never taught either in public or in private; at least of that morality which instructs us how to fulfil all the duties attached to our social relations, and which regard us as candidates for a future and more happy existence. Instead of such lessons of morality, the precepts first instilled into their hearts, are cruelty, murder, and rapine. The first step the young savage is taught to take, is in blood; and is it any wonder that when manhood nerves his arm, we should see him grasp the tomahawk and the scalping knife, and his savage heart thirst for blood!

Amongst others of their customs which appeared to me singular, I observed that it was a part of their hospitality, to offer the guest, who takes up his residence in their lodges, one of the females of the family as a bedfellow; sometimes even one of their wives, daughters, or sisters, but most usually a maid-servant, according to the estimation in which the guest is held, and to decline such offer is considered as treating the host with some disrespect; notwithstanding this, if it be remarked that these favours are uniformly declined, the guest rises much higher in his esteem. Self control, in the midst of temptations which overpower the common mind, being thought, even amongst these people, to indicate a superior character. Our common boatmen soon became objects of contempt, from their loose habits and ungovernable propensities. To these people, it seemed to me that the greater part of their females, during our stay, had become mere articles of traffic; after dusk, the plain behind our tents, was crowded with these wretches, and shocking to relate, fathers brought their daughters, husbands their wives, brothers their sisters, to be offered for sale at this market of indecency and shame. I was unable to account for this difference from any people I had ever heard of; perhaps something may be attributed to the inordinate passion which had seized them for our merchandize. The silly boatmen, in spite of the endeavors of the leaders of our parties, in a short time disposed of almost every article which they possessed, even their blankets, and shirts. One of them actually returned to the camp, one morning entirely naked, having disposed of his last shirt—this might truly be called *la derniere chemisse de l'amour*.

Seeing the chief one day in a thoughtful mood, I asked him what was the matter—"I was wondering," said he, "whether you white people have any women amongst you." I assured him in the affirmative. "Then," said he, "why is it that your people are so fond of our women, one might suppose they had never seen any before?"

About two miles on this side of the first village, my attention was attracted by a number of small scaffolds, distributed over several acres of ground on the slope of a hill. I soon discovered that this was a depository of the dead. The scaffolds were raised on forks about ten feet, and were sufficiently wide to contain two bodies; they were in general covered with blue and scarlet cloth, or wrapt in blankets and buffaloe robes; we did not approach near enough to examine closely, this frightful Golgotha, or place of human skeletons, but we could see a great number of valuable articles which had been left as offerings to the manes of the deceased. Several crows and magpies were perched upon them; we could not but experience a sensation of horror, when we thought of the attraction which brought these birds to this dismal place. Some of the scaffolds had nearly fallen, perhaps overturned by the wind, or the effect of decay, and a great number of bones were scattered on the ground underneath. This mode of exposing the dead has something peculiarly horrible in it. The wolves of the prairie, the birds of the air, and even the Indian dogs, are attracted to the place, and taught to feed on human flesh.

21

Connecticut's Canaan in the Western Reserve, 1821

The details of the life of Zerah Hawley are meager. He was born in 1781, apparently in Connecticut, where he received an excellent education. Yale conferred a Bachelor's degree on him in 1803 and a Master's degree in 1808. By profession he was a physician. When nearly forty years of age, he undertook an extended journey across New England and New York to Ohio,

The Frontier Moves West

where in Ashtabula County, in the northeastern corner of the Western Reserve, he remained for a year during 1820–21. He thereupon returned home
to Connecticut, published the account of his experiences, A Journal of a Tour
(*New Haven, 1822*), lived out the remainder of an uneventful life, and died
in 1856.

A Journal of a Tour *is not an unbiased account of life in northeastern
Ohio, and it must be regarded in the light of the author's own prejudices.
That he regarded westerners much in the same manner as President Dwight
of Yale is apparent. Their manners were bad and their morals little better.
The fabled account of wealth and prosperity was hugely overdrawn. It is apparent that the good doctor wished he had never gone West and that his fellow-citizens in Connecticut would be well advised not to go either. Certainly
his strict Calvinist opinions viewed the more lax religion of the frontier with
dismay, and life in the land of steady habits had not prepared him for raw
frontier settlements. Possibly forty years of age was too old to make the
necessary adjustments. Nevertheless, despite Hawley's querulousness, his account was a valuable antidote to some of the overexuberant "frontier fever,"
and he noted and jotted down many observations which did not ordinarily
find their way into print.*

On Sept. 30, I crossed the State line and entered Ohio, the *fabled region*
of the West. I say *fabled region,* because more, much more has been said
about the State, than has any foundation in truth. It has been compared to
Canaan, and even extolled above it. It has been called the *Garden* of America,
and many other high sounding titles have been given to it, which it is needless and superfluous to mention.

Today I rode to Harpersfield to see a sick woman, through the woods
about a mile; the road so bad in consequence of the abundance of stumps,
roots and mud, that I could only ride upon a slow walk; and entered for
the first time in my life into a log-house with one room without any fire-
place, the log being laid against the logs of the house and the fire built in
front.

In consequence of this manner of building the fire, some of the logs were
entirely burnt in two, and many were much injured by the fire. The furniture of the house consisted of a bed, laid upon a bedsted made of saplings
of suitable size, (having bark on) with holes bored to receive the legs which
were made of the same materials.—Three or four indifferent chairs, a chest
or two, a few articles of hollow ware, two or three shelves made by boring
holes into the logs of the house, into which were inserted pins of wood upon
which rough boards were laid, forming the whole pantry of the house, con-

{ 296 }

taining a few articles of crockery. Furniture for the fire consisted of two stones which answered the purpose of andirons, and a wooden poker which performed the double office of shovel and tongs. A large hole through the roof, answered the two-fold purpose of a vent for the smoke, and the admission of light. The house was also lighted and ventilated by many large cracks or spaces between the logs, which in winter are sometimes filled with clay, and many times are left without filling through the year, for the purpose (perhaps) of preventing pestilential diseases, as in many cases little pain is taken to keep their habitations cleanly, and in all it is utterly impossible that neatness should exist in consequence of the continual falling of clay from the crevices between the logs, and of bark with which the roof is in many instances covered, and the constant accumulation of mud which is brought into the only room in the house in great profusion. This is not an exaggerated picture; but a reality, and will in most particulars answer for a general description of most of the houses in this part of the country; others there are, a few comfortable framed houses, and some far worse than what I have described, as I shall presently show.

Most of the log houses which have two rooms, more resemble two houses standing near to each other, and covered by one roof, than one house, having a space of about six feet between them, so that in passing from one to the other, you have always to go into the open air, which every one may imagine to be very pleasant and comfortable, especially in a cold stormy winter night. In this hall are usually placed the *swill-barrel, tubs, pots, kettles, &c.* Here the hogs almost every night dance a hornpipe to a swinish tune, which some one or more musicians of their own number play upon the pots and kettles, while others regale themselves at the swill-barrel, and add to the music, by upsetting it, which produces *liquid* music by the discharge of its contents into the Hall! To this music the whole assembly join in a grunting chorus. Now the whole Assembly leave their dancing, and repair to the feast, which is widely and profusely spread upon the ground of the Hall.

I will add that almost all of the houses, whether log or framed, are built without a cellar, and the framed houses are, in this case, built on large piles, as stones are not sufficiently plenty in many towns on the Reserve for this purpose.

A block-house differs from a log one in this particular; in the former the logs are hewn square, so that they are smooth within and without, and the latter are hewn only within, having the bark on the outside. In general also blockhouses are shingled in the ordinary manner, but most of the log houses are covered with long shingles, which are kept in place by means of three or four large poles laid from one end of the roof to the other, which are prevented from slipping off, by small billets of wood placed at right angles with them at certain intervals.

A shanty is a tenement (if it may be so called) built of logs split through the centre, having the plain surface inwards, and the bark without. They are generally about ten or twelve feet square, with a roof on one side, in the manner that horse-sheds are frequently built; consequently they have no chamber at all. In some there is a chimney, in others none, the smoke escaping through an opening at one corner of the roof, or else diffusing itself through the whole apartment, and finding its exit through the large openings between the logs. The door, in order that all the room in the building may be saved for use, always opens outwards, and is hung on wooden hinges, and is usually fastened when the family goes abroad, by a stick of wood leaning against it. This is as full a description of such a building as it merits.

I will finish by giving you some account of *titled men and their habitations*. In riding through the country, you come to a log or block house; on enquiring to whom it belongs, you are surprised to hear that it belongs to Judge ———. The whole establishment consists of one room, in which all the family, with their guests, eat, sleep, and perform all the domestic operations. You proceed a little farther, and arrive at a similar mansion, and are informed that it belongs to Esquire ———, who you find is a miller, and a man who has had no other advantage for acquiring information than an ordinary school education.

Soliciting information respecting another residence, you are told that it is the property of a Representative or a Senator of the Legislature of the State of Ohio. In this villa, containing also but one room, is found a bed in two corners, in another a cup-board, in the fourth a swill-barrel, and on one side of the room a wooden clock without a case, and by one window a three-cornered piece of a looking-glass, set in a little wooden frame of domestic manufacture and on the other side may be seen the Major Z—— at work at shoes. You will find another similar residence belonging to Colonel such a one.

These things are all well enough; but if such are the residences of the Honourable, what must be those of the vulgar.

The furniture of most houses is scanty. Few families have more than one indifferent table, and chairs of the plainest kind, and most of them either broken or worn out, just sufficient to accommodate the family; so that, should company call to see them, the guests or some part of the family must either stand, or sit on the bed, or some stool or block of wood which is most convenient.

The furniture for the table is equally scanty and inconvenient. I once had occasion to dine with a family in Harpersfield, in Ashtabula county, where six of us set at the table. There was a plate for each of us, a large dish in the middle of the table contained the food. I had the good fortune to obtain a decent knife and fork, one of the family had a shoe-knife and a fork, another (if I mistake not) an old raisor-blade with a wooden handle, and the other three were content with forks only. This was a family which has been here for *seventeen* years, and have had time to be in a better condition.

The articles of crockery are also very few and indifferent. Many people brought here with them, a good supply of good crockery, which is mostly broken, and its place partially supplied with very indifferent ware. Many broken-nosed tea-pots are to be seen, and others without a handle, the use of which is supplied by means of a bail made of iron wire, which is inserted into holes drilled through the earthen pot at opposite sides.

For want of a glass, or other convenient vessel, from which to drink, if you are offered whiskey, (which is the principle drink here,) the bottle is presented to you, or a bowl, or tea-cup containing the liquor.

Iron ware is no less scarce than other articles, sometimes a pot answering the four-fold purpose of pot, dish-kettle, tea-kettle, and brass-kettle. In other cases the tea-kettle or the dish-kettle answer the same purposes. In some cases the only tea-kettle, which is to be found in a house is destitute of lid, and one ear, so that the bail applies to the inside of the kettle, which is used in this manner. All articles of iron manufactured in this part of the country are very heavy, and easily broken.

I will now attempt to give as accurate an account of the manners of the people as is in my power.

In general, the manners of the inhabitants are very rude and uncultivated. To this remark there are a few exceptions, though not numerous. But to be more particular; when any man or boy enters a house, he does it almost invariably with his hat on, and forgets to take it off his head during his stay, unless you ask him, and then generally excuses himself from so doing, by saying, *"it is no matter about it."* This is the mode in which ninety-nine in a hundred always enter an house. Whether they do not know enough to think it is proper to take off their hats when they enter a house, or suppose that the head is the most convenient place to hang their hats, it is not for me to determine.

When the person is seated, it is as likely as any way, even if he come on urgent business, that he will say nothing for the space of half an hour, unless to answer a question, laconically, by the monosyllables, yes or no, and many times you have to learn his business by asking it directly. During all this time of silence, there is a vacant kind of stare about every part of the room and the furniture, as if they would say when there is any article of furniture which they have not been accustomed to see, "what do you call that?"

When persons have got within the door, it is common for them to stand as near it as they can, till they are invited forward, staring wildly upon every article in the house, some, especially of the children, turning quite round to see if there is nothing behind them which they have not already discovered.

When leaving the room, after the business on which they came is dispatched, upon arriving at the door, they will, in many instances, turn round again, to take another survey, very frequently departing without any ceremony or inclination of the head. For this perhaps they are not to blame, as for aught I will assert, they may be troubled with a stiffness of the back.

When females enter a room, it is in much the same manner, frequently coming in without knocking, especially on the Sabbath after meeting, when half a dozen come in upon you without any previous notice, or being bid to enter, huddling in and standing behind each other, till you have time to dispose of them in some orderly manner. They have the same stare of astonishment as the male part of the community.

A stranger is to them as much an object of curiosity, to appearance, as would be any common animal.

These manners and customs, perhaps you will say, are innocent and harmless, as they do not affect the morals of the people. To this I agree; but there are others not so free from censure. One custom in particular I shall mention, which cannot be denied or excused, which is very indelicate, and has a very demoralizing tendency. It is this. Sleeping *promiscuously* in one room. In almost every house, parents and children, brothers and sisters, brothers and sisters-in-law, strangers and neighbours, married and unmarried, all ages, sexes and conditions, lodge in the same room, with out any thing to screen them from the view of each other. This I affirm, is not the case in a solitary instance; but it is a general practice, not in the poorest families only, but among the richest and most respectable, as the inhabitants themselves will tell you. And this is done in some cases which I could particularize, where there is not the slightest shadow of necessity; even in houses where there are apartments sufficient to accommodate each sex separately, adult brothers and sisters, and young men and women, no ways related, sleep in the same bed-chamber.

Of the indelicacy of this practice, every one who has been accustomed to a more polished mode of living, will, I think, agree in opinion.

Of the immoral tendency, I think also, every one is well satisfied. Those who are in the practice of this custom, where there is no existing necessity,

I think could hardly say in sincerity, "Lead us not into temptation." Of its immoral effects I could mention some instances, if it were advisable. Of the existence of this practice, I do not write from report; but from my own knowledge, and I do not exaggerate in the description.

People here possess a great share of curiosity, especially in one particular, *i.e.* a great desire to be acquainted with the business of others; so much so, that any thing uttered in a manner supposed to be secret, will, some how or other, be known in a few days time to almost every individual, in a dozen towns, and you are wholly at a loss to determine in what manner, the information could have been communicated. Frequently when a person has mounted his horse, and has set out on some business of his own, he is, without ceremony, bluntly asked, "where are you going?" If he inform the inquirer, he will add, "what are you going there for?" If he satisfies him in this particular, he proceeds to inquire, "what are you about to do?" &c.&c. appearing to feel as much or more interest in his affairs than he does himself, or than he does in his own.

If one could be convinced that this solicitude, concerning his affairs, originated in a desire to promote his interest, or from any motives of friendship, it would be gratifying enough; but when it is known that curiosity is the cause of all this apparent solicitude, it is extremely disgusting and odious, and highly reprehensible. There is still another thing. I never knew, so far as my recollection serves me, a person in *haste.* All appear at ease, whether their business drives or not, and it is a notorious fact, that people (in many towns) are very deficient in industry. It is not an uncommon circumstance, but happens to many, I believe, every year, that a part at least, of their pumpkins, corn, and potatoes, remain in the fields, until snow falls, and thus are lost, for the want of a little more industry.

Instead of preparing wood for the summer, in winter, as is the custom in the Eastern States, men frequently meet in considerable numbers, and spend half the day in idle chit-chat, or invidious remarks concerning their neighbours, each of whom, if you were to believe the assertions of some one individual, is either a *debauchee,* a *drunkard,* a *cheat,* or a *swindler.*

The people here in general are very fond of *borrowing,* it is no matter what, is it any thing you have which they fancy they want, so that you must expect to lend all your crockery, should it chance to be wanted, and if it is broken, they will be *very* sorry, and in a short time, you will have neither any to lend or use yourself. They are, in turn, very good to lend also, and are not in the habit of refusing you any thing you need, if they can spare it as well as not.

It is evident to any impartial observer, that one generation after another, degenerate in a wonderful manner. You may in many cases observe, that the grandparents are people of good manners, and generally improved minds. These, it must be remembered, are immigrants from various parts of the old Atlantic States, and have brought all their improvements with them, which they still retain.

The children of these immigrants, who came into the country with their parents, partake, in some degree, of the manners of their progenitors, although gentility of behaviour is much adumbrated. The grand children, for want of the example and instruction which their parents enjoyed, are degenerated still more, so much so, that politeness, ease of manners, and every kind of grace, is almost entirely lost or obliterated.

Whiskey is the principal drink used in all this western country, and is drunk in great abundance, and is more generally used in liberal portions, than any or all kinds of spirituous liquors, in any other part of the country with which I am acquainted. The principal reason of this is, probably, the want of a market for their surplus quantity of grain, which induces the inhabitants to convert it into whiskey, which is very cheap in consequence of its great abundance.

If we are to judge of the characters of men, by the report of their neighbours, I do not know of more than two or three honest men among all those whom I am acquainted with, or concerning whom I have received any information; but almost all, according to fame, have been guilty of some heinous transaction, and it is remarked by some, that "when people get here, they appear to think that they have got away from all restraint of law and conscience."

Two days ago, I was conversing with a gentleman, who was lately justice of the peace in Ashtabula county, respecting the state of society and morals, who remarked to me, "that when he was on the grand jury about two years since, that it was proved before them, that there were in this county, *twenty-eight* men married to women here, who had left their wives living in the Eastern States, and afterwards he learnt that there were a number more, that they did not know of at that time," so that probably the number of men living in this state of adultery, may not be less than fifty. You will remark that the population of this county, according to the census of last year, is less than seven thousand two hundred.

Schools in this part of the country, are necessarily, very indifferent. Young men and women, in many cases, can read and write, but very badly.

I knew two young men, one of nineteen, the other twenty-one years old, conversing with each other respecting the points used in writing. One remarked to the other, that "that is a comma," "the semicolon is the pause between two syllables," &c. &c. which, by their manner of speaking, they appeared to have just learned, and expressed as much pleasure in knowing these things, as children of eight years old would have done. These were the sons of one of the most wealthy farmers in the town where they resided.

If you inquire of the people, if they have seen or read such and such books, which are most common in New-England, they will reply in most cases, that they have never heard of them, and the library of most families, consists of, (at most,) three or four volumes.

Schools in this part of the country are taught, (if kept up at all,) by females about three months for the Summer term, who teach merely the rudiments of reading, writing, and plain sewing. In many cases these schools are not taught more than eight weeks, and some not more than six, and compensation for teaching is made in almost all cases in such articles as the country affords, and not in money, so that teachers of much erudition, cannot be prevailed upon to undertake the business of teaching the rising generation.

In the winter term, men teach the same branches as are taught by the females in the summer, with the addition of a little Arithmetic, and the exclusion of sewing during about three months.

From this method of teaching, and the short time the schools are kept, and the long intervals that intervene between the terms, it will readily be conceived, that the children forget nearly as much as they learn, and it is very common to meet with young men and women, who cannot read, better than children in Connecticut, of six years of age, and even with less propriety than some with which I am acquainted.

Their knowledge of Geography, Grammar &c. is confined to a few, who may have the privilege of occasionally attending the few academies which are established here; or to those very few, who have property sufficient to send their children abroad. Yet those who have property sufficient to give their children a good education, and are disposed to do so, cannot at this time procure cash sufficient to pay the expense of such an education.

22

A Roving Reporter on the Frontier: The
Ohio and Mississippi, 1837

Edmund Flagg appears never to have stayed in one place or at one job long. Born in Wiscasset, Maine, in 1815, and graduated from Bowdoin at twenty, he followed the course of many other New Englanders by migrating to the West. If, indeed, he had one place of residence, it was Louisville, Kentucky; and, if he worked in one capacity more than another, it was as a newspaperman. In the course of a life which extended to 1890, he traveled much and produced plays, poems, newspaper articles, criticism, and novels. At one period he was even United States consul at Venice.

The Far-West, which he wrote for the Louisville Journal, *and published in book form in 1838, was the result of a trip, taken the year previous, down the Ohio River from Louisville into the Missouri and Illinois country. The two volumes are overconsciously "literary," and the material is often badly organized and diffuse. Unhappily, Flagg appears to have felt that, the more purple-colored adjectives were stacked against a noun, the more effective was the resulting description. Yet he undeniably did see much, especially in the more intimate life of the people; and, after an appropriate amount of blue-penciling and rearrangement, he exhibited an accurate and telling portrayal of frontier conditions.*

A drizzly, miserable rain had for some days been hovering, with proverbial tenacity, over Louisville, the "City of the Falls," while the quay continued to exhibit all that wild uproar and tumult which characterizes the steamboat commerce of the Western Valley. The landing at the time was thronged with steamers, and yet the incessant "boom, boom, boom," of the high-pressure engines, the shrill hiss of scalding steam, and the fitful port-song of the negro firemen rising ever and anon upon the breeze, gave notice of a constant augmentation to the number. Some, too, were getting under way, and their lower guards were thronged by emigrants with their household and agricultural utensils. Drays were rattling hither and thither over the rough pavement; Irish porters were cracking their whips and roaring alternate staves of blasphemy and song; clerks hurrying to and fro, with fluttering note-books, in all the fancied dignity of "brief authority"; hackney-coaches dashing down to the water's edge, apparently with no motive to the nervous man but noise; while at intervals, as if to fill up the pauses of the Babel, some incontinent steamer would hurl forth from the valves of her overcharged boilers one of those deafening, terrible blasts, echoing and re-echoing along the river-banks, and streets, and among the lofty buildings.

To one who has never visited the public wharves of the great cities of the West, it is no trivial task to convey an adequate idea of the spectacle they present. The commerce of the Eastern seaports and that of the Western Valley are utterly dissimilar; not more in the staples of intercourse than in the mode in which it is conducted; and, were one desirous of exhibiting to a friend from the Atlantic shore a picture of the prominent features which characterize commercial proceedings upon the Western waters, or, indeed, of Western character in its general outline, he could do no better than to place him in the wild uproar of the steamboat quay.

Steamers on the great waters of the West are well known to indulge no violently conscientious scruples upon the subject of punctuality. Hour after hour, therefore, still found us and left us amid the untold scenes and sounds of the public landing. It is true our doughty steamer ever and anon would puff and blow like a porpoise or a narwhale; and then would she swelter from every pore and quiver in every limb with the ponderous laboring of her huge enginery, and the steam would shrilly whistle and shriek like a spirit in its confinement, till at length she united her whirlwind voice to the general roar around; and all this indicated, indubitably, an intention to be off and away; but a knowing one was he who could determine *when*.

It was not until the afternoon was far advanced that we found ourselves fairly embarked. The finest site from which to view the city we found to be the channel of the Falls upon the Indiana side of the stream, called the *Indian* chute, to distinguish it from two others, called the *Middle* chute and the *Kentucky* chute. The prospect from this point is noble, though the uniformity of the structures, the fewness of the spires, the unimposing character of the public edifices, and the depression of the site upon which the city stands, give to it a monotonous, perhaps a lifeless aspect to the stranger.

The view of the Falls from the city, on the contrary, is one of beauty and romance. They are occasioned by a parapet of limestone extending quite across the stream, which is here about one mile in width; and when the water is low the whole chain sparkles with bubbling foam-bells. When the stream is full the descent is hardly perceptible but for the increased rapidity of the current, which varies from ten to fourteen miles an hour.* Owing to the height of the freshet, this was the case at the time when we descended them, and there was a wild air of romance about the dark rushing waters: and the green woodlands upon either shore; while the receding city, with its smoky roofs, its bustling quay, and the glitter and animation of an extended line of steamers, was alone necessary to fill up a scene for a limner.

Long before the dawn on the morning succeeding our departure we were roused from our rest by the hissing of steam and the rattling of machinery as our boat moved slowly out from beneath the high banks and lofty syca-mores of the river-side, where she had in safety been moored for the night, to resume her course. Withdrawing the curtain from the little rectangular window of my stateroom, the dark shadow of the forest was slumbering in calm magnificence upon the waters; and glancing upward my eye, the stars were beaming out in silvery brightness. The hated clang of the bell-boy was soon after heard resounding far and wide in querulous and deafening clamour throughout the cabins, vexing the dull ear of every drowsy man. The mists of night had not yet dispersed, and the rack and fog floated quietly upon the placid bosom of the stream.

There is not a stream upon the continent which, for the same distance rolls onward so calmly, and smoothly, and peacefully as the Ohio. Danger rarely visits its tranquil bosom, except from the storms of heaven or the reckless folly of man, and hardly a river in the world can vie with it in safety, utility, or beauty. Though subject to rapid and great elevations and depressions, its current is generally uniform, never furious. The forest-trees which skirt its banks are the largest in North America, while the variety is endless. Its allu-vial bottoms are broad, deep, and exhaustlessly fertile; its bluffs are often from three to four hundred feet in height; its breadth varies from one mile to three, and its navigation, since the improvements commenced, under the authority of Congress, by the enterprising Shreve, has become safe and easy. The classification of obstructions is the following: *snags,* trees anchored by their roots; fragments of trees of various forms and magnitude; *wreck-heaps,*

---

* It is only at high stages of the river that boats even of a smaller class can pass over the Falls. At other times they go through the "Louisville and Portland Canal."

consisting of several of these stumps, and logs, and branches of trees lodged in one place; *rocks,* which have rolled from the cliffs, and varying from ten to one hundred cubic feet in size; and *sunken boats,* principally flat-boats laden with coal. The last remains one of the most serious obstacles to the navigation of the Ohio. Many steamers have been damaged by striking the wrecks of the *Baltimore,* the *Roanoke,* the *William Hulburt,* and other craft, which were themselves snagged; while keel and flat-boats without number have been lost from the same cause.

Several thousands of the obstacles mentioned have been removed since improvements were commenced, and accidents from this cause are now less frequent. Some of the snags torn up from the bed of the stream, where they probably for ages had been buried, are said to have exceeded a diameter of six feet at the root, and were upwards of an hundred feet in length. The removal of these obstructions on the Ohio presents a difficulty and an expense not encountered upon the Mississippi. In the latter streams, the root of the snag, when eradicated, is deposited in some deep pool or bayou along the banks, and immediately imbeds itself in alluvial deposit; but on the Ohio, owing to the nature of its banks in most of its course, there is no opportunity for such a disposal, and the boatmen are forced to blast the logs with gunpowder to prevent them from again forming obstructions. The cutting down and clearing away of all leaning and fallen trees from the banks constitutes an essential feature in the scheme of improvement. The construction of stone dams, by which to concentrate into a single channel all the waters of the river, where they are divided by islands, or from other causes are spread over a broad extent, is another operation now in execution. When all improvements are completed, it is believed that the navigation of the "beautiful Ohio" will answer every purpose of commerce and the traveller, from its source to its mouth, at the lowest stages of the water.

Thump, thump, crash! One hour longer, and I was at length completely roused from a troublous slumber by our boat coming to dead stop. Casting a glance from the window, the bright flashing of moonlight showed the whole surface of the stream covered with drift-wood, and, on inquiry, I learned that the branches of an enormous oak, some sixty feet in length, had become entangled with one of the paddle-wheels of our steamer, and forbade all advance.

We were soon once more in motion; the morning mists were dispersing, the sun rose up behind the forests. We passed many pleasant little villages along the banks, and it was delightful to remove from the noise, and heat, and confusion below to the lofty *hurricane deck,* and lounge away hour after hour in gazing upon the varied and beautiful scenes which presented themselves in constant succession to the eye. Now we were gliding quietly on through the long island chutes, where the daylight was dim, and the enormous forest-trees bowed themselves over us; then we were sweeping rapidly over the broad reaches of the stream, miles in extent; again we were winding through the mazy labyrinth of islets which fleckered the placid surface of the stream, and from time to time we passed the lonely cabin of the emigrant

A STORM ON LAKE ERIE

beneath the venerable and aged sycamores. Here and there, as we glided on, we met some relic of those ancient and primitive species of river-craft which once assumed ascendency over the waters of the West.

In the early era of the navigation of the Ohio, the species of craft in use were numberless, and many of them of a most whimsical and amusing description. The first was the barge, sometimes of an hundred tons' burden, which required twenty men to force it up against the current a distance of six or seven miles a day; next the keel-boat, of smaller size and lighter construction, yet in use for the purposes of inland commerce; then the Kentucky flat, or broad-horn of the emigrant; the enormous ark, in magnitude and proportion approximating to that of the patriarch; the fairy pirogue of the French voyageur; the birch caique of the Indian, and log skiffs, gondolas, and dug-outs of the pioneer without name and number. But since the introduction of steam upon the Western waters, most of these unique and primitive contrivances have disappeared; and with them, too, has gone that singular race of men who were their navigators.

During the morning of our third day upon the Ohio we passed, among others, the villages of *Rome, Troy,* and Rockport. The latter is the most considerable place of the three, notwithstanding *imposing* titles. Here terminates that series of beautiful bluffs commencing at the confluence of the mountain-streams. A new geological formation commences of a bolder character than any before; and the face of the country gradually assumes those features which are found near the mouth of the river. Passing Green River with its emerald waters, its "Diamond Island," the largest in the Ohio, and said to be *haunted,* and very many thriving villages, among which was Hendersonville, for some time the residence of Audubon, the ornithologist, we found ourselves near midday at the mouth of the smiling Wabash, its high bluffs crowned with groves of the walnut and pecan. The confluence of the streams is at a beautiful angle; and, on observing the scene, the traveller will remark that the forests upon one bank are superior in magnitude to those on the other, though of the same species. The appearance is somewhat singular, and the fact is to be accounted for only from the reason that the soil differs in alluvial character. It has been thought that no stream in the world, for its length and magnitude, drains a more fertile and beautiful country than the Wabash and its tributaries. Emigrants are rapidly settling its banks, and a route has been projected for uniting by canal its waters with those of Lake Erie.

About ten miles below the mouth of the Wabash is situated the village of Shawneetown. The buildings, among which are a very conspicuous bank, courthouse, and a land-office for the southern district of Illinois, are scattered along upon a gently elevated bottom, swelling up from the river to the bluffs in the rear, but sometimes submerged, from this latter cause it has formerly been subject to disease; it is now considered healthy; it is the chief commercial port in this section of the state, and is the principal point of debarkation for emigrants for the distant West.

From this spot the river stretches away in a long delightful reach, studded with beautiful islands, among which "Hurricane Island," a very large one, is chief. Passing the mouth of the Cumberland River with its green island, once the rendezvous of Aaron Burr and his chivalrous band, we next reached the town of Paducah, at the outlet of the Tennessee. This is a place of importance, though deemed unhealthy.

It was sunset when we arrived at the confluence of the rivers. Though the hour was a delightful one, the scene did not present that aspect of vastness and sublimity which was anticipated from the celebrity of the streams. For some miles before uniting its waters with the Mississippi, the Ohio presents a dull and uninteresting appearance. It is no longer the clear, sparkling stream, with bluffs and woodland painted on its surface; the volume of its channel is greatly increased by its union with two of its principal tributaries, and its waters are turbid; its banks are low, inundated, and clothed with dark groves of deciduous forest-trees, and the only sounds which issue from their depths to greet the traveller's ear are the hoarse croaking of frogs, or the dull monotony of countless choirs of moschetoes. Thus rolls on the river through the dullest, dreariest, most uninviting region imaginable, until it sweeps away in a direction nearly southeast, and meets the venerable Father of the West advancing to its embrace. The volume of water in each seems nearly the same; the Ohio exceeds a little in breadth, their currents oppose to each other an equal resistance, and the resultant of the forces is a vast lake more than two miles in breadth, where the united waters slumber quietly and magnificently onward for leagues in a common bed. On the right come rolling in the turbid floods of the Mississippi; and on looking upon it for the first time with preconceived ideas of the magnitude of the mightiest river on the globe, the spectator is always disappointed. He considers only its breadth when compared with the Ohio, without adverting to its vast depth. The Ohio sweeps in majestically from the north, and its clear waters flow on for miles without an intimate union with its turbid conqueror. The characteristics of the two streams are distinctly marked at their junction and long after. The banks of both are low and swampy, totally unfit for culture or habitation. "Willow Point," which projects itself into the confluence, presents an elevation of twenty feet; yet, in unusual inundations, it is completely buried six feet below the surface, and the agitated waters, rolling together their masses, form an enormous lake. How strange that the confluence of the waters of such streams, in their onward rolling to the deep, should take place at almost the only stage in their course devoid entirely of interest to the eye or the fancy.

It was late before we had passed the confluence of the Ohio with the dark-rolling tide of the "endless river," and the darkness became gradually so dense that doubts were entertained as to the prudence of attempting to stem the mighty current of the Mississippi on such a night. These, however, were overruled; and sweeping around the low peninsula of Cairo, our steamer met the torrent and quivered in every limb. A convulsed, motionless struggle ensued, in which the heavy laboring of the engine, the shrill whistle of the safety-valve, the quick, querulous crackling of the furnaces, the tumultuous rushing of the wheels, and the stern roar of the scape-pipe, gave evidence of the fearful power summoned up to overcome the flood. At length we began very slowly to ascend the stream. Our speed was about five miles an hour, and the force of the current nearly the same, which so impeded advancement that it requires as long to ascend from the confluence to St. Louis as to descend to the same point from the Falls, though the distance is less than half. All night our steamer urged herself slowly onward against the current, and the morning found us threading a narrow channel amid a cluster of islands, from whose dense foliage the night-mists were rising and settling in dim confusion. Near the middle of the stream, above this collection, lays a very large island, comprising eight or ten thousand acres, called English Island. The stream here expands itself to the breadth of four miles.

A company of emigrants, in course of the morning, were landed from our boat at a desolate-looking spot upon the Missouri shore; men, women, and little ones, with slaves, household stuff, pots, kettles, dogs, implements of husbandry, and all the paraphernalia of the backwood's farm heaped up promiscuously in a heterogeneous mass among the undergrowth beneath the lofty trees. A similar party from the State of Vermont were, during our passage, landed near the mouth of the Wabash, one of whom was a pretty, delicate female, with an infant boy in her arms. They had been *deck-passengers,* and we had seen none of them before; yet their situation could not but excite interest in their welfare.

It was yet early in the morning of our first day upon the Mississippi that we found ourselves beneath the stately bluff upon which stands the old village of Cape Girardeau, and some thirty miles further on, the waters of the Muddy River enter the Mississippi from Illinois.

A few miles above the Big Muddy stands out from the Missouri shore a huge perpendicular column of limestone, of cylindrical formation, about one hundred feet in circumference at the base, and in heighth one hundred and fifty feet, called the "Grand Tower." Upon its summit rests a thin stratum of vegetable mold, supporting a shaggy crown of rifted cedars. This is the first of that celebrated range of heighths upon the Mississippi usually pointed out to the tourist, springing in isolated masses from the river's brink upon either side, and presenting to the eye a succession of objects singularly grotesque. There are said to exist, at this point upon the Mississippi, indications of a huge parapet of limestone having once extended across the stream, which must have formed a tremendous cataract, and effectually inundated all the alluvion above. At low stages of water ragged shelves, which render the navigation dangerous, are still to be seen. The whole region bears palpable evidence of having been subjected, ages since, to powerful volcanic and diluvial action; and neither the Neptunian or Vulcanian theory can advance a superior claim.*

For a long time after entering the dangerous defile in the vicinity of the *Grand Tower,* through which the current rushes like a racehorse, our steamer writhed and groaned against the torrent, hardly advancing a foot. At length, as if by a single tremendous effort, which caused her to quiver and vibrate to her centre, an onward impetus was gained, the boat shot forward, the rapids were overcome, and then, by chance, commenced one of those perilous feats of rivalry frequent upon the Western waters, A RACE. Directly before us, a steamer of a large class, deeply laden, was roaring and struggling against the torrent under her highest pressure. During our passage we had several times passed and repassed each other, either boat was delayed at the various wood-yards along the route; but now, as the evening came on, and we found ourselves gaining upon our antagonist, the excitement of emulation flushed every cheek. The passengers and crew hung clustering, in breathless interest, upon the galleries and the boiler deck, wherever a post for advantageous view presented; while the hissing valves, the quick, heavy stroke of the piston, the sharp clatter of the *eccentric,* and the cool determination of the pale engineer, as he glided like a spectre among the fearful elements of destruction, gave evidence that the challenge was accepted. A dense mist came on, and the exhausted steamers were hauled up at midnight beneath the venerable trees upon the banks of the stream. On the first breakings of dawn all was again in motion. But alas! alas! in spite of all the strivings of our valorous steamer, it soon became but too evident that her mighty rival must prevail, as she came rushing up in our wake. Like a civil, well-behaved rival, she speeded on, hurling forth a triple bob-major of curses at us as she passed, doubtless by way of salvo, and disappeared behind a point. When to this circumstance is added that a long-winded racer of a mail-boat soon after swept past us in her onward course, and left us far in the rear, I shall be believed when it is stated that the steamer on which we were embarked was distinguished for anything but speed.

As we were passing Ste. Genevieve an accident occurred which had nearly proved fatal to our boat, if not to the lives of all on board her. A race which took place between another steamer and our own has been noticed. In some unaccountable manner, this boat, which then passed us, fell again in the rear, and now, for the last hour, had been coming up in our wake under high steam. On overtaking us, she attempted, contrary to all rules and regulations

---

* [A reference to two conflicting opinions among early geologists as to the causes of changes in the earth's surface.—ED.]

for the navigation of the river provided, to pass between our boat and the bank beneath which we were moving; an outrage which, had it been persisted in a moment longer than was fortunately the case, would have sent us to the bottom. For a single instant, as she came rushing on, contact seemed inevitable; and, as her force was far superior to our own, and the recklessness of many who have the guidance of Western steamers was well known to us all, the passengers stood clustering around upon the decks, some pale with apprehension, and others with firearms in their hands, flushed with excitement, and prepared to render back prompt retribution on the first aggression. The pilot of the hostile boat, from his exposed situation and the virulent feelings against him, would have met with certain death; and he, consequently, contrary to the express injunctions of the master, reversed the motion of the wheels just at the instant to avoid the fatal encounter. The sole cause for this outrage, we subsequently learned, was a private pique existing between the pilots of the respective steamers.

However this may be, our passage seemed fraught with adventure, of which this is but an incident. After the event mentioned, having composed the agitation consequent, we had retired to our berths, and were just buried in profound sleep, when crash—our boat's bow struck heavily against a snag, which, glancing along the bottom, threw her at once upon her beams, and all the passengers on the elevated side from their berths. No serious injury was sustained, though alarm and confusion enough were excited by such an unceremonious turn-out.

One bright morning, when all the others of our company had bestowed themselves in their berths because of the intolerable heat, I took occasion to visit the sooty Charon in the purgatorial realms over which he wielded the sceptre. "Grievous work this building fires under a sun like that," was the salutation, as my friend the fireman had just completed the toilsome operation once more of stuffing the furnace, while floods of perspiration were coursing down a chest hairy as Esau's and as brawny. Hereupon honest Charon lifted up his face, and drawing a dingy shirt sleeve with emphasis athwart his eyes, bleared with smut, responded, "Ay, ay, sir; it's a sin to Moses, such a trade"; and seizing incontinently upon a fragment of tin, he scooped up a quantity of the turbid fluid through which we were moving, and deep, deep was the potation which went gurgling down his throat.

It was a bright morning, on the fifth day of an exceedingly long passage, that we found ourselves approaching St. Louis. At about noon we were gliding beneath the broad ensign floating from the flagstaff of Jefferson Barracks. The site of the quadrangle of the barracks enclosing the parade is the broad summit of a noble bluff, swelling up from the water, while the outbuildings are scattered picturesquely along the interval beneath. Passing the venerable village of Carondelet, with its white-washed cottages crumbling with years, and old Cahokia buried in the forests of the opposite bank, the gray walls of the Arsenal next stood out before us in the rear of its beautiful esplanade. Sweeping onward, the lofty spire and dusky walls of St. Louis Cathedral, on rounding a river bend, opened upon the eye, the gilded crucifix gleaming in the sunlight from its lofty summit; and then the glittering cupolas and church domes, and the fresh aspect of private residences, mingling with the bright foliage of forest-trees, recalled vividly the beautiful "Mistress of the North." For beauty of outline in distant view, St. Louis is deservedly famed. The extended range of limestone warehouses circling the shore give to the city a grandeur of aspect, while the dense-rolling forest-tops stretching away in the rear, and the funereal grove of steamboat-pipes lining the quay, altogether make up a combination of features novel and picturesque. As we approached the landing all the uproar and confusion of a steamboat port was before us, and our own arrival added to the bustle.

23

"We Air an Almighty People": The Old Northwest, 1848

*J*ohn L. Peyton was born near Staunton, Virginia, in 1824. He received *a degree in law from the University of Virginia in 1844. Four years later he was traveling through the Old Northwest and in 1853 took up a three-year residence in Illinois. Two books resulted from these western sojourns: A*

Statistical View of the State of Illinois (*1855*) *and, much later,* Over the Alleghanies (*1869*), *from which the present excerpts are taken. When the Civil War broke, Peyton, like so many southerners, opposed secession but stood loyally by his state when it left the Union. He acted as agent for North Carolina in England and, after the war, chose to remain in England until 1876. His subsequent career was largely literary; he wrote no less than six works, most of which are ephemeral, though the two-volume* American Crisis (*1867*) *is more substantial. He died in 1896.*

Over the Alleghanies *is an excellent account of life and manners in the Old Northwest in 1848. Written with humor, it offers the comments of a good observer without any pretensions to profundity or subtlety. Despite the fact that it was written twenty years after the events described, though from notes made at the time, it captures vividly a sense of being "on the spot," at the moment of writing.*

A STAGE COACH JOURNEY ACROSS OHIO

The Xenia station, where I secured a ticket by the first train to Columbus, was a rude shed constructed of timber, and everything connected with the spot indicated the haste in which it was built. Approaching, I discovered seated upon a log a well-dressed, grey-haired gentleman of about fifty, with a florid complexion and *retroussé* nose. Saluting me with characteristic western politeness, he inquired somewhat abruptly, "where I was bound?" Replying Chicago, he seemed unexpectedly surprised and pleased, saying, "I shall be your travelling companion, as it's my own destination."

From Xenia we travelled to Columbus, the capital of the state, and thence to Tiffin, a small town which had recently sprung up like a mushroom amid the decaying logs and stumps of a forest. From this point to Sandusky on Lake Erie, there was no railway, only a stage coach. These Ohio coaches were something between a French diligence and a London omnibus, and the particular one in which we now took our seats, was neither wind nor water-tight. It was incrusted with mud until its original colour could no longer be discovered. The leather aprons, to cover the open panels in bad weather, where they are secured on buttons, were so dried and shrivelled by alternate wet and heat, that they scarcely covered half the opening. Had they been of sufficient length they could not have been buttoned—the buttons were gone, and the button-holes split. The door was an inch too small on every side for the aperture it was designed to close. This, however, was not considered important, as the four panes of glass which formed the upper half were broken. During the previous night it had rained, and the vehicle having been exposed without cover to the storm, the seats were soaked with water and were now dripping like a wet sponge. The wind being high and squally, coming over the plain, which extends from the lake shore, the curtains flapped in our faces every moment, literally giving us gratis a shower bath. In all probability we should have had a plunge bath also, but for several holes in the floor which let the water escape. The prospect was none of the pleasantest, far from cheerful, but the Illinoisian seating himself in a corner, upon the top of his carpet bag, and drawing his overcoat around his person, prepared for whatever might follow. For myself, I preferred a seat by the driver. The other passengers having made themselves "snug," according to the advice of the driver, we dashed forward to the music of his voice, the screeching of wheels, and the flapping of the aged curtains.

Pursuing what was called our road, though the traces of a road were slight, we soon found that we were in the midst of a dense forest, with no guide but the blazes, or cut spots upon the sides of the trees. After going about fifteen miles, all such slight traces as existed of the road were lost, and to add to our embarrassment the blazes forked or diverged in opposite directions. The driver now acknowledged that he had taken the wrong road.

We set off again over roots and stumps, across creeks and swamps, up hill and down hill, and by following the blazes of the trees finally returned to the main road. No sooner out of one difficulty, however, than we plunged into another. At this point one of our wheels gave way, and we were turned into the road to think of an expedient for getting on with three. The driver was not at all disconcerted, seemed quite at home in the emergency, and proceeded at once to supply the defect. Felling a small tree, he took from it a log ten feet long, one end of this was, with the assistance of the passengers, secured upon the front axle, and passed back so as to hold up the body of the coach sufficiently high to admit of the wheel on the opposite side turning upon its spindle. This done, the passengers were coolly informed that it would be necessary for them to make the residue of the journey, a distance of twenty-five miles, on foot. To my surprise, every one took this announcement with perfect good temper, whereupon the journey was resumed. At the end of three miles we came upon a farmhouse, and here the driver borrowed a wheel from the farmer's ox-cart, which was placed upon our coach, and we found ourselves unexpectedly seated once more in the vehicle. It must be confessed, too, after our walk of three miles, it seemed decidedly more comfortable. And this, though we soon entered upon "a corderoy-road," on which the jolting is truly formidable. A corderoy-road, as all Western travellers know, consists of small trees stripped of their boughs, and laid across the road, touching one another, and without any covering of earth. As the marsh underneath is of various degrees of solidity, the whole road assumed a kind of undulating appearance.

Somewhat in this fashion we made the entire journey of forty miles to Sandusky, having had three upsets and one turn-over. No lives were lost, no limbs broken, and consequently no one thought seriously of such an every-day accident. Arrived at Sandusky, we were informed that the boat from Buffalo for Detroit, in which we purposed sailing, would not be in port till the following morning. The clerk of the hotel offered us a pen, and we proceeded, in accordance with the custom of the country, to register our names, abodes, and destinations. The knight of the carpet-bag, taking the pen, wrote his name thus: *Buckner S. Morris,* Chicago, Illinois. Thus for the first time I became acquainted with the name of my travelling companion, as he with mine.

The country round about Sandusky is monotonous and uninteresting, resembling the salt marshes of the sea coast. The town itself was so new that it amounted to little more than a hamlet of scattered houses for the most part built of boards and timber. Everything about the spot looked bald, naked and raw, and there was a disagreeable angular freshness about the newly built houses. The fences round the fields in the neighbourhood were built of rails, (rifted logs) with the green, sappy bark clinging to them, the ground under tillage was still rife with trees, tall as heretofore, but shorn of their verdant tops by the process of girdling, which puts an end to vegetable life, but allows the trunk and branches to remain like so many ghosts in the wilderness: undrained swamps stagnated in the midst of corn-fields; and the roads were barely passable, except towards the centre of the town and near the port. No attention was paid to neatness and finish of any kind, and comfort, indoors or out of doors was impossible. Its chief importance arose from the harbour, where vessels navigating the lakes occasionally called. Good, firm roads however were projected, and had been commenced in town and the immediate neighbourhood. Some villas had already been erected, and others were rising, and while Sandusky was a comfortless place, it was obvious that she only awaited her share of the immense bodies emigrating west, to become a place of no small consequence. The monotonous character of the surrounding scenery, the existence during a certain portion of the year of intermittent fevers and ague, and the necessity for drainage, deterred many from stopping here, who would otherwise have been glad to cut short a western journey.

While there, for the steamer not arriving at the appointed time, we were detained two days, I walked much in the neighbourhood. On one occasion I entered the neat, comfortable house of a mechanic. Here I saw a tall handsome German, of about twenty-five years of age, trembling and shuddering with the chill which precedes the fever in the ague. He was a miserable, woe-begone looking object, or rather a fine object under distressing circumstances. In half an hour when I returned to the house, his chill had passed and his face was flushed with fever. He informed me that he had been induced to leave an excellent situation in Pennsylvania, in ignorance of the real state of things in Ohio. That he believed from the pictures drawn of it, that it was the true *El Dorado,* and had found himself a dupe, with the ague for his pains. He did not, however, intend to return, but on the opening of the next spring, when his family would join him, to proceed further west, and when he had secured a healthy situation to "squat" as a frontiersman, sports-

THE WESTERN STAGE

man and farmer. "The want of health was," he said, "the only difficulty in the way of the early improvement and rapid progress of this portion of Ohio."

"You will not find," he continued, "precious stones or metals here, but innumerable dangers, discomforts and toil; but these are inseparable from a new country, and if surmounted by industry any man can accumulate a fortune. The soil is of extraordinary fertility, and the facilities for market by the lake are all that could be desired."

I quite agreed with the young German, and saw at once that he possessed the judgment and perseverance which insure success. In the course of our conversation, he informed me that he was a native of Dresden in Saxony—that his name was Otto Paul, and that he had received a liberal education, but was so infatuated by a desire for travel, and by a fondness for hunting and shooting, and was of such an adventurous disposition that he had determined to emigrate to America. Before taking this step, he married a girl to whom he had been long attached. Sailing from Bremen they landed at Baltimore. Here he remained two years teaching in a public school, during which time his wife became the mother of two children; he then removed to Chambersburg, Pennsylvania, where his wife and children continued. In the spring they would join him, as also a brother was expected from Europe, and the party would then proceed together to the far west. Their means were small, but he had sufficient to make himself comfortable, and should make the soil contribute the rest. The history of this young man is that of thousands of others who have sought homes on the western prairies of America.

FRONTIER MISSOURI

An unexpected and singularly good opportunity presenting, I determined to avail myself of it to see something of the interior of Missouri, or "Misery," as disappointed emigrants call the State.

Mr. Bates was about to attend a session of the Court at Jefferson, and not only invited, but urged me to accompany him, which I consented to do. Going aboard a steamer destined for Jefferson, we found the deck crowded with passengers, consisting, in addition to a few legal gentlemen, of Indians and emigrants. One of these red-men was an Osage chief, returning with a deputation of his tribe from a visit to their great father, the President of the United States. He was an interesting and striking object, was six feet high, straight as an arrow and perfect in his proportions. On the top of his head he wore a tuft of hair, (the rest of the head was bare) with a cord tightly tied around it in which were stuck some bright coloured feathers, selected from a peacock's tail, intermixed with the bristles of the porcupine. Like the rest of his companions, he wore a dark green toga or hunting shirt, yellow leather breeches, a little the worse for wear—no stockings, and high-laced moccasins. Near him was one of his trusted companions, a chief also, dressed in the same style, and as handsome a lad of sixteen as I ever remember to have seen, his son and successor. These three chiefs constituted a separate group. The rest of the picturesque looking deputation were smoking and soon some were sleeping on the open deck, as if it were the middle of the night. Taciturn and reserved, they presented a sad picture, and no one could look on their vacant countenances without feeling that they were a melancholy and expiring race. Thus they were proceeding towards their homes, in the track of the setting sun, which, unlike their sinking fortunes, was going down to rise again.

Quite different in their countenances, but even more squalid in their poverty, was a party of savage-looking German immigrants, who had recently arrived in New York, and had been dispatched to the far West to find homes in the solitude of the prairies. The head of this party was a short, stout Bavarian, who wore a blue tail-coat, covered with grease, without a single button and only a remnant of one tail. A pair of ancient cazinet trousers, in tatters at the feet, patched in the rudest manner on the knees, and unpatched in unmentionable parts where they ought to have been—an ancient leather waistcoat and an apology for a pair of boots. Scarcely any of the men, women or children in this party were better dressed, but they had been supplied in New York and St. Louis with a few agricultural implements and carpenters' tools, and expected before winter to build themselves comfortable timber houses, and to get a considerable body of land prepared for a spring crop. Fortunately they were to join a party of their countrymen who had preceded them by two years and were prospering in their new home. Notwithstanding, therefore, their poverty and present distress, they were cheered by the hope of something better, and consequently unlike the poor Indians, their rough bearded faces shone through their dirt with cheerfulness. A half-dozen raw-boned Kentuckians, with iron constitutions and nerves apparently of whip cord, their wives and children, were also emigrating. A few natives of the West made up the list of passengers.

The Kentuckians were of the farmer class, and men of some means, of hard heads, and probably harder hearts, determined to succeed. Whittling and whistling, they passed their time in a "devil-may-care" style, which seemed to gain them admirers. It soon became evident that they would turn both German and Indian to their account. Before we had gone half the distance, two of the Germans with their families had abandoned their party and joined the Kentuckians, who promised them shelter and immediate wages. One of the Kentuckians spoke German with tolerable facility, and another managed to communicate with the Indians, and they smoked the calumet together incessantly—the calumet, too, loaded with Missouri tobacco, the most potent and, to me, the most offensive in the world. From these appearances, I did not doubt but that these children of the woods would be made in some way useful to the native-born citizens. This could not be done, however, without at the same time bettering their own condition, and advancing the common country of all.

Notwithstanding the force of the current, the numerous islands, the snags, sawyers, and other obstructions, our gallant boat, under the impetus of a high pressure engine, kept steadily upon her course, and in due time we arrived at our destination, Jefferson City, the capital of Missouri, Tuesday the 24th of October, 1848.

Landing, we proceeded to the principal hotel, and found it entirely deserted. Entering the public room, and seeing no bell, or other means of announcing our arrival, we rapped loudly upon the inner doors hoping to attract attention. Disappointed in this, we proceeded to the back yard, where we encountered a superannuated negress hastening to the rescue, who invited us to re-enter the house and make ourselves at home. She apologised for the state of affairs, saying that every one belonging to the establishment was absent at a camp meeting. The hotel was flanked by two rows of one story timber rooms, and in one of these rows we were each accommodated with a separate chamber, the negress hospitably inviting us to occupy those we liked best. About the time we had indicated our choice, the landlady appeared with her daughters—there was no landlord in the case. Information had reached her of the arrival of the boat, and she rushed home at the top of her speed. This worthy widow, with the aid of her daughters, and a negro porter, who belonged to the establishment, stowed our luggage away, lighted jocund fires on our hearths, and, in due season, placed a Missouri dinner upon the table-d'hote. This particular Missouri dinner consisted of boiled bacon and greens, a haunch of venison, and a wild turkey, with coffee for those who liked it, and whiskey for all.

Jefferson, distant from St. Louis, one hundred and forty miles, was one of those straggling Western villages where it was difficult to say when the village terminated and the country commenced. The streets were unpaved, six inches deep with dust in the summer, and knee deep with mud in the winter. Dust, dirt, and mud, and the effects of dust, dirt and mud were everywhere perceptible. The houses were spattered with thick layers of mud, and the people seemed for the most part to have wallowed in the mire. The session of Court attracted a considerable number of country people to the town, and these were principally collected about a miserable, naked-looking edifice made of mud in the form of brick, called the Court House, where a set of half educated muddy-headed lawyers, make a muddle in attempting to make the "wrong side appear the better cause." A rougher set of citizens, whether regarded with reference to dress, manners or physical appearance, separately or combined, could not be imagined. Bear-skin caps, Mackinaw blankets, leather leggings, old Bess rifles and hunting knives, entered into their dress and equipments. Tall, square-shouldered, broad-chested, stout men, made up of bone and gristle, they drank whiskey, chewed tobacco, and while waiting for the opening of Court, engaged in athletic sports in front of the temple of Thetis. These sports consisted of throwing heavy weights, jumping, wrestling, and boxing. These powerful men, thus encountering each other in trials of physical strength, recalled the athletes of old. Their general good humour, and the excellent temper with which they bore their reverses was admirable, until towards evening, when fiery liquor caused many to lose their heads.

A more cheerless, comfortless, wretched place cannot be imagined than the Court House, which, however, was soon filled after the judge took his seat. The Court was not unfrequently adjourned for a buffalo hunt, and the business of the day was always despatched, that the judge and bar might spend a part of the afternoon pitching quoits. Their evenings were passed over the whist-table, or in political discussions conducted amidst clouds of tobacco smoke. In these after dinner discussions, they often indulged in roseate views of the future of the United States, and prognosticated as time developed the power, of what the Editor of the Jefferson paper, Mr. Windett (a Yankee importation), called "our Almighty country," universal dominion for her. The general form of expression with this knight of the quill, who was leading the Western mind through his Missouri organ, was,

"Yes, sir, we *air* an Almighty *people.*"

CHICAGO

In the afternoon Mr. Shirley called with his "trap" and a pair of Morgan horses to drive me about the city, and point out the sights of Chicago. The city is situated on both sides of the Chicago river, a sluggish, slimy stream, too lazy to clean itself, and on both sides of its north and south branches, upon a level piece of ground, half dry and half wet, resembling a salt marsh, and contained a population of 20,000. There was no pavement, no macadamized streets, no drainage, and the three thousand houses in which the people lived, were almost entirely small timber buildings, painted white, and this white much defaced by mud. I now recall but a single exception to this rule, in a red brick, two story residence in the north division, surrounded by turf, and the grounds ornamented with trees and shrubbery.

The city was not yet lighted with gas, and the gardens were open fields where I often saw horses, cows and animals of inferior dignity, sunning themselves, instead of what I expected to see, shrubs and flowers. To render the streets and sidewalks passable, they were covered with deal boards from house to house, the boards resting upon cross sills of heavy timber. This kind of track is called "the plank road." Under these planks the water was standing on the surface over three-fourths of the city, and as the sewers from the houses were emptied under them, a frightful odour was emitted in summer, causing fevers and other diseases, foreign to the climate. It not unfrequently happened that from the settling or rolling of a sleeper, that a loose plank would give way under the weight of a passing cab, when the foul water would spurt into the air high as the windows.

On the outskirts of the town where this kind of road terminated, the highways were impassable, except in winter when frozen, or in summer when dry and pulverized into the finest and most penetrating of dust. At all other seasons they were little less than quagmires. As may be imagined, the communication with the interior was principally carried on in canoes and batteaux. Of architectural display there was none. The houses were built hurriedly to accommodate a considerable trade centering here, and were devoid of both comforts and conveniences. Every one in the place seemed in a hurry, and a kind of restless activity prevailed which I had seen no where else in the West, except in Cincinnati. A central point in the western route of emigrants, it was even at this inclement season animated by passing parties. In summer, I understood emigrant parties went through daily. Those whom I now saw, were wild, rough, almost savage looking men from North Germany, Denmark and Sweden—their faces covered with grizzly beards, and their teeth clenched upon a pipe stem. They were followed by stout, well-formed, able-bodied wives and healthy children. Neither cold nor storm stopped them in their journey to the promised land, on the frontiers of which they had now arrived. In most instances they followed friends who had prepared a resting place for them.

Chicago was already becoming a place of considerable importance for manufactures. Steam mills were busy in every part of the city preparing lumber for buildings which were contracted to be erected by the thousand the next season. Large establishments were engaged in manufacturing agricultural implements of every description for the farmers who flocked to the country every spring. A single establishment, that of McCormick, employed several hundred hands, and during each season completed from fifteen hundred to two thousand grain-reapers and grass-mowers. Blacksmith, wagon and coachmaker's shops were busy preparing for a spring demand, which, with all their energy, they could not supply. Brickmakers had discovered on the lake shore, near the city and a short distance in the interior, excellent beds of clay, and were manufacturing, even at this time, millions of brick by a patent process, which the frost did not hinder, or delay. Hundreds of workmen were also engaged in quarrying stone and marble on the banks of the projected canal; and the Illinois Central Railway employed large bodies of men in driving piles, and constructing a track and depot on the beach. Real estate agents were mapping out the surrounding territory for ten and fifteen miles in the interior, giving fancy names to the future avenues, streets, squares and parks. A brisk traffic existed in the sale of corner lots, and men with nothing but their wits, had been known to succeed in a single season in making a fortune—sometimes, certainly, it was only on paper.

Wishing to change a few American (gold), eagles, for I had provided myself with this kind of solid currency for my Western tour, my friend Shirley accompanied me to a timber-shed, or shanty, bespattered with mud and defaced by the sun and storm, where the great banking establishment of those days was conducted by George Smith and Co. When there, placing my eagles upon the counter, Mr. Willard, the manager, a lean, yellow, thick-skinned, but shrewd man of business from the East, though I hardly think he could be classed among the wise men, returned me notes of the denomination of one, two, three and four dollars, which read as follows:

The Bank of Atlanta, Georgia, promises to pay the bearer on demand, one dollar, when five is presented at their banking-house at Atlanta.

GEORGE SMITH, *President.*

WILLARD, *Cashier.*

I objected most decidedly to receiving this currency, because Atlanta was by the usual route of travel nearly two thousand miles distant; because when the notes were presented, the bank of Atlanta might pay them in the currency of another "wild cat" bank, probably conducted by Tom Mackenzie in Texas or New Mexico, and because they would only pay them in particular amounts of five dollars, a sum, I said ironically, which a judicious man was not likely to accumulate in his hands of this kind of currency. Stating these objections, both Messrs. Willard and Shirley smiled at my ignorance and inexperience, my "old fogyism," and explained that these notes were as current in Chicago and the State of Illinois as gold; and much more plentiful, thought I to myself. Nevertheless, on their assurances I accepted them, with a mental reservation, however, that I would divest myself of the trash before my departure.

We now left the bank for a ramble about the "Garden City," as Chicago was then and is now called, from the fact that the houses were very small and the gardens enormous. Returning to the hotel, Mr. Rossiter informed me that my bank notes (and my pocket was stuffed with them) were called "wild cat money," and such institutions as that at Atlanta "Wild Cat Banks"; but he said the circulating medium of the United States was so far below the actual wants of the people, that they were compelled to resort to such systems of credit to get on rapidly and improve the country, and as long as farmers would take the money (as they now did) there would be no difficulty.

"Why, sir," said Mr. Rossiter, looking around his establishment with pride, "this hotel was built with that kind of stuff, and what is true of 'The American,' is very nearly true of every other house in Chicago. I will take 'wild cats' for your bill, my butcher takes them of me, and the farmer from him, and so we go, making it pleasant all round. I only take care," continued Mr. Rossiter,

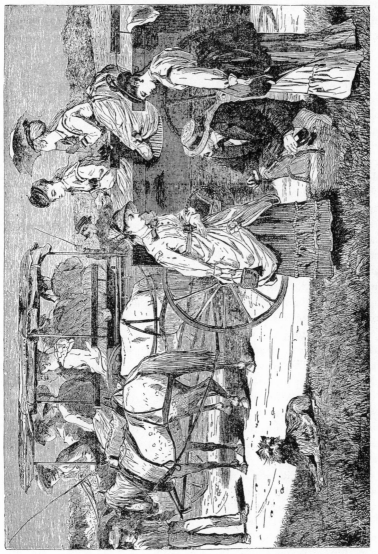

PICNIC EXCURSION

"to invest what I may have at the end of a given time in corner lots. Then I'll be prepared, I guess, for the deluge, or crash, when it comes, and sooner or later it must come, as sure as the light of day. Mr. Smith has already in circulation six millions of his wild cat currency, and in order to be prepared for contingencies—to be out of the way of a hempen collar and Chicago lamp-post, when people are ruined by his financiering devices—he remains in New York and carries on his operations through Mr. Willard and his 'lambs,' as the clerks are called. On this kind of worthless currency, based on Mr. Smith's supposed wealth and our wants, we are creating a great city, building up all kind of industrial establishments, and covering the lake with vessels—so that suffer who may when the inevitable hour of reckoning arrives, the country will be the gainer, Jack Rossiter will try, when this day of reckoning comes, to have 'clean hands' and a fair record, and I would advise you, on leaving Illinois, to do likewise—wash your hands of Smith and Co. A man who meddles, my dear sir, with wild cat banks is on a slippery spot, and that spot the edge of a precipice."

It required no persuasion to make me follow the sensible advice of my host, and when I afterwards stepped on the steamer which was to bear me across the lake on my return, I divested myself of the last note—which had come into my possession in the way of change—a note of small denomination, by presenting it to the hotel-porter as a gratuity for what one was not then likely to get from Western "helps," a little common civility. Pat was delighted to receive the shin plaster, and gave "yer 'onour" many thanks.

Mr. Shirley drove me to the Chicago Theatre, where Hamlet was played that night—a promising young Western actor, named Perry, taking the principal part. The Theatre was then owned by the manager, Mr. Rice, who was a good actor and a pleasant man. The house was well attended, and the play a decided success. After the performance, we accepted an invitation and went to Mr. Rice's residence in Wabash Avenue, where a number of his friends and some of the principal members of the company were assembled for supper. Here the evening passed rapidly amidst the sparkle of wit, humour and champagne.

The morning following my attendance at the theatre, I found Chicago covered with snow two feet deep on a level, and at places where it was drifted from thirty to forty feet deep! The population was stirring, however, like a hive of bees to open a pathway, by throwing it from the trottoirs into the streets before it became so frozen as to be immovable, except with enormous labour. By mid-day the pavements were tolerably comfortable, but we seemed to be moving in a trench—the shops on one side and the snow upon the other. The snow thrown into the streets raised their level about four feet, so that as we walked on the side-walk, the feet of the horses pulling the sleighs were almost even with our shoulders. Becoming as the season advances more and more firmly frozen and compactly beat down, the streets are smooth and slippery to a degree, forming admirable roads for sleighs, in which every one not on foot moves about, and they furnish delightful means of locomotion. Coach bodies are placed upon sleds, and ladies go to make morning calls in them as also to parties and picnics.

Picnicking was by the by one of the Chicago winter amusements, and they are sometimes very amusing. They are organised somewhat after this fashion. A hotel from ten to fifteen miles in the country is secured for a particular evening and dinner prepared for six or seven o'clock, as the case may be. By this hour sleighs arrive from Chicago, driven by the beaux and freighted with the belles and their chaperons nestling under buffalo robes and other furs. After dinner, dancing commences, the services of one of the numerous German bands in Chicago having been previously secured. Dancing is usually kept up till eleven when the sleighs reappear and taking up their "freight," one by one disappear in the night.

From our dinner table, the day following the pic-nic, we adjourned to the Tremont House, to a ball given by the bachelors. These balls occurred once a week during the winter, and were called the "Bachelors' Assembly Balls," and were intended as a return by the *brave garçons* of Chicago to the community, for the lavish hospitalities bestowed upon them by managing mammas. The rooms were large, handsomely decorated, brilliantly lighted and enlivened, and embellished by a dashing company. The music was all that could be desired, and the supper beyond praise.

Everything passed off the evening of my attendance agreeably, and as this was usually the case, these assemblies were decidedly popular. In the company there were many young married ladies, and even those who could lay claims to being "fair, fat and forty." I soon discovered that Chicago society in its freedom from restraint and easy sociability was more French than English, and more American than either. Many of the handsomest, gayest and most desirable-looking ladies were mothers, and in the same room mothers and daughters were often "tripping the light fantastic toe." This I thought entirely as it should be, and admirable evidence of the healthfulness of the north-western climate. It was also a refutation, complete and perfect of the common error—I might almost say popular superstition in England—that American ladies fade at forty and go off at fifty. Frail creatures, they are not quite so frail and fleeting in their charms as their British sisters imagine, certainly not in Chicago.

24

The American Spirit in the West, 1856

J. Milton Mackie (see p. 232), though he journeyed mostly through the West Indies and the Southern States, managed a river trip up the Mississippi to St. Louis. The following extract gives his impression of the ebullient spirit of the western country. However St. Louis may consider itself geographically today, or textbooks persist in referring to it as "border territory," the city, though it possessed southern characteristics, was essentially frontier and "western," even as late as 1856. Mackie was quite correct in thinking of it from such a point of view and in suspecting that this "western" spirit was representative of a goodly portion of the "American" spirit.

It was late on a rainy evening that I arrived at the great Western city of St. Louis. On entering the hotel which had been recommended to me, I found the hall filled like a merchant's exchange, and made my way to the office, not without some difficulty. The clerks were all too busy to notice my arrival. I was not asked to register my name in the hotel book, but did so without invitation. After waiting some little time, however, I succeeded in catching the eye of a clerk, when we held the following conversation:

"Have you a room for me?"

"Not a room in the house, sir."

"Well, give me a cot, then."

"Not a cot in the house, sir."

"But I am ill, and can go no farther. You may give me a sofa—anything."

"Not a sofa in the house, sir. Nothing in the house, sir."

And the clerk passed on, to say the same thing to another applicant for hospitality—and to another—until he was so tired of refusing, that he did it without pity, or even politeness. I turned toward one of the bystanders, a good Samaritan, who picked me up in my hour of need, and gave me a cot in his empty parlor.

I then learned that I had arrived at the wrong hour in the day. In the great Western hotels, the tide of travel ebbs and flows twice in the twenty-four hours. After nine o'clock in the morning, rooms are easy to be had; after nine in the evening they can rarely be obtained for money, and never for love. The hospitality of the house ceases at nine P.M. The civility of the clerks is completely exhausted by that time. Travellers arriving later than that are a nuisance to all the officials, from landlord to chambermaid. The cold, inhospitable looks the belated comer gets all round seem to say to him, "Why did you not arrive earlier in the day, sir?" If it would do any good, you might easily account for the lateness of your getting to town, and show that the blame rested on other shoulders than your own; but it will be of no avail. You can have as many apartments as you please tomorrow morning; but to-night you must get your sleep on three chairs, or walking the hall, if you happen to be a somnambulist.

So it is year in and year out. A porter gifted with a strong pair of lungs is kept pretty constantly perambulating the halls of the house, and bawling out, loud enough to waken every sleeper and stun every waker, "all aboard! all aboard! Omnibus ready for the cars!" A person accustomed to the quiet of his own mansion may be annoyed by this; but before he has lived forty days in the hotel, he pays no more attention to them than to the hand organ which nightly grinds its grist of melodies under his windows. Not less embarrassing are the piles of luggage heaped up in the halls and passage ways, against which one is constantly liable to run his nose or bark his shins. And when the trunks are loaded on the backs of hurrying porters, the risk of a collision is still greater; for poor Paddy, with half a ton of trunks to his back, is blind as a bat, and sees nothing but the main chance of the open doorway. The traveller is more in danger of being run down in his hotel than on the river, or the rail. Porters, waiters, guests, all are in quick motion; and one or the other is pretty sure to knock him over. Indeed, the society of a Western hotel is in a constant flux. The universe, in the Hegelian philosophy, is not more fluid. Every man is either just in from Cincinnati or Chicago, or he is just starting for one of these places. Unless he makes his hundred miles between breakfast and dinner, he counts himself an idler, and talks of growing rusty. A great deal of his business he transacts "aboard the cars," or the steamboats; some of it at the hotels; and all of it on his feet, and ready to "bolt." The dinner table, too, is an exchange for him. Business before soup—it is the first course of the dinner, and the last. Between fish and pudding he will sell a prairie. With every mouthful of bread he will engage to deliver ten thousand

THE "S.S. JACOB STRADER," OF THE LOUISVILLE MAIL COMPANY

bushels of wheat. The "upset price" is knocked hard down on the table with the end of his knife handle; and the bargain is clinched by the help of the nut cracker or the sugar tongs. If he sees his next neighbor prefer mutton, he at once offers to sell him sheep by the thousand; if he dines on pork, he will invite him to go into a speculation in hogs. His railroad shares he will dispose of at the price of peanuts; and his State bonds he will give away to any one who will pay his champagne bill, and the piper generally; or rather, he would do so a few years ago.

I was not so ill as to prevent my getting down to the table at mealtime. This was the chief amusement of my day, being as good a high-low comedy as may be seen on any stage, at least west of the Alleghanies. The table groans with good things. Here are the veritable solids, and none of what the Frenchman calls *les choses maigres*. The waiters drop fatness, literally. Your plate is brought to you heaped up with roast beef. Every third man has his pudding. The waiters hand about the iced cream in slices, which suggest the resemblance of small prairies. And, finally, the dinner goes off, like the finale of a display of fireworks, with "Jenny Lind cake," "vanities," "cookeys," "lady fingers," "jelly snips," and "pecans."

The only difficulty is in getting little enough of anything you may call for. Just a bit of a thing—*un morceau*—is an impossibility. A thin cut can't be had. A man, therefore, with a delicate stomach, is entirely out of place here, where the arrangements are all designed for persons who are ready to "go the whole animal." When I came down in the evening, to get a cup of tea and a bite at a biscuit, I never could escape the everlasting "Have a beef-steak, sir?" of the waiters. 'Tis a great country out West, and the men who live in it are feeders to correspond. They want their meat three times a day, as regularly as poor Pat does when he leaves his potato island and arrives in this land of beeves and buffaloes. Even their horses have freer access to the corn crib than negroes do in Virginia. The Western man expects to see plenty around him. Nothing is too good for him. He never stops to count the cost. Corn and wine are his—honey, and the honeycomb. The cattle on a thousand acres are his also. The prairies are white with his flocks; the eye follows the waving grain to the horizon; the buffalo yields him its tongue, the bear its haunches, and the buck his saddle; the wild turkey is brought in from the forests, the canvas-back duck from the bays, and the pinnated grouse from the prairies; the salmon trout is caught at Mackinaw, the whitefish fill the lakes, and oysters "hermetically sealed" arrive by express from the seaboard, every day in their season.

The society one meets in a Western hotel consists principally of the gentlemen of the road. I mean the railroad men, so called—road builders and road owners. There are, also, the men of real estate, who deal in prairie and river bottoms. There are grain and lumber merchants. There are speculators of every kind. But all have only one thought in their minds. To buy, sell, and get gain—this is the spirit that pervades this house, and the country. The chances of making fortunes in business or speculation are so great, that everybody throws the dice. Five years hence every man expects to be a nabob. I saw in the West no signs of quiet enjoyment of life as it passes, but only of a haste to get rich. Here are no idlers. The poor—if any such there be—and the wealthy are all equally hard at work. Beyond the Alleghanies the day has no siesta in it. Life is a race, with no chance of repose except beyond the goal. The higher arts which adorn human existence—elegant letters, divine philosophy—these have not yet reached the Mississippi. They are far off. There are neither gods nor graces on the prairies yet. One sees only the sower sowing his seed. No poets inhabit the savannas of Iowa, or the banks of the Yellow Stone. These are the emigrants' homes. Life in the valley of the Mississippi is, in fact, but pioneering, and has a heavy pack to its back. At present, the inhabitants are hewing wood and drawing water—laying the foundations of a civilization which is yet to be, and such as never hath been before. This they are doing with an energy superior to that which built Carthage or Ilium. Though men do not write books there, or paint pictures, there is no lack, in our Western world, of mind. The genius of this new country is necessarily mechanical. Our greatest thinkers are not in the library, nor the capitol, but in the machine shop. The American people is intent on studying, not the beautiful records of a past civilization, not the hieroglyphic monuments of ancient genius, but how best to subdue and till the soil of its boundless territories; how to build roads and ships; how to apply the powers of nature to the work of manufacturing its rich materials into forms of utility and enjoyment. The youth of this country are learning the sciences, not as theories, but with reference to their application to the arts. Our education is no genial culture of letters, but simply learning the use of tools. Even literature is cultivated for its jobs; and the fine arts are followed as a trade. The prayer of this young country is, "Give us this day our daily bread"; and for the other petitions of the Pater Noster it has no time. So must it be for the present. We must be content with little literature, less art, and only nature in perfection. We are to be busy, not happy. For we live for futurity, and are doing the work of two generations yet unborn.

Everything is beautiful in its season. What is now wanted in this country is, that all learned black-smiths stick to their anvils. No fields of usefulness can be cultivated by them to so great advantage as the floor of their own smithy. In good time, the Western bottom lands will spontaneously grow poets. The American mind will be brought to maturity along the chain of the great lakes, the banks of the Mississippi, the Missouri, and their tributaries in the far Northwest. There, on the rolling plains, will be formed a republic of letters, which, not governed, like that on our seaboard, by the great literary powers of Europe, shall be free indeed. For there character is growing up with a breadth equal to the sweep of the great valleys; dwarfed by no factitious ceremonies or usages, no precedents or written statutes, no old super-

EXPLOSION ON BOARD THE "HELEN MCGREGOR"

stition or tyranny. The winds sweep unhindered, from the lakes to the gulf, from the Alleghanies to the Rocky Mountains; and so do the thoughts of the Lord of the prairies. He is beholden to no man, being bound neither head nor foot. He is an independent world himself, and speaks his own mind. Some day he will make his own books, as well as his own laws. He will not send to Europe for either pictures or opinions. He will remain on his prairie, and all the arts of the world will come and make obeisance to him, like the sheaves in his fields. He will be the American man, and beside him there will be none else.

Of course, one does not go to the West to study fashions or manners. The guests of a Western hotel would not bear being transported to Almack's without some previous instruction in bowing and scraping, or some important changes of apparel. Foreign critics, travelling in pursuit of the comical, do not fail of finding it here in dress, in conversation, in conduct: for men here show all their idiosyncrasies. There are no disguises. Speech is plump, hearty, aimed at the bull's eye; and without elegant phrase or compliment. On the road, one may meet the good Samaritan, but not Beau Brummell. Anything a Western man can do for you, he will do with all his heart; only he cannot flatter you with unmeaning promises. You shall be welcome at his cabin; but he cannot dispense his hospitality in black coat and white cravat. His work is too serious to be done in patent leathers. He is, in outward appearance, as gnarled as his oaks, but brave, strong, humane, with the oak's great heart and pith. The prairie man is a six-foot animal, broad shouldered and broad fore-headed; better suited to cutting up corn than cutting a figure in a dance, to throwing the bowie knife than to thrumming the guitar. In Europe, a man always betrays a consciousness of the quality of the person in whose presence he is standing. If he face a lord, it is with submission; if a tradesman, with haughtiness; if a servant, with authority; if a beggar, with indifference. At the West, two persons meeting stand over against each other like two door-posts. Neither gives signs of superiority or inferiority. They have no intention of either flattering or imposing upon each other. Words are not wasted. So is the cut of each other's coat a matter of perfect indifference. Probably the man who is "up for Congress" wears the shabbier one of the two. If disposed to make a show at all, the Western gent is more apt to be proud of his horses than his broadcloth. His tread may occasionally have something in it indicative of the lord of the prairie; but he has little or no nonsense about him. The only exception is, perhaps, a rather large-sized diamond pin in his shirt bosom.

The Western cockney differs considerably from him of New York. He has more of the "ready-made-clothing" appearance about him, and wears his hat drawn closer down over his left eye. Sometimes his cigar is in his buttonhole, and sometimes in his cheek. He chews tobacco. He vibrates between sherry cobblers and mint juleps. His stick is no slight rattan, but a thick hickory or buckeye, and has a handle large enough to allow of its being carried suspended from his shoulder. His watch chain is very heavy—lead inside, and gold out. He is learned in politics, and boasts that a United States senator from his State once put his arm around his neck, and slapped him familiarly between the shoulders. When he was in Washington, he messed and slept with the Western members of the House. He knows, personally, all the Western judges and generals in Congress; bets at all the elections; and makes money out of them, let whichever party conquer. He also goes in the steamboats whenever there is to be a race; plays "poker" on board, and lives on the profits. He has a small capital in wild lands, likewise, and owns a few corner lots in Cairo, and other cities laid down in his maps. These he will sell cheap for cash. He affects the man of business, and ignores ladies' society. His evenings are spent at a club house, having the name of "Young America" blazoned on its front in large gilt letters. He dines at the crack hotel of the town, and, having free passes over all railroads, he keeps up his importance in the world by going to and fro, and putting on the airs of a man owning half the Western country.

IMMIGRANTS CROSSING THE PLAINS

Part IV

WESTWARD THE COURSE
OF EMPIRE

American interest in the Far West was of long duration, as the popularity of the Lewis and Clark expedition and the fame of Dana's *Two Years before the Mast* or Parkman's *Oregon Trail* clearly testified. Yet it was an interest at first more or less sporadic and certainly never fully sustained until near the middle of the nineteenth century. This was due, in part, to the fact that the area was not originally an American possession and, in part, to the fact that the territories nearer the Mississippi were still primitive, open to occupation, and sufficiently bizarre to satisfy the longings of the romantically inclined. With the acquisition of the Oregon country (1846) and the cession of the Southwest and California from Mexico (1848), together with a population sufficient to create a tier of states in the hitherto unoccupied areas just west of the Mississippi, American concern in the Far West markedly quickened. The sensational discovery of gold in 1849 made the interest permanent.

Travelers wrote of the routes to the Pacific Coast and about what they found there on arrival. Three main routes were ordinarily followed: the Santa Fé Trail to the Southwest, the California Trail, and the Oregon Trail. Until the late forties and early fifties, accounts were largely by emigrants in company with other emigrants and are not quite "travel" books within the ordinary meaning of the word. Once population had moved in, however, the observer made a quick appearance, and thereafter travelers' accounts began to multiply.

They were interested in all manner of things and people, as good travelers should be: alkali deserts, Indians, gold and silver deposits, the mining camps, and the prospects of wealth. In a lesser degree they described cowboys, ranchers, fur-traders, and giant trees; but, more than anything else, they wrote minutely and at length of fabulous, romantic, spectacular San Francisco, of California, and of the way thither. The Oregon country, particularly the Columbia River region, received some attention; but, rather surprisingly, the Southwest came in for only minor recording. By and large, the travelers' accounts of the Far West do not deal so analytically, or probe so deeply into economic and social phenomena, as do those of the eastern states or the Cotton Kingdom. But for sheer entertainment and readability the books on this section are unsurpassed.

In the end the West became "tamed," though never by 1900 so completely as to lose its fascination. Transcontinental trains naturally brought in a different type of tourist from that which horse and coach had conveyed. Nevertheless, by the close of the century, the West commanded better observers and better observations than was the lot of the rest of the nation.

THE COURSE OF EMPIRE

25

Outfitting a Santa Fé Expedition, 1844

Josiah Gregg, who was born in Overton County, Tennessee, in 1806, is the classic historian of the Santa Fé trade. Before he was twenty-one he had settled at Independence, Missouri, from which, for motives of health, he began in 1831 his many journeys with the southwestern traders. Well educated, a keen observer, and armed with copious notes, he wrote down the sum of his experiences in his Commerce of the Prairies, *published in two volumes in New York in 1844. It went through many editions in his own day and has remained popular for a century. His last visit to Santa Fé was made in 1849, after which he engaged in an ill-fated expedition to California. Worn out from unparalleled sufferings, he died on his return in 1850.*

People who reside at a distance have generally considered St. Louis as the emporium of the Santa Fé trade; but that city, in truth, has never been a place of rendezvous, nor even of outfit, except for a small portion of the traders who have started from its immediate vicinity. The town of Franklin on the Missouri River, about a hundred and fifty miles farther to the westward, seems truly to have been the cradle of our trade; but as the navigation of the Missouri River had considerably advanced towards the year 1831, and the advantages of some point of debarkation nearer the western frontier were very evident, whereby upwards of a hundred miles of troublesome land-carriage over unimproved and often miry roads might be avoided, the new town of Independence, but twelve miles from the Indian border and two or three south of the Missouri River, being the most eligible point, soon began to take the lead as a place of debarkation, outfit, and departure, which in spite of all opposition it has ever since maintained. It is to this beautiful spot, already grown up to be a thriving town, that the prairie adventurer, whether in search of wealth, health, or amusement, is latterly in the habit of repairing about the first of May, as the caravans usually set out some time during that month. Here they purchase their provisions for the road, and many of their mules, oxen, and even some of their wagons—in short, load all their vehicles and make their final preparations for a long journey across the prairie wilderness.

As Independence is a point of convenient access (the Missouri River being navigable at all times from March till November), it has become the general port of embarkation for every part of the great western and northern "prairie ocean." Besides the Santa Fé caravans, most of the Rocky Mountain traders and trappers, as well as emigrants to Oregon, take this town in their route. During the season of departure, therefore, it is a place of much bustle and active business.

Among the concourse of travelers at this starting point, besides traders and tourists a number of pale-faced invalids are generally to be met with. The prairies have, in fact, become very celebrated for their sanative effects—more justly so, no doubt, than the more fashionable watering-places of the North. Most chronic diseases, particularly liver complaints, dyspepsias, and similar affections, are often radically cured; owing, no doubt, to the peculiarities of diet and the regular exercise incident to prairie life, as well as to the purity of the atmosphere of those elevated unembarrassed regions. An invalid myself, I can answer for the efficacy of the remedy, at least in my own case. Though, like other valetudinarians, I was disposed to provide an ample supply of such commodities as I deemed necessary for my comfort and health, I was not long upon the prairies before I discovered that most of such extra preparations were unnecessary, or at least quite dispensable. A few knick-knacks, as a little tea, rice, fruits, crackers, etc., suffice very well for the first fortnight, after which the invalid is generally able to take the fare of the hunter and teamster. Though I set out myself in a carriage, before the close of the first week I saddled my pony; and when we reached the buffalo range I was not only as eager for the chase as the sturdiest of my companions, but I enjoyed far more exquisitely my share of the buffalo than all the delicacies which were ever devised to provoke the most fastidious appetite.

The ordinary supplies for each man's consumption during the journey are about fifty pounds of flour, as many more of bacon, ten of coffee and twenty of sugar, and a little salt. Beans, crackers, and trifles of that description are comfortable appendages, but being looked upon as dispensable luxuries, are seldom to be found in any of the stores on the road. The buffalo is chiefly depended upon for fresh meat, and great is the joy of the traveler when that noble animal first appears in sight.

The wagons now most in use upon the prairies are manufactured in Pittsburg; and are usually drawn by eight mules or the same number of oxen. Of late years, however, I have seen much larger vehicles employed, with ten or twelve mules harnessed to each and a cargo of goods of about five thousand pounds in weight. At an early period the horse was more frequently in use, as mules were not found in great abundance; but as soon as the means for procuring these animals increased, the horse was gradually and finally discarded, except occasionally for riding and the chase.

Oxen having been employed by Major Riley for the baggage wagons of the escort which was furnished the caravan of 1829, they were found, to the surprise of the traders, to perform almost equal to mules. Since that time, upon an average, about half the wagons in these expeditions have been drawn by oxen. They possess many advantages, such as pulling heavier loads than the same number of mules, particularly through muddy or sandy places; but they generally fall off in strength as the prairie grass becomes drier and shorter, and often arrive at their destination in a most shocking plight. In this condition I have seen them sacrificed at Santa Fé for ten dollars the pair; though in more favorable seasons they sometimes remain strong enough to be driven back to the United States the same fall. Therefore, although the original cost of a team of mules is much greater, the loss ultimately sustained by them is usually less, to say nothing of the comfort of being able to travel faster and more at ease. The inferiority of oxen as regards endurance is partially owing to the tenderness of their feet; for there are very few among the thousands who have traveled on the prairies that ever knew how to shoe them properly. Many have resorted to the curious expedient of shoeing their animals with moccasins made of raw buffalo-skin, which does remarkably well as long as the weather remains dry; but when wet, they are soon worn through. Even mules, for the most part, perform the entire trip without being shod at all; though the hoofs often become very smooth, which frequently renders all their movements on the dry grassy surface nearly as laborious as if they were treading on ice.

The supplies being at length procured and all necessary preliminaries systematically gone through, the trader begins the difficult task of loading his wagons. Those who understand their business take every precaution so to stow away their packages that no jolting on the road can afterwards disturb the order in which they had been disposed. The ingenuity displayed on these occasions has frequently been such that after a tedious journey of eight hundred miles the goods have been found to have sustained much less injury than they would have experienced on a turnpike road, or from the ordinary handling of property upon our western steamboats.

The next great difficulty the traders have to encounter is in training those animals that have never before been worked, which is frequently attended by an immensity of trouble. There is nothing, however, in the mode of harnessing and conducting teams in prairie traveling which differs materially from that practiced on the public highways throughout the states, the representations of certain travelers to the contrary notwithstanding.

At last all are fairly launched upon the broad prairie—the miseries of preparation are over—the thousand anxieties occasioned by wearisome consultations and delays are felt no more. The charioteer as he smacks his whip feels a bounding elasticity of soul within him, which he finds it impossible to restrain; even the mules prick up their ears with a peculiarly conceited air, as if in anticipation of that change of scene which will presently follow. Harmony and good feeling prevail everywhere. The hilarious song, the *bon mot,* and the witty repartee go round in quick succession; and before people have had leisure to take cognizance of the fact, the lovely village of Independence with its multitude of associations is already lost to the eye.

It may be proper to observe here for the benefit of future travelers that in order to make a secure shelter for the cargo against the inclemencies of the weather, there should be spread upon each wagon a pair of stout Osnaburg sheets, with one of sufficient width to reach bottom of the body on each side, so as to protect the goods from driving rains. By omitting this important precaution many packages of merchandise have been seriously injured. Some preferred lining the exterior of the wagon-body by tacking a simple strip of sheeting all around it. On the outward trips especially a pair of Mackinaw blankets can be advantageously spread betwixt the two sheets, which effectually secures the roof against the worst of storms. This contrivance has also the merit of turning the blankets into a profitable item of trade by enabling the owners to evade the custom-house officers, who would otherwise seize them as contraband articles.

But after this comes the principal task of organizing. The proprietors are first notified by proclamation to furnish a list of their men and wagons. The latter are generally apportioned into four divisions, particularly when the company is large—and ours consisted of nearly a hundred wagons, besides a dozen of dear-borns and other small vehicles and two small cannons (a four and six pounder), each mounted upon a carriage. To each of these divisions a lieutenant was appointed, whose duty it was to inspect every ravine and creek on the route, select the best crossings, and superintend what is called in prairie parlance the "forming" of each encampment.

Upon the calling of the roll we were found to muster an efficient force of nearly two hundred men, without counting invalids or other disabled bodies, who, as a matter of course, are exempt from duty. There is nothing so much dreaded by inexperienced travelers as the ordeal of guard duty. But no matter what the condition or employment of the individual may be, no one has the smallest chance of evading the common law of the prairies. The amateur tourist and the listless loafer are precisely in the same wholesome predicament —they must all take their regular turn at the watch. There is usually a set of genteel idlers attached to every caravan, whose wits are forever at work in devising schemes for whiling away their irksome hours at the expense of others. By embarking in these trips of pleasure they are enabled to live without expense; for the hospitable traders seldom refuse to accommodate even a loafing companion with a berth at their mess without charge. But then these lounging attachés are expected at least to do good service by way of guard-duty. None are even permitted to furnish a substitute, as is frequently done in military expeditions, for he that would undertake to stand the tour of another besides his own would scarcely be watchful enough for the dangers of the prairies. Even the invalid must be able to produce unequivocal proofs of his inability, or it is a chance if the plea is admitted. For my own part, although I started on the sick list, and though the prairie sentinel must stand fast and brook the severest storm (for then it is that the strictest watch is necessary), I do not remember ever having missed my post but once during the whole journey.

The usual number of watches is eight, each standing a fourth of every alternate night. When the party is small the number is greatly reduced, while in the case of very small bands they are sometimes compelled for safety's sake to keep one watch on duty half the night. With large caravans the captain usually appoints eight sergeants of the guard, each of whom takes an equal portion of men under his command.

The wild and motley aspect of the caravan can be but imperfectly conceived without an idea of the costumes of its various members. The most fashionable prairie dress is the fustian frock of the city-bred merchant furnished with a multitude of pockets capable of accommodating a variety of extra tackling. Then there is the backwoodsman with his linsey or leather hunting-shirt—the farmer with his blue jean coat—the wagoner with his

CROSSING THE PECOS

flannel-sleeve vest—besides an assortment of other costumes which go to fill up the picture.

In the article of firearms there is also an equally interesting medley. The frontier hunter sticks to his rifle, as nothing could induce him to carry what he terms in derision "the scatter-gun." The sportsman from the interior flourishes his double-barreled fowling-piece with equal confidence in its superiority. The latter is certainly the most convenient description of gun that can be carried on this journey; as a charge of buck-shot in night attacks (which are the most common) will of course be more likely to do execution than a single rifle-ball fired at random. The repeating arms have lately been brought into use upon the prairies and they are certainly very formidable weapons, particularly when used against an ignorant savage foe. A great many were furnished beside with a bountiful supply of pistols and knives of every description, so that the party made altogether a very brigand-like appearance.

When caravans are able to cross in the evening they seldom stop on the near side of a stream—first, because if it happens to rain during the night it may become flooded and cause both detention and trouble; again, though the stream be not impassable after rain, the banks become slippery and difficult to ascend. A third and still more important reason is that, even supposing the contingency of rain does not occur, teams will rarely pull as well in cold collars, as wagoners term it—that is, when fresh geared—as in the progress of a day's travel. When a heavy pull is just at hand in the morning wagoners sometimes resort to the expedient of driving a circuit upon the prairie before venturing to take the bank.

For the edification of the reader, who has, no doubt, some curiosity on the subject, I will briefly mention that the kitchen and table wares of the traders usually consist of a skillet, a frying-pan, a sheet-iron camp-kettle, a coffee-pot, and each man with his tin cup and a butcher's knife. The culinary operations being finished, the pan and kettle are set upon the grassy turf, around which all take a lowly seat and crack their gleesome jokes while from their greasy hands they swallow their savory viands—all with a relish rarely experienced at the well-spread tables of the most fashionable and wealthy.

The insatiable appetite acquired by travelers upon the prairies is almost incredible, and the quantity of coffee drunk is still more so. It is an unfailing and apparently indispensable beverage, served at every meal—even under the broiling noon-day sun the wagoner will rarely fail to replenish a second time his huge tin cup. Every year large parties of New Mexicans, some provided with mules and asses, others with *carretas* or truckle-carts and oxen, drive out into these prairies to procure a supply of buffalo beef for their families. They hunt like the wild Indians, chiefly on horseback and with bow and arrow, or lance, with which they soon load their carts and mules. They find no difficulty in curing their meat even in mid-summer, by slicing it thin and spreading or suspending it in the sun; or, if in haste, it is slightly barbecued. During the curing operation they often follow the Indian practice of beating or kneading the slices with their feet, which they contend contributes to its preservation.

Here the extraordinary purity of the atmosphere is remarkably exemplified. The caravans cure meat in the same simple manner, except the process of kneading. A line is stretched from corner to corner on each side of a wagon-body and strung with slices of beef, which remains from day to day till it is sufficiently cured to be stacked away. This is done without salt, and yet it very rarely putrefies. In truth, as blow-flies are unknown here, there is nothing to favor putrefaction. While speaking of flies I might as well remark that after passing beyond the region of the tall grass between the Missouri frontier and Arkansas River, the horse-fly, also, is unknown. Judging from the prairies on our border we had naturally anticipated a great deal of mischief from these brute-tormentors; in which we were very agreeably disappointed.

Upon encamping, the wagons are formed into a hollow square (each division to a side), constituting at once an enclosure (or *corral*) for the animals when needed, and a fortification against the Indians. Not to embarrass this cattle-pen, the camp fires are all lighted outside of the wagons. Outside of the wagons, also, the travelers spread their beds, which consist, for the most part, of buffalo-rugs and blankets. Many content themselves with a single Mackinaw; but a pair constitutes the most regular pallet; and he that is provided with a buffalo-rug into the bargain is deemed luxuriously supplied. It is most usual to sleep out in the open air, as well to be at hand in case of attack as, indeed, for comfort; for the serene sky of the prairies affords the most agreeable and wholesome canopy. That deleterious attribute of night air and dews so dangerous in other climates is but little experienced upon the high plains: on the contrary, the serene evening air seems to affect the health rather favorably than otherwise. Tents are so rare on these expeditions that in a caravan of two hundred men I have not seen a dozen. In time of rain the traveler resorts to his wagon, which affords a far more secure shelter than a tent; for if the latter is not beaten down by the storms which so often accompany rain upon the prairies, the ground underneath is at least apt to be flooded. During dry weather, however, even the invalid prefers the open air.

Prior to the date of our trip it had been customary to secure the horses by hoppling them. The fore-hopple (a leather strap or rope manacle upon the fore-legs), being most convenient, was more frequently used; though the side-line (a hopple connecting a fore and hind leg) is the most secure; for with this an animal can hardly increase his pace beyond a hobbling walk; whereas, with the fore-hopple, a frightened horse will scamper off with nearly as much velocity as though he were unshackled. But better than either of these is the practice which the caravans have since adopted of tethering the mules at night around the wagons, at proper intervals, with ropes twenty-five or thirty feet in length tied to stakes fifteen to twenty inches long driven into the ground; a supply of which, as well as mallets, the wagoners always carry with them.

26

California on the Eve of Conquest, 1847

One readily believes that Henry A. Wise was a very charming man, for he wrote a very charming book. He was born in the Brooklyn Navy Yard in 1819, and his whole life was connected with the United States Navy. During the Mexican War he was assigned to duty in California waters, and in Los Gringos he gives a record of his travels around the Horn, of South America, and of California. Whatever the Mexican War may have been like in other theaters, it appears to have been in California largely a matter of Mexican beauties, fandangos, and hunting expeditions. The account is told with fresh-ness and verve and portrays beautifully the idyllic character of California before it was to be turned upside down in the rush for gold two years later.

The rain came down in a steady drizzle, as we anchored in our new haven, but as the falling water thinned, and rolled partially along the land, we discerned an endless succession of green gentle slopes and valleys, with heights of just a medium between hills and mountains, rising gradually from the shores of the bay, clothed and crowned with magnificent vegetation.

The town of Monterey, if it could be dignified by the title, we found a mean, irregular collection of mud huts, and long, low, adobie dwellings, strewn promiscuously over an easy slope, down to the water's edge. The most conspicuous was the *duana*—Custom House—a spacious frame building near the landing, which unquestionably had in times past been the means of yielding immense revenues to the Mexican exchequer, but now its roomy storehouses were empty and silent. Neither men nor merchandise disturbed its quiet precincts. Notwithstanding the rain, numbers of us resolved to dare the moisture, and I, for one, would wade about on land, up to my neck in water, at any time to get quit of a ship after forty days aquatic recreation; but here there was no resisting the gratefully green appearance of the shores around us: we were soon stowed in a boat—the oars dipped smart and strong in the water, and we went merrily towards the land. Indeed I have invariably observed that men-of-war's men are wont to use their arms with much vigor, on first pulling on shore in a strange port; a physical characteristic which I am led to attribute to a desire on their part to test the virtues of any liquid compounds to be met with in the abodes of hospitable publicans. The anchorage was barely half a mile from the shore, and in a few minutes we disembarked at a little pier, that only partially served to check the rolling swell from seaward; but what's a wet foot in a fit of enthusiasm, or a heavy shower! Nothing, certainly, so we scrambled up the slimy steps, and while on the point of giving a yell of delight, to announce our arrival in California, my pedal extremities flew upwards and down I sank, making a full length *intaglio* in the yielding mud—this was my first impression, but after getting decently scraped by Jack's knives, I became less excitable, and took intense delight during the course of the afternoon, in beholding my companions going through precisely the same performances. By cautious navigation we reached the main street, then our progress was dreadfully slow and laborious. The mud—a sticky, red pigment, lay six good inches on the dryest level, and at every step our feet were disengaged by a powerful jerk, and a deep, guttural noise from the slippy holes; occasionally, too, we were forced to climb ungainly barricades of timber, with here and there a piece of ordnance gazing ferociously out into the surrounding country. Although a casual observer might naturally have supposed that the mud would have offered a sufficient barrier to all the armies ever raised, still, as trouble had been brewing, and

most of the garrison withdrawn for an expedition into the interior, these pre-
cautions were quite an imposing display, which was, no doubt, all intended.
At last, by dint of perserverance, we attained a firm foothold in the barracks,
and then had breath and leisure to look around.

Monterey, before the war, contained about five hundred people, but on our
advent there was scarcely a native to be seen: all the men had gone to join
their belligerent friends in the southern provinces, leaving their property and
dwellings to be guarded by their wives and dogs; even their ladies bore us no
good will, and our salutations were returned by a surly *adios,* extorted from
closed teeth and scowling faces. The dogs were more civil, and even when
showing their fangs, were sagacious enough to keep beyond the chastening
reach of Yankee arms. There were a goodly number of sentinels on the alert,
prowling about, with heavy knives in their girdles, and the locks of their
rifles carefully sheltered from the rain; and at night it became a matter of
some bodily danger for an indifferent person to come suddenly in view of
one of these vigilant gentlemen, for with but a tolerable ear for music he
might detect the sharp click of a rifle, and the hoarse caution of "Look out,
thar, stranger"; when if the individual addressed did not speedily shout out
his name and calling, he stood the merest chance of having another eyelet-
hole drilled through his skull.

The time passed rapidly away. The rainy season had nearly ended,—we
were only favored with occasional showers, and by the latter part of February, the early spring had burst forth, and nothing could exceed the loveliness
of the rich, verdant landscape around us. After the treaty and capitulation
had been signed by the Picos at Los Angeles, their partizans dispersed, and
all who resided in Monterey shortly returned to their homes. Every day
brought an addition to the place—great ox-cart caravans with hide bodies,
and unwieldy wheels of hewn lumber, came screaming along the roads, filled
with women and children, who had sought refuge in some secure retreat in
the country. Cattle soon were seen grazing among the hills. The town itself
began to look alive—doors were unlocked and windows thrown open—a
café and billiards emerged—pulperias, with shelves filled with aguadiente
appeared on every corner—the barricades were torn down—guns removed—
and the Californians themselves rode blithely by, with heavy, jingling spurs,
and smiling faces—the women, too, flashed their bright eyes less angrily upon
their invaders—accepted pleasant compliments without a sneer, and even
Doña Augustia Ximénes, who took a solemn oath upon her missal a few
months before, never to dance again, until she could wear a necklace of
Yankee ears, relented too, and not only swept gracefully through waltz and

contra danza, but when afterwards one of our young officers became ill with fever, she had him carried from the tent to her dwelling, watched him with all a woman's care and tenderness, as much as though she had been the mother that bore him, until he was carried to his last home.

Gradually these good people became aware that the Yankees were not such a vile pack of demonios as they first believed, and thus whenever guitars were tinkling at the fandangos, or meals laid upon the board, we were kindly welcomed, with the privilege of making as much love, and devouring as many *frijoles* as may have been polite or palatable. Upon visiting the residences of the townspeople, true to the old Spanish character there was no attempt made in show or ostentation—that is always reserved for the streets or alemeda, but a stranger is received with cordiality, and a certain ease and propriety to which they seem to the "manor born." With the denizens of Monterey, even the wealthiest, cleanliness was an acquirement very little appreciated or practised, and I should presume the commodity of soap to be an article "more honored in the breach than the observance." For being given to cold water as a principal of lady-like existence I was something shocked on one occasion, to find a nice little Señorita, to whom I had been playing the agreeable the night previous, with a chemisette of a chocolate hue peeping through a slit in her sleeve; her soft, dimpled hands, too, made me speculate mentally upon the appearance of her little feet, and I forthwith resolved, in the event of becoming so deeply infatuated as to induce her papa to permit a change of estate, to exact a change of raiment in the marriage contract.

The occasion of inspecting the arcana of this young woman's vestments was during a visit to her portly mamma, and I may as well, by way of example, describe my reception. The dwelling was a low, one story pile of adobies, retaining the color of the primitive mud, and forming a large parallelogram; it enclosed a huge pen, or corral, for cattle, over which guard was carefully mounted by crowds of *gallinazos*. There were divers collections of Indian families coiled and huddled about beneath the porticos and doorways, each member thereof rejoicing in great masses of wiry shocks of hair, quite coarse enough to weave into bird cages on an emergency; there were some bee-hive shaped ovens also, from the apertures of which I remarked a number of filthy individuals immersed neck deep, taking, no doubt, balmy slumber, with the rain doing what they never had the energy to perform themselves—washing their faces. This much for externals—men and beasts included, merely premising that the whole affair was situated in a quiet detachment by itself, a few hundred yards in the rear of the village. My guide, though a good pilot, and retaining a clear perception of the road, was unable to convoy me safely to the house, without getting stalled several times in the mire; however, I reached terra firma, thankful to have escaped with my boots overflowing with mud, and then we marched boldly into the domicile. We entered a large, white-washed *sala,* when, after clapping hands, a concourse of small children approached with a lighted tallow link, and in reply to our inquiries, without further ceremony, ushered us by another apartment into the presence of the mistress of the mansion. She was sitting *a la grande Turque,* on the chief ornamental structure that graced the chamber—namely, the bed, upon which were sportively engaged three diminutive brats, with a mouse-trap—paper cigarritos—dirty feet, and other juvenile and diverting toys. The Doña herself was swallowing and puffing clouds of smoke alternately—but I must paint her as she sat, through the haze. "Juana," said she, calling to a short, squat Indian girl, *"lumbrecita por el Señor,"*—a light for the gentleman—and in a moment I was likewise pouring forth volumes of smoke. I saw but little of her figure, as she was almost entirely enveloped in shawls and bed clothes; the arms, however, were visible, very large, round and symmetrical, which of themselves induced me to resign all pretensions to becoming her son-in-law. She excused herself on the plea of indisposition for not rising, and it being one I surmised she was a martyr to every year or so, I very readily coincided, but in truth I found the Señora Mariqueta sensible, good-humored, and what was far more notable, the mother of fourteen male and five female children—making nineteen the sum of boys and girls total, as she informed me herself, without putting me to the trouble of counting the brood; and yet she numbered but seven and thirty years, in the very prime of life, with the appearance of being able again to perform equally astonishing exploits for the future. After an hour's pleasant chat we took leave, with the promise on my part of teaching the eldest daughter, Teresa, the Polka, for which I needed no incentive, as she was extremely graceful and pretty.

One morning, at break of day, I left Monterey for a tramp among the hills; the natives by this time had become pacifically disposed, and there was no serious apprehensions of getting a hide necklace thrown over one's head, in shape of the unerring lasso, if per chance a Yankee strayed too far from his quarters. With a fowling-piece on my arm, and a carbine slung to the back of an attendant, we pursued a tortuous path, through a gap in the hills, to the southward, and after a four or five miles' walk we found ourselves at the Mission of Carmelo. It is within a mile of the sea, protected by a neck of land, close to a rapid clear stream of the same name. A quaint old church, falling to decay, with crumbling tower and belfry, broken roofs, and long lines of mud-built dwellings, all in ruins, is what remains of a once flourishing and wealthy settlement. It still presents a picturesque appearance, standing on a little rise, above a broad fertile plain of many acres, adjacent to the banks of the river, and at the base a large orchard of fruits and flowers. Following up the stream for some leagues, through the same rich level, crossing and re-crossing the pure running water, with noble salmon flashing their silver sides at every fathom, we soon bagged as much game as we could stagger under: wild ducks, quail, partridges, hares of a very large size, and rabbits. By this time we had penetrated so far from ravine and hill as to have completely lost our bearings, and becoming quite bewildered, I began to entertain serious ideas of seeking some place of shelter for the night but I espied a horseman slowly winding his way beneath us in the gorge. By discharging a barrel of my piece, and continued shouts, we soon attracted attention, and thus being encouraged by the sight of a fellow-being, we sprang briskly down the steep. I heard a shrill voice crying, *"Que es lo que quiere?"* "We are lost," I replied; "will you assist us?" With many a wary glance and movement, he at last came frankly towards us, and I then discovered an intelligent little fellow, about ten years of age astride a powerful animal, which he guided by a single thong of hide. On learning our situation he gladly volunteered to guide us, and told me that we had described a wide circuit around the hills, and were within a short league of the Mission. This last was highly gratifying information, and mounting my worn-out attendant on the horse, our little guide took the bridle, and led the way towards the valley. It was quite dark on reaching the stream, and I felt thoroughly knocked up, but a few minutes bathe in the chill water gave me new life, and shortly after we were housed in the great hall of the Mission.

It chanced to be Sunday evening, moreover, during carnival, and there were preparations for a more brilliant fandango than the usual weekly affair produced. A few horses were picketted about the great *patio,* and two or three ox-carts with hide bodies were serving as boudoirs to damsels, who had come from afar to mingle in the ball. But the company had not yet assembled in the old hall, that had once served the good *frayles* for a refectory; and on entering I was kindly welcomed by the Patrona Margaria, and her handsome coquettish daughter, Domatilda, who were the liege and lady hostess of the Carmelo Mission. With her own hands the jolly madre soon prepared me an *olla podrida* of tomatoes, peppers, and the remains in my game bag. Then her laughing nymph patted me some *tortillas:* and after eating ravenously, and draining a cup of aguadiente, the hospitable old lady tumbled me into her own spacious couch, which stood in an angle of the hall, and giving me a hearty slap on the back, shouted, *"Duerme usted bien hijo mio hasta la media noche"*—Sleep like a top until midnight. I needed no second bidding, and in a moment was buried in a deep sleep.

Unconscious of fleeting hours, I was at length restored to life, but in the most disordered frame of mind; suffering under a most complicated attack of nightmare, of which bear-hugs, murders, manacles and music present but a slight idea of my agony; and indeed, when after pinching myself, and tearing my eyelids fairly open, I had still great difficulty in recalling my erring faculties. I found my own individual person deluged with a swarm of babies, who were lying athwart ships, and amid ships, fore and aft, heads and toes, every way; and one interesting infant, just teething, was suckling vigorously away on the left lobe of my ear, while another lovingly entwined its little fingers in my whiskers. Nor was this half the bodily miseries I had so innocently endured. A gay youth, with a dripping link, nicely balanced against my boots, was sitting on my legs, with a level space on the bed before him, intently playing *monté,* to the great detriment of the purses of his audience. On glancing round, I beheld the lofty apartment lighted by long tallow candles melted against the walls, whose smoke clung in dense clouds around the beams of the lofty hall; the floor was nearly filled, at the lower end, with groups of swarthy Indians and paisanos, sipping aguadiente, or indulging in the same exciting amusement as the gentleman sitting on my feet. On either side were double rows of men and women, moving in the most bewildering mazes of the contra danza: turning and twisting, twining and whirling with unceasing rapidity, keeping time to most inspiriting music, of harps and guitars; whilst ever and anon, some delighted youth would elevate his voice, in a shout of ecstacy, at the success of some bright-eyed señorita in the dance. It took me but an instant to appreciate all this; and then, being fully roused to my wrongs, I gave one vigorous spring, which sent the *monté* man, candle, cards, and coppers, flying against the wall, and bounding to my feet I made a dash at the Patrona, drank all the *licores* on the tray, and seizing her round the waist, away we spun through the fandango. Long before rosy morn I had become as merry and delighted as the rest of the company. I bought a dirty pack of cards for a rial, and opened a monte bank, for coppers and paper cigars and I comprehended by their guttural exclamations that their *compadre* was not so verdant a person as they at first imagined. I busied myself swearing love, and sipping *dulces* with the brunettas; vowing friendship with the men; drinking strong waters; promising to redress all grievances, to pay all claims out of my own pocket for the government; and ending by repudiating the Yankees, and swearing myself a full-blooded Californian.

Sunday, the Fourth of July, we attended church. The building was oblong, painted roughly in fresco, and decorated with a number of coarse paintings, and lots of swallow-tailed, green and yellow pennants dangling from the ceiling. During service an indefatigable cannonier, outside, gave frequent *feux de joie,* from a graduated scale of diminutive culverins—made of brass in shape of pewter porter pots, half filled with powder, and the charge rammed down with pounded bricks—this with music of kettle-drums, cymbals and fiddles made a very respectable din; there were two gentlemenly priests of the order of Saint Francisco who preached each a brief sermon with eloquence and force. Among the congregation were all the belles and dandies of the valley; the former kneeled demurely on little rugs or bits of carpet in the nave of the church; but the latter were lounging near the doors—their gala costume quite in keeping with Andalusia—and one handsome fellow at my side took my eye, as I have no doubt he did that of many a brighter. He was dressed in a close-fitting blue cloth jacket; sky-blue velvet trowsers, slashed from the thigh down, and jingling with small filagree silver buttons, snow-white laced *calçoncillos,* terminated by nicely stamped and embroidered *botas;* around the waist was passed a heavy crimson silk sash; a gay woollen serapa hung gracefully over the shoulder; in one hand a sugar-loafed, glazed sombrero, bound with thick silver cords; and in the other, silver spurs of an enormous size, each spike of the rowels two inches long: all these bright colors—set off by dark, brilliant eyes, jetty black locks, and pliant figure—would have made him irresistible anywhere. Turning towards me, he asked me, smilingly, *Porque no sirve ud à la Misa?* Why don't you kneel at the Mass?—*Tengo pierna de palo,* quoth I, quite gravely: glancing at my pins with much interest, to discover if they were of timber, he seemed to relish the joke, and we then sidled out of the church, and became firm friends on the spot.

On Saturday evenings, crowds of degraded Indians, of both sexes, after laboring during the week, and feeding on locusts or grasshoppers, were accustomed to congregate on the outskirts of the town, where, with gaming and arguadiente, they were enabled to remain torpid all the following day. Their favorite amusement was a game called *escondido*—hide and seek—played with little sticks; and their skill was exerted by trying to discover in whose hands they were: seating themselves on the ground, around a huge blazing fire, separate parties were ranged on opposite sides; then beginning a low, wild chaunt, moving their bodies to and fro, groping with their hands within the serapas before them, until the perspiration starts in streams down their naked sides, after a strange succession of deep, harsh, guttural grunts and aspirations, they suddenly terminate their exertions by giving a sharp yell, and pointing to one of the opposite party, who, if rightly detected, pays forfeit. When one set of players becomes exhausted, others supply their places, and thus they keep it up the live-long night.

Among the Californians an agreeable pastime, much in vogue, is the *me-*

rendar—Anglice, pic-nic. They are usually given on the patron saint's day of some favorite señora or señorita, by their admirers. A secluded, pleasant spot is selected a few miles away from the presidio, where provisions, wine and music are collected beforehand; then each cavalier, with arm thrown affectionately around his sweetheart, on the saddle before him, seeks the rendezvous. Guitars and choral accompaniments soon are heard, and the *merenda* begins, and is kept up with the greatest possible fun and spirit: dancing, frolicking and love-making. There are two or three singular dances of the country: one, called the *Son,* where a gentleman commences, by going through a solo part, to quick, rattling music, then waving a handkerchief to a damsel, who either pays the same compliment to another favored swain, or merely goes through a few steps, without relieving the first comer, who, in turn, is obliged to continue the performance until a lady takes pity on him. It not unfrequently happens, that when a particularly graceful girl is on the floor, making her little feet rapidly pat the ground, like castanets, to the inspiriting music, that some enthusiastic *novio* will place his sombrero on her head, which can never be reclaimed without a handsome present in exchange. But, Heaven help us! the pranks and mischief indulged in on the return home; the tricks and tumbles, laughter and merriment; even the horses appear to enter into the play, and when a cluster of gay lads and lassies have jostled one another from the saddles, the waggish animals, fully appreciating the joke, stop of their own accord. The last affair of this kind I attended, was given by the best-hearted little fellow in the territory; and I am prepared to prove it— Señor Verde, he was an universal favorite, as well with old as young; for he was at different times taking a short *pasear* on every horse, laughing with the madres, and kissing the shy doncellas—*valgame dios*—but I had work in getting him into Monterey that night, for my caballo carried weight—besides a big overgrown dame and myself, Verde hung on to the tail.

We were many weeks in Monterey. But at last we began to tire of foggy mornings, damp nights, tough beef, lounging under the Consul's piazza, sweltering dust, catching fleas, playing monté, and fandangos at Carmelo. The time was drawing near for our departure.

27

California Exchanges Latin Civilization
for American, 1846–49

Joseph Warren Revere, with an ancestry as distinguished as his name, was born in Boston in 1812. Until 1850 his early years were connected with the United States Navy, and he saw service in the Pacific, the Carribean, the Mediterranean, the Baltic, the China Seas, and finally, in 1845, the California coast. He was present during the brief conflict of the Mexican War which changed the ownership of California from Mexico to the United States and himself raised the American flag at Sonoma, July 9, 1846. He returned home in 1848 but came back to California during the gold rush of 1849. His account as a traveler covers vital and significant years. He saw California when it was a sleepy, half-settled community; he witnessed its transfer to the United States; he observed the radical and swift change which occurred with the influx of the Forty-niners. In a short space of time he covers the period when Lieutenant Wise saw California to when Bayard Taylor wrote down his observations. The account possesses generally neither the geniality of the one nor the romanticism of the other. Yet there is, especially in the documents he includes, an aspect of sober and accurate reality in his volume.

When the Civil War broke out, Revere joined the army rather than the navy. He got into difficulties, however, when he removed troops without orders. Though he was a brigadier general, and his previous career had been distinguished, he was court-martialed and dismissed. Lincoln revoked the order, but Revere thereupon resigned. He died in Hoboken, New Jersey, in 1880.

SUTTER'S FORT

Emerging from the woods lining the banks of the river, we stood upon a plain of immense extent, bounded on the west by the heavy timber which marks the course of the Sacramento, the dim outline of the Sierra Nevada appearing in the distance. We now came to some extensive fields of wheat in full bearing, waving gracefully in the gentle breeze like the billows of the sea, and saw the whitewashed walls of the fort situated on a small eminence commanding the approaches on all sides.

We were met and welcomed by Capt. Sutter and the officer in command of the garrison; but the appearance of things indicated that our reception would have been very different had we come on a hostile errand.

The appearance of the fort, with its crenulated walls, fortified gateway, and bastioned angles; the heavily bearded, fierce-looking hunters and trappers, armed with rifles, bowie knives and pistols; their ornamented hunting shirts, and gartered leggins; their long hair turbaned with colored handkerchiefs; their wild and almost savage looks, and dauntless independent bearing; the wagons filled with golden grain; the arid, yet fertile plains; the "caballados" driven across it by wild shouting Indians, enveloped in clouds of dust, and the dashing horsemen, scouring the fields in every direction;—all these accessories conspired to carry me back to the romantic East. Everything bore the impress of vigilance and preparation for defense—and not without reason.

The fame of Capt. Sutter and his fort is so extended, that some account of that distinguished person may be interesting to my readers.

John A. Sutter is a Swiss by birth and a soldier by profession; and, like many of his countrymen, he early sought in the service of a foreign sovereign, that advancement in the career of arms which he was unlikely to find at home, accepting the post of Lieutenant in one of the Swiss regiments of infantry in the service of France, during the reign of Charles X. At the period of the revolution of 1830, and the consequent dethronement of that monarch, he was with his regiment in garrison at Grenoble. Even after the revolution was under full headway, and the tri-color flying in the town, the brave Swiss, with their proverbial fidelity, kept the white flag of the Bourbons displayed over the citadel; nor was it until the revolution was consummated, and Charles a fugitive, that they consented to capitulate. On the disbanding of their corps, which took place shortly afterwards. Sutter came to the United States, became a citizen, and after spending several years in different States of our Union, engaging in various pursuits, and undergoing many vicissitudes of fortune, he concluded to emigrate to Oregon, whence he went to California. With adventurous daring he resolved to take up his abode, alone and unsupported, in the midst of the savages of the frontier; for at that time not a single white man inhabited the valley of the Sacramento. His first attempt to ascend that river was a failure, he having lost his way among the interminable "slues"; but still persevering, he arrived at his present location, established alliances with several tribes of Indians in the vicinity, acquired a great ascendancy and power among them, took some of them for soldiers and instructed them in the mysteries of European drill, built his fort on the most improved frontier model, and boldly made war upon the refactory tribes in the vicinity. I doubt if a more remarkable instance of individual energy, perseverance and heroism, has ever been displayed under similar circumstances. This unceremonious way of settling down in a strange country, and founding a sort of independent empire on one's "own hook," is one of those feats which will excite the astonishment of posterity. In times past men have been deified on slighter grounds.

At length the influence and power of Sutter attracted the attention of the Mexican government; but as he was too remote, as well as too strong, to be punished or betrayed, they thought it their wisest plan to conciliate him. He was, therefore, made military commandant of the frontier, with full authority and absolute power, extending to life itself, within the limits of his jurisdiction. In this office he continued for several years, trading with the Indians, teaching them the rudiments of manufactures, agriculture and arms, and acquiring an extensive influence in the valley. He always, however, had a decided leaning towards his adopted country, and hospitably received and entertained, even to his own detriment, such parties of Americans as came near his retreat; and, I regret to add, that many of our countrymen made but a poor return for this kindness and liberality. Finally, the Mexicans seeing that the Americans, emboldened by his example, began to settle in the valley, and growing jealous of his influential position, endeavored to remove him, and as an inducement to give up his border fortress to a Mexican garrison, offered him the beautiful and improved mission lands of San José, near the pueblo of that name, and the sum of fifty thousand dollars; proving their eagerness to get rid of him by actually providing security for the money, a practice almost unknown in Mexican financiering, which generally consists of promises intended to be broken. But not an inch would Sutter budge from his stronghold, sagaciously looking forward, with the eye of faith, to the time when the United States should acquire possession of the country—a consummation which he devoutly hoped for, and hailed with delight when it came to pass.

The fort consists of a parallelogram enclosed by adobe walls, fifteen feet high and two feet thick, with bastions or towers at the angles, the walls of which are four feet thick, and their embrasures so arranged as to flank the curtain on all sides. A good house occupies the centre of the interior area, serving for officers' quarters, armory, guard and state rooms, and also for a kind of citadel. There is a second wall on the inner face, the space between it and the outer wall being roofed and divided into work-shops, quarters, &c., and the usual offices are provided, and also a well of good water. Corrals for the cattle and horses of the garrison are conveniently placed where they can be under the eye of the guard. Cannon frown (I believe that is an inveterate habit of cannon,) from the various embrasures, and the *ensemble* presents the very ideal of a border fortress.

THE DISCOVERY OF GOLD

It was reported that gold had been found in the valleys of the rivers which flow into the Tulé Lakes. I profess to know nothing of these gold deposits from my own observations, and perhaps Mr. Benton is right in pronouncing them a curse to California. Certain it is, that a land to which nature has been so prodigal might well dispense with them, and perhaps a hundred years hence it will be apparent that the true wealth of California did not lay in her shining sands. Whether the same eminent Senator will be right in predicting that those treasures will prove ephemeral no man can determine. The probability is, that large quantities of gold will be found for many years to come, and it is not unlikely that the value of that precious metal will be seriously affected by the vast additions which will be made to the currency of the world in the course of the next ten years.

What is to be the moral effect of this well-founded mania in the present anomolous condition of California, it is fearful to contemplate. She is without government, without laws, without a military force, while tens of thousands of adventurers from all parts of the earth are pouring into her golden valleys. Among these there must be many lawless and dangerous men; and it is to be feared that thousands who go out respectable, law-abiding citizens, will be transformed by the evil spirit of avarice and by associating on familiar terms with the vicious and depraved, into knaves and men of violence. It will not be surprising to hear at any moment of the most atrocious robberies and murders in the gold region, and it is to be hoped that the heterogeneous mass congregated in the valley of the Sacramento and elsewhere, will pause for a moment in their greedy pursuit of gold, and organize an association for the preservation of law and order. In the present state of affairs, it is apparent from the official documents, that it would be in vain to send troops to California. Our very men-of-war appear to be infected with insubordination as soon as they approach the magic shores of California, and ere this time a large fleet of merchantmen are rotting in the harbor of San Francisco. Where all this is to end, heaven only knows; and the most effective counteracting measure, would be to immediately quiet the land titles, and hold out inducements to settlers to turn their attention to the cultivation of the soil.

The most reliable and intelligent accounts of the gold deposits are to be found in the public documents, and the probability is, that they will continue to furnish the most authentic data respecting the auriferous regions. It is very certain that I could have written nothing so complete and graphic as the account furnished by the accomplished temporary governor, Col. R. B. Mason. His admirable report has been copied all over the world—published in every newspaper, and reprinted in ten thousand catch-penny pamphlets. But it still remains the most accurate and authentic history of the discovery of the gold deposits, and of the early operations of the gold collectors. It ought to be preserved in all the books which treat of California, and familiar as it is, I shall republish it in preference to any second-hand statement of my own. I shall also add the despatches of Lieut. Larkin and Commodore Jones, which will be found extremely interesting.

I begin these interesting extracts with the standard authority—the celebrated report of Col. Mason. Such valuable documents never grow stale.

"HEADQUARTERS 10TH MILITARY DEPOT
"MONTEREY, CALIFORNIA
"Aug. 17, 1848

"SIR:

"I have the honor to inform you that, accompanied by Lieutenant W. T. Sherman, I started on the twelfth of June last, to make a tour through the northern part of California. My principal purpose, however, was to visit the newly-discovered gold 'placer'* in the Valley of the Sacramento. We reached San Francisco on the twentieth, and found that all, or nearly all its male inhabitants had gone to the mines. The town, which a few months before was so busy and thriving, was then almost deserted.

"On the evening of the twenty-fifth, the horses of the escort were crossed to Sousolito in a launch, and on the following day we resumed the journey to Sutter's Fort, where we arrived on the morning of the second of July. Along the whole route, mills were lying idle, fields of wheat were open to cattle and horses, houses vacant, and farms going to waste. At Sutter's there was more

---

* This word has now become naturalized among us. It is pronounced in the singular as if written "plarthair," and in the plural as if written "plarthair-ess."

MINING IN CALIFORNIA

life and business. Launches were discharging their cargoes at the river, and carts were hauling goods to the fort, where already were established several stores, a hotel, &c. Captain Sutter had only two mechanics in his employ, (a wagon-maker and blacksmith), to whom he was then paying ten dollars a day. Merchants pay him a monthly rent of one hundred dollars per room; and while I was there, a two-story house in the fort was rented as a hotel for five hundred dollars a month.

"At the urgent solicitation of many gentlemen, I delayed there to participate in the first public celebration of our national anniversary at that fort, but on the fifth resumed the journey and proceeded twenty-five miles up the American fork, to a point on it known as the Lower Mines, or Mormon Diggings. The hill-sides were thickly strewn with canvass tents and bush arbors; a store was erected, and several boarding shanties in operation. The day was intensely hot, yet about two hundred men were at work in the full glare of the sun, washing for gold—some with tin pans, some with close-woven Indian baskets, but the greater part had a rude machine, known as the cradle. This is on rockers, six or eight feet long, open at the foot, and at its head has a coarse grate, or sieve; the bottom is rounded, with small cleets nailed across. Four men are required to work this machine: one digs the ground in the bank close by the stream; another carries it to the cradle and empties it on the grate; a third gives a violent rocking motion to the machine; while a fourth dashes on water from the stream itself.

"The sieve keeps the coarse stones from entering the cradle, the current of water washes off the earthy matter, and the gravel is gradually carried out at the foot of the machine, leaving the gold mixed with a heavy fine black sand above the first cleets. The sand and gold mixed together are then drawn off through auger holes into the pan below, are dried in the sun, and afterwards separated by blowing off the sand. A party of four men thus employed at the lower mines averaged one hundred dollars a day. The Indians and those who have nothing but pans or willow baskets, gradually wash out the earth, and separate the gravel by hand, leaving nothing but the gold mixed with sand, which is separated in the manner before described. The gold in the lower mines is in fine bright scales, of which I send several specimens.

"As we ascended the north branch of the American fork, the country became more broken and mountainous; and at the saw-mill, twenty-five miles above the lower washings, or fifty miles from Sutter's, the hills rise to about a thousand feet above the level of the Sacramento plain. Here a species of pine occurs which led to the discovery of the gold. Captain Sutter, feeling the great want of lumber, contracted in September last with a Mr. Marshall to build a saw-mill at that place. It was erected in the course of the past winter and spring—a dam and race constructed—but when the water was let on the wheel, the tail race was found to be too narrow to permit the water to escape with sufficient rapidity. Mr. Marshall, to save labor, let the water directly into the race with a strong current, so as to wash it wider and deeper. He effected his purpose, and a large bed of mud and gravel was carried to the foot of the race.

"One day Mr. Marshall, as he was walking down the race to his deposit of mud, observed some glittering particles at its upper edge; he gathered a few, examined them, and became satisfied of their value. He then went to the fort, told Captain Sutter of his discovery, and they agreed to keep it secret until a certain grist-mill of Sutter's was finished. It, however, got out, and spread like magic. Remarkable success attended the labors of the first explorers, and in a few weeks hundreds of men were drawn thither. At the time of my visit, but little over three months after the first discovery, it was estimated that upwards of four thousand people were employed. At the mill there is a fine deposit, or bank of gravel, which the people respect as the property of Captain Sutter, although he pretends to no right to it, and would be perfectly satisfied with the simple promise of a pre-emption, on account of the mill, which he has built there at considerable cost. Mr. Marshall was living near the mill, and informed me that many persons were employed above and below him; that they use the same machines at the lower washings and that their success was about the same—ranging from one to three ounces of gold per man, daily. This gold, too, is in scales a little coarser than those of the lower mines.

"From the mill Mr. Marshall guided me up the mountain on the opposite, or north bank, of the south fork, where, in the bed of small streams or ravines, now dry, a great deal of coarse gold has been found. I there saw several parties at work, all of whom were doing very well; a great many specimens were shown me, some as heavy as four or five ounces in weight, and I send three pieces. You will perceive that some of the specimens accompanying this, hold mechanically pieces of quartz; that the surface is rough, and evidently moulded in the crevice of the rock. This gold cannot have been carried far by water, but must have remained near where it was first deposited from the rock that once bound it. I inquired of many people if they had encountered the metal in its matrix, but in every instance they said they had not; but that the gold was invariably mixed with washed gravel, or lodged in the crevices of other rocks. All bore testimony that they had found gold in greater or less quantities in the numerous small gullies or ravines that occur in that mountainous region.

"On the seventh of July I left the mill, and crossed to a stream, emptying into the American fork, three or four miles below the sawmill. I struck this stream (now known as Weber's creek) at the washings of Sunol & Co. They had about thirty Indians employed, whom they pay in merchandise. They were getting gold of a character similar to that found in the main fork, and doubtless in sufficient quantities to satisfy them. From this point, we proceeded up the stream, about eight miles, where we found a great many people and Indians; some engaged in the bed of the stream, and others in the small side valleys that put into it. These latter are exceedingly rich, and two ounces were considered an ordinary yield for a day's work. A small gutter, not more than a hundred yards long by four feet wide and two or three feet deep, was pointed out to me as the one where two men—William Daly and Parry McCoon—had, a short time before, obtained seventeen thousand dollars' worth of gold. Captain Weber informed me that he knew that these two men had employed four white men and about a hundred Indians, and that, at the end of one week's work, they paid off their party, and had left ten thousand dollars' worth of this gold. Another small ravine was shown me, from which had been taken upwards of twelve thousand dollars' worth of gold. Hundreds of similar ravines, to all appearances, are as yet untouched. I could not have credited these reports had I not seen, in the abundance of the precious metal, evidence of their truth.

"Mr. Neligh, an agent of Commodore Stockton, had been at work about three weeks in the neighborhood, and showed me, in bags and bottles, over two thousand dollars' worth of gold; and Mr. Lyman, a gentleman of education, and worthy of every credit, said he had been engaged, with four others, with a machine, on the American fork, just below Sutter's mill; that they had worked eight days, and that his share was at the rate of fifty dollars a day; but hearing that others were doing better at Weber's place, they had removed there, and were then on the point of resuming operations. I might tell of hundreds of similar instances; but, to illustrate how plentiful the gold was in the pockets of common laborers, I will mention a simple occurrence which took place in my presence when I was at Weber's store. This store was nothing but an arbor of bushes, under which he had exposed for sale goods and groceries suited to his customers. A man came in, picked up a box of Seidlitz powders, and asked the price. Captain Weber told him it was not for sale. The man offered an ounce of gold, but Captain Weber told him it only cost fifty cents, and he did not wish to sell it. The man then offered an ounce and a half, when Captain Weber *had* to take it. The prices of all things are high, and yet Indians, who before hardly knew what a breech-cloth was, can now afford to buy the most gaudy dresses.

"On the eighth of July I returned to the lower mines, and on the following day to Sutter's, where, on the nineteenth, I was making preparations for a visit to the Feather, Yubah, and Bear rivers, when I received a letter from Commander A. R. Long, United States Navy, with orders to take the sloop of war, Warren, to the squadron at La Paz. In consequence I determined to return to Monterey, and accordingly arrived here on the seventeenth of July. Before leaving Sutter's, I satisfied myself that gold existed in the bed of the Feather river, in the Yubah and the Bear, and in many of the smaller streams that lie between the latter and the American fork; also, that it had been found in the Cosumnes to the south of the American fork. In each of these streams the gold is found in small scales, whereas, in the intervening mountains, it occurs in coarser lumps.

"The principal store at Sutter's fort, that of Brannan & Co., had received, in payment for goods, thirty-six thousand dollars' worth of this gold, from the first of May to the tenth of July. Other merchants had also made extensive sales. Large quantities of goods were daily sent forward to the mines, as the Indians, heretofore so poor and degraded, have suddenly become consumers of the luxuries of life. I before mentioned that the greater part of the farmers and rancheros had abandoned their fields to go to the mines. This is not the case with Captain Sutter, who was carefully gathering his wheat, estimated at forty thousand bushels. Flour is already worth, at Sutter's thirty-six dollars a barrel, and soon will be fifty. Unless large quantities of breadstuffs reach the country, much suffering will occur; but as each man is now able to pay a large price, it is believed the merchants will bring from Chili and Oregon a plentiful supply for the coming winter.

"The most moderate estimate I could obtain from men acquainted with the subject, was, that upwards of four thousand men were working in the gold district, of whom more than one-half were Indians; and that from thirty to fifty thousand dollars' worth of gold, if not more, was daily obtained. The entire gold district, with very few exceptions of grants made some years ago by the Mexican authorities, is on land belonging to the United States. It was a matter of serious reflection to me, how I could secure to the government certain rents or fees for the privilege of procuring this gold; but upon considering the large extent of country, the character of the people engaged, and the small scattered force at my command, I resolved not to interfere, but to permit all to work freely, unless broils and crimes should call for interference. I was surprised to learn that crime of any kind was very infrequent, and that no thefts or robberies had been committed in the gold district.

"All live in tents, in bush arbors, or in the open air; and men have frequently about their persons thousands of dollars worth of this gold, and it was to me a matter of surprise that so peaceful and quiet state of things should continue to exist. Conflicting claims to particular spots of ground may cause collisions, but they will be rare, as the extent of country is so great, and the gold so abundant, that for the present there is room enough for all. Still the government is entitled to rents for this land, and immediate steps should be devised to collect them, for the longer it is delayed the more difficult it will become.

"The discovery of these vast deposits of gold has entirely changed the character of Upper California. Its people, before engaged in cultivating their small patches of ground, and guarding their herds of cattle and horses, have all gone to the mines, or are on their way thither. Laborers of every trade have left their work-benches, and tradesmen their shops. Sailors desert their ships as fast as they arrive on the coast, and several vessels have gone to sea with hardly enough hands to spread a sail. Two or three are now at anchor in San Francisco with no crew on board. Many desertions, too, have taken place from the garrisons within the influence of these mines; twenty-six soldiers have deserted from the post of Sonoma, twenty-four from that of San Francisco, and twenty-four from Monterey. For a few days the evil appeared so threatening, that grave danger existed that the garrisons would leave in a body. I shall spare no exertions to apprehend and punish deserters, but I believe no time in the history of our country has presented such temptations to desert as now exist in California.

"The danger of apprehension is small, and the prospect of high wages certain; pay and bounties are trifles, as laboring men at the mines can now earn in *one day* more than double a soldier's pay and allowances for a month, and even the pay of a lieutenant or captain cannot hire a servant. A carpenter or mechanic would not listen to an offer of less than fifteen or twenty dollars a day. Could any combination of affairs try a man's fidelity more than this? I really think some extraordinary mark of favor should be given to those soldiers who remain faithful to their flag throughout this tempting crisis. No officer can now live in California on his pay, money has so little value; the prices of necessary articles of clothing and subsistence are so exorbitant, and labor so high, that to hire a cook or servant has become an impossibility, save to those who are earning from thirty to fifty dollars a day. This state of things cannot last forever. Yet from the geographical position of California, and the new character it has assumed as a mining country, prices of labor will always be high, and will hold out temptations to desert. If the government wish to prevent desertions here on the part of men, and to secure zeal on the part of officers, their pay must be increased very materially.

"Many private letters have gone to the United States giving accounts of the vast quantity of gold recently discovered, and I have no hesitation now in saying that there is more gold in the country drained by the Sacramento and San

Joaquim rivers, than will pay the cost of the present war with Mexico a hundred times over. No capital is required to obtain this gold, as the laboring man wants nothing but his pick and shovel and tin pan, with which to dig and wash the gravel; and many frequently pick gold out of the crevices of the rocks with their butcher-knives, in pieces from one to six ounces.

"Mr. Dye, a gentleman residing in Monterey, and worthy of every credit, has just returned from Feather River. He tells me that the company to which he belonged worked seven weeks and two days, with an average of fifty Indians, (washers), and that their gross product was two hundred and seventy-three pounds of gold. His share, (one seventh), after paying all expenses, is about thirty-seven pounds, which he brought with him and exhibited in Monterey. I see no laboring man from the mines who does not show his two, three, or four pounds of gold. A soldier of the artillery company returned here a few days ago from the mines, having been absent on furlough twenty days. He made by trading and working during that time one thousand five hundred dollars. During these twenty days he was travelling ten or eleven days, leaving but a week, in which he made a sum of money greater than he receives in pay, clothes, and rations during a whole enlistment of five years. These statements appear incredible, but they are true.

"The 'placer' gold is now substituted as the currency in this country; in trade it passes freely at sixteen dollars per ounce; as an article of commerce its value is not yet fixed. The only purchase I made was at twelve dollars the ounce. That is about the present cash value in the country, although it has been sold for less. The great demand for goods and provisions made by the sudden development in wealth, has increased the amount of commerce at San Francisco very much, and it will continue to increase.

"I have the honor to be, your most ob't. serv't,

"R. B. MASON
"*Colonel First Dragoons, Commanding*"

"BRIGADIER GENERAL R. JONES,
"*Adjutant General U. S. A., Washington, D.C.*"

EXTRACT FROM A LETTER FROM MR. LARKIN TO MR. BUCHANAN

"SAN FRANCISCO, UPPER CALIFORNIA
June 1, 1848

"A few men have been down to the boats in this port, spending twenty to thirty ounces of gold each—about three hundred dollars. I am confident that this town has one-half of its tenements empty, locked up with the furniture. The owners—storekeepers, lawyers, mechanics and laborers—all gone to the Sacramento with their families. Small parties, of five to fifteen men, have sent to this town, and offered cooks ten to fifteen dollars per day for a few weeks. Mechanics and teamsters, earning the year past five to eight dollars per day, have struck and gone. Several United States volunteers have deserted. United States bark Anita, belonging to the army, now at anchor here, has but six men. One Sandwich Island vessel in port lost all her men; engaged another crew at fifty dollars for the run of fifteen days to the Islands.

"One American captain having his men shipped on this coast in such a manner that they could leave at any time, had them all on the eve of quitting, when he agreed to continue their pay and food; leaving one on board, he took a boat and carried them to the gold regions—furnishing tools and giving his men one-third. They have been gone a week. Common spades and shovels, one month ago worth one dollar, will now bring ten dollars at the gold regions. I am informed fifty dollars has been offered for one. Should this gold continue as represented, this town and others would be depopulated. Clerks' wages have risen from six hundred to one thousand per annum, and board; cooks, twenty-five to thirty dollars per month. This sum will not be any inducement a month longer, unless the fever and ague appears among the washers. The *Californian,* printed here, stopped this week. The *Star* newspaper office, where the new laws of Governor Mason, for this country, are printing, has but one man left. A merchant, lately from China, has even lost his China servants. Should the excitement continue through the year, and the whale-ships visit San Francisco, I think they will lose most of their crews. How Colonel Mason can retain his men, unless he puts a force on the spot, I know not.

"I have seen several pounds of this gold, and consider it very pure, worth, in New York, seventeen to eighteen dollars per ounce; fourteen to sixteen dollars, in merchandize, is paid for it here. What good or bad effects this gold mania will have on California, I cannot foretell. It may end this year; but I am informed it will continue many years. Mechanics now in this town are only waiting to finish some rude machinery, to enable them to obtain the gold more expeditiously, and free from working in the river. Up to this time, but few Californians have gone to the mines, being afraid the Americans will soon have troubles among themselves, and cause disturbance all around. Although my statements are almost incredible, I believe I am within the statements believed by everyone here. Ten days back, the excitement had not reached Monterey.

"I have the honor to be, very respectfully,

"THOMAS O. LARKIN"

"HON. JAMES BUCHANAN
   "Secretary of State, Washington"

28

Eldorado: California and the Forty-niners, 1849

*P*erhaps the most sensational news ever to break in nineteenth-century America was the discovery of gold in California. At once—around the Horn, over the Isthmus, across the continent—poured a hungry multitude in search of the golden grains and quick riches. They came from all walks of life and from every section of the nation. Jammed in together in the gold regions of California, they transformed the sleepy Latin civilization of the natives and ratified in fact the Treaty of Guadalupe-Hidalgo written on paper two years before. If life was lawless, it was also picturesque. And to the sensation of get-rich-quickness were added lurid accounts of desperadoes, gamblers, prosti-tutes, and every other element that was at once damnable or interesting.

An insatiable demand for news of California swept through the East, and the New York Tribune *could have selected no person better qualified to re-port the story than Bayard Taylor. Born in 1825 in Kennett Square, Pennsyl-vania, Taylor was by instinct and inclination a reporter and a traveler. Though he regarded himself as a poet and a novelist, the world does not to-day, nor did it much in his own time, regard these aspects of his career seri-ously. But as a wanderer with a keen eye for what was interesting, it was an-other matter. He had already published one travel book,* Views Afoot *(1846), with great success. He now spent some five months in California, in the first flush of the gold discoveries, and produced* Eldorado *(1850) with equal suc-cess. He added to his popularity by long lecture tours, filling many a lyceum and theater stage with verbal accounts of his experiences, often garbed in the costume of the people of whom he talked, and thus brought to the staid mid-*

dle classes a sense of romance and adventure. His account of California clearly seeks to capture the dramatic, the sensational, and the colorful. With sober matters of economics he was little concerned. But there is no reason to believe that, if his picture seems one-sided, it is not also accurate, for he was, after all, dealing with a bizarre and melodramatic society.

FIRST IMPRESSIONS OF SAN FRANCISCO

At last the voyage is drawing to a close. Fifty-one days have elapsed since leaving New York and now we are in front of the entrance to San Francisco Bay. The mountains on the northern side are 3,000 feet in height, and come boldly down to the sea. As the view opens through the splendid strait, three or four miles in width, the island rock of Alcatraz appears, gleaming white in the distance. There is a small fort perched among the trees on our right, where the strait is narrowest, which might be made as impregnable as Gibraltar. The town is still concealed behind the promontory around which the Bay turns to the southward, but between Alcatraz and the island of Yerba Buena, now coming into sight, I can see vessels at anchor. High through the vapor in front, and thirty miles distant, rises the peak of Monte Diablo, which overlooks everything between the Sierra Nevada and the Ocean. On our left opens the bight of Sousolito.

At last we are through the Golden Gate—fit name for such a magnificent portal to the commerce of the Pacific! Yerba Buena Island is in front; southward and westward opens the renowned harbor, crowded with the shipping of the world, mast behind mast and vessel behind vessel, the flags of all nations fluttering in the breeze! Around the curving shore of the Bay and upon the sides of three hills which rise steeply from the water, the middle one receding so as to form a bold amphitheatre, the town is planted and seems scarcely yet to have taken root, for tents, canvas, plank, mud and adobe houses are mingled together with the least apparent attempt at order and durability. But I am not yet on shore. The gun of the Panama has just announced our arrival to the people on land. We glide on with the tide, past the U.S. ship Ohio and opposite the main landing, outside of the forest of masts. A dozen boats are creeping out to us over the water; the signal is given—the anchor drops—our voyage is over.

I left the Panama, in company with Lieut. Beale, in the boat of the U.S. ship Ohio, which put us ashore at the northern point of the anchorage, at the foot of a steep bank, from which a high pier had been built into the bay. A large vessel lay at the end, discharging her cargo. We scrambled up through the piles of luggage, and among the crowd collected to witness our arrival, picked out two Mexicans to carry our trunks to a hotel. The barren site of the hill before us was covered with tents and canvas houses, and nearly in front a large two-story building displayed the sign: "Fremont Family Hotel."

As yet we were only in the suburbs of the town. Crossing the shoulder of the hill, the view extended around the curve of the bay, and hundreds of tents and houses appeared, scattered all over the heights, and along the shore for more than a mile. A furious wind was blowing down through a gap in the hills, filling the streets with clouds of dust. On every side stood buildings of all kinds, begun or half-finished, and the greater part of them mere canvas sheds, open in front, and covered with all kinds of signs, in all languages. Great quantities of goods were piled up in the open air, for want of a place to store them. The streets were full of people, hurrying to and fro, and of as diverse and bizarre a character as the houses: Yankees of every possible variety, native Californians in *sarapes* and sombreros, Chilians, Sonorians, Kanakas from Hawaii, Chinese with long tails, Malays armed with their everlasting creeses, and others in whose embrowned and bearded visages it was impossible to recognize any especial nationality. We came at last into the plaza, now dignified by the name of Portsmouth Square. It lies on the slant side of the hill, and from a high pole in front of a long one-story adobe building used as the Custom House, the American flag was flying. On the lower side stood the Parker House—an ordinary frame house of about sixty feet front—and towards its entrance we directed our course.

Our luggage was deposited on one of the rear porticos, and we discharged the porters, after paying them two dollars each—a sum so immense in comparison to the service rendered that there was no longer any doubt of our having actually landed in California. There were no lodgings to be had at the Parker House—not even a place to unroll our blankets; but one of the proprietors accompanied us across the plaza to the City Hotel, where we obtained a room with two beds at $25 per week, meals being in addition $20 per week. I asked the landlord whether he could send a porter for our trunks. "There is none belonging to the house," said he; "every man is his own porter here." I returned to the Parker House, shouldered a heavy trunk, took a valise in my hand and carried them to my quarters, in the teeth of the wind. Our room was in a sort of garret over the only story of the hotel; two cots, evidently of California manufacture, and covered only with a pair of blankets, two chairs, a rough table and a small looking-glass, constituted the furniture. There was not space enough between the bed and the bare rafters overhead, to sit upright, and I gave myself a severe blow in rising the next morning without the proper heed. Through a small roof-window of dim glass, I could see the opposite shore of the bay, then partly hidden by the evening fogs. The wind whistled around the eaves and rattled the tiles with a cold, gusty sound, that would have imparted a dreary character to the place, had I been in a mood to listen.

Many of the passengers began speculation at the moment of landing. The most ingenious and successful operation was made by a gentleman of New York, who took out fifteen hundred copies of The Tribune and other papers, which he disposed of in two hours, at one dollar apiece! Hearing of this I bethought me of about a dozen papers which I had used to fill up crevices in packing my valise. There was a newspaper merchant at the corner of the City Hotel, and to him I proposed the sale of them, asking him to name a price. "I shall want to make a good profit on the retail price," said he, "and can't give more than ten dollars for the lot." I was satisfied with the whole-sale price, which was a gain of just four thousand per cent!

I set out for a walk before dark and climbed a hill back of the town, passing a number of tents pitched in the hollows. The scattered houses spread out below me and the crowded shipping in the harbor, backed by a lofty line of mountains, made an imposing picture. The restless, feverish tide of life in that little spot rendered it singularly impressive. Every new-comer in San Francisco is overtaken with a sense of complete bewilderment. One knows not whether he is awake or in some wonderful dream. Never have I had so much difficulty in establishing, satisfactorily to my own senses, the reality of what I saw and heard.

It may be interesting to give here a few instances of the enormous and unnatural value put upon property at the time of my arrival. The Parker House rented for $110,000 yearly, at least $60,000 of which was paid by gamblers, who held nearly all the second story. Adjoining it on the right was a canvas-tent fifteen by twenty-five feet, called "Eldorado," and occupied likewise by gamblers, which brought $40,000. On the opposite corner of the Plaza, a building called the "Miner's Bank," about half the size of a fire-engine house in New York, was held at a rent of $75,000. A friend of mine, who wished to find a place for a law-office, was shown a cellar in the earth, about twelve feet square and six deep, which he could have at $250 a month. A citizen of San Francisco died insolvent to the amount of $41,000 the previous Autumn. His administrators were delayed in settling his affairs, and his real estate advanced so rapidly meantime, that after his debts were paid his heirs had a yearly income of $40,000.

The prices paid for labor were in proportion to everything else. The carmen of Mellus, Howard & Co. had a salary of $6,000 a year, and many others made from $15 to $20 daily. Servants were paid from $100 to $200 a month, but the wages of the rougher kinds of labor had fallen to about $8. Yet, notwithstanding the number of gold-seekers who were returning enfeebled and disheartened from the mines, it was difficult to obtain as many workmen as the forced growth of the city demanded. A gentlemen who arrived in April told me he then found but thirty or forty houses; the population was then so scant that not more than twenty-five persons would be seen in the streets at any one time. Now, there were probably five hundred houses, tents and sheds, with a population, fixed and floating, of six thousand. People who had been absent six weeks came back and could scarcely recognize the place. Streets were regularly laid out, and already there were three piers, at which small vessels could discharge. It was calculated that the town increased daily by from fifteen to thirty houses; its skirts were rapidly approaching the summits of the three hills on which it is located.

A curious result of the extraordinary abundance of gold and the facility with which fortunes were acquired, struck me at the first glance. All business was transacted on so extensive a scale that the ordinary habits of solicitation and compliance on the one hand and stubborn cheapening on the other, seemed to be entirely forgotten. You enter a shop to buy something; the owner eyes you with perfect indifference, waiting for you to state your want; if you object to the price, you are at liberty to leave, for you need not expect to get it cheaper; he evidently cares little whether you buy it or not. One who has been some time in the country will lay down the money, without wasting words. The only exception I found to this rule was that of a sharp-faced Down-Easter just opening his stock, who was much distressed when his clerk charged me seventy-five cents for a coil of rope, instead of one dollar. This disregard for all the petty arts of money-making was really a refreshing feature of society. Another equally agreeable trait was the punctuality with which debts were paid, and the general confidence which men were obliged to place, perforce, in each other's honesty. Perhaps this latter fact was owing, in part, to the impossibility of protecting wealth, and consequent dependence on an honorable regard for the rights of others.

About the hour of twilight the wind fell; the sound of a gong called us to tea, which was served in the largest room of the hotel. The fare was abundant and of much better quality than we expected—better, in fact, than I was able to find there two months later. The fresh milk, butter and excellent beef of the country were real luxuries after our sea-fare. Thus braced against the fog and raw temperature, we sallied out for a night-view of San Francisco, then even more peculiar than its daylight look. Business was over about the usual hour, and then the harvest-time of the gamblers commenced. Every "hell" in the place, and I did not pretend to number them, was crowded, and immense sums were staked at the monte and faro tables. A boy of fifteen, in one place, won about $500, which he coolly pocketed and carried off. One of the gang we brought in the Panama won $1,500 in the course of the evening, and another lost $2,400. A fortunate miner made himself conspicuous by betting large piles of ounces on a single throw. His last stake of 100 oz. was lost, and I saw him the following morning dashing through the streets, trying to break his own neck or that of the magnificent *garañon* he bestrode.

Walking through the town the next day, I was quite amazed to find a dozen persons busily employed in the street before the United States Hotel, digging up the earth with knives and crumbling it in their hands. They were actual gold-hunters, who obtained in this way about $5 a day. After blowing the fine dirt carefully in their hands, a few specks of gold were left, which they placed in a piece of white paper. A number of children were engaged in the same business, picking out the fine grains by applying to them the head of a pin, moistened in their mouths. I was told of a small boy having taken home $14 as the result of one day's labor. On climbing the hill to the Post Office I observed in places, where the wind had swept away the sand, several glittering dots of the real metal, but, like the Irishman who kicked the dollar out of his way, concluded to wait till I should reach the heap. The presence of gold in the streets was probably occasioned by the leakings from the miners' bags and the sweepings of stores; though it may also be, to a slight extent, native in the earth, particles having been found in the clay thrown from a deep well.

SACRAMENTO CITY

The plan of Sacramento City is very simple. It is laid out in regular right-angles, in Philadelphia style, those running east and west named after the alphabet, and those north and south after the arithmetic. The limits of the town extended to nearly one square mile, and the number of inhabitants, in tents and houses, fell little short of ten thousand. The previous April there were just four houses in the place! Can the world match a growth like this?

The original forest-trees, standing in all parts of the town, give it a very picturesque appearance. Many of the streets are lined with oaks and syca-mores, six feet in diameter, and spreading ample boughs on every side. The emigrants have ruined the finest of them by building camp-fires at their bases, which, in some instances, have burned completely through, leaving a charred and blackened arch for the superb tree to rest upon. The storm which occurred a few days previous to my visit, snapped asunder several trunks which had been thus weakened, one of them crushing to the earth a canvas house in which a man lay asleep. A heavy bough struck the ground on each side of him, saving his life. The destruction of these trees is the more to be regretted, as the intense heat of the Summer days, when the mercury stands at 120°, renders their shade a thing of absolute necessity.

The value of real estate in Sacramento City is only exceeded by that of San Francisco. Lots twenty by seventy-five feet, in the best locations, brought from $3,000 to $3,500. Rents were on a scale equally enormous. The City Hotel, which was formerly a saw-mill, erected by Capt. Sutter, paid $30,000 per annum. A new hotel, going up on the levee, had been already rented at $35,000. Two drinking and gaming-rooms, on a business street, paid each $1,000, monthly, invariably in advance. Many of the stores transacted business averaging from $1,000 to $3,000 daily. Board was $20 per week at the restaurants and $5 per day at the City Hotel. But what is the use of repeating figures? These dead statistics convey no idea of the marvellous state of things in the place. It was difficult enough for those who saw to believe, and I can only hope to reproduce the very faintest impression of the pictures I there beheld. It was frequently wondered, on this side of the Rocky Mountains, why the gold dust was not sent out of the country in larger quantities, when at least forty thousand men were turning up the placers. The fact is, it was required as currency, and the amount in circulation might be counted by millions. Why, the building up of a single street in Sacramento City (J street) cost *half a million,* at least! The value of all the houses in the city, frail and perishing as many of them were, could not have been less than $2,000,000.

It must be acknowledged there is another side to the picture. Three-fourths of the people who settle in Sacramento City are visited by agues, diarrhoeas and other reducing complaints. In Summer the place is a furnace, in Winter little better than a swamp; and the influx of emigrants and discouraged miners generally exceeds the demand for labor. A healthy, sensible, wide-awake man, however, cannot fail to prosper. In a country where Labor rules everything, no sound man has a right to complain. When carpenters make a strike because they only get *twelve dollars* a day, one may be sure there is room enough for industry and enterprise of all kinds.

The city was peopled principally by New-Yorkers, Jerseymen and people from the Western States. In activity and public spirit, it was nothing behind San Francisco; its growth, indeed, in view of the difference of location, was more remarkable. The inhabitants had elected a Town Council, adopted a City Charter and were making exertions to have the place declared a port of entry. The political waters were being stirred a little, in anticipation of the approaching election. Mr. Gilbert, of the Alta California, and Col. Stewart, candidate for Governor, were in the city. A political meeting, which had been held a few nights before, in front of the City Hotel, passed off as uproariously and with as zealous a sentiment of patriotism as such meetings are wont to exhibit at home.

The city already boasted a weekly paper, the Placer Times, which was edited and published by Mr. Giles, formerly of the Tribune Office. His printers were all old friends of mine—one of them, in fact, a former fellow-apprentice—and from the fraternal feeling that all possess who have ever belonged to the craft, the place became at once familiar and home-like. The little paper, which had a page of about twelve by eighteen inches, had a circulation of five hundred copies, at $12 a year; the amount received weekly for jobs and advertising, varied from $1,000 to $2,000. Tickets were printed for the different political candidates, at the rate of $20 for every thousand. The compositors were paid $15 daily. Another compositor from the Tribune Office had established a restaurant, and was doing a fine business. His dining saloon was an open tent, unfloored; the tables were plank, with rough benches on each side; the waiters rude Western boys who had come over the Rocky Mountains—but the meals he furnished could not have been surpassed in any part of the world for substantial richness of quality. There was every day abundance of elk steaks, unsurpassed for sweet and delicate flavor; venison, which had been fattened on the mountain acorns; mutton, such as nothing but the wild pastures of California could produce; salmon and salmon-trout of astonishing size, from the Sacramento River, and now and then the solid flesh of the grizzly bear. The salmon-trout exceeded in fatness any fresh-water fish I ever saw; they were between two and three feet in length, with a layer of pure fat, quarter of an inch in thickness, over the ribs. When made into chowder or stewed in claret, they would have thrown into ecstacies the most inveterate Parisian gourmand. The full-moon face of the proprietor of the restaurant was accounted for, when one had tasted his fare; after living there a few days, I could feel my own dimensions sensibly enlarged.

Sacramento City was one place by day and another by night; and of the two, its night-side was the most peculiar. As the day went down dull and cloudy, a thin fog gathered in the humid atmosphere, through which the canvas houses, lighted from within, shone with a broad, obscure gleam, that confused the eye and made the streets most familiar by daylight look strangely different. They bore no resemblance to the same places, seen at mid-day, under a break of clear sunshine, and pervaded with the stir of business life. The town, regular as it was, became a bewildering labyrinth of half-light and deep darkness, and the perils of traversing it were greatly increased by the mire and frequent pools left by the rain.

To one, venturing out after dark for the first time, these perils were by no means imaginary. Each man wore boots reaching to the knees—or higher, if he could get them—with the pantaloons tucked inside, but there were pitfalls, into which had he fallen, even these would have availed little. In the more frequented streets, where drinking and gambling had full swing, there was a partial light, streaming out through doors and crimson window-curtains, to guide his steps. Sometimes a platform of plank received his feet; sometimes he skipped from one loose barrel-stave to another, laid with the convex-side upward; and sometimes, deceived by a scanty piece of scantling, he walked off its further end into a puddle of liquid mud. Now, floundering in the stiff mire of the mid-street, he plunged down into a gulley and was "brought up" by a pool of water; now, venturing near the houses a scaffold-pole or stray beam dealt him an unexpected blow. If he wandered into the outskirts of the town, where the tent-city of the emigrants was built, his case was still worse. The briery thickets of the original forest had not been cleared away, and the stumps, trunks and branches of felled trees were distributed over the soil with delightful uncertainty. If he escaped these, the lariats of picketed mules spread their toils for his feet, threatening entanglement and a kick from one of the vicious animals; tent-ropes and pins took him across the shins, and the horned heads of cattle, left where they were slaughtered, lay ready to gore him at every step. A walk of any distance, environed by such dangers, especially when the air was damp and chill, and there was a possibility of rain at any moment, presented no attractions to the weary denizens of the place.

A great part of them, indeed, took to their blankets soon after dark. They were generally worn out with the many excitements of the day, and glad to find a position of repose. Reading was out of the question to the most of them when candles were $4 per lb. and scarce at that; but in any case, the preternatural activity and employment of mind induced by the business habits of the place would have made impossible anything like quiet thought. I saw many persons who had brought the works of favorite authors with them, for recreation at odd hours, but of all the works thus brought, I never saw one read. Men preferred—or rather it grew, involuntarily, into a custom —to lie at ease instead, and turn over in the brain all their shifts and manoeuvres of speculation, to see whether any chance had been left untouched. Some, grouped around a little pocket-stove, beguile an hour or two over their cans of steaming punch or other warming concoction, and build schemes out of the smoke of their rank Guayaquil *puros*—for the odor of a genuine Havana is unknown. But, by nine o'clock at farthest, nearly all the working population of Sacramento City are stretched out on mattrass, plank or cold earth, according to the state of their fortunes, and dreaming of splendid runs of luck or listening to the sough of the wind in the trees.

There is, however, a large floating community of overland emigrants, miners and sporting characters, who prolong the wakefulness of the streets far into the night. The door of many a gambling-hell on the levee, and in J and K streets, stands invitingly open; the wail of torture from innumerable musical instruments peals from all quarters through the fog and darkness. Full bands, each playing different tunes discordantly, are stationed in front of the principal establishments, and as these happen to be near together, the mingling of the sounds in one horrid, ear-splitting, brazen chaos, would drive frantic a man of delicate nerve. All one's old acquaintances in the amateur-music line, seem to have followed him. The gentleman who played the flute in the next room to yours, at home, has been hired at an ounce a night to perform in the drinking-tent across the way; the very French horn whose lamentations used to awake you dismally from the first sweet snooze, now greets you at some corner; and all the squeaking violins, grumbling violincellos and rowdy trumpets which have severally plagued you in other times, are congregated here, in loving proximity. The very strength, loudness and confusion of the noises, which, heard at a little distance, have the effect of one great scattering performance, marvellously takes the fancy of the rough mountain men.

Some of the establishments have small companies of Ethiopian melodists, who nightly call upon "Susanna!" and entreat to be carried back to Old Virginny. These songs are universally popular, and the crowd of listeners is often so great as to embarrass the player at the monte tables and injure the business of the gamblers. I confess to a strong liking for the Ethiopian airs, and used to spend half an hour every night in listening to them and watching the curious expressions of satisfaction and delight in the faces of the overland emigrants, who always attended in a body. The spirit of the music was always encouraging; even its most doleful passages had a grotesque touch of cheerfulness—a mingling of sincere pathos and whimsical consolation, which somehow took hold of all moods in which it might be heard, raising them to the same notch of careless good-humor. The Ethiopian melodies well deserve to be called, as they are in fact, the national airs of America. Their quaint, mock-sentimental cadences, so well suited to the broad absurdity of the words—their reckless gaiety and irreverent familiarity with serious subjects—and their spirit of antagonism and perseverance—are true expressions of the more popular sides of the national character. They follow the American race in all its emigrations, colonizations and conquests, as certainly as the Fourth of July and Thanksgiving Day. The penniless and half-despairing emigrant is stimulated to try again by the sound of "It'll never do to give it up so!" and feels a pang of home-sickness at the burthen of the "Old Virginia Shore."

At the time of which I am writing, Sacramento City boasted the only theatre in California. Its performances, three times a week, were attended by crowds of the miners, and the owners realized a very handsome profit. The canvas building used for this purpose fronted on the levee, within a door or two of the City Hotel; it would have been taken for an ordinary drinking-house, but for the sign; "EAGLE THEATRE," which was nailed to the top of the canvas frame. Passing through the bar-room we arrive at the entrance; the prices of admission are: Box, $3, Pit, $2. The spectators are dressed in heavy overcoats and felt hats, with boots reaching to the knees. The box-tier is a single rough gallery at one end, capable of containing about a hundred persons; the pit will probably hold three hundred more, so that the receipts of a full house amount to $900. The sides and roof of the theatre are canvas, which, when wet, effectually prevents ventilation, and renders the atmosphere hot and stifling. The drop-curtain, which is down at present, exhibits a glaring landscape, with dark-brown trees in the foreground, and lilac-colored mountains against a yellow sky.

The overture commences; the orchestra is composed of only five members, under the direction of an Italian, and performs with tolerable correctness. The piece for the night is "The Spectre of the Forest," in which the celebrated actress, Mrs. Ray, "of the Royal Theatre, New Zealand," will appear. The bell rings; the curtain rolls up; and we look upon a forest scene, in the midst of which appears Hildebrand, the robber, in a sky-blue mantle. The foliage of the forest is of a dark-red color, which makes a great impression on the spectators and prepares them for the bloody scenes that are to follow. The other characters are a brave knight in a purple dress, with his servant in scarlet; they are about to storm the robber's hold and carry off a captive maiden. Several acts are filled with the usual amount of fighting and terrible speeches; but the interest of the play is carried to an awful height by the appearance of two spectres, clad in mutilated tent-covers, and holding spermaceti candles in their hands. At this juncture Mrs. Ray rushes in and throws herself into an attitude in the middle of the stage: why she does it, no one can tell. This movement, which she repeats several times in the course of the first three acts, has no connection with the tragedy; it is evidently introduced for the purpose of showing the audience that there is, actually, a female performer. The miners, to whom the sight of a woman is not a frequent occurrence, are delighted with these passages and applaud vehemently.

In the closing scenes, where Hildebrand entreats the heroine to become his bride, Mrs. Ray shone in all her glory. "No!" said she, "I'd rather take a basilisk and wrap its cold fangs around me, than be clasped in the hembraces of an 'artless robber." Then, changing her tone to that of entreaty, she calls upon the knight in purple, whom she declares to be "me'ope—me only 'ope!" We will not stay to hear the songs and duetts which follow; the tragedy has been a sufficient infliction. For her " 'art-rending" personations, Mrs. Ray received $200 a week, and the wages of the other actors were in the same proportion. A musical gentleman was paid $96 for singing "The Sea! the Sea!" in a deep bass voice. The usual sum paid musicians was $16 a night. A Swiss organ-girl, by playing in the various hells, accumulated $4000 in the course of five or six months.

The southern part of Sacramento City, where the most of the overland emigrants had located themselves, was an interesting place for a night-ramble, when one had courage to undertake threading the thickets among which their tents were pitched. There, on fallen logs about their camp-fires, might be seen groups that had journeyed together across the Continent, recalling the hardships and perils of the travel. The men, with their long beards, weather-beaten faces and ragged garments, seen in the red, flickering light of the fires, made wild and fantastic pictures. Sometimes four of them might be seen about a stump, intent on reviving their ancient knowledge of "poker," and occasionally a more social group, filling their tin cups from a kettle of tea or something stronger. Their fires, however, were soon left to smoulder away; the evenings were too raw and they were too weary with the day's troubles to keep long vigils.

SAN FRANCISCO REVISITED

When I had climbed the last sand-hill, riding in towards San Francisco, and the town and harbor and crowded shipping again opened to the view, I could scarcely realize the change that had taken place during my absence of three weeks. The town had not only greatly extended its limits, but actually seemed to have doubled its number of dwellings since I left. High up on the hills, where I had seen only sand and chapparal, stood clusters of houses; streets which had been merely laid out, were hemmed in with buildings and thronged with people; new warehouses had sprung up on the water side, and new piers were creeping out toward the shipping; the forest of masts had greatly thickened; and the noise, motion and bustle of business and labor on all sides were incessant. Verily, the place was in itself a marvel. To say that it was daily enlarged by from twenty to thirty houses may not sound very remarkable after all the stories that have been told; yet this, for a country which imported both lumber and houses, and where labor was then $10 a day, is an extraordinary growth. The rapidity with which a ready-made house is put up and inhabited, strikes the stranger in San Francisco as little short of magic. He walks over an open lot in his before-breakfast stroll—the next morning, a house complete, with a family inside, blocks up his way. He goes down to the bay and looks out on the shipping— two or three days afterward a row of storehouses, staring him in the face, intercepts the view.

A better idea of San Francisco cannot be given than by the description of a single day. Supposing the visitor to have been long enough in the place to sleep on a hard plank, in spite of the attacks of innumerable fleas, he will be awakened at daylight by the noises of building, with which the hills are all alive. The air is temperate, and the invariable morning fog is just beginning to gather. By sunrise, which gleams hazily over the Coast Mountains across the Bay, the whole populace is up and at work. The wooden buildings un-lock their doors, the canvas houses and tents throw back their front curtains; the lighters on the water are warped out from ship to ship; carts and porters are busy along the beach; and only the gaming-tables, thronged all night by the votaries of chance, are idle and deserted. The temperature is so fresh as to inspire an active habit of body, and even without the stimulus of trade and speculation there would be few sluggards at this season.

As early as half-past six the bells begin to sound to breakfast, and for an hour thenceforth, their incessant clang and the braying of immense gongs drown all the hammers that are busy on a hundred roofs. The hotels, restaurants and refectories of all kinds are already as numerous as gaming-tables, and equally various in kind. The tables d'hôte of the first class, (which charge $2 and upwards the meal,) are abundantly supplied. There are others, with more simple and solid fare, frequented by the large class who have their fortunes yet to make. At the United States and California restaurants, on the plaza, you may get an excellent beefsteak, scantily garnished with potatoes, and a cup of good coffee or chocolate, for $1. Fresh beef, bread, potatoes, and all provisions which will bear importation, are plenty; but milk, fruit and vegetables are classed as luxuries, and fresh butter is rarely heard of. On Montgomery street, and the vacant space fronting the water, venders of coffee, cakes and sweetmeats have erected their stands, in order to tempt the appetite of sailors just arrived in port, or miners coming down from the mountains.

By nine o'clock the town is in the full flow of business. The streets running down to the water, and Montgomery street which fronts the Bay, are crowded with people, all in hurried motion. The variety of characters and costumes is remarkable. Our own countrymen seem to lose their local peculiarities in such a crowd, and it is by chance epithets rather than by manner, that the New-Yorker is distinguished from the Kentuckian, the Carolinian from the Down-Easter, the Virginian from the Texan. The German and Frenchman are more easily recognized. Peruvians and Chilians go by in their brown ponchos, and the sober Chinese, cool and impassive in the midst of excitement, look out of the oblique corners of their long eyes at the bustle, but are never tempted to venture from their own line of business. The eastern side of the plaza, in front of the Parker House and a canvas hell called the Eldorado, are the general rendezvous of business and amusement —combining 'change, park, club-room and promenade all in one. There, everybody not constantly employed in one spot, may be seen at some time of the day. The character of the groups scattered along the plaza is oftentimes very interesting. In one place are three or four speculators bargaining for lots, buying and selling "fifty varas square" in towns, some of which are canvas and some only paper; in another, a company of miners, brown as leather, and rugged in features as in dress; in a third, perhaps, three or four naval officers speculating on the next cruise, or a knot of genteel gamblers, talking over the last night's operations.

The day advances. The mist which after sunrise hung low and heavy for an hour or two, has risen above the hills, and there will be two hours of pleasant sunshine before the wind sets in from the sea. The crowd in the streets is now wholly alive. Men dart hither and thither, as if possessed with a never-resting spirit. You speak to an acquaintance—a merchant, perhaps. He utters a few hurried words of greeting, while his eyes send keen glances on all sides of you; suddenly he catches sight of somebody in the crowd; he is off, and in the next five minutes has bought up half a cargo, sold a town lot at treble the sum he gave, and taken a share in some new and imposing speculation. It is impossible to witness this excess and dissipation of business, without feeling something of its influence. The very air is pregnant with the magnetism of bold, spirited, unwearied action, and he who but ventures into the outer circle of the whirlpool, is spinning, ere he has time for thought, in its dizzy vortex.

But see! the groups in the plaza suddenly scatter; the city surveyor jerks his pole out of the ground and leaps on a pile of boards; the venders of cakes and sweetmeats follow his example, and the place is cleared, just as a wild bull which has been racing down Kearney street makes his appearance. Two vaqueros, shouting and swinging their lariats, follow at a hot gallop; the dust flies as they dash across the plaza. One of them, in mid-career, hurls his lariat in the air. Mark how deftly the coil unwinds in its flying curve, and with what precision the noose falls over the bull's horns! The horse wheels as if on a pivot, and shoots off in an opposite line. He knows the length of the lariat to a hair, and the instant it is drawn taut, plants his feet firmly for the shock and throws his body forward. The bull is "brought up" with such force as to throw him off his legs. He lies stunned a moment, and then, rising heavily, makes another charge. But by this time the second vaquero has thrown a lariat around one of his hind legs, and thus checked on both sides, he is dragged off to slaughter.

The plaza is refilled as quickly as it was emptied, and the course of business is resumed. About twelve o'clock, a wind begins to blow from the north-west, sweeping with most violence through a gap between the hills, opening towards the Golden Gate. The bells and gongs begin to sound for dinner, and these two causes tend to lessen the crowd in the streets for an hour or two. Two o'clock is the usual dinner-time for business men, but some of the old and successful merchants have adopted the fashionable hour of five. Where shall we dine to-day? the restaurants display their signs invitingly on all sides; we have choice of the United States, Tortoni's, the Alhambra, and many other equally classic resorts, but Delmonico's, like its distinguished original in New York, has the highest prices and the greatest variety of dishes. We go down Kearney street to a two-story wooden house on the corner of Jackson. The lower story is a market; the walls are garnished with quarters of beef and mutton; a huge pile of Sandwich Island squashes fills one corner, and several cabbage-heads, valued at $2 each, show themselves in the window. We enter a little door at the end of the building, ascend a dark, narrow flight of steps and find ourselves in a long, low room, with ceiling and walls of white muslin and a floor covered with oil-cloth.

There are about twenty tables disposed in two rows, all of them so well filled that we have some difficulty in finding places. Taking up the written bill of fare, we find such items as the following:

SOUPS.

Mock Turtle $0 75
St. Julien 1 00

FISH.

Boiled Salmon Trout, Anchovy
   sauce 1 75

BOILED.

Leg Mutton, caper sauce 1 00
Corned Beef, Cabbage 1 00
Ham and Tongues 0 75

ENTREES.

Fillet of Beef, mushroom sauce $1 75
Veal Cutlets, breaded 1 00
Mutton Chop 1 00
Lobster Salad 2 00
Sirloin of Venison 1 50
Baked Maccaroni 0 75
Beef Tongue, sauce piquante 1 00

So that, with but a moderate appetite, the dinner will cost us $5, if we are at all epicurean in our tastes. There are cries of "steward!" from all parts of the room—the word "waiter" is not considered sufficiently respectful, seeing that the waiter may have been a lawyer or merchant's clerk a few months before. The dishes look very small as they are placed on the table, but they are skilfully cooked and very palatable to men that have ridden in from the diggings. The appetite one acquires in California is something remarkable. For two months after my arrival, my sensations were like those of a famished wolf.

In the matter of dining, the tastes of all nations can be gratified here. There are French restaurants on the plaza and on Dupont street; an extensive German establishment on Pacific street; the *Fonda Peruana;* the Italian Confectionary; and three Chinese houses, denoted by their long three-cornered flags of yellow silk. The latter are much frequented by Americans, on account of their excellent cookery, and the fact that meals are $1 each, without regard to quantity. Kong-Sung's house is near the water; Whang-Tong's in Sacramento Street, and Tong-Ling's in Jackson street. There the grave Celestials serve up their chow-chow and curry, besides many genuine English dishes; their tea and coffee cannot be surpassed.

The afternoon is less noisy and active than the forenoon. Merchants keep within-doors, and the gambling-rooms are crowded with persons who step in to escape the wind and dust. The sky takes a cold gray cast, and the hills over the bay are barely visible in the dense, dusty air. Now and then a watcher, who has been stationed on the hill above Fort Montgomery, comes down and reports an inward-bound vessel, which occasions a little excitement among the boatmen and the merchants who are awaiting consignments. Toward sunset, the plaza is nearly deserted; the wind is merciless in its force, and a heavy overcoat is not found unpleasantly warm. As it grows dark, there is a lull, though occasional gusts blow down the hill and carry the dust of the city out among the shipping.

The appearance of San Francisco at night, from the water, is unlike anything I ever beheld. The houses are mostly of canvas, which is made transparent by the lamps within, and transforms them, in the darkness, to dwellings of solid light. Seated on the slopes of its three hills, the tents pitched among the chapparal to the very summits, it gleams like an amphitheatre of fire. Here and there shine out brilliant points, from the decoy-lamps of the gaming-houses; and through the indistinct murmur of the streets comes by fits the sound of music from their hot and crowded precincts. The picture has in its something unreal and fantastic; it impresses one like

GAMBLING SCENE AT SAN FRANCISCO

the cities of the magic lantern, which a motion of the hand can build or annihilate.

The only objects left for us to visit are the gaming-tables, whose day has just fairly dawned. We need not wander far in search of one. Denison's Exchange, the Parker House and Eldorado stand side by side; across the way are the Verandah and Aguila de Oro; higher up the plaza the St. Charles and Bella Union; while dozens of second-rate establishments are scattered through the less frequented streets. The greatest crowd is about the Eldorado; we find it difficult to effect an entrance. There are about eight tables in the room, all of which are thronged; copper-hued Kanakas, Mexicans rolled in their sarapes and Peruvians thrust through their ponchos, stand shoulder to shoulder with the brown and bearded American miners. The stakes are generally small, though when the bettor gets into "a streak of luck," as it is called, they are allowed to double until all is lost or the bank breaks. Along the end of the room is a spacious bar, supplied with all kinds of bad liquors, and in a sort of gallery, suspended under the ceiling, a female violinist tasks her talent and strength of muscle to minister to the excitement of play.

The Verandah, opposite, is smaller, but boasts an equal attraction in a musician who has a set of Pandean pipes fastened at his chin, a drum on his back, which he beats with sticks at his elbows, and cymbals in his hands.

The piles of coin on the monte tables clink merrily to his playing, and the throng of spectators, jammed together in a sweltering mass, walk up to the bar between the tunes and drink out of sympathy with his dry and breathless throat. At the Aguila de Oro there is a full band of Ethiopian serenaders, and at the other hells, violins, guitars or wheezy accordeans, as the case may be. The atmosphere of these places is rank with tobacco-smoke, and filled with a feverish, stifling heat, which communicates an unhealthy glow to the faces of the players.

We shall not be deterred from entering by the heat and smoke, or the motley characters into whose company we shall be thrown. There are rare chances here for seeing human nature in one of its most dark and exciting phases. Note the variety of expression in the faces gathered around this table! They are playing monte, the favorite game in California, since the chances are considered more equal and the opportunity of false play very slight. The dealer throws out his cards with a cool, nonchalant air; indeed, the gradual increase of the hollow square of dollars at his left hand is not calculated to disturb his equanimity. The two Mexicans in front, muffled in their dirty sarapes, put down their half-dollars and dollars and see them lost, without changing a muscle. Gambling is a born habit with them, and they would lose thousands with the same indifference. Very different is the demeanor of the Americans who are playing; their good or ill luck is betrayed at once by involuntary exclamations and changes of countenance, unless the stake should be very large and absorbing, when their anxiety, though silent, may be read with no less certainty. They have no power to resist the fascination of the game. Now counting their winnings by thousands, now dependent on the kindness of a friend for a few dollars to commence anew, they pass hour after hour in those hot, unwholesome dens. There is no appearance of arms, but let one of the players, impatient with his losses and maddened by the poisonous fluids he has drank, threaten one of the profession, and there will be no scarcity of knives and revolvers. Frequently, in the absorbing interest of some desperate game the night goes by unheeded and morning breaks upon haggard faces and reckless hearts. Here are lost, in a few turns of a card or rolls of a ball, the product of fortunate ventures by sea or months of racking labor on land.

There had been a vast improvement in the means of living since my previous visit to San Francisco. Several large hotels had been opened, which were equal in almost every respect to houses of the second class in the Atlantic cities. The Ward House, the Graham House, imported bodily from Baltimore, and the St. Francis Hotel, completely threw into the shade all former establishments. The rooms were furnished with comfort and even luxury, and the tables lacked few of the essentials of good living, according to a "home" taste. The sleeping apartments of the St. Francis were the best in California. The cost of board and lodging was $150 per month—which was considered unusually cheap. A room at the Ward House cost $250 monthly, without board. The principal restaurants charged $35 a week for board, and there were lodging houses where a berth or "bunk"—one out of fifty in the same room—might be had for $6 a week. The model of these establishments —which were far from being "model lodging-houses"—was that of a ship. A number of state-rooms, containing six berths each, ran around the sides of a large room, or cabin, where the lodgers resorted to read, write, smoke and drink at their leisure. The state-rooms were consequently filled with foul and unwholesome air, and the noises in the cabin prevented the passengers from sleeping, except between midnight and four o'clock.

The great want of San Francisco was society. Think of a city of thirty thousand inhabitants, peopled by men alone! The like of this was never seen before. Every man was his own housekeeper, doing, in many instances, his own sweeping, cooking, washing and mending. Many home-arts, learned rather by observation than experience, came conveniently into play. He who cannot make a bed, cook a beefsteak, or sew up his own rips and rents, is unfit to be a citizen of California. Nevertheless, since the town began to assume a permanent shape, very many of the comforts of life in the East were attainable. A family may now live there without suffering any material privations; and if every married man, who intends spending some time in California, would take his family with him, a social influence would soon be created to which we might look for the happiest results.

Towards the close of my stay, the city was as dismal a place as could well be imagined. The glimpse of bright, warm, serene weather passed away, leaving in its stead a raw, cheerless, southeast storm. The wind now and then blew a heavy gale, and the cold, steady fall of rain, was varied by claps of thunder and sudden blasts of hail. The mud in the streets became little short of fathomless, and it was with difficulty that the mules could drag their empty wagons through. A powerful London dray-horse, a very giant in harness, was the only animal able to pull a good load; and I was told that he earned his master $100 daily. I saw occasionally a company of Chinese work-men, carrying bricks and mortar, slung by ropes to long bamboo poles. The plank sidewalks, in the lower part of the city, ran along the brink of pools and quicksands, which the Street Inspector and his men vainly endeavored to fill by hauling cart-loads of chapparal and throwing sand on the top; in a day or two the gulf was as deep as ever. The side-walks, which were made at the cost of $5 per foot, bridged over the worst spots, but I was frequently obliged to go the whole length of a block in order to get on the other side. One could not walk any distance, without getting at least ancle-deep, and although the thermometer rarely sank below 50°, it was impossible to stand still for even a short time without a death-like chill taking hold of the feet. As a consequence of this, coughs and bronchial affections were innumerable. The universal custom of wearing the pantaloons inside the boots threatened to restore the knee-breeches of our grandfathers' times. Even women were obliged to shorten their skirts, and wear high-topped boots. The population seemed to be composed entirely of dismounted hussars. All this will be remedied when the city is two years older, and Portsmouth Square boasts a pavé as elegant as that on the dollar side of Broadway.

The effect of a growing prosperity and some little taste of luxury was readily seen in the appearance of the business community of San Francisco. The slouched felt hats gave way to narrow-brimmed black beavers; flannel shirts were laid aside, and white linen, though indifferently washed, appeared instead; dress and frock coats, of the fashion of the previous year in the At-lantic side, came forth from trunks and sea-chests; in short, a San Francisco merchant was almost as smooth and spruce in his outward appearance as a merchant anywhere else. The hussar boot, however, was obliged to be worn, and a variation of the Mexican sombrero—a very convenient and becoming headpiece—came into fashion among the younger class.

The steamers which arrived at this time, brought large quantities of newspapers from all parts of the Atlantic States. The speculation which had been so successful at first, was completely overdone; there was a glut in the market, in consequence whereof newspapers came down to fifty and twenty-five cents apiece. The leading journals of New-York, New-Orleans and Boston were cried at every street-corner. The two papers established in the place issued editions "for the Atlantic Coasts," at the sailing of every steamer for Panama. The offices were invaded by crowds of purchasers, and the slow hand-presses in use could not keep pace with the demand. The profits of these journals were almost incredible, when contrasted with their size and the amount of their circulation. Neither of them failed to count their gains at the rate of $75,000 a year, clear profit.

My preparations for leaving San Francisco, were made with the regret that I could not remain longer and see more of the wonderful growth of the Empire of the West. Yet I was fortunate in witnessing the most peculiar and interesting stages of its progress, and I took my departure in the hope of returning at some future day to view the completion of these magnificent beginnings. The world's history had no page so marvellous as that which has just been turned in California.

29

An Editor Visits the Mormons, 1859

*H*orace Greeley was born in 1811 in Amherst, New Hampshire. Though
his career was varied, he is today chiefly associated with the New York
Tribune. Under his skillful guidance, that newspaper, in the twenty years
after 1841, became the best known and perhaps most influential publication
in the United States. Nor are the causes hard to find. Greeley was a man of
exceptional integrity and the warm champion of all kinds of "causes." He
held strong convictions and possessed a sturdy American sense of his right
to express them, whether they were popular or not. Consequently, his newspaper was not, like the majority of them today, a namby-pamby effort to
conciliate all shades of interests. It relied, too, for its popularity not upon
scandalous sensation but rather upon a strong sense of public and social
responsibility.

His Overland Journey, made in 1859, was typical of such an editor. He was
accompanied by Henry Villard and Albert D. Richardson, the latter of whom
has left us a parallel account of the journey. Greeley pried into odd corners
for interesting material; he looked below the surface to discover the truth;
and his observations are stated with all the candor expected of such an author.
Greeley did not like proslavery Democrats, and ridiculed them; he did not
like land speculators, and exposed them; he thought the Mormons less vicious
than they were painted, and justified their works if not their theology; he
had no mawkish sentiment about Indians; and he thought young men better
advised to dig the soil for crops than for gold, and said so. One has

little difficulty in following his trail across the continent to Denver, Salt Lake City, through Nevada, to San Francisco. The observations are interesting, for they come in the years between the first discoveries of gold and the building of the transcontinental railways.

In 1872 Greeley was the unhappy presidential candidate of the Liberal Republicans and, ironically, of the Democrats. He would probably not have made a successful President, though it is hard to believe that he would have made a worse one than the Republican victor in that election. He died shortly after his defeat.

Salt Lake City wears a pleasant aspect to the emigrant or traveler, weary, dusty, and browned with a thousand miles of jolting, fording, camping, through the scorched and naked American Desert. It is located mainly on the bench of hard gravel that slopes southward from the foot of the mountains toward the lake valley; the houses—generally small and of one story—are all built of adobe (sun-hardened brick), and have a neat and quiet look; while the uniform breadth of the streets (eight rods) and the "magnificent distances" usually preserved by the buildings (each block containing ten acres, divided into eight lots, giving a quarter of an acre for buildings and an acre for garden, fruit, etc., to each householder), make up an *ensemble* seldom equaled. Then the rills of bright, sparkling, leaping water which, diverted from the streams issuing from several adjacent mountain cañons, flow through each street and are conducted at will into every garden, diffuse an air of freshness and coolness which none can fail to enjoy, but which only a traveler in summer across the Plains can fully appreciate. On a single business street, the post-office, principal stores, etc., are set pretty near each other, though not so close as in other cities; everywhere else, I believe, the original plan of the city has been wisely and happily preserved. Southward from the city, the soil is softer and richer, and there are farms of (I judge) ten to forty or sixty acres; but I am told that the lowest portion of the valley, nearly on a level with the lake, is so impregnated with salt, soda, etc., as to yield but a grudging return for the husbandman's labor. I believe, however, that even this region is available as a stock-range—thousands on thousands of cattle, mainly owned in the city, being pastured here in winter as well as summer, and said to do well in all seasons. For, though snow is never absent from the mountain-chains which shut in this valley, it seldom lies long in the valley itself.

The pass over the Wahsatch is, if I mistake not, eight thousand three hundred feet above the sea-level; this valley about four thousand nine hundred. The atmosphere is so pure that the mountains across the valley to the south seem but ten or fifteen miles off; they are really from twenty to thirty. The lake is some twenty miles westward; but we see only the rugged mountain known as "Antelope Island" which rises in its center, and seems to bound the valley in that direction. Both the lake and valley wind away to the north-west for a distance of some ninety miles—the lake receiving the waters of Weber and Bear Rivers behind the mountains in that direction. And then there are other valleys like this, nested among the mountains south and west to the very base of the Sierra Nevada. So there will be room enough here for all this strange people for many years.

My friend Dr. Bernhisel, late delegate in Congress, took me this afternoon, by appointment, to meet Brigham Young, President of the Mormon Church, who had expressed a willingness to receive me at two P.M. We were very cordially welcomed at the door by the president, who led us into the second-story parlor of the largest of his houses (he has three), where I was introduced to Heber C. Kimball, General Wells, General Ferguson, Albert Carrington, Elias Smith, and several other leading men in the church, with two full-grown sons of the President. After some unimportant conversation on general topics, I stated that I had come in quest of fuller knowledge respecting the doctrines and polity of the Mormon Church, and would like to ask some questions bearing directly on these, if there were no objection. President Young avowing his willingness to respond to all pertinent inquiries, the conversation proceeded substantially as follows:

H. G.—Am I to regard Mormonism (so-called) as a new religion, or as simply a new development of Christianity?

B. Y.—We hold that there can be no true Christian Church without a priesthood directly commissioned by, and in immediate communication with the Son of God and Saviour of mankind. Such a church is that of the Latter-Day Saints, called by their enemies Mormons; we know no other that even pretends to have present and direct revelations of God's will.

H. G.—Then I am to understand that you regard all other churches professing to be christian as the Church of Rome regards all churches not in communion with itself—as schismatic, heretical, and out of the way of salvation?

B. Y.—Yes, substantially.

G. H.—Apart from this, in what respect do your doctrines differ essentially from those of our Orthodox Protestant Churches—the Baptist or Methodist, for example?

B. Y.—We hold the doctrines of christianity, as revealed in the Old and

New Testaments—also in the Book of Mormon, which teaches the same cardinal truths and those only.

H. G.—Do you believe in the doctrine of the Trinity?

B. Y.—We do; but not exactly as it is held by other churches. We believe in the Father, the Son, and the Holy Ghost, as equal, but not identical—not as one person [being].* We believe in all the bible teaches on this subject.

H. G.—Do you believe in a personal devil—a distinct, conscious, spiritual being, whose nature and acts are essentially malignant and evil?

B. Y.—We do.

H. G.—Do you hold the doctrine of eternal punishment?

B. Y.—We do; though perhaps not exactly as other churches do. We believe it as the bible teaches it.

H. G.—I understand that you regard baptism by immersion as essential?

B. Y.—We do.

H. G.—Do you practice infant baptism?

B. Y.—No.

H. G.—Do you make removal to these valleys obligatory on your converts?

B. Y.—They would consider themselves greatly aggrieved if they were not invited hither. We hold to such a gathering together of God's people, as the bible foretells, and that this is the place, and now is the time appointed for its consummation.

H. G.—What is the position of your church with respect to slavery?

B. Y.—We consider it of divine institution, and not to be abolished until the curse pronounced on Ham shall have been removed from his descendants.

H. G.—Are any slaves now held in this territory?

B. Y.—There are.

H. G.—Do your territorial laws uphold slavery?

B. Y.—Those laws are printed—you can read for yourself. If slaves are brought here by those who owned them in the states, we do not favor their escape from the service of those owners.

H. G.—Am I to infer that Utah, if admitted as a member of the Federal Union, will be a slave state?

B. Y.—No; she will be a free state. Slavery here would prove useless and unprofitable. I regard it generally as a curse to the masters. I myself hire many laborers, and pay them fair wages; I could not afford to own them. I

* I am quite sure that President Young used here the word "person" as I have it; but I am not aware that christians of any denomination do regard the Father, Son and Holy Spirit, as one person.

can do better than subject myself to an obligation to feed and clothe their families, to provide and care for them in sickness and health. Utah is not adapted to slave-labor.

H. G.—Let me now be enlightened with regard more especially to your church polity: I understand that you require each member to pay over one-tenth of all he produces or earns to the church.

B. Y.—That is a requirement of our faith. There is no compulsion as to the payment. Each member acts in the premises according to his pleasure, under the dictates of his own conscience.

H. G.—What is done with the proceeds of this tithing?

B. Y.—Part of it is devoted to building temples, and other places of worship; part to helping the poor and needy converts on their way to this country; and the largest portion to the support of the poor among the saints.

H. G.—Is none of it paid to bishops, and other dignitaries of the church?

B. Y.—Not one penny. No bishop, no elder, no deacon, nor other church officer, receives any compensation for his official services. A bishop is often required to put his hand into his own pocket, and provide therefrom for the poor of his charge; but he never receives anything for his services.

H. G.—How, then, do your ministers live?

B. Y.—By the labor of their own hands, like the first apostles. Every bishop, every elder, may be daily seen at work in the field or the shop, like his neighbors; every minister of the church has his proper calling, by which he earns the bread of his family; he who cannot, or will not do the church's work for nothing is not wanted in her service; even our lawyers (pointing to General Ferguson and another present, who are the regular lawyers of the church), are paid nothing for their services; I am the only person in the church who has not a regular calling apart from the church's service, and I never received one farthing from her treasury; if I obtain anything from the tithing-house, I am charged with, and pay for it, just as any one else would; the clerks in the tithing-store are paid like other clerks; but no one is ever paid for any service pertaining to the ministry. We think a man who cannot make his living aside from the ministry of Christ unsuited to that office. I am called rich, and consider myself worth two hundred and fifty thousand dollars; but no dollar of it was ever paid me by the church, nor for any service as a minister of the ever-lasting Gospel. I lost nearly all I had when we were broken up in Missouri, and driven from that state. I was nearly stripped again, when Joseph Smith was murdered, and we were driven from Illinois; but nothing was ever made up to me by the church, nor by any one. I believe I know how to acquire property, and how to take care of it.

H. G.—Can you give me any rational explanation of the aversion and hatred with which your people are generally regarded by those among whom they have lived and with whom they have been brought directly in contact?

B. Y.—No other explanation than is afforded by the crucifixion of Christ and the kindred treatment of God's ministers, prophets and saints, in all ages.

H. G.—I know that a new sect is always decried and traduced—that it is hardly ever deemed respectable to belong to one—that the Baptists, Quakers, Methodists, Universalists, etc., have each in their turn been regarded in the infancy of their sect as the offscouring of the earth; yet I cannot remember that either of them were ever generally represented and regarded by the older sects of their early days as thieves, robbers, murderers.

B. Y.—If you will consult the contemporary Jewish account of the life and acts of Jesus Christ, you will find that he and his disciples were accused of every abominable deed and purpose—robbery and murder included. Such a work is still extant, and may be found by those who seek it.

H. G.—With regard, then, to the grave question on which your doctrines and practices are avowedly at war with those of the Christian world—that of a plurality of wives—is the system of your church acceptable to the majority of its women?

B. Y.—They could not be more averse to it than I was when it was first revealed to us as the Divine will. I think they generally accept it, as I do, as the will of God.

H. G.—How general is polygamy among you?

B. Y.—I could not say. Some of those present (heads of the church) have each but one wife; others have more: each determines what is his individual duty.

H. G.—What is the largest number of wives belonging to any one man?

B. Y.—I have fifteen; I know no one who has more; but some of those sealed to me are old ladies whom I regard rather as mothers than wives, but whom I have taken home to cherish and support.

H. G.—Does not the Apostle Paul say that a bishop should be "the husband of one wife"?

B. Y.—So we hold. We do not regard any but a married man as fitted for the office of bishop. But the apostle does not forbid a bishop having more wives than one.

H. G.—Does not Christ say that he who puts away his wife, or marries one whom another has put away, commits adultery!

B. Y.—Yes; and I hold that no man should ever put away his wife except for adultery—not always even for that. Such is *my* individual view of the matter. I do not say that wives have never been put away in our church, but that I do not approve of the practice.

H. G.—How do you regard what is commonly termed the Christian Sabbath?

B. Y.—As a divinely appointed day of rest. We enjoin all to rest from secular labor on that day. We would have no man enslaved to the Sabbath, but we enjoin all to respect and enjoy it.

Such is, as nearly as I can recollect, the substance of nearly two hours' conversation, wherein much was said incidentally that would not be worth reporting, even if I could remember and reproduce it, and wherein others bore a part; but as President Young is the first minister of the Mormon Church, and bore the principal part in the conversation, I have reported his answers alone to my questions and observations. The others appeared uniformly to defer to his views, and to acquiesce fully in his responses and explanations. He spoke readily, and not always with grammatical accuracy, but with no appearance of hesitation or reserve, and with no apparent desire to conceal anything, nor did he repel any of my questions as impertinent. He was very plainly dressed in thin summer clothing, and with no air of sanctimony or fanaticism. In appearance, he is a portly, frank, good-natured, rather thick-set man of fifty-five, seeming to enjoy life, and to be in no particular hurry to get to heaven.

His associates are plain men, evidently born and reared to a life of labor, and looking as little like crafty hypocrites or swindlers as any body of men I ever met. The absence of cant or snuffle from their manner was marked and general; yet, I think I may fairly say that their Mormonism has not impoverished them—that they were generally poor men when they embraced it, and are now in very comfortable circumstances—as men averaging three or four wives apiece certainly need to be.

The degradation (or, if you please, the restriction) of woman to the single office of child-bearing and its accessories, is an inevitable consequence of the system here paramount. I have not observed a sign in the streets, an advertisement in the journals, of this Mormon metropolis, whereby a woman proposes to do anything whatever. No Mormon has ever cited to me his wife's or any woman's opinion on any subject; no Mormon woman has been introduced or has spoken to me; and, though I have been asked to visit Mormons in their houses, no one has spoken of his wife (or wives) desiring to see me, or his desiring me to make her (or their) acquaintance, or voluntarily indicated the existence of such a being or beings. I will not attempt to report our talk on this subject; because, unlike what I have given above, it assumed somewhat the character of a disputation, and I could hardly give it impartially; but one remark made by President Young I think I can give accurately, and it may serve as a sample of all that was offered on that side. It was in these words, I think exactly: "If I did not consider myself competent to transact a certain business without taking my wife's or any woman's counsel with regard to it, I think I ought to let that business alone." Another feature of President Young's remarks on this topic strikes me on revision. He assumed as undeniable that outside of the Mormon church, married men usually keep mistresses—that incontinence is the general rule, and continence the rare exception. This assumption was habitual with the Mormons, who, at various times, discussed with me the subject of polygamy.

Since my interview with Brigham Young, I have enjoyed opportunities for studying the Mormons in their social or festive and in their devotional assemblies. Of private social intercourse—that is, intercourse between family and family—I judge that there is comparatively little here; between Mormons and Gentiles or strangers, of course still less. Their religious services (in the tabernacle) are much like those that may be shared or witnessed in the churches of most of our popular sects; the music rather better than you will hear in an average worshiping assemblage in the states; the prayers pertinent and full of unction; the sermons adapted to tastes or needs different from mine. They seemed to me rambling, dogmatic, and ill-digested; in fact, Elder Orson Pratt, who preached last Sunday morning, prefaced his harangue by a statement that he had been hard at work on his farm throughout the week, and labored under consequent physical exhaustion. Elder John Taylor (a high dignitary in the church) spoke likewise in the afternoon with little or no pre-meditation. Now, I believe that every preacher should be also a worker; I like to see one mowing or pitching hay in his shirt-sleeves; and I hear with edification an unlettered but devout and earnest evangelist who, having worked a part of the week for the subsistence of his family, devotes the rest of it to preaching the gospel to small school-house or wayside gatherings of hearers, simply for the good of their souls. Let him only be sure to talk good sense, and I will excuse some bad grammar. But when a preacher is to address a congregation of one to three thousand persons, like that which assembles twice each sabbath in the Salt Lake City Tabernacle, I insist that a due regard for the economy of time requires that he should prepare himself, by study and reflection, if not by writing, to speak directly to the point. This mortal life is too short and precious to be wasted in listening to rambling, loose-jointed harangues, or even to those which severally consume an hour in the utterance, when they might be boiled down and clarified until they were brought within the compass of half an hour each.

The two discourses to which I listened were each intensely and exclusively Mormon. That is, they assumed that the Mormons were God's peculiar, chosen, beloved people, and that all the rest of mankind are out of the ark of safety and floundering in heathen darkness. I am not edified by this sort of preaching.*

The spirit of the Mormon religion appears to me Judiac rather than Christian; and I am well assured that Heber C. Kimball, one of the great lights of the church, once said in conversation with a Gentile—"I *do* pray for my enemies: I pray that they may all go to hell." Neither from the pulpit nor elsewhere have I heard from a Mormon one spontaneous, hearty recognition of the essential brotherhood of the human race—one generous prayer for the enlightenment and salvation of all mankind. On the other hand, I have been distinctly given to understand that my interlocuters expect to sit on thrones and to bear rule over multitudes in the approaching kingdom of God. In fact, one sincere, devout man has to-day assigned that to me as a reason for polygamy; he wants to qualify himself, by ruling a large and diversified family here, for bearing rule over his principality in the "new earth," that he knows to be at hand. I think he might far better devote a few years to pondering Christ's saying to this effect, "He who would be least in the kingdom of heaven, the same shall be greatest."

I was undeceived with regard to the Book of Mormon. I had understood

---

* [Six years later, Samuel Bowles (see p. 746), editor of the *Springfield Republican,* made the following report verbatim of a sermon by Heber C. Kimball, first vice-president and chief prophet of the church:

"Ladies and gentlemen, good morning. I am going to talk to you by revelation. I never study my sermons, and when I get up to speak, I never know what I am going to say only as it is revealed to me from on high; then all I say is true; could it help but be so, when God communicates to you through me? The Gentiles are our enemies; they are damned forever; they are theives and murderers, and if they don't like what I say they can go to hell, damn them! They want to come here in large numbers and decoy our women. I have introduced some Gentiles to my wives, but I will not do it again, because if I do, I will have to take them to my houses and introduce them to Mrs. Kimball at one house, and Mrs. Kimball at another house, and so on; and they will say Mrs. Kimball such, and Mrs. Kimball such, and so on, are whores. They are taking some of our fairest daughters from us now in Salt Lake City, damn them. If I catch any of them running after my wives I will send them to hell! and ladies you must not keep their company, you sin if you do, and you will be damned and go to hell. What do you think of such people? They hunt after our fairest and prettiest women, and it is a lamentable fact that they would rather go with them damned scoundrels than stay with us. If Brother Brigham comes to me, and says he wants one of my daughters, he has a right to take her, and I have the exclusive right to give her to who I please, and she has no right to refuse; if she does, she will be damned forever and ever, because she belongs to me. She is part of my flesh, and no one has a right to take her unless I say so, any more than he has a right to take one of my horses or cows.

"We have our apostolic government. Brigham Young is our leader, our President, our Governor. I am Lieutenant-Governor. Aint I a terrible feller? Why, it has taken the hair all off my head. At least it would, if I hadn't lost it before. I lost it in my hardships, while going out to preach the kingdom of God, without purse or script."—ED.]

that it is now virtually discarded, or at least neglected, by the church in its services and ministrations. But Elder Pratt gave us a synopsis of its contents, and treated it throughout as of equal authority and importance with the Old and New Testaments. He did not read from it, however, but from Malachi, and quoted text after text from the prophets, which he cited as predictions of the writing and discovery of this book.

The congregation consisted, at either service of some fifteen hundred to two thousand persons—more in the morning than the afternoon. A large majority of them (not including the elders and chief men, of whom a dozen or so were present) were evidently of European birth; I think a majority of the males were past the meridian of life. All gave earnest heed to the exercises throughout; in fact, I have seldom seen a more devout and intent assemblage. I had been told that the Mormons were remarkably ignorant, superstitious, and brutalized; but the aspects of these congregations did not sustain the assertion. Very few rural congregations would exhibit more heads evincing decided ability; and I doubt whether any assemblage, so largely European in its composition, would make a better appearance. Not that Europeans are less intellectual or comely than Americans; but our emigrants are mainly of the poorer classes; and poverty, privation, and rugged toil plow hard forbidding lines in the human countenance elsewhere than in Utah. Brigham Young was not present at either service.

Do I regard the great body of these Mormons as knaves and hypocrites? Assuredly not. I do not believe there was ever a religion whereof the great mass of the adherents were not honest and sincere. Hypocrites and knaves there are in all sects; it is quite possible that some of the magnates of the Mormon Church regard this so-called religion (with all others) as a contrivance for the enslavement and fleecing of the many, and the aggrandizement of the few; but I cannot believe that a sect, so considerable and so vigorous as the Mormons, was ever founded in conscious imposture, or built up on any other basis than that of earnest conviction. If the projector, and two or three of his chief confederates are knaves, the great body of their followers were dupes.

A party of us visited the lake on Saturday. It is not visible from this city, though it must be from the mountains which rise directly north of it; Antelope, Stansbury, and perhaps other islands in the lake, are in plain sight from every part of the valley. The best of these islands is possessed by "the church," (Mormon) as a herd ground, or *ranche,* for its numerous cattle, and is probably the best tract for that purpose in the whole territory. That portion of the lake between it and the valley is so shallow, that cattle may, at most seasons, be safely driven over to the island; while it is so deep (between three and four feet) that none will stray back again, and it would be difficult and dangerous to steal cattle thence in the night, when that business is mainly carried on. So the church has a large and capital pasture, and her cattle multiply and wax fat at the least possible expense. The best cañon for wood near this city is likewise owned by "the church"—*how* owned, I can't pretend to say—but whoever draws wood from it must deposit every third load in the church's capacious yard. (On further inquiry, I learn that Brigham Young personally is the owner; but, as he is practically the church, the correction was hardly worth making.) These are but specimens of the management whereby, though the saints are generally poor, often quite poor, so that a saint who has three wives can sometimes hardly afford to keep two beds—"the church" has a comfortable allowance of treasures laid up on earth. And her leading apostles and dignitaries also, by a curious coincidence, seem to be in thriving circumstances. It looks to me as though neither they nor the Church could afford to have the world burnt up for a while yet.

Crossing, just west of the city, the Jordan (which drains the fresh waters of Lake Utah into Salt Lake, and is a large, sluggish creek), we are at once out of the reach of irrigation from the northern hills—the river intercepting all streams from that quarter—and are once more on a parched clay-plain, covered mainly with our old acquaintance, sage-brush and grease-wood; though there are wet, springy tracts, especially toward the southern mountains and near the lake, which produce rank, coarse grass. Yet this seeming desert has naturally a better soil than the hard, pebbly gravel on which the city stands, and which irrigation has converted into bounteous gardens and orchards.

I rejoice to perceive that a dam over the Jordan is in progress, whereby a considerable section of the valley of that river (which valley is forty miles long, by an average of twenty broad) is to be irrigated. There are serious obstacles to the full success of this enterprise in the scarcity of timber and the inequality of the plain, which is gouged and cut up by numerous (now dry) water-courses; but, if this project is well-engineered, it will double the productive capacity of this valley.

In the absence of judicious and systematic irrigation, there are far too many cattle and sheep on this great common, as the gaunt look of most of the cattle abundantly testifies. Water is also scarce and bad here; we tried several of the springs which are found at the bases of the southern mountains, and found them all brackish, while not a single stream flows from those mountains in the five or six miles that we skirted them, and I am told that they afford but one or two scanty rivulets through the whole extent of this valley. In the absence of irrigation, nothing is grown or attempted but wild grass; of the half-dozen cabins we have passed between the Jordan and the lake, not one had even the semblance of a garden, or of any cultivation whatever. A shrewd woman, who had lived seven years near the lake, assured me that it would do no good to attempt cultivation there; "too much alkali" was her reason. I learn that, on the city side of the Jordan, when irrigation was first introduced, and cultivation attempted, the soil, whenever allowed to become dry, was covered, for the first year or two, with some whitish alkaline substance; but this was soon washed out and washed off by the water, so that no alkali now exhibits itself, and this tract produces handsomely.

That this lake should be salt, is no anomaly. All large bodies of water into which streams discharge themselves, while they have severally no outlet, are or should be salt. I am told that three barrels of this water yield a barrel of salt; that seems rather strong, yet its intense saltness, no one who has not had it in his eyes, his mouth, his nostrils, can realize. You can no more sink in it than in a clay-bank, but a very little of it in your lungs would suffice to strangle you. You make your way in from a hot, rocky beach over a chaos of volcanic basalt that is trying to the feet; but, at a depth of a yard or more, you have a fine sand bottom, and here the bathing is delightful.

The water is of a light green color for ten or twenty rods; then "deeply, darkly, beautifully blue." No fish can live in it; no frog abides it; few birds are ever seen dipping into it. The rugged mountains in and about it have a little fir and cotton-wood or quaking-asp in their deeper ravines or behind their taller cliffs, but look bare and desolate to the casual observer; and these cut the lake into sections and hide most of it from view. Probably, less than a third of it is visible from any single point.

These Mormons are in the main an industrious, frugal, hard-working people. Few of them are habitual idlers; few live by professions or pursuits that require no physical exertion. They make work for but few lawyers—I know but four among them—their differences and disputes are usually settled in and by the church; they have no female outcasts, few doctors, and pay no salaries to their preachers—at least the leaders say so. But a small portion of them use tea and coffee. Formerly they drank little or no liquor; but, since the army came in last year, money and whiskey have both been more abundant, and now they drink considerably. More than a thousand barrels of whiskey have been sold in this city within the last year, at an average of not less than eight dollars per gallon, making the total cost to consumers over two hundred and fifty thousand dollars, whereof the Mormons have paid at least half. If they had thrown instead, one hundred and fifty thousand dollars in hard cash into the deepest part of Salt Lake, it would have been far better for them. The appetite they are acquiring, or renewing will cling to them after the army and its influx of cash shall have departed; and Saints who now drink a little will find themselves as thirsty as their valley, before they suspect that they care anything for liquor. And yet, I believe, they have few or no drunkards.

Utah has not a single export of any kind; the army now supplies her with cash; when that is gone, her people will see harder times. She ought to manufacture almost everything she consumes, or foreign debt will overwhelm her. Yet, up to this hour, her manufacturing energies have been most unhappily directed. Some two hundred thousand dollars was expended in preparations for iron making at a place called Cedar City; but the ore, though rich, would not flux, and the enterprise had to be totally abandoned, leaving the capital a dead loss. Wool and flax can be grown here cheaply and abundantly; yet, owing to the troubles last year, no spinning and weaving machinery has yet been put in operation; I believe some is now coming up from St. Louis. An attempt to grow cotton is likely to prove a failure. The winters are long and cold here for the latitude, and the Saints must make cloth or shiver.

Sugar is another necessary of life which they have had bad luck with. They can grow the beet very well, but it is said to yield little or no sugar— because, it is supposed, of an excess of alkali in the soil. The sorghum has not yet been turned to much account, but it is to be. Common brown sugar sells here at sixty cents per pound; coffee about the same; in the newer settlements, they are of course still higher. All sorts of imported goods cost twice to six or eight times their prices in the states; even quack medicines (so-called) and yellow-covered novels are sold at double the prices borne on their labels or covers.

Doubtless this city is far ahead of any rival, being the spiritual metropolis and the earliest settled. Its broad, regular streets, refreshed by rivulets of bright, sparkling, dancing water, and shaded by rows of young but thrifty trees, mainly locust and bitter cotton-wood, are already more attractive to the eye than those of an average city of like size in the states. The houses (of *adobe* or merely sun-dried brick) are uniformly low and generally too small; but there is seldom more than one family to a dwelling, and rarely but one dwelling on a lot of an acre and a quarter. The gardens are well filled with peach, apple, and other fruit trees, whereof the peach already bears profusely, and the others begin to follow the example. Apricots and grapes are grown, through not yet abundant; so of strawberries. Plums are in profusion, and the mountain currants are large, abundant and very good. Many of the lots are fenced with cobble-stones laid in clay mortar, which seems to stand very well. The wall of Brigham Young's garden and grounds is nine or ten feet high, three feet thick at the base, and cost some sixty dollars per rod. Undoubtedly, this people are steadily increasing in wealth and comfort.

Still the average life in Utah is a hard one. Many more days' faithful labor are required to support a family here than in Kansas, or in any of the states. The climate is severe and capricious—now intensely hot and dry; in winter cold and stormy; and, though cattle are usually allowed to shirk for themselves in the valleys, they are apt to resent the insult by dying. Crickets and grasshoppers swarm in myriads, and often devour all before them. Wood is scarce and poor. Irrigation is laborious and expensive; as yet, it has not been found practicable to irrigate one-fourth of the arable land at all. Ultimately, the valleys will be generally irrigated, so far as water for the purpose can be obtained; but this will require very costly dams and canals. Frost is very destructive here; Indian corn rarely escapes it wholly, and wheat often suffers from it. Wheat, oats, corn, barley, rye, are grown at about equal cost per bushel—two dollars may be taken as their average price; the wheat crop is usually heavy, though this year it threatens to be relatively light. I estimate that one hundred and fifty days' faithful labor in Kansas will produce as large an aggregate of the neccessaries of life—food, clothing, fuel—as three hundred just such days' work in Utah. Hence, the adults here generally wear a toil-worn, anxious look, and many of them are older in frame than in years.

I do not believe the plural-wife system can long endure; yet almost every man with whom I converse on the subject, seems intensely, fanatically devoted to it, deeming this the choicest of his earthly blessings. With the women, I am confident it is otherwise; and I watched their faces as Elder Taylor, at a social gathering on Saturday night, was expatiating humorously on this feature of the Mormon system, to the great delight of the men; but not one responsive smile did I see on the face of a woman. On the contrary, I thought they seemed generally to wish the subject passed over in silence. Fanaticism, and a belief that we are God's especial, exclusive favorites, will carry most of us a great way; but the natural instinct in every woman's breast must teach her that to be some man's third or fourth wife is to be no wife at all. I asked my neighbor the name of a fair, young girl who sat some distance from us with a babe on her knee. "That is *one* of Judge Smith's ladies," was his quiet, matter-of-course answer. I need hardly say that no woman spoke publically on that occasion—I believe none ever speaks in a Mormon assemblage—and I shall not ask any one her private opinion of polygamy; but I think I can read an unfavorable one on many faces.

Yet polygamy is one main pillar of the Mormon church. He who has two or more wives rarely apostatizes, as he could hardly remain here in safety and comfort as an apostate, and dare not take his wives elsewhere. I have heard of but a single instance in which a man with three wives renounced Mormonism and left for California, where he experienced no difficulty; "for" said my informant (a woman, no longer a Mormon,) "he introduced his two younger wives (girls of nineteen and fourteen) as his daughters, and married them both off in the course of six weeks."

I am assured by Gentiles that there is a large business done here in *un*-marrying as well as in marrying; some of them assure me that the church exacts a fee of ten dollars on the marriage of each wife after the first, but charges a still heavier fee for divorcing. I do not know that this is true, and I suspect my informants were no wiser in the premises than I am. But it certainly looks to me as though a rich dignitary in the church has a freer and fuller range for the selection of his sixth or eight wife than a poor young man of ordinary standing has for choosing his first. And I infer that the more sharp-sighted young men will not always be content with this.

Since the foregoing was written, I have enjoyed opportunities for visiting Mormons, and studying Mormonism, in the home of its votaries, and of discussing with them in the freedom of social intercourse, what the outside world regards as the distinguishing feature of their faith and polity. In one instance, a veteran apostle of the faith, having first introduced to me, a worthy matron of fifty-five or sixty—the wife of his youth, and the mother of his grown-up sons—as Mrs. T., soon after introduced a young and winning lady of perhaps twenty-five summers, in these words: "Here is another Mrs. T." This lady is a recent emigrant from our state, of more than average powers of mind and graces of person, who came here with her father, as a convert, a little over a year ago, and has been the sixth wife of Mr. T. since a few weeks after her arrival. (The intermediate four wives of Elder T. live on a farm or farms some miles distant.) The manner of the husband was perfectly unconstrained and off-hand throughout; but I could not well be mistaken in my conviction that both ladies failed to conceal dissatisfaction with their position in the eyes of their visitor, and of the world. They seemed to feel that it needed vindication. Their manner toward each other was most cordial and sisterly—sincerely so, I doubt not—but this is by no means the rule. A Gentile friend, whose duties require him to travel widely over the territory, informs me that he has repeatedly stopped with a bishop, some hundred miles south of this, whose two wives he has never known to address each other, nor evince the slightest cordiality, during the hours he has spent in their society. The bishop's house consists of two rooms; and when my informant staid there with a Gentile friend, the bishop being absent, one wife slept in the same apartment with them rather than in that occupied by her double. I presume that an extreme case, but the spirit which impels it is not unusual. I met this evening a large party of young people, consisting in nearly equal numbers of husbands and wives; but no husband was attended by more than one wife, and no gentleman admitted or implied, in our repeated and animated discussions of polygamy, that *he* had more than one wife. And I was again struck by the circumstance that here, as heretofore, no woman indicated, by word or look, her approval of any arguments in favor of polygamy. That many women acquiesce in it as an ordinance of God, and have been drilled into a mechanical assent of the logic by which it is upheld, I believe; but that there is not a woman in Utah who does not in her heart wish that God had *not* ordained it, I am confident. And quite a number of the young men treat it in conversation as a temporary or experimental arrangement, which is to be sustained or put aside as experience shall demonstrate its utility or mischief. One old Mormon farmer, with whom I discussed the matter privately, admitted that it was impossible for a poor working-man to have a well-ordered, well-governed household, where his children had two or more living mothers occupying the same ordinary dwelling.

Though Brigham has buried eight sons and two daughters, he has fifty surviving children and several grandchildren.* His wives number about thirty; he increases the list by one or two additions yearly. The first and eldest is matronly and well-looking; all the later ones I saw are exceedingly plain and unattractive, though some of their daughters are pretty, winning and graceful. Among the present generation of Mormons, the men are far more intelligent and cultivated than the women.

The Gentiles relate many stories at the expense of the leading patriarch of the church. He is the grand Supreme Court of all his people; to him they carry their troubles for relief, and their difficulties for adjustment. There is a legend that one day a woman went to Brigham for counsel touching some alleged oppression by an officer of the church. Brigham, like a true politician, assumed to know her; but when it became necessary to record her case, hesitated and said:

"Let me see, sister—I forget your name."

"My name!" was the indignant reply; "Why, I am your wife!"

"When did I marry you?"

* [These concluding paragraphs are taken from the account of Greeley's companion, A. D. Richardson.—ED.]

The woman informed the "President," who referred to an account-book in his desk, and then said:

"Well, I believe you are right. I *knew* your face was familiar!"

The Gentile women recognize and visit only the first wives. The first wife deems herself superior to the rest, sometimes refusing to associate or speak with them, or to recognize the legitimacy of their marriage.

"Are you Mr. ———'s only wife?" asked a Gentile of a Mormon sister.

"I am," was the reply; "though several other women call themselves his wives!"

We are told of one poor fellow, with a pair of wives in a single house containing two rooms. When he brought home his second wife, the first indignantly repudiated him, and would no longer even speak with him. Soon after, the second wife also refused to serve him further; and there the poor wretch was, sleeping alone upon the floor of his cabin, and doing his own cooking, washing and mending, while his consorts were at least agreed in hating him cordially.

But the wives are sometimes very amiable, even toward each other. We dined at the house of a leading Saint, whose two consorts, present at the board, but only as waiters, were dressed precisely alike, and seemed to regard each other as sisters. One portly brother has a wife in nearly every village; so whenever he makes the annual tour of the territory, with Brigham, he can always stay in his own house and with his own family! Polygamy is at least self-sustaining; the women are expected to support themselves.

The Saints' theatre is the grand material wonder of Salt Lake City. It was built by Brigham, and will cost, when completed, a quarter of a million dollars. Its walls are of brick and rough stone, to be covered with stucco. It will seat eighteen hundred persons, and is the largest building of the kind west of New York, except the Cincinnati and Chicago opera houses. The proscenium is sixty feet deep. In the middle of the parquette is an armed rocking-chair, which Brigham sometimes occupies, though his usual place is one of the two private boxes. It is open three nights in the week, when the parquette is filled almost entirely by the families of the leading polygamists. One often sees a dozen of Brigham's wives side by side, and long seats quite filled with his children. The scenery, all painted in Salt Lake, and the costumes, all made there, are exquisite. The wardrobe is very large and rich, varied enough for the standard and minor drama, from the sables of Hamlet to the drapery of the *ballet* girl. With two exceptions, the company are all amateurs—Mormons, who perform gratuitously, and with whom it is a labor of love and piety. It is a novel way of increasing one's chances of heaven; but Brigham is the church, and they do unquestioningly whatever the church requires.

On the whole the theatre is the rarest feature of the rare city, in view of its location, twelve hundred miles from the steamboat and the railroad. During the day the performers are engaged in their regular pursuits, as clerks, mechanics, etc.; and they rehearse only in the evening. Last season the receipts averaged eight hundred dollars per night, and once, thirteen hundred dollars were taken at the box-office. Mrs. Julia Deane Hayne, who was playing a most successful star engagement, had trained the amateurs until they played exceedingly well, producing entertainments in all respects better than one finds anywhere else in the Union, save at three or four leading metropolitan theatres. It was a novel place for the best actress in the United States.

At first she found the audiences curiously excitable, and inexperienced, composed very generally of persons who had never seen a theatre before. When she played the last act of Camille, one old lady left her seat, passed through the private entrance and rushed upon the stage with a glass of water for the dying girl. Another declared, in a voice audible throughout the house: "It is a shame for President Young to let that poor lady play when she has such a terrible cough!"

Brigham shows unequalled sagacity in strengthening the church and putting money in his purse, by the same operation. He says: "The people must have amusement; human nature demands it. If healthy and harmless diversions are not attainable, they will seek those which are vicious and degrading." Therefore he built this Thespian temple, which spiritually refreshed all the Saints of Utah, and increases his personal income fifty thousand dollars annually.

30

Northwest and Southwest, 1866

Though he was not a professional man of letters, James F. Rusling deserves better to be remembered than some who were. He was born in Washington, New Jersey, in 1834, graduated from Dickinson College in 1854, and earned his living as a lawyer. His career was moderately distinguished—at least he was a trustee of several educational institutions. He apparently harbored a taste for creative writing. He wrote for the most distinguished periodicals in America—Harper's, the Atlantic, and Century—and published a variety of books, mostly on occasional topics. He served with distinction in the Civil War and was breveted a brigadier general before its conclusion. In his military capacity he was sent, soon after the close of the conflict, on a tour of inspection through the West, and the result was embodied in his one outstanding volume, Across America.

He covered an amazing amount of ground, and all that he saw he recorded faithfully, with much humor, with discernment, and with perspicacity. It is hard to discover in his professional career of the law the background which could produce so humane a work; and one certainly does not associate with the army the cultivated tone and objectivity with which he wrote. However inexplicable it may be, he achieved one of the most graphic travel accounts of mid-nineteenth-century America.

THE MINING TOWN OF BOISE

Idaho, one of the latest of our new Territories, was formed by lopping off the eastern prolongations of Oregon and Washington, and calling the incipient state by that euphonious name. Lewiston, the head of navigation then, *via* the Columbia, was originally its capital; but the "shrieks of locality" demanded a more central position, and so Boisè City secured the honor. We found it a mushroom town of log and frame buildings, but thoroughly alive in every way. Three years before, there was nothing there but the Boisè bottoms, and a scattered ranch or two. Now she boasted three thousand inhabitants, two daily newspapers, stage-lines in all directions, and ebullient prosperity. A hotel, of large capacity, that was to "take the shine" out of all the rest, was just being completed. The Episcopalians and Presbyterians already had their churches up, and the Methodists were expecting soon to build theirs, though then worshipping temporarily in the Court House. Excellent free-schools, to accommodate all the children and more, abounded, and the sermon we heard on Sunday was chiefly a "pitching into" Brigham Young, largely for the want of these. The preacher had been down to Salt Lake, spying out the land for missionary purposes, and had returned filled with hearty unction against the whole system of Mormonism.

Boisè City was then the centre of the mining regions of Idaho, though not *of* them—like Denver, as related to Colorado. The mines were chiefly miles away, at Owyhee, Ruby, Idaho City, and Silver City; but all business sprang from and converged here at Boisè, as the most central point, all things considered, and most of the "bricks" dropped first into her lap. Mining operations were mostly over for that season, and the streets and saloons of Boisè were thronged with rough miners, *en route* from the Columbia, or even California, to winter and return. They claimed they could save money by this temporary exodus—the price of living was so high in Idaho—and at the same time escape the rigor of the climate. With expensive hats, clad chiefly in red-shirts, and "bearded like a pard," every man carried his bowie-knife and revolver, and seemed ready for any emergency. They were evidently a rougher crowd, than the Colorado miners, and in talking with them proved to be from California, Arizona, Nevada, Oregon, Frazer's River, Montana, and about everywhere else, except Alaska. Your true miner is a cosmopolite who has "prospected" everywhere, from the British Dominion to Mexico, and he is all ready to depart for any new "diggings," that promise better than where he is, on half a day's notice, no matter how far. His possessions are small, soon bundled up or disposed of, and he mocks at the old maxim, "A rolling stone gathers no moss," though usually he is a good exemplification of it.

The chief business of Boisè, just then, seemed to be drinking whiskey and gambling. The saloons were the handsomest buildings in town, and were thronged at all hours of the day and night. The gamblers occupied corners of these, and drove a brisk trade unmolested by anybody. The restaurants were also important points of interest, and gave excellent meals at not unreasonable prices, all things considered. Here at Boisè, our U.S. greenbacks for the first ceased to be "currency," and the precious metals became the only circulating medium. It did one's eyes good to see our old gold and silver coins in use once more, though gold and silver "dust" was also recognized as a medium of exchange. All the stores, restaurants, and saloons kept a delicate pair of scales, and their customers carried buck-skin or leather bags of "dust," from which they made payment, and into which they returned their change. Disputes now and then arose, from the "dust" offered not being up to standard, but these were usually settled amicably, unless the "dust" proved basely counterfeit, and then the saloons sometimes flashed with bowie-knives, or rung with revolvers.

Here, also at Boisè, for the first time, we met John China-man. Quite a number of the Celestials had already reached Idaho from California, *via* the Columbia, and were scattered through the towns, as waiters, cooks, launderers, etc. A few had sought the mines, but not many, as they preferred the protection of the towns. Along with the rest, these Chinese miners were migrating to the Columbia and beyond; and as they paid their stage-fare and rode, while many others footed it to the "River," of course, we augured well of them.

The imbecile, brutal, and barbarous laws of the whole Pacific Coast, where Chinamen are concerned, it appeared, however were still in force in Idaho. A good illustration of their practical workings had just occurred over in Owyhee, or somewhere there, and should be recorded here. Three or four ruffians over there, it appears, had set upon an unoffending Chinaman at work in the mines, and had first abused and insulted him, and then robbed and killed him. Other miners, hearing of the circumstances, arrested the murderers and took them before an Idaho Dogberry, who promptly liberated them on the ground, that no Anglo-Saxon was present at the transaction, and that the Chinamen (who were) were incompetent as witnesses, as against white men! This was good Idaho law and justice, no doubt. But it was too strong for the indignant miners, and the same day Judge Lynch amended it by *hanging* all the miscreants in the nearest gulch. This was rude law, and rough justice, no doubt; but was it not infinitely better, than the absurd and inhuman code of the Pacific Coast?

PORTLAND, OREGON

A ride of six miles down the Columbia, on the little steamer *Fanny Troup,* and then twelve miles up the Willamette, landed us at Portland, the metropolis of all that region. Here we found a thrifty busy town, of eight or ten thousand people, with all the eastern evidences of substantial wealth and prosperity. Much of the town was well built, and the rest was rapidly changing for the better. Long rows of noble warehouses lined the wharves, many of the stores were large and even elegant, and off in the suburbs handsome residences were already springing up, notwithstanding the abounding stumps nearly everywhere. The town seemed unfortunately located, the river-plateau was so narrow there; but just across the Willamette was East Portland, a growing suburb, with room plenty and to spare. A ferry-boat, plying constantly, connected the two places, and made them substantially one. Portland already boasted water, gas, and Nicholson pavements; and had more of a solid air and tone, than any city we had seen since leaving the Missouri. The rich black soil, on which she stands, makes her streets in the rainy season sloughs or quagmires; but she was at work on these, and they promised soon to be in good condition. Several daily papers, two weekly religious ones, and a fine Mercantile Library, all spoke well for her intelligence and culture, while her Public School buildings and her Court-House would have been creditable anywhere. The New England element was noticeable in many of her citizens, and Sunday came here once a week, as regularly as in Boston or Bangor. The Methodists and Presbyterians both worshipped in goodly edifices, and the attendance at each the Sunday we were there was large and respectable.

Being the first city of importance north of San Francisco, and the brain of our northwest coast, Portland was full of energy and vigor, and believed thoroughly in her future. The great Oregon Steam Navigation Company had their headquarters here, and poured into her lap all the rich trade of the Columbia and its far-reaching tributaries, that tap Idaho, Montana, and even British America itself. So, also, the coastwide steamers, from San Francisco up, all made Portland their terminus, and added largely to her commerce. Back of her lay the valley of the Willamette, and the rich heart of Oregon; and her wharves, indeed, were the gateways to thousands of miles of territory and trade, in all directions. Nearer to the Sandwich Island and China, by several hundred miles, than California, she had already opened a brisk trade with both, and boasted that she could sell sugars, teas, silks, rice, etc., cheaper than San Francisco. Victoria, the British city up on Puget Sound, had once been a dangerous rival; but Portland had managed to beat her out of sight, and claimed now she would keep her beaten. It was Yankee Doodle against John Bull; and, of course, in such a contest, Victoria went to the wall!

It seemed singular, however, that the chief city of the northwest coast should be located there—a hundred miles from the sea, and even then twelve miles up the little Willamette. Your first thought is, Portland has no right *to be* at all, where she now is. But, it appears, she originally got a start, from absorbing and controlling the large trade of the Willamette, and when the Columbia was opened up to navigation rapidly grew into importance, by her heavy dealings in flour, wool, cattle, lumber, etc. The discovery of mines in Idaho and Montana greatly invigorated her, and now she had got so much ahead, and so much capital and brains were concentrated here, that it seemed hard for any new place to compete with her successfully. Moreover, we were told, there are no good locations for a town along the Columbia from the ocean up to the Willamette, nor on the Willamette up to Portland. Along the Columbia, from the ocean up, wooded hills and bluffs come quite down to the water, and the whole back country, as a rule, is still a wilderness of pines and firs; while the Willamette up to Portland, they said, was apt to overflow its banks in high water. Hence, Portland seemed secure in her supremacy, at least for years to come, though no doubt at no distant day a great city will rise on Puget Sound, that will dominate all that coast, up to Sitka and down to San Francisco. From want of time, we failed to reach the Posts on Puget's Sound; but all accounts agreed, that—land-locked by Vancouver's and San Juan islands—we there have one of the largest and most magnificent harbors in the world. With the Northern Pacific Railroad linking it to Duluth and the great lakes, commerce will yet seek its great advantages; and the Boston, if not the New York, of the Pacific will yet flourish where now are only the wilds of Washington. The Sound already abounded in saw-mills, and the ship-timber and lumber of Washington we subsequently found famed in San Francisco, and throughout California. She was then putting lumber down in San Francisco, cheaper than the Californians could bring it from their own foothills, and her magnificent forests of fir and pine promised yet to be a rare blessing to all the Pacific Coast.

The Portlanders, of course, were energetic, go-ahead men, from all parts of the North, with a good sprinkling from the South. Outside of Portland, however, the Oregonians appeared to be largely from Missouri, and to have retained many of their old Missouri and so-called "conservative" ideas still. All through our Territories, indeed, Missouri seemed to have been fruitful of emigrants. Kentucky, Indiana, Illinois, were everywhere well represented; but Missouri led, especially in Idaho and Oregon. This fact struck us repeatedly, and was well accounted for by friend Meacham's remark (top of the Blue Mountains), "the left wing of Price's army is still encamped in this region."*The tone of society, in too many places, seemed to be of the Nasby

* [An allusion, probably, to the Confederate raider in Missouri, Sterling Price.—Ed.]

order, if not worse.* No doubt hundreds of deserters and draft-sneaks, from both armies, had made their way into those distant regions; and then, besides, the influence of our old officials, both civil and military, had long been pro-slavery, and this still lingered among communities, whom the war had not touched, and among whom school-houses and churches were still far too few. Of course, we met some right noble and devoted Union men everywhere, especially in Colorado; but elsewhere, and as a rule, they did not strike us as numerous, nor as very potential. In saying this, I hope I am not doing the Territories injustice; but this is how their average public opinion impressed a passing traveller, and other tourists we met *enroute* remarked the same thing.

Here at Portland, John Chinaman turned up again, and seemed to be behaving thoroughly well. At Boisè, we found these heathen paying their stage-fare, and riding down to the Columbia, while many Caucasians were walking, and here at Portland they appeared alike thrifty and prosperous. Their advent here had been comparatively recent, and there was still much prejudice against them, especially among the lower classes; but they were steadily winning their way to public favor by their sobriety, their intelligence and thrift, and good conduct generally. Washing and ironing, and household service generally, seemed to be their chief occupations, and nearly everybody gave them credit for industry and integrity. Mr. Arrigoni, the proprietor of our hotel (and he was one of the rare men, who know how to "keep a hotel"), spoke highly of their capacity and honesty, and said he wanted no better servants anywhere. One of them, not over twenty-one, had a contract to do the washing and ironing for the Arrigoni House, at a hundred dollars per month, and was executing it with marked fidelity. He certainly did his work well, judging by what we saw of the hotel linen. In walking about the town, we occasionally came upon their signs, over the door of some humble dwelling, as for example, "Ling & Ching, Laundry"; "Hop Kee, washing and ironing"; "Ching Wing, shoemaker"; "Chow Pooch, doctor"; etc. As far as we could see, they appeared to be intent only on minding their own business, and as a class were doing more hearty honest work by far, than most of their bigoted defamers. We could not refrain from wishing them well, they were so industrious, and orderly; for, after all, are not these the first qualities of good citizenship the world over?

THE CALIFORNIA CHINESE

We found the Chinese everywhere on the street and in the houses, in pretty much all occupations except the highest, and were constantly amazed

* [I.e., Petroleum V. Nasby, the American humorist.—ED.]

at their general thrift and intelligence. Out of the hundred thousand or so on the Coast, perhaps half were massed in San Francisco and its suburbs.

All wore the collarless Chinese blouse, looped across the breast, not buttoned—that of the poorer classes of coarse blue stuff, but of the richer of broadcloth. Otherwise, they dressed outwardly chiefly as Americans. Here and there a Chinese hat, such as you see in the tea-prints, appeared, but not often—the American felt-hat being the rule, stove-pipes never. A good many still wore the Chinese shoe, wooden-soled, with cotton uppers; but the American boot and shoe were fast supplanting this, especially among the out-door classes, such as mechanics and laborers. Pig-tails were universal, generally hanging down, but often coiled about the head, under the hat, so as to be out of the way and attract less attention. In features, of course, they were all true Mongolians; but here and there were grand faces, worthy of humanity anywhere. Their food consists chiefly of fish and rice; but the wealthier classes indulge freely in poultry and beef, and the Chinese taste for these was constantly on the increase. The old stories of their dog and rat diet are evidently myths, at least here in America. Intelligent Californians laugh at such reports as antediluvian, and say their Chinese neighbors are only too glad to eat the very best, if they can only get it.

Everybody gave them credit for sobriety, intelligence, and thrift, the three great master qualities of mankind, practically speaking; and without them the industry of the Pacific Coast, it was conceded, would soon come to a stand-still. All are expert at figures, all read and write their own tongue, and nearly all seemed intent on mastering English, as quickly and thoroughly as possible. When not at work or otherwise occupied, they were usually seen with a book in their hands, and seemed much given to reading and study.

Their chief vices were gambling, and opium-smoking; but these did not seem to prevail to the extent we had heard, and appeared really less injurious, than the current vices of other races on the Coast, all things considered. The statistics of the city and Coast somehow were remarkably in their favor, showing a less percentage of vagrancy and crime among these heathens, than any other part of the population, notwithstanding the absurd prejudices and barbarous discriminations against them.

Their quickness to learn all American ways, even when not able to speak our tongue, was very surprising. They engaged in all household duties, ran errands, worked at trades, performed all kinds of manual labor, and yet as a rule, their only dialect was a sort of chow-chow or "Pigeon English." "Pigeon" is said to be the nearest approach a Chinaman can make to *"business,"* and hence "Pigeon English" really means *business* English. Most of the words are English, more or less distorted; a few, however, are Chinese Anglicized. They always use *l* for *r*—thus *lice* for "rice"; *mi* for "I," and abound in terminal "ee's." *Chop-chop* means "very fast"; *maskee,* "don't mind." If you call on a lady, and inquire of her Chinese servant, "Missee have got?" he will reply, if she be up and about, "Missee hab got topside"; or if she be still asleep, "Missee hab got, wakee sleepee." Not wishing to disturb her, you hand him your card, and go away with, "maskee, maskee; no makee bobbery!"

We had seen a good deal of the Chinese generally, but on the evening of Dec. 31st were so fortunate as to meet most of their leading men together. The occasion was a grand banquet at the *Occidental,* given by the merchants of San Francisco, in honor of the sailing of the *Colorado,* the first steamer of the new monthly line to Hong-Kong. All the chief men of the city—merchants, lawyers, clergymen, politicians—were present, and among the rest some twenty or more Chinese merchants and bankers. The Governor of the State presided, and the military and civil dignitaries most eminent on the Coast were all there. The magnificent Dining-Room of the *Occidental* was handsomely decorated with festoons and flowers, and tastefully draped with the flags of all nations—chief among which, of course, were our own Stars and Stripes, and the Yellow-Dragon of the Flowery Empire. A peculiar feature was an infinity of bird-cages all about the room, from which hundreds of canaries and mocking-birds discoursed exquisite music the livelong evening. The creature comforts disposed of, there were eloquent addresses by everybody, and among the rest one by Mr. Fung Tang, a young Chinese merchant, who made one of the briefest and most sensible of them all. It was in fair English, and vastly better than the average of post-prandial discourses. This was the only set speech by a Chinaman, but the rest conversed freely in tolerable English, and in deportment were certainly perfect Chesterfields of courtesy and propriety. They were mostly large, dignified, fine-looking men, and two of them—Mr. Hop Kee, a leading tea-merchant, and Mr. Chy Lung, a noted silk-factor—had superb heads and faces, that would have attracted attention anywhere. They sat by themselves; but several San Franciscans of note shared their table, and everybody hob-nobbed with them, more or less, throughout the evening. These were the representatives of the great Chinese Emigration and Banking Companies, whose checks pass current on 'Change in San Francisco, for a hundred thousand dollars or more any day, and whose commercial integrity so far was unstained. There are five of these Companies in all, the Yung-Wo, the Sze-Yap, the Sam-Yap, the Yan-Wo, and the Ning-Yung. They contract with their countrymen in China to transport them to America, insure them constant work while here at fixed wages, and at the expiration of their contract return them to China again, dead or alive, if so desired. They each have a large and comfortable building in San Francisco, where they board and lodge their members, when they first arrive, or when sick, or out of work, or on a visit from the interior. Chinese beggars are rare on the Coast, and our public hospitals contain no Chinese patients, although John before landing has always to pay a "hospital-tax" of ten dollars. This is what it is called out there; but, of course, it is a robbery and swindle, which the Golden State ought promptly to repeal. These great Companies also act, as express-agents and bankers, all over the Coast. In all the chief towns and mining districts, wherever you enter a Chinese quarter or camp, you will find a representative of one or more of them, who will procure anything a Chinaman needs, from home or elsewhere; and faithfully remit to the Flowery Kingdom whatever he wants to send, even his own dead body. Both parties appear to keep their contracts well—a breach of faith being seldom recorded. Here, surely, is evidence of fine talent for organization and management—the best tests of human intellect and capacity—and a hint at the existence of sterling qualities, which the English-speaking nations are slow to credit other races with. Such gigantic schemes, such far-reaching plans, such harmonious workings, and exact results, imply a genius for affairs, that not even the Anglo-Saxon can afford to despise, and which all others may ponder with profit. A race that can plan and execute such things as these, must have some vigor and virility in it, whatever its other peculiarities.

Some days after the Banquet, we were driven out to the Mission Woolen Mills, where Donald McLennan, a Massachusetts Scotch-Yankee, was converting California wool into gold. The climate being so favorable to sheep, the wool-product of the coast was already large, and everywhere rapidly increasing. I mention all these things in order to emphasize the fact, that out of the 450 persons then employed about these Mills, 350 were Chinamen. For the heavier work, Americans or Europeans were preferred; but the more delicate processes, we were assured, Chinamen learned more quickly and performed more deftly, besides never becoming drunk, or disorderly, or going on a "strike." We saw them at the looms, engaged in the most painstaking and superb pieces of workmanship, and they could not have been more attentive and exact, if they had been a part of the machinery itself. And yet, these one hundred Anglo-Saxons were paid $2,95 per day, coin, while the three hundred and fifty Chinamen received only $1,10 per day, coin, though the average work of each was about the same. Without this cheap labor of John Chinaman, these Mills would have had to close up; with it, they were run at a profit, and at the same time were a great blessing and credit to the Pacific Coast in every way. So, also, the Central Pacific Railroad was then being pushed through and over the Sierra Nevadas, by some ten thousand Chinamen, working for one dollar per day each, in coin, and finding themselves, when no other labor could be had for less than two dollars and a half per day, coin. It was simply a question with the Central directors, whether to build the road or not. Without John, it was useless to attempt it, as the expense would have bankrupted the company, even if other labor could have been had, which was problematical. With him, the road is already a fact accomplished; and in view of possible contingencies, nationally and politically, who shall say we have completed it an hour too soon? Here are practical results, not shadowy theories—of such a character, too, as should give one pause, however anti-Chinese, and ought to outweigh a world of prejudices.

Not long afterwards, we were invited to join a party of gentlemen, and make a tour of the Chinese quarter. Part were from the East, like ourselves, bent on information, and the rest Pacific-Coasters. We started early in the evening, escorted by two policemen, who were familiar with the ins and outs of Chinadom, and did not reach the *Occidental* again until long after midnight. We went first to the Chinese Theatre, an old hotel on the corner of Jackson and Dupont streets, that had recently been metamorphosed into an Oriental playhouse. We found two or three hundred Chinese here, of both sexes, but mainly males, listening to a play, that required eighty weeks or months—our informants were not certain which—to complete its performance. Here was drama for you, surely, and devotion to it! It was a history of the Flowery Kingdom, by some Chinese Shakespeare—half-tragedy, half-comedy, like most human history—and altogether was a curious medly. The actors appeared to be of both sexes, but we were told were only men and boys. Their dresses were usually very rich, the finest of embroidered silks, and their acting quite surprised us. Their pantomime was excellent, their humor irresistible, and their love-passages a good reproduction of the grand passion, that in all ages "makes the world go round." But it is to be doubted, if the Anglo-Saxon ear will ever become quite reconciled to John's orchestra. This consisted of a rough drum, a rude banjo or guitar, and a sort of violin, over whose triple clamors a barbarous clarionet squeaked and squealed continually. Japanese music, as rendered by Risley's troupe of "Jugglers," is much similar to it; only John's orchestra is louder, and more hideous. Much of the play was pantomime, and much opera; some, however, was common dialogue, and when this occurred, the clash and clang of the Chinese consonants was something fearful. Every word seemed to end in "ng," as Chang, Ling, Hong, Wung; and when the parts became animated, their voices roared and rumbled about the stage, like Chinese gongs in miniature. The general behavior of the audience was good; everybody, however, smoked —the majority cigars and cigarritos, a very few opium. Over the theatre was a Chinese lottery-office, on entering which the Proprietor tendered you wine and cigars, like a genuine Californian. He himself was whiffing away at a cigarrito, and was as polite and politic, as a noted New York ex-M.C. in the same lucrative business. Several Chinamen dropped in to buy tickets, while we were there; and the business seemed to be conducted on the same principle, as among Anglo-Saxons elsewhere.

Next we explored the famous Barbary Coast, and witnessed scenes that Charles Dickens never dreamed of, with all his studies of the dens and slums of London and Paris. Here in narrow, noisome alleys are congregated the wretched Chinese women, that are imported by the ship-load, mainly for infamous purposes. As a class, they are small in stature, scarcely larger than an American girl of fourteen, and usually quite plain. Some venture on hoops and crinoline, but the greater part retain the Chinese wadded gown and trousers. Their chignons are purely Chinese—huge, unique, indescribable— and would excite the envy even of a Broadway belle. They may be seen on the street any day in San Francisco, bonnet-less, fan in hand, hobbling along in their queer little shoes, perfect fac-similes of the figures you see on lacquered ware imported from the Orient. They are not more immodest, than those of our own race, who ply the same vocation in Philadelphia and New York; and their fellow-countrymen, it seemed, behaved decently well even here. But here is the great resort of sailors, miners, 'long-shoremen, and the floating population generally of San Francisco, and the brutality and bestiality of the Saxon and the Celt here all comes suddenly to the surface, as if we were fiends incarnate. Here are the St. Giles of London and the Five Points of New York, magnified and intensified (if possible), both crowded into one, and what a hideous example it is for Christendom to set to Heathendom! San Francisco owes it to herself, and to our boasted civilization, to cleanse this Augean stable—to obliterate, to stamp out this plaguespot—to purge it, if need be, by fire—and she has not a day to lose in doing it. It is the shameful spectacle, shocking alike to gods and men, of a strong race trampling a weaker one remorselessly in the mud; and justice will not sleep forever, confronted by such enormities.

The same evening we took a turn through the Chinese gambling-houses, but did not find them worse than similar institutions elsewhere. Indeed, they were rather more quiet and respectable, than the average of such "hells" in San Francisco. They were frequented solely by Chinamen, and though John is not averse to "fighting the tiger," he proposes to do it in his own *dolce far niente* way. They seemed to have only one game, which consisted in betting whether in diminishing steadily a given pile of perforated brass-coins, an odd or even number of them would at last be left. The banker with a little rod, drew the coins, two at a time, rapidly out of the pile towards himself, and when the game was ended all parties cheerfully paid up their losses or pocketed their gains. The stakes were small, seldom more than twenty-five or fifty cents each, and disputes infrequent. A rude idol or image of Josh, with a lamp constantly burning before it, appeared in all these dens, and indeed was universal throughout the Chinese quarter.

The Chinese New Year comes in February, and is an occasion of rare festivities. It began at midnight on the 4th that year, and was ushered in with a lavish discharge of fire-crackers and rockets, to which our usual Fourth of July bears about the same comparison as a minnow to a whale. The fusilade of crackers continued, more or less, for a day or two, until the whole Chinese quarter was littered with the remains. It takes them three days to celebrate this holiday, and during all this period there was a general suspension of business, and every Chinaman kept open house. Their leading merchants welcomed all "Melican" men who called upon them, and the Celestials themselves were constantly passing from house to house, exchanging the compliments of the season. I dropped in upon several, whom I had met at the Banquet, and now have lying before me the unique cards of Mr. Hop Kee, Mr. Chy Lung, Mr. Fung Tang, Messrs. Tung Fu and Co., Messrs. Kwoy Hing and Co., Messrs. Sun Chung Kee and Co., etc. Several of these understood and spoke English very well, and all bore themselves becomingly, like well-to-do gentlemen. Like the majority of their countrymen, many were small; but some were full-sized, athletic men, scarcely inferior, if at all, to our average American. Their residences were usually back of their stores, and here we everywhere found refreshments set out, and all invited to partake, with a truly Knickerbocker hospitality. Tea, sherry, champagne, cakes, sweetmeats, cigars, all were offered without stint, but never pressed unduly. For three days the whole Chinese quarter was thus given up to wholesale rejoicing, and hundreds of Americans flocked thither, to witness the festivity and fun. John everywhere appeared in his best bib and tucker, if not with a smile on his face, yet with a look of satisfaction and content; for this was the end of his debts, as well as the beginning of a new year. At this period, by Chinese custom or law, a general settlement takes place among them, a balance is struck between debtor and creditor, and everything starts afresh. If unable to pay up, the debtor surrenders his assets for the equal benefit of his creditors, his debts are sponged out, and then with a new ledger and a clean conscience he "picks his flint and tries it again." This is the merciful, if not sensible, Bankrupt Law of the Chinese, in force among these heathen for thousands of years—"for a time whereof the memory of man runneth not to the contrary"—and its humane and wise provisions suggest, whether our Christian legislators, after all, may not have something to learn, even from Pagan Codes.

The Chinese temple, synagogue, or "Josh House," of which we had heard such conflicting reports, stands near the corner of Kearney and Pine streets, in the heart of the city. It is a simple structure of brick, two or three stories high, and would attract little or no attention, were it not for a plain marble slab over the entrance, with "Sze-Yap Asylum" carved upon it, in gilt letters, and the same repeated in Chinese characters. It was spoken of as a "Heathen Synagogue," a "Pagan Temple," etc., and we had heard much ado about it, from people of the William Nye school chiefly,* long before reaching San Francisco. But, in reality, it appeared to be only an asylum or hospital, for the unemployed and infirm of the Sze-Yap Emigration Company; with a small "upper chamber," set apart for such religious services, as to them seemed meet. The other companies all have similar hospitals or asylums, but we visited only this one. The first room on the ground-floor seemed to be the business-room or council-chamber of the company, and this was adorned very richly with crimson and gold. Silk-hangings were on the walls, arm-chairs elaborately carved along the sides, and at the end on a raised platform stood a table and chair, as if ready for business. The room adjoining seemed to be the general smoking and lounging room of the members of the company. Here several Chinamen lay stretched out, on rude but comfortable lounges, two smoking opium, all the rest only cigarritos— taking their afternoon siesta. Back of this were the dining-room, kitchen, etc., but we did not penetrate thither. A winding stairs brought us to the second floor, and here was the place reserved for religious purposes,—an "upper chamber" perhaps twenty by thirty feet, or even less. Its walls and ceiling were hung with silk, and here and there were placards, inscribed with moral maxims from Confucius and other writers, much as we suspend the same on the walls of our Sunday-school rooms, with verses on them from *our* Sacred writings. These mottoes, of course, were in Chinese; but they were said to exhort John to virtue, fidelity, integrity, the veneration of ancestors, and especially to admonish the young men not to forget, that they were away from home, and to do nothing to prejudice the character of their country in the eyes of foreigners. A few gilded spears and battle-axes adorned either side, while overhead hung clusters of Chinese lanterns, unique and

* [A reference to the American humorist, Edgar Wilson Nye, whose writings were published under the name of "Bill" Nye.—ED.]

beautiful. Flowers were scattered about quite profusely, both natural and artificial—the latter perfect in their way. At the farther end of the room, in "a dim religious light," amid a barbaric array of bannerets and battle-axes, stood their sacred Josh—simply a Representative Chinaman, perhaps half life-size, with patient pensive eyes, long drooping moustaches, and an expression doubtless meant for sublime repose or philosophic indifference. Here all orthodox Chinamen in San Francisco, connected with the Sze-Yap company, were expected to come at least once a year, and propitiate the deity by burning a slip of paper before his image. There was also some praying to be done, but this was accomplished by putting printed prayers in a machine run by clock-work. Tithes there were none—at least worth mentioning. Altogether, this seemed to be a very easy and cheap religion; and yet, easy as it was, John did not seem to trouble himself much about it. The place looked much neglected, as if worshippers were scarce, and devotees infrequent. A priest or acolyte, who came in and trimmed the ever-burning lamp, without even a bow or genuflection to Josh, was the only person about the "Temple," while we were there. The dormitories and apartments for the sick and infirm, we were told, were on this same floor and above; but we did not visit them. This Josh-worship, such as it is, seemed to be general among the Chinese, except the handful gathered into the various Christian churches; but it did not appear to be more than a ceremony. The truth is, John is a very practical creature, and was already beginning to understand, that he is in a new land and among new ideas. Surely, our vigorous, aggressive California Christians stand in no danger from such Pagan "Temples," and our all-embracing nationality can well afford to tolerate them, as China in turn tolerates ours.

LATINS AND GERMANS IN SOUTHERN CALIFORNIA

We anchored off the old wharf, then fallen to decay, at San Diego, where in other days the Panama steamers had floated proudly, and after rowing well in, were carried ashore on the shoulders of Mexican peons. San Diego was three miles off up the bay. Formerly numbering two or three thousand inhabitants, and a pretty stirring place, it now had only about two or three hundred. Its buildings, of course, were all one-story adobe, but partly inhabited, and these were grouped about a squalid Plaza, that reminded one of Mexico or Spain, rather than the United States. Being the county-seat, of course, it had a court-house and a jail, the one, a tumble-down adobe, the other, literally a cage, made of boiler-iron, six or seven feet square at the farthest. The day we were there three men were brought in, arrested for horse-stealing, or something of the sort; but as the jail would accommodate only two—and crowded at that—the judge discharged the third, with an appropriate reprimand. At least, we supposed it "appropriate"; but as it was in Californicé, and the judge a native, we could make nothing of it. In hot weather, this iron jail-cage must be a miniature tophet; but, no doubt, it remains generally empty. On a hill just back of the town, commanding it and the harbor, were the remains of Fort Stockton, which our Jersey commodore of that name built and garrisoned with his gallant Jack-Tars, during the Mexican war, and held against all comers. Beyond it still, were the ruins of the old Mexico Presidio, with palm and olive trees scattered here and there, but all now desolate and forsaken. The general broken-down, dilapidated, "played out" appearance of the town, was certainly most forlorn. And yet, the San Diegoans, like all good Californians, had still a profound faith in their future, and swore by their handsome bay as stoutly as ever. All united in pronouncing the climate simply perfect, though a little warm in summer; and, I must say, it really seemed so, when we were there. They declared the thermometer never varied more than twenty degrees the year round, and maintained people never died there, except from the knife or bullet. When reminded of a Mr. S. who had died that morning, they replied, he came there too late—a confirmed consumptive; otherwise, he would have got well, and in the end have shrivelled up and evaporated, like the rest of their aged people.

As to business, the town really seemed to have none, except a little merchandising and whiskey-drinking, and these only gave signs of life, because it was "steamer-day." The country immediately about the town was dull and barren, from want of water to irrigate and cultivate it. The great ranches were at a distance, and these depended on streams from the Coast Range, that mostly disappeared before reaching the harbor. Here horses, cattle, and sheep were raised in considerable numbers; but the breadth of valuable land was not considered large, and the population of the section seemed to be on the stand-still, if not decrease. The splendid harbor, however, is there—the second as I have said, on the California Coast—and it will be passing strange, if the future does not evolve something, that will give it vitality and importance.

Los Angelos itself proved to be a brisk and thriving town. It is the county-seat of a large county of the same name, and probably contained then some five thousand inhabitants—about one-third Americans and Europeans, and the balance native Californians and Indians. The Americans seemed to own most of the houses and lands, the Europeans—chiefly Jews—to do the business, the native Californians to do the loafing, and the Indians to perform the labor. It had mail communication with San Francisco twice a week by stage, and twice a month by steamer *via* San Pedro, and telegraphic communication *via* San Francisco with the whole coast and country. It boasted two or three very fair hotels, a fine old Spanish church, and quite a number of brick and frame residences, that would have been called creditable anywhere. The town seemed steadily increasing in wealth and population, as more and more of the surrounding Plains were brought under cultivation, and already had a substantial basis for prosperity in its vineyards and fruit-orchards, aside from its flocks and herds. It was also doing a considerable business with Utah, Arizona, and Southern California, for all which regions it was then largely a mart and entrepôt. Its climate was mild and equable, reminded one more of Italy and the Levant, than America, and already it was quite a resort for invalids from all parts of the Coast. Then in February, and again in May, when we returned there from Arizona, the air really seemed like the elixer of life, and quickened every sense into new life and power of enjoyment. As in all Spanish Americans towns, however, Sunday seemed to be the chief day for business and pleasure. A few stores and shops were closed; but the majority kept open, the same as any other day. The native Californian and Indian population of the surrounding country flocked into town that day, in holiday attire and, after a brief service at the old church (dedicated "To the Queen of the Angels,") assembled in the Plaza, to witness their customary cock-fights. There were several of these, which men and women, priests and people—alike eager and excited—all seemed to enjoy; but to us, Eastern-bred, they seemed cruel and barbarous. The poor fowls pecked away at each other, until some fell dead, and others dropped exhausted, when the survivors were borne away in triumph.

At Anaheim, we found quite a settlement of Germans, fresh from the Rhineland, engaged chiefly in wine-making. It appears, they had clubbed together in San Francisco, and bought a thousand acres of the Los Angelos Plains, bordering on the Santa Anna river, whose waters they now used for irrigating purposes. This they divided into twenty-acre lots, with a town-plot in the centre and convenient streets, each lot-holder being also owner of a town-lot of half an acre besides. Here were some five hundred or more Germans, all industriously engaged, and exhibiting of course their usual sagacity and thrift. They had constructed acequias, and carried the hitherto useless Santa Anna river everywhere—around and through their lots, and past every door; they had hedged their little farms with willows, and planted them with vines, orange, lemon, and olive trees; and the once barren plains in summer were now alive with perpetual foliage and verdure. Of course, there had consequently been a great rise in values. The land had cost them only two dollars per acre in 1857; but now in 1867, it was rated at one hundred and fifty dollars, with none to sell. We drove through the clean and well-kept avenues and streets, scenting Rhineland on every side; and, indeed, this Anaheim itself is nothing but a bit of Germany, dropped down on the Pacific Coast. It has little in common with Los Angelos the dirty, but the glorious climate and soil, and was an agreeable surprise every way. We halted at the village-inn, which would have passed very well for a Wein-Haus in the Fatherland, and were entertained very nicely. The proprietor was also the village-schoolmaster, and his frau was one of the brightest and neatest little house-keepers, we had seen on the Coast. They gave us bologna sausage and native wine for supper, as well as excellent tea; and when bed time came, we were conducted to apartments unimpeachable every way. In the course of the evening, half the village seemed to drop in for a sip of wine or glass of beer (they kept both, of course), and the guest-room became so thick with smoke, you could have cut it with a knife. The next morning they gave us some wine for our trip.

ARMY POSTS AND ARIZONA SAND

At Anaheim we bade good-bye to civilization, and at last were fairly off for Arizona. The distance from Wilmington to Yuma is about three hundred miles, and we hoped to make it in ten days at the farthest. We got an early start from Anaheim, and crossing the Santa Anna river through a congeries of quicksands rode all day (by ambulance), with the Coast Range to the right of us, and another serrated ridge ten or twelve miles off to the left, through what was mostly arid and sterile plain, though here and there it was broken up into ravines and "arroyas," or dry water-courses, abounding in cottonwood and live-oaks. Just at sunset, we crossed a divide, and before us lay a sheet of water, five miles long by two wide, reposing like a sea of silver, skirted by wide plateaus, and these in turn flanked by outlying ranges of mountains. This was Laguna Grande, the pet lake of all that region. Draining a wide extent of country, it always remains a large body of water, though in summer much of it disappears, and the balance becomes brackish from alkali. It continues palatable, however, for horses and cattle, and accordingly here we found a great hacienda, one of the largest south of Los Angelos.

The proprietors were two brothers Machado, who here owned leagues square of land, from the summit of one mountain range to the other, including the Laguna. They lived in a rude adobe hut, with three rooms, that no common laborer East would think of inhabiting; but they numbered their live-stock by the thousand, and esteemed their rude home a second paradise. They raised a little barley and some beans on a few acres, bordering on the lagoon; but devoted the great bulk of their broad acres to stock-raising. Señor Delores Machado met us at the door, as we drove up; but as he could speak no English, and we no Spanish, there seemed to be a predicament. Before leaving Los Angelos, we had anticipated this, knowing the old Mexican or Spanish-speaking population still prevailed over most of Southern California and Arizona, and had provided ourselves with "Butler's method of learning to speak Spanish quickly," accordingly. We had conned this over several days, selecting the phrases that would apparently be more useful, and now assailed Señor Machado with everything we could summon. Imagine our disgust, when he looked wild at our attempted Spanish, and responded to every phrase, "No sabe, Señors!" Our driver, Worth, at last came to our rescue, with some mongrel Spanish he had picked up, when soldiering formerly down in Arizona; and when Señor M. understood we only wanted entertainment for the night, he smilingly replied, "O, Si! Señors! Si! Si!" "Yes! Yes!" with true Castilian grace, and invited us into his abode. He gave us a rough but substantial meal, of coffee, frejoles, and mutton; and when bedtime came, allowed us the privilege of spreading our blankets on the softest part of the only board floor in the house. He and his wife occupied a rude bed in one corner of the same room, while his brother slept on one in another. There was not, and never had been, a pane of glass in the house, notwithstanding they were such large-landed proprietors. The breeze stole in at the broken shutter, that closed the only window in the room, and all night long we could count the stars through the dilapidated roof.

Thence to Buena Vista, we passed through a succession of small valleys, between the same general mountain ranges before mentioned. Though wanting in water, yet these all had small streams of some sort flowing through them, which if carefully husbanded could be made to irrigate thousands of fertile acres all through here. We were detained here a day, by a severe rain that set in at nightfall, just after our arrival, and continued for twenty-four hours; but as it gave us and our team a bit of rest, we did not greatly regret it. Thence to Villacito, the valley opened broader and wider, and the grand San Bernardino peak—which day after day had dominated the landscape off to the right—its outlines sharply defined against that exquisite sky—dropped gradually out of sight.

Here we struck the southern California or great Colorado Desert, and thence on to Yuma—one hundred and fifty miles—we might as well have been adrift on the Great Sahara itself. Until we reached this point, the country consisted chiefly of arid plains, it is true; but broken, more or less, into ravines or valleys, with some semblance of life, or at least capacity for supporting life hereafter, should sufficient intelligence and labor ever drift that way. But as we approached the Desert, all this ceased, and the very genius of desolation seemed to brood over the landscape. We descended into it through a narrow rocky cañon, so rough and precipitous, that T. and I both got out and walked down, leaving the driver to navigate the empty ambulance to the foot, the best he could. Jolting and jumping from rock to gully, now half upset, with wheels spinning in the air, and now all right again, he got down safe and whole at last, and we augured well of our wheels and springs, after such a rugged experience.

Quitting Villacito, we found the road sandy and heavy, the air sultry and hot, and the nearest water eighteen miles off at Carissa Creek. The country was one dreary succession of sand and gravel, barren peaks and rocky ridges, with arroyas now and then, but no signs of humidity anywhere. It was not, however, such a perfect desert, as we had anticipated; for here and there were clumps of chemisal, mescal and cactus, and these somewhat relieved the general dreariness of the landscape, poor apologies as they were for trees and shrubbery. The flora, as we proceeded southward, constantly became sparcer and thornier; but the fauna continued about the same—the chief species being jack-rabbits and California quails—the latter a very handsome variety, with top-knots, never seen east. The rabbits were numerous, and the quails whirred across our road in coveys quite frequently, until we were well into the Desert, when both mainly disappeared. We reached Carissa Creek, with its welcome though brackish water, about 2 P.M.; but as it was thirty-three miles yet to the next certain water at Laguna, with only uncertain wells between (dug by the Government), concerning which we could get no definite information, we concluded to halt there till morning.

From there on, the first few miles were about the same as the day before. Then we ascended an abrupt bluff, that looked in the distance like an impassable castellated wall, and suddenly found ourselves on an elevated *mesa* or table-land, the very embodiment of dreariness and desolation. On all sides, it was a vast, outstretched plain, of coarse sand and gravel, without tree, or shrub, or living thing—even the inevitable mescal and cactus here disappeared. Behind us, to the north and east, there was a weird succession of grand terraces and castellated mountains, reminding one of portions of Wyoming. On our right, to the west, the ever present Coast Range loomed along the landscape, barren and ghostly. To the south, all was a dead level, panting and quivering beneath the sun, as he neared the zenith, except where here and there a heavy mirage obscured the view, or vast whirlwinds careered over the desert, miles away—their immense spirals circling upward to the very sky. These last, on first sight, we took for columns of smoke, so erect and vast were they. But soon they rose all along the southwestern horizon, one after another, like mighty genii on the march, and our driver bade us look out for a Yuma sand-storm. We had already here and there found the sand drifted into ridges, like snow-banks, where sand-storms had preceded us, and had heard ugly accounts of them before leaving Wilmington; but, fortunately, we escaped this one—the whirlwinds keeping away to the southwest, where they hugged the Coast Range, and in the course of the afternoon obscured the whole landscape there. This was now the Colorado or Yuma Desert in earnest, without bird, or beast, or bush, or sign of life anywhere—nothing, in fact, but barrenness and desolation, as much as any region could well be. A large portion of it is so low, that the overflow of the Colorado often reaches it during spring freshets, and remains for weeks. In travelling over this portion, now baked dry and hard beneath the sun, we had frequent exhibitions of mirage, on a magnificent scale. One day in particular, we had been driving since early morning, over a heavy sandy road, with the sun blazing down upon us like a ball of fire, with no water since starting, our poor mules panting with heat and thirst, when long after noon we observed—apparently a mile or so ahead—what seemed like a great outspread pond or lake, with little islands here and there, their edges fringed with bushes, whose very images appeared reflected in the water. The scene was so perfect, that the driver and T. both insisted it must be water; however, I inclined to believe it mirage, as it afterwards turned out, but the optical illusion was so complete in this and other instances, that when later in the day we really did approach a veritable sheet of water at Laguna, we all of us mistook this for a mirage also. Here, however, we found a body of water a mile long by half a mile wide, surrounded by a rank growth of coarse grass, and covered with water-fowl—a perfect oasis in the desert. This was also a part of the overflow of the Colorado, there being a depression in the Desert just here, which holds the water like a cup. The quantity is so large, that it lasts for two seasons; but after that, is apt to dry up, if the overflow does not come. But as this usually happens every year, this Laguna (Spanish for *lagoon* or *lake*) becomes a perfect god-send to the traveller here. On its southern margin, a Mr. Ganow from Illinois had established a ranch, and already was acquiring a comfortable home. His horses and cattle found ample subsistence in the brakes, on the borders of the lagoon, and the passing travel to and from California and Arizona made him considerable patronage in the course of the year.

Thence past Alamo to Pilot Knob, where we rounded the corner of the mountains, and struck the valley proper of the Colorado, the country continued more or less an unbroken desert. The roads were heavy and dusty, the air hot and stifling, the landscape barren and monotonous; and when, at last, we made Pilot Knob, and struck the river, eight or ten miles below Fort Yuma, we rejoiced heartily, that the first stage of our tour was so nearly over. The Colorado flowed by our side, red and sluggish, but of goodly volume; the breeze came to us cool and moist across its broad bosom; and as we neared the post, the garrison-flag floating high in the air seemed to beckon us onward, and welcome us beneath its folds. Starting long before daylight, and lying by in the middle of the day, we had driven fifty-three miles that day, over a country that equals, if it does not surpass Bitter Creek itself; and when at last we drew rein at Fort Yuma, we were thoroughly jaded ourselves, and our poor animals quite fagged out. We had made the distance from Wilmington in nine driving days, instead of ten; but they seemed the longest we had ever driven.

Fort Yuma is popularly believed to be in Arizona, but is in reality in the extreme southeastern corner of California. The fort itself stands on a high bluff, on the west bank of the Rio Colorado, which alone separates it from Arizona, and is usually occupied by two or three companies of U.S. troops. Directly opposite, on the east bank of the Colorado, stands Arizona City, a straggling collection of adobe houses, containing then perhaps five hundred inhabitants all told. Here and at Yuma are located the government storehouses, shops, corrals, etc., as the grand depot for all the posts in Arizona. Hence, considerable business centres here; but it is chiefly of a military nature, and if the post and depot were removed, the "City" as such would speedily subside into its original sand-hills. Being at the junction of the Gila and Colorado, where the main route of travel east and west crosses the latter, it is also the first place of any importance on the Colorado itself; and hence would seem to be well located for business, if Arizona had any business to speak of. The distance to the mouth of the Colorado is one hundred and fifty miles, whence a line of schooners then connected with San Francisco two thousand miles away *via* the Gulf of California. From the head of the Gulf, light-draught stern-wheel steamers ascend the Colorado to Yuma, and occasionally to La Paz, and Fort Mojave or Hardyville—one hundred and fifty, and three hundred miles, farther up respectively. Sometimes they had even reached Callville, some six hundred miles from the Gulf, but this was chiefly by way of adventure, as there was no population or business sufficient to justify such risks ordinarily.

March 2d, while still at Arizona City, inspecting the depot there, we saw something of a Yuma sand-storm. The whirlwinds we had observed in the distance, when crossing the Colorado Desert a day or two before, seemed to have been only its precursers. It struck Yuma on the 2d, and promised to be only a passing blow, lulling away at eventide; but on the 3d, it resumed its course, with increased violence, and all day long rolled and roared onward furiously. We had heard much of these Yuma sand-storms, and on the whole were rather glad to see one, disagreeable as it proved. The morning dawned, hot and sultry, without a breath of air anywhere. Along about 9 A.M., the wind commenced sweeping in from the Desert, and as it increased in power uplifted and whirled along vast masses of sand, that seemed to trail as curtains of tawny gossamer from the very sky. As yet, it was comparatively clear at Yuma, and we could see the sweep and whirl of the storm off on the Desert, as distinctly as the outlines of a distant summer shower. But, subsequently, the Desert itself seemed to be literally upborne, and sweeping in, on the wings of the wind. The heavens became lurid and threatening. The sun disappeared, as in a coppery fog. The landscape took on a yellowish, fiery glare. The atmosphere became suffocating and oppressive. Towards noon, the wind rose to a hurricane; the sand, if possible, came thicker and faster, penetrating into every nook and cranny; the air became absolutely stifling, until neither man nor beast could endure it passably. People kept within doors, with every window closed, and animals huddled in groups with their noses to the ground, as if the only place to breathe. As night approached, the tempest ceased, as if it had blown itself out; but it followed us on a minor scale, for a day or two afterwards, as we journeyed up the Gila. The ill-defined horror, and actual suffering of such a day, must be experienced to be appreciated. Out on the Desert, in the midst of the storm, the phenomenon no doubt would amount much to the same thing as the simoons of the Sahara. Travellers or troops caught in these sand-storms have to stop still, and instances are not rare where persons have lost their lives, in attempting to battle with them. They obliterate all sign of a road, whirling the sand into heaps and ridges, like New England snow-drifts; and the next travellers, who chance along, have either to go by compass, or employ a guide, who understands the lay of the mountains, and country generally.

These sand-storms, it appears, are pretty much the only *storms* they ever get at Yuma, and they would not be unwilling there to dispense with even these. In the spring and summer, they frequently prevail there, sweeping in from the south and southwest, and they are simply execrable. They have done much to make the name of Fort Yuma proverbial on the Pacific Coast, as the hottest place in the Union.*

* [James F. Meline, in his *Two Thousand Miles on Horseback* (New York, 1867), pp. 53–54, tells the following story of Fort Yuma's heat:

"I listened to a discussion, last evening, on the comparative merits, or rather demerits, of the various military posts.

The Frontier Moves West

The Post stands on a high gravel bluff, facing to the east and south, exposed to the blazing sun throughout the day; and, subsequently, becoming saturated through and through with heat, retains it for months together. Hence, in the summer months, for weeks together, the thermometer there ranges from 100° to 125° in the shade, and the chief end of the garrison becomes an effort to keep cool, or even tolerably so. A tour of duty there was commonly regarded on the Coast, as a kind of banishment to Botany Bay; and yet we found the officers a very clever set of gentlemen, and spent some days there quite delightfully.

The Post here was established about 1857 to overawe the Yumas, then a stalwart and numerous tribe of Indians, occupying both banks of the Colorado for a few hundred miles or more. Though much reduced, they still numbered over a thousand souls; and physically speaking, were the finest specimens of aborigines we had seen yet. They cultivate the river-bottoms to some extent, and raise barley, wheat, beans, melons, etc.—for their surplus of which, when any, they find a ready market at Fort Yuma and Arizona City. Some chop wood for the river-steamers, and others indeed we found employed on the steamers themselves, as deck-hands, firemen, etc. Altogether, these Yumas seemed to have more of the practical about them, than any savages we had met yet, and no doubt they might be saved to the race for generations to come, were proper efforts made to protect and care for them. They had been peaceable for years, and scores of them thronged the Post and the depot, every day we were there.

The men wore only a breech-cloth, with long ends fluttering fore and aft; the women but little more, though some of them affected a rude petticoat. Both sexes, as a rule, were naked from the waist up, and many of each were

---

" 'Boys, did ever any of you hear of Fort Yuma?'

"Not one of them.

" 'Well, Fort Yuma is clear over beyond Arizona, where nothing lives, nor grows, nor flies, nor runs. It's the hottest post, not only in the United States, but in all creation, and I'll prove it to you.

" 'You see I was ordered to Fort Yuma six years ago, and hadn't been on duty two weeks in the month of August, when two corporals took sick. Well, they both died, and where do you think they went?'

"No one could possibly imagine.

" 'Why, I'll tell you; they both went straight to hell!'

"Profound astonishment in the auditory.

" 'Yes, but they hadn't been gone forty-eight hours—hardly time to have their descriptive-lists examined and put on fatigue duty down below—when, one night at twelve o'clock, the hospital steward at the Fort was waked up in a hurry, and there he saw the two corporals standing by his bedside.'

" ' "What do you want?" says he. You know them hospital stewards always get out of temper at a soldier's ever wanting any thing. "What do you want?" says he.'

" ' "We want our blankets," says they!'

" 'After that, you needn't talk to me about any post being hot as Yuma!' "—ED.]

superb specimens of humanity; but all seemed corrupted and depraved, by contact with the nobler white race. The open and unblushing looseness and licentiousness of the riff-raff of Arizona City, with these poor Indians, was simply disgusting, and it is a disgrace to a Christian government to tolerate such orgies, as frequently occur there, under the very shadow of its flag. Great blame attaches to the army, in former years, for ever admitting these poor creatures within the precincts of the Post at all. Some time before, it was said, the commanding officer sent for Pasquol, their head-chief, and bade him order his squaws away.

"*My* squaws?" he indignantly responded; "no *my* squaws now! White man's squaws. Before white man come, squaws good—stay in wigwam—cook—fish—work in field—gather barley—heap good. But now squaws about Fort all day—City all night—and Yumas no want 'em. White man made squaws a heap bad. White man keep 'em!"

And with this, old Pasquol, a stately savage, wrapped his blanket about his shoulders, and strode haughtily away.

With a host of "adios" and "good-byes," from our Yuma friends, we swung out of Arizona City late that morning, through knee-deep sand, and thus were fairly off for Tucson. The roads proved heavy all that day, and the remains of the sand-storm kept us company; yet we succeeded in making thirty-one miles, and went into camp before night-fall on the banks of the Gila. Some twenty miles out we passed Gila City, consisting of two adobe huts and an abandoned mine. Thence on to Maricopa Wells, indeed all the way from Arizona City, the road ascends the south bank of the Gila, and confines itself pretty closely to it, except here and there where it strikes across the mesas, to avoid some bend in this most tortuous of streams.

The Gila itself ordinarily is an insignificant river, apparently famed more for quicksands than water; but just now its banks were full with the spring freshet, and its usual fords dangerous if not impassable. Its valley is of uncertain breadth, from one to five miles, though its river-bottoms—its only really valuable land—are of course much narrower.

Beyond the valley, on either side, are high mesas or plateaus, covered often with barren volcanic rocks, like the table-lands of Idaho; and, beyond these still, are substantial mountain-ranges. The range on the north, day after day, was a constant wonder and delight. Instead of ridges and peaks, it seemed to be rather a succession of domes, and towers, and castellated ramparts, sharp and well-defined against a peerless sky, chief among which was Castle Dome—a superb domelike mountain, that dominated the landscape for two or three days together. The dome-shaped mountains are a feature of Arizona, and abound everywhere in the Territory, especially in the northern part of it.

A few miles west of Gila Bend, we passed a group of rocks, that interest everybody, but which nobody seemed to know much about. They stand near the roadside, and consist of smooth red porphyry, or some such stone, curiously carved with figures of men, birds, beasts, fishes, etc. Many of the figures are now quite indistinct, but sufficient remain to show what they were, and their very indistinctness—coupled with the hardness of the stone— proves their great antiquity. The rocks themselves, when struck, ring like genuine clink-stones; and, it would seem, only the sharpest and hardest of instruments could make much impression on them. The place is called "Painted Rocks," and we had only time for a cursory examination; but the sculpturing seemed too remote for Spanish times, and was generally attributed to the days of the Aztecs. However this may be, they appeared to be there as a species of hieroglyphics, and doubtless have a story to tell, that some future Champollion may unfold. It may be that the ancient travel for Mexico left the Gila here, or about here, and struck across the country for the Santa Cruz and so south, flanking the Maricopa Desert, and that these sculptured rocks record the place as the starting point—as a sort of finger-board or mile- stone. This is only a conjecture; but here, at least, is work for the archaeolo- gist and antiquarian, as well as at so many points in Arizona.

At Maricopa Wells, and thence up the Gila, we found a large settlement of the Maricopa and Pimo Indians. The Maricopas, it seems, are an offshoot of the Yumas, and number less than a thousand souls. The Pimos foot up five or six thousand, and from them are sprung the Papagos—a great tribe dominating all southern Arizona. The Maricopas and Pimos have a Reserva- tion here together, some twenty-five miles long by four or five wide, embrac- ing both sides of the Gila, and live in twelve different villages scattered over it. Two of these are occupied by Maricopas—the rest, by Pimos.

Both tribes are a healthy, athletic, vigorous-looking people, and they were decidedly the most well-to-do aborigines we had yet seen. Unlike most Indians elsewhere, these two tribes are steadily on the increase; and this is not to be wondered at, when one sees how they have abandoned a vagabond condition, and settled down to regular farming and grazing. They have constructed great acequias up and down the Gila, and by means of these take out and carry water for irrigating purposes, over thousands of acres of as fine land as anybody owns. Their fields were well-fenced with willows, they had been scratched a little with rude plows, and already (March 9th) they were green with the fast springing wheat and barley. In addition, they raise corn, beans, melons, etc., and have horses and cattle in considerable numbers. One drove of their live stock, over two thousand head, passed down the road just ahead of us, subsequently when *en route* to Tucson, and we were told they had many more. The year before, these Indians had raised and sold a surplus of wheat and corn, amounting to two millions of pounds, besides a large surplus of barley, beans, etc.

Their wigwams are oval-shaped, wicker-work lodges, made of poles, thatched with willows and straw, and this in turn overlaid with earth. An inverted wash-bowl, on an exaggerated scale, would not be a bad representation of one of them. They are usually five or six feet high in the centre, by fifteen or twenty in diameter, and would be very comfortable dwellings, were it not for their absurd doors. These are only about thirty inches high, by perhaps twenty wide, and consequently the only mode of entrance is on your hands and knees. While halting at the Pimo villages for a day, we managed to crawl into one, for the sake of the experience; but the smoke and the dirt soon drove us out. There was a dull fire in the centre, but with no means of exit for the smoke, except the low doorway. Rush or willow mats covered the rest of the floor, and on these three or four Pimos lay snoozing, wrapped in hides and blankets. Various articles of rude pottery, made by themselves, were stowed away under the eaves of the roof; and at the farther side, suspended from a roof-pole in a primitive cradle, was a pretty papoose sound asleep.

These Indians had long been quiet and peaceable, and it would seem are already on the road to civilization. What they need is school-houses and religious teachers.

Tucson we found to be a sleepy old town, of a thousand or so inhabitants, that appeared to be trying its best to take things easy, and succeeds in doing so. It was formerly, and is now again, the capital of Arizona, and the largest town in the territory. It is reputed to be some two hundred years old, and its appearance certainly justifies its reputation.

The town itself is built wholly of adobe, in thorough Mexican or Spanish style, and its population fluctuated. It was then only about a thousand or so, as above stated, of whom fully two-thirds or more were Mexicans, originally or by descent. Its streets are unpaved, and all slope to the middle as a common sewer, as in Spain. It boasted several saloons, one rather imposing, and some good stores; but had no bank, newspaper, school-house, or church, except a rude adobe structure, where a Mexican padre officiated on Sunday to a small audience, with much array of lights, images, drums and violins, and afterwards presided at the customary cock-fight.

As specimens of ruling prices, grain (barley and wheat) sold at $3 per bushel, hay at $40 per ton, lumber at $250 per thousand, all coin, and other things in proportion. The lumber came from the Santa Rita Mountains, fifty miles away, and was poor and scarce at that.

The basis of Tucson's existence, it appears, is the little Santa Cruz river, which flows along just at the edge of the town, and irrigates some hundreds of surrounding acres. There is a good breadth of fine land here, and near here, and the river ought to be made to irrigate the whole valley. No doubt with proper husbanding and utilizing of the little stream, thousands of acres might be cultivated, and the whole region, both above and below Tucson, be made to produce largely. Peach-trees were in bloom down by the river side when we were there; the grape, the orange, and the olive appeared in many gardens; and both climate and soil seemed all the most fastidious could wish. But Tucson lacks energy and capital, and besides, it seemed, the Apaches claim original, and pretty much undisputed, jurisdiction over most of the country there. Merchants complained that the Apaches raided their teams and trains *en route,* and ranchmen that the wily rascals levied contributions regularly on their live stock, as soon as it was worth anything, and did not hesitate to scalp and kill, as well as steal. Farming or grazing under such circumstances, it must be conceded, could hardly be called very lucrative or enticing, and the Tucsonians are entitled to the benefit of this explanation.

The liveliest and most energetic things, however, that we saw about Tucson were its innumerable blackbirds, that thronged the few trees about the streets, and awoke us every monring with their multitudinous twittering and chattering. What a relief they were to the dull and prosy old town! The men and women, wrapped in their serapes or blankets, sunned themselves by the hour in the doorways. The dogs and cats, the goats and pigs, slept on in the streets, or strolled about lazily at will. But these plucky birds sung on and on, with all the heartiness and abandon of the robin or mocking-bird in the East; and Tucson should emulate their intrepidity, and zeal. She should shake off somewhat of the spirit of Rip Van Winkle, and remember she is under Yankee government now, and in the latter half of the nineteenth century.

A Bibliographical Note

There is no general bibliography of books of travel in America. Though one such was projected by the American Historical Association, and some progress made on it, work has long since been suspended. An account of this plan, and the problems inherent in it, is to be found in Solon J. Buck, "The Bibliography of American Travel: A Project," in the *Papers of the Bibliographical Society of America*, XXII, Part I (1928), 52–59.

In lieu of any complete, general bibliographical guide for the whole United States, there exist a few lists, varying in degree of completeness and value, which are nonetheless useful. None of them, however, relates solely to American travelers in America, intermixing foreign accounts with native; and very few of them make any rigid distinction between books of travel and books of description. The great bibliographical compilations of books printed in America by Evans, Sabin, and Roorbach are rewarding but, by their very nature, unwieldy. For travel accounts specifically, the most complete are in the *Literary History of the United States*, edited by Robert E. Spiller *et al.*, Volume III: *Bibliography* (New York: Macmillan Co., 1948), pages 245–83; the *Cambridge History of American Literature*, edited by William P. Trent *et al.* (New York: G. P. Putnam's Sons, 1917–21), Volume I: *Travellers and Observers, 1763–1846*, pages 468–90; Volume IV: *Travellers and Explorers, 1846–1900*, pages 681–728; and Seymour Dunbar, *A History of Travel in America* (Indianapolis: Bobbs-Merrill Co., 1915), IV, 1447–81. Within its special field, William Matthews, *American Diaries: An Annotated Bibliography of American Diaries Written Prior to the Year 1861* (Berkeley and Los Angeles: University of California Press, 1945), is of special value. Helpful, too, are Edward G. Cox, *A Reference Guide to the Literature of Travel* (Seattle: University of Washington, 1938), Volume II: *The New World*, though the listings go only to the year 1800 with any completeness; Charles W. Plympton, "Select Bibliography on Travel in North America," in the *New York State Library Bulletin,* Bibliography No. 3 (May, 1897), pages 35–60, which describes as well as lists; and Joseph P. Ryan, "Travel Literature as Source Material for American Catholic History," in the *Illinois Catholic Historical Review,* Volume X, No. 3 (January, 1928), and No. 4 (April, 1928). More limited in value are Edward Channing, Albert B. Hart, and Frederick J. Turner, *Guide to the Study and Reading of American History* (Boston: Ginn & Co., 1912), pages 89–102; Josephus N. Larned (ed.), *The Literature of American History: A Bibliographical Guide* (Boston: Houghton Mifflin & Co., 1902), the Index of which lists works of travel; and Justin Winsor (ed.), *Narrative and Critical History of America* (Boston: Houghton Mifflin & Co., 1884–89), VIII, 489–94, which lists travel accounts only to 1820.

Unique, and written entertainingly, is Henry T. Tuckerman's *America and Her Commentators: With a Critical Sketch of Travel in the United States* (New York: Charles Scribner, 1864). Not only is the work a valuable bibliographical contribution, but the discussion of the travelers is pertinent and penetrating. Chapter x is devoted entirely to American travelers.

For the separate geographic sections of the United States the amount of bibliographical matter is uneven. For the Northeastern States no bibliography exists, though the guides for the entire United States noted above offer considerable aid. For travel in the Southern States, for its limited period, E. Merle Coulter, *Travel in the Confederate States: A Bibliography* (Norman: University of Oklahoma Press, 1948), is a model work, compiled with scholarly competence and furnished with critical and descriptive notes. The Middle West has four bibliographies of use: Solon J. Buck, "Travel and Description, 1765–1865," in the *Illinois State Historical Library Collections,* Volume IX ("Bibliographical Series," Vol. II [1914]), relates specifically only to Illinois, but, since travelers in that state usually went beyond its borders, the work has a larger value than its place of publication would suggest; Dorothy A. Dondore, *The Prairie and the Making of Middle America* (Cedar Rapids, Iowa: Torch Press, 1926), offers an interpretive text as well as bibliographical aid; Ralph L. Rusk, *The Literature of the Middle Western Frontier* (New York: Columbia University Press, 1925), gives an extended bibliography in Volume II (pp. 96–144); and R. W. G. Vail, *The Voice of the Old Frontier* (Philadelphia: University of Pennsylvania Press, 1949), whose lists extend, however, only to the year 1800. The Southwest and the Pacific West have two bibliographical guides to their travel literature of surpassing excellence: Jesse L. Rader, *South of Forty: From the Mississippi to the Rio Grande. A Bibliography* (Norman: University of Oklahoma

The Frontier Moves West

Press, 1947), and Henry R. Wagner, *The Plains and the Rockies: A Bibliography of Original Narratives of Travel and Adventure, 1800–1865. Revised and Extended by Charles L. Camp* (San Francisco: Grabhorn Press, 1937).

PRINTED IN U·S·A